*The New England Merchants in the
Seventeenth Century*

Massachusetts Shipping, 1697–1714
(with Lotte Bailyn)

Education in the Forming of American Society

The Ideological Origins of the American Revolution

The Origins of American Politics

The Great Republic
(coauthor)

The Ordeal of Thomas Hutchinson

*The Peopling of British North America:
An Introduction*

Voyagers to the West

Faces of Revolution

On the Teaching and Writing of History

To Begin the World Anew

Atlantic History: Concepts and Contours

Edited and Coedited Works

The Apologia of Robert Keayne

Pamphlets of the American Revolution

*The Intellectual Migration:
Europe and America, 1930–1960*

Law in American History

The Press and the American Revolution

*Strangers Within the Realm:
Cultural Margins of the First British Empire*

The Debate on the Constitution
(2 vols.)

*Soundings in Atlantic History:
Latent Structures and Intellectual Currents, 1500–1830*

The Barbarous Years

THE PEOPLING OF
BRITISH NORTH AMERICA

THE BARBAROUS YEARS

The Conflict of Civilizations

1600–1675

Bernard Bailyn

ALFRED A. KNOPF   NEW YORK
2012

THIS IS A BORZOI BOOK
PUBLISHED BY ALFRED A. KNOPF

www.aaknopf.com

Knopf, Borzoi Books, and the colophon are registered trademarks
of Random House, Inc.

Bailyn, Bernard.
The barbarous years : the peopling of British North America : the conflict of
civilizations, 1600–1675 / Bernard Bailyn.—1st ed.
p. cm.
"This is a Borzoi Book—T.p. verso."
Includes bibliographical references and index.
ISBN 978-0-394-51570-0
1. United States—History—Colonial period, ca. 1600–1775.
2. Canada—History—To 1763 (New France) 3. Immigrants—North America—
History—17th century. 4. North America—Civilization—17th century.
5. Great Britain—Colonies—America—History—17th century. I. Title.
E191.B35 2012
973.2—dc23   2012034223

Jacket design by Jason Booher

Manufactured in the United States of America
First Edition

FOR
LOTTE

Contents

WITHDRAWN

Maps and Illustrations

Introduction

THIS BOOK IS a major part of a project I set out some years ago, to give an account of the peopling of British North America in the seventeenth and eighteenth centuries. Publication began with a sketch of aspects of the subject as a whole (*The Peopling of British North America: An Introduction*), which traced the broad outlines of the European population movements that resulted in the repeopling of the eastern borderlands of North America. That book concluded with a view of an emerging North American society that mingled barbarism and gentility, and that contained strange, at times bizarre, distensions of familiar European forms of life.

There followed a study of the movements of some ten thousand immigrants from Britain to America in the years 1773–76. The statistical base of that book, *Voyagers to the West: A Passage in the Peopling of America on the Eve of the Revolution*, was made possible by the survival of a complete register of departures from the British Isles in those pre-Revolutionary years. From the register's 350 closely written folio sheets one could reconstruct the predominant socioeconomic characteristics of this entire migrant population, the geographical contours of their wanderings, the new communities they formed, modeled on what they recalled of those they had left behind, and the transatlantic communication networks they created.

The present book precedes *Voyagers* in time. It first sketches the world of the native Americans in eastern North America before the arrival of significant numbers of Europeans, then recounts in regional narratives the first great transit of people from Britain, Europe, and Africa, and concludes with a sketch of the transformed world of British North America after seventy-five years of conquest. It is an account of the fortunes of the founding generations of Europeans and their conflicted involvements with the indigenous peoples. But though contemporary population estimates and local censuses of particular groups appear throughout the book, it has no comprehensive statistical base. The data do not exist. Much is known, however, of the migrants', and to a lesser degree the natives', backgrounds, behavior, enterprises, and common experiences; and in the scattered sources one can find some evidence, however fragmentary, of their inner lives, their motives, beliefs, fears, and aspirations.

Of one characteristic of the immigrant population there can be no doubt. They were a mixed multitude. They came from England, the Netherlands, the German and Italian states, France, Africa, Sweden, and Finland; and they moved out to the western hemisphere for different reasons, from different social backgrounds and cultures, and under different auspices and circumstances. Even those who came from England—the majority of the immigrant population of the founding years—fitted no distinct socioeconomic or cultural pattern. They came from all over the realm, bearing with them diverse lifestyles. They came from the commercialized, modernizing southeast, especially the great conurbation of London; from remote, isolated farmlands in the north still close to their medieval origins; from enterprising towns in the midlands, the south, and the west; from dales, fens, grasslands, and wolds; and they represented the entire spectrum of Christian communions, from Counter-Reformation Catholicism to Anglican Episcopacy, Puritan Calvinism, Arminianism, Anabaptism, Millenarianism, and semimystical Quakerism. For England in the seventeenth century was composed of a multitude of regional and religio-ideological subcultures, which would meld and re-form in the open environment of the colonies. And the English mingled with other Europeans, clashed at times savagely with the indigenous peoples whose worlds they exploited but did not understand, and formed networks of association stretching from the Appalachian Mountains to western Europe, Latin America, the Caribbean, and Africa, all part of the immense socio-economic structure of Atlantic civilization.

HERBERT BUTTERFIELD REMARKED that history should be both a study and a story. What follows are studies within stories, long familiar stories and new stories of the early years of British North America—narratives of how the land was peopled and then repeopled and with what results. I have attempted to tell these stories with new details of individual lives, however obscure, and within a broad pan-Atlantic framework. At the heart of these narratives is the struggle of the Europeans, low and high born, to re-create, if not to improve, in this remote and, to them, barbarous environment, the life they had known before. But their experiences were not mainly of triumph but of confusion, failure, violence, and the loss of civility as they sought to normalize abnormal situations and to recapture lost worlds, in the process tearing apart the normalities of the people whose world they had invaded. In this, British and Dutch America was not different from Spanish or Portuguese America. The British and Dutch overseas conquests were as brutal as those of the other conquering nations, in certain places and at certain times as genocidal. All the people involved— native Americans, Europeans, latterly Africans—struggled for survival with outlandish aliens, rude people, uncultured in what mattered. All—native Americans, Europeans, and Africans—felt themselves dragged down or threatened with descent into squalor and savagery. All sought to restore the civility they once had known.

Later generations, reading back into the past the outcome they knew, would gentrify this early passage in the peopling of British North America; but there was nothing genteel about it. It was a brutal encounter—brutal not only between the Europeans and the native peoples, despite occasional efforts at accommodation, and between Europeans and Africans, but among the Europeans themselves, as they sought to control and prosper in the new configurations of life that were emerging around them. In the process they created new vernacular cultures and social structures similar to but confusingly different from what had been known before, yet effective in this outback of European civilization.

My aim is to recount their experiences as simple narratives that have beginnings and developments but no inevitable outcomes; to identify individuals wherever possible, their personalities, appearances, fortunes, and passions; to reach back into their prior experiences; and to suggest the involvements of this emerging world with the larger scenes of Atlantic history.

B. B.

PART I

Foundations

CHAPTER 1

The Americans

1

T HEY LIVED crowded lives. Few in number by modern demographic standards, even before European diseases tore through their villages like the wrath of God, their world was multitudinous, densely populated by active, sentient, and sensitive spirits, spirits with consciences, memories, and purposes, that surrounded them, instructed them, impinged on their lives at every turn. No less real for being invisible, these vital spirits inhered in the heavens, the earth, the seas, and everything within. They drove the stars in the sky and gave life and sensibility to every bird, animal, and person that existed, and they were active within the earth's materials—rocks, hills, lakes, and rivers—and in the wind, the cold, the heat, and the seasons.

These purposeful, powerful spiritual forces that crowded the Indians' world required respect; care had to be taken not to offend them. One must act prudently, obey ancient precepts, learn complex prescriptions, and take advice from the gracious and sage. There were right ways and wrong ways. There were life-giving empowerments and tangles of prohibitions. When the rules were broken, people suffered.[1]

The earth's generosity, on which survival depended, could be jealously withheld. Profligacy, waste, irreverence could offend. Though a community's life depended on the success of the hunt, one might not slaughter animals recklessly. They too were protected by patron spirits, by "elder brothers," by soul spirits of their kind capable of retribution for insults and wanton killings; they too had rights to life and, properly, only limited reasons for dying. Hunting therefore had its rituals: was in itself a form of ritual—a religious, at times a mystic, rite essential not only for survival but also for the maintenance of order and balance in the world. So the Micmacs in Nova Scotia, out of respect for their prey, strove to prevent any drop of beaver blood from falling on the ground, and when that animal's flesh was boiled into soup, they were careful never to allow the broth to drip into the fire. They refused to eat the embryos of moose for fear of their mothers' retribution. Bones had to be disposed of with care. To treat these remains crudely, to throw them to the dogs or toss them about randomly, would offend the animals' kin and their presiding spirits, who would thereafter prevent their easy capture. So too the creative spirits, who watched jealously over the success of procreation, might resent the punishment of children and remove them from human hands; children were treated indulgently.[2]

Since the myriad, immanent spirits were everywhere alert, everywhere sensitive and reactive, the whole of life was a spiritual enterprise, and the rules of behavior had to be finely drawn. Propitiating the anima of beavers, who were greatly respected, was especially demanding, and there were significant distinctions: those that were trapped had to be treated differently from those that were otherwise killed. There were special rules for dealing with birds and animals caught in nets; the sex of captured animals mattered in their treatment. Respectful of the animals' spirits, Penobscot hunters would not eat the first deer or moose they killed each season, the Chipaways in the north offered up to ritual the first fish caught in a new net, and Eastern Abenaki boys had to give away their first kill, however small. And everywhere great attention had to be given to the ways that bears, patrician animals, were killed and consumed. Before or after bears were slain (it made no difference which, since in either case their spirits were alive), they had to be addressed with ceremonial honor and with apologies for the necessity of killing them; their carcasses had to be disposed of reverentially.[3]

In this magico-animist world taboos abounded. To obey them would minimize offenses and so help maintain stability; to violate them would lead to disaster. The possible effects of women's "uncleanliness" and their procreative processes had to be strenuously controlled. When menstruating, Micmac women were not allowed to eat the flesh of beavers, whose spirits would be insulted, nor drink out of common kettles. Huron women, when pregnant, were excluded from the area of the hunt since they would frustrate the capture of any animals they happened to glance at. And childless women were banished when bear meat was being brought in and consumed.[4]

The universe in all its elements, animate and inanimate, was suffused with spiritual potency—*manitou*, the Algonquian peoples called it—that empowered each entity to function in its distinctive way and that embraced all of life's diversity in an ultimately unified and comprehensive state of being. Children, Calvin Martin writes, were taught "that nothing was profane." There were few gradations in value or levels of superiority among animate things; nor were any species truly alien or any objects completely insensate. Animals no less than men belonged to "nations," lived in communal dwellings, conferred together sociably, danced and played together, fought in familiarly human ways, and acted in everything they did according to rules and precepts no less judicious and spiritually self-protective than those that shaped the behavior of men. The dignity of trees had to be acknowledged when they were felled, sometimes by sprinkling tobacco, which had peculiar powers, on the ground around them. The west wind—the seasons—thunder—too had purposes.[5]

In such a world, reciprocity was the key to stability, to happiness, in the end to survival. Injuries had to be requited, insults repaid, losses recovered. Raids were launched, wars were fought, over the failure of reciprocal trade, and to capture prisoners who might replace deaths or abductions incurred in previous conflicts ("mourning wars") and to restore lost dignity and pride. Body parts—severed heads or hands—of warriors who had fought improperly might be offered to victims' families to maintain the stability of tribal relations. Village life and political alliances were based on reciprocity: the fear of supernatural retribution was in itself a form of social control. Productive land had to be left fallow to recover the nourishment of which it had been robbed; rich fishing grounds had to be vacated to prevent irreversible depletion; girls given in marriage had somehow to be replaced, by compensation to a woman's family "for the loss of her valuable labor and child-bearing potential."[6]

But reciprocity, the maintenance of equilibrium, the restoration of balance—among people, between people and their environment, and among the elemental forces of life—was a complex process, full of mysteries that people struggled to comprehend. When the world went wrong—when there were droughts, epidemics, unaccountable wars, frustrated hunts—familiar remedies could be resorted to: well-known rituals, sanctioned patterns of self-abasement and self-denial, symbolic gestures, cunning exhortations. But often the sources of disturbance, of the insults to the system, were hidden; only direct communication with the ultimate powers could help, and that was the work of experts: doctors of esoteric lore and divination, shamans, magi, sorcerers.

The shamans, authoritative cosmologists and custodians of the myths of creation, could make personal contact with the immanent powers, penetrate the mysteries of lost balances, identify forgotten violations of taboo or offenses that demanded apologies, and recommend the proper forms of recovery. They could even diagnose the ultimate causes of physical illnesses that defied herbal cures, and find remedies in magical chants, amulets, rattles, and sucking procedures that rid the body of the disbalancing, destructive spirit. For they, above all others, knew that physical nature was only part of the great universe whose ultimate forces were spiritual. So in these emergencies, the shamans, the powwows, the sorcerers and soothsayers transcended physicality—in trances, by hallucinogenic drugs, by hypnotic, mind-blinding incantations, perhaps in epileptic seizures—in order to penetrate the deeper recesses of being and connect with spiritual sources. They emerged from these encounters with mandates that could be strange, at times frightening, entailing everything from symbolic gestures and prayerful dances to warfare, torture, and cannibalism.[7]

But ordinary people too had an avenue of direct access to the controlling anima, though it was an erratic, at times perplexing route requiring imaginative interpretation—through dreams.

Centuries would pass before European civilization would match the Indians' understanding of the importance of dreams. They were not seen as random, superficial ephemera that expired with the light of day, but as cold reality, profoundly meaningful experiences that had to be understood. The Hurons and Senecas, a Jesuit reported in 1649, believed that, quite beyond one's conscious wishes,

> our souls have other desires, which are, as it were, inborn and concealed. These, they say, come from the depths of the soul, not through any knowledge, but by means of a certain blind transporting of the soul to

certain objects; these transports might, in the language of philosophy, be called *desideria innata*, to distinguish them from the former, which are called *desideria elicita*. Now they believe that our soul makes these natural desires known by means of dreams, which are its language. Accordingly, when these desires are accomplished, it is satisfied; but . . . if it be not granted what it desires, it becomes angry . . . [and] often it . . . revolts against the body, causing various diseases, and even death.

Dreams were probes of ultimate realities, and anticipations of the future. Correctly understood they could guide one's behavior into safe channels, prevent disasters to oneself or to one's people, and ease anxieties that could not be consciously acknowledged.

Dreams as portents made demands. To ease one's latent troubles, to satisfy one's guiding spirit, or to anticipate some approaching disaster, a dream might clearly require one to do things that appeared bizarre but that were logical in the greater system of which the palpable world was only a part. A dream might oblige one to find sexual gratification with two married women; to sacrifice ten dogs; to burn down one's cabin; even to cut off one's finger with a sea shell, to fulfill symbolically a nightmare dream of torture. The worst nightmares were experienced by the young, groping apprehensively for maturity; by warriors, who knew that capture in warfare often ended in torture; and by the old, facing sickness and death—from all of whom society demanded fortitude and stoic endurance. A warrior who dreamed of being burned alive by his captors had his people singe him repeatedly with torches, but then, hoping that a symbol might substitute for his agonies and life, killed a dog, roasted it, and ate it in a public feast in the way sacrificed enemies might be eaten. Another, driven to accomplish a dream of captivity, had himself stripped naked, dragged through his own village, ridiculed and reviled, and tied up for execution; but then, having sung his death song, he stopped, hoping that this proximate enactment would be acceptable as suffering enough.

Sometimes, however, the true meanings and mandates of dreams were not obvious, but hidden, lying deep beneath manifest appearances. Expert analysts—the shamans—would be called in to penetrate the mysteries and prescribe the right courses of action. But not only the shamans: village elders, concerned for the fate of their people, might join in the search for a dream's meaning. There were even rites by which a whole community might gather to probe the riddle of an individual's mysterious dream, combining forces to discover its meaning and the correct, the relieving, course of action.[8]

Dreams could be deeply disturbing, upsetting the balance of life by their portents and the demands they made. But for people crowded and jostled by exigent spirits, stability—psychological as well as social—was in any case a fragile achievement. The psychological pressures, especially on men, could be intense. They were expected to be proud, courageous, resourceful, independent, defiant in the face of savage adversity, and at the same time devout in their reverence for the animating forces of the world and for their personal guardian spirits. Above all, they were hunters and warriors, and they were expected to excel as both. It was not merely courage that was required in hunting and warfare but reckless courage, heedless courage. Danger was not to be feared and evaded, but sought: it provided the ultimate tests of manhood. So their vivid war paint, whose color and design conveyed specific meanings—brilliant daubs of red for battles—was meant to startle the enemy, intimidate him, and weaken his confidence, but it also had the effect of heightening a warrior's visibility and declaring his fearlessness and his disdain for danger.[9]

A man who failed conspicuously as a hunter—whose technical skills were inadequate, whose nerve gave way at a crucial moment, who lacked the stamina for month-long searches in snow and ice—would be shamed, publicly disgraced, his humiliation destructive of status and of economic, even marital, prosperity. Against such outcomes they were trained from early childhood. As boys they were carefully instructed in the skills and fortitude of hunters and warriors, and their courage was tested in puberty rites. In some regions these passages from childhood were vague in structure, mild and diffused, though they usually involved some form of ritual self-abasement to invoke one's guardian spirit, whose presence would ever thereafter be represented in the pouch of charms one carried with one. In other regions, however, puberty rites were rigorous and severe. Nothing could be more demanding than the Powhatans' *huskanaw*, a process required of adolescent sons of leading families that could last for several months and was calculated to be so physically devastating as to wipe out all memory of earlier life, with its emotional ties of dependence. Some did not survive the ordeal of beatings, starvation, drug-induced bouts of madness, confinement in narrow "sugar-loaf" cages, and the tortuous recovery through contrived setbacks. Among those who, at the end of it all, failed to show the expected marks of total transformation and were made to repeat the procedure, death was not uncommon. So Europeans who heard vaguely of the ordeal, but who never actually witnessed or understood the whole of it, concluded that the natives indulged in human sacrifices to the feared god of evil, punishment, and power, Okse.[10]

The Powhatans' *huskanaw* initiated males into a crowded, delicately balanced, and perilous world, the stability of which might easily be upset and which might end in the devastation of military defeat. That ultimate threat was always there, even among such peaceful peoples as the horticulturists and fishing folk of New England. Among the Powhatans of the Virginian plain, battling furiously against or as allies of a would-be native overlord, and among the aggressive Iroquois and their Huron and Algonquian victims in upcountry New York and the eastern Great Lakes, warfare, with all its personal horrors, was commonplace. Raiding parties, seeking revenge, tribute, or restitution, devastated whole villages, pillaging stores of food, destroying crops and habitations, butchering the wounded, and carrying off the women, children, and defeated warriors. The women and children who survived were often adopted as replacements for the victors' recently deceased kinfolk, but the captured warriors were brought home as trophies, along with severed hands, feet, and heads. Beaten continuously, the prisoners were often maimed—fingers chopped or bitten off to incapacitate them for further warfare, backs and shoulders slashed—then systematically tortured, by women gashing their bodies and tearing off strips of flesh, by children scorching the most sensitive parts of their immobilized bodies with red-hot coals—while judgment was passed on whether they would live as dependents, in effect as slaves, or die. If spared, their lives as slaves involved brutal humiliation, complete repudiation of their former lives, and changes of name. While they might eventually rise to prominence in their new society, they were seldom free of the stigma of subjection. If condemned, they would most likely be burned to death after disembowelment, some parts of their bodies having been eaten and their blood drunk in celebration by their captors. This was the ultimate test, for which warriors had fearfully prepared. But it was not so much death they feared as shameful death, a cringing, pitiful death in which one begged for life. Those who died properly were those who withstood the agony not only uncomplainingly but defiantly, mocking, singing, laughing at their torturers until the end.[11]

• • •

SOME, for certain stretches of time, lived placid lives, blessed with abundant sources of food, moving peacefully with the seasons for safety and ecological advantage, deeply familiar with the physical world as well as with the neighbors they were likely to encounter and with the crowded universe of animating spirits that surrounded them. They found enjoyment in ordinary village life, in games—ball games, stick games, field sports—above all in dance. And festivals of all sorts were frequent.[12]

But none of these people, however isolated and well established, were secure—not the Beothuks on the remote fringes of Newfoundland, nor the tribes on the outer banks of the Carolinas, nor the Lenapes on the Chesapeake's Eastern Shore, nor the Monongahelas in the mountains of western Pennsylvania. None were free from the threat of violence—the unpredictable and uncontrollable violence of the natural world, the unfathomable violence of inner lives that exploded so strangely in dreams, the violence of border wars that erupted repeatedly, year after year, and the psychological violence endemic in cultures that demanded heroic invincibility and endurance and that familiarized children with excruciating cruelty.

Deep strains of anxiety tinged their lives. As adults they were often taciturn—that was the style of responsible maturity—but far from the model of nerveless, marmoreal stolidity that would later become their popular image, they were commonly sensitive and edgy—"touchy and vindictive," as the Powhatans are known to have been. So much could go wrong. They were fearful of possible shame, loss, and defeat. There was no end to the conflicts in their lives: at all levels "an injury demanded revenge, which was considered by the other side as an injury that demanded revenge in turn." And their valor, or lack of it, was always on display. For who they were was what they did, as the succession of their names, which were often descriptive, made clear.[13]

A person was given a public name at birth and also commonly a private pet name; later he or she might acquire another name to mark the emergence from childhood or exceptional promise or an early achievement; still later a new public name might be bestowed for some distinguished exploit; and others might be added that in effect suggested roles one had successfully played. "Pocahontas," the English discovered after the young woman converted to Christianity, was a childhood pet name; her people commonly called her Matoaka (playful), though her formal name was Amonute. These were agreeable names, appropriate for a paramount chief's daughter; but one could also be given a rueful, even a shameful name, or one that was conspicuously lacking in distinction or dignity or honor, or worst of all, a name of derision, such as those imposed on captives by masters who spared their lives.[14]

SENSITIVELY ATTUNED TO both the physical world and the ruling spiritual forces, and familiar with a complex array of procedures by which to adjust these external elements to serve their personal needs, the Americans experienced life as a delicate balance, which had to be carefully maintained. But though they were psychologically and spiritually tense and calculating, their inner lives crowded by forces and spirits of intense meaning and great power, they played out their physical lives freely and loosely in immense territories whose spaciousness was as necessary as the intricacy of their religion.

2

The sector of North America that the English adventurers and settlers would come to know in the course of the seventeenth century stretched from North Carolina to Nova Scotia and west to the Appalachians and the eastern Great Lakes—a domain five and a half times the size of England. Much of this land was heavily wooded. Mixed deciduous and coniferous growths covered huge tracts, darkened whole mountain ranges with rich, dense foliage. But though in some places the forests crowded the coasts and lined the river banks, there were innumerable patches of grassy meadowland along the coasts, as well as riverside and lakeside clearings and open fields in the interior. Many of these bare stretches had developed naturally, but others were the results of deliberate burnings and small-scale efforts at brush removal and deforestation. On these open plots and in satellite encampments near them lived a population whose remote Asian ancestors had moved east from the Bering Strait to settle on the Atlantic slope ten or fifteen thousand years before.

How numerous they were on the eve of permanent English settlements we do not know. We can only guess, and there are wild discrepancies among even the best-informed guesses that have been made. It may be reasonable, though, to estimate that the total population of this northeastern woodland area was around 300,000, a density of approximately one person per square mile, but with highly uneven distributions.[15] Large spaces were completely uninhabited, or so thinly peopled that one could travel for days without encountering a soul. But certain small regions were well populated. The ten towns and associated hamlets of the Iroquois people probably had a combined population of between 20,000 and 30,000, though these communities were scattered in a broad band stretching 150 miles west of the Hudson River to Lake Ontario; some of the Iroquois towns may have had populations of 2,000. It is likely that the settlements on the lower Hudson River basin, including northern New Jersey and Delaware, together had a population of just over 50,000—a density that approached eight people per square mile, roughly comparable to that of modern South Dakota. The population density of central Connecticut was probably about five per square mile; that of the Powhatan tribes on the coastal plain of Virginia—a population of over 14,000—approximately two per square mile, increasing to over three in the most populous region between the Potomac and Rappahannock rivers. There were no urban centers. Communities of 2,000, like those of a few of the Iroquois tribes, were extremely rare; most villages had no more than 200 or 300 inhabitants, and some communities, such as the Lenapes in the lower Delaware River valley, were simply bands of less than 50 related individuals, little more than extended families, loosely affiliated with other kinship groups nearby which together formed a distinctive cultural unit.[16]

The low ratio of people to land meant open space, freedom to move freely over large areas, which was vital to the Indians' existence. No one was completely sedentary. Most villages were only seasonally occupied. Though practices differed from place to place, most people remained in their "home" villages only through the spring and summer months, and even then wandered out from time to time in small bands to coastal and riverside fishing areas located fifteen, sometimes twenty-five, even fifty miles away. The exact location of the habitations that comprised a village had little permanence. Small dwellings lightly built of arched or propped saplings covered with bark or hides could easily be moved or simply abandoned and replaced elsewhere. And villages were moved and abandoned, frequently—in New England on average every dozen years or so—because the fertility of the surrounding fields, planted with the staples of corn, beans, and squash, declined; or because firewood became scarce; or because enemy raids drove the villagers to more defensible ground; or because blights devastated the local vegetation.[17]

"Home" was not, therefore, a village of fixed location to which one might have sentimental or ancestral attachments, but a spacious area, a territorial zone within which clusters of dwellings could shift location, fields could be cultivated and abandoned, and satellite hamlets erected overnight. The cultivation of fields did not bind one to the land. Though there were some groups, like the Lenapes and the Eastern Abenakis on the Maine coast, who were hunters and gatherers, horticulture was crucial for the survival of most of these people, but the cultivation of the soil was superficial. The land, which was worked by the women assisted by the children, was not plowed but simply scratched and punctured, with sticks and shells. The crops were planted together in hummocks formed amid surviving trees, stumps, and half-burned roots; the beans grew in twists around the cornstalks, and the squash and other gourds appeared helter-skelter alongside patches of weeds. Seemingly wild tangles of growths, these were in fact produce gardens, which provided a high percentage of the Indians' caloric intake and much of the bulk of their consumption. But the cultivation of these fields, which were not renewed or fertilized but in time abandoned, did not engage one's pride or challenge one's skills. And it did not confine one's attention or limit one's sense of spatial horizons.[18]

For village life and horticulture occupied only a part of the Indians' yearly cycle. After the early fall harvests, the villagers began moving off to inland hunting camps, where they spent at least the early part of the winter, leaving behind only a small cadre of elders and children to maintain the original site. The pattern of these movements varied from region to region. A typical New England sequence was two long sojourns in interior camps from mid-October to mid-March and then four or five short trips to coastal fishing camps between May and September. Some more sedentary horticulturists divided their lives between main villages and outlying farmsteads, from both of which groups moved out to special camps for fishing, fowling, and hunting.[19]

The hunting camps were widely scattered. The range of a single community's winter dispersal could cover large spaces. Individual family units of both the Western Abenakis, in present-day Vermont, and the Delawares occupied hunting territories estimated at two hundred square miles each, informally divided into subareas, some for immediate use, some reserved, to prevent the depletion of game. A more precise measure—of the Iroquois hunting territories, based on careful estimates of the annual consumption of deer meat and deer skins on the one hand and deer herd densities on the other—reveals similarly that a village of two hundred inhabitants required for survival a hunting area of 272 square miles, or approximately 175,000 acres.[20]

Though particular hunting areas were identified with particular peoples and incursions of any kind could touch off wars, there were no formal, linear boundaries, which in any case could not have restrained hunters on active chases. There were only rough natural demarcations like recognizable environmental zones (forest types, drainage areas) or at best hills or mountain ranges or "systems of trails related to water-courses," often separated by buffer zones. Rivers, for example, which often served as important borders, were also centers of community life, with housing clustered on both banks. But they were nevertheless part of a system of inexact but effective territorial parameters in a world that did not know possession.[21]

No one possessed—"owned"—land. "Ownership"—exclusive posses-sion, with the publicly approved right to sell as a commodity or other-wise alienate and use as one saw fit—was unknown. Land was held and used communally, by the "larger corporate groups, and ultimately the tribe, that discharge a proprietary or controlling function over territory and thus resources." The "ownership" of the land that communities were collectively entitled to control and use was vested in their sachems and those who advised them, but these leaders were only symbolic owners of collective rights in which individuals shared. Individuals possessed only things they used—farming tools, hunting equipment, cooking utensils. Similarly what they possessed of the land was what they could use of it. They had no private and absolute rights in the land, only rights of use derived from membership in the group—rights that were never exclusive, were commonly shared with others, and were impermanent. There were no permanent private property boundaries: a market in real estate was inconceivable. There was only access to the wealth that the land con-tained. Since most groups were structured and statuses differed, indi-viduals played different roles in the life of the community and enjoyed different degrees of wealth, but their affluence or eminence bore no rela-tion to the land as such. They engaged with it as they did with the air, the lakes, and the sea—freely, as part of their total environment, physical and spiritual. And like the rest of their environment, the land was familiar to them. Within its wide and vague boundaries the territory they inhabited and controlled was well known, well mapped in their mind's eye; its terrain features, its dangers, and its strange numinous places—caves, whirlpools, deep springs, huge hollow trees: thresholds of other worlds—were registered in tribal lore and contemporary experience.[22]

They knew the land, however spacious, because it lay within their grasp. Villages and tribes in these broad regions were bound together by efficient communication systems. The Powhatans, dominant over almost all of the Virginia plain from the Rappahannock south to North Carolina and west to the Piedmont and its hostile tribes, could move quickly over the entire six thousand square miles of their territory by means of the rivers that flowed eastward into Chesapeake Bay and the complex of footpaths and tributaries leading north and south that linked the rivers into a single network. Similarly, the river system of Pennsylvania and western New York—formed by the Susquehanna, Delaware, and Allegheny rivers and their contributing streams—constituted a transportation system that covered thousands of square miles, from Lakes Ontario and Champlain south to Chesapeake Bay and west to the Allegheny Mountains. Between these rivers, brooks, and creeks, as between the rivers in the Virginia plain, forest pathways formed intricate grids that rendered the whole region familiar: "eastern Pennsylvania and all of New York were linked into one great system of intercourse by canoe and trails through the valleys." A modern scholar has identified 131 separate Indian paths within the present state of Pennsylvania, a communication system certainly more elaborate and efficient than that of eighteenth-century Scotland and probably than those of the rural areas of most of western Europe.[23]

These were east-coast networks, but they were not isolated on the coast. They were linked, by footpaths and rivers that ran through and around the Blue Ridge and Appalachian mountains, to an arterial system in the backcountry and the farther west. The central highway—later called the Great Catawba War Path, or the Iroquois, Cherokee, or Tennessee Path—began at the Allegheny River in western New York and ran south through western Pennsylvania, West Virginia, the Carolinas, Kentucky, and Tennessee. In effect, through its lateral linkages, it extended from Canada to Florida and west into the Mississippi Valley.[24] How wide in the end the extent of the coastal Indians' geographical aware-

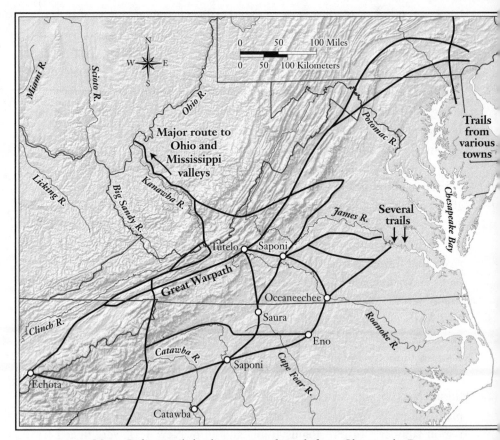

Major Indian trails leading west and north from Chesapeake Bay

ness was, what sense they had of ultimate spatial magnitudes, is difficult to discover. But they were well aware that their hunting parties traveled one hundred miles or more in normal course, that warriors from Iroquoia regularly raided their enemies in North Carolina, who as regularly reciprocated, and that trade goods traveled great distances, by successive relays. Most of the copper ornaments that the Atlantic coastal and southern Indians prized were known to be produced by the Ottawas who lived near the Great Lakes, and conversely most of the marine shell beads treasured by Appalachian tribes and Iroquois peoples in the north and west were products of craftsmen working on the Atlantic beaches, especially those in the Chesapeake Bay area, who sent their goods northward up the Susquehanna River and its tributaries, through intermediaries like the Massawomecks in western Pennsylvania and New York. The Mohawks and Oneidas in upstate New York had access to Atlantic salmon, and it was common practice for the Wabanakis in the maritime provinces of Canada to send war parties on coastal sea voyages to southern Massachusetts and Rhode Island. The sources of Ontario's most exotic trade goods were particularly far-flung: slaves and marine shells from Florida and the lower Mississippi, copper from Lake Superior, and volcanic glass and pipestone from the Dakotas and Wyoming. Beyond those far-distant rims of common experience lay remote realms, imagined, legendary worlds that blended into the invisible universe of spirits that ruled the Indians' everyday lives.[25]

3

Thus their lives were played out in open, spacious landscapes, and their long-distance travel and trade, generous hospitality to friendly strangers, and regular adoption of war captives led to a sense of cosmopolitanism and to genetic intermixing as well.[26] Yet these were village people, born into small communities and keenly aware of parochial identities and local cultural differences. Any sense of themselves as "Indians"—that is, as members of a single vast racial group distinct from any other—was inconceivable. The differences among them mattered greatly, however well they were able to tolerate and absorb them, and the differences in some respects were extreme.

Modern scholars identify two large language groups among the eastern woodlands peoples, Algonquians and Iroquois, the former dominant along the Atlantic coast from the Canadian Maritimes to North Carolina and irregularly but not very deeply inland, the latter prevalent in an irregular inland band stretching south from the eastern Great Lakes and the Mohawk Valley through western Pennsylvania and the Chesapeake Piedmont to central North Carolina and Tennessee. But as living languages the similarities within these two major blocs are largely technical and theoretical. Evolving unselfconsciously over centuries, following the movement and spread of peoples along the river routes and major valley trails, the two stem languages had branched out into separate dialects; eighteen have been identified among the eastern Algonquians, sixteen among the Iroquois.

The result, as these innovations spread and became stable, was geographical patterns of graduated distinctions such that most sublanguages or dialects were recognizable to their immediate neighbors, especially within separate river drainages, but less and less familiar to those more distant from them. So Munsee, spoken in the upper Delaware and lower Hudson drainages, was similar but not identical to Unami, spoken by people of the lower Delaware region. Similarly the thirty tribes of Powhatan's empire in Virginia spoke different Algonquian dialects, but most, having developed in close association with each other along adjacent river valleys, found their languages mutually intelligible. Not all, however: geographical proximity did not always in itself create linguistic kinships. The language of the defiant Chickahominies, who lived in the midst of the Powhatans' territory, and that of the Nansemonds, just to the south, may have differed from that of the regional majority. Even more different to the Powhatans was the language of their bitter enemies in the nearby Piedmont—the Manahoacs and Monacans; their speech was probably Siouan, one of several dialects of a language system extending south through the Atlantic backcountry, but it may have been an Algonquian dialect of such ancient origin and such isolated development as to be foreign to people only a few miles to the east. So too Cherokee, a language spoken by Iroquois people in the inland southeast, was as different from the rest of the surrounding Iroquois languages, experts report, as Romanian is from Spanish or Icelandic from Dutch.[27]

Language, in its differentiated forms, reinforced and helped shape boundaries that determined group identities. These were local people; they knew who they were and where they belonged. They lived as family bands and "tribes"—that is, closely interacting, coresidential clusters who shared not only dialects but also distinctive patterns of behavior and sets of deeply meaningful symbols. Their group names reflect, in complex ways, their sense of separate identity. *Lenape* is a self-definition that means "our men" or "real, common," or "original people"; *Onondaga* means "people of the hill"; *Powhatan* means "town at the falls"; *Abenaki* means "dawnland people" or "easterners." Of four autonomous groups that lived along the Delaware River, the northernmost, at the New York–New Jersey border, were *Minsi* or *Minisinks* ("people of the stony country"); the next, just to the south, were the *Unalimi* ("people up the river"); next, the *Unami* ("people down the river"); and finally, those at the mouth of Delaware Bay, the *Unalachtigo* ("people near the ocean"). So they were known, by themselves and by others. But tribal nomenclature could work in several dimensions: internal and external identifications could differ.

The Mohawks, in their own Iroquoian dialect, called themselves "people of the flint," but *Mohawk* itself is a south coastal word that means, in Narragansett, "man-eaters," in Unami "cannibal monsters." The Oneidas identified themselves as "people of the erected stone," but within the Iroquois League they were referred to as "they of the big tree." The Senecas called themselves "people of the great hill," but the Oneidas called them "bird people" and the Munsees "red-tailed hawks."[28]

Names, either self-referential or external, set groups apart, but names were only the outer expressions of social and behavioral differences. The Powhatans' world was hierarchical, centralized, and structured in three tiers: towns grouped into chiefdoms dominated by a paramount chiefdom. While it was not a vertically integrated authority system (Powhatan's personal authority was neither complete, consistent, nor everywhere compelling, and he, and the lesser rulers, were beholden to the priests), the district chiefs had life-and-death power. A hierarchy of ascribed statuses was elaborately expressed in dress, ritual, and various signs of affluence, and the flourishing horticultural and hunting economy was dominated by a savage tribute system that resulted in an elitist redistribution of resources that was arbitrary with respect to need or productivity. Powhatan, the paramount chief, had created an "empire" by military force, but like other, smaller, less stable, and less well-organized groupings, the peripheries of his domain remained fluid, likely to dissipate in loyalty and merge with alien groups. So Powhatan was frequently at war to keep his power intact, raiding and punishing those who resisted his authority, and annihilating whole tribes when they could not be disciplined.[29]

The Powhatans' world was "one of the most complex societies . . . then extant in eastern North America." But other peoples in southern Virginia and northern North Carolina (the Nansemonds and Chowans, for example) had something of the same sociocultural structure, while still others in the same general region (the Tuscaroras, Nottoways, and Meherrins) were essentially egalitarian, their distinctions achieved not ascribed, their decisions arrived at by consensus, and their goods shared or pooled. The Lenapes, who lived just to the north of the Virginia plain, along the lower Delaware River and its tributaries, were pacific people, neither horticulturists nor enterprising hunters but foragers, who lived in small unprotected kinship bands scattered along the river terraces. Their economy was primitive, their social and political order egalitarian, their unplanned villages scarcely more than temporary encampments of family units entirely lacking in central authority. To the north of them—in the more densely populated area of northern New Jersey, the lower Hudson River valley, western Long Island, and southern New England—were more sophisticated people. They lived in well-organized villages, or in dispersed farmsteads surrounded by fields; they cultivated gardens that stretched out into the countryside, and maintained consensual governments, independent of regional coordination or central domination. The Shinnecocks of Long Island were radically egalitarian—at times almost anarchically democratic. Still farther north, in the thinly populated maritime region of northern New England reaching into southeastern Canada and Nova Scotia, were Eastern Abenaki tribes closely identified with the coastal rivers and streams on which they were entirely dependent. They were peaceable, riverine fisher folk, hunters and gatherers; their political organization was as undeveloped as their economy. Subsisting largely on fish supplemented by wild plants and game, they lived in a primitive survivors' world distinctly different from that of the tribes to the west—the prosperous villagers who lived on the floodplains of the Connecticut River valley, the Mahican fishermen, horticulturists, and hunters in relatively secure palisaded villages built on hilltops along the upper Hudson River valley, and the Western Abenakis in present-day New Hampshire and Vermont. The last, whose settlements centered on the Champlain valley and for whom horticulture was a mere supplement to hunting and gathering, had a civil chief and a war chief, a Great Council of chiefs and elders, and a General Council to decide on questions of war. And still farther to the west—west of the Hudson and Catskill divide—was the contrasting world of the Iroquois.[30]

The five tribes in the Mohawk Valley and the Finger Lakes district of western New York who had joined in the late fifteenth century to form the nonaggression coalition known as the Iroquois League—the Mohawks, Oneidas, Onondagas, Cayugas, and Senecas—were politically the most sophisticated people in the eastern woodlands and militarily the most powerful and the most feared. Fierce warriors perpetually organized for war, whose savage treatment of captives created terror wherever it was known, the Iroquois were the scourge of their neighbors and rivals. The Western Abenakis' panic fear of the Iroquois tribe closest to them, the Mohawks, has been described as "almost psychotic"; the Hurons might realistically have anticipated that one day the neighboring Iroquois would utterly destroy them.

The Iroquois League's ten populous towns and associated hamlets were bustling, well-organized, and well-fortified communities, constructed not at river edges but on hilltops, from which all approaches could be seen. The major towns were surrounded by two or three rings of palisades—solid barriers of upright logs enclosing two to sixteen acres—constructed within outer ranks of ditches and earth mounds and complete with inner galleries and weapons platforms. In each of these spacious, fortified compounds were several dozen longhouses, bark-covered structures with arched roofs, some two hundred feet long and twenty feet high, built in parallel rows. Each such dwelling was divided into family compartments, with raised sleeping platforms and ample storage space, the whole interior heated by fireplaces located at regular intervals. And beyond the town walls and barriers were fields of the staple crops—corn, beans, and squash—cultivated by women and children. English visitors understandably called these compounds "castles."

The Iroquois' political organization was no less highly evolved and far more fully structured than that of the Algonquians to the south and east. The league was not a state or a statelike confederation but a council of fifty sachems whose purpose was to preserve peace among the autonomous tribes through elaborate ceremonies and exchanges of ritual gifts, and to keep the league's traditions and purposes alive. Similarly elaborate ceremonies were shared with tribes outside the league in order to maintain goodwill, and within the individual villages consensus was sought among kin groups by chiefs guided by councils of senior leaders, women as well as men. Unlike the Powhatan chieftains, the Iroquois village chiefs lacked coercive power; they were chosen for their negotiating skill and oratorical powers as well as for their personal stature and influence. Their political system—essentially a religious, ceremonial process rather than the working of formalized public institutions—was a delicate, ritualistic balancing of sensibilities, a constant search for reciprocity in which conflict and consensus were paradoxically braided. Invidious losses could not be tolerated nor undue advantages sustained.[31]

In much of this, the Iroquois were unique. The forms of community life and the practice of politics differed markedly from region to region, from tribe to tribe. So within the Iroquois villages women played a key role, precipitating wars, dominating councils, selecting male leaders, and largely deciding the fate of prisoners. But other communities (the southern New England tribes) were mainly male dominated. Among some people (the Pequots, Mashpees, and other New Englanders) leadership and family life were largely patrilineal; in others (the Mahicans, Susquehannocks, Munsees, and Lenapes), matrilineal; in still others (the Powhatans), leadership descended through both male and female lines. In New England success in leadership depended on charisma and persuasion; in the Powhatans' chiefdoms sheer power, reinforced by priestly authority, decided people's fates. In parts of northern New England, men provided the basic staple of life, game; in southern New England, women, working in the fields, produced an estimated 90 percent of all caloric consumption. Priestly—shamanistic—roles were important everywhere, but in some places, like the Virginia plain and the Pequot region of Connecticut, the shamans shared in, if they did not dominate, the ultimate group decisions.[32]

This was a diverse world—polylingual, polyethnic, regionally disparate in political and social structure, and economically multiform. Yet below these manifest differences lay the common civilization of people who lived at a distinctive level of culture. North and south, east and west, they were all villagers, most of them horticulturists, who lived in similar multifamily dwellings, acquired and prepared food in similar ways, dressed similarly in clothes of similar material, recognized similar signs of status, practiced the same division of labor, and fought wars in similar ways. Above all, they coped with their environment with similar skill.[33]

4

They had developed remarkable dexterities, highly refined skills. They fought principally with bows and arrows; these were not crude instruments. Their bows, five or six feet long, were deadly weapons. A typical bow, taken in Massachusetts in 1660, had a "pull" of forty-six pounds—less than that of English longbows but powerful nevertheless. With a maximum range of close to two hundred yards, the arrows, three feet or more in length, could be shot with great accuracy up to at least fifty yards. Their triangular projectile points, flaked from dense rock to razor sharpness, could tear through the hides of bears or moose, let alone human flesh; they penetrated deeply, were difficult to extract, and were likely to produce hemorrhages. An arrow that killed a Frenchman on Cape Cod in 1606 went through him and pinned his dog to his body. The arrows, made by craftsmen knowledgeable of both woods and minerals, could be shot one after another in rapid succession: seven could be released in the time it took a matchlock musketeer, propping his heavy, muzzle-loading weapon on a stand and igniting the powder charge to fire, to shoot once. Ordinary bowmen could hit racing deer and birds in flight "without a standing pause or left eye blinking." And the weapons they used for close fighting were as effective as any in Europe: hatchets with heads of chipped stone tightly lashed to long hafts, war clubs topped with wooden balls studded with pointed stones, and knives, in effect elongated arrowheads, as lethal as steel daggers or finely pointed stilettos. And they knew about armor. The Mohawks and Munsees used wooden helmets, arrow-proof tunics of closely woven reeds, and wooden or moose-hide shields.

The craftsmanship in all this weaponry was highly refined, the raw materials subject to what might be called quality control. The favored woods for bows were hickory, ash, and witch hazel; for arrows, elder. The proper felsite or quartz for arrowheads might be brought in lots from distant quarries, to be selected on the basis of reliable knowledge of mineralogy. The bowstrings, made of sinews or twisted strips of deer hide, were strong, and all the joinings—of string to bow, of feathers and projectiles to arrow shafts, of hatchet heads and knife blades to handles—were done with precise windings of fine gut, secured with glue of melted horn.[34]

This devotion to patient craftsmanship carried over to all the vital work of life. The first European settlers marveled at the Indians' skill in boat building. Large dugout canoes, made from trees felled by axes and fire, were fashioned by burning and chipping away the center, the smoldering fire limited by wet clay, until only a substantial shell was left. These narrow, round-bottomed troughs, some as long as fifty feet, could carry ten to twenty people; some were said to hold forty. Though blunt-ended and heavy, they could be paddled with speed, and though they rolled almost like logs, they were commonly used for spear fishing by men who managed to keep them in balance while standing and hurling harpoons. But it was the birchbark canoe, made in the north where paper birch trees were available, that commanded the Europeans' greatest admiration. They wrote about these remarkable vessels again and again and described how they were made.

The bark of giant paper birch trees, pried off in sheets under special weather conditions, was wrapped around a frame of white cedar, whose gunwales were spread apart by thwarts fitted into drilled notches. Stakes held the bark sides upright while the sections were sewed and glued together, then folded over the gunwales and joined at the pointed ends. Every joint was tightly bound and glued. Fine adjustments were made for weight and balance, the seams waterproofed with deer fat, and the result was a vessel of extraordinary speed, capacity, and adaptability. Birchbark canoes could bear remarkably heavy loads but were light enough for one man to carry: two could carry a canoe that held ten or twelve men. With three paddlers, it was noted, they could outrace an English longboat with eight oarsmen. They were wonderfully maneuverable, slipping through rapids, swinging around rocks and whirlpools. More fragile than dugouts, easily torn by jagged debris, they were nevertheless durable if handled properly; a well-made canoe could last ten years, and if sunk, it could be repaired and reused even after long submersion.[35]

Bark, in the hands of even ordinary craftsmen, was a substance of many uses. Everywhere in the North American woodlands it was used, along with skins and rush matting, for the outer covering of all three of the most common dwellings—the elongated, high-arched longhouses, the small, conical tepees, and the hemispheric wigwams. Light, waterproof, durable sheathing, bark could easily be stripped off the house frames and tied into rolls for reuse when villages were relocated. It could be fashioned into large carry-alls, into buckets, even into cooking pots, with heat provided by hot rocks dropped into soups or stews.[36]

Their ingenuity and craft skills were especially refined in their provisions for basic subsistence. They were ingenious fishermen. Their needle-sharp fishhooks made of bone or antler were weighted by rock sinkers notched or drilled for the fastening of lines. Their bone harpoon points, wedged into, but detachable from, long shafts, were tied to ropes to haul in catches of sea bass, bluefish, even seals and whales—not only drift whales but whales active in the offshore waters. They constructed stone and reed weirs to catch fish during spawning runs; trawling nets, some seventy or eighty fathoms long; hemp screens to hook fish by their gills; sieves to catch them descending through rapids; and hand nets to scoop them up as they battled their way upstream against the falls. They fished at night, by torchlight; in winter, through ice holes, with lines and spears.[37]

They were no less ingenious as hunters. Individual bowmen and spear throwers were skillful in hiding, lurking, tracking, and killing—and practiced in imitating animal calls and in disguising their human shape and sound and smell. They constructed traps of all kinds—deadfall traps of logs that could crush a bear to death; snares of bent saplings which when sprung could snatch anything up to the size of a deer in its thongs and fling it aloft, alive or dead. And they organized cooperative, mass game hunts: some, in which all the animals in a large area were driven between mile-long fences in the shape of a V, to be killed as they crowded through the narrow apex; others, in which the prey was forced over precipices or into creeks or rivers; still others, in which deer were terrorized into help-less packs by narrowing rings of fire.[38]

Food was thus produced—crops grown, fish and game caught, roots, nuts, berries, and fruit gathered—and it could be preserved. They froze meat in pine troughs, ice, and straw, as efficiently as later Americans would do, up to the age of refrigeration. The fish they did not eat they smoked for future use. And food of all kinds was preserved in storage pits, some seven or eight feet deep and five feet in diameter, lined with straw and bark or with stones and baked clay and periodically fumigated by smoke to kill off vermin and reharden the walls. With similar skill, they made wells to draw spring water by driving hollow tree trunks into the ground, tapped maple trees for their sap, and turned pine gum into tar and turpentine.[39]

Their ingenuity, their craftsmanship, reached into all areas of every-day life. They turned rough animal skins into soft leather, which, with furs, provided the clothes they needed. They made thread and cord from hemp, sinews, and vegetable fibers; sewing needles from horn; combs, tweezers, hairpins, hand tools, pottery, and baskets. Perhaps their most intricate technical accomplishment lay in turning the shells of the qua-hog, or hardshell clam, into the beads that came to be known as wampum. Carefully differentiating white from blue or purple shells, color having highly charged symbolic meanings, they perforated rectangular pieces of clamshell lengthwise with extremely thin wooden drills, threaded these blanks on strings of hemp, and then worked them through grindstone grooves to smooth off the edges and form them into short tubes or discs of uniform size. Patience and great manual skill were required to turn out these beads, which, when woven together into belts of various lengths, at five per inch on each strand, were objects of great value, the "diamonds of the country." The sheer difficulty of producing them limited their num-ber enough for them to serve as currency.[40]

Every measure that historians have been able to devise indicates successful adaptation to the environment. These were people skillful in producing what they needed—food, clothing, and shelter. Subsistence could at times be meager, forced tributes by demanding rulers like Powhatan could impoverish productive farmers and hunters, and overemphasis on starch and carbohydrates in some regions could have damaging effects. But most people were well fed: their diets—high in grains, fibers, and protein, lacking in sugar and milk products—were generally nutritious, much better balanced than that of the English, who lacked fruits and vegetables for much of the year. Starvation was not unknown, but it was rare, far less common than in the main population centers of Europe, notorious for filth, disease, crowding, and misery. They knew how to avoid polluted water, poisonous plants, and dangerous insects; in some areas they bathed frequently, and everywhere they found ways to inure themselves against the rigors of the climate—commonly protecting their bodies against cold in winter and insects in summer with thin rubbings of animal fat. And they did not overburden the natural resources available to them; nor did they disbalance their economies by excessive demands. Their mobility allowed them to travel seasonally to the available food sources and thus to take maximum advantage of ecological diversity—diversity that meant for them "abundance, stability, and a regular supply of the things that kept them alive." Mobility also made it possible for them to avoid exhausting the soil. They preserved resources of all kinds, with important demographic consequences. The Western Abenakis, by limiting hunting to subdivisions of the territory physically available to them, "maintained their populations at about 25 percent of actual carrying capacity" and thus created "a margin of safety against potential hard times; it is unlikely that they would ever face starvation, as might have been the case had their populations been closer to carrying capacity."[41]

Protective of the environment, sensitively attuned to ecological patterns, reasonably well fed, clothed, and sheltered, these were healthy people, by early modern standards, who impressed the first Europeans who met them by their robustness, their enormous physical endurance, their freedom from deformities, and their stature.[42] Archaeologists, studying ossuary deposits, present a more complicated picture, but one not inconsistent with overall health. Because of high infant mortality—an estimated 30 percent before the age of five (not much higher than rates in many parts of Europe)—life expectancy at birth was only 21 to 23 years (it has been estimated at 23.5 for Paris in the early eighteenth century), but those who survived to age 15 could expect to live to 35—not much less than their English contemporaries. They were taller than Europeans, though not as much as the first settlers claimed, and they were largely free of rickets and other bone diseases that crippled so much of the European population. In some places, at certain times, some among them suffered from tuberculosis, dysentery, influenza and pneumonia, arthritis, and various kinds of bacterial and parasitical infections. But the spread of these diseases was quite confined; the attacks were relatively benign; herbal remedies were in part effective; and the worst killers that devastated the European population in great waves of epidemics—smallpox, plague, cholera, yellow and scarlet fever, diphtheria, chicken pox, whooping cough—were absent, as were the immunities that might limit their effect.[43]

5

How can one describe this world? For those who experienced it, it was spiritually hyperactive and crowded; it was integrated, from the cosmos to every animate and inanimate object within it; it was diverse—linguistically, ethnically, politically, and socially; and it was skillful in stone-age technology and competent in managing available resources and ensuring survival. None of this, however, was fixed, immemorial, or static. Explorers from abroad may have thought they had found a timeless world, frozen in an early stage of human development, awaiting its deliverance into modernity. In fact what they had found were societies very much within history—their own history—living on the wing of change, facing new challenges, adjusting, learning, gaining, and losing. It was still largely a traditional world, but a world, in Nancy Lurie's phrase, "in a process of growth, elaboration, and internal change."[44]

Among the many forces of change that had been building up in the years before the settlement at Jamestown and that were reshaping American domestic history, two were preeminent. Their effects were radiating out into ever larger realms.

The first, dominating the Virginia plain, was the brutally expansive "empire" of Powhatan. That dominant chiefdom had emerged only in the recent past, sometime between the 1550s and 1580s, and was still in the process of expansion and consolidation when the English arrived in 1607. Inheriting six chiefdoms on the upper James and York rivers, Powhatan had expanded the area of his control by sheer conquest, defeating or intimidating one neighboring group after another, absorbing their warriors into his own band, and turning his enlarged army on other neighbors who resisted his demands for tribute and subjection. There was constant opposition, especially at the southeastern extremities. It was only in 1596 or 1597 that Powhatan succeeded in conquering the powerful Kecoughtans, on the north shore of the James where it meets Chesapeake Bay, a hundred miles from Powhatan's home village. He killed the Kecoughtans' chief and most of the warriors, took the survivors captive, and repopulated the territory with loyalists. A decade later, just as the Virginia Company's first fleet was preparing to sail to its colony, Powhatan was waging his greatest campaign, to destroy the Chesapeakes, on the south shore of the James, just south of the present Norfolk. Hoping to frustrate his priests' prophecy that his empire would be destroyed by people advancing from the bay, he turned on the Chesapeakes with fury and obliterated the entire community. Still there was no peace. Warlike, ethnically alien people hemmed him in on the west and raided his people repeatedly. The northern and eastern fringes of his territory were only weakly held; the groups there were eager to break away, and they were capable of doing so if given any effective support. And there were pockets of resistance even in the midst of Powhatan's central domain, the most important of them the Chickahominies, near the present site of Richmond.[45]

There was nothing settled, final, consolidated, or secure in Powhatan's realm on the Virginia coastal plain. It was a fluid world, a world in motion, with small-scale alliances forming and dissolving, skirmishes breaking out unexpectedly, and bloody repression imposed at points of chronic discontent. But however unsettled the results, Powhatan's ambitions were powerful, and they affected, at least indirectly, even the outer fringes of peoples across Chesapeake Bay and north along the Maryland-Pennsylvania border. The main northern groups, the Piscataways and the Patuxents, pressed by the Powhatans in the south, were at the same time beginning to be even more directly affected by a second field of force radiating out in all directions from the Iroquois tribes in the distant northwest.

The long-term prehistory of the Iroquois peoples is a remarkable tale of scattered, autonomous villages and camps in west-central New

York and northern Pennsylvania coalescing, after centuries of bitter, violent feuding, into a cooperating confederation of Five Nations. By 1600 they had long been acquainted with certain European goods, which had reached them indirectly, through successive relays—in part from the fishermen of many nations working off the shores of Newfoundland and Cape Breton, and in part from a succession of explorers and traders visiting the Chesapeake-Susquehanna watershed. Continuing imports from European traders in the later sixteenth century, negotiated through traditional trade contacts with coastal tribes, had stimulated a passionate desire for the glass beads on offer, which they identified with wampum and its spiritual power, and for copper and brass pendants, bracelets, and necklaces, "non-'utilitarian' in form and function . . . which were perceived and received as analogous to traditional, indigenous substantial metaphors of cultural value." Even the first practical commodities to reach them—kettles, metal ax-heads, and cloth in various forms—also "had a cultural or ideational efficacy, vastly disproportionate to whatever utilitarian function to which they were initially put." By 1600 they had learned how to pay for such goods, and they were beginning to develop "adaptive strategies" to cope with the first evidences of epidemic diseases and demographic decline that resulted from these early, indirect contacts. But their main effort was to overcome their isolation from the initial transactions and their exclusion from the best routes of trade. At the turn of the seventeenth century they were engaged in a massive, and massively disruptive, campaign to control the developing, still poorly understood, commerce.[46]

They were at war with a succession of Algonquian, Montagnais, and Huron peoples who dominated the St. Lawrence waterway route, with its increasingly important French trading stations. And at the same time they were driving the Susquehannocks, who had left Iroquois territory for a new location in Pennsylvania directly athwart the Chesapeake trade corridor, farther and farther to the south. And as they pressed, with deeply unsettling effect, southeast against the Susquehannocks and northeast against the St. Lawrence tribes, they mounted lesser campaigns for similar reasons against the Western Abenakis in Vermont, against the Algonquians in western Connecticut, and in scattered forays far to the south, against some of the backcountry tribes of Virginia and the Carolinas.

The spread of tribal warfare in the Iroquois' world was the clearest manifestation of something general and profound that was developing

on the eve of English settlement in North America. Emerging slowly at
a latent level were the beginnings of fundamental alterations in native
culture that, within a single generation after 1600, would prove to be
destructive beyond any contemporary imagining. In most places, the cultural malignancy was as yet scarcely visible; where it was visible, its force
was not fully revealed; and among those who saw the symptoms clearly,
there was hope for recovery. But this was a deadly disease.

The specific virus, unmistakable in the case of the Iroquois, was the
fur trade. Where, in scattered places, its effects were beginning to be felt,
it led to strange cultural inversions. In Newfoundland first, then in Nova
Scotia, in Maine, on the shores of the St. Lawrence waterway, and south
along the east coast, the market for furs, initiated randomly by the first
European traders, grew with increasing velocity at the end of the sixteenth
century, in ways that could not be accommodated within the natives' traditional culture. No new skills were required to collect furs, but the trapping of large numbers of small fur-bearing animals whose pelts brought
the best return took much time and effort, especially when the most obvious sources were exhausted, and it did not produce the nutrition provided
by larger game. Concentration on fur hunts upset the ancient pattern of
shifting seasonal activities, led to the neglect of horticulture, and since
women were increasingly involved in the preparation of pelts, disturbed
the traditional division of labor between the sexes. Further, a new and
disruptive sense of territoriality was engendered in those who competed
for both control of the richest trapping grounds and exclusive relationships with trading stations, where rivalries meant lower prices. Competition led to bickering, then to skirmishes, then to warfare among peoples
otherwise peaceful. Here and there along the coast and at the mouths of
the interior river systems, wherever the early fur traders were active, local
groups were beginning to organize into hitherto unknown combinations
to control the trade, and sought to become monopolists and middlemen
to the inland fur-producing tribes. So certain groups among the Eastern Abenakis joined to control the trade of the Penobscot drainage, the
Narragansetts took control in Rhode Island, the Pequots in Connecticut,
the Mahicans on the Hudson, and the Susquehannocks in the Delaware
Valley. The wars that erupted between these middlemen and their inland
suppliers led to population concentrations in fewer but larger palisaded
villages; and the conflicts were self-intensifying. Loss of warriors and the
captivity of women and children touched off retributive "mourning wars"

and gradually, among the Iroquois, an increase in the incidence and savagery of cannibalism. A religious as well as a military ritual, practiced with ever more horrifying cruelty, cannibalism served to propitiate the dominant spirits, ostensibly to gain military success, latently to help stabilize the social disruptions and uncertainties of severe and unpredictable economic competition.[47]

It was the start of a degenerative spiral. As more and more effort was devoted to hunting for furs, and horticulture was less strenuously pursued, the traditional dietary balances were increasingly upset. So the health of whole regions was placed at risk, and when the first, still peripatetic Europeans brought with them unfamiliar diseases, the result was the first wave of massive epidemics. In the last decades of the sixteenth century, in the years just preceding the first English settlements, measles, smallpox, and other virulent diseases were beginning to sweep through the most exposed groups and were carried by them into the interior. Shamans, medicine men, witch doctors were brought in to cure the sick and protect the tribes against further illness, but the traditional remedies proved futile, and the authority of those leaders, always dependent on success, was alarmingly and increasingly undermined.

Yet however disturbing these signs of decay, change, and social pathology, they were only scattered through the fringes of an immense territory that was still largely traditional, still familiar. The question for the leaders of the native American peoples on the eve of the English settlements—still confident, still hopeful for the future—was not how to destroy the invaders and wipe out the pathologies they brought with them, but how to use the strangers and their goods within the traditional culture, how to absorb the apparent benefits of European civilization, which they had so far found merely attractive but which would soon become useful, and ultimately indispensable.

PART II

Conquest: The Europeans

CHAPTER 2

꙳

Death on a Coastal Fringe

1

I T WAS INTO this still-traditional though changing, animist, violently competitive, and delicately poised world, constantly beset by disbalancing shocks, that a small contingent of Englishmen arrived in 1607. They were people whose way of life, sensibilities, assumptions, skills, knowledge, social relations, and aspirations—their entire experience and view of the world and the universe—could scarcely have been more different from those of the people who watched their arrival from the shores of Chesapeake Bay.

Though contentious in religious doctrine and organization, the English were monotheists, devoted to the belief that there was a hierarchy of being—that though touched by God, civilized mankind existed below the divine order but above and apart from crude nature and "natural" people, whom they were destined to convert and to rule, as they were to have "dominion over . . . all the earth, and over every creeping thing that creepeth upon the earth." Spirit existed, mind existed, not as a part of the shared physical world but apart from it; these were unique attributes of humanity.[1] Patriarchalist in social and political organization, they were sophisticated in the advanced technologies of warfare and in economic production and distribution, and they lived in a literate culture, within complex, highly articulated systems of law, dominated by monarchical authority. They enjoyed relative security, protected as they were by the sea from major disruptions from abroad, a temperate climate, and a physical environment that they had anciently learned, in some degree, to control. Since transportation and communication were still largely unchanged from what they had been for centuries, there were deep regional differences in subcultures and the economy, and there were enclaves of semiprivate political jurisdictions.

They were people who lived on the land—only an estimated 8 percent lived in communities of over five thousand, and many of the town dwellers were partly involved in agriculture. Their relation to the land was the heart of their world. It shaped the structure of social and political relations; it was the basis of the economy; and it was "the chief measure of wealth, prestige, and political influence." While most people were manorial tenants, others "held land by a bewildering variety of tenures" ranging from freehold, which was close to outright ownership, through copyhold and leasehold, to villeinage, the last a fast-disappearing status that tied people to the land in perpetuity without claim of any sort to the property itself. But beneath all the tenurial variations lay the concept and the experience, direct or indirect, of land as a possession, a commodity to be personally owned, leased, loaned, sold, or otherwise disposed of.[2]

They were a mobile people. Though most lived out their lives in their native parishes, there were short-distance movements everywhere, as marginal and ambitious people in the countryside sought security and stability. Young people commonly circulated as servants among households of higher or equal status, while unattached farmworkers and vagrants—propelled by population growth (35 percent in Elizabeth's reign, 1558–1603), by decline in real wages, and by the extension of commercial farming—roamed the local countrysides seeking employment. Some went longer distances—eight to twenty miles, distances short enough to allow easy return—to reach provincial towns and cities, which grew steadily in these years. And beyond all of those local and regional movements there was a growing drift of people moving long distances, mainly south and east, into the great catch basin of London. While the total population of the seventeen leading provincial towns grew to about 160,000 in 1640, London continued its explosive growth. Its population rose to 200,000 in 1600; it would reach 350,000 by 1650 and 575,000 by the end of the century. In 1600, 5 percent of England's population (roughly equivalent to the entire native population of the North American eastern woodlands) lived within London's conurbation; it would rise to 10 percent by 1700. The city devoured people. Disease devastated its slums—almost a quarter of the city's population died in the last year of Elizabeth's reign—but new-comers from all over the realm restored the losses. It has been estimated that about an eighth of all those who survived infancy outside London migrated to London in the early seventeenth century, rising to a sixth later in the century. Plague deaths of some 15 percent of the total would be made up within two years.[3]

Above all, there were energetic, enterprising, and ambitious elements within the English population. The nation's horizons in recent years had widened out into the broad Atlantic world, dominated by Spain and Por-tugal, and its capacities and aspirations were developing quickly. In Eliza-beth's long reign the English had rarely entered formally and officially into adventures abroad, but informally—in privateering, coastal raids on Spanish-American towns, and the release of English troops to serve under European commanders—they were adventurous, eager, and fiercely competitive. Their boldest outreach, driven by deep-lying forces within the domestic economy, stimulated and directed by the skill and vigor of suddenly enriching entrepreneurs, lay in the field of international com-merce. It had been expanding for half a century. While agriculture and domestic trade and industry rose and fell within a generally ascending curve, the growth and increasing concentration of capital accruing from agricultural surpluses and textile sales fed a sudden spurt in investments in overseas enterprise, and a greater awareness of possibilities abroad. But more was involved than commercial exuberance. England's expansionist tendencies were driven too by its sense of responsibility for the survival of Protestantism abroad, by the dawning of a "*British* ideology of empire" based on the "composite monarchy" of England, Scotland, and Ireland, by the promotional skills of the geographer Richard Hakluyt and publi-cists like Samuel Purchas, and by the ambitions of "projectors" for whom colonization was "a project among projects"—all of whom had visions of England's future as a colonial power that radiated through the higher echelons of government.[4]

The dominant energizing force in the early seventeenth century, however, was the newly empowered commercial organizations: the pro-vincial trading associations in Newcastle-upon-Tyne, Bristol, Exeter, Southampton, Chester, and Hull, the Merchant Adventurers of London, the Muscovy or Russia Company, the Eastland Company, the Levant Company, and finally, the great East India Company (1600). At their head, directing the expansion of these sophisticated, Crown-chartered monopoly companies—overseas trading guilds, in effect—was a small circle of financial magnates, who controlled large sums of capital, sat in various combinations on numerous corporate boards, and were close to the key figures in the government. Though not alien from the great landed interests, these merchants were a distinct force in English life, secure in their control of large-scale commerce, eager to expand their operations.[5]

Though the companies they owned and managed were conservative organizations within which individual investment groups operated in monopolized trading areas, they were well aware of the risky, experimental exploration and colonizing efforts that certain landed interests had launched before the outbreak of the Spanish war: Sir Humphrey Gilbert's failed attempt to establish England's claim to Newfoundland and plant a colony in the area of New England and Sir Walter Raleigh and his friends' short-lived colony at Roanoke on the coast of North Carolina. The merchants understood the financial demands such ventures made and the disastrous consequences of the failure to quickly locate commodities that would yield returns on investments.[6] And they shared the strangely mingled visions of the native peoples of the Caribbean and North America that had been forming for over a century.

THE IMAGE THAT informed Englishmen had of the American Indian population on the eve of permanent settlement in America was an inconsistent blend of notions derived from scattered sources, all of which reinforced an assumption of immense European superiority in religion, culture, power, and capacity. From some of the many Spanish accounts that reached English readers in the course of the sixteenth century came a view of an original population of prosperous, even wealthy natives, gifted in mechanical arts, sophisticated in speech and manners, rich in precious metals and agricultural production, living in well-designed and well-appointed cities built, in jungle clearings, of stone, and managed by well-organized political systems. Yet they were clearly barbarians: some were said to be cannibals, and all of them worshipped satanic gods whose priestly agents, frightening in themselves, imposed merciless, bloodthirsty demands on an obsequious populace. Though valiant warriors, the native Americans, the Spanish had discovered, could be defeated by small contingents of European soldiers and thereafter reduced to servility and forced to serve in the exploitation of American wealth.[7]

But from other sources—mainly English adventurers who had made contact with the North American Indians in the 1570s and 1580s—came a different picture: of barbarous people, natural, uncorrupted, and simple; unsophisticated people who had not yet emerged from the early stages of human development into the later phases that might lead, ultimately, to the fully evolved civilization of Elizabethan England. So John White added to his eyewitness paintings of the placid, agreeable-looking North Carolina natives he encountered at Roanoke in 1585 a set of vivid, wildly imaginative depictions of pre-historic Picts, ferocious, naked, blue-painted head-hunters. These startling images of monstrous savages were reproduced in popular engravings "for to showe," the legend explained, "how that the inhabitants of the great Brettanie have bin in times past as savvage as those of Virginia." The message was clear: if the naked, murderous Picts, shown holding aloft their enemies' dripping heads, were the ancestors of Elizabethan gentlefolk, what could not the homey Algonquians become? And since the Roanoke natives were pagans, they were undoubtedly susceptible to the tutelage of Christian missionaries, who could promise them advancement through salvation, if they accepted the Word.[8]

The most immediate, vivid, and best-known image of native peoples came, however, from neither of these sources but from the transfer, the extrapolation, of England's grim experiences with the Irish. The English had been actively struggling and failing to conquer or otherwise control Ireland for over half a century, and had found there a people whose apparent baseness set a universal standard for savagery. The "wild Irish" were said by would-be colonizers in the 1560s to be godless. They "blaspheme, thei murder, commit whoredom, hold no wedlocke, ravish, steal, and commit all abomination without scruple . . . matrimonie emongs them is no more regarded . . . than conjunction betwene unreasonable beasts, perjurie, robberie and murder [are] counted alloweable." For such people—"more uncivill, more uncleanly, more barbarous and more brutish in their customs . . . then in any other part of the world"—no treatment could be too severe; any brutality would be justified if it resulted in "the suppressing and reforming of the loose, barbarous and most wicked life of that savage nation." To reform "so barbarous a nation," by whatever forceful means, could only be "a goodly and commendable deede," but until that reformation might happen, they could be dealt with best by expulsion beyond a pale around the English settlements, which would at least protect the English settlers from succumbing to Ireland's barbarous ways. And there was for Elizabethans a natural conflation of the "wild Irish" and the American natives because many of the leaders of the first settlements in North America were also landowners and military officers in Ireland and could themselves see the ostensible similarities between the two native peoples—in social practices, and pagan rituals, "bestial" feeding habits, flimsy housing, and sexual promiscuity. The similarities were unmistakable.[9]

These mingled images of natives in the alien lands of the Atlantic world—advanced but satanic people whose wealth and labor could easily be exploited; simple, innocent, natural folk whose resources were as yet unknown and who could presumably be led, through Christianity, to higher stages of civilization; and brutish, debased people condemned by their animal-like wildness to live beyond an exclusionary pale—such visions had little in common except barbarousness, paganism, and the threat of dark mysteries as yet unrevealed. The inconsistency of these images would in itself prove to be a force in race relations in North America.

For the English, the native American world remained exotic, bizarre; it had none of the everyday familiarity it had acquired for the Spanish and Portuguese, who had lived and struggled, prospered and governed, in the western hemisphere for a century. The English venturing to the west had no fixed sense of what to expect, except that they were to encounter strange people, perhaps sophisticated, perhaps simple, undoubtedly savage. But despite all the strangeness, they would find that the two peoples had some things in common, and these common elements in their lives, along with the differences, would help shape the history of their violent interaction.

THEY BOTH LIVED in worlds that were at least in part experienced as magical. In England Christianity, even Protestantism, had not driven out ancient beliefs in occult forces; in magic, white and black; in the power of soothsayers, conjurors, cunning men, wizards, diviners, and witches; in the ever-present threats of sorcery and devilish disturbances to the equilibrium of life; in the power of charms, curative rituals, and fortune-telling; and in ghosts, apparitions, and walking spirits. For the

English, magic and witchcraft were not abnormal and extraordinary but commonplace and realistic, and that would be especially true in North America, for that distant land was known to be "one of the dark places of the earth," one of the "wild partes" ultimately ruled by Satan and his minions; there the native priests were known to be "no other but such as our witches are."[10]

For both peoples, the environment, human and physical, was unpredictable, threatening, and miraculous, despite time-honored ritualistic forms of intervention. For most Englishmen, neither traditional counter-magic, science, nor technology had significantly mitigated the randomness of human misfortune. Like the American natives, they were destined to struggle against hidden, occult forces, to seek to obliterate the malevolent powers, and to match their capacity to manipulate the esoteric forces of life with that of their adversaries.

Both peoples, too, lived precariously on the irregular bounty of the land. In good years England could support its growing population, but not all years were good, and in England as in America there were repeated harvest disasters—three devastating dearths in the sixteenth century—which led to periods of near famine. Both knew how fragile prosperity could be, how quickly security could be wiped out, how easily the balance required for survival could be destroyed—how vulnerable people were.[11]

Both peoples, further, were familiar with man-made disasters—wars, massacres, and scorched-earth vengeance driven by fear and the passions of religious belief. Both believed in their own inherent military and cultural superiority and their capacity to absorb conquered adversaries into their own world and to "civilize" barbarous aliens.[12] And both knew the horrors of physical cruelty. If the Indians sanctioned the torture of enemies and the most agonizing forms of execution, so too did the English. Ordinary crimes were punished by public floggings that could be severe, confessions were extracted by torture, and those convicted of treason and some felonies were hanged before large and enthusiastic crowds, cut down while still alive, disemboweled, castrated, beheaded, and hacked into quarters for display. Women were not mutilated, but for heresy, treason, or killing husband or master they could be burned at the stake, though compassionate executioners might strangle them before lighting the fire. And some of the most serious offenders were broken on the wheel—that is, spread-eagled in public spectacles, their bones smashed, their bodies eviscerated before final execution, their heads and quartered bodies displayed prominently in public places. England was spared some of the more "unspeakable litanies of suffering" that were known to be inflicted on judicial victims in central and eastern Europe—blinding, tearing with red-hot tongs, flaying, crushing into pointed stakes, sawing off of limbs. But in England too witches and heretics, like the Indians' captives, were burned alive—not in rare instances, but commonly. Mary Tudor, in her reign of five years, burned nearly three hundred men and women for their Protestantism (technically, heresy); Elizabeth executed almost the same number for their Catholicism (technically, treason).[13]

The fires of Smithfield and other places of execution burned deep into the awareness of sixteenth- and early seventeenth-century English people, as did the terror, theatrically enhanced, of public, celebratory hangings and quarterings. John Foxe's vast martyrology *Actes and Monuments of . . . the great persecutions & horrible troubles that have bene wrought and practised by the Romishe Prelates . . .* (1563, reprinted four times before 1600) was one of the most popular publications of the era. By 1684 some ten thousand copies had circulated, more than any other book except the Bible. It conveyed to generations of Protestants the fearful physical agonies, the tortures and persecutions, suffered by those who were loyal to their faith. The tale of Archbishop Cranmer recanting his earlier repudiation of Protestantism by putting his offending hand first into the fire so that "all the people might see it burnt to a coal before his body was touched" was the most famous, though not the most lurid, of the stories of martyrdom Foxe told in his 2,500 folio pages.[14]

2

It was from this advanced, modernizing world, still in many ways close to its medieval origins, that the first English colonists in North America were drawn. They were sent by the Virginia Company, one of the most ambitious of the enterprises in the burst of colonizing activity that followed the end of the Spanish war in 1604. A supervisory, guild-like organization, the company was chartered by the Crown to oversee the work of two investment groups formed to explore the east-coastal regions of North America for commercial possibilities, to set up trading stations at strategic points, and to discover access routes to the Pacific Ocean and the Far East. One group, agents of West Country gentry investors, sailed to the northern region, "Norumbega," built a small fort at the mouth of the Kennebec River in Maine, and began trading with the natives. A severe New England winter, Indian attacks, dissension within the leadership, and a disastrous fire destroyed that enterprise within a year.[15]

The second group, 104 passengers on three small vessels, were agents and employees of a syndicate of London merchants and their affiliates, major figures in late Elizabethan overseas commerce, who had taken over the rights to Raleigh's abandoned settlement in the "Roanoke" region to the south and were intent on reviving it. After a troubled, quarrelsome, grimly protracted voyage of thirteen weeks, the three ships finally entered the broad expanse of Chesapeake Bay, then turned into the mouth of the James River, and began, warily, a slow reconnaissance into the unknown and mysterious interior of the land along that narrowing stream.

They were a strange lot, these early English settlers in North America—not a cohort of settling immigrants but a band of adventurous gentlemen, younger sons of distinguished families, drawn to what seemed a fascinating adventure in an exotic land and a possible source of personal gain and national prestige, together with a small group of veteran soldiers of fortune and a contingent of artisans and laborers. Of sixty-eight arrivals in this first shipment to Virginia whose names survive in the records, thirty-seven were either gentlemen or military and maritime "captains." Only twenty-seven were identified as artisans, laborers, and "boyes." The status and high-level connections of the leaders were remarkable. Among the gentlemen were George Percy, brother of the Earl of Northumberland, then imprisoned for involvement in the Gunpowder Plot, and closely connected with Sir Walter Raleigh and his adviser, the scientist, linguist, and explorer Thomas Hariot, who had participated in the settlement at Roanoke in 1585 and written the first account of the region's people, flora, and fauna; John Martin, son of the Lord Mayor of London and Master of the Mint, and brother-in-law of the highest law lord, the Master of the Rolls; and three members of the Gosnold family, prosperous Suffolk and Essex landowners and London lawyers, related to the Virginia Company's merchant financiers and connected both to Richard Hakluyt, the geographer and colonial promoter, and to the family of Sir Francis Bacon, king's counsel, later attorney general and Lord Chancellor.[16]

They were forerunners of other members of highly placed, gentle or noble families who would follow to the obscure, often miserable riverside

George Percy

colony in the years directly ahead. Among those who appeared in Virginia in the next dozen years were four sons of Thomas West, Second Baron De La Warr and his wife, a first cousin, once removed of Queen Elizabeth; Christopher Davison, the son of Queen Elizabeth's secretary, William Davison, MP and privy councilor; Sir Francis and Haute Wyatt, sons of substantial Kent gentry and grandsons of Thomas Wyatt, who had led the rebellion of 1554 against Queen Mary; George Sandys, the exceptionally well-educated and well-traveled son of the Archbishop of York and brother of Sir Edwin Sandys, a man of great influence in London who would become governor of the Virginia Company; George Thorpe, a former MP and Gentleman of the Privy Chamber, as deeply invested in Virginia property as he was in the conversion of the Indians; and John Pory, another former MP and official in several embassies in Europe and the Near East, whose services as an "intelligencer" disseminating news and up-to-date information would prove as valuable in Virginia as they had been in London.

George Sandys

Well connected, these adventurers of the upper gentry and aristocracy were educated and sophisticated. Davison, like Martin trained in the law, was a poet in a family of poets. Thorpe was a "student of Indian views on religion and astronomy." Francis Wyatt wrote verses and was something of a student of political theory. Alexander Whitaker, MA, author of *Good Newes from Virginia* (1612), was the worthy heir "of a good part of the learning of his renowned father," the master of St. John's College and Regius Professor of Divinity at Cambridge. Pory, MA, who would become the speaker of Virginia's first representative assembly, "protege and disciple of Hakluyt," a translator from Italian and Arabic and formerly a teacher of Greek in Cambridge University, assured his patron, in a letter from Virginia sprinkled with Latin, that "nexte after my penne," in "the solitary uncouthnes of this place," he was determined "to have some good book alwayes in store" and begged for copies of the publications he was missing. And George Sandys, a member of Lord Falkland's literary circle, continued, while in Virginia, to work on his translation of Ovid's *Metamorphoses*.[17]

In the first years of Virginia's European history these representatives of England's affluent intelligentsia would explore the Indians' world, report on it, attempt to understand it and to conceive ways of exploiting it. And they would naturally attempt to assume leadership roles in the colony appropriate to their status. But in the first, desperate years of the colony's founding, they were not the sole governors. The colony's officially designated governing council included men of a different kind: tough, experienced soldiers of fortune who had volunteered for, or were drawn into, this open-ended project in search of employment, adventure, and ultimately perhaps exotic riches. They would discover adventure enough, but for most of them, as for most of the entire first generation of Englishmen in Virginia, instead of fame and fortune they would find early graves in the tidewater land.

The freebooting style of these soldiers of fortune, all of them war veterans, "headstrong, giddy, and insubordinate," their abrasive egos, and their explosive tempers, set them apart in the history of English colonization. It is less surprising that the annals of their sojourn in America record endless turmoil and conflict—that they were hopelessly improvident and constantly engaged in quarrels among themselves and in deadly warfare with the natives—than that the settlement they led survived at all.

Nothing, for example, in the early career of Capt. George Kendall promised a tranquil contribution to overseas settlement. A veteran of seven years of warfare in the Low Countries, five times wounded, he had a zest for intrigue, having served as one of Lord Salisbury's spies among the continental Catholics plotting to subvert England's Protestant regime, and he was probably at the same time informing on the English for Spain. As one of the seven appointed councilors in the initial settlement of Virginia, he was no less an intriguer. He plunged into the plots and counterplots that soon distracted the colony's leadership, was suspected of planning to desert the colony or defect to the Spanish, and was convicted of mutiny and perhaps treason. Six months after the ships' arrival he was executed by gunshot on order of a drumhead tribunal.

The fleet's "vice-admiral," Capt. Christopher Newport, had no less adventurous and rough a background. He had sailed with English free-

THE PORTRAICTUER OF CAPTAYNE IOHN SMITH / ADMIRALL OF NEW ENGLAND .

Ætat 37.
A° 1616

These are the Lines that shew thy Face; but those
That shew thy Grace and Glory, brighter bee :
Thy Faire-Discoueries and Fowle-Over throwes
Of Salvages, much Civilliz'd by thee⸗
Best shew thy Spirit; and to it Glory Wyn;
So, thou art Brasse without, but Golde within .

JOHN SMITH

He may seem "Brasse without," Smith tells his viewers, but he is "Golde within"—and a discoverer and civilizer of "Salvages."

booters to Brazil, joined Sir Francis Drake as an apprentice in his famous raids on Spanish vessels and territories, served for years as a captain of privateering vessels, lost his right arm, or hand, in a firefight with Mexican treasure ships, and then continued in a long career of plundering off the coasts of north and west Africa and in the Caribbean. An expert in assaults on Spanish American coastal towns, he was a prize employee for the London merchants who turned from privateering to commercial investments and overseas enterprises when the Spanish war ended. As "a mariner well practised for the westerne parts of America," the grizzled Newport was an obvious choice to command the Virginia fleet of 1606.

The key organizer behind much of that project, linking the lure of exotic exploration with commercial enterprise, was Capt. Bartholomew Gosnold, senior to the two other Gosnolds aboard the vessels of 1607 and another former privateer. Drawing on the contacts of his well-connected family, stimulating particularly the interest of his powerful kinsman, Sir Thomas Smith, governor of the East India Company as well as of the Virginia Company, Gosnold, who had led an exploratory voyage to New England in 1602, brought together the "first movers" of the enterprise, principally his elegant cousin, Edward Maria Wingfield—one of the company's original patentees, a veteran of wars in Ireland and the Netherlands—and a recent acquaintance, Capt. John Smith.[18]

The exploits of that extraordinary soldier of fortune, as Smith himself related them, were so wildly flamboyant, so bombastic and improbable, that generations of historians would later dismiss them as fiction. But we now know that his autobiographical accounts, though boastful and fancifully embroidered, are largely accurate. It is true, as he said, that as a teenager, having schooled himself in the art of war, he had fought against the Spanish in the Low Countries, thereafter had seen service in France, toured the Mediterranean on a piratical merchant vessel, and finally had joined the Austrian forces fighting the Turks. In Transylvania he had killed and perhaps had beheaded three Turkish officers in dramatic jousting duels (a feat he later blazoned on his coat of arms), was captured and enslaved by the Turks, but after noting carefully the way of life of the Turks, he managed to escape by murdering his owner with a threshing bat, and then made his way back to western Europe via Russia, Poland, and the German and Czech lands. Failing to find further military employment either in Europe or North Africa, he returned to England in 1604 where, through Gosnold, he was caught up in the plans for the colonization of Virginia.

Courageous, exuberant, imaginative, impatient, ruthless, highly articulate, fiercely resentful of privileged authority, and endlessly ambitious, Smith was destined to struggle for leadership, to succeed in command of dangerous situations, and to trample on everyone's sensibilities in the process. Before the initial voyage to Virginia was half over, in the cramped quarters of the pitching and rolling *Susan Constant*, he had come to despise the refinements and presumptions of the shipboard aristocrats like Percy and Wingfield, whom he knew to be incompetent, and to dispute the authority of the fleet commander, Newport. Fearful that his abrasive and insubordinate ways would lead to serious trouble—he might "usurpe the government, murder the Councell, and make himselfe Kinge"—the expedition's leaders arrested him for mutiny and restrained him "as a prisoner." They released him on landing, despite their belief that he was, as Percy wrote, "an ambitious[,] unworthy[,] and vayneglorious fellowe, attempteinge to take all mens authoreties from them . . . and ingrose all authorety into his owne hands." But it would be he, in the few months of his ascendancy in Jamestown, who saved the colony from utter collapse, and it would be he who would secure for posterity a triumphalist interpretation of the colony's founding and of his role in it, in his *True Relation* (1608) and his *Generall Historie of Virginia* (1624).[19]

3

Such were the founders of 1607. The story of their fortunes and of those who would follow them until the colony was abandoned in 1610 begins with the instructions and advice issued by the company's directors to the expedition's leaders. The instructions were logical and reasonable, but they bore little relation to reality in Virginia and compounded the chaos that the settlers struggled to survive.

First, they were told, if you have a choice of rivers to follow into the interior, choose the one "which bendeth the most towards the northwest, for that way shall you soonest find the other sea." Choose a fertile, wholesome, and secure place to settle, clear of surrounding forests, preferably as far up the river as a barque of fifty tons will sail—or if possible, one hundred miles from the entrance. If the natives turn out to be "blear eyed and with swollen bellies and legs," the place is unhealthy; if "the naturals be strong and clean made it is a true sign of wholesome soil." Leave a small crew at the river's mouth with a light boat, to warn the main settlement of impending trouble, and clear the intervening area of the natives, for no matter what you do, "they will grow discontented with your habitation" and will assist any invaders who plan to assault your settlement.

The main object, the company wrote, was to discover the source of whatever river they entered. If it proves to be a lake, it might give access to "the East India Sea," for it was well known that the famous Volga, Don, and Dvina rivers fall from a single source into three different seas. As to the "naturals," try not to offend them, and be sure to trade for food before they realize "you mean to plant among them." Take care that native guides not lose you in the wilderness, and if you have to shoot them, choose your best marksmen, for if you miss "they will think the weapon not so terrible and thereby will be bould." And never let them know that any of your people are killed or become sick lest "they perceive they are but common men." Build public facilities before private, and set the houses in straight lines off a central marketplace so that by a few centrally located "feild pieces you may command every street." And "lastly and cheifly," devote yourselves to "the good of your country and . . . serve and fear God the giver of all goodness."[20]

Pious thoughts were probably far from the minds of the adventurers as they made their first contacts with the land and its people. They sailed slowly and cautiously around the entrance of Chesapeake Bay, probing for a channel into the James River. Exploring short distances inland, they found an exceptionally attractive terrain: "faire meddowes and goodly tall Trees," George Percy reported, fresh water that "ravished" them, and such oddities as "fine and beautifull Strawberries, foure times bigger and better than ours," and near still-smoldering campfires they came on "Mussels and Oysters, which lay on the ground as thicke as stones," some of which, Percy reported, contained pearls, and they came on a forty-five-foot-long "cannow . . . made out of the whole tree." Everything was exotic, much was unimaginable. Especially the people.[21]

At the outset they were intrigued and puzzled by the people they found. They fitted none of the main stereotypes. As the first exploratory group was returning to their ship they were attacked by Indians who crept "from the Hills like Beares, with their Bowes in their mouthes," but their arrows had little effect and they withdrew when the English fired their muskets. Some sign-language communication with a few stray Indians on the north shore of the river led to what they took to be an invitation to visit a nearby village, Kecoughtan. There they were treated to a feast of strange food and honored by a performance of singing and dancing ("shouting, howling, and stamping against the ground, with many anticke tricks and faces, making noise like so many wolves or devils"). It was the first of several ceremonial meetings as they rowed and sailed deeper into the land, and came on Indian villages, strange at first sight, with which they were soon to become intimately familiar.

Passing the site of what would become Jamestown, they came to the village of Paspahegh, where they were welcomed, and treated to a long oration by the chief—the *werowance*—which no one could understand but which all felt was impressive. There, a rival chief from across the river arrived, to show his displeasure at this dalliance with the Paspaheghs. He invited the strangers to his own village, Quiyoughcohannock, and there they were startled by the fantastic appearance of the chief in full dress. They marveled at his headdress of red deer's hair and a copper crown, at his body painted crimson and his face solid blue with silver flecks, and at his ears hung with pearls and bird's claws. He moved solemnly, they reported, with "great majestie," and he entertained the visitors "in good humanitie."

But by then they realized, as they continued their slow exploration, that they were likely to be caught up in Indian rivalries, and that they would inevitably face violent hostility. At Appomattoc, deeper inland, near the present Petersburg, "many stout and able savages" armed with bows and arrows and also with swords or clubs "beset with sharp stones and pieces of yron able to cleave a man in sunder," confronted them, blocked their passage, but then relented "and let us land in quietnesse." But the threat was clear, and they turned back.

Five days later, drifting back downstream, they finally selected the site for their settlement. It was a narrow, two-mile-long peninsula of swampy land about sixty miles inland from the mouth of the river, connected to the shore by a sandbar that could easily be blocked. The water at the outer edge was deep enough for ships to dock against the shore and tie up to the nearby trees. They called this quasi-island Jamestown, and on May 14, 1607, they unloaded their men and equipment, threw together tents and huts behind a brushwood barrier, and set about building "a triangular palisade of posts, rails, and poles, with bulwarks at the corners where cannon were mounted."[22]

4

The three years that followed was a period of violent dissension within the tiny palisaded settlement, confusion of purpose, physical devastation, and the emergence of a permanent pattern of race conflict. Death was everywhere.[23]

When the settlers opened their instructions they discovered that they were to be governed by an appointed council of seven—Newport, when he was in residence, Gosnold, Wingfield, and Captains Martin, Kendall, Smith, and Ratcliffe, the last a tempestuous veteran of the Low Countries' wars. Wingfield was elected president, and the rivalries and disagreements began. By September Wingfield, arrogant, pompous, and incompetent, had stirred up a storm of opposition and was deposed; a "jury" condemned him to pay heavy damages for his offenses. His successor, Ratcliffe, who had led the opposition, was no more successful; he too was deposed. Factions within the small leadership group continued, forming and re-forming; the councilors bickered, competed for domination, and sent to England for support. Orders from designated and insecure leaders with no natural or legal authority would not be obeyed.

Partly the confusion was generated by conflicts of purpose. Some struggled vainly to fulfill the company's mandate to find the transmontane passage to the South Sea, to locate deposits of gold or other valuable commodities, to find the survivors of Raleigh's Roanoke venture, and to establish—by force if necessary—the legal sovereignty of the English Crown over whatever native "princes" could be found. But others—led by Smith—insisted on providing first for the settlement's long-term survival by building secure fortifications and housing, planting crops, and establishing reliable trading relations with the Indians or coercing them into supplying the colonists' basic needs.

In the best circumstances these conflicts would have threatened the survival of the settlement, but the circumstances could hardly have been worse. The settlers had arrived at the peak of an extended drought in the lower Chesapeake region, which in itself, for natives and immigrants alike, created poor harvests that led to famine conditions, a toxic water supply, and a devastating disease environment.[24] The summer was hot and their English clothes were no more suitable for the damp heat than for the winter that followed. Their supplies, much of them consumed by Newport's sailors who remained for eight weeks, ran out. The daily rations in the small riverside fort were soon reduced to "a small can of barlie sod [soaked] in water to five men." The beer was quickly consumed, and the river water they were forced to drink was salty and putrid: "full of slime and filth, which was the destruction of many of our men." For months their only shelters were tents and light lean-to shacks. They slept on bare ground. There were outbreaks of dysentery, typhus, salt poisoning, and nutritional-deficiency diseases.[25]

By August, three months after the expedition's arrival, the settlers in their small encampment were facing annihilation. The indispensable and inspirational organizer Bartholomew Gosnold died on August 22, one of dozens whose names George Percy recorded despondently day after day—victims, he explained, "of the bloudie flixe . . . of the swelling . . . of a wound"—in sum, of many "cruell diseases . . . and by Warrs . . . but for the most part they died of meere famine." The groans "in every corner of the fort [were] most pittifull to heare," he wrote; it made one's heart "bleed to heare the pittiful murmurings and out-cries of our sick men." Some fled to the Indians to avoid starvation, but soon straggled back from that strange world. For six weeks, until some relief came in from the Indians, three or four died each night, and "in the morning their bodies [were] trailed out of their cabines like dogges to be buried." By September, 46 of the 104 settlers had died, and among the survivors there were not 6 able-bodied men. By January 2, 1608, when Newport arrived back from England in one of the two vessels of the "first supply," only 38 were still alive—and only barely alive.[26]

Newport brought with him, in this first relief shipment, 120 new settlers, again a mixture of adventurous gentlemen (33) and employee-laborers. Among them, however, reflecting the London Company's rising expectations stirred by Newport's enthusiasm, were not only six tailors and two apothecaries but eleven artisan specialists, among them a jeweler, two goldsmiths, two "refiners" (to make assays of the gold and other precious materials that the investors expected to find), a perfumer, a surgeon, a gunsmith, and a "tobacco-pipe-maker." The newcomers outnumbered the survivors of 1607 almost four to one and would in any case have had difficulty cramming themselves into such shelters as existed. But even that was denied them when, three days after their arrival, the entire fort and all but three of the shelters within it, together with all the supplies and ammunition, were destroyed by fire.[27]

Many of the relief supplies Newport had carried with him were consumed by his sailors, who remained in and around Jamestown for four-teen weeks. When in April the second vessel of the "first supply" arrived with thirty more settlers, conditions were only slightly better, and in October a "second supply," again led by the shuttling Newport, arrived with seventy passengers. This time Newport had with him, besides the usual gentlemen and laborer-employees, two women and eight "Dutch-men" and Poles, hired to build a glassworks and to produce pitch, tar, and potash. At that point the population may have reached two hun-dred, and John Smith had become president of the Council, successor to Ratcliffe.[28]

By then, thanks mainly to Smith, much more was known about the land they had invaded and about its native peoples than had been known before, but very little of the news was hopeful for the success of the com-pany or the survival of the colony.

Seeking fresh food supplies, knowledge of the Indians, and possible routes north and west, Smith set out on a series of explorations, roaming first west along the James to the Falls, near the site of the present city of Richmond, beyond which he discovered not a mountain leading to the South Sea but the threatening Monocans, deadly enemies of the coastal tribes with whom the English were attempting to establish useful rela-tions. He then went north, overland, a short distance, to capture desper-ately needed corn supplies from the semi-independent Chickahominies, and followed the Chickahominy River to its sources. In early 1608 he led a further series of expeditions up into Chesapeake Bay, reaching north to Delaware and southern Pennsylvania. At that point he encountered the Susquehannocks, whose iron tools and weapons, Smith realized, could only have come from French Canada, and he learned about their fear of enemies pressing down on them from the northwest.

Having penetrated that far north—almost three hundred miles from Jamestown—Smith turned west and south, crossing the upper Potomac River beyond the site of present-day Washington, where he tangled dangerously with groups of Rappahannock warriors. Returning south, with his barge now ringed with protective shields of tightly woven reeds, he ended his explorations with a tour of the south shore of the James River, before returning to the fort, to begin his year-long, controversial term as president of the resident Council.[29]

He had traced a huge circle west, north, and south of the Jamestown settlement and discovered the geographical boundaries and contours of

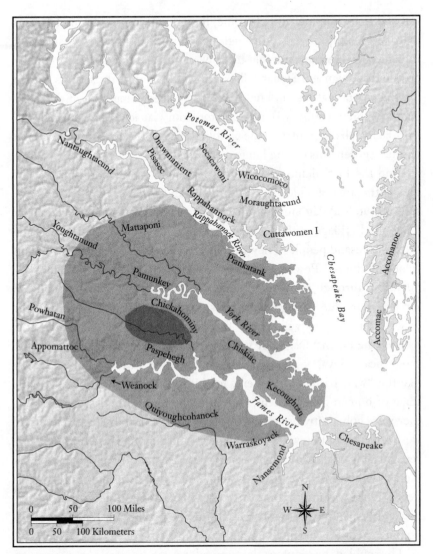

Tsenacommacah—the center of the Powhatan chiefdom. The independent Chickahominy tribe is shown in dark shading.

the tidewater region that the Virginia Company had entered, stretching from south of the James River north to the Potomac and from the Atlantic coast west to the Piedmont. He knew that neither the sources of the coastal rivers he had found—the James, York, Rappahannock, and Potomac—nor of Chesapeake Bay itself, lay in mountain lakes whose western outlets would flow into the South Sea. He had learned that the entire coastal lowland, and especially its tidewater edge, was fertile in its soil and rich in animal and plant life, though not in precious metals, and that it was easily traversed through its intricate network of streams and Indian trails. He knew too that there were human boundaries, formed by hostile Iroquoian and Siouan tribes that would confine the settlers as they did the coastal natives, and he therefore grasped something of the great demographic pressure system reaching from Canada south through the Appalachian backcountry to the Carolina coastal region that enclosed the obscure settlements on the James.

And the local demographic environment was now unmistakable. In the central area of Tidewater Virginia he knew there was a scattering of several hundred Algonquian villages, organized into some thirty chief-doms, each village with less than one hundred souls, totaling perhaps fifteen thousand people. They were led, with imperfect authority, by the "chief of chiefs," Powhatan and his warrior brother Opechancanough, operating through subordinate chiefs from whom tribute and military service were due. And Smith knew that Jamestown's survival would depend on the goodwill or the forceful subjection of these tidewater natives, the Powhatans. They were, he knew, in no way like the sophisti-cated Incas, Maya, or Aztecs; nor were they utterly savage and barbarous like the "wild Irish." They were, for him, primitive pagans at an early stage of human development, culturally inferior to the last degree. But they were coherently organized for civil and political discourse, and they were effective in the warfare they knew. Their mores were primitive but recognizably civil, if in some ways mysterious, and they understood com-merce, within their own value system, and could be useful trading part-ners when it was in their own interest. But Smith was never in doubt of his, and his people's, superiority and the inevitability of their successful dominance of Powhatan's empire.[30]

Untroubled by doubts, determined to subordinate the natives to English rule, and driven by the fear that the Jamestown settlement faced annihilation, Smith swept into the Powhatans' world like a tor-nado, beginning a campaign to extract from the natives, themselves on short supply, sufficient food to keep the settlers alive.[31] The Powhatans in turn tried to assess his purposes and the benefits and dangers he and the other Englishmen might bring. They had dealt with threatening incur-sions before, especially from harassing border tribes raiding from north and west, and they knew of Spanish threats in the south and of vague dangers from the remnants of the Roanoke settlement closer to hand.

Their fear was not simply that they might face brutal attacks but, in a deeper sense, that the equilibrium of their lives would be permanently upset, subject to shattering disturbances. Their response was not only to defend themselves but to retaliate in ways that would restore the balance of their lives. They would return violence for violence, but they did not need or seek the annihilation of their enemies. Their wars were rarely genocidal. What they fought for, however savagely and cruelly, was the restoration of the equilibrium of forces, human and spiritual, that formed the inner stability of their world. The English, whose mere presence was disbalancing and whose designs were unknown, would have to be tested and constrained—not destroyed, for their goods were peculiarly valuable, but contained within and subordinated to the larger native system.[32] For Powhatan himself, the need to contain the intruders was especially urgent. He was tormented by his priests' prophecy that his rule would one day be ended by people invading from Chesapeake Bay, and he was determined at all costs, and in any way he could think of, to keep this from happening.[33] The English too did not seek destruction for its own sake. They would be content with accommodation, so long as they were free to plant, to explore, and to exploit independently with the natives contained within and subordinated to England's larger system.

Two episodes, minuscule events in a confused world, seemingly mere curiosities in the bloody struggles for survival, reveal the mutuality, the parallelism, of hopes and expectations, reasonable in themselves but that would prove to be contradictory, ultimately the source of bitter conflict.

Late in 1607 Smith, on a foraging trip with two companions, was captured by Opechancanough. After several weeks of marches and countermarches and obscure ceremonial maneuvers, Smith, despite establishing his magical power by displaying his compass and demonstrating the effect of written communication, was brought before Powhatan, the first Englishman to meet the dominant chief face-to-face. By then elderly, the dominant chief was still impressive. "Of a tall stature, and cleane lymbes," William Strachey wrote, "he hath bene a strong and able saluadge, synowie, active, and of a daring spirit, vigilant, ambitious, subtile to enlarge his dominions." His cruelty had served, Strachey noted, "to stryke a terrour and awe" even into his loyal subordinates.[34]

In three days of elaborate ceremony and elusive conversation, fending off Powhatan's question of the colonists' purpose in settling, Smith was urged, on behalf of his people, to acknowledge Powhatan "as their lord" and to accept for himself the role of a subordinate chief. This, of course, to the extent that he understood the proposal, he ignored, but in the end, symbolically at least, he had no choice. After being feasted "in their best barbarous manner" and treated like a defeated enemy about to be slain, he was brought to what appeared to be an execution block, surrounded by warriors "ready with clubs to beate out his braines." Then at the final moment he was suddenly released, and he thereby, in the Indians' eyes, symbolically entered a new life, adopted as a subordinate *werowance*, and by extension his people were symbolically enclosed within the constraints of Powhatan's regime. Never, of course, experiencing these events as acts of subordination, and declining the benefits offered, Smith recorded the story of his captivity at first briefly and with little drama (he "procured his owne liberty"), then elaborated it in retelling, finally embellished it as an elaborate ceremony centered on the tale of how Pocahontas "the King's dearest daughter" (who was eleven at the time) "got his head in her armes, and laid her owne upon his to save him from death."[35]

The parallel effort to subordinate and control barbarous and threatening people, at least symbolically, was played out reciprocally by the English the next year. Smith and Newport, on orders from London, led a troop of musketeers to present Powhatan with a plethora of gifts, including copper objects, a bedstead and bedclothes, a red coat, and a copper crown, the last a gift heavily freighted with symbolism from the great King James. When with difficulty they managed to place the crown on Powhatan's forcibly bowed head, the ceremonial reduction of the chief of chiefs to the status of a vassal or local lord of King James was complete, symbolically confined within England's sovereign power.[36]

These were calm passages in a tumultuous sea of uncertainty and conflict. And there were others. Young boys were exchanged on both sides, to learn the languages, the "designs," and the ways of life of the other people. Thomas Savage, Samuel Collier, and Henry Spelman, entering into the lives of the "naturals," were expected to serve ultimately as interpreters of the Indians' languages and culture. Similarly Powhatan gave Newport his trusted Namontack, already a willing guide to the settlers; Newport took him to England and returned him with the "third supply." There were exchanges of food for gifts, and some of the celebrations that followed were so bounteous in food and so magnificent in body paint, costuming, and dance that the articulate Smith confessed that he lacked the power to describe them.[37]

But the savage conflict that had begun in the first days intensified. Two weeks after the Jamestown settlement was established, two hundred warriors had assaulted the half-built fort, killing two and wounding ten. Only the guns on the docked vessels had kept the encampment from complete destruction. Random skirmishes to confine and contain the settlement had continued—attacks on exploring teams distant from the fort, ambushes of individuals working outside the palisades or wandering in the woods. The first two settlements outside Jamestown—at the Falls fifty miles upstream of Jamestown, and on an island in the Nansemond River at the mouth of the James—were attacked so severely that they had to be abandoned. Vulnerable settlers were spared nothing. A captured workman accompanying Smith on his journey to the Chickahominies was tortured to death in ways familiar to the Indians but not to Englishmen, despite their knowledge of terror-inducing public executions. At a leisurely pace, his extremities were cut off with mussel shells and tossed into the fire before him; he was flayed—the skin was torn from his face and head—then disemboweled while still alive; and finally burned to ashes. In the same way, before long, would the cantankerous Captain Ratcliffe meet his death.[38]

Smith, in his Elizabethan love of drama and pageantry, may have relished the feasts and ceremonies, but most of his contacts with the natives were ruthless raids on their villages to extract corn and other supplies for the starving settlers. When his demands were not met, he threatened murder, took hostages at gunpoint, "negotiated" by intimidation, and without hesitation seized from the natives precious supplies that were necessary for their tribes' survival. Believing the Indians to be inherently barbarous, he attributed to them deceits and plots they did not have and provoked them in ways they did not understand.

So on one foraging raid, after laying out his demands for food in high-blown speeches, Smith realized that he and his men were outnumbered and likely to be ambushed. To head that off and gain coveted corn supplies, he challenged Opechancanough, as years earlier he had his Turkish adversaries, to a personal duel, the two of them to fight on equal terms ("my body shall bee as naked as yours") on an island in the river. "Our game," he later recalled of the "plaine tearmes" he offered the Indian, who was probably less fearful than bewildered, "shall be, the conquerour take all." When nothing came of this, he simply grabbed the warrior chief "by his long locke," jammed a pistol into his chest, and assured the surrounding warriors, in another florid oration, that if they "shed one drop of bloud of any of my men" he would not only kill their chief on the spot but wipe out every living soul of their "nation." "You promised to fraught [freight] my ship ere I departed," he declared, "and so you shall, or I meane to load her with your dead carcasses." The threat subsided, and Smith obtained the supplies he had come for.[39]

5

By such means a marginal survival was preserved, reinforced by the arrival in August and October 1609 of a contingent of the "third supply"— probably around three hundred people, who were part of a storm-tossed complement of five hundred, the remnants of whom would finally assemble in Virginia a year later.[40] But the newcomers were destined to suffer through one of the worst episodes in Anglo-American history. They arrived toward the end of Smith's presidency of the Council (1608–9), which had seen some promising improvements. The fort at Jamestown was restored and reinforced; a church and some houses were built; thirty to forty acres of the island were planted; a glassworks was constructed nearby; timber was cut up into clapboards for shipment home; some tar, pitch, and soap ashes were made; pigs and chickens were deposited on Hog Island, five miles below Jamestown, and were beginning to multiply; and the two auxiliary settlements—west at the Falls and east on Nansemond Island—were provided with garrisons and some supplies.

But when Smith left for England in October 1609 the signs, as winter approached, were ominous. Indian attacks were multiplying, the outer settlements were destroyed, and stragglers, foragers, and exploring parties were routinely killed. Supplies for the expanded population dwindled, especially after rats devoured much of the corn reserve. Diseases continued to ravage the settlers. Several of the "Dutchmen" assigned to build a house for Powhatan created great confusion by deserting to the Indians and abandoning the glass furnace. Above all, despite Smith's stringent rule that only those who worked would eat, most of the settlers remained what he called "distracted lubberly gluttons" who would trade everything they had for some of the Indians' food rather than pitch in to life-sustaining labor.[41]

Besieged over an especially bitter winter by a tightening ring of hostile Indians, the Jamestown band, in Percy's phrase, began to feel the "sharpe pricke of hunger." The scene within the palisades grew desperate. As the weeks passed the survivors were forced to eat the horses, then, Percy recorded, "vermin as doggs[,] Catts[,] Ratts[,] and myce"—even eventually "Bootes[,] shoes[,] or any other leather some Co[u]lde come by." Those who found starch left in their ruffs, Smith wrote, "made a gluey porridge of it." Frantic men robbed the storehouse; they were caught and executed for their crime. Grubbers searching the nearby woods for edible snakes and roots were killed by arrow shots before they could return. Then the ultimate catastrophes began. A few of the "gastely and pale" inhabitants of the fort—we do not know how many—did "those things w[hi]ch seame incredible, as to digge upp deade corp[s]es outt of graves and to eate them . . . and some have Licked upp the Bloode w[hi]ch hathe fallen from their weake fellowes." And even beyond that, Percy wrote, one man murdered his wife, "Ripped the Childe outt of her woambe . . . Chopped the Mother in pieces and sallted her for his foode." Forced to confess "by torture haveinge hunge by the Thumbes w[i]th weightes att his feete a quarter of an howere," the murderer was executed. Many of those who "To eate . . . did Runn away unto the Salvages" fared no better: "we never heard of [them] after."[42]

By May 1610, when the remainder of the delayed flotilla of 1609, including the new interim governor, Sir Thomas Gates, finally arrived in Virginia, only sixty of the four hundred of the previous spring and summer were still alive, and they were, Percy wrote, "so leane thatt they looked lyke anotannes [skeletons], cryeinge owtt, We are starved, We are starved. Others goeinge to bedd as we imagined in healthe weare fownd deade the nexte morneinge." Gates was horrified by what he saw. Jamestown, he reported, appeared more like "the ruins of some auntient [for]tification" than a place living people might inhabit:

the pallisadoes . . . tourne downe, the portes open, the gates from the hinges, the church ruined and unfrequented, empty howses . . . rent up and burnt, the living not hable, as they pretended, to step into the woodes to gather other fire-wood.

The Indians were not even bothering to attack the protected blockhouse since they assumed the people within it would shortly perish.

And so they would have, if Gates had not rescued them. But he was experienced in the ways of survival (he had served on Drake's marauding expeditions and fought in the Dutch wars); he knew that the supplies he had would quickly be consumed, and he saw that no help would come from the natives. He therefore gathered up the remnants of the James-town community, loaded them together with his own people aboard his vessels, and after cautiously preventing the men from burning the rem-nants of the town to the ground ("we knowe nott butt that as honeste men as our selves may come and inhabitt here"), on June 10, 1610, "giv-ing a farewell with a peale of small shott," abandoned the Jamestown settlement.[43]

꙰

CHAPTER 3

The "Hammerours'" Regime

1

I T WAS no doubt a remarkable coincidence that Gates, moving down-stream with his rescue party and the survivors of Jamestown, met the advance boats of the rest of the delayed fleet of 1609, including the new governor, the third Baron De La Warr. But the three ships and a pin-nace then approaching—"w[i]th many gentlemen of quallety and thre hundrethe men[,] besydes greate store of victewles[,] municyon[,] and other p[ro]vissyon"—would in any case have reestablished the colony.[1] They—and two additional fleets that arrived a year later with more than five hundred men, women, and children—were the product of a basic restructuring and refinancing of the Company in London and of its stren-uous efforts at population recruitment. As a result, by 1618 Tidewater Virginia was transformed. Race relations were still not resolved—savage conflicts mingled with signs of accommodation—but the vague outline of a new civic order, based on an unexpected and still uncertain economy, had emerged after years of brutal coercion and social confusion.

THE POWER BEHIND the life-saving reinforcements that arrived in the fleet of 1609–10 was generated by the company's major investors, led by its governor, Sir Thomas Smith. That domineering merchant—at one time or another the governor or director of all the major overseas trading companies and some of the lesser—had led the Virginia Company of London from its inception. By 1609 Newport's and others' accounts of the internal squabbles in Jamestown and race conflicts in Virginia, together with the failure of the settlers to produce valuable goods or a new route to the Pacific, led Smith and his coinvestors to recast the entire venture. Their original idea of a fort, trading station, and base camp for exploration would never succeed. A permanent, self-supporting, and productive colony was needed, and they drew up plans to achieve it. The land would be owned by the company and worked by servants sent out and maintained at the company's expense. The company would have a complete monopoly of all marketing of goods shipped home and would establish a severely coercive regime in the colony to overcome any future factionalism and enforce an effective work regime.[2]

The success of all of this would depend, in the end, on the recruitment of labor. Company servants were needed in much larger numbers than before—and they had to be people of the right sort. "Idle and wicked persons," a company spokesman wrote, escaping from shame or fear, would ruin the place: they are "the weedes and ranknesse of this land who . . . must needes be the poison of [a new social body] so tender, feeble, and as yet unformed." The colonists would have to be responsible working people, "families, of wife, children and Servants, to take fast holde and roote in that land." Such a migration would not harm England by depletion. On the contrary, it would benefit the home country "by transplanting the rancknesse and multitude of increase in our people, of which there is left no vent but age, and evident danger that the number and infinitenesse of them will out-grow the matter whereon to worke for their life and sustentation, and shall one infest and become a burthen to another."[3]

Such recruitment would cost money and would require tight managerial control. The Company, therefore, in a chartered reorganization of 1609, was transformed from the earlier loose investment group under Crown supervision into an independent joint-stock corporation able to direct its own affairs and to solicit investments in the form of shares. Under the auspices of this new corporation, whose land grant was enlarged to stretch two hundred miles north and south of the mouth of the James and from the Atlantic to the Pacific, a short northern transatlantic route to Virginia was quickly charted; a well-educated soldier-politician, Lord De La Warr, "whose Honour nor Fortune needs not any desperate medicine," was chosen to serve as the all-powerful, "*absolute*" resident governor in chief; and a carefully detailed list of the kinds of people desired as settlers, their "faculties, arts and trades," was published.

Besides ordinary laborers and four "honest and learned ministers," artisans in thirty-three specified occupations were listed as necessary for the colony's success. The most urgently needed were sawyers, fishermen, and "iron men for the furnace and hammer": ten of each were required. Then came blacksmiths, carpenters, shipwrights, gardeners, fowlers, coopers, and vine-dressers—six of each; then turners, brickmakers, rope makers, pitch boilers, and "sturgeon dressers and preservers of the caveary [caviar]"—four each; and all the rest, including surgeons, druggists, "minerall men," "planters of sugar-cane," and "pearle drillers"—two each.[4]

To attract the investments needed to recruit such a population, transport it, and supply it until it could become self-sustaining and commercially profitable, the company issued a glittering prospectus—one of several that would follow—entitled *Nova Britannia*. It justified, morally and legally, England's claim to the land of North America; lavishly praised the richness of Virginia—an "earthly paradise"—and the immense profits that would flow from it; explained how the colony would contribute to England's growing greatness in the world; and offered specific incentives for investors and settlers. In a distribution of the company's assets after seven years, the pamphlet explained, stockholders, who would have voting rights in the company's general meetings, would receive, in addition to a prorated proportion of the company's profits, parcels of land in similar proportions. As for settlers, in an eventual land distribution "every individual, man or woman, and every child of twelve years and upwards," would receive the value in land of one share of stock; and "persons of extraordinary character"—officials, justices, knights, gentlemen, physicians, and others "who are able to render very special services to the colony"—would be given provisions to help them settle "in proportion to the quality of each one" and eventual dividends in profits and land "according to the amount at which their persons and their services were estimated."[5]

These enticements were broadcast throughout the nation. Every effort was made to raise capital. Former subscribers were dunned for renewals, and specific appeals were directed to the principal towns of England, to bishops, noblemen, and gentry, and to the Lord Mayor and livery companies of London. At first the campaign worked reasonably well. The

Thomas West, Third Lord De La Warr

company's new corporate charter, when issued in May 1609, listed as subscribers the names of 56 London companies and 659 individuals. In all, between 1609 and 1612 the company attracted 1,152 investors—ten times the number of subscribers to either the East India Company or the Levant Company in the same years. By 1611, £18,000 in subscriptions had been pledged, and it was this first flush of financial interest in the renewed Virginia enterprise that made possible the two rescue fleets of 1609 and 1610. The nine vessels in that flotilla were a sensation as they sailed, with more than six hundred people aboard, slowly out of the Thames.[6]

But the majority of the passengers aboard were far from the company's ideal. The flow of well-connected, adventurous men "of birth and quality" continued, but the company's efforts to recruit "sufficient, honest, and good artificers" still showed few results. The company had been obliged to solicit the magistrates of London and other cities to encourage some of their "swarme of unnecessary inmates" who otherwise "must lye in the streetes" to join the emigration. And indeed the majority of those who reported to Smith's office in Philpot Lane "to proffer their service in this action" were still of that "idle crue . . . of lascivious sonnes . . . bad servants . . . and ill husbands" who would "rather starve for hunger than lay their hands to labor." But in addition to these "unruly youths . . . of most leaud [lewd] and bad condition," casual laborers, rural vagrants, and urban drifters, there was added, by deliberate recruitment, a large contingent (perhaps as many as 150) of "old soldiers trained up in the Nether-lands" with experience in English military operations. Veterans not only of the Dutch wars but also of the savage campaigns in Ireland, typical of the plundering, half-vagabond troops of the time who were traded among commanders like cattle and whose service was likely to be cut short by death under degrading conditions, they would soon earn, in their time in Virginia, Hakluyt's description of them as "hammerours" who would know how to "prepare" the Indians for "our preachers' hands."[7]

2

With this unpromising mixture of "quality," unruly, idle vagrants, and combat veterans, De La Warr began his effort to rebuild the colony. He set out the rules of government and sent some men to fish, others to revive the neglected cornfields and gardens; he saw to it that Jamestown's church, palisades, and some of the houses and barracks were rebuilt. He also started the construction of two forts near the mouth of the James River and sent out expeditions to find provisions. In that, he was somewhat encouraged. The land, he found, was rich, and if the "mischeivous" Indians stood in the way of the company's harvesting the nearby grain fields, he would master them "ere long, and . . . thresh it out on the flores of our barnes when the time shall serve," for he was "irreconsilable" in recalling the Indians' "late injuries and murthering of our men." But the workers he had available, he wrote, were such "deboisht [debauched] hands . . . of such distempered bodies and infected mindes" that no example of goodness or threat of punishment "can deterr [them] from their habituall impieties or terrifie from a shameful death." In their apathy, bewilderment, and disorientation—driven to labor as they never had been before and under punishing physical conditions—they quickly succumbed to despair and disease. In the first six months after De La Warr's arrival, one-third of the settlers had sickened and died or were killed by the Indians.[8]

Conflict with the natives began almost immediately, when the governor demanded that Powhatan stop his attacks on the English settlements and that the warriors who had recently killed four settlers be punished or handed over, together with all captives and stolen arms. He was careful to remind the paramount chief that he was a subject of King James. When Powhatan ignored the message and ordered the English to remain confined in Jamestown or be killed, and when a captured soldier was tortured to death before his companions' eyes, conflict erupted and quickly escalated.[9]

DE LA WARR ORDERED Gates to take revenge on the Kecoughtans, which he did with guile and savagery. His soldiers, mimicking an Indian gesture of hospitality, lured the Kecoughtan villagers into the open with the piping, dancing, and drumming of a young taborer, then killed fourteen of the men, women, and children who had come out to watch, and looted their lodges and fertile maize fields. A month later De La Warr sent Percy and seventy men to avenge the Paspaheghs' failure to return arms and captives. Nothing and no one was spared. Percy's troops killed fifteen or sixteen natives on the spot, burned down the village houses, and destroyed the crops. Returning downriver with the tribe's "queen," her children, and a male Indian captive in tow, Percy, criticized by his troops for burdening them with these encumbrances, "cawsed the Indians heade to be Cutt of[f]," and then was persuaded by his troops to allow them to kill the children, which they did by throwing them overboard and "shotingge owt their Braynes in the water." The queen, for the time, was spared. After a foray inland to burn another village's houses and crops and to destroy their "Spacyous Temple, cleane and neatly kept" though it was, Percy arrived back in Jamestown, to be told that the governor was "discontente" because the queen had not been disposed of. De La Warr thought it best, Percy was told, "to Burne her." But "haveinge seene so mutche Blood shedd thatt day," Percy "desired to see noe more," and in any case, burning, he felt, was not "fittinge." He therefore decided that if the queen was to be murdered it should be "by shott or Sworde to give her a quicker dispatche." So Capt. James Davis, a remorseless "taskmaster" at the forts, took the woman into the woods and "putt her to the sworde." The next episode in the series of summer raids was an expedition north, to the Chickahominies, whose houses the attackers burned and whose corn they confiscated. Then, quickly turning back across the James, they did the same to a nearby tribe on the south side of the river.[10]

After these initial strikes, a troop of soldiers and some of the colony's miners were sent west in search of a river passage to the South Sea and the location of rumored mines. Far from their base and from possible reinforcements, they came under constant attack and were lured to a feast among the Appomattocs. There, unsuspecting, they were attacked and either slain or badly wounded. Only the drummer boy of the Kecoughtan raid escaped. The fighting escalated, and the atrocities multiplied. When De La Warr suspected that some natives visiting the Jamestown fort were spies, he "caused one to have his hands cutt of[f], and so sentte [him] unto his fellowes to geve them warneinge for attemptinge the lyke." By 1611 the conflict had taken on the aspects of a crusade, as religious fervor inflamed the already heated fears and passions. The Powhatans, for their part, appealed to their god of war, Okee, for support and for rescue from the fearful prophecy of extinction by an alien force from the east. The English, increasingly convinced that the natives were impelled by devilish spirits, attempted to redeem Christianity itself against "the gates of hel" and targeted especially "sathan's owne brood," the shamans, while tearing into the "temples" or whatever other religious manifestations they could find. But the Powhatans continued their deadly raids, celebrating their victories and mocking the cries of their tortured captives. Signs of mutiny appeared. When a group of miners was found to be conspiring to flee the colony, De La Warr promptly hanged the ringleader. But his effectiveness was weakening as his health deteriorated. When in March 1611 he became seriously ill, he left the colony, turning over control to Percy until the newly appointed deputy governor, Sir Thomas Dale, could join Gates in the new leadership.[11]

The devastation continued. Before that year was out, seven more vessels arrived on the James River with 630 newcomers, bringing the total immigration from the beginning of settlement to just over 1,500, but the total population was only 450. In 1612 at least 122 new arrivals can be identified; in 1613, 30; in 1614, 40; in 1615, 65. By 1616 approximately 2,000 people had arrived under the company's auspices, but the population had declined to 351.[12]

Small as it was, the English population in 1616 was scattered among

Sir Thomas Dale

several settlements and encampments. Dale, upon his arrival, attempted to combine the dirt-raw farms and nascent plantations into five main population centers along the James River, between the coast and the Falls. To realize this plan he moved the center of the colony inland, away from the swampy, vulnerable island of Jamestown to higher, more remote and safer ground. Fifty miles west of Jamestown, at what he called Henrico (near the later Richmond), he built a palisaded village complete with fort, storehouses, and a number of small houses. Three years later it had a few streets, the foundation of a substantial church, and a flourishing field of corn. Across the river from Henrico he established Coxendale, enclosing, within a palisade guarded by four corner towers, one hundred acres of high ground, on which, he hoped, would later be built a parsonage, a retreat, and an infirmary. Further, using traditional English designations in a very un-English setting, he founded several "hundreds" and two "cities." To the east, near Jamestown, he grouped together a cluster of small riverside clearings ("Diggs His Hundred," the Upper and the Nether Hundreds, Rochdale Hundred, and West's Shirley Hundred) to form a unit he called "Bermuda [later Charles] City." By 1616 Bermuda City, designed as "an impregnable retreat against any forraign invasion, how powerful so ever," contained 119 people and was the most active and productive center of the colony; it served at times as the colony's administrative headquarters. Then, at the mouth of the James River, he founded what he called "Elizabeth City," built out of the two rudimentary forts centered on the site of the Indians' Kecoughtan, which the natives had had to abandon. And across Chesapeake Bay, on the southern tip of the Eastern Shore, he set up an isolated fishing station which he named "Dale's Gift," together with a small salt works.[13]

3

While Dale sought to bring order into the scattering of new farms by clustering them into nominal communities, he directed his energies mainly to two other goals, for the attainment of which his military experience proved crucial. For he was, even more than others who had led the colony, a professional soldier. He had served in the Dutch wars, rising from the ranks to a captaincy; then fought in France under Henry IV; then in Ireland under the Earl of Essex; and finally again in the Netherlands, where he commanded an English company in Dutch service and was favored with a knighthood. In both Ireland and the Netherlands he had served together with Gates; at one point both were in active service with the future Lord De La Warr. Thus broadly connected with the Virginia promoters and strongly supported by his patron, Robert Cecil, Lord Salisbury, Dale was an obvious choice, in the company's reorganization of 1609, to be appointed the provost of the colony—that is, the military commander and in effect the chief of police—as well as deputy governor.[14]

His whole life having been spent in the military (he would die in Java in 1619, after leading a naval victory over the Dutch), Dale, like De La

Warr and Gates, believed that the problems Virginia faced could best be solved by military means. The company's instructions to the new governor and his deputies supported this idea. Not only were they given "full and absolute power and aucthority to correct, punishe, pardon, governe and rule" all the company's "subjects," agreeably with the laws and policies of England, but when faced with rebellion, mutiny, and cases of "necessity," they were to "proceede by martiall lawe," without bothering with "the nicenes and lettre" of ordinary English law, and in adjudication they were free to act on natural right and equity as a chancellor, rather than a judge, might do.[15]

With this mandate, the new leaders were determined to turn Virginia's ragged and often despairing "crue" of "disordered Persons, so prophane, so riotous, so full of mutenie and treasonable Intendments," into a disciplined workforce capable of sustaining and defending itself. To do this and to make profitable this wretched "parcell" of humanity, who had been snatched from "riotous, lasie [lazy] and infected places," whose bodies were now so "diseased and ill used" by sea and climate as to "render them unhable, fainte, and desperate of recoverie," they proceeded to devise a strict, quasi-military regime. Gates, upon his arrival, published a prepared set of thirty-seven regulations covering everything from attendance at church to murder, blasphemy, sodomy, slander, rape, illegal trade, "disgraceful words," unauthorized slaughter of animals, dumping of dirty laundry water and doing "the necessities of nature" close to the palisades, failing to keep houses and streets clean, running off to the Indians, failing to report to work "upon the beating of the drum," robbing gardens, stealing laundry, failing to pay debts, and falsifying weights and measures. The penalties for violations were severe. In eighteen cases the punishment was death; in the others, whipping, tying together of head and heels, branding, loss of ears, and a familiar but seldom used punishment for incorrigibles, who thereby became "slaves"—service in the galleys. That in fact there were no galleys in the American coastal waters and few in England was beside the point. The severity of punishment extended to the limits of punitive imaginings, and the propriety of using English criminals, army deserters, rogues, and vagabonds as galley slaves had recently been reiterated in English law.[16]

To Gates's rules Dale, as provost, added fifty-one provisions of the martial law, regulating every conceivable aspect of a soldier's life, violation of which in almost every case was to be punished by death. And Dale laid out in addition separate sets of detailed instructions for the behavior and duties of colonels, captains, ensigns, sergeants, corporals, and private soldiers. The whole compilation ended in an elaborate prayer to be delivered morning and evening by the captain of the watch or his deputy.[17]

The two together—Gates's civil regulations and Dale's drastic code of martial law—comprised the famous *Laws Divine, Moral, and Martiall*, which the company published in 1612. Though separated into the civil and military areas of life, in practice the *Laws* merged into a single body of draconian rules. Civilian settlers in this regime were to be, in effect, soldiers under military discipline; soldiers were to be workers—carpenters, sawyers, farmers, and fishermen—in the company's common cause.

This merging of soldiers and civilians and the use of degrading punishments were not unique. Martial law was used in other situations believed to be analogous to the settlement in Virginia—in England's most violent borderlands, Ireland and the Welsh and Scottish marches. And in England itself severe, degrading punishments were commonly used to discipline the unfree, the servile, the base dependents who lacked full legal rights and survived on the benevolence of others. So, conceiving of Virginia's "wretched and untoward people" as subject to the discipline of martial law and the familiar degradation of the unfree, it was no great leap for Dale to propose, as he did in a letter to Lord Salisbury, that the colony's servile population be supplemented by a cohort of truly degraded people: convicts under sentence of death.[18]

If somehow, Dale wrote Salisbury, he could get two thousand more men with supplies for six months, he would not only achieve all the company's goals but in addition take "full possession of Powhatan's countrie," which, cleared of its native population, would open up "many excellent seates for many a thowsand householders." Let the Crown, he wrote, send to Virginia all of England's convicts awaiting execution, and let that be continued for three years. There would be nothing unusual in that. That was the way, he believed, the Spanish were peopling the Indies, and one need not fear the results. Convicts condemned to death were not always "the worst kinde of men" in terms of "birth, spiritts, or bodie." And such reprieved convicts, unlike the present "crue" who grieved at being in Virginia, would welcome the chance to be there since they would be escaping with their lives, even though they had been justly condemned, and therefore would be happy "to make this their new countrie, and plant and inhabite herein with all diligence, cheerfullnes, and comfort."[19]

His appeal, which, when renewed in later years by others in different circumstances, would produce remarkable results (fifty thousand convicts would eventually be shipped to America), went unanswered. Gates and Dale proceeded with the people they had. Consistent with the goals of the *Laws*, they organized Virginia's population into companies "to be exercised and trayned up in martiall manner and warlike discipline." Each person was assigned specific duties, to be enforced by their company captains. People were to be called to work by drumbeat, leave their work by drumbeat, be led to church by drumbeat, and after prayers and a meal, be summoned again by drumbeat to work until evening prayers. And they were to be punished for infractions as specified in the *Laws*. How consistently or fully these drastic rules were enforced we do not know, but Percy's eyewitness account shows that Dale had no hesitation in putting some of the most severe of them into effect. A group of men, "idile and not willeinge to take paynes," attempted to desert to the Indians. When caught, some were "apointed to be hanged, some burned, some to be broken upon wheles, others to be staked, and some to be shott to deathe. All theis extreme and crewell tortures [Dale] used and inflicted upon them to terrefy the reste for attempteinge the lyke." And then, Percy grimly reported, there were those who robbed the supply store: Dale caused them "to be bownd faste unto trees and so sterved them to deathe."[20]

But there were limits to Dale's ferocity when directed to the English settlers since his ultimate aim was to preserve them and make their labor profitable. He was less limited in dealing with the Indians. His plan, he explained to Lord Salisbury, was to "over master the subtile-mischeivous Great Powhatan" in such a way as to establish English superiority beyond all doubt. He would allow the paramount chief "no roome in his countrie," leaving him with the choice of subordinating himself and his people to the English or seeking refuge in a "straunger countrie" among "the neighbour salvadges [now] confining him." No longer thinking, as Smith had done, simply of the desperate need for life-saving supplies, Dale, a participant in the ruthless slaughter of noncombatants in Ireland on the ground that "terrour . . . made short Warrs," launched a program of deliberate military provocation and savage harassment. His campaign to reduce the natives to the status of subject people and drive them off the most valuable lands was part of what has been called England's "First Anglo-Powhatan War (August 1609 to April 1614)." That series of bloody clashes, Frederick Fausz, the war's most careful analyst, writes, "translated England's *ad terrorem* tactics from the Irish wars of the late sixteenth century—specifically the use of deception, ambush, and surprise, the random slaughter of both sexes and all ages, the calculated murder of innocent captives, and the destruction of entire villages . . . [The attacks] neither discriminated between combatant and noncombatant victims nor between hostile and friendly tribes." Once launched, the struggles intensified, driven by atavistic impulses—by the natives' passion to maintain the right, hence moral, balance of existential forces and by the invaders' equally passionate belief in their right to dominate primitive, satanic peoples and take possession of their land.[21]

But in their desperate struggles with the Indians the English came to fear that they might be descending into the debased state of their enemies. The fear of a decline into barbarism, as the savagery increased, haunted them, and the more thoughtful among them sought to alleviate their fears. They were not bloodthirsty brutes like the Spanish, whose barbarism they knew from recent translations of Bartolomé de Las Casas—avaricious, murdering looters butchering their way through peaceful civil societies. Even Dale, in the midst of his most punitive raids, felt the need to distinguish his English warriors from Spanish predators and to keep his people free from the charge of hypocrisy, which would "give cause of laughter to the Papists who desire their ruin." However fierce their attacks, as humane Englishmen they were benefactors and parental guides to the benighted. Their aim was ultimately to bring these savage people out of darkness into light, to Christianize them for their own good, and to do this by force if need be. Force itself was not an evil, William Strachey, who witnessed the bloodshed of 1610–11, wrote in his *Historie of Travell into Virginia Britania*. A father is not barbarous if he beats his child "to bringe him to goodnes." What would have happened to the people of Britain, he asked, people as savage in their origins as the bloody Picts, if the Romans had not violently forced upon them civilized ways? "We might yet have lyved overgrowne Satyrs, rude and untutred, wandring in the woodes, and dwelling in Caves, and hunting for our dynners . . . prostituting our daughters to straungers, sacrificing our Children to our Idolls." So a civilizing end justified barbarous means.[22]

The need for some such rationale grew with the escalation of conflict. Analysis of the five-year war Gates and Dale pursued reveals twenty distinct encounters—skirmishes, ambushes, sieges, raids, and direct confrontations—in which at least 350 Englishmen were killed (a number

equivalent to almost 20 percent of all the immigrants between 1607 and
1614) and 250 Indians. The settlers' strike force of well-equipped combat
veterans began by attacking the least militant and weakest tribes within a
twenty-mile radius of Jamestown. Dale first sent an invincible contingent
of veteran musketeers east against the Nansemonds to secure access to
the James River once and for all. They decimated the band of native warriors that opposed them and again ravaged the land. He then sent an even
larger force once more to the west, this time finally to command beyond
dispute the area around Henrico and to penetrate past that point, to the
villages of the Appomattocs, whose fertile tribal lands seemed right for
seizure. The troops in the west were constantly beset by bands of bowmen,
but the "faceless mass of steel-coated musketeers moving methodically
against most targets at will" demoralized the natives and evoked ever
more direct appeals for spiritual and magical aid. One of their warriors,
whom the English called "Jack-of-the-Feathers," went into combat not
with the usual red and black body paint but in his own unique protective armor, which his people believed made him "shot-free": "all Covered over w[i]th feathers and Swans wings fastened unto his showlders as
thowghe he meante to flye." His luck, for the moment, held, but there
was no flight from the steady advances of the English.[23]

Having succeeded, however, in gaining these major goals and in creating terror among the Indians, Dale drew back in 1612–13 to secure his
victories and develop a strategy for the next moves. The English received
an unexpected advantage when, in March 1613, they captured Pocahontas and found her susceptible both to conversion to Christianity and to
John Rolfe's romantic, and missionary, interest. Meanwhile Dale and the
other leaders mobilized their forces for a conclusive invasion of Powhatan's heartland. In March 1614 an English flotilla sailed up the York River
directly into the core of Powhatan's "empire" and were poised to con-
front several hundred warriors protecting the inner home territory. The
two forces faced each other, menaced each other, and were at the edge of
attack when Dale drew back, confident that he had shown an intimidating
force and willing to defer an actual battle until the significance of Pocahontas's pending conversion to Christianity and her possible marriage to
Rolfe played themselves out. A truce was arranged when the marriage
actually took place, and it held, in the months that followed, well enough
to constitute an apparent peace.

Apparent, at best: it was an unstable arrangement of fragile compromises and basic misunderstandings. The English assumed that Powhatan's momentary willingness to tolerate the presence of a few hundred ruthless soldier-settlers constituted a willing subordination to and acceptance of future English immigration and the expansion of settlement. And they saw in Pocahontas's acceptance of Christianity the harbinger of mass conversion. The Indians believed that Dale's withdrawal was a significant victory for them; that they remained undefeated, their superiority maintained despite the slaughter of their people and the ravaging of their fields and villages; and that the "gift" of Powhatan's daughter to the English and their acceptance of her were, in a very traditional sense, a seal of agreement and a sign of peaceful intentions.[24]

Some kind of reciprocity had been achieved. But the Indians saw it as the end of a process; the English saw it as a beginning.

4

For the company in London, intent on populating their American estate to make it profitable, news of what appeared to be a victorious end of hostilities came when it was most needed. While Gates and Dale were clamping a rigorous work routine on the colony's settlers and while their "hammerours" were bringing devastation and terror to the Powhatans, the company's fortunes at home had badly declined. The embattled settlers had managed to send back some useful products—furs, timber, sassafras, soap ashes, silk grass—but only in small quantities and with no indication that a truly lucrative staple would be forthcoming that would satisfy investors. Stockholders, therefore, reluctant to send good money after bad, increasingly failed to pay the installments of their subscriptions, and new investors were hard to find.

By 1612 the company was in serious financial trouble and began to cast about for new departures to keep the enterprise afloat. At the same time, by a systematic evolution, a significant and permanent change was emerging from within the confusion of the settlements on the James. These new developments, in London and Virginia, converged to determine much of the future population history of the first permanent English colony in America.

In London, to stimulate the languishing finances of the company, Thomas Smith and his leadership group decided to take drastic measures. They would sue for the unpaid subscriptions, seek a public lottery to raise

funds, and reorganize the company's structure to give more power, hence
encouragement, to the ordinary stockholders. The organizational change
was formalized, in 1612, in a third company charter, which extended
the company's boundaries east into the Atlantic to include the Bermuda
islands, whose value had been assessed by the part of the fleet of 1609 that
had been shipwrecked there. To manage that part of the company's property a separately financed joint stock, subsidiary to the company's main
stock fund, was formed from among the company's investors.

But the company continued to find it almost impossible to replen-
ish the main stock fund. Lawsuits failed to force subscribers to pay their
installments, and the yields of the lotteries were disappointing, as were the
results of various experiments undertaken in the colony (to grow grapes,
oranges, pineapples, silkworms, and tobacco and to produce iron). Therefore Smith and his closest allies, especially his son-in-law, the powerful
London alderman Robert Johnson, having created the Bermuda group,
formed another subsidiary company that was virtually failure-proof. The
colonists had to eat and be clothed, armed, and otherwise equipped, and
they would pay anything for those supplies. Therefore a separate joint
stock company for the sole purpose of supplying the colonists, in exchange
for a monopoly of whatever trading goods were returned, would surely
turn a profit. The Magazine, as it was called, hiving off from the parent
company for the benefit of its separate investors but still legally within
the parent company, proved to be a model for a broad range of ad hoc
subsidiaries—especially small partnerships able to send over workers to
develop the investors' "private plantations"—that could flourish even
while the company itself floundered. In this way the "publique" character
of the company as a controlling, quasi-governmental body similar to the
East India Company eroded, while small private enterprises within the
colony multiplied.

The process of privatization on the English side would in the end
dovetail with a major development in the colony itself. In 1614 the
seven-year labor contracts of the initial settlers of 1607 came to an end.
Freed from their obligations, some of the surviving workers immediately
returned to England, but most remained and received from Dale small
individual plots of land to be held as tenant farms. By 1615 there were
said to be eighty-one such farms in the colony—as yet primitive clearings
in the first, crude stages of cultivation—and the numbers were destined
to grow as in successive years other laborers reached the end of their

contracted terms. Since it was increasingly difficult for the company to finance further recruitment and emigration to the colony, the number of laborers working for the "publique" dwindled until by 1618 they had all but disappeared. And this process of distributing company land to private groups and individuals was intensified when in 1616 the company's seven-year joint stock of 1609 was terminated. Lacking funds to issue as dividends, the company gave stockholders fifty acres of Virginia land per share for their personal, private development, with the prospect of more for future investments. At the same time independent planters in the colony would also receive fifty acres for having committed themselves personally to developing the colony.

The policy quickly created its own dynamic. Shortly thereafter the company, seeking the maximum use of land for population growth, announced its willingness to grant fifty acres to every adventurer, resident or absentee, who transported an individual to the colony. In this way the "headright" system of land distribution, which would last for a century, came into being.[25]

At that point most of the elements of a system that would, within the next fifty years, account for the immigration to the Chesapeake lands of some seventy thousand people, had come together. What was still missing was a dynamic force in the form of a profitable commodity to drive the process forward.

The first, failing experiments that had been made in growing tobacco were not of the native, local plant known to the Indians but of a Spanish variety imported from Trinidad, for which a market was known to exist in Europe. Two years later John Rolfe's efforts to produce the plant that grew natively in the Chesapeake region were beginning to look promising, though the quality of the tobacco shipped was still judged too poor for English consumption. It was, however, easily produced on partly cleared land, and the farmers, desperate for some kind of cash crop, persisted. The quality of the crop gradually improved, especially as a result of experiments carried on by experts sent to Bermuda, and production rose in every planting season. In 1616, a mere 1,250 pounds were shipped to England; in 1617, almost 10,000 pounds; in 1618, almost 25,000; in 1620, almost 60,000. In all, by 1621 over 100,000 pounds of Virginia tobacco were sent to England; by 1625, almost 400,000.

These large quantities of tobacco were not produced on the company's land, and the laborers necessary to produce these crops were not, as originally planned, employees of the Virginia Company. They were contract workers, on an increasing number of "private plantations" created by the company's new land policy, and tenant farmers of absentee landowners, assisted by indentured servants. By 1617 a model structure had emerged. Adventurers due land for their investments began to pool their grants to create larger and more efficient units of production. "Smith's Hundred," founded that year, which combined the land claims of leading figures in the company, became a virtual colonizing company of it own, financed by a terminable joint stock and complete with a private labor force of indentured servants and a domain of land far larger than what could then be cultivated.

But "Smith's Hundred," which had entitlement to some 80,000 acres north of the James, up into Chickahominy country, and in which over £6,000 would be invested, underwent a change in title that reflected a basic transformation in the entire Virginia enterprise. That private plantation had been named for the longtime head of the Virginia Company, Sir Thomas Smith, who was also, along with Sir Edwin Sandys, its leading investor. By 1618 the company's stockholders still had no substantial returns for their investments, the company still failed to attract new subscribers to its stock, and Smith's leadership of the company had come under attack. After bitter factional fighting, Sandys ousted Smith from the company's leadership, took over the enterprise with an extremely ambitious program of development, and along the way changed "Smith's Hundred" to "Southampton's Hundred," to honor his patron and chief coinvestor, the Earl of Southampton, now the titular head of the company.[26] At that point the company entered its final phase, which for a few short years seemed to be leading to the brilliant success so long delayed. But it was a false dawn that led to another dark passage of bloodshed and terror—which might have been predicted.

CHAPTER 4

✿

Recruitment, Expansion,
and Transformation

1

S IR EDWIN SANDYS, having taken control, realizing that the company faced bankruptcy and the colony itself ruin and annihilation, seized on initiatives undertaken by Smith and developed them into a comprehensive rescue campaign. He had first to convince the public at large that Virginia was not only a going concern but held enormous possibilities for the future. He had then somehow to settle the increasingly confused problem of land tenure in Virginia; get rid of Dale's now notorious regime of martial law, yet maintain some discipline in the settlers' lives; cut down on the colony's growing reliance on tobacco; and force the farmers to diversify their production. Above all, most urgently and quickly, he had to find ways to increase the population—by enticements of all sorts, by coercion if necessary.[1]

A Declaration of the State of the Colonie was Sandys's principal public appeal. The English colony in Virginia, the pamphlet stated, was a "noble action" for the Christian religion and the people of England. "The countrey is rich, spacious, and well watered," temperate in climate, "very healthfull, after men are a little accustomed to it," abounding in "all Gods naturall blessings," and capable of producing a vast range of commodities that England is now obliged to buy, at great expense, from abroad. Everything flourishes in the colony: the cattle grow bigger than at home, "*does* of their *deere* yeelde two fawnes at a birth, and sometimes three," the fish are as plentiful as those off Newfoundland, wheat grows wonderfully, and everything from drug plants to cotton and sugar can eventually be produced "in abundance." As for management and the organization of public life, everything is now in order. Martial law has been eliminated, and the normal processes of English law and governance transferred to the colony. The land tenure system is regularized, with entitlements adjusted to length of service in the colony; indentured servants guaranteed half-profits during their term of service and fifty acres as freedom dues; and tradesmen promised a house and land for their contribution. Further, income from the company lands is being set aside to provide for the expenses of church, state, and education; a regular system exists for the creation of more private plantations, and the colonists are well on their way to building "publique guest houses for intertaining of new men upon their first arrivall."[2]

Heralded by such propaganda, advanced by skillful promotion within London's political and financial community, and mobilized by energetic entrepreneurship, Sandys's campaign to rescue the faltering colony and enrich the company's investors took off in a whirlwind of activity. It was true, the colony's resident secretary, John Pory, wrote from Virginia in 1619, that the colony was "nowe contemptible," its only assets being the tobacco it produced and the servants it could buy and sell, but it would soon become "a flourishing estate" because of the English crops it could produce, the vineyards it could cultivate, and the cattle it could raise. Within seven years, he was persuaded, "the governor's place here may be as profitable as the lord deputies in Ireland."[3]

A multitude of schemes appeared overnight, all of them requiring the recruitment of workers. Within a year the company drew up plans to establish three ironworks, and to produce cordage and linen, potash, soap-ash, pitch, tar, timber, silk, vines, and salt. Ironworkers—at least 150—were sent over, together with a contingent of "skilfull vignerons" expert in growing grapevines, and four "Dutch" [German] carpenters with orders to erect sawmills. In 1621 one private plantation owner imported twenty skilled ironworkers for his own projects; another, an enterprising Englishman who had settled in Ireland, joined with a friend, Captain

William Newce, to bring over an advance party of fifty Irishmen and a small herd of cattle, which they sold to the Virginia Company at a good profit; they called their private plantation "New Porte Newce" (Newport News). Shortly thereafter twenty-five shipwrights were enlisted, along with a carpenter and five apprentices taken on to build the East India Company's projected "free school" in the colony. Nine more ironworkers contracted to "make iron by a bloomery"; and a group of skilled glassworkers was hired to renew the glassworks that had been abandoned years before. The company's original plan for "the university and colledge"— a "college for the *infidels* children"—was revived, and land was set aside for the project, but construction of the "fabricke" (the building) was put off until the rental of the lands granted to the college produced sufficient income for the work.[4]

The proliferating projects involved recruitment from all over Europe. The vignerons were French, from "Languedock"; the experts in salt manufacture came from "Rochell"; some of the wine producers were brought in from the Rhineland; "Polackers" were hired to make potash, soap, pitch, and tar; the shipbuilders and sawmill operators came from Hamburg; the glassworks were manned by Italians (one of them a murderous wife beater, George Sandys wrote, the whole lot "a more damned crew hell never vomited"); and there were Walloons (from modern Belgium), who together with a group of French made up a prospective shipment of 55 men, 41 women, and 129 children. But the overwhelming number of emigrants were English, recruited in desperation by the company from whatever sources and by whatever means available. The result was a further scattering of half-organized, socially inchoate clusters of strangers drawn disproportionately from certain segments of English society, seeking, in the crude, stump-filled tobacco farms of this subtropical lowland, to re-create a world they had known.

The company's coercive power was directed mainly at the most vulnerable element in Jacobean society, the vagrant children. How many hundreds of children and petty criminals the company managed to collect from the streets and public institutions of London is not precisely known, but some of the numbers were recorded. Between August 1618 and August 1620 the company obtained from Bridewell Hospital, a detention center and jail for vagrant children, "idle wastrels, petty thieves, and dissolute women," at least 337 of its charges to be sent to Virginia as "apprentices."[5]

Transporting vagrant children to Virginia was a process greatly facilitated—indeed, mandated—by London's Common Council, whose Lord Mayor was an investor in the Virginia Company. In 1619, responding to a petition of the company and drawing on its "superfluous multitude," the city sent over to Virginia, at a cost to itself of £5 each, 99 children—75 boys and 24 "wenches"—between the ages of eight and sixteen, to serve as apprentices in the colony and to receive, in their maturity, fifty acres of land each. By early January 1620 the city was even more active in the cause. It ordered the constables of all of the city's wards to "walk the streets . . . [and] apprehend all such vagrant children, both boys and girls, as they shall find on the streets and in the markets or wandering in the night" and send them to Bridewell, with the clear implication that they were to be shipped to Virginia. And further, the aldermen were to instruct all churchwardens to visit the houses of the poor, to inquire whether these households were "overcharged and threatened with poor children," and if so, to ask if they would agree to have these children, twelve years or older, sent to Virginia, thereby easing the families' burdens and providing for the children's "good education and future maintenance." And if the poor householders were uncooperative, the churchwardens were to point out that if they "deny or refuse such order . . . they [will] receive no further relief from the parish wherein they inhabit." There were other sanctions too. A revolt of some of the Bridewell children, despite—or perhaps because of—the company's assurance that "under severe masters they may be brought to goodness," was put down on order of no less a body than the king's Privy Council, which authorized the city to imprison and punish those who remained "obstinate" in refusing to go to the colony.[6]

The result, by the late spring of 1620, was a shipment of at least sixty-five more children, twelve years and older, now on somewhat different terms. The city would still pay the company £5 each for costs, but after their apprenticeship the children were to serve as tenants on the company's land for seven years and only then receive some land, now reduced to twenty-five acres. But still more children were needed, and so the company petitioned twice again, and succeeded once more, in 1622, in obtaining a shipment of one hundred. By then Sandys's ambitions, and need, had risen ever higher. In 1621 he turned to Parliament and requested a law ordering every parish in England to send its poor to Virginia, at its own expense. Nothing came of this, but here and there in the countryside the possibilities were seized by hard-pressed parishes, and ruthless operators moved in. In Somerset, in October 1618, a justice of the peace found that one Owen Evans, equipped with fake credentials, had commanded the constables of various hundreds "to press him divers maidens, to be sent to the Bermudas or Virginia," offering money to some authorities (five or twelve shillings a head) and threats to others for their cooperation. Evans was thrown in jail and "fell upon his knees and humbly confessed his fault," but not before his "undue proceedings" had created "such terror to the poor maidens as forty of them fled out of one parish into such obscure and remote places as their parents and masters can yet have no news what is become of them."[7]

2

So it was that day after day, month after month, crowds of London's vagrant children, "out of the multitudes that swarm there," were collected, subjected to official punishment if they caused "any disorder," jumbled together with assorted thieves, "nippers," "lewd boy[s] that will not be ruled by [their] parents," and miscellaneous servants, and distributed among the vessels headed for Virginia or the associated colony of Bermuda. Of their character and condition little was said, but the little that was said reveals something of the desperation of the company's recruitment. "You shall doe verie well," George Thorpe wrote the company in 1621, to appoint qualified physicians and surgeons to screen the prospective servants "concerning the health and soundness of theire bodies." Two of the boys assigned to labor for him on the college lands, he reported, were "soe diseased with olde solcers [ulcers] in their leggs . . . that I doe dispaire of theire abilitie to woorke." One was close to death, another "broken-bellied [ruptured], a fourth . . . is maymed in one of his hands," a fifth was "soe diseased in his who[le] body that he hath not bine able to help himself." Many of the new recruits, both men and boys, he wrote, "have died in this countrey of incurable maladies that they brought with them."[8]

But there was no medical screening, and the number of recruits constantly rose. In the first year of Sandys's regime the company itself and the merchants and planters resident in the colony brought to Virginia some 400 settlers and thereby doubled the colony's population. In the spring of 1619, 1,261 more were sent, with supplies and cattle. By 1622, 3,500 had been transported to the settlements along the James; by 1624, more than 4,000.[9]

Most arrived on small vessels, which began to crowd the makeshift docks at the entrance of the Chesapeake Bay and along the shores of the James and York rivers. In his first five months in Virginia in 1619 Pory reported the arrival of eleven vessels. March 19, 1619, seems to have been a particularly busy day on the Virginia wharves. Both the *Gift of God* and the *Sampson* apparently arrived that day with approximately three hundred passengers for Martin's Hundred, while the *George* and the *Diane* also docked, the former with one hundred settlers (fifty to labor on the governor's land), the latter with eighty to one hundred London children, said to have been starving in the streets. Among the arrivals in August of that year was the Dutch man-of-war that sold to the colony "20 and odd Negroes" (Angolan natives, they were not the first Africans to appear in the colony's records: thirty-two—fifteen men and seventeen women—were listed in a muster of March 1619 as "in ye service of severall planters").[10] At any one time three or more vessels could be seen unloading their jumbled passengers and supplies and beginning the slow process of reloading with goods for the return to England. One could also see the sailors, temporarily adrift in these crude settlements, doing what they could, by way of private barter, socializing, and entertainment, to pass the time until they sailed again.

The number of shipments continued at the same high level. In 1620 at least 10 vessels docked along the James, one of them the *Duty*, with 51 boys, referred to thereafter as "duty boys"; in 1621, at least 9; in 1623, at least 11. In all, in Sandys's years as the company's leader (1618–23), there is evidence of 96 separate ship arrivals, most of them small vessels carrying a few dozen passengers; only a small number transported 100 or more; only one—the *Abigail* of 1621—bore as many as 230.[11]

There is no record of the identity of the hundreds of passengers these vessels carried, but it is clear that they were not groups of like-minded, socially or culturally homogeneous people drawn from similar backgrounds, moving together in neighborhood clusters. They were a miscellaneous collection of disparate people, most expecting to be tenants on half profits until they could acquire independent stakes in the land, or servants committed to various terms of indenture. But there is evidence that the company's enticements were beginning to attract elements of somewhat higher strata of society. The *Bona Nova* of 1619 carried 92 prospective tenants, who came from 27 English counties and from Wales; 19 of them claimed to be husbandmen (substantial farmers), the rest claimed specific skills in a great variety of trades, in construction, food, and apparel; 2 were identified as goldsmiths, 7 claimed to be gentlemen. And at least 14 were traveling with kin. Of the 103 passengers on the *James* (1622), more than half were financially independent, traveling with wives, servants, and children.[12]

The effort to recruit from the more respectable elements of society was reflected in the company's extraordinary program to attract proper women to the colony, the lack of whom, the company declared, was threatening the success of the enterprise. If the settlers were dejected and sought to return to England, it was, they said, because of the lack of "the comforts without which God saw that man could not live contented-lie, noe not [even] in Paradize." Lacking wives and children, the settlers viewed Virginia simply as a source of quick profit, ignoring all long-term goals and commitments. Therefore "to tye and roote the planters myndes to Virginia by the bonds of wives and children," a number of company investors contributed to a joint stock to subsidize the shipping of "young, handsome and honestlie educated maides . . . to be disposed in marriage to the most honest and industrious planters" willing and able to repay the investors the cost of the women's passages.

How "handsome and honestlie educated" the young women were we cannot know, but the identity and something of the background of fifty-seven of those shipped to Virginia in 1620 and 1621, as well as the supplies provided for their journeys, can be found in the company's surviving records.

Most of the women were unmarried orphans in their early twenties or late teens, committed to service or unemployed, adrift in a patriarchal world. All gave evidence of respectability (eight claimed connections with the gentry), presenting the company with written testimonials to their good character, respectable connections, industry, and correct "carriage" (behavior). Thus the recommendations for the twenty-five-year-old daughter of a gentleman and niece of a knight; for the twenty-one-year-old daughter of "a gentleman of good meanes"; for a "cosen once removed" of an attorney at the law; for the twenty-three-year-old sister (and servant) of "the king's crossbow maker"; and for the twenty-five-year-old daughter of "gentelfolke of good esteeme" said to

Recommendations for women shipped to Virginia, 1620–21, with a list of the apparel and bedding sent with them

1   Joane ffletcher widdowe aged 25 daughter of John Egerton gentleman
    brother to S[i]r Ralph Egerton Knight borne at Morely house neare to
    Bridge Stafford in Chessheire this is testifide ~~certified~~ by Mr. Gibson dwell-
    ing neare to the three Nunns w[i]thout Algate.

2   An Hramer mayde aged 21 yeares daughter to Mr Harmer of Baldock a
    gentleman of good meanes nowe lyvinge her Mothers names was Kempton
    Mr Undwell and Mr ffartlow Grocers in Bucklersbury are her kinsemen ~~and~~
    affirme all this and com[m]end her to the Company.

3   Lettice King Maide aged 23 borne at Newebury in Barkshire her father is
    deade her brother an Atturney at the Lawe S[i]r Wm Udall is her Cosen
    once removed shee hath been in div[er]s good services whene shee cometh
    recom[m]ended.

4   Allice Burges mayd aged 28 her parent deade were countire ffolke dwelling
    at Linton come out of service and recommended.

5   Katherine ffinch: aged 23 borne in Mardens parish in Herfordshire her ffa-
    ther and Mother are dead shee was in service with her brother Mr Erasmus
    ffinch the kings Crossbow maker who brought her and com[m]ended her
    to the Company She was likewise com[m]ended by her other two brothers
    Edward ffinch goldsmith and John ffinch Crossbow maker all three dwell-
    ing in the Strand.

A noate of the ~~provisions~~ *Apparaile &*
bedding that the Adventurers have bestowed
uppon each of the younge woemen now sente

1 Petticoate.
1 Wastcoate.
2 payre of stockings
1 payre of garters
2 smocks
1 payre of gloves
1 hatt and bande
1 round bande
1 Apron
2 payre of shoes
1 Towell
2 Coyfe 1 Croscloath
Worsted to worke them
and yarne to knitt stockings
There is more for them
~~A Rugg~~
6 payre of sheetes packed
6 Canvas bedds & bolster
6 Ruggs.
6 Course sead bedds

} All theese things were delivered them

~~All w[hi]ch apparaile together w[i]th~~
~~besides this apparaile they have~~
This apparaile there transportation and
other provisions have stoode in above
eleven poundes neere twelve.

be somehow related to Sir Edwin Sandys. Most, like the twenty-year-old woman presented by her widowed mother who swore to her daughter's "honest Carriage" and capacity to do all kinds of work, were servants, lacking parental protection (in only five cases out of the fifty-seven is it clear that both parents were alive), with poor prospects, attracted by the company's advertising.

The company said it would, and did, make every effort to provide for the welfare of these certified young women. They issued clothes, bedding, food, and other supplies and gave instructions for their careful treatment upon arrival in the colony. And though they were to be sold as soon as possible only to "honest and sufficient" planters for at least 150 pounds "of the best leafe tobacco" (c. £22), the company conceded to wayward sensibilities. Since they "dare not infrindge" on the "libertie of mariadge" they allowed the husband of any woman who "unwarily or fondly bestow[ed] herself . . . uppon such as shall not be able to give present sattisfaccon" to postpone payment until he could pay, that debt to have precedence over all other obligations. But romance seems to have played little part in these transactions. The women were snapped up by the more affluent planters, bought at such high rates, it was said, that poor men never got near them, and for a time—before Indian attacks and a starving season in the years immediately ahead—they must have considered themselves fortunate.

How attractive was the company's appeal to these young, insecure, vulnerable women is indicated by the geographical spread of their origins. Only between a quarter and a third can be said to have had their origins in or around London; the rest came from nineteen of England's thirty-nine counties, ranging from Yorkshire to Dorset; four of the women came from Wales. In their geographical diversity they were typical of the company's recruitment at large.[13]

The English immigrants of the Sandys era came from no one region of the country, no one subculture, no one economic environment. The company was boasting when it declared that most of the settlers it sent were "choise men, borne and bred up to labour and industry," but it stated the truth when it noted, in its *Declaration*, that while many of the hundreds came from Devonshire, Warwickshire, Staffordshire, and Sussex, most came "dispersedly out of divers shires of the realm."[14]

Nor was there uniformity of religion among the English. Between 1618 and 1621, three contingents of radical dissenters, parts of the diaspora of English separatists exiled in Holland, settled in Virginia. The first was headed by Christopher Lawne, a fiery theological polemicist, who led a group to what he named "Lawne's Plantation," south of the James—an isolated spot that he wrongly believed could be defended against the Indians. Within a year he was joined in that exposed area by a more numerous and better-financed group of dissenters sponsored by Edward Bennett, an affluent member of the Virginia Company who was also an elder of the separatist church in Amsterdam. His plantation, Bennett's Welcome, adjoining Lawne's, had all the advantages that money could supply, but it too was perilously perched on the southern frontier. Bennett's son Richard led that Puritan settlement, which would eventually move again, in search of a more tolerant regime.[15]

The third group of Anglo-Dutch religious radicals to settle in Virginia was initially the most tragic. Of the 180 passengers whom the embattled Elder Francis Blackwell led from Amsterdam to Virginia, no fewer than 130, including Blackwell himself, died on that voyage of seven months. They had been "packed together," it was reported, "like herrings; they had amongst them the flux, and also want of fresh water, so as it is here [London] wondered at that so many are alive, than that so many are dead." Yet by 1622 religious dissent—both radical separatism and more moderate Puritanism—was well established in Virginia, though vulnerable to pressure ecclesiastically from Anglican churchmen and physically from resentful Indians.[16]

The horror of Blackwell's notorious voyage was only an extreme example of the miseries of the transportation and resettlement process of those years. For most of the voyagers, emigration was a shocking experience; for some it was as deadly as it was for Blackwell's pilgrims. The Virginia Company published guidelines for the supplies necessary for such voyages but did nothing to enforce them, with the result that the provisions on board were so poor that they became a subject of complaint to the Privy Council. The voyages on these small, ill-equipped, rocking vessels lasted two to three months; food and drink were bad ("stinckinge beere") in quality and short in quantity; sanitation was primitive; and sickness swept through the passengers like deadly storms. Each year, each shipping season, many died at sea: most of the carefully recruited ironworkers were lost on a single voyage. The survivors were so weakened by disease and exhaustion that they quickly fell victim to debilitating attacks of dysentery and other afflictions. Whole shiploads that had been sent over to work on various "publique" enterprises had to be transferred to whatever private plantations would take them simply to assure their survival. And the "guest houses," of which Sandys spoke so happily, did not exist. Only one building—forty feet by twenty—is known to have been built for that purpose, and so, since "it is mortall for new comers to ly [on] the ground," the hundreds of new arrivals had to be added to the crowds that already filled the small, flimsy dwellings that were being hastily constructed. Even that might have been tolerable if the timing of the voyages had been right. But despite bitter protests from Virginia, the vessels typically left England early in the spring and arrived at the worst possible time: at the beginning of the hot season and before the year's harvest had come in.

The constant, often unexpected arrivals of shipload after shipload of sickly, disoriented passengers in a climate that was debilitatingly hot and humid, lacking supplies to carry them over the first phase of resettlement, destined to be housed in crowded huts until they could be distributed, often to places other than their intended destinations—all of this brought repeated outcries from the resident leaders. "I pray sir," Governor George Yeardley (1618–21) wrote Sandys, "give me both tyme to provide meanes and to build and settell" before you send one load after another. At least, he said, he must be warned: "had not your zealous desires over hasted you and the passage at sea bin soe unfortunate . . . whereby I had no warning at all given to provide for these people, I should have bine able to have done much better than now I can." But, sponsored more by private developers than by the company, lot after lot of new settlers continued to arrive—vagrant children, convicts, artisans, farmers, and farmhands from all over England—utterly unfamiliar with conditions in semitropical lowlands. They suffered diseases for which they had no immunities, and moved off, those who survived the first shock, to nascent farms scattered along one hundred miles of riverside land.[17]

3

These farms, increasingly "private plantations," multiplied remarkably—dangerously as it proved—in the years of Sandys's ascendancy. In 1618 there had been sixteen settlements, mainly clustered in the middle area near Jamestown and in the western district, around Bermuda

City and Coxendale. In 1619 eleven more were founded; in 1620, three more; in 1621, four; in 1622, nine. These new plantations were given names—mostly personal, often romantic and alliterative, sometimes mysterious: Jordan's Journey, Pace's Paines, Causey's Care, Chaplaine's Choice, Archer's Hope, Martin's Brandon, Tanks Weyanoke, Curls, Warrascoyack (or Bennett's Welcome). They were scattered randomly about the extensive riverside lands and were widely separated: in fact the company required the new settlements to be spaced ten miles apart.[18]

Some were staked out at immense scale. The patent for Berkeley Hundred, a speculative venture sponsored by five of the company's major investors and designed, ultimately, to provide homes for "many land-hungry people" in Gloucestershire, contained twelve and a half square miles, with four miles of frontage on the James. Martin's Hundred, an "enormous corporate settlement" led by the company's lawyer, Richard Martin, and Sir John Wolstenholme, "one of the City's greatest merchants," was said by some to contain 21,500 acres, by others 80,000, by still others 800,000, and it was generally known to have ten miles of riverfront. Southampton's (or Smith's) Hundred was patented at 80,000 acres.[19]

In these major properties, great efforts were made to establish lucrative farming communities and fortified compounds. The owners, in combinations typical of an emerging pattern of merchant-planter partnerships, sent over men, equipment, cattle, supplies, arms and armor, and plans for cultivation and construction on the patented lands, some of which would be farmed by, or more likely for, the owners themselves, most of which would be rented out to tenants in small parcels. The most successful of these enterprises represented very sizable investments. Recruiting, fully equipping, and transporting one man to Virginia with supplies for his settlement in the colony cost approximately £20. Thus the backers of Berkeley Hundred spent over £2,500 to send over ninety people in 1619 and 1620, and it took over £6,000 to establish Southampton Hundred. The results in such exceptional cases, we know from the work of archaeologists, were not merely tobacco plantations but scattered agricultural communities. Governor Yeardley's Flowerdieu Hundred, for example, on the south shore of the James, a year after its sale in 1624 to Capt. Abraham Peircey, supported a population of fifty-seven (among them seven blacks: four men, two women, and a child), organized into ten "musters" or separate households. Each of these farming units within the Flowerdieu patent, increasingly tobacco producers, possessed its own store of basic food supplies, equipment, and arms. The main farm, Peircey's, included thirty-six servants, ten dwelling houses, three storehouses, four tobacco sheds, two boats, a windmill, twenty-five cattle, and nineteen swine, plus three hundred bushels of corn and peas on hand, thirteen hundred pounds of fish, six pieces of ordnance, numerous firearms with powder and lead, two "murderers" (breech-loaded cannon), fifteen suits of armor, and twenty swords. Most of the Flowerdieu houses were palisaded, and "ye whole necke [of land] is well railed in."[20]

Of one of the more substantial establishments in the years of Sandys's leadership, Shirley Hundred, much is known. Financed and settled by Francis, John, and Nathaniel West, the younger brothers of Lord De La Warr, the property was located partly on an island in the James and partly on the river's north shore. In 1625 an incomplete inventory listed sixty-one people at Shirley Hundred, living on seventeen farms. Five of the farm units were worked by nuclear families, with or without servants, who claimed seven houses. Nine units were farmed by adult males, who had among them seven houses, nine servants, and eight "partners"; three units were headed by widows, one of whom had two servants, while another had none. Most of the farms had some kind of fortification, and the most prosperous of them were well staffed and supplied. Richard Biggs's household included his wife, who had followed him to Virginia after eight years, an infant son, two young cousins who had followed after six years, and four recently arrived servants. Biggs's farm had three buildings, one boat, supplies of corn, peas, and fish, six firearms with powder and lead, two "compleate" suits of armor, eight cattle, twenty-one swine, and thirty poultry.

Evidence of initial affluence has been unearthed at the Shirley site: fragments of imported Chinese (Wan Li) porcelain, delftware pottery, medicine vials, window glass, and some silver utensils. But most of the houses consisted of a single dirt-floored room and loft, some of them adjacent to a tobacco storage house or other farmyard shelters. A third of Shirley's adult population, whose leaders were well-connected gentlemen, were bonded servants—a rough, contentious lot drawn from some of the most deprived elements of English society. One, the son of a London porter, was convicted of raping four girls in Virginia and was executed; another was one of the very few survivors of the shipment of one hundred children from the Bridewell correctional hospital; a third sustained such injuries in a shipboard fight just before landing that he died shortly after his arrival.[21]

But the most elaborate private entitlement in Sandys's time, and the most fully developed, was Martin's Hundred. Between 1618 and 1621 its ambitious sponsors sent over at least 280 settlers on seven vessels—220 in 1618 alone—complete with a large quantity of equipment, supplies, farm animals, arms, and building materials. Its satellite farms were scattered through several miles of north shore territory, but its core lay in "Wolstenholme Town," a farming compound that archaeologists have recovered in great detail and that has been depicted in a vivid modern painting.

Wolstenholme Town was in effect a rudimentary farming village of fifty or sixty people—perhaps one-quarter of the Hundred's total population at its height. The town contained a fenced-in company compound (a longhouse and store), a sizable company barn for storage of goods before shipment, at least one adjacent cottage-homestead, and several nearby, all dominated by a palisaded fort. That key structure, an irregular rectangle with parapets and a watchtower-gun platform with a clear view downriver, was modeled on an Irish "bawn" and contained the leader's house and sheds. Its quarter-acre enclosure provided protective shelter for the villagers, and perhaps their animals, if the settlement came under attack.

Yet Wolstenholme Town, a model construction of the ambitious Sandys years, was a primitive affair. The fields of this riverside clearing were still pocked with tree stumps, and its dozen or so buildings, like most of Virginia's structures in this era, were lightly constructed of wattle-and-daub walls (panels of woven sticks plastered over with clay, between posts sunk a few feet into the ground) and covered with roofs of thatch. They were small. A typical servant's house was nothing more than an enlarged hut: overall fourteen by twelve feet. The original "longhouse" measured only twenty by eighteen; the leader's "big house," perhaps thirty-six by nineteen. They were dirt floored and poorly lit and ventilated. The leaders, of gentry origins like those at Shirley Hundred, brought with them some decorative crockery of European manufacture and in addition fancy spurs and elegant swords and armor. There is archaeological evidence of glazed delftware tiles, glass bottles, ornamental fireplace tongs, and enough window glass and lead strips to suggest that, while most buildings had shutters or oiled paper to cover wall openings, at least one had proper windows. But these fineries were residues, emblems of a better existence than that of scattered frontier encampments in which life was so precarious that the population could not begin to reproduce itself.[22]

The death rate in these larger properties, as well as on the ordinary farms, continued to be devastating. We do not know how many of the 280 settlers sent over to Martin's Hundred survived the journey, but approximately half of those who did were dead by the end of 1621. A year after 34 men were sent to Berkeley Hundred to join 4 already on the property, 31 were reported dead, 2 of them "slayne." Of the 120 men and boys sent on the *Seaflower* to Bennett's Welcome in 1621, only 10 were alive in 1623, and more than half of the deaths were the result of disease, exhaustion, and malnutrition.

Optimists among the settlers—and there continued to be such—groped for explanations of the colony's miseries that might relieve the concerns of the colony's backers. George Thorpe, the enthusiastic, evangelizing leader of the Berkeley plantation, wrote late in 1620 that he had never been in better health than he was then, after almost seven months in the colony. There was no shortage of good food in the colony, he insisted, nor even of good drink, for, he reported, they had found a way of making such excellent liquor out of Indian corn that he preferred it to "good stronge Englishe beare." "More doe die here of the disease of theire minde," he insisted, "then of theire body by havinge this countrey['s] victualls over-praised unto them in England," and they suffer too by "not knowinge they shall drinke water here." The colony was prospering, he wrote, and his mission to improve the lives and spiritual estate of the Indians was succeeding. He hoped his wife and children would join him, and he advised his close friend, John Smyth, steward of the Berkeley Hundred in Gloucestershire and a sponsor of the Berkeley plantation, to send his younger son to Virginia, well equipped with servants and cattle.

It was bad advice. Thorpe's optimism betrayed him. He was dead by early 1622—murdered by the Indians, and mutilated. He was decapitated, John Smith reported in his *Generall Historie*, his body hacked to pieces "with such spight and scorn . . . as is unfitting to be heard with civill eares."[23]

CHAPTER 5

🙣

"A *Flood,* a *Flood* of *Bloud*"

1

R ACE RELATIONS HAD TAKEN a strange turn after the ambiguous
"peace" of 1614. Powhatan's personal dominance, essentially mod-
erating if not conciliatory, quickly faded. Uncertain and confused in his
relations with the English, he withdrew from the leadership of his people
in 1617 and died the next year. His successor, his more belligerent, enterprising, and realistic brother Opechancanough, understood the mortal
threat to the tidewater tribes that the expansion of English settlements
implied. In 1618, the year that Sandys took over control of the company in London, he began planning for a coordinated attack, by all the
tribes he could assemble, that would reassert the Powhatans' control of
the coastal region and with it their sense, if not of their superiority over
the aggressive English, then of the autonomy they seemed to have lost.
He did not intend to drive the English off the land, to exterminate them
in genocidal warfare. The English were useful, if properly confined, kept
within a careful balance of forces; the problem was how to confine them
and thus reestablish the coherence of life that was being destroyed by
English expansionism. His aim was to strike a single, devastating blow, a
violent coup that would drive the English into a limited eastern enclave
from which they might conduct their trade. The situation that devel-

oped between 1618 and 1622 was therefore paradoxical, for the company, under Sandys, was also developing a plan for future race relations—an ostensibly benevolent plan but one no less ethnocentric and no less dangerous to their opponents' survival.

Sandys, a son of the Archbishop of York, had taken holy orders at Oxford, and though a merchant and man of affairs, he never abandoned his religious commitment. Under his vigorous leadership, the elaborate plans for the development of the colony and the rationale for its promotion were cast increasingly in terms of rescuing the Indians from paganism and thereby converting them to European civility. The conversion of the Indians had been one of the company's stated goals from the beginning, and the Anglo-Powhatan War of 1609–14 had been seen by many of the English involved as a holy war fought "under the banner of Jesus Christ." But though missionary zeal had surfaced repeatedly in the colony over the years—as in Rolfe's passionate justification of his marriage to Pocahontas as a holy obligation "to make her a Christian" (a passion, he insisted, in no way contaminated by an "unbridled desire of carnall affection")—it had faded amid the turmoil of war, disease, and the expansion of settlement.[1]

Sandys and his colleagues, determined to devise the broadest possible appeal for increased funding, and sincere in their religious commitments, reawakened the gospel mission and issued a flood of pronouncements aimed at making the advancement of the colony not only a national cause but a religious crusade. Governor Yeardley was instructed to set aside ten thousand acres for "the building and planting of a college for the training up of the children of those infidels in true religion, moral virtue, and civility, and for other godly uses." Thorpe, deeply sympathetic to the Indians, determined to see them treated with kindness and understanding, and convinced that they were "very loving, and willing to parte with their children" for conversion, was made the overseer of the college and its lands. The instructions to Governor Wyatt in 1621 went beyond institutional projects. He was told to see to it that "no injurie or oppression bee wrought by the English against any of the natives of that countrie wherby the present peace may be disturbed"; he was also to find Indian children for conversion and education in preparation for the college; and above all, he was "to converse" with the natives and "labor amongst them . . . that therby they may growe to a likeing and love of civillty and finallie bee brought to the knowledge and love of God and true religion."

For such benevolent purposes, private donors were eager to contribute. An anonymous benefactor ("Dust and Ashes") gave first £550 in gold for the conversion of the Indians and their subsequent apprenticeship in trade, then followed that with £450 for the company to send eight or ten Indian children to England for education, to be clothed "as the children of Christes Hospitall do." Another gave £300 for the education of ten Indians and an annual stipend for settlers who would supervise their preparatory education. The shipboard preaching of the Rev. Patrick Copland led the crew and passengers of one East India ship to raise over £70 to support a collegiate school in Virginia, and the mariners of another gave over £66. By 1620 such contributions totaled over £2,000. And the company, to advance the cause of Anglo-Powhatan conciliation, voted support for the abandoned Indian women who had accompanied Pocahontas to London, made careful selection of the plantations permitted to house Indian children, prohibited Indian children from being transported to the alien climate of England, and dispatched to America ministers who could be relied on to "allure the heathen people to submit themselves to the scepter of Gods most righteous and blessed kingdome."

But however useful the gospel appeal was for fund-raising in England, it did little to divert the settlers in Virginia from expanding tobacco planting as far and as quickly as they could. With tobacco prices high in England, with private plantations being started up on both sides of the James, from Chesapeake Bay to Henrico, and with immigrants flooding in to serve as tenants and general laborers, acre after acre of private land was scratched open to cultivation in a pell-mell rush for quick profits, with little regard to physical protection, company projects, or public welfare. Each of the new plantations added to the encroachments on Indian land, yet not systematically and not comprehensively. There were no sharp boundaries. The two worlds permeated each other. New clearings sliced into tribal lands, to be surrounded by Indian camping and hunting grounds. The English commonly visited Indian settlements, and the natives wandered among the scattered plantations, where they were welcomed for trade. In many settlements they were fed at the settlers' tables, and they were even reported to be "commonly lodged in [the colonists'] bed-chambers."[2]

Contact between the races was thus continuous and, despite occasional raids and skirmishes, relatively peaceful. The stability was ostensibly reinforced by the terms of a "peace" and "league" that Opechancanough confirmed with Governor Yeardley in 1621, which was extended in a series of remarkable concessions the Indian leader agreed to. Opechancanough promised to encourage trade with the settlers, to assist in the search for the South Sea and "certaine mynes," to come to terms on mutual defense, to permit the exchange of families, to give up the mysterious *huskanaw* ceremony ("makinge their children black boyes"), and since, he told the receptive Thorpe, God apparently "loved us [the English] better then them," to take instruction in the Christian religion.

Thorpe felt justified in his proselytizing labors, though it was uphill work. The heathens, he wrote Sandys, "live round aboute us and are dayly con[v]ersant amongst us & yeat there is scarce any man amongst us that doth soe much as affoorde them a good thought in his hart." Most in fact "give them nothinge but maledictions and bitter execrations." A fierce misapprehension has developed, he noted, "that these poore people have done unto us all the wronge and iniurie that the malice of the Devil or man can affoord, whereas in my poore understandinge if there bee wronge on any side it is on o[u]rs who are not soe charitable to them as Christians ought to bee, they beinge (espetiallye the better sort of them) of a peaceable and vertuous disposition." So he did what he could, indulging the Indians in every way possible. If the English attack dogs frightened them, he had the animals killed; if the dominant chief's dwelling was too crude, he had "a faire house" built for him "after the English fashion"—all in an effort to reach them personally in the hope of their conversion.

The agreements with Opechancanough were heartening but no less ambiguous than the earlier peace treaty with Powhatan had been. For the English, Opechancanough's concessions meant, or implied, freedom to expand tobacco planting limitlessly, without fear of attack, and to explore more deeply than before into Indian territory. For Opechancanough they meant a period of stability in which to rally his forces and organize a massive assault that alone, he correctly understood, might save his people's way of life and guarantee their physical survival. Anticipating this momentous event, he identified himself with the coming military victory by adopting a new name, Mangopeesomon, presumably a war name, and mobilized the forces available to him.[3]

2

By the time the tidewater Indians returned from their winter hunt early in 1622, Opechancanough's plan was in place. A combination of ten tribes in

the western areas, north and south of the James River, would produce an
initial strike force, backed up by other groups in the north. The warriors
would wander, casually and unarmed, with provisions to sell, into English
settlements where they were well known, and then at a given time they
would grab any object they could find—spade, ax, gun, knife, rock, log,
tong—and murder every person they could reach, man, woman, or child,
and they would burn all the buildings and crops.[4]

The utter violence of the plan, its bloodthirstiness and mercilessness,
expressed not only a pent-up passion for revenge and fear of destruction
but something deeper, something obscure and elementally compelling,
which, it has been suggested, may have been related to the death, in late
1621 or early 1622, of the proud, charismatic warrior Nemattanew—"Jack
of the Feathers." His claim to invulnerability, associated with the protection of the gods and dramatized in his magical armor of feathers and wings,
had inspired Indian fighters since the beginning of the Anglo-Powhatan
struggle. His continuing survival in battle after battle instilled confidence
and courage in the face of firearms and steel-clad soldiers and testified to
the power of tribal deities. But he was fatally shot—shot rather casually,
John Smith explained in his *Generall Historie*—by two young servants of
a settler whom Nemattanew was thought to have murdered. As he died,
Smith wrote, hoping, in this ultimate humiliation, to preserve the myth
of his invulnerability and all that it implied, Nemattanew begged the servants to hide the fact that he had been killed by a bullet and to bury him
among the English. His death was a deeply unsettling blow to Opechancanough, both for the resulting loss of military leadership and for what
it suggested about divine protection. On March 22, 1622, he took his
revenge in what the poet John Donne called "a *Flood*, a *Flood* of *Bloud*."[5]

WHAT WOULD HAVE HAPPENED if one or more semi-Christianized
Indians had not warned the Jamestown villagers of Opechancanough's
plan just before the attack can only be imagined. The warning probably
saved Jamestown and also Pace's Paines and several other plantations
nearby. But elsewhere the assault went much as planned. In plantation
after plantation from west to east, north and south of the James, the
Indians turned on their unsuspecting hosts, in some places while sharing
"breakfast with people at their tables," and with axes, hammers, shovels,
tools, and knives slaughtered them indiscriminately, "not sparing eyther
age or sexe, man, woman, or childe; so sodaine in their cruell execu-

tion that few or none discerned the weapon or blow that brought them to destruction." Those in the fields or otherwise at work were tracked down and murdered "contrary to all lawes of God and men, of nature & nations." And the horror was compounded by the attackers "defacing, dragging, and mangling the dead carkasses into many pieces, and carrying some parts away in derision, with base and bruitish triumph."

Houses were burned to the ground, crops were plundered, equipment wrecked, animals killed, maimed, or driven off. And the Indians' protectors and advocates among the settlers were, it seems, singled out for attack, as if the acculturation they had sought, with its assumption of divine sanction, was a special danger that had to be utterly obliterated. So the murder of Thorpe—which he faced stoically, "void of all suspition" and confident that the Indians meant him no harm—came to be seen as an act of Christian martyrdom and proof of the irredeemable savagery, the satanic evil, and "unnaturall bruitishnesse" of the Powhatan peoples, while for the natives the murder, mutilation, and utter obliteration of this agent of forced acculturation and alien doctrines was "an act of catharsis," and a symbol of liberation.

The colony was devastated. In a few hours, in the western and central areas of the colony, between 325 and 330 English men, women, and children were killed. Of the four "corporations" into which the colony had been divided, Henrico, sixty miles west of Jamestown, was most vulnerable and was severely hit: 61 lay dead; the ironworks, in which £5,000 had been invested, was in ruins; and most of the workers killed, as were the tenants on the college lands. From this blow the "sacred bussiness" of the Indian college never recovered. Just to the east, in the relatively well-fortified Charles City Corporation, nineteen sites were attacked and 142 people were killed. Among the devastated plantations were Berkeley, Southampton, and Flowerdieu Hundreds, and among the dead were four members of the colony's council of state. In James City Corporation 139 were killed; one of the five sites attacked was the model plantation, Martin's Hundred, with its core settlement at Wolstenholme Town. There 74 colonists were killed—more than were slain at any other single location—and at least 15 women were taken prisoner. The town itself was burned to the ground, never to be rebuilt, and though the plantation itself was reoccupied some months later, its population, a year after the massacre, had fallen from 140 to 22, and of the buildings two houses and "a peece of a church" were left. Only the easternmost corporation, Elizabeth City, was spared, not only because Opechancanough's forces were weakest there and farthest from their base but also because that much of the colony might be tolerated as a confined enclave.[6]

The scenes of individual struggles—frenzied, bloody, deadly hand-to-hand fights—would never be forgotten by those who survived them, and they were made vivid to others in letters and publications that conveyed in apocalyptic terms the carnage wrought by those whom John Smith, in his widely circulated account of the massacre, paraphrasing the colony's official *Relation of the Barbarous Massacre*, called a "viperous brood," "hell-hounds," "more fell than lions and dragons."

Captain Nathaniel Powell, one of the original settlers in the colony, well known to the natives whom he had favored, was slain, along with his family, decapitated, and his body "butcher-like, hagled" (mangled). The veteran soldier Nathaniel Causey, one of the few survivors of the "first supply" of 1608, was "cruelly wounded," Smith wrote, but somehow managed to grab an ax, "did cleave one of their heads," and drove off the rest of the attackers. Hugh Baldwin, at Bennett's Welcome, to save his wife who "lay for dead" and others in his house, kept shooting off his musket randomly, until the Indians turned away. Nearby the Indians set fire to a tobacco shed and, as the men ran out to quench it, "shot them full of arrowes, then beat out their braines." Thomas Hamor escaped because he had delayed going to the fire in order to finish writing a letter. When he finally went out he was shot in the back, raced back to the house, barricaded himself, and then, when the house was set on fire, fled with eighteen women and children under cover of gunfire to the Baldwin place. His brother Ralph, who had lived in the colony for thirteen years, came late to the scene but once there defended himself with "spades, axes, and brickbats," and with the help of a party of armed mariners that suddenly appeared, escaped, rescued his brother, and with the others at Baldwin's farm, ran to the safety of Jamestown, passing on the way the smoldering ruins of Martin's Hundred.[7]

But the devastation of the massacre was not only physical; it was psychological as well, and in the end political. The Indians, one planter said, had "burst the heart" of those who had survived. Wandering amid the charred ruins and unburied bodies, the wrecked equipment and broken barricades, was a reduced population in shock. In despair, overcome

This depiction (1634) of the Virginia Massacre of 1622, by the prolific engraver and publisher Matthaeus Merian in Frankfurt, Germany, is a work of imagination, but it must have been based in part on Edward Waterhouse's *Declaration of the state of . . . Virginia: With a relation of the barbarous massacre . . .* (London, 1622), since it illustrates precisely some of the details described in that pamphlet and conveys accurately Waterhouse's sense of the wild frenzy of the attack and the settlers' complete surprise. Jamestown in the background is entirely fanciful.

with fear and sorrow, devastated by having "to stand and gaze at our distressed brethren fryinge in the furie of our enimies and could not relieve them," they strugged to explain how the catastrophe could have happened.

The dispersal of settlement, mandated by the company, had clearly invited trouble: *"wee are like quicksilv[er] throwne into the fire,"* the scholarly George Sandys wrote, *"and hardlie to bee found in so vast a distance.*

The English throughout this wild countrye [Sandys wrote a year after the massacre] planted dispersedlie in small familyes, far from neighbours, . . . covetous of large poss[ess]ions (larger than 100 tymes their number were able to cultivate) . . . lyve like libertines out of the eye of the magistrate, not able to secure themselves nor to bee releived by others upon any occasion . . . if they had had anie knowledge of the purpose of the Indians, the most part could not possiblie have prevented their treacheries, but must either have beene beseiged in their houses (and consequentlie famished) or cut of[f] as they followed their labours.

Further, the whole colony had been weakened by the company's sending over large numbers of people before provision could be made for their maintenance or safety, and transporting them on overloaded ships "for the lucre & gayne . . . of the owners." In addition, Sandys reported, tenants sent over to work "*on that so absurd condition of halves*" cannot live on half of what they produce and must therefore become so "dejected with their scarce provisions, and finding nothing to answeare their expectacion, that [they] give themselves over and die of melancholye, the rest running so farre indebt as keepes them still behind hand, and manie (not seldome) looseing their crops whilst they hunt for their bellyes." But beyond all of that, beyond all the errors and evils of the company and of the settlers themselves, the major cause of the massacre, it was universally agreed, was what they called the sheer barbarousness, the ingratitude, duplicity, treachery, and satanism, of the native American people.[8]

The rage against the Indians wiped out all thoughts of benevolence and any immediate prospect that the gospel mission would soon be renewed. These "wyld, naked natives," Edward Waterhouse, the Virginia Company's secretary and chief publicist, wrote, were instigated by the devil, which they worship out of fear and cowardice characteristic of a people who "flye as so many hares" at the mere sight of a woman holding an unloaded gun. But so shallow is their understanding that they do not see that in the end all of this bloodshed will be for the good of the colony. For, Waterhouse continued in a passage that anticipated the ten-year war that would follow, previously the colonists' hands "had been tied with gentlenesse and faire usage," but the treacherous violence of the Indians had now untied the knot. No longer would they be confined to scraps of the Indians' wasteland: now "by right of Warr and the law of nations" they would turn "the laborious mattocke into the victorious sword," invade the Indian country, "destroy them who sought to destroy us," confiscate the most fruitful land, and prevent the Indians from enjoying their indiscriminate hunting. In dealing with such "rude, barbarous, and naked people," Waterhouse noted, civility has too slow and uncertain an effect. They must be taken "by force, by surprize, by famine in burning their corne, by destroying and burning their boats, canoes, and houses, by breaking their fishing weares, by assailing them in their huntings . . . by pursuing and chasing them with our horses and blood-hounds . . . and mastives to seaze them . . . [and] by driving them (when they flye) upon their enemies, who are round about them, and by animating and abetting their enemies against them." Thus "may their ruine or subjection be soone effected."

All of this the company in London, once the promoter of racial harmony and peaceable conversion, firmly endorsed. Justice cries out for revenge, the company told the governor and council in Virginia, and wisdom demands security. Therefore "roote out from being any longer a people so cursed a nation, ungratefull to all benefitts and uncapable of all goodnesse . . . let them have a perpetuall Warr without peace or truce and . . . without mercie too." Spare only the children, who might later provide good labor and profitable service and whose minds, "not overgrowne with evill customes," may be reduced to civility and eventually Christianity. So

> pursue and follow them, surprisinge them in their habitations, intercepting them in theire hunting, burninge theire townes, demolishing theire temples, destroyinge their canoes, plucking upp theire weares, carying away theire corne, and depriving them of whatsoever may yeeld them succor or relief, by which meanes in a very short while both your just revenge and your perpetuall security might be certainly effected.

Public opinion in England supported this mandate for vengeance and racial warfare, which it rationalized in terms of religious obligation. A Christian crusade, a holy war "leaving not a creature / that may restore such shame of man and nature" was justified in flaming sermons, pamphlets, essays, and poems, in which Thorpe's martyrdom was a centerpiece.[9]

3

Disorganized, shocked, and still fearful, but determined to save the colony and turn on the Indians in a punishing campaign of revenge, the
colonists began to reorganize the settlements for protection and future
strength. Seven plantations were abandoned, the fortifications of another
seven were strengthened for future defense, and the demographic weight
shifted eastward. As panicked refugees fled to the safety of Jamestown
and the eastern plantations, commissions were issued to local commanders giving them absolute war powers, and an overall structure of military
command began to take form.

By late spring, two months after the massacre, the war of revenge was
well in motion, and it took the form, already seen in the earlier phases of
Anglo-Powhatan warfare, of "feedfights," which have been described as
"the 'fieringe and wastinge' of the enemy's food supply, field crops, and
habitations to promote dislocation, confusion, and starvation." Backup
raids in the late fall were designed to destroy irreplaceable corn supplies
before winter set in. Any canoes that were found were wrecked to reduce
the possibility of the Indians' importing food from outside. Every effort
was made to break up the alliance responsible for the massacre, while
support was given to the enemies of the combatant tribes in an effort to
press the target people between two aggressive fronts.

No tactic, however ruthless, was ruled out. In May 1623 one Captain Daniel Tucker was commissioned to negotiate the release of prisoners and conclude a peace treaty with the Patawomeke Indians along the
Potomac River, who had wiped out a trading mission led by the colony's
best interpreter, Henry Spelman. Tucker succeeded in his mission, and
then, to toast the peace, he gave the Indians poisoned wine, which had
apparently been prepared for the occasion by the colony's Dr. John Pott.
"Some tooe hundred weare poysned," the Puritan Robert Bennett wrote
his brother Edward from Bennett's Welcome, after which, he reported,
Tucker circled back to the same area and "killed som 50 more and
brought hom parte of ther heades . . . Soe this beinge done yt wilbe a
great desmayinge to the blodye infidelles." Bennett himself planned to go
after other tribes as soon as his tobacco and corn could be harvested, "to
cute downe ther corne and put them to the sorde. God sende us vyctrie,
as we macke noe question [of] God asistinge."[10]

But if God was assisting in the grinding war of attrition, He was not helpful in the domestic plight of the settlers. The usual early spring planting had been impossible in the weeks that followed the massacre, a food shortage quickly developed and deepened despite the supplies plundered from the Indians, and disease began to spread as new shiploads of servants and planters, responding to the growing passion for quick tobacco profits, arrived steadily. Close to nine hundred newcomers disembarked from fifteen vessels between March and the end of December, far more than could be effectively housed and supplied. They were easy victims to infectious diseases and the ravages of malnutrition. And then in December, when some signs of recovery could be seen, the *Abigail* arrived.

Sent out by the company as a relief ship bearing Lady Margaret Wyatt, the governor's wife, and some two hundred passengers, the *Abigail* proved to be a carrier of death. The ship, Lady Wyatt wrote, "was so pesterd wth people & goods that we were so full of infection that after a while we saw little but throwing folkes over boord." The shipboard epidemic, said to have been caused initially by contaminated beer, spread quickly among the passengers and through the colony after the survivors arrived and scattered among the settlements. The colony's leaders, desperate not for people they could not support, even healthy people, but for food supplies, arms, and equipment, were outraged. George Sandys, in the course of a savage indictment of the company for its persistent mismanagement, hoped that the brewer responsible for the noxious drink could be hanged and lamented the "extreame sicknes and unheard of mortalitie" that was devastating the land. The death rate rose beyond anyone's ability to gauge it. At one point Sandys said that five hundred had died in the year after the massacre, "*the lyveing being hardlie able to bury the dead*," at another that "the mortalitie of this year . . . hath dobled the nomber of those wch were massacred." The mortality continued. An official enumeration listed by name 360 people who had died in the nine months after 1623, leaving a total of 1,274 still alive. It was reasonable to believe, as one planter wrote, that "the Lordes hand hath ben more heavie by sicknes and death then by the sword of our enemyes."[11]

Just how heavy was the hand that blighted the land, how desperate was the state of the colony as it pursued its struggle with the Indians and its scramble for tobacco profits, can be seen in the savage indictment written by Capt. Nathaniel Butler, the departing governor of Bermuda who stopped off in Virginia en route to England. A partisan of the Smith faction in London, an enemy to Sandys's governing group now reinforced by the Earl of Warwick, Butler had no incentive to look kindly on the scene he found, but his charges, though perhaps exaggerated, were essentially true. The colony, he reported to the company, was set in "infectious boggs and muddy creeks and lakes" that generated disease. New arrivals came at the worst time of year and had no shelter or assistance, "soe that many of them by want herof are not onely seen dyinge under hedges and in the woods, but, beinge dead, ly some of them for many dayes unregarded and unburied." (Others would claim that the dead were "so litle cared for that they have lien untill the hogs have eaten theyr corps.") The price of food was astronomical, largely because of engrossing by the leaders who controlled the Indian trade. "Their howses are generally the worste that ever I sawe, the meanest cottages in England beinge every way equall (if not superiour) wth the moste of the best"; they were located "improvidently and scatteringlie" and lacked "the least peec of ffortificacion." All of the industrial projects had collapsed, and people simply "laughed to scorne" the company's ambitious prospectuses. "Tobacco onely was ye buisines," and no one gave a thought to anything else. Government was capricious, and anyone who urged conformity to English laws and customs was held in contempt. If nothing was done, and soon, to clear up the mess, the colony "will shortly gett ye name of a slaughter house."[12]

Replies to Butler's stinging eyewitness account were immediately drawn up, one by "divers of the planters that have long lived in Virginia" together with several mariners who had recently been there, another officially by the company itself. But the charges, though partisan, could not easily be refuted and in fact were substantiated by private correspondence that reached the company—despairing letters, like that of Thomas Niccolls who, besides cursing the lack of food and the false expectations the servants had arrived with, explained that the overpriced women did nothing but devour food without doing a decent day's work. Laundering had therefore been neglected, and poor tenants "dye miserablie through nastines, & many dep[ar]te the world in their own dung for want of help in their sicknes." Women should be sent over, he wrote, "whether they marry or no," just to clean the place up and tend to the sick.[13] But the letters of the young Richard Frethorne, one of the passengers on the *Abigail* who had contracted to work as an indentured servant on Martin's Hundred, convey something of the inner experiences of the servant population struggling to survive.

Two months after his arrival in Virginia, Frethorne—literate and eloquent, of a respectable family, and with reason to hope for social advancement—wrote one of his sponsors in England that he was in a "most miserable and pittiful case both for want of meat and want of cloathes." The starving servants on the plantation when he had arrived "fell to feedinge soe hard of our provision that itt killed them . . . as fast as the scurvie & bloody fluxe did kill us new Virginians." A pint of meal had to serve a man three days, he reported. He had only one ragged shirt left, one pair of hose and shoes, and one suit of clothes. "I am like to perish for want of succor & releife," and he begged his sponsor, amid flurries of citations of the Bible, "to redeeme me," "have mercy uppon me," or at least take up a collection in the parish to send him what he needed or to purchase his freedom.

To his parents he was more explicit. Servants like him "must worke hard both earelie and late for a messe of water gruell and a mouthfull of bread and beife." They lived in constant terror of attacks by the Indians, who now could use guns as well as the English could, and in any attack the plantation people would be completely outnumbered. Half of the servants aboard the *Abigail* who had shipped with him to Martin's Hundred were already dead, and two more were at death's door. "Ther is nothing to be gotten here but sicknes and death." He was in rags; his cloak had been stolen by someone who sold it for food; he was eating in the course of an entire week what he ate at home in one day. The one person who had befriended him "much marvailed that you would send me [as] a servaunt . . . he saith I had beene better knockd on the head." If you love me, he wrote, "redeeme me suddenlie, for wch I doe intreate and begg," and if that can't be done, "then for Gods sake" take up a collection to send food. "Good ffather, doe not forget me, but have mercie, and pittye my miserable case . . . if you love or respect me as yor child, release me from this bondage, and save my life." And then in a long afterthought, he said that his master, William Harwood, had warned the servants that he might not be able to provide for them all and might have to set them loose.

> Then wee shalbe turned up to the land and eate barks of trees or moulds of the ground. Therefore with weeping teares I beg of you to helpe me. O that you did see [my] daylie and hourelie sighes, grones, and teares, and [the] thumpes that I afford mine owne brest, and rue and curse the

time of my birth with holy Job. I thought no head had beene able to hold so much water as hath and doth dailie flow from mine eyes.

If Frethorne was ever sent the "succor & releife" he asked for, it came too late. He died within a year.[14]

4

Death was everywhere. Race warfare ground on relentlessly, and the new arrivals who survived "seasoning" struggled with disease and disability. None of Sandys's prized enterprises succeeded—not silk production, iron or glass manufacture, grape growing, or timber development. Nor could the workers assigned to company lands to produce sustenance for officials of church, schooling, or state be kept from slipping off to private plantations where conditions were somewhat better. And the private planters increasingly ignored the company's—and indeed the Crown's—pleas for agricultural diversity and concentrated more and more on the one clearly successful cash crop, tobacco.[15]

When in 1624 the company was forced to acknowledge its bankruptcy and its charter was annulled, the cost in human lives of its great adventure could, in part at least, be estimated. A polyglot, polyethnic collection of more than 8,000 men, women, and children from various parts of England, the continent of Europe, and Africa had arrived in Virginia under the company's auspices. A census of 1625 listed 1,218 still alive. In the single year 1622 close to 1,000 had died of disease or starvation or had been killed by the Indians. More than twice as many people died of disease that year than were killed in the massacre. The death toll among the natives would never be known, but thousands of Indian villagers, whose people had lived for centuries along the banks of the James and Chesapeake Bay, had been driven into the interior. The near-complete success of their desperate, bloody campaign against the English had initially restored their confidence and given them hope. Though increasingly pressed between the English on the east and ancient enemies on the north and west, they continued to resist and desist in alternating cycles, ultimately planning for another, final, apocalyptic assault on the invaders of their land and the challengers to their spiritual security.[16]

The English, who both repelled and attracted the Indians as they probed their exposed borders, continued to lead fragile, disordered lives in an unfamiliar, dangerous environment, pressing against threatening people no less disoriented and fearful than themselves. The settlers were still sheltered in small, lightly built, dirt-floored dwellings scattered haphazardly amid crudely cultivated, stump-filled tobacco fields and cattle farms, some with produce gardens and small fields of corn and other crops, cut out of Indian hunting grounds. Most of them were servants—"slaves," they were frequently called—working off their indentures, often side by side with their masters, hoping eventually to acquire a parcel of tobacco land of their own or return to their original homes. The Africans among them—twenty-three in 1625—were of indeterminate legal status since they had no contracts, and their social status, though debased, was unclear.[17] The social order as a whole, in the struggling colony's pell-mell scramble for survival and profits, was chaotic.

Some representatives of England's ancient, highly structured civil order remained: one of the original four adventurous sons of the West family, for example. And a few more such arrived: George Harmar, brother of Oxford's professor of Greek; Nathaniel Littleton, son of North Wales's chief justice and brother of the chief justice of common pleas; Edmund Scarborough, of Norfolk gentry. But the romantic, highly placed adventurers of earlier years were gone. George Percy had fled as early as 1612; the learned Whitaker had drowned; the benevolent Thorpe, who had been welcomed in the colony as "*an Angell* from heaven," had been murdered; the scholarly, worldly Pory, pining for his books and intellectual fellowship, had abandoned Virginia's "solitary uncouthnes"; and the litterateur George Sandys, as soon as his brother's governorship of the company ended, had returned from what he called his "exile," published his translation of Ovid, resumed his place among Lord Falkland's circle of poets, wits, and scholars ("one of the last great societies of England's golden age"), and became a Gentleman of the Privy Chamber.[18]

In place of these well-educated, well-connected adventurers, and in place too of the soldiers of fortune like Smith, Kendall, and Newport and the battalion of mercenary "hammerours" whom the company had sent out to drive back the Indians, a new generation of local leaders was emerging in Virginia. They were the first of the successful tobacco farmers and small-time Indian traders whose positions rested on their ability to wring material gain from the wilderness. Some, like Samuel Mathews, started with large initial advantages, but more typical were George Menefie and

John Utie, who began as independent landowners by right of transporting themselves and only one or two servants. Abraham Wood, who would
become famous for his explorations and, like Menefie and Utie, would
possess a large estate and important offices, appears first as a servant boy
on Mathews's plantation. Adam Thoroughgood, the son of a country
vicar, also started in Virginia as a servant, aged fourteen. William Spencer is first recorded as a yeoman farmer without servants.

Such men as these—Spencer, Wood, Menefie, Utie, Mathews—were
becoming the most important figures in Virginia at the end of the company period, engrossing large tracts of land and dominating the government. But their successes were not independent achievements. With the
collapse of the Virginia Company, the major figures in large-scale English
corporate enterprise lost interest in the colony. In their place as financial
backers and commercial managers came a new generation of small-time
English merchants, who plunged into the now highly competitive, still
small-scale free-for-all of colonial exploitation. Some of the newcomers had prospered in the English provinces, some were City shopkeepers, some were ship captains, some lesser City merchants excluded from
the monopolized overseas trades. And a few had themselves once been
planters in Virginia; prospering moderately, they had begun marketing
their own products by joining forces with traders operating in London.
At the same time, small-time shippers in England took advantage of the
headright system to acquire land in the colony by shipping servants and
thereby became absentee plantation owners and codevelopers with associates in the colony. The planters in Virginia and their new commercial
collaborators in England, linked in various kinds of associations, pressed
for increased production, which meant increases in the amount of land
under cultivation, and that in turn meant a constant increase in the size
of the labor force. The intensifying pressure to populate the land was a
measure of their escalating ambitions.

The whole enterprise was wide open. By 1634 there were 175 London
merchants in the Virginia trade; by 1640, there were 330. They and their
hustling collaborators in the colony—some formal partners, some family
associates, some simply ad hoc trading affiliates—were close to the actual
work of production and marketing and were aware of the profits that
could be realized by quick escalation of tobacco production and aggressive pursuit of the Indian trade.[19]

By 1630 the outlines of this new planter-merchant regime were clear.

But in no traditional sense were men like Spencer, Wood, Menefie, Utie, and Mathews, who were patenting large tracts of land and controlled Virginia's Council, a ruling class. Like the suddenly elevated and universally despised Governor Yeardley, mocked for his plebeian origins and his vulgar display after receiving a knighthood, or like the public-spirited William Peirce, whose "capacitie . . . is not to bee expected in a man of his breedinge," they lacked the kind of social authority, the "personall aucthoritye & greatness," the "eminence or nobillitye" that in this post-Elizabethan society would lead "everye man subordinate . . . to yeild a willing submission wthowt contempt or repyning."[20] Only with the greatest difficulty, if at all, could distinction be expressed in a genteel style of life. Their status was never beyond competition. Mathews may have created a flourishing tobacco estate and Menefie had fruit gardens, but the great tracts of land that such men claimed were almost entirely, in European terms, raw wilderness.[21] They had risen to their positions, with few exceptions, by brute labor and shrewd manipulation; they had personally shared the burdens of settlement. They succeeded not because of, but despite, whatever gentility they may have had. A few were educated, some were illiterate; but what counted was their common capacity to survive and flourish in frontier settlements. They were unsentimental, quick-tempered, crudely ambitious men concerned with profits and increased landholdings, not the grace of life. They roared curses, drank exuberantly, and gambled for their servants when other commodities were lacking. Rank had its privileges, and these men were the first to claim them, but rank itself was unstable, and the lines of class and status were fluid. There was no insulation for even the most elevated from the rude impact of frontier life.

By the early 1630s the more aggressive among them had seized control of the colony's government to assure themselves of constant increases in land grants, despite the Indians' resistance, and of free access to the Indian trade. They had also begun to move west to open trading camps along the middle and upper reaches of the York, Rappahannock, and Potomac rivers while they consolidated their control of the coastal plain. In 1634 they sealed off the entire coastal territory, enclosing some three hundred thousand acres by means of a six-mile-long palisade that stretched between the James and York rivers approximately forty miles inland from the Bay. The barrier, built of wooden planks behind a six-foot ditch and maintained by settlers granted fifty acres for their work on the palisade, was never an effective fortification. Within a decade the boards were rotting and the ditch was overgrown, but the palisade was important nevertheless. It served as a declaration of the English conquest of Powhatan territory and as a symbol of English exclusivity; it was an unmistakable line to be maintained between the once intermingled English and Indian worlds. Cleared of the presence of Indians, the newly opened boundary area—the Middle plantation, it was called—quickly attracted ambitious planters, whose crude initial clearings would in time become the town of Williamsburg.[22]

Among the most aggressive of the new planter-traders driving the expansion forward was the young William Claiborne, a Cambridge-educated son of a Kentish merchant family, who had arrived in 1621 with the lucrative commission as Virginia's surveyor of lands. Elevated to the ruling Council and to the post of secretary of the colony, he quickly acquired several patents of land for himself—a total of one thousand acres, at Kecoughtan and on the Eastern Shore—and a license to trade with the Indians. In a scouting expedition north along the upper shores of the Bay, he found a surprising number of private traders at work, perhaps as many as one hundred; some of them were mariners temporarily engaged in petty barter with the natives. Suspecting that the ultimate sources of much of the furs on offer were far inland, Claiborne conceived of a major enterprise based on large-scale trade with the Susquehannock Indians. These tribes, reaching south from deep inland to the head of Chesapeake Bay, drew on sources of furs as far north as Canada. Claiborne's imagination soared: he envisioned a "vast fur-trading and colonial provisioning network up and down the Atlantic coast." It would be centered on a spacious island he found at the northern end of Chesapeake Bay, which he named Kent Island, with an annex on the smaller Palmer's Island fifty miles farther north, at the mouth of the Susquehanna River. He would draw furs via the Susquehannocks from deep interior sources to Kent Island and trans-ship from there to markets in all the colonies and in England and the Continent as well.[23]

With this elaborate plan in mind, he returned to England in 1629 and put together a partnership that was as strong in funds as it was in political connections. The key figures were William Cloberry, already deep in the Newfoundland and Guinea trades and in marketing American tobacco; Cloberry's father-in-law, Humphrey Slaney, a founder of the Newfoundland Company and an investor in half a dozen major trading companies in Europe and the Middle East; Sir William Alexander, secretary of state for Scotland and proprietor of Nova Scotia, already engaged in the Canadian fur trade; and Claiborne's kinsman, the great London merchant Maurice Thomson. Backed by this powerful team of investors, Claiborne returned to Kent Island in 1631 with a start-up staff of twenty servants, over £300 worth of supplies, and a royal commission to trade in New England and Nova Scotia. He quickly "acquired" the fifteen-thousand-acre island from the friendly Metapeake Indians and began clearing the land and constructing a fort, houses, wharves, mills, warehouses, gardens, and marketplaces.[24]

BUT AS HE and his affluent London affiliates began populating Kent Island 120 miles north of Jamestown, they came into conflict with a new, unexpected influx of migrants to the upper Chesapeake lands, which, unknown to Claiborne, had been officially designated Maryland.

CHAPTER 6

❧

Terra-Maria

1

IN THE GENERATION after the Virginia Company sent its first settlers to America, England and its relation to the western hemisphere
were transformed. Though in the countryside England was still very
much a traditional society, the regional growth of trade and industry
and the accompanying expansion of the provincial towns, together with
the extraordinary growth of London, were creating economic and social
innovations throughout the land and stimulating mobility and a propensity to emigrate to a level that had not existed before.

Increasingly urban and mobile, modernizing in various sectors of
life, its most progressive elements enterprising and ambitious, England
was far from stable or secure. No one could have predicted the upheaval
that would tear the country apart in the 1640s, but social and political
strains were visible two decades earlier. Serious economic problems had
developed—partly as a result of the volatility of the all-important textile
industry, especially in East Anglia and the West Country, which in the
1620s fell into a depression, and partly because of falling wages, high food
prices, and disasters like plague, fires, and failed harvests. At the same time
religious dissent grew fierce and defiant in the face of official pressure for
conformity, and political animosities deepened as court patronage bal-

looned, generating increasingly bitter opposition. All of these domestic dislocations and discontents played into the emerging world overseas.

For while economic changes were loosening the ties of thousands to their native roots, propelling them out across the land in search of employment and security, and while the demands of an increasingly intolerant established church were forcing both Protestant and Catholic dissenters to search for escape and refuge, England's transoceanic possessions were becoming known to increasing numbers of people throughout the realm. The east coasts of Newfoundland, Nova Scotia, and northern New England had long been familiar to West Country fishermen, and news of developments in the Chesapeake lands and the West Indies had been widely circulated not only officially by the Virginia and Bermuda companies but informally by friends and families of the thousands who had ventured there and by the hundreds who had invested in American land rights and in trade in colonial products. It was well known in non-conformist circles that a contingent of the radical dissenters exiled in the Netherlands had followed Lawne and the Bennetts to America but had ended up not in Virginia but on the shores of Massachusetts, where they had found a safe though spartan refuge for their small conventicle. And the success of the settlements in the West Indies, especially those in Bermuda, challenged the imagination of entrepreneurs who thought seriously of investing in transoceanic trade and were ambitious enough to hope for a share of the profits that were beginning to flow from the sale of American tobacco at home and in the European markets.

Impelled by discontents and dislocations at home and drawn by opportunities that had suddenly appeared overseas, emigration from the British Isles and resettlement in the colonies became a significant demographic phenomenon in the 1630s.[1] The flow of emigration, which would continue with shifting intensities for two centuries, can be seen for what it was, a new and dynamic force in European, American, and African population history. What mattered most was not the emergence of specific English colonies, whose identities had not yet formed, but the beginning of a general westward diaspora of the peoples of the British Isles and their contacts—strange, varied, often bloody—with the indigenous Americans.

England's nascent colonies in the west, the products of individual and private group initiatives, formed no coherent unit. But however scattered and unrelated, these settlements created in England a general sense that there existed in the west a vast, largely unknown territorial periphery to which access was possible. These outer lands—barbaric islands and coastal fringes of an unknown continent—seemed to offer strange, dangerous, but promising opportunities. In the years when the Virginia Company's directors were pouring funds and lives into a failing effort to earn corporate profits from settlements on the James River, they and others were investing also in settlements in Bermuda and in Ireland—especially in Ireland. It was Ireland in fact that was Britain's fastest-growing colony throughout the early seventeenth century. Large regions in northeastern and southeastern Ireland were seized from their inhabitants, plantations created or resumed, the natives forced west into infertile hill country, and great parcels of land declared open for resettlement by veterans of the Irish wars and migrants from abroad. The result was a burst of westward migration far more powerful than any that lay behind the settlements in the western hemisphere. In the twelve years after 1630, 120,000 Englishmen and Scots are estimated to have migrated to Ireland, double the number of those who went to the West Indies in those years, six times more than went to New England.[2]

It was the beginning, in the British Isles, of an extraordinary period of emigration, a demographic phenomenon that would not be matched until the 1760s, when again there was a sense that an entire new world had suddenly been flung open for settlement by land-hungry migrants.[3] While in the years of the Virginia Company and the two decades that followed Scottish Presbyterians and Covenanters settled by the thousands in the six counties of Ulster, other English nonconformists, in smaller numbers, settled elsewhere in the farther colonial borderlands: on Providence Island off the coast of Nicaragua and on the shores of southern New England. At the same time, on the upper reaches of Chesapeake Bay another group of English adventurers struggled to found a settlement new in concept and design which would create a distinctive element in North American population history.

2

Their sponsors and leaders were Catholics, dissenters on the "right," a standing challenge to England's Episcopal establishment. Caught in the great religious struggles of the sixteenth century, they were thought likely to be associated with foreign powers that threatened England's sovereignty, and they had been forced to withdraw from public life. Subject to penal laws for public profession of their faith, susceptible to charges of treason, their worship necessarily private and their priests hunted and often imprisoned or exiled, England's and Wales's sixty thousand Catholic worshippers—approximately 1 percent of the population—were split into several groups, with "the backbone of the community . . . in the ranks of the armigerous gentry." They were quietist though active in public life and flexible in adjusting to the complex restrictions they lived under—restrictions that were neither annihilatory nor superficial. They worshipped privately, most often under the protection of gentry and noble families, and they came to accept that the religion of subjects need not be the same as that of rulers and states. They formed a community that was carefully pragmatic, shy of publicity that might imperil the privacy they were allowed, reluctant to break out of the paternalistic protection they enjoyed, geographically scattered, and not easily mobilized as a community.[4] That they came to sponsor the resettlement of an area strategically located on the east coast of North America was largely the result of the imagination of a retired public official whose religious commitment was as profound as his entrepreneurial spirit was unbounded.

GEORGE CALVERT, born into the Catholic gentry of northern Yorkshire, had conformed to the Church of England at least from the age of fourteen, when he entered Oxford University. After his years there, followed by study at the Inns of Court and travel abroad, he became a dutiful and successful public servant. Prominent at the court of James I, he took on more and more responsibilities, ultimately reaching the great office of secretary of state. But, more a reliable bureaucrat than an imaginative statesman, and lacking in the skills of a political infighter, he lost out to more adroit politicians when he stubbornly continued to support the failed diplomatic project of marrying the Prince of Wales to the Spanish Infanta, which included plans to relieve English Catholics of legal disabilities. In 1625, politically bypassed and isolated, he sold his office and left public service, bearing with him the King's "princely approbation and . . . good grace," the income from the sale of his office, and the parting royal gift of the Irish barony of Baltimore.[5]

Once freed from official duties, Calvert, now the Baron Baltimore, openly reclaimed his Catholicism, made contact with Catholic laymen and regular priests, and turned to projects of overseas settlement, with which he had been marginally involved for years. As early as 1609, he had invested in both the Virginia Company, to whose leaders he had family connections, and the East India Company. In 1620 he had bought land in Newfoundland; and in 1622 he had supported the New England Company. At the same time he had received substantial land grants in Ireland, which became his principal residence. Thus associated with overseas enterprises east and west, he turned to the least developed, Newfoundland, which engaged him most actively in the early 1620s. It was there that he began his active career in colonization, and it was there that he developed the ideas that would shape a unique segment of North American population history.[6]

In 1621 he sent a small party of settlers, mainly Welshmen, to Ferryland, the harbor of his property in the jutting southeastern promontory of Newfoundland. Despite the forbidding terrain ("nothing but rocks, lakes, or mosses, like bogs") they erected some buildings, sowed crops, and began the construction of a quarry, a forge, and a salt manufactory. Two years later, in 1623, Calvert received a royal charter for an enlarged territory—a broad band of over two million acres stretching west from the Atlantic coast—which he called the Province of Avalon. Legally a palatinate, the grant gave Calvert vice-regal powers to make his own laws within this domain, consistent with the Crown's sovereignty. And though the charter required adherence to "God's holy and true Christian religion," it omitted any restriction on Roman Catholicism. In 1625, with the colony boasting an English population of one hundred and "a broode of horses, kowes, and other bestial," Baltimore advertised for "any that will adventure with him, or serve under him." He appointed a Catholic, Sir Arthur Aston, to head the colony, and allowed a Carmelite priest, Father Simon Stock, to establish in Avalon "a missionary outpost . . . to which priests could venture forth both to convert the Indians and to offset the increasing Puritan presence." And if a northwest passage through the continent opened up, Father Stock looked forward to using the Ferryland mission as a base for the Church's penetration of Asia.[7]

Aston arrived with a small party of co-religionists; and Baltimore himself, on two trips to the colony, brought with him two secular priests, one of whom remained to establish the first Catholic mission in British America, and then, along with most of his family and another priest, about forty other Roman Catholics—some Irish, some Yorkshire recusants. But by 1629 the outlines of one of the problems that would later beset the

Calverts in Maryland became clear. The majority of the settlers proved to be Protestants who had their own preacher and did not share Baltimore's hopes that the two communions could or should live together peaceably. The Anglican minister was shocked by the open practice of Catholicism on English territory and reported his dismay to the authorities at home.[8]

Locked in controversy with "that knave, [the Anglican Rev.] Stourton," and harassed, in addition, by marauding French men-of-war in the coastal fishing waters, Baltimore faced a bitter winter in which his house became a hospital for fully half the colony. By the spring, he despaired of "this wofull country, where with one intolerable wynter were we almost undone," and decided to relocate his community to the south, in or near Virginia, where, on "some good large territory" he hoped "to lay my bones."

But the Avalon experiment, though a costly failure (an estimated loss of £20,000 to £30,000), had been useful. Baltimore had known from childhood how difficult it was in England for Catholics and Protestants to live together, but he had now learned of further, possibly disastrous, complications when the problem was transferred to fragile settlements in the remote Atlantic borderlands. In addition, he had come to appreciate the extraordinary ambitions and passionate zeal of the Catholic missionaries, especially the regular priests, which, however honorable, could threaten any regime in an era of confessional struggles and of volatile relations with the American natives. Above all, he had learned the necessity, if he was to succeed in establishing a colony safe for Catholics, of somehow transcending the prevailing doctrine of *cuius regio, eius religio*—for each regime, its own (exclusive) religion. His colonial domain would have to be something different—a regime that tolerated people of all Christian confessions, the government itself committed to none.[9]

How necessary this would be became even clearer to him the moment, in 1629, he brought his party from Newfoundland to Virginia, the colony to which he had had connections for twenty years, to seek out a site for his new colony. Fearful of competition and echoing the antipopery of the metropolis, the Virginia authorities under Governor John Pott—the doctor who had prepared the poison for the Indians six years before—denied them entry when, as Catholics, they refused to swear the oath of supremacy.

Baltimore spent the next two years—his last—at home, maneuvering for a charter for a colony just north of Virginia where he might realize his dreams. He had the favor and support not only of influential court-iers and officials but of Charles I himself. The monarch, who had sup-ported Baltimore's Newfoundland adventure, remembered favorably his "former services and late indeavors," though he warned him that men of "your condition and breeding" were fitter for other employments than the framing of new plantations, which commonly had rugged and labo-rious beginnings and that required greater resources than most private subjects could command. Thus cautioned but supported by the Crown, Baltimore carefully worked his charter through the bureaucracy, but died two months before the legalities were complete. It was left to his dutiful son Cecilius, the second Baron Baltimore, to carry the project through. The young Calvert spent the rest of his life managing the project his father had designed, preserving it through great vicissitudes, struggling and stumbling, failing and recovering, with energy, patience, imagina-tion, and political skill. By the time he died in 1675 he had laid a durable foundation. A Catholic population survived, and his descendants, years later, especially the profligate sixth baron (d. 1771), would inherit wealth from the Maryland palatinate that the first baron could scarcely have imagined.[10]

The charter, modeled on the earlier Avalon grant, gave Baltimore a princely territory of ten to twelve million acres stretching north from the Potomac River to the fortieth parallel (thus including what would later be southern Pennsylvania), west to the sources of the Potomac, and includ-ing most of the Eastern Shore of Chesapeake Bay. And the proprietor was given the powers of a palatine lord, powers that had not been granted since the fourteenth century, when the Welsh and Scottish marchland jurisdictions had been created. He had absolute power to use or dispose of the land, defend and administer the province, and govern the popula-tion, whose legal status, technically, was not that of subjects of the king but tenants of the lord proprietor. Writs were to run in his name, not the king's. And Baltimore was specifically authorized to create manors, each with its own local governing powers—a provision vital, he believed, for the recruitment of wealthier planters and for the re-creation of the enclaves of privacy that had sheltered Catholics at home. Above all, noth-ing in the charter prevented Baltimore from recruiting a population of his own choosing, Catholics as well as Protestants, clerics as well as laymen.[11]

The entire enterprise depended on population recruitment, and on this Baltimore moved cautiously. While the Crown, in its geopolitical calculations, was particularly interested in creating a buffer between Virginia and the Dutch, who were moving south from the Hudson River area, Baltimore increasingly thought of Maryland not only as a source of profit and achievement for himself and the nation but as a refuge for Catholics, who were under growing pressure in England. But he knew from the start that he would be dependent on a general population of Protestant farmworkers, artisans, and tenants. And he knew too that the survival of his charter would always be in question, vulnerable as it was to attacks, on the one hand, in England, by antipapists in combination with certain Virginia Company stockholders with claims to northern Chesapeake lands and, on the other hand, in Virginia, by the emerging colonial leaders eager to expand their landholdings and trade. So, carefully and guardedly, he gathered a small party of investors—twenty in all, fifteen of them Catholics, thirteen either members of the Calvert family or close acquaintances—and, discreetly, welcomed prospective emigrants at a recruitment office he set up in London. To help in all his planning, advertising, and recruiting, and especially to help him realize his religious mission in America, he applied to the Jesuit authorities for members of their order to join him in his enterprise. Though few in number, the Jesuits—"the best organized, most numerous, and most militant of England's priests," zealous proselytizers led by the "prickly scholar" Father Andrew White—proved to be key figures in the first group of settlers, who arrived in Chesapeake Bay in March 1634.[12]

This first of Baltimore's expeditions to the Chesapeake was the occasion for him to express his hopes and imaginings, his justification and goals in launching a settlement of English people in a distant, exotic world. His aim, he (or Father White) wrote in his initial recruitment leaflet, was, principally, "to bring to Christ [Maryland] and the countreys adjacent, which from the beginning of the world to this day, never knew God." It would be no intrusion of unwelcome aliens, no subjugation of an unwilling population. For, he wrote, he had studied the accounts of other plantations and explorations, and he knew with a certainty that "the Indians themselves [were] sending farre and nigh for teachers to instruct and baptize them." He had no doubt that thousands, many thousands, would happily be brought to Christianity. They simply needed the agency, which he hoped to provide.

But God, he believed, worked in wonderful ways. Establishing a Christian mission in Maryland had the further advantage, he wrote, of enlarging Charles I's overseas "empire and dominions," a goal Baltimore strongly and loyally endorsed; and beyond that, the colony would serve the more mundane interests of those ordinary people who "are not so noble-minded" as to seek mainly "great and glorious" satisfactions but are drawn by "pleasure, wealth, and honour." So that lower as well as higher inducements might not be wanting, God had provided great potential wealth in Maryland, which men of ordinary inclinations might, while serving higher ends, gainfully exploit. There was abundant timber, all sorts of minerals, an infinity of fish and animals, and rich farming land that might be possessed by smallholders as well as by magnates, and there were vast beaver supplies, which in the previous year alone, he wrote, had yielded a profit of £10,000.[13]

There was in all of this a tone of benevolence blended with opportunism which Baltimore and his colleagues would soon amplify in a series of pamphlets explaining and promoting his nascent colony. From the start the whole enterprise was loftily conceptualized and personalized to benefit Baltimore himself and his embattled Catholic community. He knew there would be protests against the project, and in 1633 he issued a paper to identify and refute all the possible objections. An easy exodus of Catholics would *not*, he argued, frustrate England's efforts to convert them to Protestantism; his charter would *not* imply the toleration of Catholics in England; such an exodus would *not* deprive the Crown of penal revenues; it would *not* drain wealth from England; nor would a Catholic colony attract foreign Catholics likely to threaten Protestant Virginia and New England or support the colonies' separation from England. Nothing he could think of was left to chance, least of all the social order he hoped would emerge as the colony developed.[14]

Other colonizers would project innovative ideas onto what they took to be the American tabula rasa—new designs, conceptual beacons lighting the way forward out of a dark past. But Baltimore's social views were idealistic in a different way. They were nostalgic and regressive, hearkening back to the fading world in which Catholicism had flourished, a world of rentier landlords with servants and tenants, societies of legal privilege and ordained disparities of wealth—a social order whose hierarchical structure would secure all people in their rightful, functional places. The manor, consistent with the values and visions of a premodern culture, would in his imagining be the institutional foundation of the new-old order—a way of "raising some nobility" from among the manor lords, who would receive political appointments, titles of honor, and "no small share in the profits of trade"—presumably the profits of the joint-stock company he created to exploit the fur trade. To anyone willing to join the first settlement at his own expense and bring with him five able men, he offered a manor of two thousand acres with full judicial powers ("courts leet and baron") and "all such royalties and privileges as are usually belonging to mannors in England," and in addition ten acres of town land for each person transported in the capital city he planned. Later the requirement would rise to ten accompanying men, then twenty. And for those lesser folk who brought only themselves and their immediate families, including servants, there would be rights to one hundred acres for each adult and fifty acres for every child. Servants, it was assumed, and tenants to work the land would be drawn from those who came with no resources of their own. And Baltimore's own profits would be assured by annual rents he would charge on the lands he so generously granted.[15]

All of this was broadcast discreetly to the country at large. But to his brother Leonard, who would serve as the resident governor of the colony, and to the two commissioners he appointed to serve with Leonard to rule the colony, he gave more specific instructions. The first of his fifteen orders went straight to the religious question, and to Baltimore's determination to make Maryland not a Catholic colony but a colony safe for Catholics. Protestants, he commanded, were to be given no offense that might be a cause for complaint in either Virginia or England. And to that end the commissioners were to see to it that

> all acts of Romane Catholique religion [were] to be done as privately as may be, and that they instruct all the Romane Catholiques to be silent upon all occasions of discourse concerning matters of religion; and that [they] treat the Protestants with as much mildness and favor as justice will permitt.

The commissioners were to gather information on any plots against Baltimore's charter and regime. They were to avoid initial contact with Virginia, but they were to make respectful diplomatic overtures both to that colony generally and to William Claiborne, on Kent Island, specifically. Though Claiborne was considered a trespasser on Baltimore's land, he was to be left alone for at least a year while the situation was carefully canvassed. At the first settlement, located at some "healthfull and fruitfull" place, the commissioners were to read out Baltimore's legal rights and declare his interest in converting the natives to Christianity and in augmenting His Majesty's "empire and dominions in those parts of the world by reducing them under the subjection of the crowne." They were to assist the settlers to "reape the fruites of their charges," and begin planning the layout of a town and adjoining manors and farmlands.

His colony would be no random scattering of settlements, as in Virginia, no sprawl of isolated plantations, farms, and houses, dangerously exposed to Indian attacks. Streets were to be laid out carefully in a fortified town, with houses "neere adjoyning one to an other," and surveys made for the controlled distribution of farmland, with special care in reserving a proper proportion of the land for Baltimore himself. The first plantings were to be for a "sufficient quantity of corne and other provision of victuall" and for nothing else until the necessary subsistence crops were raised. Militia duty was to be required, and the possibilities of various industries scouted out. Above all, the government was "to do justice to every man without partiality," avoid all conflict with Virginia, and inform Baltimore of every development, large and small.[16]

Thus was the colony planned, and thus, with elaboration, was it promoted. Recruitment tracts—seven, in one form or other, in the 1630s, several of them written at least in part by Father Andrew White— emphasizing the opportunities in Maryland, in terms calculated to appeal to wide segments of the English population eager for independent settlement on the land, were printed and discreetly distributed. But the most remarkable and expansive treatise on the lure of Maryland's prospects circulated in manuscript.

THAT DOCUMENT IS extraordinarily revealing. It expresses at once the fierce nationalism that impelled England's colonial expansion; the idyllic aspirations of the deprived younger sons of gentry families in considering the benefits of overseas settlements; the peculiar problems of the Catholic gentry denied access to established institutions; the intense moralism of English attitudes to the American natives; and above all the passion of ordinary householders for a stake in the land. Its image of felicity in the Atlantic west would haunt the imagination of the relatively deprived English gentry for generations.

The manuscript, a romantic, self-consciously literary essay ("But soft, 'tis not my purpose . . . ") in the form of a letter to a friend contemplating emigration, was written by Robert Wintour, grandson of the Earl of Worcester and of an Elizabethan admiral who had fought with Drake, a younger son of a prosperous Gloucestershire Catholic family, and brother of the queen's secretary. Catholics all, connected by marriage to the Calvert family, they were much involved in what Wintour called the "Maryland designe." Two of his younger brothers were among the colony's first settlers. Through them and others Wintour kept in close touch with the colony's fortunes during the first few years and was able to sketch a vividly enticing image of its future.

Why should one remove to the New World generally, Wintour asked, and to Maryland specifically? To study men, he wrote, "as God and nature made them, morally good," people without the sins of "deceipt, pride, avarice, ambition, or (of all vices, the mother) sloth." Besides satisfying "all manner of curiosities" and probing "unknowen secretts," one would serve God nobly by contributing to the "conversion and civilizing [of] those barbarous heathens that live like beasts without the light of faith." Maryland's aim, as opposed to Virginia's, was not "to extirpate and destroy" the natives (who he believed were "no lesse witty and discoursive" than Europeans) but "to civilize, cherish and preserve to eternity their manners, bodies, and soules."

> Where can witt and worth be more truely exprest then in conquering nations to enrich them, subduing people to make them men, subjecting wild savages to make them free, taking nothing from them but barbarous nakednes and in counterchange adorning them with decent civility?

In joining the Maryland settlement, Wintour wrote, one would also be serving the king and state, by enlarging "our Soverraigne's dominions adding . . . much to the honor profitt and strength of his State and Realmes." It grieved his soul, he wrote, to hear England abused by those who complain of unemployment and can think of nothing else to do with themselves but in desperation to serve as mercenaries to foreign princes. "Shall the brave Englishman, the noble Brittain be the drudge to . . . those insulting strang[er]s (to whom he must crouch and fawne to gett his beggerly pay)"? England was "the garden of the earth . . . the flower of kingdomes for power and ma[jes]tie, the envy of countries for freeborne nurslings, the terror of nations for untamed spirits, the magazine of the world for trade and commerce." And so, "peopling o[u]r new colonies [is] . . . more laudable in it selfe, more convenient for our country, and every way more worthy and becoming a true English heart then any forreine service." By peopling Baltimore's new colony, England's sons could gain for themselves the name that so honored their ancient ancestors, "founders of a nation."

And then, Wintour explained to his friend, there were the material rewards. In Maryland it would be possible to achieve "a quiett life sweetned with ease and plenty," in secure possession of a "compotent estate . . . answerable to [one's] birth and calling." And he described in detail the good things of life that would in time become available in Maryland—all those benefits of life that people like himself should have had in England but didn't: "ground of our owne . . . our owne beefe and mutton . . . venison out of our owne parke[,] a partridge, a pheasant, and a cock taken in o[u]r owne Mannor . . . with a good fire in the great chamber" attended by half a dozen "blew coates [servants] . . . to bring up our meate upon Sondaies." And the gentleman settler would find "wholesome and fatt gardenage . . . a dainty river at his foote . . . delightfull walkes on every side . . . halfe a dozen or halfe a score gentlemen, his freinds and partners . . . to accompany him in his sports and consummate his felicity . . . nothing to doe but to be merry and grow fatt, eate, drinke, & recreate, and give God thanks."

How could all this be achieved? Everything would depend on the servants one could recruit. Of an investment of £500, £300 would cover the expenses of fifteen "able labouring men" whose transportation would guarantee land grants of no less than three thousand acres. Some of that land—fertile, healthful, and fit "for our English bodies"—could nicely be turned into a deer park, while the rest would provide, within the space of a mere two years, ample crops of all kinds, the profits of which could support the importation of more servants, who would produce more crops, which would make possible more servants, and so forth in an ever-ascending scale. The land would be so abundant that one could provide for the eventual homesteads of the servants once they were freed from service, and they, working their plots, would produce an income for the landowner in the form of rents.

Surely, he wrote, this was far better than remaining in England, where land was misused and scarce, where the countryside was overwhelmed with "loyterers and wasters" who "pester the earth and but few employed to convert it to best use," and where much of the land was consigned to "great men's sports or excesse." In Maryland land was abundant, and as the Jesuit Thomas Copley was soon to write, "nothinge is wanting but people. Let [Maryland] be peopled and it shall not yeeld to the most flourishing country for profitt and pleasure." And beyond all of that, there was the tolerant colonial government of Lord Baltimore, in which settlers could worship as they pleased; each freeholder would have a voice in an assembly; the leadership would be comprised of men of high birth, education, and wealth; and the servant population would be made up not, as elsewhere in the colonies, of "the scumme of the people, taken up promiscuously, as vagrants and runnewayes from their m[aste]rs, debauched, idle, lazie squanderers, jaylbirds, and the like," but of decent fellow countrymen, tenants of known landowners, loyal servants happy to share in their masters' fortunes, admitted to the colony only on "good recommenda[ti]ons and knowledge of them to be free from any taints."

How much of this Wintour himself believed cannot be known. But he must have been convinced of at least some of his imaginings because he emigrated to Maryland in 1637 with seven (not the recommended fifteen) servants and with personal property appropriate for the genteel life he anticipated. In Maryland he did indeed become a landowner and also a councilor, justice of the peace, and assemblyman. But he died within two years, leaving behind not a deer park, pheasants, and "fatt gardenage," but a complicated balance of assets and debts calculated in pounds of tobacco, an assortment of farm tools and equipment, and the remains of the finery he had so hopefully brought with him from England: seven suits of clothes, a gold ring, "an old silver belt," a small library, a painting, a parcel of printed pictures, and a dozen napkins.[17]

3

Such men as Wintour, younger sons of well-placed Catholic families, often with wives and children, began to arrive in the colony with the first shipment, on the *Ark* and the *Dove* in 1634. How many passengers those vessels carried is not precisely known—contemporaries said 200 to 300; modern estimates vary from 148 to 175. These were small vessels—the *Ark* a ship of 360 tons, the *Dove* a mere pinnace of 60 tons. With equipment, supplies, and animals, together with their human freight, they were dangerously overloaded, and shipboard relations, under those conditions, were exceedingly complex. For the passenger group reflected Baltimore's reliance both on the Catholic gentry and on the English working-class population, who together formed the basis of the community that would initially emerge. When the expedition left Cowes for Maryland, it included seventeen "Gentlemen of Fashion," most of them Catholic, among whom were at least eight younger sons of peers, knights, or members of Parliament. Investors in the overall settlement project, they brought with them, besides their own servants, farm equipment, supplies, and some of the finery of their gentle way of life. The rest of the passengers, most of them Protestants, were indentured or paid servants, one of them black, one a Portuguese mulatto, some artisans, and a few independent farmers. Two Jesuit priests—Andrew White and John Altham—and a lay brother completed the shipboard list. Sharply divided between gentry and laborers, most of whom were indentured servants, the first settling group conformed reasonably well to Calvert's social expectations.[18]

They arrived at the Potomac River on March 3, 1634, after a difficult three-month voyage via the West Indies and a surprisingly amicable stopover in Virginia. The landscape that met them, 180 miles north of the James River, was significantly different from what the Virginians had found on the malarial shores to the south. The well-traveled Father White reported in his enthusiastic *Briefe Relation* (1634) that the Potomac "is the sweetest and greatest river I have seene, so that the Thames is but a little finger to it." It ran, near its mouth, between terraced banks that stepped down in stages from about forty feet; and behind the shores lay woods—of oak, cedar, pine, cypress, elm, ash, and poplar. Successive burnings had long since cleared out the forest undergrowth, together with the more flammable trees, and had created small meadows, parks, and corridors leading inland, through which, White wrote, "a coach and fower horses may travale without molestation." The terraced shoreline— "noe marshes or swampes . . . but solid firme ground"—seemed fertile. One could imagine a rich agriculture developing in this well-watered land.

These first impressions were confirmed as the settlers began a slow reconnaissance of the Potomac estuary. After celebrating mass on Blackistone's Island and erecting a "great cross which we had hewn from a tree . . . as a trophy to Christ the Saviour, while the litany of the Holy Cross was chaunted humbly, on our bended knees, with great emotion of soul," they moved inland. They were determined, for both religious and commercial purposes, to avoid the catastrophe in race relations that the Virginians had endured and to engage constructively with the strange native peoples. In this, in their first encounters, they largely succeeded, in part due to the excellent guide they had to lead them into this mysterious world, in part due to the peculiar configuration of forces among the Potomac Indians—the local Piscataways and Patuxents desperate for defensive alliances against the aggressive Susquehannocks and Iroquois—and in part due to the Jesuits' boundless zeal, their rhapsodic joy in embracing this vast missionary field and the possibility it offered of bringing untold multitudes of pagans to the altar of Christ.[19]

Rumors, spread by the Virginians, had already reached the natives, who had long been familiar with European explorers and settlers, warning them that a force of vengeful Spaniards was about to invade their land; but Calvert's shrewdly acquired guide to the Indians' world helped ease the settlers' entry. Henry Fleete, son of a Kentish landowner and barrister with connections to the Virginia Company, had arrived in Virginia in 1621. Two years later he had been captured by the Potomac Indians and had spent five years with them, learning their language (which he claimed he knew better "than mine own"), their lore, and the details of intertribal relations. In England after his release, he had acquired backers (perhaps associated with the Kent Island venture) for a deep exploration of the fur supplies in the Potomac region. In 1631–32, when Baltimore was negotiating for his charter, Fleete was exploring every creek and inlet and Indian settlement along the Potomac waterway, voyaging with a small team on flatboats and pinnaces as far west as the site of the present District of Columbia and soaking up all the information he could find on the natives, the sources of furs and food supplies, and the possibilities of bringing both out into the European markets. When Calvert's vessels appeared, Fleete was working at several bartering centers in what was legally Maryland territory. Both a rival and an associate of Claiborne, he was brought into the Maryland project by the promise of manorial lands and trading rights. He led Calvert's party on an inspection of the lands he knew so well at the mouth of the Potomac and, cautiously, on a slow voyage up into that river, to come to terms with the natives.[20]

That initial encounter with the Potomac Indians, which introduced the relative ease in race relations that would follow, comes to us first through the eyes of Father White, determined to reach sympathetically into the souls of the pagan people. In *A Briefe Relation*, sent home two months after the *Ark* arrived, he wrote of the governor's decision to pay his respects to the tribal "Emperour" at Piscataway, 120 miles upriver. The goodwill of this dominant figure, it was assumed, would pave the way with the other, lesser chiefs. The aim would be to convince this headman of their sincere intention "to teach them a divine doctrine, whereby to lead them to heaven," and also to enrich them with the "ornaments" of European culture.

They stopped along the way, however, at "Patomacke towne," half-way up the river. There Father Altham delivered the first of the Jesuits' sermons to the Indians, firmly informing the local chief of "his [religious] errours in part, which he seemed to acknowledge," though, White had to admit, they did not really get far on religion, probably, he thought, because the interpreter was a Protestant. They finally reached the "Emperour" at Piscataway, eased his fears and those of his "500 bow-men," convinced him of their good intentions, and extracted from him "leave to us to sett downe where we pleased."[21]

They found an even warmer reception downriver when, under Fleete's and some local Indians' guidance, they selected a choice spot for their settlement—the site of one of Fleete's makeshift trading posts, on the ele-vated shores of a tributary stream, St. Mary's River, close to the mouth of the Potomac. The resident Indians, the Yoacomacos, were already plan-ning to abandon the site, with its village and cleared fields, and willingly gave the English the whole region in exchange for a supply of axes, hoes, and cloth. White never doubted what was happening. God, he explained, was disposing things to the advantage of those who were bringing "the light of his holy law to these distressed, poore infidels." He had seen to it that, just at the right moment, the belligerent Susquehannock tribes had threatened to exterminate the local tribes, causing them to fear for their lives and, "like lambes, [to] yeeld themselves, glad of our company, give-ing us houses, land, and liveings for a trifle. *Digitus dei est hic.*"

Thus encouraged by the finger of God, White was endlessly intrigued by his benign charges, and he carefully described his impressions. Their appearance, he said, was utterly bizarre. Their body paint was weird, the cut of their hair was outlandish, they wore necklaces of eagles' claws and "the teeth of beasts," their clothes were made of skins and furs; and he noted their strange weapons and their skill in using them, their houses, diet, conjugal habits, and taciturnity; above all, their dark, barbarous, pagan worship. He had to confess that after a month of contact with them he had not quite penetrated their spiritual life, but his confidence persisted: once these people became Christians, "they would doubtlesse be a vertuous and renowned nation."[22]

4

So, on the well-watered open area above St. Mary's River, Baltimore's party dug in. While still living aboard the anchored vessels, they threw together a square moated fort, which quickly became a two-and-a-half-mile-long palisaded village. From the "rough habitations" that were hastily built within the walls, farmworkers walked out to a "crazy quilt of plots" in the cleared fields the Indians had left behind. This open-field farming around a nuclear settlement lasted for three growing seasons. Then, in 1637, when the settlers felt secure in their immediate environment, when they had inspected the land for miles around, and when the leadership had drawn up the information needed for the distribution of manorial and headright land, the dispersal began.

The major adventurers blocked out manors southeast of the town. Together with Governor Calvert they claimed fifteen thousand acres and set aside five thousand adjacent acres for later manorial sites. At the same time the Jesuits, seeking to engage the Indians directly, moved nine miles north and established three manors close to the Indian villages along the Patuxent River, which ran parallel to the lower Potomac. There, on land given them by the Patuxent "King" Maquacomen, they opened their first missions and built the storehouse for their entire conversion enterprise. Others were moving north too—the merchant Justinian Snow, whose Snow Hill Manor, just north of St. Mary's Town, was surveyed at six thousand acres; and Richard Garnett, whose St. Richard's Manor, abutting the Jesuits at Mattapany, was his reward for transporting himself, his wife, four children, and two servants. Meanwhile Fleete, followed by lesser claimants including three of his brothers and a number of freed indentured servants, turned west, to open a four-thousand-acre manor across St. Mary's River. A scattering of raw farms was marked out beyond Fleete's property, west along the north shore of the Potomac, culminating in Dr. Thomas Gerard's St. Clement's Manor, which would ultimately stretch across fourteen thousand acres on the neck of land between the Wicomico River and St. Clement's Bay.[23]

By the early 1640s, less than a decade after the arrival of the first settlers, the outer fringes of the lower Potomac were transformed. Crude farms and temporary habitations—little more than huts—appeared here and there over much of the wedge of land between the Potomac and Patuxent rivers as they sloped into Chesapeake Bay and through a twenty-mile stretch of the lower Potomac's north shore. Nowhere were there significant concentrations of people. Vessels bearing newcomers were arriving frequently at the docks at St. Mary's, though not in numbers approaching those that had been drawn to Virginia in Sandys's years.

BALTIMORE'S RECRUITMENT CAMPAIGN, always subdued and weakly financed, had limited though significant results. The small group of Catholic gentlemen who had helped Baltimore organize and launch the project had no large population of mobile co-religionists to draw into the colony as indentured servants, tenants, or freeholders. And neither the mobile, unemployed population that did exist nor restless Protestants of higher status were eager to flock to a Catholic enterprise, especially when conditions in Virginia and the Caribbean were thought to be improving. There was no hope for public support for a Catholic venture in the form of lotteries or municipal mobilization of the poor, and appeals could not be broadcast from the pulpit. Still, slowly, in small numbers, highly placed venturers continued to arrive in the 1630s and early 1640s, bringing with them indentured servants and wage laborers. They claimed manors or lesser properties on the basis of headrights, and, amid increasing contention, joined in the governance of the colony and its economic development.

The original seventeen "Gentlemen of Fashion" aboard the *Ark* and the *Dove* had been led not only by the proprietor's brother Leonard but also by his counselors Thomas Cornwallis and Jerome Hawley. Both, like Governor Calvert, were Catholics, well-educated younger sons, and affluent. Cornwallis, son of a member of Parliament and grandson of the ambassador to Spain who was also treasurer for the Prince of Wales, was related by marriage to the Calverts and had invested heavily in the *Dove* and in the colony's commercial joint stock. Describing himself as in "good consiens a real Catholick," he brought with him twelve servants, quickly established a manor which he called Cornwallis's Cross, laid claim to several others, and became a major tobacco producer, Indian trader, merchant, soldier, and politician. He also became one of the main importers of laborers. Between 1643 and 1657 he brought over at least seventy-one

servants. Hawley, brother of the governor of Barbados and himself formerly an official at the court of the queen, fared less well. Owner of two
of the first Maryland manors—St. Jerome and St. Helen—he died in
Maryland after an office-seeking trip to England, in 1638.[24]

Other adventurers of similar background followed these first settlers,
seeking the glowing benefits that Wintour and the colony's official promoters had so vividly described. John Lewger had been a college mate
of the future Lord Baltimore at Oxford. With three degrees from that
university, he had become an Anglican priest, then converted to Catholicism and as a consequence lost his teaching and preaching offices. In 1637
he emigrated to the colony with his family and seven servants. Commissioned by Baltimore as the colony's secretary, he quickly brought over
other servants—twenty-seven in all—acquired other offices, received
two manorial grants (one of which, St. John's, has been the subject of
meticulous archaeological reconstruction), and became a leading official
and politician.

The Brent family, arriving in 1638—four siblings: Giles and Fulke,
Margaret and Mary—were adult children of the sheriff of Gloucestershire, friends if not relatives of the Calverts, well educated and ambitious.
They brought with them gentry status, some wealth, excellent connections, and enough servants to entitle them to numerous large land grants.
Both brothers quickly became councilors and acquired major estates.
Giles, lord of the Fort Kent Manor, soon married (reputedly with an eye
to future land grants) the daughter of the Piscataway "emperor," who had
been sent to live with the English at the age of seven. He would serve
as acting governor at a critical time. His sister, the spinster Margaret,
would prove to be one of the most remarkable women of the era. Fiercely
litigious in protecting her rights and unusually successful in innumerable
lawsuits, she owned and managed properties throughout the colony and
served as both executor of Governor Calvert's estate and as Lord Baltimore's attorney in the colony. In these capacities it fell to her to face the
demands of Calvert's soldiers for pay they had been denied. When the
soldiers' anger seemed to threaten the colony's existence, she appeared at
the Assembly with the remarkable demand that she be given two votes,
one for herself and one as Lord Baltimore's legal representative, hoping
that with her influence the Assembly would vote the soldiers' pay. But
there were impassible limits, even on this chaotic frontier, to women's
public roles, and when her demand was rejected, she promptly sold off

not only all of Leonard Calvert's property to pay the soldiers but also the movable property of his brother, the absent proprietor, Lord Baltimore.

Baltimore's fury at this unauthorized move at his expense drove the Brent family across the bay to Virginia, though they maintained property and family connections in Maryland. But as the Assembly officially acknowledged, no one but Margaret could have managed the chaotic situation, commanding as she did the respect of all for her tough business and diplomatic skills and the civility due a woman. She deserved, they wrote to the proprietor, "favour and thanks" rather than "bitter invectives." She had saved the colony not only for his family but for a number of ambitious immigrants eager to establish themselves as gentry in this area of the Chesapeake tobacco lands.

Thomas Gerard, lord of St. Clement's manor, also arrived in 1638, with his family and five servants: by 1648 he had imported forty more servants, whose headrights became the basis of the claim to his manorial estate. Similarly affluent and well connected among the first settlers were John Boteler, nephew of the governor of Bermuda and Providence Island; William Braithwaite, a Calvert relation, grandson of the chief clerk of His Majesty's Rolls; and John Langford, son of the paymaster of the Royal Navy and personal agent of Lord Baltimore. But these leaders of the earliest years were drawn from a very small segment of the English gentry, and they were never numerous. Some, like William Blount and Col. Francis Trafford, left the colony within a year of their arrival, and those who remained left few traces. By 1638, twelve of the seventeen original Gentlemen of Fashion were dead, and of the remaining five, none left known descendants.[25]

Yet, by the end of the first decade, Baltimore might well have felt, in respect to social organization, that he had at least some grounds for satisfaction. A social profile of some seven hundred individuals whose names appear in Maryland's first provincial court papers suggests a traditional hierarchical order. The colony was dominated by six or seven manorial lords, foremost among whom were Governor Calvert, Cornwallis, Gerard, and Lewger. This small Catholic elite owned most of the property and, with the Jesuits, had imported 60 percent of the bound laborers, who for the terms of their indentures had been their servants. The top 10 percent of landowners in St. Mary's County owned 69 percent of the patented land; 79 percent of all freemen owned no land, hence were tenants, wage laborers, and sharecroppers.[26]

But in fact there was no traditional manorial regime, or anything close to it. Only one estate, St. Clement's, functioned as a proper manor "worked by tenants and governed by manorial arrangements," and it soon succumbed to the general pressures. Beneath the hierarchical structure of formal land titles lay a frontier world of great confusion.[27] It was a jumble, a scramble, of people drawn from a miscellany of English sources, shifting constantly in their locations and personal relations, living in crude encampments only beginning to be developed into respectable farms, seizing, legally or not, whatever land they could claim.

Baltimore had expected the capital site, St. Mary's City, to be a comfortable fortified community with a proper residence for himself, a chapel, regular streets, and houses built "one by another" in a "decent and uniform" manner. And indeed there is evidence that the town had originally been designed as a "Baroque planned city," so conceived by the colony's councilors, who as Catholics had of necessity been educated in Europe and were familiar with its urban designs. In fact the "city" proved to be a five-mile riverside sprawl of small, half-cultivated farms with no urban character. By 1641 the original palisade walls, beginning to rot, were being torn down. The official fur trade was only a limited success, and the manorial lords turned out to be, not social and juridical eminences presiding loftily over a stable, respectful population of tenants, but hustling, labor-poor tobacco planters and frontier land developers living in conditions not very different from that of the ordinary farmers.[28]

The first dwellings in the early years were small and crude, much like the "thatch roofed huts set on crotches and raftered with a covering of brush" that had been built earlier on Kent Island. The settlers inside the original fort at St. Mary's lived in what remained of shelters left by the Indians and their own crude "cottages." These were "earth-fast" buildings, structures built by driving thick posts into the ground and forming walls between them with wattle and daub. The thatched roofs were tied down with ropes; the chimneys were made of timber, also filled with wattle and daub, hence highly flammable. Most windows were covered with wax paper, cloth, or shutters. As to size, the typical huts varied from ten to fifteen feet square.

The first attempt to build more durable housing was made by Thomas Cornwallis, who in 1638, hoping *"toe encourage others toe follow my example, for hithertoe wee live in cottages,"* built a sawn timber framed house one and a half stories high, with a cellar and brick chimneys. But even such medieval-style English dwellings, though more substantial than the common huts, remained small and crude through most of the century. Nor were the houses of the wealthy very large or comfortable during the first two decades. Probably the largest house in the 1630s was that of Lewger, built around 1638. It measured fifty-two by twenty feet and had a stone foundation and a central chimney that divided the house into two large rooms: a hall where meals were prepared and eaten and where all domestic activity took place; and a parlor for sleeping and more formal events. The garret of the wood-framed house, one and a half stories high, was used to store corn. Lewger's "large" house was the only place spacious enough to hold all the members of the legislature, which met here regularly during the 1640s. Similarly, Justinian Snow's house at Snow Hill, built around 1639, had a wooden floor, a corn loft, a closet, brick chimneys, and framed glass casement windows, but the roof was so fragile, it was quickly blown off in the first storm.[29]

Falling roofs notwithstanding, these more substantial houses were improvements over the first crude cottages. In these second-phase constructions, riven clapboards replaced wattle-and-daub walls, and wooden shingles replaced thatch. Some of the floors were of wooden planks, and the buildings were almost twice the length of the original cottages. But even these improved dwellings were small, averaging sixteen by twenty feet. They had at most two rooms and a loft and were furnished simply, with a bed or more commonly a mattress of some sort laid on the floor, a few rugs or mats, a chest or two, some kitchenware (kettles, skillets, pots, spoons, bowls, and linens) and the necessary farm tools (axes, hoes, sieves, saws, spades, pails, hammers, and rakes). Though later the houses of the wealthy became more elaborate, most people continued to live in these small two-room, hall-and-parlor houses. There were advantages, though, in these easily constructed, impermanent "wooden boxes" where mobility and uncertainty were common and where most of people's energy was spent raising tobacco.[30]

Baltimore's injunction against reliance on tobacco—echoed by Cornwallis ("I came not hither for toe plant . . . this stincking weede of America")—was ignored. Within a decade tobacco had become the major crop (100,000 pounds of the leaf were said to have been marketed in 1639), and it was the money of account as well, though almost anything of value—livestock, servants, beaver, and Indian "peake" (wampum)—was also common tender. Almost everyone was a planter, even if they had other skills. Combinations such as merchant-planter, mariner-planter, or carpenter-planter appear regularly in the early court records, as do such occupational references as "repairer of tobacco houses," "seller of tobacco," "tobacco shipper," and "tobacco inspector."[31]

To support this still primitive tobacco economy, everyone lived by borrowing, even when they were creditors. Giles Brent, the manor lord of Kent Fort Manor, owed, at various times, his sister Margaret, Edward Packer, Calvert, and the considerable sum of 10,000 weight tobacco (roughly £42 sterling) to Lord Baltimore. He paid off the £110 sterling he owed his sister by giving her all his lands, goods, cattle, chattels, and servants and all the debts owed him. Trading, borrowing, lending, and sharing were necessary for survival. Many, if not most, of the court cases in this early period are concerned with debts not paid. Some involved three or more parties. John Wortley paid John Dandy the 42 pounds of tobacco that John Robinson owed Dandy, and when Robinson died, his estate owed Wortley.

Property transactions—sales, subdivisions, leases, and rentals of still largely wild land—also crowded the pages of the first court records in tangles of complex dealings, as tracts were patented, surveyed, added to, divided, abandoned, and reissued to others. Everyone wanted a piece of land to grow tobacco and corn. Desperate efforts were made to identify boundaries and secure ownership. The manorial lord Thomas Gerard, one of his tenants testified, bought and sold land "without survey by instruments, bounding by guess from heads of creeks to heads of creeks or other parts . . . sometimes by paths, some times mentioning courses & distances and sometimes not."[32]

Thus, typically, the land claims of the twenty-nine-year-old Thomas Adams. Born in the village of Bodenham, Herefordshire—lush meadow-land on the Welsh border whose parcels of ownership had been defined for centuries[33]—he had migrated to London where he became a book-keeper for Cloberry & Co., the backers of the Kent Island settlement, and then migrated to that outpost at the head of Chesapeake Bay. There he became the company's storekeeper, an Indian trader, and a local public official. Having brought with him to Maryland five servants, in 1640 he claimed and received one thousand acres called "Prior's Manor"—whose boundaries he defined as, on the west, "Prior's Creek," on the south, Chesapeake Bay, and on the north, a line drawn from the head of Prior's Creek to "Adams' Bite."

Such vague and ephemeral designations became sources of controversy as the land claims and grants multiplied, were sold, inherited, and
divided, and as the original boundary markers shifted or disappeared.
So Giles Basha claimed a parcel called "Peare's Plantation," bounded by
Oyster Creek, Chesapeake Bay, and a line drawn from "Basha's Branch
of Oyster Creek to the north of the dwelling house to the Bay." The land
claims of the Brent family form an archive in themselves. Giles Brent may
have received none of the land he had hoped for from his marriage to the
Piscataway "princess," renamed Mary, but having brought over eleven
servants, he claimed three thousand-acre plots plus two town plots in St.
Mary's City, the boundaries of which he attempted to describe by such
markers as "St. Mary's Forest." Seemingly permanent physical features
were favored—"the northern point of St. Inigo's Creek," "St. George's
Island." But how firm a designation was "a swamp in St. George's River
called Key Swamp" or "a line from the head of Weston's Creek to David's
well" or "a creek called Stent's branch"? The boundary lines in one sector
of Gerard's manor were such a tangle that the district was called Bedlam's
Neck. Everything, even the all-important property claims, was transitory,
shifting, and insecure.

If property claims were imprecise and ephemeral, even less secure were
community structures and social cohesion. How could it have been otherwise with a population drawn across the Atlantic from all over England
and from several foreign countries and then scattered over open, uncultivated fields in groups few of whose members had prior attachments to
each other? Some were driven by dire need, some sponsored by corporate
and personal agencies. Cloberry & Co. sent ninety-three indentured servants to Kent Island, in addition to agents, wage laborers, and independent
settlers.[34] Thirty-six settlers in Maryland before 1645 were listed as having imported servants to the colony, but some of the sponsors operated
rather blindly from afar. The bizarre, passionate Catholic convert Elizabeth Cary, Viscountess Falkland—cantankerous, fearsomely learned, and
argumentative, a lady, the Earl of Clarendon wrote, "of a most masculine
understanding," whose stubborn adherence to Catholicism endangered
the political career of her Protestant husband—managed to sponsor the
transportation of five servants to her co-religionists' colony.[35]

Drawn from such scattered sources, the settlers shared no distinctive
geographical subculture, and they were all equally alien to the environment they faced. St. Mary's few hundred settlers can be traced back to

villages in Gloucestershire, Kent, Essex, and Yorkshire, mingling with others from Newcastle, London, and Portugal. St. Michael's inhabitants, even fewer in number, came from Cumberland, Norfolk, Devonshire, Northumberland, Lancashire, Buckinghamshire, Northamptonshire, and Ireland. Kent Island had people from London and fourteen English counties living together with Frenchmen, Irishmen, Welshmen, mulattoes, and (in very small numbers) blacks.

While most of the settlers had no choice but to become farmworkers, they claimed a great variety of vocational skills. Among the population of St. Mary's County, there were approximately thirty different occupations. Those living at St. Mary's City included mariner-merchants, a "licentiate in physick," three barber-surgeons, a glover-skindresser, a surveyor, a boatwright, builders of all kinds (carpenter, sawyer, brickmaker, etc.), and a midwife. Elsewhere there were seamen, millwrights, attorneys, coopers, millers, and laundresses. The inhabitants of Kent Island listed twenty-eight different occupations. It took a wrenching adjustment for these artisans, craftsmen, and urban service workers to survive in the still-experimental, unformed, tobacco and aboriginal trading world.

Everything was awkward, skewed, unlikely. Households, as they formed and reformed, were often strange in composition. Heavily male, they were frequently not familiar family clusters but work groups of recently arrived young men, many of whom lived in small quartering houses—"outhouses": barracks, in effect. Not uncommon were households of "mates"—men who formed partnerships with one another to work a leasehold, and who held property in common and worked for equal shares. Thus Henry Bishop, John Bryant, and Joseph Edlow jointly leased land in 1637 and shared a house at Mattapany. Each legally owned a one-third share of the house and crops. Living with them were Bryant's wife and his servant, Elias Beach. Within the year, Bryant was killed by a tree he was felling, and the mateship broke up. Bishop moved across the Patuxent River to St. Leonard's and set up another mateship with Simon Demibiel (who had recently left another joint venture) and Leonard Leonardson. Edlow moved south of the Patuxent area to St. Mary's Township and set up a mateship with Christopher Martin.[36]

By 1642 most of the original indentured servants, whose terms of service were limited to four or five years, had gained their freedom and were trying to establish themselves as independent farmers, claiming land of their own. A few, in these early years, made the transition to independence easily and successfully, some spectacularly. Thus Daniel Clocker, an illiterate seventeen-year-old son of Westmoreland miners, drifted into London where in 1636 he was taken up as one of Cornwallis's indentured servants. Having survived his service in the colony, he used his freedom dues to buy an initial parcel of land, married one of Margaret Brent's servants, raised five children, and prospered as a small householder and justice of the peace. He died possessed of movables worth £71 sterling and a freehold of 230 acres. More successful was Cuthbert Fenwick, also brought to Maryland as a servant by Thomas Cornwallis. Freed after four years of service and immediately referred to as "gentleman," he married Cornwallis's daughter, became his overseer, steward, and attorney, held numerous public offices, played a major role in provincial politics, and died the lord of a two-thousand-acre manor. Among his possessions were six blacks who had come to him as part of a marriage settlement. Similarly Henry Adams, one of Lady Falkland's indentees, became a planter, merchant, judge, and legislator; his property at his death, forty-seven years after his arrival, totalled £569 sterling, and included eight hundred acres, five servants, one slave, and twenty-eight books.[37]

Such successes were rare. For most, servitude and the transition to freedom and independence were struggles, profusely documented in the records of the first provincial court. As in Virginia, servants were bought and sold, pledged as security on debts, even risked in gambling—something, an observer noted, not done even by "Turk or Barbarian, and not becoming Christians." Their worth was closely calculated, upon sale or in estate inventories. In Justinian Snow's inventory, his servant Samuel Barrett was valued at eight hundred pounds of tobacco (about £6.6 sterling); one of Lady Falkland's transportees was priced at one thousand pounds; Edward Westbee was bought for four milk cows; John Cockshott's inventory included a maidservant worth seven hundred pounds of tobacco. Contracts were flexible. Some servants earned wages (and like Robert Edwards and Rowland Vaughan sued for overdue payment; the one claimed his master owed him "1 breeding sow," the other eleven hundred pounds of tobacco). Some struck extraordinary bargains. The bricklayer Cornelius Canedy extracted from Thomas Gerard for three years of service not only the usual food, clothes, and lodging but, as freedom dues, "200 acres of land . . . with a sufficient house upon the same of twenty-five foot long and sixteen foot wide, two cowes or heifers with calfe, two sowes with pigg, two goats with kid, five barrells of corne, a bed fill'd with feathers or flocks, a pillow, and one rugg, two dishes, one pott, and six spoons." Thomas Todd bought out his indenture with John Lewger by providing fifty deerskins each year for three years. William Naufin's relation to his master, the romantic Robert Wintour, was strange. Wintour recorded that he brought Naufin to Maryland "to keepe him company, and to breed him up at schoole." Another unusual contract recorded in the Maryland court was that of Anne Fletcher. The arrangement she had with Edmund Plowden, proprietor of his own failed colony, "New Albion," adjacent to Maryland, committed her to revocable service, "from yeare to yeare," as a "waitingmaid" to Plowden's wife and daughters, with wages of £4 a year in commodities; if she disliked the country she could quit Plowden's service at year's end but would be obliged to pay for her return passage. A few, like Robert Cooper, were given special rewards: "a cow calf because he had been a good servant." Some argued about the terms of their servitude: John Genallis refused to work on Saturday afternoons; Humphrey Chaplin insisted that he was bound for four not five years and to prove it took his master to court. Servitude—its flexible forms, its conditions, personnel, problems, and benefits—was a pervasive condition of life in the nascent colony.[38]

The recruitment of labor was a dynamic process, and the resulting demographic situation was inherently unstable. A steady state required more than a one-for-one replacement of freed servants, since many of the increasing number of former indentees themselves soon needed one or more servants. While efforts to keep up a flow of English servants under indentures succeeded through the first generation, search for a more reliable and permanent labor force was inevitable. Within a decade there were signs of an interest in supplanting the free, transient labor force with involuntary permanent workers, but it would be many years before there would be an overwhelming demand for slaves, however defined, or the resources to purchase them in significant numbers, or a reliable system for importing them.[39]

5

By the end of the first decade of settlement, the colony, its European society still in disarray, was primitive—it would be described as primitive for years to come. Its population of some three to four hundred Europeans in 1642 was growing only slowly, and internal divisions within that

population were beginning to appear. Within a decade of the first arrivals, the animosities became abrasive, then deadly. By the early 1640s,
the scattered community, small as it was, was being torn apart by bitter disputes that could be resolved only by absolute victory and absolute
defeat. These internal struggles within a fragile European outpost at the
edge of a boundless aboriginal world threatened the survival not only of
Baltimore's chartered proprietorship but of the physical existence of his
colony. The turmoil completed the disarray of the hoped-for social order
begun by the jarring circumstances of migration and resettlement.

THE JESUITS, whom Baltimore had deliberately recruited,[40] proved to
be an especially bitter and unexpected source of disorder. Their benevolent and initially supportive ambitions created a potentially deadly contradiction in the colony's goals and procedures.

The priests—especially the learned Father Andrew White—had
served Baltimore well. They had shared in the fashioning of the colony
and had been leaders in the initial explorations and settlement decisions
of 1634. Once the colony was under way, they looked forward to launching one of the greatest conquests of paganism in the history of Christianity. They would conduct, with their passion, discipline, and energy, a
veritable crusade, a sweeping harvest of souls, radiating out from what
they imagined would be "a semi-autonomous Catholic community of
English colonists and Indians living on Jesuit-owned manorial estates
governed by ecclesiastical courts and exempt from the taxation and much
of the jurisdiction of the civil government."[41]

Things began well. The Mattapanian Indians, hoping for military
support, gave the Jesuits a site on the southern border with the aggressive
Susquehannocks. With their storehouse secure at that northern location,
the Jesuits awaited reinforcements from home and permission from the
governor to penetrate the Indians' world. The former they never ade-
quately received, and the latter was slow in coming.

At no time during the eleven years during which the Jesuits were active
in Maryland were there more than five priests on the scene. Though the
fame of the colony and its missionary ambitions spread throughout the
Order's European centers, and though at least twenty-three priests at
the Jesuit college at Liège fervently sought permission to join their brethren in distant Maryland, only eleven priests and three assistants ("coadju-
tors") were ever sent to the colony; eight died there (of yellow fever, of

untreated abcesses, of Indian violence, of a gunshot accident), and four left quickly. Some were men of exceptional ability: the learned White, his two successors as head of the mission (Thomas Copley, an able businessman and estate manager, and the "prudent" and experienced Ferdinand Poulton). And there was also the young Roger Rigbie, a gifted linguist and scholar. But some were not considered to be capable of handling the work. And the entire venture was caught up in the cross-currents of religious politics in England and the global demands on the Order's available personnel.[42]

Nor was the governor immediately supportive. For four years he kept the Jesuits from venturing into the Indians' lands, fearful of the eastward spread of diseases said to be afflicting the tribes, fearful even more of stirring up Indian attacks that might threaten the settlements, and hopeful that the Jesuits might usefully devote themselves to converting some of the colony's Protestant heretics.[43] Finally, in 1638, permission to visit the natives was granted. While Copley kept charge of the Order's headquarters at St. Mary's, the others moved out into the fertile fields of the benighted: Altham to Kent Island, Poulton to Mattapany and its surroundings, and White 120 miles north to the Piscataway village of the "emperor" Kittamaquund, whose conversion, they were sure, would open the spiritual floodgates.

Though White failed in his first effort at conversion of the nearby "King of Patuxent" (such, he explained, were "the inscrutable judgments of God"), he appeared to succeed with the ruling tayac of Piscataway. For that uneasy leader, suffering nightmares after murdering his brother in a struggle for dominance, had dreamed that White and Altham, whom he remembered from their exploratory visit of 1634, would bring him peace of mind. And in another dream he had seen White in the company of a beautiful god "surpassing the snow in whiteness," in contrast to an image of "a most hideous demon" in company with the threatening Protestant trader Justinian Snow. These premonitions and insights, reinforced by White's providential cure of the tayac's "serious disease" by application of "a certain powder . . . mixed with holy water," convinced the chief of the "errors of their former life." Thus illuminated by "the light of Heaven," the tayac, who insisted that White live with him in his "palace," forthwith exchanged his furs and skins for European clothes, put away his concubines, abstained from meat as instructed, forswore all worldly goods in favor of "knowledge of the only true God," began the study of English, and instructed, first his wife and two daughters, then "a convention of other rulers," to cast aside the "stones and herbs" they had formerly worshipped (symbolically flinging a stone aside and kicking it with his foot) and "embrace the profession and practice of Christianity," which alone would save one's "immortal soul . . . from eternal death."

Such a conversion, reinforced by vivid tales of other miraculous interventions by the Holy Spirit in the Indians' lives, proved to the Jesuits beyond any doubt that these Indians, though of all the people on earth the most "abject in appearance," had souls "for which a ransom has been paid by Christ, and which are no less precious than those of the most cultivated Europeans." Yes, they had vices, "though not so many, considering the darkness of their ignorance, their barbarism, and their unrestrained and wandering mode of life"; but they were willing to accept the concept of one Superior Being and are "readily swayed by reason, nor do they obstinately withhold their assent from the truth when it is placed distinctly before them."

White and his colleagues, their labor rewarded by the sight of converts "in crowds" and hopeful that a "most desireable harvest" would soon follow, staged a dramatic baptism of the converted tayac and his family. In a bark chapel built for the occasion, a formal baptism was performed, after which the tayac and his wife were properly married, their names changed (to the royal Charles and Mary), and a "great cross" was borne aloft and fixed at a proper place with the physical help of the tayac, the governor, and the colony's secretary, while Fathers White and Altham "chanted before them the Litany of Loreto in honor of the Blessed Virgin."[44]

But frustrations and disappointments began to weigh heavily on the mission. The harvest of souls at Piscataway, which spread to the central Potomac village of Portobacco and was said to bring appeals for conversion from the Anacostans farther up the river, had to be curtailed when White fell ill and returned to St. Mary's and when Altham died of a foot infection that spread through his body. Further, a famine drained the vitality of the Piscataways and their neighbors; their tayac, whose conversion had so vivified the entire mission, died in 1641; and the hoped-for reinforcements were never sent from England. Severely restricted in manpower, confessedly slow in learning the natives' difficult languages despite White's efforts to compile a dictionary and grammar, the missionaries could no longer hope to set up a network of inland stations from which the Word might be spread, and so they resorted to "excursions."[45]

In these flying visits, as described in the missionaries' annual reports, a priest, an interpreter, and a servant would set off in a pinnace, two of them rowing when the wind fell, carrying with them food, holy water, and "the sacred utensils," including a makeshift altar for performing the mass and wine for the ceremony. They carried too a chest filled with "little bells, combs, fishing-hooks, needles, thread" to be given to the Indians "to gain their good will." Arriving near a village in the evening, they would set up camp on the river shore, light a fire, erect a tent or hut if it rained, seek out the local people, entice them with trinkets, and begin the preaching they hoped would end in conversion. Given the size of the territory they hoped to cover they could not tarry long at any one spot, and so bringing pagans to Christianity in this fleeting manner and with the "humble fare and hard couch" they had to endure was difficult, especially as they still could not themselves speak directly with the Indians. Even their interpreter was "so imperfectly acquainted with their language that he sometimes excites their laughter." At times they were tempted to despair, but, they reported to their superiors in England, "by patience we make progress with them and are gradually bringing them over to what we desire."[46]

But there were deeper problems than the difficulty of conversing in the Algonquian dialects and failing to share the Indians' lives for extended periods. The Jesuits' whole missionary enterprise, especially its material foundation and legal status, came into question before the first decade was out, and the main challenger was their erstwhile patron, Lord Baltimore himself. The financial security of his colony and his family's personal fortune rested on his ownership of the colony's land, and that in turn rested on the survival of his chartered rights, increasingly likely to be questioned by the rising tide of anti-Catholicism at home.

Anticipating challenges, he had long since ordered full toleration for all Christian worship and had required Catholicism to be practiced privately. But the Jesuits posed special and very difficult problems. Not only did they actively proselytize among the colony's Protestants, a practice that was quickly reported to the authorities in England, but they insisted on having all the privileges their order was accorded in Catholic Europe and Hispanic America: that as a society they be allowed to own property, that they be free of ordinary taxation, and that they be subject only to the laws and courts of the Church. The problem was compounded by the fact that they had been responsible for bringing over a very large number of servants—perhaps sixty-five—which led to claims to 28,500 acres, and also by the fact that the Indians had given them the land on the Patuxent that they called "Conception," bypassing the proprietor's ownership and authority.[47]

As a result, while the ordinary settlers struggled with a multitude of problems, the colony's leaders, Catholics all, were embroiled in conflict with the Jesuits and the higher authorities of the order in England and Rome. Antagonisms rose, friendly relationships soured, and bitterness seeped into the leadership of the Catholic enterprise as Baltimore realized how seriously the Jesuits "threatened the delicate balance that he sought between English and Catholic loyalties." We are suffering, the Jesuits insisted, "from those from whom we rather expected aid and protection, who in anxiety for their own interests, have not hesitated to violate the immunities of the Church." Lord Baltimore's increasingly hostile attitude might be excused, they said, as an excess of material self-interest, but Lewger, the colony's secretary and Baltimore's personal agent, was, it was observed, a recent convert and no doubt was still driven by deep-seated Protestant prejudices. Their land threatened with confiscation and taxation and their claims forced into the secular courts, they appealed for support to the Society of Jesus's Vice-Provincial of England, who in turn appealed, in an eloquent memorial, to the Sacred Congregation *de Propaganda Fide* in Rome.

The Jesuits in Maryland, the English vice-provincial, Father Henry More, wrote to his superiors, are in worse danger than their brethren in England, situated as they were between the Protestant strongholds of Virginia and New England, and confronted by hordes of savages "who live after the manner of wild beasts." Lewger, he reported, no doubt still infused with "the leaven of Protestantism," had submitted a twenty-point exposition of precisely "those dogmas so justly offensive to Catholic ears" and then, consistent with them, had attempted to enact laws "repugnant to the Catholic faith and ecclesiastical immunities," the essence of which was that "no ecclesiastic shall enjoy any privilege . . . nor to gain anything for the Church except by the gift of the Prince." When Maryland's priests had challenged such rulings, More wrote, Lewger fell into a rage and turned Baltimore against them. The Catholic baron, fearing a precedent that would deprive him of his property and income, had confiscated the land that the Indians had freely given the Jesuits and had appealed to the Sacred Congregation to recall Maryland's suffering fathers and to replace them as missionaries with secular priests. The Jesuits, More assured the authorities in Rome, were obedient; they would never "refuse to make way for other labourers." But, he asked, was it expedient

> to remove those who first entered into that vineyard at their own expense, who for seven years have endured want and sufferings, who have lost four of their *confrères*, labouring faithfully unto death, who have defended sound doctrine and the liberty of the Church with odium and temporal loss to themselves, who are learned in the language of the savages, of which the priests to be substituted by the Baron Baltimore are entirely ignorant?

Father Poulton, superior of the Maryland mission, wrote an equally impassioned appeal from the scene of contention. Impoverished, with no help from anyone in America, the Jesuits in the colony, he wrote, now feared that the entire mission might be abandoned. "Certainly the very thought of recalling us or of not sending others to help us in this glorious work of the salvation of souls would in a manner assail our faith in the Providence of God and His care for His servants." For his own part, he declared, he

> should prefer to work here among the Indians for their conversion, and, destitute of all human aid and reduced by hunger, to die lying on the bare ground under the open sky, than even once to think of abandoning this holy work of God through any fear of privation.

The bitterness mounted. The struggle between Baltimore, keenly aware of the threat of England's Long Parliament, and the passionate Jesuits could not be resolved. In the end, after all the charges and countercharges had been filed and all the urgent appeals to the centers of power in London and Rome had been heard, the papal authorities, seeking to avoid further confrontations with England, found it expedient to support Baltimore's cautious policies. His seizure of the Jesuits' property on the Patuxent was approved, however reluctantly, and while the fathers in Maryland were not recalled from their mission, they were thereafter

subject to the secular power in the colony, except for corporal punishment, just as they were in England; and Baltimore was assured that no
additional Jesuits would be sent without his approval.[48]

BUT THIS CONTROVERSY, which tore at the ideological heart of the
colony, was genteel next to another series of conflicts that developed
through these early years, conflicts that reduced the colony to a cockpit
of "insolencies, rapines, murthers, & other barbarous cruelties."[49]

Calvert's caution in dealing with the local Indian tribes had eased
the initial encounters and, with the support of the Jesuits, had accounted
for a short period of easy, though vigilant, intermingling of the races.
The natives, Father White wrote, were entirely cooperative, instructing
the settlers in hunting, fishing, and food preparation; "their women and
children came very frequently amongst them." But the Jesuits' efforts at
converting, hence "civilizing," the Indian villagers touched only a few
points on the fringe of the natives' world, and those contacts were at
best superficial. The apparent welcome the missionaries received, and
the general ease in race relations at the start, were largely the result of a
temporary configuration of forces that the English only gradually came
to understand.[50]

They had settled at the embattled core of the Piscataway "empire," a
group of loosely affiliated tribes whose domain, centered on the populous
village of Moyaone (near the present Mount Vernon), stretched across a
broad inland strip on the north shore of the Potomac, from as far west as
the present District of Columbia east to Chesapeake Bay and across the
Bay into Maryland's Eastern Shore. When the English arrived at this confederation of palisaded villages, which may have contained seven thousand
tribute-paying inhabitants, it was under severe pressures from all sides
and threatened with destruction. On the south, from Virginia, they were
repeatedly attacked by their traditional rivals, the Patawomekes, whose
raid, a decade earlier, had been supported by ninety militiamen from Virginia who hoped, with the Patawomekes' help, to encircle the Powhatans
from the north. On the northwest and northeast, Iroquois tribes harassed
the Piscataways' border areas—Senecas, Eries, and Nacotchtanks coming in from the west to hit the villages along the upper Potomac and to
press the Susquehannocks, at the mouth of the Susquehanna River, down
both sides of the Bay. And as the Susquehannocks, linked to the League

Iroquois on the Great Lakes, pressed south into the Eastern Shore, they drove the Nanticokes, themselves aggressive raiders, west across Chesapeake Bay into the Potomac entrance of the Piscataways' "empire."[51]

For a few years the English settlers, welcomed by the Piscataways as valuable allies, helped sustain a balance of power in this tangle of belligerent forces. But by the early 1640s, the stability was weakening. Trouble started at the margins—on the north along the Patuxent; on the Eastern Shore; and west around St. Clement's. There and elsewhere the settlers' "cattle" (mainly hogs), allowed to roam freely in search of food, foraged around Indian encampments and were killed as game. Charges were brought against such depredations; repayment was demanded; and fencing—which violated the natives' most elemental sense of the proper use of land—was demanded at the exposed borders. In 1638, in response to the Nanticokes' murder of a Virginia trader, Calvert sent a force to the Eastern Shore to impose justice.

With charges and countercharges and sporadic retaliation multiplying between people lacking shared values, laws, or customs, a sense of violation rose on both sides. Random murders of isolated traders—Richard Thompson's entire family, wife, child, and seven servants, living alone on Poplar Island, south of Kent, was wiped out—and demands for punishment further heightened tensions, which grew more dangerous as traders began to roam through the whole region. Their operations spread quickly, out of control. Baltimore's legal right to license all Indian traders and the requirement that traders post bond for good behavior were ignored; there was no way that the thousands of square miles of the Maryland colony could be policed. Traders were everywhere, ruthless in their search for furs, ready to peddle not only trinkets and clothes but liquor and guns. Some were isolated individuals, some worked in partnerships, some in biracial teams. Most traders set up movable bartering camps, some so deep into the interior that the authorities in St. Mary's knew of them only by rumor. Father White's proposal that all trade be confined to three official trading posts could not be seriously undertaken. A few of the most active in the gun trade worked their way north from Virginia into Maryland; others came south from Swedish settlements on the Delaware and from Dutch Manhattan. But most of the illegal traders were associated in one way or another with Claiborne's private trading center on Kent Island.[52]

Claiborne—irrepressible, tireless, ruthless, a freebooting entrepreneur—

had become a key figure in the life of the Susquehannock Indians, controlling as he did the fur trade at the head of the Bay and supplying a local network of tribes and their affiliates far inland with European goods on which they were increasingly dependent. His settlement on Kent Island had quickly expanded, first into a busy trade center, then into a plantation, then into a biracial community that included approximately 175 English men and women. Radiating out from the Kent Island headquarters, Claiborne's contacts stretched across the Atlantic world, from the mercantile exchanges in London to the Hurons' fur traps on the shores of the Great Lakes.

As the years passed Claiborne proved to be a bristling phenomenon in the emerging world of Anglo-American exploitation, a relentless infighter, an insidious intriguer, and a fierce partisan, determined to keep possession of his island and its trade. Financed by his London sponsors, he became a frontier baron, as easy in the company of the gentry of Kent and sophisticated Londoners as he was with the Susquehannocks he courted.[53] Though his claim to Kent Island was clearly in violation of the terms of Baltimore's charter, he continued to defy the Maryland authorities, violently when necessary. A climax was reached in 1638 when he attacked a Maryland vessel trading along the Eastern Shore, killing one of the crewmen. Calvert promptly charged him with piracy, murder, and treason and took the opportunity to seize Kent Island by military force. He then confiscated property that Claiborne estimated at £10,000 and hanged one of his island associates. Escaped to England, Claiborne lined up support from the victorious Parliamentary forces and their Puritan merchant supporters, thus aligning himself with the new, revolutionary establishment. Back in Virginia, he reestablished contact with his allies there, on Kent Island, and among the Susquehannocks. It was his influence, in all probability, that convinced that tribe in 1642 to launch a brief war against his Maryland enemies.[54]

They did not need much convincing. Raw from harassment by Iroquois raiders from the north and alarmed by fears of what Maryland's influence might do to the trade they had developed with Claiborne, the Susquehannocks tore into the Piscataway-Maryland borders at two especially sensitive points. They attacked first the central Piscataway village of Moyaone, wiped out the people at the Jesuit mission there, and made off with all the supplies. That blow, which destroyed the Jesuits' most promising post, was repeated at their plantation on the Patuxent. When on top of that, settlers only eight miles from St. Mary's Village were killed and eight others elsewhere in the colony were also picked off and their property ravaged, Calvert declared Susquehannocks, Wicocomocos, and Nanticokes official enemies of Maryland, banned all Indians from entering the colony's territory, and authorized the settlers to shoot any Indians who entered the borders. Elaborate precautions were then taken to defend the colonists against attack. A warning system was devised, routes of escape from attack and "resident fortresses" were created, and officers were appointed to enforce martial law when necessary. Though a small militia army was formed under the command of Cornwallis and Lt. William Lewis, the Jesuits' zealous chief steward, Indian raids continued, with bloodshed on both sides. On one occasion and at small cost, these troops routed an ambushing force of Susquehannocks, said to number 250 warriors, but then in 1644 they were defeated. Fifteen Maryland militiamen were captured, and tortured. They were dropped twice into a raging fire intensified by bear fat and pitch, a contemporary reported, then taken out, bound to flaming poles, and slowly roasted until a designated "devil chaser" tore the flesh from their faces, cut out their tongues, cut off their fingers and toes, which he threaded on strings for necklaces and knee bands, and finally tied them to burning bundles of reeds while boys "with a great noise" shot arrows into their smoldering bodies.[55]

The fighting continued, intermittently, inconclusively, with more hit-and-run raids by the Indians and such indiscriminate shootings by the colonists that Calvert had to withdraw his earlier punitive orders. Large-scale campaigns were planned but failed to materialize. The fighting ground on, though the lines of affiliation began to blur. By 1644 the still-loyal Piscataways were threatening to collaborate with the Susquehannocks and were said to be making approaches to the Virginia tribes which, under Opechancanough, were planning the second great massacre in that colony. The likely outcome, in the late 1640s, was unclear. If the Piscataways submitted to the Susquehannocks and joined with them in an assault on the colony, the result would be devastating even if the colony were fully mobilized and closely unified. But in fact the opposite was true. While Indian affairs remained potentially explosive, demanding close attention and carefully considered decisions, the English were embroiled in a series of tumultuous domestic struggles.[56]

THE "PLUNDERING TIME" of the mid-1640s, though brief, was one of the most barbarous passages in Maryland's history. The turmoil was in part the result of personal animosities among adventurers freed from normal social constraints, and in part a reflection and extension of the political upheaval of England's Civil War. But it was also, and in large part, an expression of the resistance of the ordinary Protestant planters to the colony's Catholic establishment and to the manorial system that the first Lord Baltimore had so carefully designed.

It began with the bombast of a violently tempestuous thirty-three-year-old mariner and tobacco trader, Richard Ingle—a "mad Captain" to officials in the Admiralty—who had been shipping goods to and from the Chesapeake for a decade. In 1642, as the conflict between Parliamentary and royalist forces was rising to a climax in England, Ingle, anchored at a port in Virginia, declared himself a fervent Parliamentarian, denounced all royalists as "rattleheads," and threatened local officials who protested with a poleax and cutlass. Avoiding arrest, he visited several Maryland ports repeating his abuse of the king and his government. A year later he was back in Maryland, even more passionate in his political fervor, reportedly refusing in the name of Parliament to disembark when ordered to do so, declaring that King Charles was no king, and threatening to cut off the head of anyone who tried to board his ship. Charged with treason by the acting governor, Giles Brent, he arranged for a postponement of his trial and returned to England, only to reappear with a letter of marque permitting him to seize vessels hostile to Parliament. By then he had cast himself as the savior of Maryland's Protestants in their struggle "against the said tyrannicall governor, and Papists, and malignants his adherents," who, he declared, intended "to execute a tyrannicall power against the Protestants and such as adhered to the Parlyament, and to presse wicked oathes uppon them, and to endeavuor their extirpation."[57]

Using his letter of marque as a general license to prey on royalists anywhere, he mobilized a gang of "most rascally fellows" in Virginia and prepared to invade Maryland, probably in alliance with Claiborne. That frustrated and vengeful entrepreneur judged the time was ripe for him to recover his control of Kent Island and his extensive properties there. Late in 1644 he gathered a ragtag contingent of "troops" and returned to the island expecting to raise a popular insurrection of Protestants against the proprietor and to restore his assets. In this he failed, succeeding only in creating great confusion among the people living on the island and forcing Governor Calvert, who had returned to the colony, to respond by mobilizing his own troop of soldiers to restore order.

The colony was clearly under threat, and in February the threat was fully realized. Sailing up the Chesapeake to Maryland's northern shore, Ingle seized a large Dutch trading vessel as personal booty and set about plundering the colony. Ruthless and violent, he drew to his side as he swept through the colony a motley crowd of the discontented. Most were obscure, identifiable only as names scattered through the records. Some were disreputable: the illiterate Thomas Bradnox, for example, himself a former servant, notorious for his vicious treatment of servants, who became known as "captain of the rebels," and Thomas Sturman, a cooper sent over by Claiborne's backers, distinguished by his remarkable zeal in ransacking houses. But some were quite respectable—ambitious planters, Protestants all, seeking greater security and autonomy within a Catholic colony: Thomas Baldridge, for example, who though originally a servant, had served under Calvert as assemblyman, sheriff, coroner, and lieutenant in the militia before becoming "captain and commander" of the rebels; and most notably Nathaniel Pope. Arriving as a freeman, Pope bought Calvert's house and transformed it into an inn and the site for the Assembly's meetings; from this connection he drew subsidies and opportunities for profit, which he fully exploited. "Pope's fort" became the main rebel stronghold and Pope himself the respected face of the Protestant resistance.[58]

Picking up such followers as he moved into the colony, Ingle aimed to seize St. Mary's City but turned first to Cornwallis's recently built and well-fortified Cross House, the finest dwelling in the colony, which, he said, he was obliged to confiscate lest it be used as a royalist fort against him. Though Cornwallis had been his business partner and friend, Ingle looted the house of everything of value, down to the hardware on the doors and windows, reducing it to "a most pitifull ruines, spoiled and defaced," which he used as a warehouse for his plundered goods and a holding station for captured Catholics. (Cornwallis would later value the loss and damage at £2,623.) After pillaging farm after farm and confiscating whole storehouses of tobacco, Ingle turned to the Brents' property, on Kent Island and elsewhere, ransacked it thoroughly (Giles Brent would estimate the loss at £1,254), burned the books ("them Papist divells"), and arrested Brent himself in the name of Parliament, along with Lewger and other Catholic leaders, all of whom he took back with him to England as prisoners. Fathers White and Copley he transported in chains. Meanwhile his gangs tore into the Catholics' manor houses, such as they were, and seized whatever of value they could lay their hands on. Ingle usually kept for himself the tobacco and whatever silver plate he found, leaving the rest to his followers. The Jesuits were particular targets. All of their substantial property was confiscated—cattle, furnishings, linens, books, ceremonial objects, and luxury items of gold and silver. As the raids continued, many of the settlers in the affected areas fled across the Potomac for refuge in Virginia, while Ingle began compiling charges against his victims to use at home as justification for his looting.[59]

Ingle's personal rampage was brief; he left for England in 1645. But the rebellion wore on, and the damage deepened, leaving a trail of ravaged and stolen property, disordered lives, and social disarray. Ingle had not meant to destroy the colony nor to plunder every farm and household. His main goal had been to make a killing in trade, licit or illicit, and to profit from the political upheaval. So he was selective in his raids in Maryland, targeting Catholics and anyone he could describe as a royalist. As a result the damage in the colony went deeper than simply the loss of property and social disorder. The raids gave expression to the resentments of indentured servants, debtors, and tenants seeking independence from manorial landowners; they weakened the authority of the manor lords; and they threw the legitimacy of Baltimore's proprietorship into question.

By the late summer of 1645 Calvert was in Virginia raising an invasion force while a makeshift group of Protestants claimed to be governing Maryland, and a petition was circulating in England for the annulment of Baltimore's charter. There, first in the admiralty courts, then in the civil courts, Ingle's fortunes were thrown into confusion. His claims for the ownership of the property he had looted were met by effective counterclaims, his petitions by counterpetitions. Nothing worked in his favor. The Dutch ship was returned to its owners; his prisoners were freed (though Father White languished in prison for a time); his loot was declared illegal; and he ended up defending himself against the Catholics' countersuits. At the same time Baltimore, in an adroit political and legal campaign, managed to retain the legal control of his great proprietorship.

It was left to Calvert, however, encouraged and instructed by his brother, Lord Baltimore, to begin the colony's restoration. Despite the fact that many of Maryland's militiamen had sympathized with the rebels and refused to support the government, Calvert gradually reassembled a small but reliable armed force to supplement the troops he had gath-

ered in Virginia. After issuing a general pardon for all who submitted
to Baltimore's authority, he mollified dissidents on Kent Island as well
as on the mainland, co-opted the popularly elected provincial Assembly,
and moved quickly to make up the demographic losses. But the basis of
any true recovery lay in resolving the religious conflict that had been so
viciously and deliberately exacerbated by Ingle. So Calvert did what he
could to temper the "ill-governed zeale" of the most passionate Catholics, criminalizing their "offensive & indiscrete speech," appointed
Protestants, not Catholic manor lords, to a new ruling Council, guaranteed the Assembly freedom to speak and debate as before, and on his
deathbed enacted Baltimore's risky appointment of William Stone to
the governorship.

A Protestant Virginia planter connected to the Parliamentary forces
in England, son of an influential London merchant close to the Puritan
leaders, and in minor ways an associate of both Claiborne and Ingle, Stone
swore an oath, on taking office, not to molest Catholics and to recruit
new settlers to the colony. At that point Baltimore, in an effort to secure
his control of the colony and maintain peace and order in the future, took
two major steps. He devised a series of oaths requiring all officeholders,
Protestant and Catholic, to attest their loyalty to the Crown, to agree not
to molest any Christian in the practice of religion, and to pledge fealty to
himself as the colony's proprietor. And in addition, "for the more quiett
and peaceable government of this province," he issued his famous Act
Concerning Religion.[60]

That document was radical in the context of the time since it protected "conscience in matters of religion" and the free right to worship,
and urged people of differing confessions to live together in peace under
the same government and avoid using inflammatory terms like "heritick,
scismatick, idolator, puritan, . . . prespiterian, popish prest, . . . jesuited
papist, Lutheran, Calvenist, anabaptist, brownist . . . sepa[ra]tist, or any
other." Yet in a larger sense the act was conservative. Its toleration was
limited to trinitarian Christians (the Maryland Assembly added clauses
mandating death to those who denied the trinity) and it in no way stated
the principle of the separation of church and state or of total freedom of
religious thought. A pragmatic effort to allow people of different Christian
confessions to live together in peace, the act, which extended Baltimore's
original instruction on freedom of religion, explicitly acknowledged the

Puritans' dominance in England and the Protestant majority in Maryland while protecting the colony's Catholics.[61]

Consistent with Baltimore's views of toleration and the urgency to increase the colony's population, he sent a delegation to Boston—which the Jesuits denounced as the seat of the "most bigoted" sectarians—to solicit prospective farmers for his province. In this he was unsuccessful, but five years later, in 1648, Governor Stone, in the same spirit, invited the Bennetts' community of Puritans, long settled on the Nansemond River in Virginia but now harassed by the Anglican regime of that colony, to migrate to Maryland as a body and take up residence there. Well connected to important Puritan merchants in England and devoted to creating their own ideal community free from "the wild boar" of corruption that would "destroy the Lord's vineyard"—a Jerusalem free of all those foul influences that would pollute "the waters of the Sanctuary"—most of these Chesapeake Puritans, devoted to living and expanding the godly life, took up residence at a remote spot on the Severn River some seventy miles north of St. Mary's City. There they formed a self-governing community of several hundred—perhaps six hundred—souls, which they called Providence. Industrious, well-organized, and competent, they quickly and systematically staked out their land claims and plunged into the colony's politics. They were determined to set the world right, especially in this papal enclave, and promptly sent seven burgesses to the Assembly, one of whom would soon become speaker.

But if Baltimore and his deputies thought that a Protestant governor, loyalty oaths, a toleration act, a Protestant majority in the Assembly and Council, and an influential Puritan enclave would save the colony from further trouble in England, they were badly mistaken. The Council of State in England included Maryland in its declaration of 1649 asserting Parliament's authority over England's dominions beyond the seas, and it created a commission to "reduce" any authorities that resisted.[62]

Most active among the commissioners in Maryland were the leader of the Providence Puritans, Richard Bennett, and the ubiquitous William Claiborne, still determined to recover Kent Island and the trading empire he had created. When Stone insisted on maintaining the proprietor's authority on the island, the commissioners, in the name of the Commonwealth of England, promptly dismissed him and his Council from office, replaced them with Puritans, and led the Assembly in repeal-

ing the Act Concerning Religion, disfranchising all Catholics and denying them freedom of worship.

Stone, reinforced by word from England that Baltimore's chartered
rights had been vindicated, resisted and mobilized his army of some 250
men. His efforts at persuasion and negotiation, as he moved north, failed.
When his men were asked to show their authorization, a Commonwealth pamphleteer sardonically reported, "They would in a proud bravado clap their hands on their swords and say, Here is a commission."
They approached the Puritan headquarters on the Severn on March 25,
1655, the writer continued, shouting "*Come ye rogues, roundheaded dogs*" to
hastily gathered Puritan troops, who were "crying to the Lord of Hosts
and King of Sion for counsel, strength, and courage." When the order
was given to the Puritan troops, "*In the name of God, fall on; God is our
strength,*" the pamphleteer continued, the Marylanders replied "*Hey for
Saint Maries.*" Each side accused the other of firing the first fatal shot.
The outcome was perhaps determined, as some alleged, by the "glorious presence of the Lord of Hosts manifested in and towards his poor
oppressed people," since an armed merchantman from New England
suddenly appeared on the Severn and blocked Stone's retreat from direct
enemy fire. Surrounded and fired on from three sides, his troops were
quickly subdued and taken prisoner, their arms and supplies seized.
About fifty men were said to have been killed or wounded in the action.

If, as Bennett's Puritans proclaimed, God was "the onely worker of
this victory and deliverance," He was not a very merciful victor. Stone's
men had surrendered upon promise of quarter, but ten were immediately
condemned to death and four were actually executed. William Lewis, the
Catholic zealot whose "indiscrete speech" Calvert had sought to temper,
was "shot to death . . . in cold bloud," Stone's wife reported to Baltimore,
"the like barbarous act was never done amongst Christians." The others
were saved, it was said, only by "the incessant petitioning and begging
of some good women . . . some being sav'd just as they were leading out
to execution." Stone himself survived only as a result of the pleas of "the
enemies owne souldiers." But his property and that of all the leading proprietary men was sequestered. Loyalty oaths were repudiated and plunder followed. The houses of the few surviving Jesuits were ransacked,
the priests themselves forced to flee to a miserable exile in Anglican Virginia, and property throughout the colony was confiscated. The upheaval
continued until in 1657 Baltimore, maneuvering in the swirling poli-

tics of Cromwellian England, was able to recover his province from the Puritan insurrectionists who had ruled the colony in the name of a vengeful God.[63]

THE "PLUNDERING TIME" and the battle with and triumph of the Puritans had devastating effects. Property, just beginning to be developed and cultivated, had been destroyed; savage animosities had exploded with deadly results; the entire basis of the struggling colony—political, legal, and social—had been undermined. Baltimore's hoped-for manorial aristocracy, already eroded before 1645, had largely disappeared. Some of the manor lords had died and had not been replaced; some had fled the turmoil of Ingle's rebellion; some had become ordinary farmers. Most of the designated manors had proved to be ragged tobacco farms, short on labor and capital and indistinguishable from other tobacco farms that were multiplying along the river banks and the interior waterways. By 1652 the lands of even the most successful manor, Thomas Gerard's St. Clement's, were being sold off in small freeholds instead of being held for eventual leasing, and current leaseholders began purchasing their farms.[64]

There was no security or firmly established way of life. The future was entirely unpredictable. The possibility that a concerted Indian attack, like that of 1622 in Virginia, would destroy the outnumbered Europeans and reduce their farms to rubble was real. Baltimore had regained his legal title to the colony, but his political and ideological opponents in England and the irredentist Virginians, led by the relentless Claiborne, were still active. There was no way of anticipating whether the flow of immigrants, necessary for the development of the economy, would continue. And if there were immigrants, who would they be? Not Catholics, surely; most likely that "scumme of the people . . . vagrants and runnewayes . . . debauched, idle, lazie squanderers, jaylbirds, and the like"—precisely those Wintour had so feared and condemned.

CHAPTER 7

⚜

The Chesapeake's New World

1

WELL BEFORE 1660, when Lord Baltimore had recovered full possession of his proprietary colony and when the most tumultuous conflicts in that colony had subsided, a pattern of life had begun to emerge throughout the Chesapeake lands different from what had been known before, far different from what the original sponsors had hoped for and designed. The most powerful propulsions were created by the knowledge, spreading throughout the British archipelago, that after all the barbarism of the initial settlements, planters—even small and middle-level planters—in the Chesapeake region were beginning to pile profit upon profit by growing tobacco; that there, and throughout the North American coastal region, land was available for private ownership and cultivation; and that the value of the land, even undeveloped land, was rising as settlement expanded. The result was rapid population growth.

In the late 1640s and the years that followed, newcomers arrived by the hundreds, then by the thousands—eight to nine thousand per decade in the 1630s and 1640s. Prominent among them, attracted by the region's widely publicized profitability, were free, independent migrants who arrived with family, one or two servants, and some small savings. They came from slightly higher levels of society than most of the indentees and were more likely to have skills, useful connections, and some small capital to rebuild their lives. Some had social pretensions. Of a sample of over four hundred such free émigrés, almost a third claimed gentry status, and 27 percent claimed to be "merchants" of one sort or another. But these were not equivalents to the aristocrats and gentry of the earliest years of settlement, for whom Virginia had been a scientific curiosity and its founding an adventure or a patriotic challenge to the claims of rival powers. These free, uncommitted emigrants, outnumbered by indentured servants by three or four to one, were impelled by the same search for security as were the servants. They too were willing to risk resettlement and labor in the tobacco world to avoid material and social decline.[1]

Locating promising sites for their settlement, they quickly began the struggle to open wild fields to cultivation. Like Robert Cole, a yeoman's son from Middlesex, England, who in 1652, with resources brought from home, settled his family on a riverside plot in St. Mary's County, Maryland, they acquired land through purchase or headrights and began providing subsistence for their families, producing goods for local trade, and growing tobacco for distant markets. Slowly, in small parcels, they took over promising lands along the main riverways and streams, settled into rigorous seasonal routines, and learned ways of coping with the vagaries of distant tobacco markets, the periodic upheavals of nature, and the isolation and lack of community life in this borderland world. In hundreds of modest farms, the planters, their families, and one or a few servants lived alone, their only regular contacts the commercial agents or more prosperous planters who managed the marketing of their tobacco crop, and their few closest neighbors five or ten miles distant. As their numbers grew and their lives became more complex with a degree of prosperity, the need had emerged for at least the most essential public institution, local courts, which were beginning to multiply within newly created county jurisdictions.[2]

The inner lives of these thousands of small and middle-level planters will never be known, but as in the case of Cole, most of whose farming records have survived, one can see the outline of their exterior lives and ordinary routines. Survival required diligence, discipline, calculation, family cooperation, and a modicum of luck. They lived frugally, but they did not assume, as they might have been expected to assume, that "some must be rich some poore, some highe and eminent in power and dignitie; others meane and in subieccion." They were ambitious—for

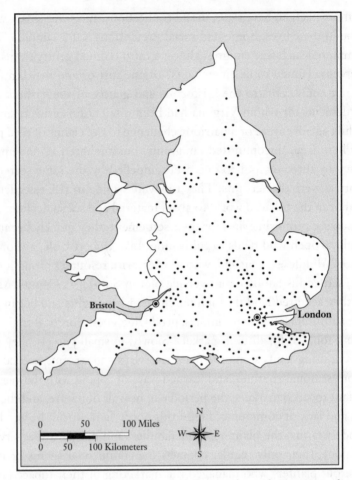

Origins of free immigrants to the Chesapeake in the seventeenth century

greater security, an increase in wealth if not income, and a higher position in life than they had had before. They took what they could as soon
as they could and in any way they could, acting, as Karen Kupperman has
remarked of their predecessors, "with barbarity toward those who were
powerless, whether they were Indians, Africans, or fellow Europeans."[3]

With the initial expectation that profits would rise in proportion to
the scale of tobacco cultivation, and with golden opportunities beckon-
ing with each cyclical boom in the fluctuating market price of tobacco,
efforts were made to acquire larger and larger plots of land and therefore
to recruit, by any means, legal or illegal, a labor force capable of working
successfully in the expanding tobacco fields.

The work, as it took standard form, was arduous. Seeds had to be planted in constructed mounds, the plants had to be topped off to enhance the leaves' growth, weeds hoed out, suckers and worms removed by hand, and the mature leaves cut off, hung up for curing, and then carefully packed for shipment. In this hard, tedious regime, which extended over the entire year, casual workers would not succeed. Strong motivation and effective discipline were needed; both were present in sufficient degree through most of the seventeenth century.[4]

The legal mechanism for securing and binding voluntary labor remained, as it had been, the contract of indenture—a legal commitment for full-time labor for four-, five-, seven-, or more year terms in exchange for maintenance, protection, and at termination some form of "freedom dues." By midcentury, notices of labor needs in the Chesapeake colonies as in the West Indies appeared everywhere in England's major port towns and the surrounding clusters of villages—posted in taverns, hawked at hiring fairs, and advertised widely by recruiters sent out through the countryside by merchants with investments in the colonies. Enticements were offered and loudly publicized: familial care, protection, and at least the prospect of land of one's own when one's bondage was completed.[5]

But propulsion was more important than enticement. With England's population growing steadily through the first half of the century (from 4.1 million to 5.3 million in those fifty years), real wages declining, periodic depressions disrupting key industries, and political upheavals unsettling development plans of all kinds, tens of thousands of unskilled laborers and insecure tradesmen and craftsmen faced unemployment and its consequences. Wandering from village to village and from farms to towns in search of employment, they intensified the population's usual mobility, and in desperation many, fearing vagrancy and destitution, chose the risks of an overseas voyage and labor in strange circumstances. Approximately one hundred thousand Britons, the great majority English, are known to have migrated to the tobacco coast in the seventeenth century. At least 70 percent of them and probably 85 percent came as indentured servants. Bonded for service, they were at work in the oldest settled areas as in the newest, arriving year after year on veritable convoys of ships from the major English ports. Middlesex County, between the Potomac and the Rappahannock rivers, a contemporary wrote, was a "sea of servants"—45 percent of that county's entire population were servants in 1668—and the same could have been said of other counties.[6]

Who were these tens of thousands of voluntarily bonded servants? Where were they from, what were their backgrounds, what were the differences and similarities among them? How did they live in this strange environment? What would become of them when they were released from service?

Leaving England at first mainly through London, then increasingly through Bristol and Liverpool, most were recorded as residents of those major port cities or of their hinterlands within a range of forty miles. But many came from distant places not only in the south of England but in the Midlands and the north country as well. Almost 40 percent of those leaving Bristol said that their homes were more than forty miles distant from the port—how distant, we do not know. And many of those who listed the ports of departure as their homes in fact came from elsewhere, from places unknown, the ports of departure being secondary or tertiary stopping points as they wandered in search of employment. Thus the migrants to the Chesapeake represented a drainage of the local "surpluses"—those dislodged in the nation's shifting economy—from "declining market towns, pastoral parishes, and proto-industrial villages." One Virginia county, York, along the Rappahannock River, had recent settlers—both bonded and free—from eleven English counties extending from Devon to Yorkshire as well as from London and Bristol, and they brought with them a variety of English subcultures, and to a lesser degree Welsh, Scottish, and Irish backgrounds as well.

Dislodged workers, caught in a buyer's market, had only their labor to offer and whatever small skills they could claim. In the early years some, perhaps half, of the male migrants could claim some skill in a craft or trade and could therefore be classified as having been drawn from middling levels of the working population. But at the point of migration all were living at the lower margins of British society. The most debased, possibly 40 percent of the total, were the youngest, the least skilled and most destitute; they shipped out without the protection of legal indentures and served therefore according to the harsh terms of extemporized contracts that followed Virginia's "local custom."[7]

Within the great flow of immigrant workers there continued to be utterly destitute vagrants picked up by recruiting agents at "beggars' fairs," where one could find "more rogues than ever . . . whipped at a cart's arse through London . . . [or] dropping out of Ireland." There were young orphans routinely disposed of to brokers by parish overseers to reduce welfare expenses. There were those "lewd and dangerous persons, rogues, vagrants, and other idle persons"—those "sturdy beggars as gypsyes and other incorrigible rogues and wanderers"—who were ordered by the Commonwealth government to be seized by the local constables, imprisoned, and unless acquitted of vagrancy, sent to the plantations "for five years under the condition of servants." And there continued to be clandestine seizures of men and boys—occasionally women as well—for forced shipment to the colonies, where their services were offered for sale. It was a brutal traffic, described in vivid accounts by victims and in court records. What had been occasional in the Virginia Company's earliest years had developed into an organized system with safe houses for confining victims until shipping could be arranged and with standardized transaction costs and procedures.

Week after week, month after month, children, male and female, were snatched from the streets of London for shipment and sale "for a slave" in Virginia. One was "an infant about foure years of age," the Middlesex County Court in London recorded, "to the endangering of his life"; another, a servant deluded and enticed by false promises; still another, an apprentice sold by his master and held on shipboard for a week before being rescued. As early as 1645, kidnapping for the servant trade in Virginia had become so notorious that the government ordered all public officers to apprehend anyone caught "stealing, selling, buying, inveigling, purloyning, conveying or receiving children so stolne." But what the Privy Council denounced as a "barbarous and inhumane" traffic continued. In 1664 Bristol sought to control the traffic by creating a registry office to record all legitimate outbound passengers and exclude all others. London later did the same. But "spiriting" could not be stopped by legislation or bureaucratic procedures. Only the decline in the market for such servants could reduce its profitability and hence its frequency. Until then stealing, buying, and inveigling children, servants, and vagrants remained a particularly vicious, if minor, part of the peopling of the tobacco lands.[8]

Vicious too, though legal, was the forced transportation to the colony of convicts, the practice that Dale had hopefully imagined would solve the labor problem. Less vicious, and greater in volume, was the traffic in prisoners of war, which flourished in the years of the Commonwealth's military campaigns. How many captured troops of the royalist armies actually reached the Chesapeake and were forced to work in the fields for seven years cannot be known. It is known, however, that after each of Cromwell's major victories—at Preston, Dunbar, and Worcester (1648–50)—hundreds of captured troops, most of them Scots, were rounded up and disposed of. Some were allowed to return to their homes, but some were handed over to local merchants in need of cheap labor, some were sent to serve as mercenaries in foreign armies, and many, below the "quality" of lieutenant or "cornet of horse," were bound to service in the plantations. At least a thousand prisoners were authorized to be shipped to Virginia and New England after Dunbar, and after Worcester 1,610 were granted to people desiring them in Virginia, upon assurance that the prisoners would be accorded "Christian usage." In all, close to three thousand war prisoners were authorized in a short period of time for shipment to the Chesapeake. And while their arrival and precise location in the colonies cannot be traced, by the late 1650s Scottish names suddenly became prominent in the land patent books. In 1665 a Scottish minister in Virginia reported that his countrymen in the colony were "living better than ever ther forfathers, and that from so mean a beginning as being sold [as] slav[e]s here, after . . . Worster fight are now herein great masters of many servants themselfs."[9]

2

Thus the workforce, flooding into the Chesapeake colonies after the boom in the tobacco industry and the expansion of land settlement, was an amalgam of people, largely English, of various geographical and subcultural backgrounds, some from provincial farmlands, some from forests and fens, some from inland towns and villages, many from the slums of the two main Atlantic ports. Some were respectable, some vicious, some hopeful; many were destitute and despairing. Yet there were measurable characteristics of this great miscellany of people. The two main surviving registers of outbound passengers—Bristol's of 1654–84 and London's of 1682–86—have made possible statistical samplings of part, at least, of this immigrant population, consisting largely of indentured servants.[10]

At the start it was preponderantly a male population of young adults, the great majority between the ages of sixteen and twenty-five. But in both characteristics, sex and age, there were basic changes as the decades passed that reflect forces at work in British society, played out against a constant if erratic demand for labor in the colonies. The socioeconomic foundations shifted. England's population growth slowed, the nation's economy stabilized after the Restoration, industry and commercial agriculture revived, and markets increased for agricultural and industrial production, hence for labor in various forms.

The results were palpable in the changes in the immigrant flows to the Chesapeake. The disproportion of incoming males decreased steadily through the mid and later years of the century, from six to one in the early years to perhaps three to one at midcentury to about 2.5 to one in 1700. And when women, largely spinsters and widows, appeared in relatively greater numbers, the average age of men declined, from only 5 percent younger than sixteen years to three times that proportion in the 1680s to perhaps eight times at the end of the century. Both changes suggest the growing difficulty of recruiting from the optimal, core population of Britain's middling working classes and the turn to the margins of society, to people less desirable to Chesapeake plantation owners: convicts, vagrants, war prisoners, orphans, and women. Increasingly there were Irish among them, despite the fact that in the West Indies, where Irish laborers had been recruited in large numbers, they had proved to be difficult, unreliable, and often rebellious, largely as a consequence of their resistance to the vicious treatment they received from the English planters, who despised them.[11]

Once debarked at the small Chesapeake ports and riverside inlets on the mainland, the incoming servants found themselves transformed into commodities—commoditized units of labor. If their service was not already committed, they—their services—were sold to the highest bidder. Most of the uncommitted were disposed of in shipboard and dockside transactions, the length of their labor determined by the terms of sale. Those who were not sold on shipboard were peddled through the countryside for sale in small numbers or individually to inland farmers, many of whom had themselves only recently been freed and were struggling to produce enough tobacco to buy a sufficient stake in the land.[12]

Though conditions had improved since the earliest, most barbarous years, mere physical survival for the newly recruited laborers was still the most immediate problem. The sudden encounter with the hot, malarial climate, especially in tidal and low-lying areas, was shocking and debilitating, and when the effect of the environment was compounded by a severe work regime, the result was devastating. Between 15 and 30 percent of male immigrants to Maryland at midcentury died within the first, "seasoning" year of their residence, and those who were alive at age twenty-two could expect to live only another twenty-three years. In one county 17 percent of the immigrant males who were alive at age twenty-two died before thirty, 41 percent by age forty, 70 percent by age fifty. In Middlesex County, Virginia, "only a minority lived to the end of their service and joined the ranks of the free."

The mortality rates were scarcely better for those born in the land. In Maryland nearly 30 percent of all infants died in their first year; overall 47 percent of the population was dead by age twenty, and those who reached that age would live, on average, only another twenty-six years. Women fared slightly better than men, but the differences were slight. The death rate was so high among both the 100,000 immigrants and the American-born Europeans that the total European population in 1700 was only approximately 87,000: fewer by 15,000 than the number of immigrants that had arrived. An estimated 34,000 people, white and black, arrived in Maryland between 1634 and 1680, but the colony's total population in 1680 was only 20,000. The demographic deficits would never be made up as long as the male preponderance among the servant population persisted and indentured women lost four or more reproductive years in service. The consequences of the devastating death rate and reproductive deficiencies transformed the structure of family life.[13]

Family life was twisted, devastated, by early death. In Charles County, Maryland, marriages lasted on average only nine years before one partner died. In Virginia most children lost at least one parent by the time they reached majority; over a third lost both. In Middlesex County a quarter of all children lost one or both parents before age five; half did so by age thirteen; and almost three-quarters by age twenty-one or by the time of marriage. Old people were rare. Few children ever knew their grandparents, and orphanage was common. Thirty percent of all children were orphans before their eighteenth birthday and were left in the care of uncles, family friends, legal guardians, godparents, and above all stepparents.

With marriages so frequently broken by the early death of one partner, second and third marriages of widows and widowers with children (serial polyandry) led to the creation of households that were complex, jumbled, unstable, at times bizarre. Had one dropped in on a typical Middlesex household in the mid-seventeenth century, that county's historians write, one would have found orphans, half-brothers, stepbrothers and stepsisters, and wards running a gamut of ages. The father figure in the house might well be an uncle or a brother, the mother figure an aunt, elder sister, or simply the father's "now-wife"—to use the wording frequently found in conveyances and wills.

Childhood, so often riven by parental loss or clouded by fears of looming disasters, scarcely existed as a time of security and nurturing. Thus the experiences of the child Agatha Vause: by her tenth birthday, she had lost a father, two stepfathers, a mother, and a guardian uncle. Stability and security might be found, in some small degree at least, in this world of transience and childhood trauma, the same historians write, not in nuclear families but in neighborhood communities of kin and quasi-kin, neighbors and friends who interacted not in formal institutions (church, parish, markets, manorial courts) but in irregular workaday encounters and on occasions of mutual help.[14]

Living conditions contributed to the brutality of life and the savage death rate. Houses on the small plantations in Maryland as in Virginia continued to be drafty wooden boxes, "dribbled over the landscape without apparent design." As in earlier years most houses consisted of a single room or at best two rooms with a loft above. Floors were usually beaten earth, the walls made of raw unpainted planks thinly chinked with clay. Normal furnishings were rolled-up mattresses for beds (bedsteads were rare), a bench and a table, a few chests for storage, and pewter and wooden dishes. Spoons and one's fingers were the only utensils for eating. There were no privies, and even chamber pots were rare. People relieved themselves outside, close to the walls, "creating stenches that must have pervaded all rooms of the house." Clothing hung from the walls or was stretched out as a space divider. The small flimsy buildings were cold in winter and hot and insect-ridden in summer; with shuttered windows, they were always dark. Above all, as the family's central place for meals, sleeping, procreation, care for the sick, and entertainment, they were crowded. Two persons per bed was the average for Maryland's ordinary families, and in this as in so many other aspects of daily life, there were few differences between servants and masters.

Most of the small farmers and their servants lived at the level of the most menial householders in England, their dwellings only "slightly larger and modified versions of flimsy English huts erected on commons and wastes," their "standard of living little different from the lowest levels of society in England." Few whose estates were worth less that £50 (the great majority of the planters) had beds to sleep on with sheets and blankets or enough furniture for all to eat at a table. And life for those at the bottom of the tobacco world was primitive. At suppertime, the leading archaeologists of seventeenth-century Virginia write, one can imagine

> a wife, husband, two children, and perhaps a servant are gathered together in the perpetual dusk of their shuttered cottage . . . their dinner is cornmeal mush boiled in an iron pot. The food is ladled into five plates or porringers, one for each person. The father sets his down on a large storage trunk which he straddles and sits on. His daughter is perched on the edge of a small chest, the only other piece of furniture in the room. The rest either stand or squat along the walls. They spoon up the food from the plates they must hold in their hands or place on the floor. They drink milk or water from a common cup, tankard or bowl passed around. No candle or lamp is lighted now or later when the room grows completely dark except for the glow of embers on the hearth. . . .While someone rinses the bowls in a bucket of water (there being only one pot) someone else drags out a cattail mattress and arranges it in front of the fire. The husband, wife, and daughter lie down there, covering themselves with a single canvas sheet and a worn-out bed rug. The son and servant roll up in blankets on the floor. For warmth all sleep in their clothes.

The wealthier planters fared better, but their houses have been compared to "modest farm cottages in England." Only the wealthiest had multi-room houses. There were no spacious brick mansions; even the upper gentry's dwellings were "small, inconspicuous, and inconsequential." The greatest of them, the Wormeleys' "Rosegill," overlooking the Rappahannock River, was only a nine-room wooden building, surrounded by small outhouses for cooking, storage, and housing servants.[15]

In theory relief might have been found in the benevolence of master-servant relations, since indentured servants were assumed to be temporary family members, protected as well as disciplined by the paternalism of the household. And so it was in many cases. But in the grinding reality of small-scale tobacco farming, where masters lived and worked intimately with servants, their clothing and appearance in no way different from those of their hirelings, relationships, however benevolently begun, easily frayed and became brutal. Some masters, especially the most marginal and desperate, drove their servants hard, stirring resistance that could become violent and that could lead to savage reprisals. Murders were reported. Women were commonly exposed to sexual exploitation: more than 10 percent of all children born to immigrant women in seventeenth-century Maryland were bastards. Women who bore illegitimate children, like those who attempted escapes and forceful resistance, were punished most commonly by extensions of service and so to still further exploitation.[16]

Yet however miserable their existence, however brutalized they may have been in service, most of the immigrant servants carried with them a sense of independence derived from the knowledge that their bondage was voluntary, contractual, and limited in time, and that they could look forward to an independent future and possibly a stake in the land. And some, like Clocker, Fenwick, and Adams in Maryland, saw their aspirations fulfilled as they advanced from servitude to freedom and acquired, with hard work and careful management, an independent if small stake in the land, with one or two servants and a place in the management of local affairs. But as hundreds of freed servants became thousands, as the most fertile coastal and riverine lands were claimed if not yet cultivated, and as a long depression in the tobacco trade compounded the problems for small farmers, the incidence and prospects of freed servants acquiring land of their own declined. By the end of the century the majority of freedmen had little choice but to move to more remote or poorer land exposed to Indian attacks, or to continue in service, now for small wages, ultimately to become lifelong tenants or sharecroppers. So in Maryland in the late seventeenth century fully one-third of all householders were tenants; in Virginia perhaps only one in ten former servants were able to establish themselves in the ranks of independent proprietors and profitable planters.[17]

Such discouraging prospects, relayed back to England by returnees and correspondents, were in themselves enough to reduce the flow of new recruits to the North American servant population. By the 1670s the decline in their numbers within increasing flows of immigrants to the region was palpable. By the 1680s it was a major problem for the established planters. Their ultimate solution, slow in coming at first but reaching fulfillment at the end of the century, was the substitution of African slaves for the familiar British and European servants—people utterly alien to the planters, of perplexing character, and believed to be barbarous by nature.[18]

3

"Negars," "negors," and Africans otherwise identified by color had begun appearing in very small numbers well before 1619, when John Rolfe noted the arrival in Virginia of "20. and odd Negroes." They were Angolans hijacked from a shipment to Spanish America and sold by their Dutch captors "for victualles." Their numbers rose very slowly, their arrivals random occurrences. The Virginia census of 1625 identified only twenty-three blacks, scattered thinly through the separate plantations. In 1640 Maryland recorded twenty blacks. But then the numbers began to rise as planters gradually, almost casually, began including them in their purchasing orders. So in 1638 Baltimore ordered his agent to buy for him—along with forty cattle, ten sows, and forty hens—"ten negroes to be transported to St. Mareys," and in 1642 Leonard Calvert offered a passing ship captain three manors or 24,000 pounds of tobacco for fourteen "negroe men-slaves, of between 16 & 26 yeare old, able & sound of body and limbs." By 1650 there were 300 blacks in Maryland; in 1660, 758; and in 1670, 1,190 (9 percent of the population), by which time Virginia's black population had reached 2,000. But there was as yet no wholesale importation of slaves. The proposal of the Royal African Company in 1664 to send one to two hundred slaves a year to Maryland had to be refused, Charles Calvert reported, because there were not "men of estates good enough to undertake such a businesse," despite the fact that "wee are naturally inclin'd to love neigros if our purses would endure it." Most if not all of those who arrived in Maryland came not directly from Africa but from the Caribbean islands, Barbados in particular, from Spanish settlements on the mainland, and from Dutch islands via New Netherland, hence people who were to some extent "seasoned" and used to life in European colonies. And they came in various statuses. Some came as freemen and remained free, though often under particular disabilities. Others could show by oral or written testimony that their service was contractually limited to a specific term, after which, like indentured servants, they were to be released.[19] And a very few, who came bound

in service, through ceaseless labor and fierce determination were able
to buy their freedom and that of their families and establish themselves
in the society at large. In 1668 nearly a third of the fifty-nine blacks in
Northampton County on Virginia's lower Eastern Shore, all of whom
had arrived bound in unlimited servitude, had acquired freedom; some
had bought property which they were able to pass on to the next generation, established effective community ties among themselves, and participated broadly in the larger white society. All blacks before 1660, Edmund
Morgan writes, "whether servant, slave, or free, enjoyed most of the same
rights and duties of other Virginians. There is no evidence . . . that they
were subjected to a more severe discipline than other servants."[20]

But the importance of the most remarkable achievers among the
blacks can easily be exaggerated. Their numbers in fact were small, they
are found only in one or two counties, they were subject to white harassment, and their claims to independence and full equality were tenuous,
contestable, and not long sustained. The great majority of Africans, even
in this most favorable period, were never viewed as fully equal to white
servants. Lacking contracts, actual or implicit, and having been bought or
seized in Africa or abroad, they were considered to be bound in servitude
for life unless otherwise identified, a condition never imposed on whites
but that seemed suitable in most Europeans' eyes. For they were black,
and color mattered. It carried with it a plethora of cultural assumptions.
To be black in north European culture, and especially in Elizabethan
and Jacobean England, was to be dark in a cultural sense—base, sinis-
ter, inferior, "grossly uncivil . . . unscrupulous, thieving, and sometimes
treacherous."[21] It was this assumption of the blacks' cultural baseness,
of their inborn inferiority in the scale of human development, and their
complete alienation from English cultural values, that, together with the
rapidly increasing demand for labor, made possible the barbarism of their
reduction to the emerging legal status of "slaves."

In Elizabethan usage, *slave* was a general term of derogation used in
offhand ways to refer to any deeply vulgar, degraded people and commonly applied to blacks held in servitude. As the economic value of servants without limit of time grew in the labor-short plantations and as
white indentured servants became less available, the term *slave*—the word
itself—acquired a salience it had not had before and, gradually, a new specific, legal meaning that would render the use of the word "scandalous," a
contemporary wrote, if it were to be applied to white servants. Something

new and vital, a newly defined legal category, began to emerge, out of the
difficulties of the labor situation, out of experience in plantation agriculture, out of necessity, and out of a sense of racial differences.[22]

There had been no preexisting legal definition of *slavery*, and no
one set out to infuse the term with a new, specific meaning. But as the
blacks' importance in the labor force grew, disputes arose over the terms
of servitude which could only be resolved through litigation, despite
the lack of legal precedents. Laws to resolve the conflicts and confine
the blacks to maximum exploitation had to be devised. Analogies were
useless. Kidnapped boys who, like Africans, arrived without work contracts were bound simply by "the custom of the country" which however
harsh allowed for eventual release. Few thought the same should apply to
blacks, or that a limited contract of some sort was *implied* where bondage
was unspecified. If *slavery* meant lifelong servitude, as in fact it most often
did, was that status heritable? Did it carry over to the slaves' offspring?
Were marriages between whites and blacks, free and unfree, Europeans
and Africans, legal? If so, were the children of such unions white or black
in the eyes of the law? Did conversion to Christianity release one from
bondage?

Answers had to be found if the planters' economy was to prosper.
What began as conditions *de facto* became statuses *de jure*, as the planters,
merchants, and lawyers sought to remedy discrepancies, resolve ambiguities, and bind into an effective and reliable labor force the growing mass
of black workers. There were some working models, if not legal precedents, that might in some degree be followed. Blacks had been enslaved
in the Caribbean islands before the Chesapeake authorities began searching for legal definitions, and slave laws had been passed there, especially
in Barbados, that were known in Virginia. So to some extent, as April
Hatfield has suggested, the emerging legalities of slavery developed as
an intercolonial "conversation." But the Barbadian laws and practices did
not cover all contingencies or fit closely the more complex economy of
the Chesapeake.[23]

So the planters, merchants, and lawyers in Virginia and Maryland
began the process of finding their own way toward a full legal definition of the Africans' bondage. Though by midcentury some clarity had
been reached, ambiguities and constraints remained—but not because of
moral concerns. There were none. To those Virginians and Marylanders
who owned slaves, bought and sold them, forced them into degrading and

perpetual labor, there were no moral constraints. Even the few planters known to have been generous to their slaves, who freed them in their wills and provided for their welfare, did not condemn slaveholding as such.[24] The English were people who denounced barbarism as they knew it, declared it to be un-Christian, uncivilized, and immoral. But sensibilities in the world they knew were blunt, and relationships between masters and servants were commonly abrasive, at times savage. Though slavery however defined was degrading and brutal, in its various forms it was familiar, venerable, and as far as the planters knew, in principle uncontested. It had existed in one form or another, defined in one way or another, for ages untold, and it flourished elsewhere in their own time: in the Middle East, in North and sub-Saharan Africa, in Iberian America, and among native tribes.[25] The question was not what the moral limits of slavery might be but how it might best be elaborated and defined in law for maximum use in the Chesapeake, and how it might relate to differences in race.

Answering these questions—even grasping their implications—was difficult, and successive efforts to reach a logical and complete resolution were halting and confused. By the 1660s and 1670s, the need for clarity in the legal status of blacks had become urgent, and laws and regulations of deepening confinement, incomplete and ambiguous though they were, followed in quick succession.

One of the most important of the early laws, an epitome of the difficulties of definition, was adopted by Maryland in 1664. It was the first statute to recognize lifelong heritable slavery as a matter of law, but strangely that was not its primary purpose. Confusing in its very title ("An Act Concerning Negroes & Other Slaves"—the latter unspecified), the law stated at the outset that all negroes or other slaves already in the colony or others who would come in the future "shall serve Durante Vita" (for life), and their children will follow their fathers' status into the same condition. That profound assertion, which went to the heart of the matter, seemed obvious to the authors of the statute, and they disposed of it quickly, without elaboration, comment, or justification. What concerned them and needed detailed comment and justification was the question of miscegenation: what to do about the "divers freeborne English women [who] forgettfull of their free condicion and to the disgrace of our nation doe intermarry with negro slaves." Conflicts had arisen "touching the issue of such woemen" that threatened "great damage" to the slaves' masters. To prevent such "shamefull matches," the law stated that in the

future white women who married blacks would become slaves of their
husbands' masters as long as their husbands lived, and that their children
would become slaves "as their fathers were." As for the children of the
white women who were presently married to negroes, they were to serve
their parents' masters "till they be thirty yeares of age and noe longer."[26]

By this statute, ambiguous and incomplete in its logic, slavery was
declared to be lifelong servitude, but this condition was not exclusively
confined to the negro race, since there could be "other slaves" as well.
Interracial marriages were fiercely condemned, but they were recognized
as legal; and derivative slavery, though absolute for slaves' children, was
limited for the white wives of black husbands and for the children of
interracial marriages that already existed. The statute ruled that the status of children of mixed marriages would follow the condition of their
fathers, which was the normal provision of the English common law. But
it would soon be seen that in the plantation world this provision would
have bizarre consequences. Slave women would be bringing up their own
children in freedom and the women's masters would be denied the benefit of their slaves' fertility. The law was therefore changed to matrilineal
descent, which became the normal American usage. And when in 1681
it was seen that the law as written might encourage planters to marry off
their white female servants to black slaves to reduce the women to slavery,
the entire statute was repealed. Even more confusing was the struggle,
not even attempted in this early statute, over how to define slaves as the
property they evidently were. Were they realty (like land and buildings)
or chattels (like horses and plows) or freehold (permanent attachments to
specific realty)?

In time, through successive revisions and expansions of the early
laws of servitude in the two colonies, such confusions, ambiguities, and
anomalies would be eliminated. Both colonies outlawed conversion to
Christianity as grounds for manumission (Virginia as early as 1667),
encouraged mating among slaves but did not recognize blacks' marriages
as legal and banished whites who married blacks, restricted slaves' movements without passes, mandated the automatic expulsion of newly freed
slaves, relieved masters of the charge of felony whose "correction" of a
slave ended in the slave's death, limited slaves' access to arms and legal
processes, and after "peculiar contortions," William Wiecek writes, "in
efforts to make a human being into a vendible thing," settled on the compromise of "chattel personal."[27]

In the end, in both colonies, though with less rigor in Maryland, the ultimate logic of chattel slavery was reached. Slavery would be, and would remain, a condition of unqualified, total, lifelong servitude, a form of bondage that would apply *only* to blacks and mulattoes, and to *all* blacks and mulattoes, except the very few who were legally free; and it would be heritable through matrilineal lines. Slaves would be chattel in the eyes of the law, to be dealt with, disposed of, as such, and any limitations in that status would only be matters of personal indulgence, the law being universally and fully enforced by constabulary authority where it existed, by vigilantism, by brute power.

There was logic but no prior design in the development of this barbarous system of human debasement, nor had it been inherited or borrowed from abroad. It had been devised in the course of three generations by ambitious planters and merchants in the Chesapeake colonies desperate for profits, familiar with human degradation, and freed from moral scruples by their deep, pervasive racism.

4

This Chesapeake upper class, an incipient gentry or aristocracy, grew quickly in the middle years of the century as the tobacco industry expanded and with it successful claims to large parcels of land. The dominant planters—dominant in the political as well as the economic life of the Chesapeake colonies—were, and would remain, a loose association of large-scale landowners and tobacco producers, not a tightly bound oligarchy with consolidated interests. Originally a small group, it emerged from two quite different sources: from among the more successful of the local, resident tobacco farmers aspiring to greater affluence, some of whom had arrived as children and servants in the 1620s, and from groups of new arrivals in the tempestuous 1640s and the three decades that followed, immigrants who carried with them more elevated statuses, better funding, and connections that would serve them well.

The former—the successful locals: Spencer, Wood, Menefie, Utie— having fought their way up step by step in difficult circumstances after the initial convulsions of settlement, and having survived Indian wars and disease, had slowly added to their property, with the help of their merchant associates, to build substantial estates, and had found their way into public office to protect their interests. By the 1640s their personal

presence was fading: Menefie died in 1647, Utie in 1640; but their properties descended as substantial estates to the following generation. Adam
Thoroughgood, the vicar's son who had begun as a servant, was able to
pass on an estate of some six thousand acres. So too William Spencer,
once a "yeoman" with a farm of only twelve acres, bequeathed, as "Wm
Spencer, Gent.," over 3,500 acres to heirs who would remain in Virginia's
ruling gentry. Maryland was no different. There too a small group, like
Clocker and Fenwick, worked their way out of servitude to achieve affluence and public authority by dint of hard work, shrewd dealings, and
luck.[28]

Thus the survivors and local successes of the first generations of
Chesapeake planters who had emerged from within the abrasions of the
earlier migrations and had managed, in crude ways, to establish a measure of economic and political control, had passed on their properties
and their statuses to successors, who would become part of a more stable
society than their predecessors had known. It was a society shaped by
the style of a new wave of immigrants of the middle years of the century,
more affluent than the earlier, self-made planters, more sophisticated,
closer to the currents of life in metropolitan Britain, and closer too to the
cosmopolitan structures of the greater Atlantic world.

IN VIRGINIA the character of the new generation of leaders was anticipated by the arrival in 1642 of Sir William Berkeley as governor. Though
more distinguished in social status and family connections than those
of the middle class, gentry, and lesser nobility who would soon follow, Berkeley exemplified their condition in two respects. Like many of
them, he had prior family connections with the colony which he hoped
to exploit, and he was a younger son of a prominent family cast off by
primogeniture from inheriting a major part of the family's fortune and
position and forced to fend for himself.

Berkeley's father, Sir Maurice, had been a substantial investor in the
Virginia Company and had played an active role in its politics. His five
sons, of whom William was the fourth, grew up surrounded by talk of
overseas ventures and investments and in contact with men who were
personally involved in colonial settlements. Like the other original investors in the defunct Virginia Company, Sir Maurice retained the hope that
something could still be retrieved from his stake in the colony, and his
awareness of that distant world, if not his material hopes, was passed on

to his sons. While the eldest, Charles, inherited the family estate, young William was forced to cast about for a suitable career. He acquired a fashionable education at Oxford, spent two leisurely years in legal studies at the Inns of Court, traveled in Europe for three years, and then accepted a fellowship at Merton College. But though highly literate, he found academic life, even for one of his social standing, which freed him from pedestrian duties, too isolated and routine, and he turned to the royal court for employment and for a path to security and prominence.

A well-educated, stylish, dilettantish young man, one of Lord Falkland's circle of litterateurs and wits, Berkeley fitted in well enough with the sophisticated life of the court. He attended to his duties as a gentleman of the king's Privy Chamber, tried his hand at fashionable playwriting (his scripts notable for their "scrappy cadences, . . . flashes of wit, [and] the pungent turn of phrase"), and served as an envoy abroad. But as his fate was increasingly linked to that of the king, his insecurities grew with the rebellious mood of the nation, and he was disappointed in his failure to achieve the prominence he sought. The Scots' invasion and the political turmoil in London that culminated in Parliament's challenge to Crown authority unsettled him, and after Strafford's execution in May 1641, he looked for ways of escape and renewal. He considered an appointment as envoy to Constantinople but dropped that when he heard of the possibility of the governorship of Virginia. Not that that post was vacant: the incumbent, Sir Francis Wyatt, was a competent and experienced governor; but the position was within the control of Berkeley's supporters at court. Once alerted he moved quickly. Mobilizing all of his family's influence at court, especially that of his eldest brother, Sir Charles Berkeley, who was close to the king, and with the additional support of both Lord Falkland and Edward Hyde, the future Earl of Clarendon, whom he had known at the Inns of Court, he was able to buy Wyatt off and secure the appointment. The transaction was formalized in July 1641. Shortly thereafter, accompanied by some three dozen servants, he sailed off to Virginia, and in March 1642 he took up his post in the colony.[29]

In the years that followed—years that at home saw the successful rebellion against the monarchy, the suppression and dispersal of Crown adherents, the triumphs and turmoils of the Commonwealth, and then the restoration of the monarchy and of England's prosperity—Virginia became a refuge for a small but influential group of royalists and a land of opportunity for members of substantial families and others with funds

Sir William Berkeley and his wife,
Lady Frances Culpeper Stephens
Berkeley Ludwell, thirty-one
years younger than he

to invest and connections to exploit. Berkeley, dismayed by the state of the colony, quickly became an active promoter of the migration of displaced royalists and ambitious younger sons. "Industriously," his friend Lord Clarendon would later recall in his *History of the Rebellion*, Berkeley "invited many gentlemen and others thither, as to a place of security" that could be defended against Parliament's forces and where they could live plentifully. As a result, "many persons of condition, and good officers in the war . . . transported themselves, with all the estate they had been able to preserve." In fact, Clarendon wrote, so confident was Berkeley that Virginia would be a secure refuge that "he writ to the King almost inviting him thither, as to a place that wanted nothing." Berkeley's confidence was misplaced; Parliament's forces quickly took control of the colony. But Virginia, perhaps because of Berkeley, continued to be thought of by some as "the onely citty of refuge left in his Majesties dominions . . . for distressed Cavallers," and a few of the most exposed royalists did arrive and settled in promising circumstances.[30]

They were a strange, rather disreputable lot, flamboyantly active for a time but no founders of a distinct "royalist" culture. They came from all over the realm—from Yorkshire, Cambridgeshire, Norfolk, Kent, Sussex, and Gloucestershire—and their interests were as diverse as their geographical origins. What distinguished them from others of the upper gentry or aristocracy was not their culture or lifestyle or folkways but their politics, their active loyalty to the Crown in a time of crisis, and their opportunistic escape to Virginia.[31]

Sir Thomas Lunsford was perhaps the most vivid personality among them. He had been imprisoned for the attempted murder of a neighbor in Sussex, had led royal troops against the Scots (boasting of having personally shot two mutineers), and had been dismissed as lieutenant of the Tower of London on Parliament's charge that he was an indebted, quarrelsome desperado contemplating a popish coup. Defeated after fighting for the Crown in several engagements, he fled to Holland, where in 1649 he managed to get a pass for himself and his family to settle in Virginia. With a reputation for sadistic violence, described by his own cousin as an outlaw given to "lewdness and dissoluteness" and proud of being known as a "swaggering ruffian," Lunsford no doubt found his appointment as the lieutenant-general of Virginia's militia a soft assignment, but it was a major position if in a minor province, and he wasted no time in taking advantage of it. Granted over three thousand acres of good tobacco land, he promptly married Ralph Wormeley's niece, the widow of the colony's influential secretary, Richard Kempe, and thus secured a connection with a prosperous, long-settled family. The connections would be further strengthened when Lunsford's daughter married Ralph Wormeley II, whose mother-in-law was his first cousin and whose wife therefore was his cousin once removed.[32]

This kind of kinship clustering was typical of the small royalist group that gathered around Berkeley. Sir Henry Chicheley, Lieutenant Colonel of Horse in Cambridgeshire, having given security that he would do nothing prejudicial to the Commonwealth government, arrived in Virginia in 1650. Within a year he had married Ralph Wormeley I's widow and had taken over her 5,200-acre estate, Rosegill, on the Rappahannock River, which became a center of the colony's higher social life. In time Chicheley would serve twice as governor and earn the description by his successor as governor, the courtier Lord Thomas Culpeper (himself a venal, profiteering adventurer, whose cousin Frances Culpeper married Berkeley), as "that lumpe, that masse of dulnesse, that worse than nothing."[33]

Chicheley had not seemed so dull or lumpish when he was first noticed in Virginia by another well-placed royalist, Maj. Henry Norwood, Berkeley's cousin, who had fought for the king at Bristol and Worcester and then fled England "as from a place," he wrote, "infected with the plague . . . to travel any where to shun so hot a contagion." The voyage of the *Virginia Merchant*, carrying him and numerous other royalist refugees, including the Majors Francis Moryson, Richard Fox, and Francis Lovelace, had been a horrendous nightmare: devastating storms, shipwreck, starvation, and possibly cannibalism. Arrived finally at the Chesapeake's Eastern Shore, Norwood made his way to the York River settlements and there came on the "feasting and carousing" at Ralph Wormeley's house, where he found "intimate acquaintance[s]," among them, besides Lunsford and Chicheley, Sir Philip Honeywood, a cavalry major disgraced with his chief, Prince Rupert, after the surrender of Bristol, and Col. Robert Hammond, former captain and governor of the Isle of Wight.[34]

How many royalists, strictly speaking—that is, Crown adherents active in defense of the king who had been forced into exile—removed to Virginia is not known; a rough estimate of "a couple of hundred" is probably high; and many of the most prominent, like Norwood, Hammond, Honeywood, and Lovelace, returned to Europe quickly, to serve in the entourage of the exiled Charles II, eventually in the Restoration court. Of those who remained, only a dozen or so became prominent and had some influence on the colony's public life, its reputation, and its social aspirations.[35]

In time their distinction as royalists of the rebellion years blurred into the more general pattern of the lives of the numerous sons and other relatives of substantial merchant and gentry families who appeared in the Chesapeake colonies in the same middle years of the seventeenth century. Some had royalist leanings, but their fortunes were not shaped by politics; nor had they been forced to emigrate. They had material interests in mind, the kind of interests that Berkeley appealed to repeatedly in person when in England, in correspondence, and in promotional publications.

False, he wrote in a memo prepared for the Council on Foreign Plantations in 1662, was the charge that only "those of the meanest quality and corruptest lives" had settled in Virginia. Its population, he said, included "men of as good families as any subjects in England," and he listed the sonorous names of the earliest years (Percys, Wests, Throgmortons) and of later times (Wyatts, Chicheleys, Morysons, Kempes). The colony was subject to many burdens, especially the unfortunate reliance on tobacco as its sole profitable product, which Berkeley appealed to the Privy Council to overcome by a policy of economic diversification. But the potential was there for great wealth in raw materials ("iron, lead, pitch, tar, masts, timber") and commodities easily produced ("flax, hemp, silk, wheat, barley, oats, rice, cotton"). It was a perfect place, he wrote, in words almost identical to those of Baltimore and Robert Wintour, for "indigent younger brothers whom the peculiar policy of this nation condemned to poverty or war." Now there was no need for them to suffer, "for a small summe of money will enable a younger brother to erect a flourishing family in a new world, and adde more strength, wealth, and honour to his native country then thousands did before, that dyed forgotten and unrewarded in an unjust war."[36]

It was to this appeal, whether delivered by Berkeley or circulated by word of mouth among knowledgeable families, especially those with earlier ties to the Chesapeake colonies, that a cohort of ambitious young men responded in the middle years of the century. Whatever their political leanings, they all saw opportunities opening before them. In time—and shortly—they combined with the successful planters of earlier years and the royalist notables who remained in the colony to create a dominant establishment that would persist, to secure its control in the eighteenth century.

Such were the Blands, whose investments in the colony dated back to 1618, three of whose sons emigrated in the 1640s and 1650s to extract what profits they could from the family's potential assets. Lewis Burwell arrived in the late 1640s to exploit his father's early subscription to the company. The first William Byrd arrived somewhat later, around 1670, to assume the Virginia properties of his mother's family, the Steggs, which dated back to the early days of the company. The Diggeses' interests stemmed from Sir Dudley Digges's and his two sons' investments, but it would be a third son, Edward, who, emigrating in 1650, established the American branch of the family. Similarly, the first of the Masons arrived in 1652 to claim assets then thirty-two years old. So too, in the ten or fifteen years either side of 1650, came the first of the Lees, the Carters, the Beverleys, the Ludwells, the Washingtons, and, a few years later, that ambitious draper's son, William Fitzhugh.[37]

The advent of similar groups in Maryland was delayed by the turmoil of the "plundering time." When that struggle subsided, the recruitment of a new gentry leadership resumed with the arrival of newcomers, fewer but no less ambitious than the new gentry of Virginia and equally able to create close networks of local kin. They too maintained close ties with England and the broadening structure of its Atlantic connections.

The Neale family's history threaded through the fabric of Maryland's emerging society. Col. James Neale, of a Catholic royalist family, had been among Maryland's first settlers; in the 1630s he had marked out Wollaston Manor, named after the family's home in Northamptonshire, on a grant of two thousand acres adjoining the Potomac River. Upon Charles I's death, he returned to England and joined the exiled court of Charles II, which he served as ambassador to Spain and Portugal, while his wife attended the queen, Henrietta Maria. At the Restoration the family, which now included several children, among them the twelve-year-old Henrietta Maria Neale, returned to the colony. At nineteen, Henrietta Maria, said to be the queen's goddaughter, began the series of marriages that would form a web among the new, scattered Maryland gentry and that conveys vividly the melding of religious confessions in this nascent, pragmatically tolerant colony.

Though a devout Catholic all her life, Henrietta Maria married first

Richard Bennet II, the son of the Puritan leader who had fled Anglican
Virginia to lead the settlement at Providence, and brought up their two
children as Catholics. Her second marriage, four years later, was to a
land-rich Anglican, Philemon Lloyd. The couple's nine children were
raised as Protestants, and eventually, together with the Bennett children,
they formed a frontier dynasty in their marriages to prominent families,
Catholic and Protestant. Henrietta Maria Neale Bennett Lloyd ("Madam
Lloyd" in her later years) died rich, or at least land rich. Among her
bequests was a gift of over eight hundred acres to the Catholic Church
in Maryland.[38]

An equivalent dynasty, closer to the Calverts, formed from the marriages of Jane Lowe, daughter of a prominent Derbyshire family of Catholics, who arrived in Maryland in 1661 with her husband, Henry Sewall,
and three children. Sewall, Lord Baltimore's personal secretary, had been
sent over as adviser to the new governor, Baltimore's twenty-four-year-old
son, Charles. Sewall died within five years and left his widow with extensive property rights and five children whose marriages, the leading historian of Maryland officialdom writes, "became the basis for Calvert's
creation of an intimate loyal Council." One year after Sewall's death, his
widow, Jane, married the young governor who had been her former husband's charge and who became the third Lord Baltimore in 1675. Among
their four children, who were brought up with the five Sewalls, was Benedict, who became the fourth Lord Baltimore in 1684 and converted to
Protestantism.[39]

By then, in part as a result of the Calverts' policy of religious toleration, the population continued to grow and to attract, in small numbers,
such substantial and well-connected men as Henry and John Darnall,
sons of one of the Calverts' main associates and nephews of the Irish Lord
Talbot. The Darnalls' progeny would spread across the colony's confessional boundaries: some remained Catholics (and were related to several
Maryland-born Jesuits), some turned Protestant; some married Diggeses,
some Lloyds, some Sewalls, some, eventually, Carrolls. And there were
other such immigrants in the century's middle years: the Tilghmans, for
example. Richard Tilghman, scion of an ancient Kentish family, who
had signed a petition for the trial of Charles I, left England at the Restoration to join his cousin, Capt. Samuel Tilghman, recently appointed
Maryland's admiral. Then a surgeon in the royal navy, Richard brought
with him his family and eighteen indentured servants. He immediately

received a thousand acres, to which, as high sheriff of Talbot County, he soon added eight thousand more, spread out over six plantations. His son, Richard II, who married the Lloyds' daughter Anna Maria, enhanced the family's prominence, which would extend through three generations, culminating in the Tilghmans of Revolutionary fame. But substantial, well-connected immigrants like the Darnalls and the Tilghmans were rare. For all his efforts at recruitment, Charles Calvert, the most constructive and long-lasting of the family's governors, felt keenly the lack of well-educated and socially prominent men in the colony.[40]

These ambitious newcomers, in Maryland as in Virginia, had means to claim land and capital to establish their families' fortunes. Many in Virginia and several in Maryland were favored by the chronology of their arrival. The most fortunate fell heirs to large areas of land that had already been brought under cultivation. The eighteen-year-old William Byrd, soon after his arrival in Virginia in 1670, inherited the developed James River estate of his uncle, the merchant-planter-councilor Thomas Stegg. Lewis Burwell inherited not only his father's land but also the developed estate of his stepfather, Roger Wingate. Some of the Carters' lands can be traced back through John Utie to a John Jefferson, who left Virginia as early as 1628. The Blands' estate in Charles City County, which later became the Harrisons' Berkeley plantation, had been cleared for settlement in 1619 by the servants of the "particular" plantation of Berkeley's Hundred. And similarly the Neales in Maryland reclaimed in 1659 the manorial property on the Potomac that they had owned since 1636 but had abandoned in 1649.[41]

5

So in the Chesapeake tobacco lands, small groups within the second and third waves of migration moved toward setting themselves off as a ruling landed gentry. That they succeeded in part was due not only to their material advantages but also to the force of their motivation. For they were in social origins close enough to secure establishment in gentility to feel the sense of deprivation most acutely. It is not the totally but the partially dispossessed who build up the most propulsive aspirations, and behind their zestful lunging at propriety and status lie not the yearnings of the disinherited but the pent-up ambitions of the gentleman *manqué*. These were neither hardheaded pioneers nor dilettante romantics but ambitious younger sons, and daughters, of middle-class families who knew well enough what gentility was and sought it as a specific objective.

Yet whatever their longings, they were not and never would be *rentiers* in the traditional mode, living securely on the income of rents produced by permanent tenants. Most of the large tracts of land they claimed remained undeveloped until, gradually, they acquired the labor, free and slave, necessary to bring them to cultivation. Tenants brought in an income, and most large planters would rent out parcels of land, though for many tenancy would prove useful less as a source of reliable income than as a cheap way of improving land held in reserve for future development or sale. They were, and could not avoid being, estate managers directly involved in crop development and marketing, labor recruitment, land sales, and bookkeeping. In time they would acquire overseers, foremen, and household assistants. But they themselves, constantly threatened with crop disasters, labor problems, and bloodshed on the borders, would be directly responsible for economic success or failure. Their fortunes would always be caught between uncontrollable fluctuations in the markets they served and the necessity of maintaining an effective labor force and of expanding into fresher, more fertile land.[42]

Especially in Maryland but also in the newly opened areas of Virginia, there was no insulation from the impact of frontier life. Even the dwellings of the emerging gentry and their standard of living, while better than those of the ordinary planters, were crude and limited by the standards of the time. Governor Berkeley's gubernatorial "mansion," Green Spring House, adjoining his five-thousand-acre plantation, grew by increments from very modest beginnings, starting as a small manor house, then doubling in size to form an odd-shaped, sprawling edifice. The houses of the other leading planters in both Maryland and Virginia were "small, inconspicuous, and inconsequential." Lord Baltimore, reporting officially in 1678, was more specific: the houses of Maryland's leaders, he wrote, built "at considerable distance from each other, were very meane and little and generally after the manner of the meanest farm houses in England." Modern historians agree: none of these dwellings "came close to matching in size, design, and quality of building materials the homes of well-to-do English squires or wealthy merchants."[43]

THUS THE CHESAPEAKE SETTLEMENTS, once the scene of squalor, murderous race warfare, and desperate, often brutal, efforts to recruit an effective labor force, had acquired a degree of stability as an agricultural production center, some normalcy in the working populations, and the beginnings of a settled aristocracy of landowners, merchants, and large-scale tobacco planters. And as this process of maturation developed, it impelled the region's contacts outward, to the expanding Atlantic networks and to the mainland colonies to the north. Of these the most important was the multicultural, polyglot farrago of Dutch New Netherland—a virtual Babel of north Europeans—pressing south against a strange collection of Swedes and Finns settled precariously along the Delaware River.

CHAPTER 8

❧❧❧

The Dutch Farrago

1

I F THE SCATTERED POPULATION on the upper Chesapeake was in many ways discordant and conflicted to the point of bloodshed, it was in a very general sense ethnically unified. Though various Europeans— Poles, Germans, French, Dutch—were brought over to Virginia and Maryland for specialized work, the great majority of the Chesapeake settlers were English in origin. But while these English—diverse regionally, occupationally, and socially; Catholics and Protestants, Jesuits and Puritans—struggled to establish some kind of order and stability in their lives and made awkward, often hostile contact with the American natives, a hundred miles to the northeast a far more heterogeneous, polylinguistic population was gathering. There, on both sides of the Delaware River and on the shores of the lower Hudson, in small numbers, Dutch, Finns, Swedes, Walloons, Flemings, Frisians, Holsteiners, Danes, Germans, and French Huguenots were settling in crude, temporary encampments, isolated trading posts, and primitive farms financed mainly by Dutch entrepreneurs involved in the far-flung effort to exploit the riches of the western hemisphere in competition with the Spanish, Portuguese, and English.

. . .

THAT THE DUTCH—so successful in the early-seventeenth-century explosion of overseas expansion—would join in the scramble for profits in America could easily have been predicted. Their mastery of overseas commerce was making their small nation the most prosperous in Europe: only their relatively slow approach to the possibilities in the Americas might have appeared surprising. But once engaged, the Netherlands became for a while a major player in the Atlantic world. Suddenly the Dutch were everywhere—in Portuguese Brazil, the islands of the Caribbean, the "Wild Coast" of Guyana, and the trading stations of West Africa—just as they were in India, Java, and Formosa, and they were effective managers of population displacements.

For the United Provinces of the Netherlands, by the early seventeenth century, was itself a melting pot of peoples from all over Europe. Though only recently freed from Spanish rule, the Dutch republic was already famous for its toleration, despite its formal church establishment, and for the opportunities it offered for entrepreneurial enterprise and high wages. To this emerging nation of fewer than two million inhabitants, especially to its coastal cities, came a flood of refugees—perhaps a hundred thousand by 1600—from the southern provinces (later Belgium) that had been reconquered by Spain and subjected to stringent enforcement of Catholic conformity. Among these refugees migrating north to the Netherlands from Flanders, Antwerp, Brabant, and Hainault were expert textile workers, ambitious entrepreneurs, and cultural leaders who would contribute to the "golden age" of Dutch cultural history. They were joined by Jews and crypto-Jews fleeing persecution in Spain and Portugal, as well as by Polish Socinians, Czech Comenians, Swiss and Prussian Baptists, and English radical separatists. In the early seventeenth century, 40 percent of the people in Amsterdam who registered for marriage were foreign born—most of them from the western German states. Of that city's 685 wealthiest citizens, 160 were Flemish or Walloon in origin, 30 were German, and there were Italian, English, and Scandinavians among them as well.[1]

While thousands of permanent immigrants were settling in family groups in the Netherlands in the early seventeenth century (their numbers would total half a million by the late eighteenth century), waves of temporary migrants were also arriving annually for seasonal work in the fertile coastal strip of Holland, Friesland, and Zeeland. Short of manpower for the summer haying season and for cutting and dredging peat, this rich littoral, only fifty kilometers wide, drew on the peasant popula-

NORTH
SEA

Groningen
Dokkum
Leeuwarden   •Groningen
Friesland
                    Assen
Heerenveen

Drenthe
                Emmen•
North
Holland
                Zwolle
Velsen
Haarlem• •Amsterdam   Overijssel

Katwijk•   Apeldoorn• •Deventer Enschede
s'Gravenhage• •Leiden   Utrecht
        South   Gelderland
        Holland   •Utrecht   Arnhem
        •Rotterdam   Nijmegen•
Dordrecht•   •Ravenstein
            •'s-Hertogenbosch
        •Breda North Brabant
Bergen op Zoom• •Tilberg
Zeeland   •Eindhoven

            Limburg
                •Roermond

                •Heerlen
        Maastricht•

0   50   100 Miles   N
                    W ✳ E
0   50   100 Kilometers   S

The Netherlands

tion of a broad hinterland stretching east and south some two to three
hundred kilometers. Summer after summer landless, impoverished farmworkers flocked singly to the Dutch coastal provinces, where for a short
time they could earn wages better than any otherwise available, then left
for home, to repeat the cycle the next season.

But it was not only agricultural needs that drew foreign laborers to the Netherlands. So too did the manpower needs of the Dutch navy and army, and above all the nation's distant colonies and trading posts after the founding of the Dutch East India Company in 1602. For thousands of north Europeans, the Dutch republic proved to be a transit center for secondary and tertiary migrations. To man the Netherlands' almost continuous wars, whole regiments were recruited from abroad, along with individual mercenaries from the German states, France, Scotland, and Ireland. Many of the tens of thousands of foreigners who worked in the Dutch fleet and the vessels of the East India Company—perhaps fifty thousand at any given time in the late seventeenth century—ended in colonial settlements in Asia. In all, in the seventeenth and eighteenth centuries, the East India Company shipped an estimated one million people to the East Indies, of whom approximately half never returned.[2]

A nation only recently formed, still very much in flux—its official boundaries still contested, its small population continuously supplemented by refugees from all over northern Europe, its official Calvinist religious culture permeated with the zest and zeal of dozens of radical sects, and its booming commercial economy protected by a large military force—the Netherlands in the early seventeenth century was entering an era of fabulous accomplishment, overseas as well as at home. Its energy was focused chiefly on its domestic economy, on its global commerce and its East Asian empire, and on the enjoyment of its affluence. But the fringes of its radiating power skirted the western hemisphere and left behind, on the shores of North America, one of the strangest assemblages of people that region would ever know.

IT BEGAN in a tentative way at the expiration of the twelve-year truce with Spain in 1609, when the Dutch East India Company sent out exploratory voyages to locate a northern passage through to the Far East. Their chief explorer, the Englishman Henry Hudson, having failed repeatedly to find a way through the ice packs north of Norway and Russia, turned west to America on his third voyage, inched along the shores of Long Island Sound, and sailed ninety miles up the river that would carry his name. The glowing reports that followed—reports not of the hoped-for river route to China but of a luxuriant land, complacent natives, and a vast population of fur-bearing animals—touched off a flurry of commercial activity. Several small-scale Dutch trading ventures began the exploitation of the lower Hudson area, followed by two cartels of Amsterdam merchants who competed for control of the Hudson-Delaware fur trade. This led to the foundation of the New Netherland Company (1615), a coalition of merchants, mainly from Amsterdam, granted a three-year monopoly of the region's Indian trade. That company built a few trading posts and undertook further exploration and mapping of the region watered by the Hudson and Delaware rivers. After its charter expired, individual barter with the Indians was resumed—scattered, random, but profitable. Then in 1621 the situation was transformed by the creation of the huge Dutch West India Company, under whose auspices the European peopling of the area began.[3]

That complex organization, similar in structure to the Dutch East India Company, consisted of five regional chambers representing five separate pools of capital, each able to act independently but governed loosely by a central board, the Heeren XIX. Thus decentralized to assure local control of investments, the company as a whole was given a complete monopoly of all Dutch trade with the western hemisphere and Africa and was empowered to maintain its own military force, to govern the territories it controlled, and to wage war and conclude peace.[4]

The company was designed as a strike force to act "in a warlike manner" against the wealth of the Iberian powers in the Atlantic world. It was not a colonizing company but a hydra-headed commercial-military machine, and it was expected to deal in shipping, trade, and commerce and to wrest, by piracy and conquest, some portion of the silver, sugar, and dyewood treasure of Spanish and Portuguese America and the precious metals, ivory, and slaves of Portuguese West Africa. So while the Netherlands' East India Company competed for the wealth of the Moluccas, Malaya, Ceylon, and India, the country's West India Company, deploying more than eighty vessels in the Atlantic waters, attacked the Iberian silver fleets in the Atlantic, seized the islands of Curaçao, St. Eustatius, and St. Maarten in the Caribbean, took over Surinam and other posts on the Essequibo River and elsewhere on the Wild Coast of Guyana, and established forts and trading stations on the coast of Africa and the Cape Verde Islands. Then, in 1630, with a force of more than seven thousand soldiers and sailors financed by the seizure of the Mexican silver fleet, the company captured from the Portuguese the northeastern Brazilian captaincies of Pernambuco, Itamaracá, and Paraíba.

That easternmost sector of Portuguese America, almost twice the size of the entire Dutch republic, was renamed New Holland. Though under the governorship (1637–44) of Count Johan Mauritz of Nassau a brilliant cultural establishment was created in that sector of Brazil, the colony as a whole remained a scene of great confusion and at times bloody chaos. Johan Mauritz built an entire new town, complete with palatial residences and strong fortifications, but New Holland proved to have little attraction for ordinary Dutch men and women and was vulnerable to insurrections by the Portuguese majority and to attacks by Portuguese fleets and exploited Indians. After two decades, New Holland was retaken by Portugal.[5]

That colony, the most extensive and costly overseas settlement effort of the Dutch West India Company, was the company's worst failure. But much remained to the company at midcentury. It had acquired a near-monopoly of the slave trade to the West Indies, islands in the Caribbean that quickly became merchandizing marts for the entire region, trading posts and plantations on the Guyana coast, and a small colony in North America that few valued.[6]

New Netherland never approached the promise, style, or glamour of New Holland; nor did it ever attract funds equivalent to those invested in that famous venture or the sophisticated leadership it enjoyed. Land claims in North America—colonization in general—had never been one of the West India Company's serious concerns. That enormously ambitious body, a trading not a settling organization, had little interest in the few primitive trading shacks that had been thrown together at the coastal edge of the mid-Atlantic forests and at a few points on the Hudson, Delaware, and Connecticut rivers; nor was it otherwise interested in territorial conquest in North America or elsewhere. But two kinds of pressures developed that, together with the growing lure of profits from the fur trade, propelled the Heeren XIX into reluctant engagement with coastal settlements in the region of Hudson's explorations.

First, refugees in the Netherlands began to press for permission to settle there. In 1620 a proposal was submitted by exiled English religious radicals, then dispersed through Rotterdam, Leiden, and southern England, to migrate to the Hudson region, and two years later the company received the settlement application of "diverse families" of Walloons and French refugees who had earlier sought to settle in Virginia. Though both petitions were denied or put off, it soon became clear that any benefit, from the fur trade or any other form of commerce, that might come to the company from its North American claims would require the establishment of clear title to the land, and that could happen only through permanent occupancy and effective use. It was for that reason—not to create a territorial settlement but to secure the Dutch claim to the land and with it access to the profitable fur trade—that in 1624 the Dutch West India Company decided to accede to the refugees' request and authorized its Amsterdam chamber to begin to populate New Netherland.

Within a few months that chamber had transported to the colony the first of a group of thirty Walloon and French families—perhaps 125 to 150 people in all—and in its provisional orders set out favorable terms for the settlers. In exchange for free passage, free land, easy credit, and freedom of private (not public) worship, the colonists—freemen, not employees of the company—agreed to the company's control of land allotments, crop selection, the marketing of furs, the allocation of food and equipment, and all relations with the native peoples.[7]

2

Who were these first "Dutch" settlers who arrived at the mouth of the Hudson in the winter and spring of 1623–24? Calvinist French-speaking Walloons and French Protestants, they were part of the rootless refugee population that had crowded Leiden, that "centre for the network of refugee churches." Many were on their third remove from their birthplaces in the Spanish Netherlands. Mingling in Leiden with the exiled English radicals, among them the Pilgrims, the Walloons had learned of the possibility of resettlement in Virginia and had petitioned for rights in that colony. Their carefully documented petition of 1621 had been written by their ambitious leader, Jesse de Forest, who himself typified the Walloons' peripatetic life. Born in Avesnes, in northeastern France, he had fled with his family to Amsterdam and finally to Leiden, where he had become a moderately successful merchant and cloth dyer. His petition, addressed to the English ambassador, was explicit in identifying the would-be Walloon emigrants and the nature of their desires. Inscribed on a "round robin" which he enclosed with the petition were the names of 228 people, including 41 heads of household, 13 single men, and 130 children—the parent group of the small company that was settling in New Netherland. Like spokes in a wheel, the names and occupations of the independent householders were written on lines radiating out from a hub that contained the text of the petitioners' promise to fulfill their obligations. An outer ring listed the numbers of children and servants associated with each of the heads of household. The whole formed a circle, a wheel, of information that was doubly revealing—of the desire that motivated the Walloon community in seeking displacement overseas, and of its family structure and occupations, hence its social character on the eve of emigration.

Except for fourteen laborers, the Walloon petitioners of 1621 were artisans—cloth, metal, and leather workers, printers, hatters, vignerons, locksmiths, bakers, shoemakers, dyers, and carpenters. A few were of more elevated status: one was a medical student who apparently qualified as a pharmacist and surgeon, another was a student of theology, and still another was a "*facteur.*" Exemplars of the Protestant artisanry that would nourish small-scale enterprise, they traveled as families. Almost all the men were accompanied by their wives, and they listed an average of slightly more than three children per household. One, a sawyer, was prepared to migrate with eight children, another with seven, two with six, five with five. Committed Protestants who had fled a hostile world, they were French speakers among the Dutch, English, and Germans in Leiden, and they sought in America a world of their own, a world apart even from other similarly minded religious refugees; a place where they could live and worship entirely as they pleased; an isolated, self-governing settlement, in which, they hoped, "no others [would be] allowed to dwell . . . unless they shall have taken letters of citizenship [*lettres de bail-lette*]." They had proposed to build, in a district sixteen miles in diameter, a fortified "city"; there they would cultivate "fields, meadows, vineyards," and they would retain the titles and amenities of traditional social ranks. Thus seeking to preserve their way of life—their own language, religion, and social structure—they sought, in 1621, to settle as a body in Virginia.[8]

But the Virginia Company, to which the petition had been forwarded, thought "otherwise." Besides the expense, which the company could not afford, it had no desire to compound Virginia's difficulties by planting in its midst a self-governing enclave of opinionated, French-speaking religious refugees from the Netherlands. The English Puritans in Nansemond County were trouble enough. The Walloons would be welcome, the Virginia Company said, but not if they insisted on settling in "one grosse bodie." They would be acceptable only if they were willing to be dispersed "by convenient nombers" among what the company fancifully described as the colony's "principall citties, borroughs, and corporacions."

Thus denied the refuge they had sought in Virginia, Leiden's Walloons gave up their community effort and proceeded in separate subgroups to relocate themselves in several of the Dutch settlements in the Atlantic world. New Netherland's fishing shacks and trading huts at the edge of an unexplored land were by no means the most attractive. The "West Indies," then thought of as the whole of Latin America, and especially the settlements at the mouth of the Amazon and on the Wild Coast of Guyana ("a beautiful paradise, where one can live well without working"), were far more alluring. It was to this exotic tropical region—in fact a bloody battleground of contending colonial powers which Dutch traders and freebooters had frequented for twenty years—that De Forest led a small party of Walloons in a search for settlement sites. They turned first to land along the Amazon delta, which proved to be remarkably crowded with English, Irish, Spanish, and Dutch traders and adventurers, then north to the more promising banks of the Oyapock ("Wyapoko") River. There, in 1624, huddled with a few companions in a village of the Yaos Indians, De Forest died, and with him died the Walloons' hopes for a settlement in the beguiling Guyanese tropics.[9]

There was nothing to distinguish this contingent of Walloons from the group of thirty Leiden families that sailed at approximately the same time to New Netherland. That region of North America was no less contested than the Amazon delta and no less controlled by native peoples whose goodwill was as necessary as it was unreliable. Knowing well the hostility of the other colonizing powers (a French vessel had immediately to be ejected from the Hudson basin) and the necessity of establishing Dutch occupancy, the experienced captain of the *Nieu Nederlandt*, Cornelis May, distributed the Walloon families strategically on each of the main rivers between the English settlements in Massachusetts and Virginia. To control the southern area he stationed four families and eight men on an island in the Delaware River just north of the site of Philadelphia. Two families and six men were sent to the mouth of the Connecticut River, and a small garrison was established on Governor's Island at the mouth of the Hudson. The rest were sent up the Hudson to reclaim the remains of an earlier Dutch trading station near present-day Albany, which they rebuilt into Fort Orange; there they began planting and trading with the Indians.[10]

In this scattering of Walloon families, the Dutch laid claim to the "unoccupied" territory of the mid-Atlantic coast. But the Walloons, in these distant outposts, had neither the community they had hoped for nor the safety they sought. In a very strange land, living in isolated encampments, they looked forward to reinforcements and a more viable plan of settlement.

Both arrived in 1625, with chaotic results. The company's relief fleet of five vessels (a sixth was captured by pirates) contained more Walloons from the Leiden community, but the majority of the newcomers were a wildly mixed company of sailors, traders, laborers, farmhands, and clerks drawn from the great ethnic melting pot of the Dutch coastal communities. Who, precisely, these newcomers were is not known: there are no records of their individual identities. What is known is that they, as opposed to the original Walloons, were almost all employees of the company or of investment groups of the Amsterdam chamber, and that they were at best "rather rough and unrestrained." They had signed on "to get rich, in idleness rather than by hard work." Why should they work? "As far as working is concerned, they might as well have staid at home . . . it was all the same what one did or how much one did, if only in the service of the company." Like so many of the transient adventurers from many lands then arriving in the West Indies, they were, Richard Pares has written, "tough guys" who "quarrelled and drank and disobeyed," wanderers easily engaged in duels, kidnappings, and rebellions, who had "to be kept at work by force." The company had no illusions. They knew these recruits, following after the respectable Walloons, were a miserable lot. But what was to be done?

> The peopling of such wild and uncleared lands demands more inhabitants than our country can supply, not so much for want of population, with which our provinces swarm, as because all those who will labor in any way here can easily obtain support, and therefore are disinclined to go far from home on an uncertainty.[11]

Such were the newcomers, 150 to 200 in all, who arrived in 1625 as reinforcements to the small Walloon contingent. They were fore-

runners of a generation of "Dutch" settler-adventurers who turned the
mid-Atlantic territory into what a contemporary called "a wild country."
And with them came a huge cargo of farm equipment, seeds, plants, flour,
trading goods, and a veritable menagerie of livestock—several hundred
horses, cattle, hogs, and sheep. In the early summer the contents of this
small fleet was disgorged, first on the Hudson harbor islands, then on the
shores of Manhattan. And in charge of all of this was a new director of the
colony, Willem Verhulst.[12]

He was the first of a succession of directors (Pieter Minuit, Wouter
van Twiller, Willem Kieft, and Petrus Stuyvesant would follow), the
chronicle of whose administrations read at times like Tacitus's annals of
imperial Rome, replete with bitter rivalries, scandalous accusations, violent encounters, assassination attempts, executions, and above all bloody
massacres of the native Indians and earth-scorching raids. The sources
of the struggles varied in detail but they share common characteristics.
The directors' authority, so far from its source, was never beyond challenge in the colony and was always susceptible to undermining at home.
Each was caught in the clash between ambitious settlers and strict orders
from the profiteering West India Company. Each was faced with random
encroachments on Indian lands that led to bloody reprisals, terror, and
fear. Each—increasingly—was harassed by boundary problems created by
aggressive foreigners invading Dutch territorial claims. And each had to
somehow come to terms with the semi-independent, semiprivate competitive jurisdiction within the colony, the patroonship of Rensselaerswyck.

3

A huge domain, perhaps a million acres, surrounding Fort Orange on
the upper Hudson, Rensselaerswyck was the one survivor of the program of patroonships projected in 1630. By then it had become clear
that while the small population of company employees and free colonists
had served to establish the Netherlands' claim to the region, they had
done little else. The huge debt the settlement had created for the company (the expeditions of 1624–25 alone had cost over 100,000 guilders)
compounded losses incurred elsewhere. Some new strategy was needed if
New Netherland was not simply to be abandoned. In 1628–29 the issue
was heatedly debated at the company's headquarters. One faction favored
withdrawing the settlers altogether and maintaining only a small trading

"factory" at New Amsterdam similar to Dutch trading stations in other exotic regions—on the coasts of Africa, India, Java, Ceylon, the Moluccas, and Formosa. Another plan, favored by the Amsterdam chamber and led by its leading merchant Kiliaen van Rensselaer and others who supported an agricultural colony, was to privatize the effort. They advocated transforming the company's role in New Netherland from that of a corporate entrepreneur—itself the financier, owner, and manager of the land and monopolist of its trade—to that of a supervising body, overseeing and profiting indirectly from the efforts of private investors who at their own risk would recruit settlers, populate the land, and make what profit they could from it. In June 1629, after a protracted controversy that reflected the company's reluctance to engage in territorial conquest, the second alternative was adopted. In a charter of "Freedoms and Exemptions," the company laid out the terms that would determine the peopling of much of the Hudson River valley for the next thirty-five years.

That document, modeled on similar "freedoms" that had authorized private colonization in company settlements on the Essequibo River in Guyana and in Tobago in the Caribbean, granted "patroons" (a newly invented term for quasi-feudal lords) "perpetual fiefs of inheritance": that is, the "free ownership" of land outside of Manhattan purchased from the Indians which might extend for twelve miles along a coast or riverside and as far inland "as the situation of the residents shall permit." The patroons, like the manor lords in Maryland, were to have "high, middle, and low jurisdiction" over their tenants but allow appeals to the company in judgments of over fifty guilders, freedom to trade anywhere along the coast from Florida to Newfoundland, and all the profits they could produce from the land, its resources, and the fisheries. In exchange, the patroons were to settle at least fifty adults on their property in four years, use only company ships at fixed freight charges, ship products for sale through Manhattan and pay duties there, and respect the company's priority in the fur trade. At the same time, individuals would receive "as much land as they can properly cultivate" and the right to hunt and fish in all public properties as well as in their own. The company promised to send military protection to the patroonships if needed, and, as long as it saw fit, "to supply the colonists with as many blacks as it possibly can."[13]

While some company members still objected to the whole idea of patroonships or any other form of territorial control, the leading advocates of the new policy sprang into action. Four major investors immediately filed plans for patroonships: Van Rensselaer, for an estate on the Hudson River; Samuel Godijn, for one on the Delaware; Albert Burgh, also for one on the Delaware; and Samuel Blommaert, for one on the Connecticut. To share the risks and limited supplies and facilities, each drew the others in as junior partners and shareholders, thus forming in effect a cartel of prospective magnates. Van Rensselaer was first off the mark, having sent scouts to block out a claim to property on the Hudson and negotiate with the Indians even before the company had officially approved the program. Throughout 1629 and 1630 he was feverishly amassing supplies, livestock, and above all colonists for his property, Rensselaerswyck. Nothing came of Burgh's and Blommaert's plans, but Godijn's project for the Delaware region began, like Van Rensselaer's, swiftly. It ended abruptly, however, in one of the worst catastrophes of the era—a testimony to the vagaries of population recruitment in such enterprises, the great cost in human lives of such projects, and the deadly complexities of race relations in coastal North America.[14]

GODIJN, head of the Amsterdam chamber of the West India Company and the dominant Dutch figure in Arctic whaling and trade with Muscovy, had general plans for colonial estates throughout the western colonies. But his major project was the patroonship he designed centered on a whaling station within an agricultural colony at the mouth of the Delaware River. He and his collaborators would surely make a fortune in whale oil in addition to other profits from trade and agriculture. An advance party selected land that stretched twenty-four miles north from Cape Henlopen along the west bank of the lower Delaware River, and induced a few Indians to agree to a "purchase." To that site, now called the patroonship of Swanendael, Godijn and his partners, late in 1630, sent two vessels. One, instructed first to reinforce another colony of Godijn's on the West Indian island of Tortuga, contained not only the granite blocks, timber, and iron equipment needed to build a fort and warehouse but also sixty Huguenot peasants and their livestock. The second carried indentured laborers, half a dozen Cape Verdean harpooners, and a load of supplies and trade goods.[15]

There was trouble from the start. The second vessel was captured by pirates, and when the first, the *Walvis*, arrived at Tortuga, it was discovered that Godijn's settlement there had been destroyed by the Spanish. The *Walvis* then proceeded to Swanendael, where it unloaded its cargo of Huguenots and building equipment. After construction began, the commander, ignoring his orders to begin whaling, left for home, to be succeeded by David de Vries, a former employee of the East India Company, a successful ship captain and privateer who had sailed and fought for years in the Far East and a typical adventurer—exuberant, expansive, and risk prone—seeking sudden wealth in the international scramble for colonial exploitation. While still preparing his relief expedition, word arrived that Swanendael had been destroyed. When in early December 1632 De Vries arrived on the Delaware to salvage what he could, he discovered, and recorded, a grim scene. The entire colony, even a guard dog, had been massacred. The fort, which turned out to have been a slim wooden palisade, had been burned, and "the skulls and bones of our people, and the heads of the horses and cows" were lying about "here and there." Through an interpreter, De Vries learned that the settlers had erected a column topped by a metal plaque bearing the arms of the United Provinces. One of the chiefs innocently stole the plaque to make tobacco pipes, which so enraged the Dutch commander that other Indians, fearing reprisals, killed the culprit and produced his head or scalp as proof. That set up a bloody reaction on the part of the murdered chief's "friends," who vowed revenge. They waited until all but two of the settlers were working in the fields, then under pretense of barter entered the fort, murdered the two men with ax blows, riddled the guard dog with arrows, and went after the people in the field, killing them one after another. One boy, hidden in deep grass, escaped.[16]

But De Vries, irrepressible, still hoped somehow to extract profit from Swanendael. Amid the rubble, and working with makeshift equipment and untrained crewmen, he rigged together the rudiments of a whaling station—windlass and cranes to lift the carcasses, ovens and boilers to refine the blubber, and a log platform for the barrels. He then took off on an exploratory voyage up the Delaware to form alliances with the natives. When he returned, at the end of the whaling season, only seven of the smallest of seventeen harpooned whales had been brought ashore, and the yield was a mere thirty-two barrels of oil. The poorly equipped and inexperienced crew was exhausted, and the investors in Holland, "one pulling this way and another that way," had no idea of what, if anything, to do next. Swanendael was abandoned, its skeletons, debris, and ruins a constant reminder of the cost of failure.

But De Vries's dreams of instant riches in colonial exploitation had not faded. Persistent and imaginative, more courageous than sage, he and a new set of partners established still another patroonship off the coast of Surinam, manned it with two dozen crewmen, thirty Germans, and refugees from the southern Netherlands, and set out to produce cotton and tobacco. But as he had been warned, the coast of Surinam was hell for everyone. Slaves, he was told, had to be forced to work by the lash, indentured field laborers were likely to rebel, the rate of mortality was fearful, and the hot, dense, wet forests were full of malevolent, vengeful runaway workers gone native. And so it proved. Two English sailors, working as field hands on De Vries's patroonship, led an uprising in his absence, seized a visiting slave ship with its full cargo, co-opted their Dutch masters with promises to share the booty, and made off for Jamaica, leaving behind a plantation in chaos. De Vries was certain that if the work had continued for another two months, the product would have yielded 150,000 guilders. "The English," he concluded, "are a villainous people, and would sell their own fathers for servants in the islands."

But even so, after all of this, De Vries was still not defeated. In the next few years he visited New Netherland repeatedly, and then remained in the colony for nearly five years after 1638. Indefatigable, still entranced by visions of bustling, enormously profitable plantations—on the Amazon, in the West Indies, on the Hudson: anywhere in this exotic Atlantic world—he once again attempted to establish a patroonship. This time he registered the whole of Staten Island in his name as patroon, and for capital drew into the venture an influential but unreliable cousin, Frederick de Vries. After putting together a small, makeshift settlement on the island, and while awaiting supplies and colonists from home that never arrived, he roamed the countryside in and around the colony looking for real estate bargains and studying the natives. Then once again, and now definitively, his hopes were blasted. The Raritan Indians, infuriated at the treatment they had received by the Dutch governor, wiped out De Vries's fragile Staten Island settlement in a single devastating raid, part of the bloody race war that raged in the early 1640s. This time there was no recovery. De Vries left America permanently in 1644, thanking God, as he returned to his native city of Hoorn, for having preserved him "through so many perils of savage heathens."[17]

BUT RENSSELAERSWYCK SURVIVED, and its growth made a significant contribution to the emergence of a uniquely complex—multiethnic and multiconfessional—population in the struggling Dutch colony and created endless jurisdictional problems for the colony's directors. Such a strange community had never been Van Rensselaer's desire. He dreamed of building in America a structured society where executive authority worked through "representatives from different orders of society . . . a republic composed of different members each of which in the first instance prevents as far as possible all acts of insolence in its own sphere" and refers "only great and important matters" to the central authority. What he did not want, what he feared above all, was a mere "loose mass of people," but that, he came to realize, was precisely what was developing, not only in the colony generally but on his own property specifically.

Faced with deadlines for populating Rensselaerswyck or losing it, Van Rensselaer hired recruiting agents and turned to the difficult task of finding people willing to accept his terms and emigrate to the Hudson as tenants and laborers. Since native Dutchmen in the more developed areas of the Netherlands were unwilling to leave, he turned to refugee groups in and around the coastal cities; to impoverished Germans, Norwegians, French, Danes, and English; to the peasants in the Dutch interior district of Utrecht, the most economically depressed area of the Netherlands; and to the tenants on his own estates, some of whom he conscripted. How, precisely, he did all this, what the mechanism was for locating and enticing those he called "poor beggars" into transatlantic resettlement, is not known. What is known is that Van Rensselaer and his agents, once they located prospective emigrants, contracted with them for service over a set number of years at higher wages than any that could be found at home—perhaps four times as high—payable in furs, tobacco, grain, livestock, and credit. Most, to judge from a sample of 174 individuals known to have come over to Van Rensselaer's property between 1630 and 1644, were single men in their late teens or early twenties. They claimed no less than thirty-two occupations, but in fact at least 60 percent of them were farmers or farmworkers. Most of the rest were construction workers—carpenters, masons, and millwrights; there were also a few tradesmen and artisans. Only approximately half of those who immigrated to Rensselaerswyck were Dutch. Mingling with farmhands from Utrecht, Gelderland, and Friesland were shepherds from Westphalia, carpenters from Denmark, Norway, and France, handymen from Germany, and bakers from England. They were a transient lot. Many failed to fulfill their contracts with Van Rensselaer, drifted off to Manhattan or to tempting possibilities in neighboring colonies, or returned to the familiar world they had left behind.[18]

4

While Van Rensselaer was striving to populate his private estate, managing to recruit perhaps a hundred people by 1643, housing them in frail, thatched, wooden dwellings along the riverbank, the company in Amsterdam was attempting to populate the colony generally. Drawing on footloose foreigners, "ne're-do-wells snatched off the streets of the city where they had drifted from the hinterland," unemployed sailors, impoverished farmers, and fringe elements among the ethnic and religious minorities, the company sought to enlarge the settlement on Manhattan and make it a more normal community. A few Africans, of uncertain legal status, taken from captured Spanish or Portuguese ships or drawn from other Dutch possessions, appeared as early as 1625 or 1626, and a major military presence was established with the arrival of the heavily armed *Zoutberg*, which carried 104 soldiers and 52 sailors, along with a contingent of construction workers brought over to rebuild New Amsterdam's fort and work on other building projects. Until they were forced into military service, the carpenters, masons, and bricklayers began the rebuilding of the original sod enclosure into a proper quadrangular stone bastion and the construction of wharves, warehouses, and mills. But all such efforts, as well as hopes for developing the Walloons' farms into an independent agricultural center, faltered for want of manpower. Again and again the company complained of the difficulty of populating the colony and bemoaned the human material they were obliged to accept. Clearly the patroonship plan had solved nothing, and the resident administration of the colony in the mid-1630s was as contentious, as prone to discord verging on violence, as it had been a decade earlier.[19]

VERHULST, the first of the regularly appointed directors, had been defeated before he was fully aware of the problems he faced. Like Yeardley in Virginia, he had been elevated to a position of authority though of inferior social status, and he lacked the administrative skills he needed. He found himself surrounded by a council of ambitious, prickly officials appointed by the company: a vice-director, a secretary, a *fiscael* (protector of the company's rights and taxes and prosecutor of crimes), a *commies* (supervisor of the company's goods and fees), and several others without specific functions. Managers of an obscure outpost of at most a few hundred people, they immediately began jostling for position. Hardly settled in, they quarrelled bitterly and denounced one another in blistering letters to the authorities at home. Verhulst, being director, was their principal target.

He did his best to follow his instructions. He had been told to withdraw the Walloon families from the Delaware, Connecticut, and upper Hudson river posts, leaving behind only small parties of traders, and to concentrate the population at the tip of Manhattan Island. Fort Orange, he was told, would remain the chief fur trading post. New Amsterdam was to be a self-contained agricultural settlement and stock farm whose produce would sustain the population. A spread of nine company farms was to be established on lower Manhattan, with a village formed around a fort at the tip of the island. Above all, he was told to treat the Indians fairly—to see that they came to no harm, that they were not deceived or even mocked, that all contracts were honest and fair, and that the Dutch were to "remain neutral" in their wars. Neither then nor at any other time in the colony's history did the West India Company propose any kind of governance of the natives, any structure of relationships with them, any purpose in dealing with them except trade. To enforce his rule over the colonists, Verhulst was told to organize a quasi-military government reminiscent of Dale's regime in Virginia a decade earlier. He was to have the power of corporal punishment and was ordered

> to expel from the colony and to send hither all adulterers and adulteresses, thieves, false witnesses, and useless persons among the Christians, likewise all the lazy persons who draw pay from the company, in order that they may be punished here according to their deserts.

A repeat offender would be dealt with severely: "in addition to forfeiting the whole of his earned wages, inclusive of tithes, etc. [he was to] be punished by the council as a common thief and be kept in prison until by the first ship returning to the fatherland he can be sent back as a rogue."[20]

But it was Verhulst and not the rogues who was shipped home in disgrace. Beset on all sides by problems he could scarcely perceive, he used his powers aggressively and became short-tempered, impatient, and autocratic. In his single year in office, he ruled "very harshly," the incoming, censorious secretary Isaac de Rasière reported, "without any legal formality, but merely upon his own authority," punishing people for what offended him "not according to law but according to his pleasure."

Everything went wrong, even in distant Fort Orange. There Daniel van Krieckenbeeck, in command of the outpost, in flat violation of company orders had undertaken "a reckless adventure" by naïvely joining the neighboring Mahican Indians in their long-standing struggle with the more powerful Mohawks, who were seeking direct access to the Dutch traders. Ambushed, Van Krieckenbeeck and three of his small party, which included two Portuguese, had been killed, one of whom had been eaten "after having [been] well roasted. The [other two] they burnt . . . The Indians carried a leg and an arm home to be divided among their families as a sign they had conquered their enemies." Hopelessly incompetent, Verhulst was confronted with demands that he resign. When he refused, he was arrested and replaced by his assistant Pieter Minuit.

Minuit should have had a better time of it, and for a while he did. A thirty-six-year-old Walloon from the German-Dutch border town of Wesel, formerly a diamond cutter and merchant in Utrecht, he was more experienced than Verhulst, of higher social standing (son-in-law of the burgomaster of Cleves), and a ruling elder or deacon of the Walloon church. Quickly fulfilling his initial orders to scout out the land and assess the possibilities of trade with the Indians, he turned to developing the colony. He regularized relations with the Indians by purchasing Manhattan Island and attempting to rein in the illegal traders who had appeared on the Hudson, sped up construction of the fort and the relocation of the colonists, and began shipping home furs, timber, grains, and plants. Though the company's profits from this nascent production were still far exceeded by its costs, more reinforcements were sent: four more vessels in 1627, then two more in 1628, all with supplies and more of the "rough and unrestrained" migrants—multilingual and multiconfessional—who were proving impossible to control.[21]

By 1630 there were some 300 "Dutch" inhabitants in New Netherland, 270 of them in or about New Amsterdam. Conditions were still primitive in the extreme. Within a loosely built wall that enclosed the end of the island were a ramshackle, sod-walled fort and a stone warehouse, thirty or so houses made "of the bark of trees," and grist and lumber mills still under construction. Beyond the palisade were six farms begun by free colonists, most of them on patches of land that had been cleared and abandoned by the Indians; they were isolated from each other and from the fort for lack of roads. Though the few officials had tolerable if crude dwellings, many of the ordinary settlers still "nestled rather than dwelt" in "hovels and cabins." Some were crowded together "with their hogs and sheep in makeshift stables without access to fresh water and dangerously exposed to the elements." Others lived in pits in the ground dug "cellar fashion, six or seven feet deep," the walls timbered for support and covered with a ceiling of "bark or green sods." Through the village's single thoroughfare, Broad Street, ran a canal which has been described as "a befouled and stinking sewer in the warm months of summer and a treacherous ice floe in the winter." And, despite hopeful remarks that the colony was beginning "to advance bravely" and to harvest its first crops, the leadership—in one of the smallest and most obscure of the many settlements scattered around the globe by Dutch entrepreneurs—was in almost constant turmoil.[22]

Verhulst's expulsion had not calmed the waters. Ordinary people—ambitious, disoriented, forced into contact with strangers from distant parts and with countrymen equally strange—cursed each other in public as "rogues and thieves," while the colony's leaders were at each other's throats. De Rasière, so censorious of others, the acting *commies* as well as the colony's secretary, himself became embroiled in a bitter and very public controversy. Gerrit Fongersz, the *ondercommies*, De Rasière charged, was determined to thwart him at every turn. Not only did he perversely claim to rank above him in Council affairs, but he insisted on marketing his own furs. When De Rasière, who was responsible for enforcing the company's monopoly of the fur trade, declared that he would confiscate any such illegal shipments and sue for return of Fongersz's wages, Fongersz replied, "I do not consider you a big enough man for that." Fongersz, De Rasière decided, was a hopeless drunk. Since Director Minuit, who could not understand where the liquor was coming from, declined to reprimand him, De Rasière did just that, telling Frongersz "to stop [drinking], both on account of its sinfulness and the scandal which it causes in the community." But it did no good. Forever drunk, Fongersz, De Rasière wrote, "shows his villainous heart, and wishes to defy me" as a person not deserving respect. "I cannot put up with much from such a drunkard and idiot," De Rasière wrote, and he begged the company "to clip the wings and check the insolence of such a half-senseless person."

Beyond all such matters, De Rasière wrote, was the simmering threat of Indian attacks, which might erupt at any time from within the natives' mysterious world. Van Krieckenbeeck's fatal folly threatened the entire community clinging to its fragile hold on lower Manhattan. The Indians, De Rasière wrote, echoing company policy, must be treated equitably. And, "much like children, [they must be] kept on friendly terms by kindness and occasional small gifts; one must be familiar with them and allow them to think that one trusts them fully, and meanwhile be on one's guard, or else things are apt to go wrong." Weird people, he wrote, everything about them was threatening and repellent: their appearance ("orange color, like the Brazilians"), their primitive dress and ornaments, their indolent way of life ("they cannot by any means be brought to work"), their smell (rank, from smeared grease), their promiscuity and lasciviousness (stimulated by eating "a sort of white salmon"), their bizarre marriage and divorce customs, and their peculiar form of government.

As for the company employees who were the majority of the small European population huddled around the fort, De Raisère declared them to be a crude, lazy crowd who drew rations but contributed little. Worse than that, they were driving fur prices up by illegal and fiercely competitive trade with the Indians. The colony's greatest need was for "sober, industrious persons" who would properly work the land and obey the law. And specialists would help—a dozen or so Norwegians, for example, would be useful in making tar and pitch.[23]

De Rasière's tempestuous term as secretary was short. He returned home in 1628, to be succeeded by Jan van Remunde, who immediately clashed with the director. He peppered the company with charges that Minuit was neglecting his office, allowing New Englanders and unlicensed Dutchmen to snatch the furs that belonged to the company while the company's sloops "lie idle and are not sent out to trade." Charges went back and forth between the two. In the midst of their embranglement, the colony's first preacher, Jonas Michaëlius, arrived, who, it was said, immediately "proceeded to stoke the growing animosities." In the end he proved to be Minuit's nemesis.[24]

MICHAËLIUS, a well-educated, scholarly minister of the Dutch Reformed Church, was no stranger to overseas ventures. Three years before he arrived in New Netherland (1628) he had served his church and nation at an obscure Dutch station, Fort Nassau, in Mouree, on the coast of West Africa. Ambitious and experienced, he threw himself into the life of the crude settlement on the Hudson and recorded his experiences in vivid letters home.

His first reaction was of shock at the "wild state" of New Amsterdam: the primitive dwellings, the roots that clogged the soil, the "hard, stale food, such as men are used to on board ship . . . beans and gray peas . . . barley, stockfish, etc., without much change . . . I shall be compelled to pass through the winter without butter and other necessities." The summers were hot and the winters so cold, one had to "cover one's self with rough furs." He was not surprised to see that some of the Walloons were returning to Holland. His personal situation could scarcely be worse. His wife, who had suffered from the nasty conditions and short fare on shipboard, had died shortly after they had arrived, leaving him with three small children to take care of with little help, "the Angola slave woman [being] thievish, lazy, and useless trash." His land allotment went unused for want of laborers, and he, a Dutch speaker, had to administer the Lord's Supper in the loft of a mill to a congregation most of whom spoke only French. The company's recently arrived employees, he wrote, were few in number, ignorant, and lazy. Even the councilors, though basically good people, were "for the most part simple and have little experience in public affairs." And they suffered from the lack of clear and consistent instructions from home. What was needed, above all, were "ten or twelve more farmers, with horses, cows, and labourers in proportion, to keep ourselves in bread, milk products, and suitable refreshments."

As for the Indians, whose conversion he had expected to accomplish, he found them

> entirely savage and wild, strangers to all decency, yea, uncivil and stupid as garden stakes, proficient in all wickedness and ungodliness, devilish men, who serve nobody but the Devil, that is, the spirit which in their language they call Menetto, under which title they comprehend everything that is subtle and crafty and beyond human skill and power. They have so much witchcraft, divination, sorcery and wicked arts that they can hardly be held in by any bands or locks. They are as thievish and treacherous as they are tall, and in cruelty they are altogether inhuman, more than barbarous, far exceeding the Africans.

He could not imagine how the Dutch had been misled into believing in the "docility of this people and their good nature." He could find "hardly a single good point" in them. Their language, full of "difficult aspirates and many guttural letters . . . formed more in the throat than by the mouth, teeth and lips," seemed impossible for others to learn. In fact, "they rather try to conceal their language from us than to properly communicate it." It was not, he concluded, a proper language at all, but something "made up, childish," a private jargon, so private that when spoken in conversation even the most experienced traders could not understand it. Given what he considered to be the Indians' stupidity, superstition, and barbarous language, it was hopeless to think of leading them to salvation. God, when described, had no reality for them (it was "like a dream"), and if one appealed to their own culture and referred instead to "one great, yea, most high sackiema" (sachem), that struck them as "a silly fable." What could one do with people like this? The only possibility he could see was to concentrate on the children: wean them away from their own people with "presents and promises" and teach them a proper language, the fundamentals of Christianity, and virtuous living, all of which they might spread among their people.

Thus Michaëlius's first impressions. Two years later his discontent took a new form. At the start his preaching, he felt, had gone well: he had had a relatively large and growing congregation. But then his hopes had suddenly been frustrated by what he called "a nefarious enterprise of wicked men, who have created serious tragedies among us." The director, Minuit, whom he had appointed to his consistory, proved, he said, to be "a slippery man, who under the treacherous mask of honesty is a compound of all iniquity and wickedness." Evil to the core, he was a fornicator, a liar, and "most cruel oppressor of the innocent"; he was given to "the most awful execrations" and favored only those who agreed with him. His Council was a cabal of "the most pestilent kind of people." Venal profiteers, they cheated the company, oppressed the innocent, lived outrageously, and propagated wickedness. Nevertheless, Michaëlius reported, he had held his tongue, expecting that the evils would become obvious to all. When that in fact happened, he wrote, Minuit tried to buy his silence with sudden friendship while secretly trying to get officials at home to fire him. Faced with this, Michaëlius had reported the whole business to the company directors, and then the storm broke.

Minuit and his toadies, the preacher wrote, turned the settlement "upside down" to persecute him and those close to him, discrediting them and even threatening their lives. Pulling strings with the directors at home, they were getting bolder all the time, "excit[ing] sundry against me, and finally . . . plot[ting] indefatigably to disperse all the fruit of my ministry and of my labours." He begged to be recalled, or that, once "this ballast [Minuit and his cronies] had been thrown overboard," honest people like himself would be left in peace. Now, having made his views public, he had no doubt that "they will attack me like mad dogs." He could only pray for God's protection.

The only protection he received was from the company. Weary of disputes they could scarcely understand, in 1631 they recalled both Minuit and the distraught preacher, sending as replacements Wouter van Twiller and as *predikant* Everardus Bogardus (Everart Bogaert), who were destined to repeat, with perfervid embellishments, the bitter struggles of their predecessors.[25]

VAN TWILLER, twenty-seven years old when appointed director, had been a clerk in the West Indies company office, but a favored clerk; he had the advantage of being Kiliaen van Rensselaer's nephew. To his rivals, he was therefore at once vulnerable on two counts, inexperience and nepotism. An upwardly mobile son of the middle class, in background he could not have been more different from the *predikant* Bogardus, who had grown up in an orphanage, had gone through some kind of mystical experience, had studied theology, had then shipped off to Guinea to serve the poor and the sick among the Dutch, and had only then been ordained and sent to New Netherland.

What the precise source of Bogardus's quarrel with Van Twiller was is not clear, but both were young, ambitious, insecure, and quarrelsome, and Bogardus, who, like Van Twiller, quickly became a considerable landowner, could only have resented the director's authority. Reacting to slights, the preacher lashed back in a manner "unbecoming a heathen, much less a Christian," and denounced Van Twiller as "a child of the devil, a consummate villain . . . to whom he [would] give such a shake from the pulpit as would make him shudder." But if to Bogardus the director was not only personally obnoxious but also incompetent, to the wandering, ubiquitous David de Vries, always searching for advantage in the colony's affairs, the source of the trouble was Van Twiller's drinking. That charge, circulating widely, was picked up by Van Twiller's uncle and sponsor in Amsterdam and reported back in alarm. Van Rensselaer had heard, he wrote his embarrassing nephew in a voluminous letter of instruction and advice, that Van Twiller, "being drunk, had run out on the street after the minister with a naked sword." And other charges, he wrote, were piling up. From outside the company, he told Van Twiller, had come stories that "you are proud and puffed up; always drunk as long as there is any wine . . . lazy and careless, hostile to the minister and no defender of religion." From inside the company had come charges that Van Twiller wrote too few reports, did not have "enough prudence and judgment to rightly discharge [his] functions," and did not keep good accounts. Van Rensselaer, thoroughly avuncular, ended with eight points of admonition: among them temperance, diligence, humility, patience, and "trust in God when you are chastened." Not, he warned, that the young man could ever expect any thanks from the colonists: "they can spit no honey," Van Rensselaer wrote, "since they have nothing but gall in their mouths."[26]

Bogardus fared little better. Surviving Van Twiller's term in office, he ended up charged by the next director, Willem Kieft, with having called him, the director, "an incompetent villain, a child of the devil whose buck goats are better than he," having also cavorted with "the greatest criminal," abused his own deacons, preached when drunk, accused the director of calling Bogardus's wife a whore—all, and other notorious acts, leading to the company's ruin, the undermining of all authority, mutiny, and rebellion. Bogardus's responses, dismissed by Kieft as "futile and absurd," seemed to pitch the director into a state of fury and to the determination to bring the preacher to court "as a rebel and contumex." Bogardus also faced a lawsuit for slander brought by one of his own deacons, the ex-soldier and now prosperous merchant Oloff Stevensen van Cortlandt.[27]

In 1647 Bogardus was finally recalled, and none too soon. He returned home on the same ship as his adversary, Kieft, and died with him when their ship was wrecked off the coast of Wales. Neither therefore could redeem his reputation, which for Kieft would have been a major undertaking. His directorship (1638–47) had been a catastrophic failure that had resulted in the butchery of hundreds of natives and the death of whole communities of European settlers, and that strained race relations for years to come.

KIEFT HAD ARRIVED on a wave of optimism inspired by the Dutch government's dawning recognition of the colony's strategic importance and the West India Company's determination to transform the crude, floundering, under-populated settlements into a flourishing province dominated by the Atlantic port city of New Amsterdam. Kieft's qualifications as manager of this renaissance must have seemed sufficient. Well educated (he would correspond with John Winthrop in Latin), grandson of one of Amsterdam's legendary magistrates, and a merchant in La Rochelle, he was determined to make his fortune in this far-flung outpost while fulfilling the company's ambitions. Perhaps, conscious as he was of his lofty heritage, he thought of his role as similar to that of Johan Mauritz of Nassau, just beginning his governorship of New Holland, or to that of Roman proconsuls, celebrated conquerors of foreign barbarians. In any case, he arrived with great expectations, despite rumors that his business in France had failed and that he had embezzled funds sent to rescue Christian prisoners of the Ottomans. "A man of unpliant temper," the nineteenth-century chronicler E. B. O'Callaghan wrote, "inflated with the idea of his own importance; ill-disposed to brook contradiction, and construing all objections to his will . . . as an attack on his prerogative," Kieft immediately set to work to revive the dilapidated settlement.

In short order he reduced the influence of his small Council, cracked down on violators of the company's fur trade monopoly, and devised severe punishments not only for "mutiny, theft, false testimony, slanderous language, and other irregularities" but also for "adulterous intercourse with heathens, blacks, or other persons." When two apparently disrespectful figures—the Rev. Francis Doughty, who had fled England and then New England in search of greater religious freedom, and the merchant Arnoldus van Hardenbergh—sought to appeal to the home courts Kieft's judgment on their land claims, they were informed that there was no appeal from the director's sovereign authority. For their presumption in seeking appeal both were fined; in addition Doughty was briefly imprisoned, and Van Hardenbergh was threatened with prison if he failed to pay his stiff fine promptly. How long Kieft could have maintained his single-minded autocracy cannot be known, since forces beyond his reach were beginning to raise issues that would overcome him and transform the community he sought to rule.

5

In the year of Kieft's arrival, the States General and the Heeren XIX of the West India Company had become convinced that population recruitment was the key to everything, especially to generating some profit from an enterprise that by 1644 would show a net loss to the company of over half a million guilders.[28]

Once again a basic restructuring was needed, and in 1638 the Amsterdam chamber, which had taken the main responsibility for New Netherland from the beginning, prodded by both the Heeren XIX and the national government, came up with a plan to solve the population problem. In its "Proposed Articles for the Colonization and Trade of New Netherland," heavily amended to satisfy the States General's views, the chamber recommended that the company throw open the fur trade to all citizens of the United Provinces, reserving to itself only an export duty of 10 percent on furs, give up its monopoly of shipping to the colony, and provide two hundred acres of free land plus hunting and fishing rights to every colonist who brought five adult family members or servants with him. The earlier free trade arrangement should be continued, and some of the privileges of the patroons should be restricted.[29]

The proposal was accepted, and it proved to be a trigger that released some of the energies of the Netherlands' independent merchants, shippers, and traders, hitherto constrained by the West India Company's monopoly of the colony's potential profits. Once this program, and especially the opening of the fur trade, was adopted, shipping to the colony increased and more settlers began to arrive. An estimated 2,200 people emigrated from the Netherlands to the colony in the fifteen years after the new policy went into effect, elevating the total population to approximately 3,500. The result, within a very few years, was a demographic diversity that astonished not only visitors but the Dutch authorities themselves. By 1646 "men of eighteen different languages" were said to live in the colony, and while only the Dutch Reformed Church was allowed to conduct public worship, there were practicing Catholics, English Puritans, German Lutherans, Anabaptists, and Mennonites.

So in the early years of Kieft's administration a surge in population began. But as it did, it created pressures that could not be contained. Many of the new arrivals, profiteering traders with no interest in settling permanently in the colony—"river-rat hustlers" they have been called—bypassed the residents in seeking out the native suppliers of furs, ignored customs duties and restraints in dealing with both Indians and local authorities, drove up the price of furs and goods, and joined a growing opposition to Kieft's autocratic regime. And the freebooting, transient newcomers were not the only agents of disorder. Resident farmers too concluded that "now was the accepted time to make their fortune" and joined in the competition for furs and valuable land. Their ambitions could not be confined. Freely if illegally they traded firearms and gunpowder for beaver skins, and some, hoping that informal personal relations with the Indians would pay off, invited them into their homes, "laying napkins before them, presenting wine to them and more of that kind of thing . . . as their due and desert, insomuch that [the Indians] were not content but began to hate when such civilities were not shown them." Others employed Indians as domestic servants, "thus exposing to them our entire circumstances." When, quickly, these Indian domestics became "weary of work" they simply walked away, taking with them "much more than the amount of their wages."[30]

As the colony expanded—rapidly and randomly—Kieft "bought" great stretches of land, mainly on Long Island and in the later Westchester County. The native occupants assumed that they would continue to live where they were, if uneasily, side by side with the Europeans, for if Kieft had "bought" the land, the natives, lacking any notion of exclusive possession, had not "sold" it; they had simply agreed to share its use. The situation quickly became confused as the influx of people continued. Increasingly the natives came to see that the fur traders' deepening forays into their hunting grounds and the constant expansion of farms and pastureland would drive them from their homeland and destroy the basis of their lives. They grew wary, then resentful, then hostile. The depredations of the colonists' cattle and hogs foraging freely in the Indians' unfenced cornfields threatened their basic food supply. They complained again and again and, receiving no relief, felt free to attack the animals at will. Given their growing fears and hostility, together with Kieft's insensitive, aggressive rule, a serious clash was inevitable.

It was touched off at two points simultaneously. In 1640, to help pay for fortification and troop support, Kieft decided to tax the tribes in the coastal regions, whom he saw as removable obstacles to the further peopling of the lower Hudson and Delaware River valleys. But when his tax collector attempted to seize one village's corn supplies and load them aboard his yacht, he was attacked by the local sachem and slashed across the face with a hunting knife. His vessel was attacked, and his party barely made it back alive to New Amsterdam. There word had arrived of the Raritan Indians' raid on De Vries's property on Staten Island, a revenge

attack by an Indian whose beaver skins had been stolen when he was
drunk. Four settlers had been killed and their houses set on fire. Kieft,
now suspecting that he faced a general uprising and confident that he had
a justification for liquidating at least some of the most troublesome tribes,
sent eighty soldiers and sailors to Staten Island with orders to impose
punishment. And he not only encouraged the colony's Indian allies to
"cut off" any threatening Raritans but also, in order "to incite them the
more," offered ten fathoms of wampum for each Raritan's head delivered
to the fort and twice that much for heads of those known to have murdered the settlers on Staten Island.[31]

Thus encouraged, his troops invaded Staten Island and killed several Indians in the Raritans' village. One zealous contingent seized the
sachem's brother, took him to one side, and tortured him—"in his private parts with a piece of split wood." They then burned some villages,
drove off the livestock, and made a traditional gesture of reconciliation.
An Indian chief appeared "in great triumph, bringing a dead hand hanging on a stick" said to be that of the murderer of the Dutch on Staten
Island.

Kieft's bloody zeal was appeased, but only for the moment. The next
year, 1641, a young warrior, to avenge the murder of his uncle—whose
spectral voice, he said, he continued to hear "in the roaring of the
storm—in the rustle of the leaves—in the sighing of the winds"—slew an
old wheelwright living alone in the north of Manhattan, decapitated him,
and plundered his house. Kieft demanded that the murderer be produced
for trial, but the local chief scoffed at this in view of the losses his people had sustained. Determined now to *wipe the mouths* of the savages,"
Kieft convened a council of leading householders and demanded to know
why they should not "ruin the entire village to which he [the murderer]
belongs." De Vries, alone among the consultants, remembering Swanendael, said no. There was "no profit," he insisted, in a war with the Indians,
and in any case the Dutch would need more people before attacking.
Their wandering cattle were vulnerable, and the settlements were too
scattered for safety. "You go to break the Indians' head," he said, "it is
our own nation you are about to destroy." But the others agreed with
Kieft, in fact petitioned for an authorization "to attack the Indians as
enemies." They recommended a surprise attack after lulling the Indians into complacency and misleading them as to their intentions. And to
add strength to the raiding party, they urged the director to organize "as

many Negroes from among the strongest and fleetest as he can conveniently spare, and provide them each with a hatchet and a half-pike." Tactical refinements were offered. Some suggested patience while they "lull the Indians to sleep" before attacking. Others urged that they waste no time and kill the Indians forthwith "so as to fill them with fear"—that if possible they simply "exterminate the savages." Everyone but De Vries agreed that "the barbarous murder must be avenged for the sake and security of our lives and cattle."[32]

And so it was. Kieft, fancying himself—De Vries later wrote—a warrior in the style of ancient heroes, deemed the campaign that he "with his co-murderers" launched "a Roman deed" and went about "committing of murders as if he were an actor in a Roman play." The genocidal scenario that followed would be debated for years and investigated at length, its origins documented in detail. The West India Company would ultimately conclude that the entire venture had been "unnatural, barbarous, unnecessary, unjust, and disgraceful."

As Kieft's attacks proceeded, the whole settlement area around New Amsterdam—thirty miles to the east and twenty or more to the north and south—went up in flames. In one raid, at Pavonia, on the Jersey side of the Hudson, the Dutch soldiers massacred eighty Indians. The gruesome scene, perhaps exaggerated in the telling by Cornelis Melyn, Kieft's worst enemy, whose account was copied by De Vries, played into the Dutch fascination with "atrocity narratives" made familiar in their long, bloody struggle with Spain:

Infants were torn from their mother's breasts [Melyn wrote], and hacked to pieces in the presence of the parents, and pieces thrown into the fire and in the water, and other sucklings, being bound to small boards, were cut, stuck, and pierced, and miserably massacred in a manner to move a heart of stone. Some were thrown into the river, and when the fathers and mothers endeavored to save them, the soldiers would not let them come on land but made both parents and children drown. . . . Some came to our people in the country with their hands, some with their legs cut off, and some holding their entrails in their arms, and others had such horrible cuts and gashes that worse than they were could never happen. . . . Did the Duke of Alva in the Netherlands ever do anything more cruel?

Later, it was said, the mother-in-law of Kieft's loyal secretary, the notorious Cornelis van Tienhoven, "amused herself in kicking about the heads of the dead men which had been brought in as bloody trophies of that midnight slaughter." In return, the Indians killed or took captive every European they could lay hands on, burned their farms, slaughtered the cattle, and drove the horrified survivors in panic to such safety as New Amsterdam's barricades ("rather a molehill," some townsmen said, "than a fort against an enemy") might provide.

One of the raids in the later Westchester County became legendary in its barbarism. There, veteran Dutch and English troops were led by Capt. John Underhill, an Anglo-Dutch military adventurer and erratic Puritan radical who had been banished from Massachusetts at least three times for serial adultery, riot, and heresy, and in 1637 had justified his reputation as a "condottiere without scruples" in the slaughter of the Pequots in New England. Now settled on Long Island and closely associated with the Dutch, he repeated his earlier military success at the village at Pound Ridge. He disposed his troops to surround the village of wigwams, killed 180 of its inhabitants as they attempted to escape, and burned the rest alive within their bark houses. Some said five hundred died in the flames, others seven hundred. "What was most wonderful," a witness remarked admiringly, was that "among this vast collection of men, women and children not one was heard to cry or to scream."

The farming settlements on Manhattan and in the surrounding areas were ruined. In letter after letter, desperate, fevered, passionate, New Netherland's popular leaders—Kieft's Council of Eight, led by Melyn—appealed for help to the West India Company and described the colonists' devastated condition. The settlers, they wrote in November 1643, were

> pursued by these wild heathens and barbarous savages with fire and sword; daily in our houses and fields have they cruelly murdered men and women; and with hatchets and tomahawks struck little children dead in their parents' arms or before their doors; or carried them away into bondage. The houses and grain-barracks are burnt with the produce; cattle of all descriptions are slain and destroyed, and such as remain must perish this approaching winter for the want of fodder.

A year later, in October 1644, they described the results:

> Our fields lie fallow and waste; our dwellings and other buildings are
> burnt . . . The crop . . . remains on the field, as well as the hay, standing
> and rotting . . . We . . . have no means to provide necessaries any longer
> for wives or children. We are seated here in the midst of thousands of
> Indians and barbarians, from whom is to be experienced neither peace
> nor pity.

But the barbarism flared on both sides. Dutch war veterans, fresh
from Europe's wartime carnage, indulged in savagery that beggared the
most sadistic imagination. Of seven unengaged Indians captured on Long
Island in 1644, Melyn reported, three were slaughtered on the spot. The
other four were brought to Manhattan's fort by boat, of whom two, towed
behind by ropes around their necks, strangled and drowned. The third,
after disputes among the impatient guards, was knifed to death. Then
"the soldiers cut strips from the live body of the other, from the hams up
the back and shoulders, and down to the knees." His genitals were cut
off and "stuck . . . into this mouth while he was still alive, and after that
[they] placed him on a mill-stone and beat his head off."[33]

Kieft's extermination policy had badly misfired, and with the colony
traumatized and himself the object of general condemnation, he sought
to shift the blame. It was all the fault of the group that had sought his
approval for attack, he declared, led by an insolent, fierce-tempered
tobacco farmer turned "freebooter" named Maryn Andriaensen, who had
clashed with Kieft on several occasions. Enraged by the accusation, Andriaensen, armed with a sword and a loaded and cocked pistol, stormed into
the director's house and demanded that Kieft admit that he had lied. Disarmed, he was led off under arrest and shipped home for trial, despite the
plea of the Council of Eight that he simply be fined and banished briefly.
But Andriaensen's loyal servant, Jacob Slangh, did attempt to carry out
the assassination that Andriaensen had threatened. He fired twice at the
director but missed his target. He was killed by a sentry, and his head was
cut off for display on Manhattan's gibbet.[34]

True peace, a permanent peace of accommodation between the
races, would never come to New Netherland, nor would there be an
end to the mutual fears and animosities. But exhaustion and the need

to provide basic sustenance required a truce. The natives withdrew, and gradually the settlers began to rebuild and further extend the range of the settlements.

6

As they did so the importance of the leadership of the "commonalty"—the town's population at large—became increasingly clear. As New Amsterdam and the surrounding towns and farms began to take on some of the familiar forms of Dutch civil society, governance by an erratic, autocratic agent of a profiteering commercial organization seemed more and more anomalous and arbitrary. By the time Kieft left on his fatal return (1647), the opposition was fully formed, led by sharp-eyed young men whose ambitions were matched by their capacity to survive and flourish in a shifting, complex situation. Some were well connected at home, some were not; some were well educated and well financed, some were not. Like the emerging groups of local leaders in Virginia and Maryland, what they had in common was the ability to seize on the immediate opportunities, exploit them and defend them, and parlay fleeting profits into sustainable advantages.

Govert Loockermans had no support to begin with. He arrived as a cook's mate, was taken on as a company servant, became a freeman, and ultimately prospered as a factor for a prominent Amsterdam firm. His brother-in-law, Oloff Stevensen van Cortlandt, a soldier employed by the West India Company, had become a storekeeper, then a prosperous brewer, merchant, and public official, and eventually burgomaster of New Amsterdam, and, through marriage, a manager of the Van Rensselaer properties. Michiel Jansz., who began as a servant of Van Rensselaer, made a small fortune in a few years on that estate and consolidated his position in New Amsterdam, as did Jacob van Couwenhoven, another of Loockermans's brothers-in-law, who turned from petty officeholding to tobacco planting, land speculation, and brewing, and joined with others as contractor for transporting two hundred emigrants to the colony. These rising leaders—among whom initially were, besides De Vries and Melyn, the latter a merchant from Antwerp who had patented all of Staten Island not claimed by De Vries but had been driven to Manhattan by Indian attacks, Jochem Kuyter, a German veteran of wars in the East

Indies, now a prominent tobacco farmer, and Jan Evertsz. Bout, the former superintendent of one of the failed patroonships.[35]

Two particularly talented and ambitious men became dominant in the growing opposition. Adriaen van der Donck and Augustine Herrman were, in Kieft's time and after, deeply engaged in the colony's public controversies, and both produced, for their immediate advantage, works that proved to be of singular historical importance, though ultimately their careers would diverge in significant ways.

THOUGH DRAWN FROM entirely different backgrounds, the two men at first had much in common, aside from their driving ambition. Both were in their twenties when they arrived in the colony; both were well educated and articulate; both had highly developed professional skills—Van der Donck in law, public and private, Herrman in commerce, including mathematics and navigational cartography; and both had family connections that helped them on their way. But they had different temperaments and different relations with authority, which would determine much of their fates in America.

Van der Donck, son of a prominent family of Breda, in Brabant, was a recent student in law from the University of Leiden when he approached Kiliaen van Rensselaer for an appointment in the administration of Rensselaerswyck.[36] A distant relation of the patroon, who was in regular touch with Van der Donck's parents, the young man saw an opportunity for profit and prominence in the colony, and Van Rensselaer, in turn, after checking on Van der Donck's character, saw an advantage in hiring him as Rensselaerswyck's *schout* (sheriff and prosecutor). He is, he wrote, "a young man of education," a person "who has good judgment," someone of stature whom he could safely put in charge of law enforcement since "human nature is such that those who have charge of another do not like to be instructed by those who are below them in rank." Trust him, he wrote optimistically to Director Kieft when Van der Donck left for New Netherland in May 1641. "He will keep up friendly intercourse with you and not treat you so impolitely as you complain others of my people have done."[37]

Within two years Van Rensselaer realized his mistake. The problem was not simply that Van der Donck—his badge of office a plumed hat and a silver-plated rapier worn at the end of an elaborate shoulder belt—had heightened the tensions between the patroon's private jurisdiction and

that of New Amsterdam. More important, he had antagonized his sponsor by the fervor of his ambition, inflamed by the opportunities he found
in the undeveloped world, by his failure to attend to the patroon's interests, and by his arrogant antagonism to others in Van Rensselaer's employ,
without respect to rank. In March 1643, in a rambling letter of some
5,500 words, written over a period of four days, Van Rensselaer let the
young man know what he thought of his performance. True, he had managed some things with "zeal and diligence," but he had decided to live
not at the entrance to the patroonship, as instructed, but at a remote spot
far from the main population center and had bought land outside the
manor to facilitate his private purchase of furs. He seemed to be acting
"not as an officer but as director," bragging that he would soon hold that
position, while failing to render the services expected of him. In addition
he claimed privilege on the basis of kinship, though the relationship was
at best remote and in any case irrelevant to advancement. "If you have
imagined that you can extort the directorship from me, [Van Rensselaer
wrote,] you will be much deceived, for that is not the way to get it." Further, his demands for supplies and funding were excessive, and his complaints to the proprietor should have been specific and not general. Nor
had his legal services been proper. "*What displeases me most in you*," Van
Rensselaer wrote with deliberate underlining,

> and what is quite the contrary of what I had expected of you is that you bring
> forward a great many charges and do not show me a single legal procedure
> against any of them, for legal practice does not consist of discourses or words but
> of formal and judicial actions and procedures.

Your instructions, he told the young *schout*,

> give you power, not to compel obedience but only to make representations in my
> interest and the words in your oath, to seek in everything my advantage and
> to protect me from loss . . . I am not without suspicion that you have indulged
> ambition too much, from which much harm has come to your and my damage:
> he who goes slowly gets farther than he who runs fast.

And in a concluding section he made clear the various levels of jurisdiction in the structure of his patroonship and lectured Van der Donck on
the paternalistic principles of political authority.[38]

No doubt Van Rensselaer was unduly controlling in his absentee management of his wilderness domain, unrealistic in hoping to squeeze substantial profits from the labor of his tenants and employees, and insensitive to the sheer brutality of life in the Indians' world. But Van der Donck's self-importance, pomposity, and supercilious disdain for his colleagues and the settlers scattered in the woods and stump-filled fields made things worse. He gained credit for some slight efforts to root out illegal trade and to chase down hirelings who reneged on their contracts. But these duties he found to be pedestrian, and he looked around for grander, more exciting possibilities. When in 1643 word reached Amsterdam that he was contemplating the purchase of a large territory in the Catskill Mountains on which to construct his own private colony, his relationship with Van Rensselaer, already embittered, came to an end.[39]

But however supercilious Van der Donck was to the settlers and his colleagues, he was almost humble in his interest in the land itself, the strange physical environment of the Hudson River valley, the climate, seasons, and plant and animal life. And he was genuinely intrigued by the native Indians, their appearance, lifeways, and languages, all of which he approached with an open and inquisitive mind, the very opposite of the crude reactions of Michaëlius. Amid the turmoil of his misbegotten efforts as *schout*, he noted with acute perception details of the land and its people—men "so stately, proud, and self-possessed that they will scarcely deign to turn their heads," women of "an attractive grace." All of this, years later, in repose three thousand miles from the wilderness scene, he would record in his notable *Description of New Netherland*.[40]

For the present, however, after a bitter dispute with Arent van Curler, Van Rensselaer's trusted nephew, who, when Van der Donck's house burned down, gave and then denied shelter to the *schout*, whom he described as "self-seeking and grasping," Van der Donck moved downriver to New Amsterdam. There he settled on a 24,000-acre tract just north of Manhattan which Kieft had allotted to him for his work in concluding a treaty with the Indians. But if his relations with Kieft began well, they ended badly. With him in his growing opposition to the distracted director was Augustine Herrman, a man of equal ambition.[41]

Well before Van der Donck had settled in his new property ("Yonkers": *Yonkheer*, the young squire), Augustine Herrman had begun his career as a leading merchant in New Amsterdam and a significant property owner in the town and the surrounding areas, including a very large plot adjacent to Van der Donck's. Little is known of his early years. A Bohemian, born in Prague, the son of a Protestant preacher, he migrated with his family first to Germany then to Holland at the outbreak of the Thirty Years War. There he had become associated with the Amsterdam firm of Peter Gabry and Sons. Stationed in New Netherland as their main agent in America, he quickly found his way into the elaborating intricacies of Atlantic commerce. He managed shipments from and to Holland and the Dutch Caribbean islands, from the Chesapeake tobacco planters to New Amsterdam and beyond, and from upriver fur traders to the markets of Europe. He would in time attempt to produce indigo in the Hudson River valley, deal in slaves shipped from Curaçao for sale in Manhattan, and invest in privateering ventures aimed at Spanish shipping. And he acquired the essentials of surveying while developing his skill in cartography. Of his personality, we know, from his dealings, that he was persistent, thorough, and unlike Van der Donck, undemonstrative and patient in negotiation. And, one may assume from his expressive portrait, probably drawn by himself, he was sharp-eyed, forceful, and assertive—qualities needed for the political battles that he and Van der Donck were beginning to wage at the end of Kieft's bloody tenure and which they would relentlessly pursue through the upheavals of his successor's directorship.[42]

BY THE TIME Van der Donck's land grant was formally issued (July 1645) the opposition to Kieft was well under way. Letters of protest were circulating privately, and in October 1644 the Council of Eight, led by Kuyter and Melyn, sent privately to the company's directors a full indictment of Kieft's regime. In it they traced the history of Kieft's "hankering after war" though previously the Indians had "lived as lambs among us"; his suppression of the meetings of the consulting group he had convened "on pain of corporal punishment"; and his unjustified claim of the right to "dispose here of our lives and properties at his will and pleasure, in a manner so arbitrary that a King dare not legally do the like." Local officials, the petition stated, should be chosen by people themselves, and their deputies should consult with the director and his Council. Only such a "different system," and a new director, would properly settle the colony's affairs.

The possibility of a "different system" would wait on events, but it was clear in the Netherlands, after receipt of the petition, that Kieft would have to go, if only "because the *wilde* [Indians] are not in any way to be pacified . . . before the director is removed." His replacement arrived in May 1647, and over the next seventeen years, until England conquered the colony, the management of its political turmoils, its economic growth, its increasingly complex peopling, its relations with other colonizing powers, and its continuing racial warfare would lie in his hands.[43]

PETRUS (PIETER) STUYVESANT was thirty-seven on his arrival in Manhattan. A Calvinist minister's son from the remote, bleak north coastal region of Friesland, he had been well educated to university level. To judge from the books he disposed of at auction, he was acquainted with, if not learned in, philosophy, theology, and some of the arts. At least one of his early poems, written at age eighteen, survives. But for reasons unknown—perhaps debt, perhaps some misdemeanor, perhaps conflict of theological views—he left the university and found a different career, as many young Dutchmen were doing, in a small corner of the nation's expanding Atlantic empire. Intelligent, self-confident, and solidly responsible, he was taken on by the West India Company and sent first, as a minor functionary, to a remote island far off the Brazilian coast, then to the newly conquered coastal town of Pernambuco, and finally in 1638 to Curaçao, then becoming the pivotal Dutch trading center just north of Venezuela. In that small but economically vital island, he flourished, first as a supply officer, then as governor, and as governor too of Aruba and Bonaire. By 1644, when he led the Dutch troops in a futile attempt to take the island of St. Maarten from the Spanish, he had become a tough, domineering politician and administrator with broad experience in the brutally competitive Atlantic world and a trusted servant of the West India Company. The disaster at St. Maarten, in which his right leg was smashed by a cannonball and amputated in the horrific procedures of the time, served to toughen him more and to secure his image as a grim, rough-mannered, short-tempered, ruthless commander capable of creating order out of chaos. But he kept his softer side; he never forsook his earlier intellectual life, maintaining a literary friendship with an English litterateur, exchanging verses with him from time to time. But to the colonists who greeted him in Manhattan in 1647 it was his grim, scowling visage, his commanding presence enhanced by his defiant display of his wooden leg, and fierce pride and formality that stood out. One of his enemies would soon call him "our great Muscovy

PIETER STUYVESANT

A short-tempered, tough commander, Stuyvesant was feared and mocked for
his ferocious manner. But he never lost his interest in literature and theology,
and alone questioned the legitimacy of wars against the Indians. He ended his
tumultuous career as a peaceful landowner in the province which he had once
ruled, now the English colony of New York.

duke"; another saw him as "a strong stickler, withal, for the prerogative."
And one of the colony's earliest historians would shrewdly comment that
"he lacked the knowledge of that valuable secret, that it is much safer not
to act at all than to become a party to other men's quarrels."[44]

It was precisely with an involvement in other men's quarrels that he
began his administration of New Netherland. He had known of Kieft's
troubles before he left Curaçao, and had sent him a contingent of soldiers to help him in the struggle with the Indians. And he knew of the
buildup of opposition to Kieft's directorship, including the petition of
1644, which Kieft himself had not seen. In the weeks before his arrival
the opposition, led by Melyn and Kuyter, had produced a string of nota-

rized testimonials laying the blame for the Indian war squarely on Kieft and had prepared a set of interrogatories directed to seven accused men, most of them company officers, including the colony's secretary, Van Tienhoven. For Stuyvesant, determined to settle the issue forthwith, these documents were inflammatory, and he asked his council whether it had ever been heard of that "vassals and subjects" should devise interrogatories for examining their superiors; whether there would not be very bad consequences if "two malignant private subjects" (Kuyter and Melyn) should be allowed to represent others in confronting their superiors; and whether indulging such "cunning fellows" would not lead to even greater opposition "to us" if our administration did not suit "their whims." His councilors—some his own men from Curaçao, some holdovers from Kieft's regime—quickly concurred. Whereupon Stuyvesant showed Kieft the commonalty's petition of 1644. Enraged, Kieft replied in detail, and his reply was forwarded to Kuyter and Melyn with the demand that they immediately reply to Kieft's denunciation of their campaign against him.

Their reply was indignant, emotional, and learned to the point of pedantry. In it they went over all of Kieft's charges against them, described the troops Kieft had assembled for his attacks, lamented the resulting "piles of ashes from the burnt houses, barns, barracks and other buildings, and the bones of the cattle," which had been so carefully nurtured, documented Kieft's boast that his power was "greater and more extensive" than that of the Prince of Orange, and reiterated the claim that the Indians had been like lambs until Kieft had attacked them and slaughtered them like "sheep." Finally they referred to the cautions of "the law of nations" in waging war and the proper terms of a just war, citing in support of their arguments Diogenes, Saint Ambrose, Aristides, and Xenophon. Far from being "pestilent and seditious persons," they were, they insisted, "good patriots and proprietors of New Netherland."

Stuyvesant was unimpressed, and after a rambling commentary of his own, quoting biblical injunctions to submit to the higher powers, and with suitable references to legal treatises on crime and punishment, he declared their petition of 1644 to be "libelous . . . false, lying and defamatory." After invoking the articles of war that required capital punishment for rebels and mutineers, he simply banished the two from the colony after imposing heavy fines. They left on the same ship that carried Kieft and Bogardus to their deaths, a fate they themselves miraculously escaped.[45]

But none of this ended the opposition to the colony's governance.

It grew with Stuyvesant's determined, authoritarian effort to repair the wreckage he had inherited and to build a proper and profitable outpost of Dutch imperialism. It was no easy task. Manhattan, Stuyvesant was shocked to discover, was a dilapidated, half-built port village around a fort whose walls had crumbled into mounds, and flimsy docks. It was overrun with a floating population of idle, brawling soldiers, sailors aimless on long layovers, and a miscellany of dockhands, many of them African. The houses were flimsy, with walls of boards and roofs of thatch, sanitation was primitive, pigs and other animals roamed the dirt streets, rummaging destructively at the base of the fort. Trash of all kinds—"rubbish, filth [sewage], ashes, oyster-shells, dead animal[s]"—was scattered about, much of it dumped into the "graft," the open ditch that drained a swampy patch into the East River. And privies had been built with openings directly onto the streets, so that hogs "may consume the filth and wallow in it." The result was so great a stench that some streets were "unfit for use."

Drunkenness was common, especially among the Indians who wandered in and out. The more respectable resident townsmen—merchants, tradesmen, servants and their families—were a mixture of Dutch, English, Germans, French, Portuguese, Swedes, Poles, and Danes, living together with Indian servants and African slaves, and the religious diversity had increased. The taverns—seventeen legal and several illegal (one-quarter of all dwellings were said to be "grog shops" in 1637)—were scenes of brawls that spilled out into the streets, ending frequently in knife fights. And there was constant fighting of another kind: legal struggles over property rights, inheritances, slander, contracts, debts, and assaults, while efforts were made to enforce the laws on theft, fornication, rape, sodomy, and bigamy.[46]

Stuyvesant, a precisionist law-and-order magistrate imbued with the austere moral code of the Dutch Reformed Church, took in this chaotic scene and demanded a quick reformation. In a stream of regulations, prohibitions, and moral dicta, he reduced the taverns' business hours (closed them and all other businesses on the Sabbath) and imposed severe fines for violations; punished knife fighters with six months of hard labor or a one-hundred-guilder fine (three hundred if wounds resulted); and levied a five-hundred-guilder charge on anyone who sold liquor to the Indians, adding corporal punishment when after a year he discovered that Indians were still "running drunk" through the streets. At the same time he demanded proper building practices to improve the ramshackle housing, banned pigpens and privies on the streets, set standards for the construction of fences, and outlawed chimneys made of wood. In addition, in an effort to restrict smuggling, he threatened to inspect outgoing cargoes and traders' account books. Finally, to finance the necessary repairs to the fort, finish the construction of the church, and reinforce the sagging piers, he imposed a tax on wines and liquors. Later, when the harvest failed, he would outlaw the use of wheat in making beer and the export of bread or its ingredients and set out standards for weight and price controls on the sale of bread.

His regulations, however imperfectly enforced, added fuel to the opposition's smoldering resentments, which intensified with Stuyvesant's effort to call in all debts owed to the company.[47] The conviction grew that the new director had the makings of a martinet likely to dominate their lives. Stuyvesant, aware of the growing opposition—indeed the threat of assassination—and the need for popular support, created a Board of Nine, chosen indirectly by the residents, presumably to share in the government's proceedings. But in selecting Herrman, Loockermans, and Van Couwenhoven among the Nine, he succeeded in giving institutional form to an otherwise amorphous opposition. And when late in 1648 he included Van der Donck in the Nine, the leadership had an effective spokesman and began a bristling offensive.

In New Amsterdam's miniature theater of politics, 1649 was a crucial year of controversy between the determined, tough-minded director who had banned all subversive writings "dangerous to the republic," and the emboldened opposition, now dedicated not only to reducing the burdens they lived under but to getting Stuyvesant removed from office. And more than that, the logic of the commonalty's demands revealed an inherent contradiction between the interests of the settlement's individual merchants and farmers and those of the absentee, profit-seeking company that governed them. What served the one disserved the other, or so it seemed, and the opposition drew the conclusion that the colony, no longer a mere trading outpost but a society of permanent residents, would prosper only when freed of the company's control and brought under the direct jurisdiction of the Dutch government.

Van der Donck, having failed to win favor with Stuyvesant, threw himself into the project of ridding the colony not only of its unbudging director but of the West India Company as well. Defiant of authority, convinced that his cause was a vindication of the rights and liberties defined by Europe's advanced thinkers, he took on the task of secretly compiling a list of particulars against Stuyvesant. Arrested and jailed when the director discovered the notes, which he denounced as "slanderous . . . injurious and defamatory," Van der Donck then turned, in what must have been a passion of literary effort, to drafting three documents addressed to the "Illustrious High and Mighty Lords States General . . . Our Most Serene Sovereigns." They were signed first by himself and Herrman, then by nine others representing the commonalty.[48]

The first was a brief formal petition itemizing the causes of the "very poor and most low conditions" of the colony, and praying for relief from the "unsuitable government" of the West India Company and from the swarms of "Schotte en chinezen" (Scots and Chinese: petty traders) who infest the land, while urging their High Mightinesses to provide a municipal government for New Amsterdam, a sufficient population of good farmers, clear borders, and soldiers to protect them against the Indians. The second was a thick bundle of "additional observations," documenting the claims of the petition in four main points with various subdivisions, the whole fortified by no fewer than eighty-seven footnotes. The third, though in form an amendment to the petitions, was in effect a veritable treatise— a "Remonstrance" of eighty-three pages, perhaps 25,000 words, that gave the petition monumentality. Van der Donck began by presenting their High Mightinesses with a bird's-eye view of the present condition of New Netherland's "fruitful and healthful land," its history, people, flora and fauna, and its ecology and contested boundaries. He then turned to an extended explanation of "why and how New Netherland is so decayed." This was the heart of the matter, and he spared no details.

There was no doubt, he wrote, as to why the colony was so "decayed" and in such "ruinous" condition. The cause was simple: "*bad government*, with its attendants and consequences.*" That was "the true and only foundation stone of the decay and ruin of New Netherland." And the cause of the bad government? It was the profit-seeking, maladroit, neglectful, narrow-minded West India Company, still the owner and governor of the province. Both the company at home and its agents in the colony had in their profiteering greed virtually destroyed the colony. They had neglected to recruit a large enough population, while throwing money away on "senseless extravagances"; they had underfunded the public's needs while keeping the settlers from taking up profitable new land. They had increased taxes while charging high prices for necessary goods. They had denied the settlers their chartered rights while failing to protect them from the Indians. They had ignored the need for establishing firm boundaries with their neighbors. They had discouraged legitimate trade while winking at contraband commerce. They had, directly or indirectly, driven the Indians to war. And they had allowed the directors to exercise "supreme authority" equal to that of the Dutch government itself.

Then, after reviewing and denouncing Kieft's and Stuyvesant's "ungovernable passions," their personal pomposities ("like a peacock's"), their cruelties, illegalities, rages, and tyrannous acts, as well as their appointments to high office of such "shrewd, false, deceitful, and . . . lying" toadies as the lascivious Van Tienhoven, forever lusting after Indian prostitutes, Van der Donck laid down the terms of necessary reform. The company's ownership and governance of the colony should be abolished; public services like orphan asylums, churches, and schools (necessary in "so wild a country, where there are many dissolute people") should be created; and above all, there must be a new, vigorous policy of population recruitment. Large numbers of farmers and farm servants must be sent over complete with supplies; all Dutch vessels voyaging to North America must be ordered to land first at Manhattan, bringing with them "as many persons as seasonably present themselves" and who can be accommodated on board the ships. True, this solution would be expensive, but it would be money well spent "if farmers and laborers with other people in straitened circumstances, of whom the Fatherland has plenty to spare, were by that means introduced, with what little they may have, into the country." The place would prosper, especially if it had the benefit of that "mother of population," generous "privileges and exemptions" (municipal government, freedom from taxes, access to all Dutch markets, and fishing rights). The main object, above all others, was to "allure every one hither."[49]

Such were the documents, composed principally by Van der Donck and endorsed by Herrman and the rest of the Nine, by which the commonalty sought to overthrow the company's governance of New Netherland and rescue the colony from ruin. It was clear that the transmission of these documents could not be entrusted to local officials, nor could the case be effectively made by documents alone. In early October Van der Donck, Van Couwenhoven, and Jan Evertsz. Bout sailed to the Netherlands to plead their case at the seat of government in The Hague. Van Tienhoven followed, armed with an elaborate "Answer" to Van der

Donck's Remonstrance and prepared to defend Stuyvesant and his interests before the government.[50]

So it was that the personal squabbles and murderous rivalries of the
settlers in the crude hamlet of New Amsterdam, surrounded by hostile natives and limitless forests, played themselves out at the heart of
Europe's most sophisticated state. At stake was the fate of the troubled
West India Company, challenged as the Virginia Company had been by
leading colonists seeking autonomy for their own emerging way of life,
and the future of the colony itself.

For weeks Van der Donck and his colleagues wound their way through
various commissions and committees; presented the authorities with gifts
of furs, fruits, and other products of the colony; pleaded privately with
influential officials; and published the Remonstrance as an appeal to
the public, supplemented with a map and an artistic townscape of New
Amsterdam. Dwelling on the miseries, bleakness, and desperation of the
mishandled settlement, they sought to discredit Van Tienhoven's argument that New Netherland was flourishing under Stuyvesant's direction.

There were ups and downs as charges and countercharges were registered with the government. In April 1650 a provisional ruling was handed
down that favored the petitioners. Although the company's jurisdiction
was not voided, it was severely criticized; New Amsterdam was accorded
a municipal government; subsidies were provided for the shipment of
prospective emigrants; and Stuyvesant was ordered to return from his
post. But the ruling was only provisional, and Van der Donck was obliged
to continue his presentations in the hope that it would be fully enacted.
Though discouraged by letters from Herrman declaring that Stuyvesant
and "that infernal swaggerer Tienhoven" had brought them all to ruin,
he made a final effort in an elaborate presentation in February 1652,
with every sign of success. But fate, in the form of rumors of war with
England, intervened. As war approached, the government's attention
turned to preparedness, and as a result the influence of the militant West
India Company rose steadily. When war broke out in July, the provisional
rulings were rescinded.

It was the end of Van der Donck's mission. He could only look forward
to returning to the colony and rebuilding his personal life with his English
wife (the daughter of the formidable Reverend Doughty) on his extensive
property north of Manhattan. He was able to send on his parents and his

Title page of Adriaen van der Donck's *Description of New Netherland*

brother's family to the colony, but for himself there were endless delays. He had made enemies. His pulsing ambition, supercilious manner, and instinctive rebelliousness had made the authorities cautious in allowing him to return to the contentious scene in Manhattan. And the ascendant West India Company, which had classified him as one of the "silly," seditious people who try "to upset every kind of government, pretending that they suffered under too heavy a yoke," wanted to see the end of him.[51]

So he waited, resumed his legal studies in Leiden, and completed and published his *Description of New Netherland*. Based on the introductory section of the Remonstrance, it went much further into a detailed description and sympathetic analysis of the exotic world he had known and left behind, a world of wonderment for him, a world of people who though "dirty, slovenly, and careless" nevertheless live by "the law of nature or of nations" and whose medical care, especially the treatment of venereal diseases, "would put many an Italian physician to shame." These taciturn, unaffected, intelligent people, still in a state of nature, and their strange but well-controlled environment, were a challenge to his imagination and an inspiration to his entrepreneurial instinct.[52]

When finally, in 1655, six years after he had left the colony, permission to return was granted, it was with the stipulation that he never again engage in politics or law: that he "accept no office whatever it may be, but rather live in private, peacefully and quietly as a common inhabitant, submitting to the orders and commands of the Company or those enacted by its director." But even that was denied him. He died in 1655, soon after his return to the colony.[53]

By then the career of his former colleague and ally, Augustine Herrman, had taken a very different path.

Within a year of Van der Donck's departure for The Hague, Herrman had overcome serious financial difficulties and had come to Stuyvesant's attention not as a "silly" malcontent but as a reliable, multilingual, energetic entrepreneur, uniquely qualified to represent him in the increasingly complex negotiations with the neighboring colonies. As the director began, haltingly, to find Herrman useful, a secure link between the two was created when in 1651 Herrman married Jannetje Verlett, whose brother had married Stuyvesant's widowed sister Anna. And equally important to Herrman's future, Jannetje's sister had married Dr. George Hack, a German who had settled on the Eastern Shore of Chesapeake Bay and had become a landowner and energetic tobacco planter. With his marriage, the forces that would determine Herrman's career—his dislike of but growing closeness to Stuyvesant and his ties to the tobacco land of Virginia's and Maryland's Eastern Shore—were in place.

In 1652 Stuyvesant sent Herrman on his first, unfortunate, mission, to Rhode Island, that "latrine of New England," whose government Stuyvesant proposed to rescue from the "rabble" and "bandits" who threatened it. A year later he sent Herrman to Boston to negotiate the difficulties of the new navigation laws that excluded the Dutch from English commerce. Then, in 1659, now Stuyvesant's "trusty agent," he was dispatched to Maryland to challenge that colony's claim to the settle-

ments on the Delaware River which the Dutch had seized in their conquest of New Sweden four years earlier.

Herrman, who undoubtedly knew something of the Eastern Shore
through the Hacks before that mission, recognized, as he traveled south
into northern Maryland, the region's great possibilities. He particularly
noted, besides the richness of the land, that the upper reaches of Chesapeake Bay were separated from the Delaware River, which was an outlet
into the Atlantic, by only a few miles. And it was also clear that this frontier region was beginning to experience a land boom as settlers moved in
to claim parcels of vacant land.

Herrman fulfilled his mission to a fault, debating vigorously and
learnedly with Maryland's governor, Josias Fendall, and the proprietor's
brother, Charles Calvert, in defense of the Dutch claim to the Delaware settlements. But increasingly he negotiated as a friend, and gladly
remained in Maryland through the winter of 1659–60. By the time he
reported back to Stuyvesant he had acquired his first plot of land in that
colony's far northeastern corner. As an affluent and sophisticated landowner and merchant he fitted perfectly Baltimore's image of a manorial
lord, and in short order he received the official title of "Lord" of his
property on the narrow neck between the Chesapeake and the Delaware
River, which he called Bohemia Manor. In 1660 he acquired rights of
denization, and in 1669 he became a naturalized English subject.

Maintaining contact with New Netherland while embracing his role
as lord of his extensive Maryland property, Herrman turned to an urgent
project. In collaboration with the Hacks and others, he arranged for
tobacco-laden vessels from the south to be secretly dragged five to ten
miles overland on ox-drawn sledges from the upper tip of Chesapeake
Bay to inlets on the shores of the Delaware River, whence they were free
to sail, in defiance of the navigation laws, to New Amsterdam or to other
Atlantic ports. When the rough trail of wooden rollers becomes a wagon
road, he wrote, journeys across the neck will be made in half a day.[54]

For years, until the English conquest of New Netherland, Herrman
not only flourished as the lord of Bohemia Manor but prospered in the
smuggling trade while expanding the outward reach of his commercial
enterprises. He increased his landholdings to about twenty-five thousand
acres and became a notable figure, a "head man," in Maryland's local government. But since land in this frontier region was as yet easily acquired,
he found it difficult to recruit reliable tenants, and the manor fell into

disrepair. Visitors in his later years found him "very miserable both in soul and body," living alone save for a small team of slaves. The invaluable Jannetje having died in 1661, he had married again, with less success. His new wife, said to be "miserable, doubly miserable," alienated his sons, one of whom, to Herrman's sadness, joined the radical Labatist sect which he had earlier favored with a grant of land. His death in 1686—forty years after he had collaborated with Van der Donck in opposing New Netherland's leadership—would not have been noteworthy had he not left behind a remarkable testimony of his skill, energy, and imagination.[55]

His original inspiration is clearly recorded. In his report to Stuyvesant in October 1659, he urged, as a primary item of business, that

> The South [Delaware] River and the Virginias, with the lands and kills between both, ought to be laid down on an exact scale as to longitude and latitude, in a perfect map, that the country on both sides may be correctly seen, . . . for some maps which the English have here are utterly imperfect and prejudicial to us. The sooner this is done, the better.

Presented at this point as a way of protecting Dutch interests, the project had broader transnational and personal implications. Herrman had already begun making sketches of the riverine configurations for his own use when Lord Baltimore subsidized the project with a special grant of land. Herrman was launched on an undertaking that would absorb his energies for ten years. When in 1670 his map of the Chesapeake region was completed, Herrman sent it for engraving to William Faithorne in London, who published it in 1673. It was entitled

VIRGINIA
AND
Maryland
As it is Planted and
Inhabited this present
Year 1670 Surveyed and
Exactly Drawne by the
Only Labour and Endeavor
Of
Augustine Herrman
Bohemiensis

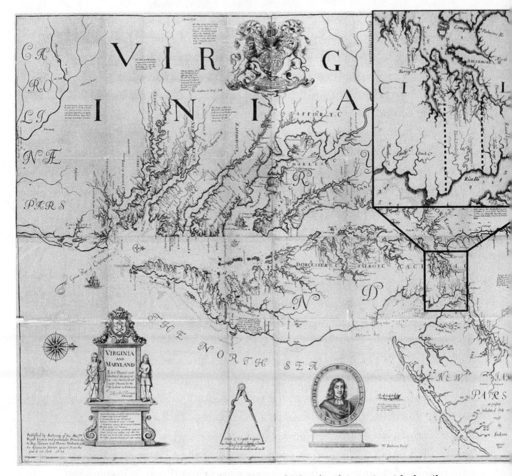

Augustine Herrman's map of Virginia and Maryland (1673), with detail
showing the portage route for smuggling tobacco from upper Chesapeake Bay
to the Delaware River. The narrowest point was an eight-mile stretch over
which vessels of twelve tons were dragged "upon sleys, or in creat carts" by
teams of oxen.

    The map, roughly thirty-one by thirty-seven inches, was elaborately
and meticulously plotted. Not only is every waterway and island along
Chespeake Bay and the Delaware River (every bay, bend, cove, neck,
kill, and overland route) depicted in exquisite detail, but hundreds of
habitations (manors, plantations, farms, and Indian encampments) are
identified, and terrain features (swamps, hills, and forests) are marked in
minuscule lettering. So fine and delicate are the tracings of the twisting

waterways that, viewed at a distance, the map seems to be an ornamental filigree rather than a functional chart.

The map's borders are crowded with sketches and commentaries on the history and prospects of the land. One marginal note comments on the mountains that lay to the west and the likelihood of passages beyond the mountains that might lead out to "the Bay of Mexico or the West Sea." The great seal of England appears at the top of the map; the coat of arms of the Lords Baltimore, somewhat to the side. And at the bottom Herrman placed his own portrait, a striking image of resolution, intelligence, and self-confidence.[56]

But the map is not only a meticulous portrayal of the Chesapeake terrain and an example of advanced cartography. In its carefully defined details, its meticulous tracings of the twists and turns of coastlines, riverways, and land routes, it reflects Herrman's profound personal engagement with this exotic land and the excitement of discovery. The map is the visual expression of the same zest and enthusiasm, the same sense of wonderment and entrepreneurial optimism, that underlay the details of Adriaen van der Donck's *Description of New Netherland*. Both documents, by the former leaders of the commonalty, the one verbal, the other visual, transcended the abrasive turmoils that had engrossed their authors, to convey a greater meaning of their endeavors, based on their shared fascination with the land and their expectations of its future.

CHAPTER 9

Carnage and Civility in a
Developing Hub of Commerce

1

THOUGH VAN DER DONCK had been suppressed and Herrman had been co-opted and then diverted by Baltimore and Maryland, and though the commonalty had in part been pacified by the grant of a municipal government for New Amsterdam, Stuyvesant had not solved New Netherland's problems. Conflict continued. Contention followed all of Stuyvesant's efforts at reform. Population recruitment remained the colony's most urgent problem, and proposals continued to be made to solve it. In 1648, the year after Stuyvesant's arrival, the colony's audit board suggested that slaves might be the key to the colony's population problem. Under the terms of their scheme, settlers who actually promoted farming and population growth in the colony would be allowed to export farm products in their own vessels directly to Dutch colonial markets, such as Brazil, and to return with shiploads of slaves. In this way Brazil and other Dutch colonies would get cheap produce and New Netherland

> would by slave labor be more extensively cultivated than it has hitherto
> been, because the [free] agricultural laborers who are conveyed thither

at great expense to the colonists sooner or later apply themselves to trade and neglect agriculture altogether. Slaves, on the other hand, being brought and maintained there at a cheap rate, various other descriptions of produce would be raised and by their abundance be reduced in price so as to allow . . . their advantageous exportation [to the Netherlands] and to other parts of Europe.

Two years later came the commonalty's urgent plea in its Remonstrance, that the government subsidize the free emigration of the Netherlands' surplus population, "farmers and laborers with other people in straitened circumstances." And indeed Van der Donck's personal efforts while in the Netherlands led to a small surge in emigration to the colony.[1]

In time there would in fact be both sizable slave imports and a significant increase in the number of immigrants from the Netherlands. But in the years immediately following Stuyvesant's arrival what mainly accounted for a sudden increase in numbers, more than offsetting those who fled the colony during and after Kieft's war, was not an organized migration from the homeland but an almost untraceable drift into the colony of a miscellany of people from outside the Netherlands: Huguenots directly or indirectly from France; Germans; Walloons; Swedes and Finns; and refugees from Brazil and the Dutch colonies in the Caribbean. Above all, and in greatest numbers, was the movement of English religious dissidents and land-hungry farmers moving south from New England into territory claimed by the Dutch in the lower Hudson River valley and especially on Long Island.

THE MIGRATION OF the English from the east and north, which would greatly shape New Netherland's population history, had been in motion since 1639, when an agent of the Earl of Stirling, who claimed possession of the whole of Long Island, began to entice New Englanders to move south and settle on the island. He turned first to a disgruntled group in Lynn, Massachusetts, who felt sufficiently "straitened" in their circumstances to look for resettlement, and brought them to the site of the later Manhasset, a mere twenty miles from New Amsterdam. Expelled from there by a troop of Dutch soldiers, they moved off one hundred miles to the far eastern tip of the island, Montauk Point, and then, disappointed with that bleak spot, settled finally at a place they called Southampton, on the southern, ocean side of the island, still far from any Dutch settlements. There, on an isolated plot eight miles square fronting the sea, thirty miles west of Montauk, they formed a self-governing New England town corporation and brought in a newly arrived preacher, Abraham Pierson, to organize a church society. The community, drawn from various parts of England as distant from each other as Buckinghamshire and Yorkshire, flourished. It soon had forty families—perhaps one hundred souls—who quickly developed bitter disputes on church polity. Within four years Pierson, once a scholar at Trinity College, Cambridge, was so deeply disappointed in the community's loose ties of church and state that he felt impelled to move once again—back across the Sound, north to the stricter Connecticut town of New Haven. But even that more rigorous devotional community disappointed him, and he gathered his remaining adherents and wandered south once more, to found what became Newark, New Jersey.[2]

Pierson's and the Lynn community's discontent in matters of religion and available land and their extraordinary mobility were typical of the impulses that brought hundreds of New Englanders south into Dutch territory. Their comings and goings made Long Island, once sparsely settled by Indians, a world in constant motion.

Thus, while Southampton was being peopled from Lynn, a contingent from New Haven, led by the proto-presbyterian Rev. John Youngs, once of Southwold, Suffolk, England, settled Southold far out on the island's north shore, where he established friendly relations with the Indians. Dissidents from the recently founded Southampton joined with immigrants from southern England to establish Easthampton, a few miles farther to the east. An English army officer, Lion Gardiner, bought and settled the island that bears his name, nestled in the eastern bay of Long Island, while a group of Barbados merchants set up a trading emporium on nearby Shelter Island.[3]

The drift of the English south to Long Island—freed servants, religious dissidents, and farmers feeling relatively deprived in their landholdings at the edge of a limitless continent—continued through the 1640s and 1650s, spreading steadily west on the island into closer and closer proximity to the Dutch settlements that were expanding east from Manhattan. New Dutch villages on the western end of Long Island—Flatbush, Breuklen, Nieuw Amersfoort (later Flatlands), named for Couwenhoven's native town, and New Utrecht—were thought of as protective barriers against English encroachment from the east. These Dutchmen soon found themselves close neighbors of some of the most radical English exiles.

It was in 1642 that the fiercely independent Rev. Francis Doughty, Adriaen van der Donck's future father-in-law, appeared, expelled from Massachusetts for his offensive ideas on baptism, to settle "Maspeth," which, as the later Newtown, would develop what has been described as a "genuine cultural pluralism." Similarly, John Throckmorton, a grocer from Norwich, England, who followed Roger Williams into exile in Rhode Island, broke off from even that utterly permissive world to settle Throg's Neck, a spit of the mainland jutting into the Sound twelve miles from New Amsterdam. At that isolated spot, his nearest neighbor, to the north, was that "woman of a ready wit and bold spirit," the notorious Anne Hutchinson, an immigrant first from Lincolnshire to Boston, then from Boston to Portsmouth, Rhode Island, and finally from Portsmouth to Pelham Bay. There, in isolation, far from the great turmoils of the Puritans' Bay Colony, she had sought peace on her own terms, only to find death, with her entire family, at the hands of marauding Indians.[4]

By the mid-1650s, English dissenters—and dissenters from dissenters—were everywhere on Long Island, west and east. The elderly Lady Deborah Moody, a wealthy, tough-minded widow, denounced as "a dangerous woman" by the church in Massachusetts for her remorseless antipedobaptism, took her many books and an entourage of thirty-nine families also "infected with anabaptism," mainly from Salem and Lynn, Massachusetts, to Gravesend on Long Island's south shore. There, protected by Kieft's grant of community autonomy, she would in time welcome other, even more extreme English radicals, including Quakers. Hempstead (Heemstede), in the center of the island, became the final home of a core group originally from Hemel Hempstead in Hertfordshire. They had settled first in Wethersfield, Connecticut, then moved to Stamford in the train of their Cambridge-educated preacher, Richard Denton—a remarkable man, Cotton Mather would later write, physically frail and half blind but mentally powerful: "an Iliad in a nutshell." While Denton sought to realize his presbyterian and yet radically democratic ideals, a company of exiled Englishmen left their refuge in Vlissingen, Holland, to settle in a like-named hamlet (later Flushing), close to the Dutch on the western end of the island. And they settled with a distinct advantage. Kieft, desperate to secure the Dutch claim to the area, granted Flushing, along with Hempstead and Gravesend, in exchange for allegiance to the States General and the West India Company, not only its own court of justice, tax-free possession of land, and hunting and fishing rights, but also rights of self-governance and "liberty of conscience"—freedom, that is, from "molestacon or disturbance from any magistrate . . . or ecclesiastical minister" on account of beliefs. Other English settlers, on their second or third removes, founded Huntington, Setauket, and Brookhaven.[5]

The Dutch exerted nominal control over only four of the near-est of these new English villages—Gravesend, Jamaica, Newtown, and Hempstead—by requiring settlers to swear an oath to the Dutch gov-ernment and claiming the right to approve the election of ministers and magistrates and to sanction the work of the town meetings. But these powers were rarely enforced, and in any case the other, quickly multiply-ing English settlements were beyond even these weak controls. By the late 1640s it was clear that the Dutch would have to assert their control over all the settlements on Long Island or concede the territory to the English. And they would also have to assert their claims to settlements at the mouth of the Connecticut River and at several points higher up along that waterway.[6]

These claims, by 1650, were thirty years old, dating back to the sta-tioning of some of the first Walloon settlers at the mouth of the Con-necticut River. But the English had long since taken command of the river's trade; had populated the river valley first with traders, then with farming families migrating from the east coast; and had threatened to cut into the Dutch fur trade centered on Fort Orange on the Hudson. Outmaneuvered and outnumbered, the few Dutch on the Connecticut River grew desperate and touched off a series of small confrontations with the English. Charges and countercharges, flung about wildly, reached the authorities in Europe where the two nations were approaching conflict, and rendered the question of colonial boundaries explosive unless some resolution were quickly found.

It was to settle this question, and at the same time to sort out the min-gling and merging of Dutch and English on Long Island, that emissaries of the two peoples met at the Connecticut River hamlet of Hartford in 1650. Stuyvesant arrived with great pomp and show, but the English, backed by greater demographic force and a distinct advantage in posi-tion, largely dictated the terms of a treaty. On Long Island, it was agreed, everything east of Oyster Bay—which included three-quarters of the island—went to the English, thus reserving to the Dutch only the towns

closest to New Amsterdam. And on the mainland the two national jurisdictions were separated by a line drawn north from Long Island Sound,
ten miles east of the Hudson River.

Many of the theoretical Dutch claims were lost, but little of the territory they had actually peopled and continued to control. The Long Island
villages closest to Manhattan remained legally Dutch, and so too was the
wide land corridor east of the Hudson. So long as these boundaries were
respected the Dutch could continue to tap into the richest sources of furs,
and their core settlement at New Amsterdam would be safely ringed with
villages dominated by their own people.[7]

But they were not safe from English encroachments. English settlers continued to populate Long Island, mingling with the Dutch even
in the towns closest to Manhattan and clamoring for proper rights and
privileges. Such rights as they had been granted could be and often
were overridden by Stuyvesant's commands. Community autonomy, as
it was known in New England, seemed entirely missing, and the governed had no representation in the government that ruled and taxed
them. Grievances mounted. Squabbles between and within the villages
multiplied, violence threatened, and the sense prevailed, among both
the Dutch and English villagers, that since their rights and properties
were not protected, the government that bound them lacked legitimacy.
When rumors circulated that Stuyvesant was conspiring with the Indians to attack the English on Long Island, John Underhill, the Indian
fighter, rose in arms. Exhilarated by the apparent crisis, he hoisted the
flag of Commonwealth England at Flushing and circulated a thirteen part
"Vindication," denouncing Stuyvesant's taxes "contrary to the privileges
of free men," his violation of liberty of conscience, his imprisonments
without trial "after the manner of a Popish inquisition," his failure to
take revenge on the murderous Indians, his "barbarous cruelty" in private encounters, and his arbitrary appointments of officers. Against this
"tyrannical yoke," Underhill declared all "honest hearts" must rise and
submit to the parliament of England.

While the countryside did not rise to defy Dutch rule, the simmering resentments, Dutch and English, were inflamed by Underhill's hero-
ics, and within six months, in December 1653, a formal convention of
aggrieved representatives—nineteen delegates from eight of the Dutch
and English villages—met in New Amsterdam to formalize their grievances in a Remonstrance addressed to the West India Company. Reminis-

cent of Van der Donck's Remonstrance of 1649, it pledged the delegates' loyalty to the company and the States General but declared that they, as provincial subjects, lacked the privileges accorded all people in the Netherlands. Repeating Underhill's charges, they stressed their fears of arbitrary government. After denouncing Stuyvesant's authoritarian regime—his dictatorial legislation "without the approbation of the country" and his denial of the rights due "every freeborn man"—they went further, to probe the fundamental principles at issue. Against Stuyvesant's insistence on divine right, on the indivisibility of established sovereignty, and on liberties merely as granted benefactions, the delegates proclaimed the primordial rights that "the laws of nature give to all men." Against Stuyvesant's fear of popular sovereignty (where every voter would choose of his own: thieves would choose thieves, smugglers smugglers) the delegates declared the natural right of all people to participate in government and to challenge officials' misuse of their powers.[8]

In the end the protest was limited. The signers did not reject the legitimacy of the Dutch government, only the misguided actions of its agents. Passions cooled as Stuyvesant held fast and as the war's end in 1654 secured Dutch claims to the colony. But the resentments did not fade. They lay simmering just below the surface, liable to flare up whenever the thin film of civic order was suddenly torn.

2

Elsewhere in the colony the forces of disorder, caused in part by the presence and ambitions of the English, could not be contained. English traders, mariners, soldiers, and land speculators appeared in all the Dutch settlements—not only in New Amsterdam and the Dutch villages on Long Island but also in the scattered farms of Rensselaerswyck 150 miles north of Manhattan, and above all in the booming but ramshackle fur-trading center, Fort Orange, at the river's edge in the midst of Van Rensselaer's property.

That northern focus for the lucrative fur trade, settled first by Walloons, then maintained by a small cadre of soldiers, and finally resettled as a trading emporium, had grown erratically over the years. Van Rensselaer, whose patroonship surrounded the fort, managed to direct some of the flow of furs from the north to his own agents, but when in 1639 the fur trade was thrown open, the strategically located fort became the key

Dutch trading station. By 1650 the settlement on the riverside floodplain, spilling out beyond the fort's dilapidated palisades, had become a tumultuous bazaar, attracting Indian fur trappers, Dutch settlers, English, French, German, and Scandinavian traders, unemployed artisans, discharged soldiers, and former tenants seeking quicker returns than farming could bring. To exert some control over this disorderly community, Stuyvesant, in 1652, designated Fort Orange an official market town independent of Van Rensselaer's jurisdiction and renamed it Beverwyck. Its government, courts, and officials were quickly organized. Rules for residency—burgher rights—and codes of law were established; townsmen patented and developed house lots; and marketing regulations were laid down.

But while such rules and agencies did create a civil society, they could not control the constant disarray. Through the frenetic trading season—officially May 1 to November 1 but concentrated in the summer months—the small riverside town was overwhelmed by Indians and strangers who came and went. They arrived

> to trade, sell seawan [wampum], bake, gamble at auctions, deliver merchandise, buy property, sue residents and other strangers for debt. The poor and the hopeful came. Youths arrived, contracting for house rental on May 1 and otherwise leaving no record of their existence. . . .Wealthy men arrived: the wholesale merchants of New Amsterdam and Holland, Hartford and Boston. . . . Outlivers [moved] back within the palisades. . . . All added to the continual and unpredictable movement of people through the town gates. Natives arrived in the hundreds. They added to the elderly natives already camped nearby, fishing the Hudson with dragnets.[9]

The most striking aspect of the long, chaotic trading season was the intimate mingling of natives and Europeans. Ordinary constraints were abandoned when several hundred Indians—four hundred settled in the area in 1659—some with wives and children, docked as many as 190 canoes along the town's river bank. To shelter these suppliers, some traders built sheds on their own property, some threw together barracks; others simply took the Indians into their homes, bedding them down where space permitted, even if, as one host wrote, one's guests were "a party of drunken savages."

The Indians were invaluable as providers of furs and skins, carrying in to Beverwyck's public auctions and private sales as many as fifty thousand beaver pelts in a single season; but they were brutally exploited. "Trading became a frenzy," as payment was demanded within twenty-four hours. In wild auctions, "a house, a consignment of goods, a yacht, a canoe," was pledged for incoming furs; a house, entire estates were mortgaged for cash to buy the Indians' wares.

Civility vanished. Drunken women roamed the streets, "strangers cavorted in all night brawls." The Indians were commonly victims of violence. Often swindled, frequently beaten and robbed, they found little relief in an alien and insensitive legal system that could not control its own people. Among the fur traders' more vicious practices was the dispatch of "factors" to intercept the Indians in the woods before they got to the competitive markets, entice them with promises of special benefits, then fleece them upon their delivery of the furs.

> They ambushed natives, bribed them to trade or, more frequently, robbed them. They molested them by "kicking, beating, and assaulting them" at will. Some they "beat severely with fists . . . and [drove] out of the woods." Breaking up the bargaining of a trader with a native, "ten or twelve of them [would] surround an Indian and drag him along, saying 'Come with me, so and so has no goods.'" At hidden trading places, natives robbed traders, while Dutch brokers violently drove natives "hither and thither" telling them lies about the merchants they "represented." . . . They enacted in the woods a lawlessness towards natives and each other that the magistrates were barely managing to control within the palisades.

For at least half the year Beverwyck was no place for the uniform enforcement of the law. "Tensions inherent in a densely configured village," the town's historian writes, "that contained a highly competitive, heterogeneous society" led to an atmosphere of radical antiauthoritarianism. The magistrates who attempted to restrain, fine, or tax the frantic fur traders were publicly vilified, denounced as "bloodhounds, dogs, villains, scoundrels, and thieves." One former magistrate heavily invested in the fur trade declared that, ordinance or no ordinance, he intended to go into the woods to beat out his competitors, and he "didn't give a damn for the magistrates," who were, he said, "a lot of perjurers." As for the ordinance, he "wiped his ass" on it.[10]

But in their own way, the Indians, however exploited and brutalized, profited too—by acquiring, in exchange for furs they did not need, clothes, household goods, weapons they greatly valued, and objects whose physical attraction and symbolic meaning escaped the awareness of Europeans.

It was this flow of furs, mainly beaver—drawn each year from hundreds of rivers, creeks, and ponds in the Iroquois and Huron lands and funneled by native intermediaries through Beverwyck to Manhattan, then to merchants' wharves in Holland, and from there to ultimate markets in England, Europe, even Russia—that largely sustained Beverwyck's, and much of the colony's, economy. Beverwyck's economy was in fact varied: the townsmen in off season produced beer, timber, tobacco, bricks, tiles, and agricultural products. But it was the fur trade that mattered most, a trade that, until its decline in the 1650s, produced large profits. The shipments through Beverwyck in the single year 1657 were valued at 327,520 guilders (approximately £34,000 sterling). A moderately successful trader in a single season could earn twelve times the annual wages of a local farmhand. But while small-time traders and speculators scrambled for a piece of the trade, the colony's majority of ordinary farmers, artisans, and laborers continued to work in traditional ways, and their numbers were in no way augmented by the success of the fur trade.[11]

3

There were, however, forces at work that were beginning to attract immigrants in larger numbers than heretofore and that would almost double the colony's population before England conquered it and transformed it into New York.

First was the slow but steady spread of land available for cultivation and the growing need for artisans and service workers in the colony's expanding port town.

In 1655—a generation after the first settlers had arrived—only a quarter of New Netherland's estimated population of 3,455 lived in New Amsterdam, and not all of them in or around the fort. In its larger dimensions, the settlements on Manhattan stretched well beyond the original fort and walled enclosure, into agricultural land newly opened for cultivation. The fertile area north of the town had become Haarlem, whose inhabitants, distributed among ten farms, were a veritable cross-section of northern Europe: French, Dutch, Walloon, Danish, Swedish, and German families had settled there. Staten Island, whose ownership had changed hands repeatedly since De Vries's patroonship had failed, had farms with about ninety inhabitants. On the New Jersey side of the Hudson there were ten farms at Bergen, the site of the mass slaughter of the Indians in Kieft's War. On Long Island, the colony's Dutch and English villages claimed approximately thirteen hundred inhabitants, some of whom were still involved in sectarian turmoils. On the upper Hudson—Rensselaerswyck, Beverwyck, and a few newly founded and still isolated farms at Wiltwyck (Esopus), Katskil, and Klaverack—there were perhaps six hundred inhabitants, mainly English and Dutch but including many other Europeans and transient Indians. And some of the colony's Dutch population had scattered to the south, to try their fortunes in the strange Swedish-Dutch-Finnish settlements along the Delaware River.[12]

While the extent of farmland grew in response to the slow increase in population, events thousands of miles from the shores of Manhattan intensified that expansion and added to the complexity of the population.

The overthrow of New Holland in Brazil in 1654, which weakened the West India Company's solvency and financial prospects, forced the directors to cast about for new initiatives in the western colonies, and it set in motion the displacement of a significant part of the Dutch-Brazilian population. Refugees from New Holland scattered to the other Dutch colonies in America—to Paramaribo in Surinam and other encampments on the Wild Coast; to St. Eustatius and Curaçao in the Caribbean; and to New Netherland. How many of the refugees ended up on Manhattan Island is not known, but notable among them—notorious, as it proved—was a very small party of Jews: twenty-three in all—four married couples, two widows, and thirteen children.[13]

Jews and crypto-Jews (conversos, New Christians, Marranos), most of them descendants of Sephardic refugees from Spain and Portugal, had long been tolerated in the Netherlands, and as tradesmen and merchants with wide international contacts, they had become valuable contributors to the Netherlands' prosperity. From Amsterdam, their main center, they had migrated, in small numbers, to the Dutch colonies in the western hemisphere. In the 1630s they had established in Recife, the capital of New Holland, their most substantial American community. It was therefore a sizable group of Dutch-Brazilian Jews—probably more than six hundred—who fled from the new Portuguese regime. Most went back to the Netherlands, some went to France (Nantes), some to the West Indies, and one shipload ended up in New Amsterdam.

It had taken that small contingent six months to reach their destination, and in that long voyage they had been reduced to abject poverty. They had gone first to French Martinique, then to Spanish Jamaica, where they were interned until released by pressure from the Dutch government; and then, together with a group of Christian refugees, they had sailed to Cuba. From there, for an exorbitant price, they had finally been taken to New Amsterdam. Arriving penniless, they sought help from two Jews who had just preceded them, and when it was found that they could not help, the refugees threw themselves on the charity of the town.[14]

There was little enough of it, either financial or social. Stuyvesant, devoted to the strict Calvinist principles of his heritage, was tolerant of the colony's ethnic diversity but utterly intolerant of religious diversity. When the Jews arrived he was in the midst of a battle with the numerous Lutherans in the colony who had petitioned to be allowed to worship publicly according to their own principles and practices. Backed by the colony's co-pastors, Dominies Johannes Megapolënsis and Samuel Drisius, Stuyvesant, torn by having to choose between offending every minority group by refusing the Lutherans' petition and violating his oath of office by accepting it, had passed the problem on to the Amsterdam directors. For them the problem was at least as difficult as it was for Stuyvesant, and so they refused to decide anything. They told Stuyvesant in the future to deflect any such petitions before they could become public controversies, and for the sake of population recruitment to allow Lutherans the right to worship as they pleased, *privately*, in their own dwellings. It was a compromise the Reformed clerics on both sides of the Atlantic continued to contest.[15]

The Lutherans, however, were at least Christians, and the differences between them and the Dutch Calvinists could be conceived of as technicalities of theology, catechism, liturgy, and religious practice. There was nothing technical about the differences with the Jews. They were, Stuyvesant wrote his superiors in Amsterdam, "a deceitful race," blasphemers who would infect the entire colony with their elemental corruption. He appealed to the West India Company for permission to expel them forthwith. The directors replied that they too deplored the Jews' "abominable religion," but they were acutely aware of the contributions Jewish merchants had made to the company's capital and were hopeful that they would do more in the future. In addition, they were subject to powerful lobbying by the most influential figures in the Dutch-Jewish community, who included in their arguments the attractive point that the refugees were likely to contribute to the growth of the colony's population. Stuyvesant's request was rejected, and he was ordered not only to receive the Jews on the tolerant terms they enjoyed in Holland but to encourage them and their co-religionists to settle permanently in the colony.

Dominie Megapolënsis then added his voice in support of Stuyvesant's appeal. The Jews, upon their arrival, he wrote to the church authorities in Amsterdam, had called on him "weeping and bemoaning their misery," but like all their brethren they were "godless rascals," and as worshippers of "unrighteous Mammon" they were notoriously rapacious. No doubt they would soon be joined by other Jews from Holland, who together would drain away the colony's good Christian property and corrupt its spiritual health. The colony had trouble enough, he pointed out, with "Papists, Mennonites, and Lutherans among the Dutch; also many Puritans or Independents and many atheists and various other servants of Baal among the English under this government, who conceal themselves under the name of Christians; it would create a still greater confusion if the obstinate and immovable Jews came to settle here." The Classis of Amsterdam was sympathetic to this appeal, but they could not move the West India Company's pragmatically tolerant position. The infuriated director and the fearful dominie were told to be content with orders to deny the Jews the right to practice their religion publicly, to confine them to separate living quarters, and to prevent them from building their own house of worship.

But Stuyvesant was not so easily defeated. Despite the company's decision, for two years he tried everything he could think of to discourage the Jews from remaining. First he forbade them to trade with the Indians; then he refused to allow them to buy land; and then he denied them the right to hold public office, to serve in the militia, and to engage in retail trade. In 1656 he finally received a flat command to stop the harassment and protect the Jews' right to enjoy the limited liberties they had in Holland.

In fact the colony's toleration did not produce the flood of new Jewish settlers that Stuyvesant and Megapolensis feared. In 1655 five affluent
Sephardic Jewish merchants from Amsterdam did arrive, and a few more
families followed. But the Jewish community in the Dutch period never
exceeded fifty souls, and many of them moved away in the 1660s. A very
small residual group remained, however, to form the basis of a larger Jewish community in later years, and to add a notable complex element to the
colony's population. For small as it was in the 1650s, the Jewish population in New Netherland included people of German, Italian, Spanish,
Portuguese, and Dutch origins.[16]

The Jews were troubling and threatening, according to the guardians
of the Dutch Reformed Church, but the dangers they posed were spiritual, not political. They were private people who kept to themselves and
avoided public controversies. More dangerous in terms of social upheavals were the English Quakers, who first appeared on the scene in 1657.
Trouble started immediately. The Quaker shipmaster who brought the
group of Quakers to the colony refused to answer any of the director's
questions and, as a typical sign of disrespect for earthly authorities, kept
"his hat firm on his head as if a goat." He and his party were quickly
sent off to Rhode Island, where, the orthodox *predikant* said, religious
cranks might safely congregate. But several were left behind, led by two
enthusiastic young women. Infused with the Holy Spirit, they fell "into a
frenzy," writhing on the ground, crying out that all must repent, for the
day of judgment was nigh. Bystanders were bewildered and ran about
the streets in confusion. No one knew what was happening. Someone
called "Fire!" The tumult subsided when the women were carried off
to prison, but the problem had scarcely yet emerged. Quakers began
turning up everywhere, especially in the Anglo-Dutch villages on Long
Island: Gravesend, Jamaica, Hempstead, and Flushing. They were relentless, irrepressible, passionate. One of their leaders, Robert Hodgson, was
arrested in an orchard where he was preparing to preach and was confined in a nearby house. When he managed still to harangue the crowd
through an open window, he was dragged off to New Amsterdam. There
he was thrown into a "dungeon full of vermin and so odious for wet and
dirt as he never saw before" and sentenced to a large fine and two years'
hard labor. That stiffened his defiance. When he refused to work he was
beaten with a tarred rope and chained to a wheelbarrow. When he still

preached to anyone within earshot, he was hung from the ceiling by his hands and whipped repeatedly. If Stuyvesant thought this would discourage other radicals, he was wrong. His strategy failed, as did his orders prohibiting all ships from bringing Quakers into the province and fining anyone who harbored them.

In response to these commands came an extraordinary document of passionate defiance from that most "infected" town, Flushing. In a flaming Remonstrance, "certainly the most important piece of theorizing about religious liberty that New Netherland produced," the townsmen declared that it was the glory of Stuyvesant's homeland that it extended "love, peace, and libertie . . . to Jews, Turks, and Egyptians"; that Christ sees God in anyone "whether Presbyterian, Independent, Baptist, or Quaker"; and that no matter what the government's orders were, the people of Flushing would welcome all men who "come in love unto us." For "wee are bounde by the Law to do good unto all men . . . the powers of this world can neither attack us neither excuse us, for if God justify who can condemn?"

Stuyvesant dismissed this fervent defiance as insubordination and promptly arrested the town's magistrates and forced them to recant. But the "infection" could not so easily be cured. For four years Stuyvesant waged a fierce campaign to stamp out all such "abominable heresies," imprisoning offenders when they could be seized, snatching off the Quakers' offending hats when they refused to remove them, and appealing to the West India Company for support.

But that, Stuyvesant discovered, was not forthcoming. The directors refused to take offense at the Quakers' doings. They too hoped the Quakers would go elsewhere, they wrote Stuyvesant, but since these wild people apparently insisted on bearing their testimonies in New Netherland, they could not be dealt with rigorously "without diminishing the population and stopping immigration, which must be favored at a so tender stage of the country's existence." He was therefore told to "shut [his] eyes, at least not force people's consciences but allow every one to have his own belief, as long as he behaves quietly and legally, gives no offence to his neighbors, and does not oppose the government." The city of Amsterdam, they wrote, had always acted in that fashion, and so it "has often had a considerable influx of people." So might New Netherland if the same toleration prevailed there.[17]

At that point New Netherland's persecution of the Quakers, after grim scenes of torment, ceased, and other Christian groups, including the Lutherans, were similarly, though gradually and reluctantly, tolerated.

THE FOUNDING OF the Jewish community was not the only consequence in New Netherland of the Dutch defeat in Brazil. New Holland's prosperity had rested mainly on the profits from sugar production, and that had involved the Dutch in the slave trade, which had grown rapidly—more than thirty-one thousand Africans were carried to New Holland between 1630 and 1651—and their labor had proved to be enormously lucrative. Immediately after the loss of Brazil, the company's directors seem, for a while, to have considered reviving the audit board's old proposal to help populate New Netherland by shipping slaves from Curaçao to the colony in exchange for foodstuffs, holding the blacks for the use of the colony and for resale and distribution throughout the western hemisphere, especially to the tobacco south. How seriously this was ever considered as a matter of official policy is not clear. As it was, the African population in the colony did increase, not systematically as a matter of policy but randomly, haphazardly, and, until the late 1650s, in small numbers.[18]

Slavery itself was nothing new. After the first mention of slaves in 1625 or 1626 and Dominie Michaëlius's denunciation, in 1628, of the Angolan slave woman as "trash," they became numerous enough for the colony to erect some kind of special camp or barracks for them five miles north of Manhattan; later many were housed together in a large building near the fort. By 1639, perhaps as many as one hundred blacks lived in the colony. In the seven years that followed, the names of seventy-seven black men, women, and children were recorded in the church records.[19]

All of these slaves, like their predecessors, had been captured at sea or taken in trade on the islands; many had Portuguese names. Property of the West India Company, they appear as farm laborers, construction and dock workers, and domestics, occasionally as artisans. But their numbers remained small and their presence unremarkable—until after the loss of New Holland. In September 1655 the first fully loaded slave ship arrived—a reeking hulk bearing three hundred Africans direct from the African coast; its cargo was auctioned off on the town's docks. Another three slave ships followed, financed by Spanish-Dutch merchants who contracted to sell off one-third of the cargo in Curaçao for £22 a head (male) before proceeding to New Netherland. Between 1660 and 1664, four hundred slaves were shipped to the colony—230 male, 170 female, almost all of them adults. And while most were sold to buyers from elsewhere, an increasing number, many of them old people, remained behind. New Amsterdam's black population, which may have numbered 150 in 1655, grew to approximately 375 in 1664—75 of them free—and constituted between 20 and 25 percent of the town's population, perhaps 4 percent of the total population of the colony. By then the slave trade, with rules for sales at auction, was so well established that Stuyvesant had blank forms printed for registering the names of all outward-bound slavers and their expected destinations on the West African coast. A 10 percent export tax levied on blacks who were sold to the English guaranteed a small supplementary income for the company.

Thus quickly after the loss of Brazil, slaves, from Africa as well as from the West Indies, became a normal part of the colony's society. Few in number in comparison with the slave populations in the other Dutch Atlantic colonies, they were widely distributed throughout the colony and owned by ordinary people as well as by the leading merchants and landowners; by French, German, English, and Jewish settlers as well as by the Dutch.[20]

But their role in New Netherland's society was entirely different from what it was in the plantation south. They were treated as bondsmen in various degrees of servitude that tended to shift toward freedom. They had legal rights little different from those enjoyed by free whites. They could give testimony in court, against whites as well as blacks, they had the right to trial, they could own movable property and be married in Christian churches, and they were paid for work done in spare time. In general they were "entitled to regular civil and criminal jurisprudence and were treated fairly, and at times with lenience." A number of those who believed they had the right to freedom for long-term faithful service were in fact freed. The company's manumission in 1644 of eleven of its slaves and their wives was recorded as due them for eighteen or nineteen years of service.

"Half-freedom" was common. It was an arrangement in which the slave, but not necessarily his children, was granted full personal liberty (certified by a pass stating the bearer to be free "as other free people") in return for an annual grant to the company and an obligation to provide service when required. This spared the company the expense of maintaining the slaves and their families while providing a reliable workforce that could be summoned at will. Some slaves were "rented out," the profits of their labor shared with their owners. By 1664, when around 10 percent of the colony's population was black, the domestics among them and some of the artisans were beginning to be housed in their owners' homes—in lofts, attics, sheds, cellars, and spare corners of the kitchens. Slaves not being uniquely necessary for the economy, there was no incentive to encourage their increase. In time, as the urban areas became more crowded, children born of slaves would become undesirable. Some Manhattan slave owners would sell their female slaves as soon as it was known that they were pregnant.[21]

As elsewhere in the colonies blacks were assumed to be different and inferior, but at this point there was no conflict between blacks and whites in New Netherland, no fear of slave rebellions or conspiracies, nor hesitation in arming them to help fight the Indians. There was no effort to define the status of slaves legally. The Dutch "left the regulation of slaves entirely to improvisation. Equity held complete sway." In the years when the planters in Virginia and Maryland were groping for ever more comprehensive and intricate legal definitions of slavery and devising ever more detailed means of deepening and perpetuating the slaves' debasement, the Dutch continued to think of slaves as people with some degree of rights, deserving of full or partial emancipation for faithful service, and capable of maintaining respectable and productive lives when freed. Criminal charges against slaves were rare. Only three came before Manhattan's courts before 1664, all for capital offenses. Later, under the English, the situation would change and measures would be taken to systematize the slave trade and codify the confinements of chattel slavery. But it was only in 1684 that New York's first law dealing with slavery was passed, though in a bill directed to the problems of servants, and only in 1703 that New York adopted a comprehensive slave code. In the years of Dutch control there had been a comity, however rough, between the races. "Despite their unequal relationship, masters and slaves had worked together at the same tasks" and lived together "on terms of easy familiarity." And the recurring problem of harboring fugitive slaves suggests an element of doubt as to the morality of slavery itself.[22]

ALMOST SIMULTANEOUSLY with the arrival of the Jews and the increase in the number of slaves came the conclusion of the First Anglo-Dutch War, which had been fought in part over England's effort to exclude the Dutch from the English commercial system. But that effort would never succeed as long as New Netherland remained a wedge in England's North American trading area. The colony therefore suddenly acquired for both the Dutch and the English a geo-economic strategic importance it had not had before. It could now be seen as a drainage valve for furs flowing from contested inland territories and as a trans-shipment and market center for the products of the English colonies north and south. Above all, it might develop into the center of an enhanced coastal and oceanic trade that could break through the barriers of England's navigation laws.

As a result of these emerging possibilities, by 1657 the once-neglected colony became the object of close attention by leading Dutch merchants and politicians. Extravagant promotional pamphlets were suddenly dashed off and published ("the epitome and most noble of all climes, a maritime empire where milk and honey flowed"). The volume of the colony's trade rose sharply; and finally emigration from Europe increased in ways that had hitherto been hoped for in vain.

Approximately four thousand immigrants arrived from abroad between 1657 and 1664. Together with approximately two thousand New Englanders who had moved south into New Netherland, they elevated the colony's total population of Europeans to about nine thousand and further increased the colony's heterogeneity. But the colony's extraordinary diversity had negative implications of which Stuyvesant became increasingly aware. The English and French colonies, he pointed out shrewdly to his superiors in Holland, are

> populated by their own nation and countrymen and consequently bound together more firmly and united, while your honors' colonies in *New-Netherland* are only gradually and slowly peopled by the scrapings of all sorts of nationalities (few excepted), who consequently have the least interest in the welfare and maintenance of the commonwealth.

And the soldiers, drawn in large numbers from the ranks of the veterans of Europe's wars—Germans, Scandinavians, English, and Swiss as well as Dutch—were even less useful as settlers. He had followed his instructions, Stuyvesant reported to the company, to give the idled troops land and goods "to animate them to remain here." But no one, he wrote, "can be kept here against his will . . . the major part of them reply, 'We have

not yet learned any trade nor farming, the sword must earn us our subsistence, if not here, then we must look for our fortunes elsewhere.'"
Some of them did remain, but many, who had enlisted in Holland, were
returning home.[23]

4

Such as it was, New Netherland's population was changing. In a sample
(27 percent) of the new arrivals from Europe, 68 percent arrived as part
of family groups. There were far fewer single men than had immigrated
previously (26 percent vs. 60 percent), and there was a small but significant percentage of single women (6 percent) ("maidens," spinsters, and
widows). Analysis of the composition of the 167 families in the sample
reveals a deeper dimension. Twenty-four percent of the families traveled with four or more children (almost twice the percentage of such
large families in the Netherlands), but 65 percent contained two or fewer
children. The latter were young families, the adults in their early twenties; the former were mature families that included young adult children.
Thus both contained people in their most vigorous years. If the heads
of the larger units are excluded, over 60 percent of all immigrants in the
sample were under twenty-five years of age.

And the colony was beginning to show signs of stability. Of a 71 percent sample of the adult males in New Amsterdam in 1664, almost
44 percent had been in New Netherland for ten years or more, 28 percent having arrived in the 1630s or earlier. Some had been born in the
colony. The sex ratio was favorable enough for the young men to find
brides among the colony's single women; most men were married and
were raising families. And the ethnic diversity was beginning to meld into
a hybrid population. Intermarriage among the European ethnic groups
was becoming common: a quarter of all marriages in the Dutch church in
New Amsterdam through 1665 were exogamous, and the church, though
theologically orthodox, welcomed Germans, Scandinavians, French, and
English to its worship. And while in 1658 there were so many French
speakers—Walloons, Frenchmen, Waldenses—in the colony that official
documents were issued in French as well as in English and Dutch, there
was a growing acceptance by all of Dutch in daily discourse.[24]

New Amsterdam, if not the colony as a whole, was becoming more
civil, more respectable, and more orderly. Though to the invading English

in 1664 the town would seem disheveled, the houses flimsy, the fort a ruin undermined by rooting hogs, and the streets "crooked and unpaved with little decency and no uniformity," there had been growth and rapid improvement. A town map of 1660 shows 354 houses (there had been 120 in 1656) on an orderly pattern of streets within a wall that stretched across the island's tip from the East River to the Hudson. Wooden chimneys had been eliminated, some houses were now made of brick, some roofs were tiled, and some streets were cobbled. There were newly built wharves and warehouses; the sides of the ragged, seeping canal that ran through the center of the town had been reinforced with bracing boards and crossed with small bridges; and the taverns, once dens of brawling drunks, were becoming exchanges for merchants, traders, and shippers.

New Amsterdam had grown into a small, enterprising port town, "firmly entrenched in an Atlantic context," one of many from Río de la Plata to Quebec, a growing hub for commerce from and to Europe through Caribbean and North American circuits, at times by way of the slave ports of Africa. Driving this growth forward were the skills, ambitions, and energy of an emerging merchant elite, dominant in government and politics as well as in trade.[25]

The origins of Manhattan's merchant leadership in the later years of Dutch rule lay partly in the survival of some of the leaders of the colony's early, tumultuous years—among them the leaders of the commonalty who had struggled so bitterly with Kieft and Stuyvesant. Theirs had been familiar names in the early annals: Jacob van Couwenhoven, Oloff Stevensen van Cortlandt, Michiel Jansz., Thomas Hall, Elbert Elbertsz., Govert Loockermans, Hendrick Kip, and Jan Evertsz. Bout. They were described by the directors' factotum, Van Tienhoven, as in origins very ordinary folk (farmhands, tailors, soldiers, cook's mates, petty traders) who owed their advancement, he said, to the company's favor. In fact, their prominence was the result of their own efforts to supply the colony's local markets, to service the coastal trade, to export fur, timber, and local crops in however small quantities, and to slowly acquire land in the colony—town land for immediate use, farm and forest land for later exploitation.

How little the West India Company contributed to the emergence of the Dutch colony's late merchant leadership is clearly indicated in the records of trading vessels dispatched from the Netherlands to New Amsterdam in the fifty-five years of Dutch control. Up to 1653, the year

Manhattan received its municipal charter, an average of just over three ships a year sailed from the home country to the colony, at least a third of which were the property of the West India Company. After 1653 there is a remarkable spike in numbers: the average tripled to about nine vessels per year, but few at the expense of the West India Company. The company hardly played any role in the colony's shipping boom in the 1650s and early 1660s. New Netherland's trade was in the hands of Manhattan's private entrepreneurs, acting most effectively as agents or associates of commercial syndicates in Holland that were driving hard, through the far-flung circuits of Atlantic trade, to reach new markets in the west and overseas sources of goods salable in Europe.

A small group who often counted on kinship ties to advance their prospects at home and abroad, these successful locals were supplemented, in the last two decades, by affluent newcomers who proved to be formidable competitors and associates. Cornelis Steenwyck was the most notable. Arriving in 1651 from Haarlem at age twenty-six, he rose rapidly in the town's newly formalizing government. He became a *schepen* (judicial magistrate and legal functionary) by 1658 and burgomaster of New Amsterdam in 1664. Like many of the leading merchants, he was flexible in his allegiance within the Protestant world and managed the transition to English rule easily, accepting the general offer of denizen rights and the promise of public office in New York and pledging loyalty to the English Crown.[26]

Behind Steenwyck's success lay a close and long association with the Van Hoornbeeck family of Amsterdam. The head of the firm, Gillis van Hoornbeeck, was "a shipowner, financier, freighter, insurance broker, and retail fur distributor" whose patronage was likely to guarantee a client's success. So too the Verbrugge Company—Gillis and his son Seth—whose sprawling trade before 1664 included twenty-seven voyages to New Netherland and fourteen to Virginia. Their kinsman Johannes Verbrugge served as their agent in the colony, as did Govert Loockermans, Van Cortlandt's brother-in-law, who married Gillis's widowed niece, a relation of the Couwenhovens. The successful Amsterdam firm of Dirck and Abel de Wolff, coinvestors with the Van Hoornbeecks, had especially effective agents in the colony. Dirck's daughter Geertruyd married Gerrit Jansz Cuyper, a Manhattanite well established in the town's trade. She joined him in managing the De Wolffs' interests in the export of the colony's furs, timber, and tobacco, in their lucra-

CORNELIS STEENWYCK

Adroit and well-connected, Steenwyck was one of the
most successful merchants and office-holders in the
late years of New Netherland, and prospered as well
under the English.

tive carrying trade, and in the distribution of manufactured goods in the
colonies. Cuyper served also as an occasional agent for the Verbrugges
and, like Steenwyck, easily managed the transition to English rule. Having become a free denizen of New York he was able to maintain the De
Wolffs' American business interests after 1664 and passed on his agency
to his son Jan de Wolff Cuyper.

The Van Rensselaers' interests in the colony also continued into the
second generation. On-site responsibility for the patroonship and the
family's Atlantic trade fell first to Kiliaen's eldest son Johannes, who had
little interest in the colony, then more effectively to a younger son, Jan
Baptiste, who arrived in the colony the same year as Steenwyck, 1651. By
1664 he was well established in the merchant leadership, and when the

English took over, he managed not only to continue the family's shipping ventures in New York but gained confirmation of the title to the family's patroonship.[27]

In 1653, two years after the arrival of Steenwyck and Jan Baptiste van Rensselaer, a young carpenter from Friesland named Vrydrich Flypsen appeared in Manhattan and began his meteoric rise as Frederick Philipse. With good connections at home, he turned to coastal trade, prospered, and then rose into prominence by his marriage to an extraordinary woman, Margaret Hardenbroeck. Probably the shrewdest, certainly the most successful, of the 134 women registered for trade in New Amsterdam, she arrived in 1659 as the twenty-two-year-old agent for her little-known Amsterdam cousin Wolter Valck. Successful as an independent trader as well as an agent, within a year she married one of the town's great burghers, Pieter de Vries. Enriched by his property when he died in 1661, she then married the fiercely ambitious Philipse. Shrewdly, she kept her own property for herself, while forming a partnership in trade with her husband. In short order their joint contacts spread from Hudson's Bay to the Caribbean and from Amsterdam to Carolina, and they managed also to profit by manipulating the colony's wampum money supply. In 1674 Philipse was said to be the richest man in New York, the owner with his wife of some 150,000 acres in New York alone. When Margaret's daughter married the eldest son of the venerable Oloff Stevensen van Cortlandt, the former young commercial agent and the former Friesland carpenter became close kin not only to the Van Cortlandts but to the Loockermanses and the Van Rensselaers as well.[28]

For some, if properly connected, New Netherland in the late Dutch period was a wide-open world in which ambitious young men could

New Amsterdam, c. 1656: the Visscher View, showing the most important buildings, from the gristmill on the left (C) past the jail (E) and the church (B) to the town inn on the right (K)

Dutch trading couple at the shoreline, mid-seventeenth century

quickly rise into the old Dutch patriciate. So the German Jacob Leisler
was only twenty in 1660 when he arrived in Manhattan, but his extensive
network of family connections quickly overcame the disabilities of youth
and ethnicity. His father, Jacob Victorian Leisler, had been a passionately orthodox Calvinist preacher who had moved from the Palatinate to
Frankfurt, where he had developed a complex of associations that spread
"all over Europe and the Atlantic world." As a "fund raising wizard" for
his church, he sought out influential co-religionists and financial benefactors in London, Hamburg, Emden, Amsterdam, Nuremberg, and
Basel, and as a high-level political mediator he was in touch with some
of Europe's chief diplomats in the negotiations of 1648. His son Jacob
moved to Amsterdam where, through some contact among the family's
"multi-layered" connections, he met and worked for Cornelis Melyn,
the notorious antagonist of Kieft and Stuyvesant and claimant to land
on Staten Island, who probably influenced his decision to seek his fortune in New Netherland. There Leisler quickly settled in. He married
promptly—a prominent merchant's widow several years his senior, stepdaughter of the ubiquitous Govert Loockermans, whose entire fortune

Leisler would inherit—and with start-up capital from his father's wealthy friends and perhaps his brothers in Europe, he turned to trade. Advised by that preeminent German entrepreneur Augustine Herrman, and perhaps also by the Gabrys, and drawing on family connections, he quickly entered the Rhine trade to Basel by shipping tobacco to his brother there for distribution to France and Italy. His dealings with the Chesapeake merchants broadened, and within a few years he managed "to combine his trade across [the] Dutch-English colonial border with transatlantic commerce." Eminent in his thirties (in 1676 only Steenwyck and Philipse were wealthier than he), if he had not become embroiled as a passionate anti-Catholic in the religio-political struggles of the late 1680s, which in the end would cost him his life, Leisler would be known only as one among a cohort of newcomers to the merchant leadership of the late Dutch years, better connected and more successful than most, and more deeply involved in religion and politics.[29]

Politics, for the merchant oligarchy, was unavoidable. If their interests were to be protected they needed control of the government, and that they held in tight rein through all these years. The high public offices—*schepens* and burgomasters—lay entirely in the hands of the great burghers—those who had "access to overseas capital, . . . [and] direct relationships with Amsterdam merchants as factors or family members." The small burghers—shopkeepers, craftsmen, petty traders—held lesser, local positions, well below the level of *schepens*. Power was concentrated. Between 1653 and 1665 only six individuals served as burgomaster. Oloff Stevensen van Cortlandt held the post for seven terms; three others served for five terms each. Twenty-four men served as *schepen*, but there was no even distribution: a Van Couwenhoven served for six terms, a Verbrugge also for six terms, a Gabry for four, while eleven men served only for one or two terms. All twenty-six of these major officeholders, burgomasters or *schepens*, knew at least something of the law as it existed and was enforced in Holland, attempted to devise rules consistent with it, and sought to maintain order and advance prosperity in what appeared to be an increasingly civil society.[30]

5

Thus the English, when they arrived in 1664, were faced with a tightly interrelated phalanx of mainly Dutch merchants in charge of the colony's trade and politics. Their increasingly diversified enterprises, capitalized from home, were spread out across the Atlantic, contributing to Holland's distinctive commerce in the West, so different from that in the East. In the Atlantic area Holland's trade was open, permeable, easily adjusted to changing circumstances, capable of seizing new opportunities—and in its totality "more important for the Dutch economy than commerce with Asia."[31] And the English knew too that New Netherland's merchants were sophisticated provincials, well aware of the style of European civility—in governance, in housing, furnishing, dress, and manners—which they increasingly sought to acquire.

But behind them, as they faced east, lay a different world which the Dutch feared but which they could neither control nor ignore. For all their skillful management and growing worldliness, there was no deepening sense of security. Their lives, like those of the other European colonists, were half genteel and half barbarous. The fear of bloody struggles with the Indians who ringed the settlements and mingled in them from time to time remained pervasive and was fed by violence that seemed to have no rational bounds.

There had been a "treaty" but no settlement with the Indians after Kieft's ferocious battles with the tribes on the lower Hudson, some of which lost over 50 percent of their population. The grievances that had fueled the atrocities of those years had not been redressed. The Europeans continued to expand their settlements into Indian lands and to fence in their own fields while allowing their animals to forage in the Indians' farmlands. The Indians continued to kill the roaming livestock as just retribution for damages done and to seek vengeance for slights and injuries, some of which the Europeans were not aware of having inflicted.

Nor had the Dutch come closer to an understanding of the Indians' world, their culture, or even their languages. While Van der Donck and De Vries wrote sympathetic accounts of the Indians, the more influential Dominie Megapolensis, active until his death in 1670, voiced the common Dutch view of the natives in his *Short Account of the Mohawk Indians* (1644). They are barbarous and stupid people, he wrote, echoing his predecessor Michaëlius, "very slovenly and dirty . . . and look like hogs," given to lasciviousness ("the women are exceedingly addicted to whoring") and to cohabitation with the devil; they eat like animals ("the blood runs along their mouths"), they exchange wives and bash them about, and they converse in languages no outsiders, even experienced traders, can possibly understand.

> One tells me a word in the infinitive mood, another in the indicative; one in the first, another in the second person; one in the present, another in the preterit. So I stand oftentimes and look, but do not know how to put it down. And as they have declensions and conjugations also, and have their augments like the Greeks, I am like one distracted, and frequently cannot tell what to do, and there is no one to set me right.

Utterly baffled, as Michaëlius had been, in his effort to learn the Indians' language, he half-believed the suggestion of the company's commissary that the reason no one could understand them was because, to fend off outsiders, by common consent they completely changed their language every two or three years.

But beyond everything else, Megapolënsis found, they were cruel. Painting their faces "red, blue, etc., and then they look like the devil himself," they bite off the fingernails of their captives, cut off their limbs, force them to sing and dance, roast them "dead before a slow fire for some days, and then eat them up. The common people eat the arms, buttocks, and trunk, but the chiefs eat the head and heart." He could not deny that the neighboring Mohawks were in fact friendly with the Dutch settlers, walking peacefully with them in the woods, sometimes sleeping in their houses. But in general, he was convinced, the Indians were capricious, given to barbarous behavior, and a constant threat to the colony's stability, even its survival.[32]

In this tense situation, in which both peoples feared for their lives and felt driven to destroy the force that threatened them—a situation in which the natives refused submission and continued to steal animals and kill exposed settlers while suffering the effects of strange diseases and the loss of their physical and cultural independence—an isolated incident could touch off a major explosion. It happened in 1655 when Stuyvesant, in the midst of his efforts to deal with religious diversity, population recruitment, political opposition, and Anglo-Dutch relations, took his soldiers south to the Delaware River to come to terms with the Swedish settlements there. In his absence, on September 15, several hundred Indians drawn from four of the northern river tribes, on their way to fight rival tribes on eastern Long Island, swarmed through the poorly guarded New Amsterdam searching for their enemies and striking terror in the town's population.[33] Driven off by a makeshift burgher militia, they withdrew to the river shore and were preparing to leave when they found that a native woman had been killed while stealing peaches. The Indians shot the alleged murderer, and the violence escalated. A vengeful crowd led by Van Tienhoven killed several natives, and in response the Indians retreated to Staten Island and the Jersey shore and there carried out a massive slaughter. At least fifty colonists were killed outright, one hundred were taken captive, and the property of at least two hundred others was completely destroyed. The surviving population fled into New Amsterdam's fort, where Stuyvesant found them on his return.

Holding off a major reprisal for want of sufficient troops, the director began negotiations to regain the captives. He appealed to the West India Company for help, three to four thousand fully armed troops, if possible; limited all visits of natives to the Dutch settlements; demanded consolidation of the scattered homesteads; and mandated the building of new blockhouses. In the course of several months, largely in exchange for powder and shot, most of the captives were recovered, and treaties were approved that set out new terms of the relationship between the races. In all of this, except for the troop request, the company concurred, agreeing that Van Tienhoven must be dismissed from his post and his influence in the colony eliminated. For, the company wrote, "with [his] clouded brains filled with liquor, he was a prime cause of this dreadful massacre." Van Tienhoven's and Stuyvesant's enemies in the commonalty heartily agreed. They had said far worse things about Van Tienhoven as far back as 1649, when they had denounced him as a clever man when sober but most of the time he was not, and for the most part he was "shrewd, false, deceitful, and given to lying; promising everyone, and when it comes to perform, at home to no one." Shamelessly lecherous, they had said, "he has run about like an Indian, with little covering and a patch before him, through lust for the prostitutes to whom he has ever been excessively addicted and with whom he has had so much intercourse that no punishment nor menaces of the Director can drive him from them." Until, they had said, Van Tienhoven, "a villain, a murderer, and a traitor" as well as a debauched satyr, was gotten rid of, "there will not be any peace with the Indians."

Whether, as alleged, Van Tienhoven had touched off the massacre of

1655 by attacking the Indians as they withdrew from New Amsterdam is not clear, though eliminating him from the scene probably contributed to the settlement of 1656. But there was no secure conclusion, only a temporary truce between parties that lacked the force, though not the desire, to destroy each other. Conflict would inevitably recur.[34]

The company recognized this and urged Stuyvesant to wage an aggressive war, but not with professional soldiers. The people, they wrote, should defend themselves by forming rural militias—an idea that Stuyvesant immediately rejected. Should burghers, farmers, and traders attack the enemy in open fields? Would the burghers of Amsterdam or Leiden do this? If the company directors had experienced the "losses, sudden attacks, unexpected murders, manslaughters, [and] different incendiary fires" that the colonists did, day after day, they would see the weakness of a local militia and favor a significant force of professional soldiers—"hammerours" who could deal properly with such enemies.

Urged not only by the company but also by the frightened settlers in the river towns to wage an aggressive war on the natives, Stuyvesant convened his Council two months after the September massacre and demanded written replies to his question of whether such a war, which he clearly opposed, could be justified according to the principles of a just war. If because of the natives' depredations an all-out war could be justified, was this the time to launch it? If so, could such a war be won? The Indians were not initially at fault, he said. "Hot-headed" settlers had touched off the violence. Some disagreed; many favored war, if not then, then later.

The immediate pressure eased, and the Dutch continued what has been called their "feline mix of cooperation, hostility, and indecisiveness." But in May 1658 the tension broke again, and this time decisively, when, at Esopus (later Wiltwyck, still later Kingston), a new farming village in the woods eighty-three miles north of New Amsterdam, a drunken Indian murdered one of the isolated Dutch farmers and burned down another's house. The settlers, fearing a wave of destruction, demanded that Stuyvesant launch a preemptive strike and wipe out the surrounding tribes. He refused and instead ordered the settlers to consolidate their scattered settlements and called a conference with the Indians. There Stuyvesant condemned them for the murder and damages and demanded the surrender of the murderer and repayment for the colonists' losses, but he assured the Esopus Indian leaders that he meant them no harm.

In reply the Indian spokesmen blamed the Dutch for selling them liquor, which, they said, lay behind all the troubles. Their young warriors could not be controlled when mad with drink and spoiling for a fight. There followed one of those strange personal challenges, reminiscent of John Smith's proposal to Opechancanough fifty years earlier, that they fight personally, hand to hand, alone, naked, on an island, to determine who should be "lord and master over all our men." If, Stuyvesant said, any of the young Indians present were really so passionate to fight, let them come forward: "I would match man with man, or twenty against thirty, yes even forty." Now was the time to fight, and with soldiers, not with helpless farmers and their families; that, he said, "was not well done," and if continued (again reminiscent of Smith's bravado), he would be compelled to lay hands on anyone and everyone in the offending tribes, "old and young, women and children . . . without regard to person." When the Indians refused the challenge and fell back into the countryside, the settlers drew together and began building a new, strongly fortified village, while Stuyvesant tried to convince the Indians to sell all the land around Esopus.[35]

A year later the sale had still not been consummated, and violence exploded again when a vigilante group from Esopus fired into a group of drunken Indian farmworkers, killing one, capturing another, and beating the rest. In return, the next day a party of thirteen settlers was ambushed; all were either killed or carried off into captivity. Fears and demands for reprisals rose on both sides. An Indian force said to number five hundred or more warriors assembled, surrounded the village, razed everything around it, killed all the exposed livestock, and locked the terrified community in a tight siege. The villagers held out until relieved, twenty-three days later, by Stuyvesant, who arrived with a ragtag army of 150 Dutchmen, Englishmen, and Long Island Indians. Complex negotiations for the conclusion of this first Esopus war came and went in the months that followed, interrupted from time to time by small-scale skirmishes. Undermanned, Stuyvesant appealed to the West India Company for help but received only a small amount of ammunition and a few soldiers, together with a good deal of advice, most of it belligerent. The issue was clear, Stuyvesant was told. When a proper occasion arose, he was to "fall upon them tooth and nail" and take revenge "on this barbarous Esopus tribe."

In fact, Stuyvesant was already planning ahead for a war with "all imaginable means." No one knew where the next attack would come, and so the whole colony became an armed camp. Raiding parties, reinforced by troops from New Amsterdam, spread out from Esopus into the near lands, killing the few Indians they could quickly lay hands on and taking eleven prisoners, who were sent off to Curaçao as slaves. Faced with the growing mobilization of Stuyvesant's army, the Esopus tribe relented and promised, in exchange for the return of their enslaved people, to sell their lands around the village, to trade in the future without arms, and to confine their drinking to areas far from the Dutch.

But the enslaved captives were not returned from Curaçao, despite the Indians' entreaties, and two years later they took their revenge. In June 1663—in a small-scale reenactment of the Virginia massacre of 1622— a large force of warriors entered the newly fortified village of Esopus ostensibly to trade, spread out among the houses, and suddenly turned on the villagers, butchered at least twenty men, captured forty-five women and children, burned the buildings to the ground, and left behind only a small group of survivors. It was a ghastly scene: "burnt and slaughtered bodies," the local dominie, Hermanus Blom, reported, "together with those wounded by bullets and axes. The last agonies and the moans and lamentations of many were dreadful to hear." The carnage, he reported, was "most frightful to behold." One immolated woman lay "with her child at her side, as if she were just delivered . . . and one corpse with her fruit still in her womb." Surely, he told his devastated congregation, the "dead bodies [lying] here and there like dung heaps on the field, and burnt and roasted corpses like sheaves behind the mower"—all this was the punishment of God, "for we have sinned against Him." In the end, however, he was certain that they would be protected by God's mighty arm; "he shall be a wall of fire around us, and require and avenge this blood on the heads of these murderous heathens."[36]

Blood vengeance was in the air, and it was left to Stuyvesant to organize it. Once again he gathered a force of Dutch, English, and Indian fighters, offering them free plunder for their services, "all the savages whom they could capture," a remission of tithes, and compensation for injuries. His force, supplemented by slaves, eventually numbered about two hundred. They set out from Esopus in a major campaign, trekking through mountainous, rocky, and swampy terrain in search of the main body of Esopus warriors. When that quarry proved elusive, they settled for destroying all the tribe's crops at their abandoned main center and burning their fortifications and huts to the ground. After a series of uncoordinated skirmishes and fruitless negotiations for the return of the captured Dutch women and children, the army finally surprised the main force of the Esopus Indians near their fort forty miles southwest of the village. Thirty or more Indians were killed or captured, twenty-three Dutch captives were freed, all the Indians' dwellings were razed, and all the goods and stores the Europeans could carry were carted off. A return party finished the job a month later. A final though still incomplete exchange of prisoners followed, ending the two Esopus wars.

But there was no end. In 1664, when the English conquered New Netherland, scattered episodes of violence still seared the margins of this small, multi-ethnic, multi-confessional, multi-linguistic colony. Some of these small-scale but bloody encounters were the work of ruthless, avaricious, fearful, or sadistic Europeans; some were the work of drunken, enraged, or vengeful Indians. Both heard rumors that the other would massacre them. Yet the two peoples continued to live close to each other; in many places they lived among each other. Natives and Dutch farmers could get drunk together, and they could be "thieves and tricksters to each other." Indian children romped on Dutch farms, and at times "beliefs and feelings," the most perceptive scholar of Dutch race relations writes, "seemed to be undergoing exchange; there were unintentional borrowings." But they had no common life. Miscegenation was rare. "Be careful," Van Rensselaer had written his agent Van Curler, "not to mix with the heathen or savage women, for such things are a great abomination to the Lord God and kill the souls of the Christians when they debauch themselves with them." And he suggested that an ordinance be passed imposing severe fines and punishment for those who had intercourse with native women.

So there were no inter-racial marriages, and the Indians mocked what they saw of Dutch worship. Perhaps not surprisingly, in view of the failure of the Dutch to develop any substantial program, religious or secular, to relate to the natives, not a single Indian was converted to Christianity. The best candidate for conversion, Megapolënsis and his colleague Drisius reported, had been tutored in Dutch and Christianity for two years and presented with a Bible to help him convert his people. But he took to drink and ended "a real beast who is doing more harm than good among the Indians." The only hope for the Indians' conversion, they concluded, lay in "subduing" them by overwhelming numbers and military power, and then showing them good examples of Christian behavior.[37]

For all the growing familiarity between the Europeans and the Native Americans, the two peoples remained fearful of each other, apprehensive, latently hostile, and uncomprehending.

CHAPTER 10

꘠

Swedes, Finns, and the
Passion of Pieter Plockhoy

1

B Y 1664, when the English conquered New Netherland, that colony was no longer simply a Dutch outpost with a complex population of north Germanic peoples. Nine years earlier it had absorbed the colony of New Sweden, a scattering of settlements on the banks of the Delaware River some hundred miles to the south. New Sweden's woodland farms, its rough log huts and dilapidated forts and trading posts housed not only Swedes but a fringe population drawn from Sweden's multi-ethnic Baltic empire and from the Netherlands, England, and the north German states. The most distinctive group were Finns—forest folk, whose cultural and geographical origins lay close to Lake Ladoga near the Russian border—the heartland of Savo-Karelia—and to Lappland in the north. Their way of life was peculiarly primitive by western European standards, and they proved to have a greater affinity to the culture of the native Americans than did any other Europeans in North America. It was they who would initiate a "frontier" style of life that would spread across the continental borderlands for generations to come.[1]

. . .

THE ULTIMATE FATE of Sweden's venture into overseas settlement was
implicit in its origins. The enterprise that left behind on the shores of the
Delaware this small population of Baltic and north European people was
a marginal, almost accidental product of Sweden's national exuberance in
what has been called its age of greatness.

A small nation, Sweden's population, including its eastern province of
Finland, numbered only a million and a half people—demographically a
fifth the size of England's, a tenth the size of France's. Yet, small as Sweden was, through most of the early and mid-seventeenth century it played
a major role in European affairs. Under the brilliant military leadership
of Gustavus Adolphus, it deployed a large army—conscripts and mercenaries perhaps 150,000 strong—in the early campaigns of the Thirty
Years War. Its Protestant forces drove deep into the heart of the territories contested between the Holy Roman Empire and its enemy states
and between Protestant and Catholic princedoms. Fighting campaigns
through central Europe as far south as the Danube, Gustavus Adolphus's
armies triumphed, but though subsidized by the French and Dutch, they
drained much of the wealth and manpower of the Swedish-Finnish state.
By 1632, when Gustavus Adolphus was killed in the Battle of Lützen in
southeastern Germany, Sweden had already become known as a nation of
soldiers' widows; at least fifty thousand men in the Swedish armies had
been lost in the decade before 1632. Its manpower was reduced, its taxes
were high, its politics oligarchic, and its economy was scarcely developed
beyond its late medieval, semifeudal origins. Much of the nation's surplus
went not to programs of development but to the uses of the landed aristocracy that controlled the government and its revenues. Still, the nation's
ambitions, buoyed by its military and diplomatic successes, ran high and
extended to plans for expansion, first at home, into the barbarous, un1 civilized frontier peoples they ostensibly ruled, the Finns in the east and the
Saamis (Lapps) in the north, then overseas, to the land of equally barbarous peoples, the Lenapes, on the shores of the Delaware River.[2]

That ambitious enterprise was a commercial venture by a few leading entrepreneurs whose ambitions transcended the Baltic trading basin
and its north European markets. Like many of Sweden's major developers the projectors were not Swedish but Dutch—merchants familiar with

investment opportunities throughout northern Europe and Scandinavia and who moved easily among the Baltic trading centers. The key figure initially was Willem Usselinx, a Walloon trained in commerce in Spain, Portugal, and the Azores. Usselinx was a schemer and dreamer of vast projects in overseas trade but never a manager or developer. Sensitive to the point of paranoia and difficult to work with, zealous in the Protestant cause and jealous of Spain's success in international trade, Usselinx had seen his plan for a Dutch West India Company come to fruition, but only after he himself had been shunted aside as an impractical dreamer by merchants with practical experience in overseas trade and with money to invest. While petitioning vainly for payment for his role in founding that enterprise, he looked abroad for more responsive and generous audiences for his ideas and turned first to Sweden.[3]

In a blur of activities—conferences, memorials, expositions, and royal audiences—Usselinx ingratiated himself with Gustavus Adolphus and his advisers and in 1627 was commissioned to establish a Swedish company to trade throughout "Africa, Asia, America and Magellanica or Terra Australia," make settlements in unoccupied areas, deal in diplomacy with foreign peoples, and raise funds by subscription. The king himself invested substantially and ordered all officials, religious as well as secular, civil as well as military, to support the effort, which he was assured would bring in great riches. But Sweden had little surplus wealth and few merchants or gentry able or willing to subscribe large amounts. Despite Usselinx's frantic efforts to raise capital, subscriptions were few and enthusiasm weakened. By 1629 what capital had become available was diverted to a ropewalk and shipyard. The South Company, as it was called, was essentially dead, and Usselinx's ambitions had once again been frustrated.[4]

But the Swedish Crown and a few of the investors were still hopeful. While Usselinx turned elsewhere for support, his effort was gradually transformed through a maze of intricate transactions, first into the United South-Ship Company (1629) and finally (1635) into the New Sweden Company.

This time there was reason to hope for substantial results, especially for success in North American trade, and specifically in the Delaware region. For chief among the investors and directors of the New Sweden Company was Samuel Blommaert, a wealthy, well-connected, and rather ruthless Dutch merchant with long experience in overseas trade. As a leading director of the Dutch West India Company, he had invested in patroonships in New Netherland and the Caribbean, most substantially in Samuel Godijn's ill-fated Swanendael on the Delaware. He also had an interest in a Swedish brass works, was a major marketer of Swedish grain and copper, and a manipulator of Sweden's foreign exchange. In 1635 he formed a close connection with Sweden's powerful chancellor, Axel Oxenstierna—the "universal, omniscient, all-competent minister"—and became the salaried Swedish commissary in Amsterdam. The Swedish West India Company would, Blommaert hoped, while creating new markets in "Guinea" for such Swedish products as copper, revive the earlier settlement at Swanendael. It was natural for him to bring into the project Peter Minuit, the German-born former director of New Netherland who knew the Delaware region well. Oxenstierna's and the government's interests were represented by Adm. Klas Fleming, who became the company's director, and by the Dutch-born official and politician Peter Spiring.[5]

THUS TIED TO and patronized by the highest leadership of the Swedish government, the Swedish West India Company began its short, strange, and well-recorded career. Its mandate was to develop trade and plant colonies on the North American coast, from Florida to Newfoundland, and specifically to conduct trade on the Delaware. A consortium of investors led by Blommaert and his friends, half of them Dutch, half Swedish, financed the first expedition, which was organized by Blommaert and Minuit in 1637.[6]

Between 1637 and 1655, the company sponsored a total of eleven expeditions (fourteen ship voyages) to the Delaware, two of which never arrived at their destination. The first expedition, which reached the Delaware in 1638, was exploratory and carried not settlers but Dutch and Swedish sailors and soldiers, twenty of whom, together with an Angolan slave, remained behind to hold the small, crude Fort Christina, which they built a few miles off the Delaware on a major Indian trading route, the Minquas Kill (creek). Two years passed before another Swedish vessel appeared on the Delaware. Then between 1640 and 1644 five expeditions (eight vessels) arrived, bearing the migrants who formed the colony's population base. But after those few years of activity, the settlement, spread thinly 120 miles up and down the shores of the Delaware, from Cape Henlopen on the south to the Schuylkill River on the north, was in effect abandoned. In the twelve years after March 1644, only four vessels arrived from Sweden with supplies and reinforcements, one of them after the Dutch had taken over the colony.[7] Only at the very end of the Swedish period was there a revival of interest in the colony and the beginning of a successful effort to increase its population. For over a decade, therefore, the Swedish colony, which never numbered more than four hundred souls—caught between the Dutch in the north and the English in the south, impoverished and riven with internal conflicts—struggled to survive in almost complete isolation from its European sources. That the settlement did survive and contributed to the pluralism of the American population was the result of its successful adaptation of Scandinavian peasant folkways to conditions in the American woodlands, the indulgence of the neighboring Lenapes, and the presence of strong, at times brutal, leadership.

The first leader was Minuit himself, who arrived with the first expedition. After renewing his acquaintance with the area, he bought, or negotiated, from the Indians, a fifty-mile stretch along the west bank of the river, drew up a detailed map of the region, and supervised the construction of the fort, its palisades, storehouses, dwellings, and barn. After four months he left for home, where he expected to organize the first group of permanent settlers, some of whom he planned to recruit in the neighborhood of his native Hanseatic town of Wesel. That disputed area on the German-Dutch border had been briefly occupied by the Dutch a few years before and had a troubled, potentially mobile population. How successful Minuit might have been in recruiting emigrants in this area can never be known since on the return voyage he was lost at sea in a storm off St. Kitts. His successor, Peter Ridder (1640–43), a Dutch- or German-born Swedish naval officer, had no such connections, and the recruitment for the second expedition, which he commanded, introduced a pattern that would persist and would determine the peculiar character of the colony's population.[8]

Fleming and Spiring made elaborate preparations for the second expedition, despite the news that the Dutch backers were pulling out for lack of immediate profits. Supplies were assembled, ships hired and outfitted, and the first effort at recruitment began. It took the form of instructions from Fleming to an officer of the new Commercial College (board of trade) and to Johan Hindricksson, the governor of the west port town and naval base of Gothenburg, to locate any likely migrants in southwestern Sweden, and especially to gather up a group of artisans in the building trades, and to include with them their wives, who would cook, make beer, and wash for the entire settlement. The same orders went out to the governor of the south-central provinces of Värmland and Dalarna, which would remain prime targets of recruitment. Similarly Måns Kling, the military commander of the first expedition who had returned to Sweden, was told to proceed to the Norwegian border region and elsewhere in the west, "to collect and hire a multitude of roving people . . . who nowhere have a steady residence and dwelling," and particularly to round up "all the forest-destroyers." If they did not come willingly he was to "capture" them and hold them for the ship departures. Hindricksson soon reported failure in locating the desired artisans, but he proposed that, instead of such respectable people who were unlikely to be dislodged from their homes, the company should seek out soldiers who had deserted or committed offenses, and send them over with their families. Fleming agreed, and the governor was told to proceed as quickly as possible—but quietly, discreetly, so as not to touch off riots. In this he succeeded, and in the four expeditions that followed, his mandate was extended to the southern Swedish and Finnish territories and to include a variety of other marginal, stigmatized groups—timber thieves and game poachers, embezzlers and adulterers, debtors and tax defaulters—as well as people who for whatever reason could be induced to settle in the colony.[9]

In New Sweden two alien groups appeared quickly. The second expedition, which arrived two years after the first, contained a contingent of Dutch families from the same impoverished province of Utrecht that had supplied immigrants to New Netherland. They settled as a separate group in the woods eighteen miles north of Fort Christina. At approximately the same time, some twenty English families—people mainly from southeastern England, but some from Yorkshire and Cornwall—subsidized by an English Delaware Company founded in New Haven, Connecticut, settled at an equal distance to the south of Christina, at Varkens Kill (later Salem, New Jersey), on the eastern shore. Then the five expeditions of 1640–44 deposited three hundred of the most diverse north European people imaginable.[10]

At least two hundred—twenty-one of them women—can be identified by name and place of origin. Some were respectable people seeking land or opportunity—a tailor and a mill maker and their families "to

begin agriculture"; "a young nobleman . . . to try his luck (or gain experience)"; a mayor's son, "an adventurer . . . to try his luck." But many
were far from respectable; not a few were convicts or refugees from the
law. From one village in Uppland, north of Stockholm, came a convict
recently reprieved from a death sentence for robbery; from another came
a deportee condemned for spreading "hard and rebellious words" against
a sheriff. From Västergötland in the south came a young cavalry officer
given the choice of death by hanging or six years in New Sweden for cutting off branches of fruit trees at the Royal Garden in Varnhem to use
as mane combs. From the island of Åland, between Sweden and Finland,
came two men condemned for adultery, one of whom had compounded
his guilt by shooting an elk without permission.

All sorts of offenses and all sorts of places of origins were recorded.
The voyagers came not only from Västergötland, Uppland, Åland,
Värmland, and Dalarna but from Södermanland and Östergötland south
of Stockholm and from Medelpad in the north. And they came from the
Netherlands and from north German towns and villages; from Saxony
and Norway; from Denmark and the Frisian coast; from Danzig and
Schleswig-Holstein. One of the sailors came from Dublin. And in all the
shipments there were Finns: Finns from Savo-Karelia near Lake Ladoga
in the east and from Kainuu near Lappland in the north; Finns from the
southern Finnish farmlands and from the islands and shorelands of the
Gulfs of Finland and Bothnia; above all, there were Finns from the hill
country of south-central Sweden to which, under official sponsorship,
they had recently migrated but from which, in the 1630s and 1640s, they
were being ruthlessly expelled. Of all the voyagers to New Sweden up to
1644 whose origins are known, at least 22 percent were Finns; by 1655
they constituted 40 percent of the colony's population.[11]

2

Ridder had presided over the first arrivals and did what he could to begin
a program of construction. The fort, which had already collapsed in three
places, was repaired; several log cottages and a windmill were built; a number of clearings were made in the forest; and a few tobacco and vegetable
patches appeared. Ridder was successful in obtaining land from the Indians that filled out the colony's territorial claims, as far north as the lower
Dutch settlements and as far south as Maryland. He established peaceful

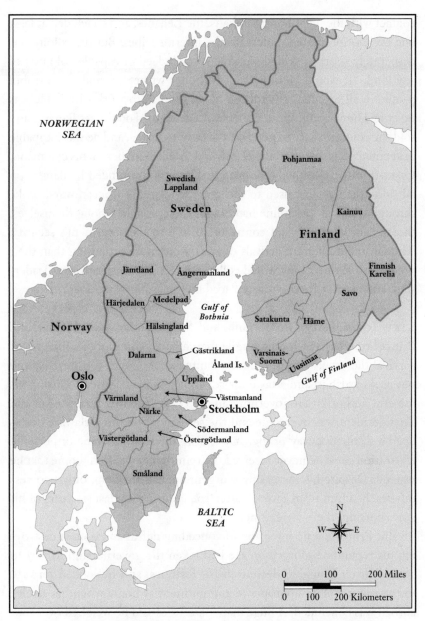

NORWEGIAN
SEA

Pohjanmaa

Swedish
Lappland

Sweden

Kainuu

Finland

Jämtland   Ångermanland

Finnish
Karelia

Härjedalen Medelpad

Savo

Gulf of
Bothnia

Hälsingland

Satakunta Häme

Norway

Dalarna   Gästrikland

Varsinais-
Suomi

Åland Is.

Uppland

Uusimaa

Oslo

Gulf of Finland

Värmland   Västmanland

Närke   Stockholm

Södermanland

Västergötland   Östergötland

Småland

BALTIC
SEA

N

W   E

S

0   100   200 Miles

0   100   200 Kilometers

Sources of Swedish and Finnish settlers on the Delaware River contact with the neighboring Indians, the Lenapes, and concluded at least one cycle of profitable trade with the interior tribes. But the colony was desperately short of skilled workmen—or indeed of capable colonists of any kind. "It would be impossible," Ridder wrote, "to find more stupid people in all Sweden" than those he was forced to work with.[12] He was beset by Dutch and English traders who descended on the settlements and sold the colonists needed goods at outrageous prices, and he was incapable of keeping peace between the Dutch and Swedish soldiers in his command. Cast off in what seemed a desolate wilderness surrounded by danger on all sides, the soldiers, used to the savagery of the European wars, broke through whatever discipline had bound them, fought among themselves, threatened desertion, and contributed little to the settlement's security. Though the immigrant arrivals of 1641 were more promising than their predecessors, the colony would collapse if it did not have stronger leadership, and in 1643 Ridder was replaced by Johan Björnsson Printz.

LIKE JOHN SMITH in Virginia and Stuyvesant in New Netherland, Printz brought to bear on a fragile marchland community scrabbling for survival the experience of military command, tolerance for brutality and physical hardship, and a taste for adventure in exotic places. During his forceful authoritarian governorship (1643–53) the initial confusion and bewilderment was overcome and the settlement on the Delaware developed a distinctive way of life. It was also, for Printz, a time of personal frustration since he never received the reinforcements from home that he needed. Despite his increasingly urgent appeals for help, only two vessels reached him from Sweden after 1644; during the last six years of his governorship, there were none.

But Printz had no intention of conceding defeat and thus of destroying his reputation altogether. He had taken the governorship in part to recover from a sudden decline in his fortunes, and he looked forward to the reward of an appropriate appointment at home when his service abroad was concluded. A huge man—De Vries said he weighed over four hundred pounds: the Indians called him "big belly"—he had a fierce temper, drank heavily, and brooked no opposition. "Very furious and passionate," John Winthrop wrote, always "cursing and swearing," Printz, he said, had "neither [a] Christian nor moral conscience"; he treated the Puritans who sought entry to the Delaware trade like criminals, denouncing them as "runagates" and personally shackling them in irons.[13]

JOHAN PRINTZ

A disgraced officer of the
Swedish army, assigned to
the governorship of New
Sweden, Printz did what
he could for the scattered,
undersupplied settlers under
pressure from the Indians,
the Dutch, and the English,
but gave up after a mutiny
and the failure of support
from home.

No one should have been surprised. Though initially intended for the
church by his highly placed clerical family and once a student of theology, Printz had become a career army officer, fighting with outstanding
bravery in a long series of battles in Germany, some of them desperate, bloody encounters, rising to the rank of lieutenant colonel. He was
always a military man. In America as in Europe, he thought like a soldier
and lived like a soldier. "For the last twenty-seven years," he wrote from
New Sweden, he had had more often "the musket and the pistol in my
hands than Tacitus and Cicero," and so he made no pretense of being
able to reply in kind to the messages in Latin he received from Governor
Winthrop in Boston. But his military career had come to a halt in 1640
when, having been forced to surrender the city of Chemnitz, he had left
Germany without either reporting the loss to his superiors or obtaining
their permission to leave. For this he was arrested, imprisoned, convicted
by court martial, and sent off to retirement in the sprawling Finnish province of Pohjanmaa that stretched north to Finnish Lappland, where he
owned property and where in earlier days he had sought army recruits.[14]

It was his sudden availability with reduced prospects, his reputation
for success as a tough commander, his familiarity with recruitment in

Finland, and above all the patronage of Per Brahe, Finland's aristocratic governor general (1637–40, 1648–54), that led to his appointment to the governorship of the obscure, forlorn colony 3,500 miles to the west.

Arriving in January 1643, he quickly took charge. He found a shockingly small population—105 adult males—severely debilitated as a result of their sea voyages and malnutrition: 26, he noted, died in the course of his first year—5 murdered by the Indians, 1 drowned, the rest victims of disease. The goods he had carried with him had rotted, almost everyone in the colony wanted to leave, and there were dangers on all sides. The local Lenapes were ostensibly friendly, exchanging not furs, which they lacked, but food, desperately needed, in exchange for European goods. But relations with the less peaceful Susquehannocks—Minquas, they were called in the colony—who lived along the Atlantic outlets of the interior rivers and hence were middlemen in the vital fur trade with the Iroquois, were much more complicated. Neither the Lenapes nor the Susquehannocks, Printz believed, could be relied on. "They do not trust us and we trust them still less." When they detect a weakness in the European defenses, he wrote, or are disappointed in the trading goods available, they strike out randomly. So without apparent provocation they slaughtered, in one place, a man and his wife "on their bed"; in another, two soldiers; in still another, a workman. Though they spoke of peace and friendly relations, they were no different from the Indians who, he was told, had recently wiped out a thousand Dutchmen in New Netherland and six hundred Christians in Virginia. The Lenapes, he said, were proud in manner, but they were in fact nothing but miserable beggars. The best thing to do, he wrote, echoing more successful appeals that had been made in Virginia, would be "to send over here a couple of hundred soldiers, and [keep them here] until we broke the necks of all of them in this river . . . Then each one could be secure here at his work, and feed and nourish himself unmolested . . . and we could take possession of the places (which are the most fruitful) that the savages now possess." That will certainly happen sooner or later, he wrote, and the sooner the better, "before they do us more harm." If he had the troops and officers he requested, he could guarantee that "not a single savage would be allowed to live in this river," and the colony would have unimpeded access to trade north and south.[15]

As for converting them to Christianity, the prospects were bleak. They simply slipped away when one tried to instruct them in the fear of the only true God; they "intimate that they are a free people and subject

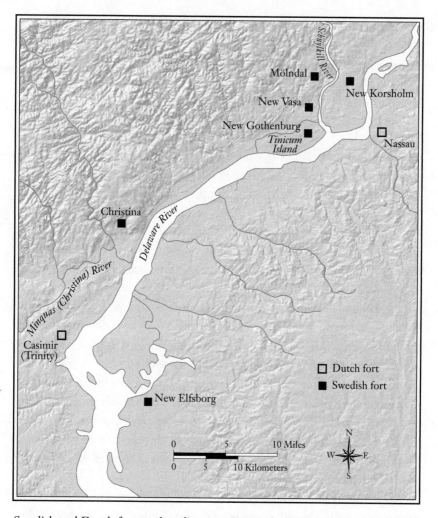

Swedish and Dutch forts and trading stations on the Delaware River, 1638–55

to no one and do what they please . . . They know nothing of God, but serve Satan." One must simply force them to accept Christianity; those who refuse should be exterminated.[16]

Soldiers were sent, but not in the numbers Printz wanted, and the settlers he needed were slow in coming. These were years of renewed warfare in Sweden: besides campaigns in Germany there was a bitter naval war with Denmark (1643–45) in which the colony's patron Fleming was killed. Thereafter there was an agricultural depression, a contraction of commercial investments, and political struggles that weakened the authority of the colony's chief sponsor, Oxenstierna. Neither resources nor attention could be spared for the colony. Four years after Printz's arrival a census revealed the presence of even fewer people than had been recorded in 1644: only 83 adult males, 183 people in all. Many had left for home, some had deserted to other colonies, and death had claimed others. But Printz made progress on several fronts, and there were indications that when the turmoil in the Baltics and northern Europe died down reinforcements and supplies would arrive.[17]

Turning to defense, Printz forced the English at Varkens Kill to switch their allegiance to Sweden and then built an earthwork fort, New Elfsborg, just below them on the eastern shore to command the entrance to the river. Then north of Fort Christina, on Tinicum Island, he built another fort, Gothenburg, as well as a residence for himself, Printzhof, which, though constructed simply of "pine beams laid one upon the other," in a world of small, dark log huts and flimsy lean-tos, was considered a princely mansion. With the Dutch he maintained a guarded amity, collaborating with them for mutual benefit and to oppose the English, but competing with them for control of the river outlets of the fur trade. While Fort Christina was well placed to receive the furs carried down Christina Kill, which reached back to the head of Chesapeake Bay, the major conduit for eastbound furs was the Schuylkill River, and to control it Printz built at its mouth a string of forts and blockhouses—New Vasa, New Korsholm, Mölndal. When the Dutch retaliated by building a blockhouse of their own in the same area, Printz constructed yet another to screen that emplacement from view.

All of this jousting, carried on when Kieft was governor of New Netherland, was civil. Though there were "offensive remarks" on both sides, and though some Dutch agents claimed to be "bloody and bruised" by the Swedes or their Indian allies, there were no outright attacks, nor were there likely to be, given the fact that Sweden and the Netherlands were allies in Europe. But the arrival of Stuyvesant on Manhattan, as formidable a combat veteran and as tempestuous a personality as Printz, altered both the tone and the substance of the contest for control and settlement of the Delaware.[18]

Dissatisfied with Printz's disdainful reaction to his claim that the Delaware was Dutch territory and fearful that the Swedes were preempting a major source of furs, Stuyvesant took action. He first sent an armed ship around the coast and up the Delaware to within a few miles of Fort Christina, and followed that with a flotilla of small vessels that sailed up and down the river "with drumming and cannonading," while he led a battalion overland to the head of the river. There he began a series of negotiations with the Indians to establish Dutch priority in the ownership of the land. When he was satisfied with the documentation, which Printz contested point by point, he simply ignored Printz and began constructing a large, well-armed fort in the center of the Swedish colony, halfway between Forts Christina and Elfsborg. He called the new fort Casimir and, while continuing what he considered a policy of nonaggression with the Swedes, made plans to send "some hundred families" to settle around the fort. By April 1653 about twenty-six Dutch families were established there. Though Printz had neither the troops nor the arms to prevent any of this, and withdrew his soldiers from the river's entrance, he was at least able to keep the Dutch from expanding farther, and turned to more urgent matters at the heart of the colony.[19]

3

By 1653 the colony's small population of independent farmers was scattered in isolated woodland encampments that were only gradually becoming cultivated. But while the freemen were more or less content to continue clearing and planting, and proceeded to construct, besides a mill of traditional Swedish design, a makeshift brewery and a small shipyard, the officials, servants, and soldiers were restless and fearful. The officials and higher-status adventurers were prevented from fully exploiting the fur trade by Printz's restrictive rule; the servants, debilitated and sickly, worked under desperate conditions with little to look forward to; and the soldiers, guarding swampy wilderness forts, were bored, beset by lurking dangers, poorly equipped, and weakly armed. All three groups were eager to escape from the colony, and some began to think enviously of what they had heard of conditions in New Netherland and Maryland. Desertions—of single servants, of isolated families, occasionally of soldiers—became a problem that had no easy solution. Printz occasionally hired Indians who, for a price, would track down the deserters, and he attempted to negotiate with Maryland for the fugitives' forced return. But the Maryland authorities, who also claimed ownership of the Delaware lands, were not likely to cooperate—were more likely, in fact, to attract the deserters and hold them as hostages for the return of Delaware land. And the hired Indians either did nothing or showed a shocking excess of zeal. In 1653 the warriors sent to bring back a group of deserters killed two of them when they resisted, cut off their heads, and brought them back to Fort Christina as proof of a job well done. Many in New Sweden thought this procedure was "too severe," not because deserters did not deserve decapitation, but because "the Indians might in that way become accustomed to slaughtering our Christians, which the Indians are only too willing to do when they have the opportunity."[20]

As the years passed with no supplies, settlers, or even communication from Sweden—the one major supply ship of the late 1640s having been shipwrecked off Puerto Rico—conditions worsened. Lacking trading goods or company funds, Printz began to lay out his own money and credit to pay the soldiers and company employees (he later claimed to have advanced 15,000 dalers, equivalent to approximately £168 sterling), which had the effect of increasing his personal domination of the colony and leading him to seize every source of profit in the colony he could possibly find. Resentment rose in volume and bitterness; desertions increased. In 1650 Printz wrote that there were not thirty men in the entire place whom he could trust. It was in fact worse than he suspected. His loyal son-in-law, Johan Papegoja, reported that not only did the settlers respond to Printz's authoritarian governance with "rebuke and ingratitude," but "the soldiers cherished secret hatred towards him and if they would find a small fault in him they would likely murder him."[21]

By 1653 the resentments exploded into open rebellion. Twenty-two settlers, Swedes and Finns, presented the governor, and indirectly the king, with a list of grievances in eleven articles. They charged Printz with brutality and avarice, with endangering "life and property," prohibiting settlers from trading freely while trafficking himself without restraint, and prohibiting them from grinding flour in the mill and from enjoying full access to fishing, timber, grass, and land. In addition he had fined one Anders the Finn a parcel of rye and other essential goods, the lack of which would probably result in the man's death from starvation and that of his wife and children.

To Printz all of this was treachery if not treason, and he knew how to handle such matters. He quickly decided that the ringleader was Anders Jönsson, a common soldier who had been personally recruited by Papegoja. He arrested him, tried him in a military court, and had him executed by firing squad. Having cleared that up, he turned to the charges against him, which would later be expanded to include exploitation of bound labor, personal beatings of irreverent Finns, and refusal to abide by jury decisions. But while he could quell the rebellion by martial law and could satisfy himself that he had refuted the accusations, he had clearly lost the trust of the colonists, and in any case he felt he had served his country well for ten years under difficult circumstances and deserved to be relieved and rewarded. Hearing no objection from home, he packed up his personal goods and a valuable cargo of furs and in October 1653, after elaborate departing ceremonies, took passage home on a Dutch ship, together with his wife, four daughters, and twenty-five soldiers and settlers. He left behind in charge of Printzhof his tough, "overbearing . . . irritable and self-willed" daughter Armegot and her husband, Papegoja. It was Papegoja's fate to see the new regime start off with the defection of fifteen more colonists to Maryland.[22]

But Papegoja was to participate in a sudden surge in the colony's fortunes, before witnessing its equally sudden demise as a Swedish enterprise. Circumstances had changed. A period of peace in the Baltic allowed investments in Sweden to return to more productive channels, and army recruitment had slackened, creating a pool of potential migrants. Word had gotten back to the most deprived and harassed people of Sweden, the Finns, that despite all its miseries New Sweden was a land of opportunity; and the colony had acquired a new civilian leader, a man with a broad vision, administrative skill, and wide experience.

Johan Risingh was a well-educated, well-traveled scholar and economist, a protégé of Oxenstierna, recently ennobled and appointed secretary of the nation's Commercial College. A learned public servant, he would leave behind a vivid account of his short tenure as governor and incorporate many of his experiences of those years into both strongly imperialist reports to the government and in *A Treatise on Commerce*, the first essay on mercantilist economics and population theory written in Swedish.

Risingh approached the colony with high expectations, both material and ideological. The colony, he wrote in a memorandum detailing his reasons for accepting the appointment, was potentially rich and hence would produce wealth for both the state and individuals. Sweden's "reputation and honor," its stature in the greater world, would be enhanced by the development of the colony, the success of which he believed was assured by promises he had received of future supplies of goods and people. And like others who might venture there as officers, he was promised advantages both occupational and financial upon his return to Sweden.[23]

The start of his voyage was promising, at least in terms of the number of emigrants. His sister ship, *The Golden Shark*, having been delayed, Risingh's *Eagle* took on an enormous load: more than 350 voyagers—passengers, crew, and soldiers—leaving one hundred behind. In February 1654 the *Eagle* left Sweden for the Delaware by way of England, the Canaries, and the Caribbean. The passengers, jammed together with their possessions, animals, and the ship's supplies in a vessel only 132 feet long and 30 feet wide, began to suffer even before they left the English Channel. There were deaths while the ship was still in the Canaries, and the transatlantic voyage, in blazing heat, with little sanitation, food, or water, was a catastrophe. Food spoiled, dysentery swept through the huddled population, lice were said to be so thick in the clothes and blankets that when beaten with clubs, blood dripped from the cloth. Disease and delirium so disoriented some people that they fell overboard and drowned. By the time the *Eagle* arrived in the Delaware, three and a half months after its departure, approximately one hundred people had died and been thrown into the sea, and of the survivors thirteen were so severely ill that not only were they unable to row the dinghies to the shore, they could not walk without assistance. And it was difficult to help the survivors on board since, Risingh reported, "the stench was so strong that one could not stand it for long."[24]

But before their painful debarkation took place, Risingh had made a decisive move that would come to be seen as the beginning of the end of New Sweden. As the *Eagle* sailed up the Delaware it came abreast of the Dutch Fort Casimir, built three years earlier. Risingh, discovering that it was guarded by only nine men who lacked effective weapons, interpreted his orders broadly and decided to capture the fort and reclaim it and the surrounding settlement for Sweden. He had no trouble. Faced with a troop of Swedish musketeers and guaranteed good treatment, the garrison quickly surrendered, and the soldiers and the nearby settlers swore allegiance to the Swedish king. There was no violence and no dispute, and Risingh's judgment seemed vindicated. But in taking the fort, which he renamed Trinity (Trefaldighet), he had laid down a direct challenge to the Dutch, which would eventually lead to a drastic response.[25]

For the moment the Dutch reaction was unknown, and Risingh turned to the manifold tasks ahead. He had to nurse his fellow passengers back to health, restore trust in the government, confirm the settlers' personal rights, rebuild the colony's decayed defenses, restore good trade relations with the Indians, work out a new land settlement policy that would be attractive to settlers, and somehow develop the colony's economic potential. There were difficulties everywhere, and everything could not be done at once. But in the sixteen months of Risingh's rule—May 1654 to October 1655—he made remarkable progress.

He first arranged for the distribution of the newcomers among the few available households and forts, and then, since the local Indians, fearing the immigrants' diseases, stayed away, he sent to New England for needed food supplies. A major question was where to settle the new colonists, who outnumbered the earlier population. His plan was both practical and strategically shrewd. He turned away from the earlier emphasis on the northern area near the Schuylkill River and gave out plots to the newcomers around Fort Christina and south from there to Fort Trinity, thus forming a continuous line of habitations on the middle and lower section of the west shore. He also distributed land west of Christina, reaching back toward the upper Chesapeake, to preempt possible encroachment by the English moving east from Maryland. Then, abandoning Fort Elfsborg, which had become a mosquito-ridden, swampy ruin, he shored up the fortifications of Christina and Trinity along with Gothenburg on Tinicum Island. The center of the colony was now clearly Fort Christina, in which he built an inn, and he had plans drawn up for a city to be constructed there, to be called Christinehamn.

The parcels of land he distributed had an important new distinction. They were outright and perpetual gifts. Recipients were to hold the land in absolute ownership for themselves and their heirs. The settlers were also allowed to acquire land directly from the Indians, and soldiers after three years of service would be given a plot in full ownership, as would servants after six years. Risingh arranged to help the settlers clear the land, and allotted them cows in exchange for future deliveries of milk products. He began construction of a sawmill, and had the decrepit gristmill repaired.

These were important material gestures. But in addition, within weeks of his arrival, Risingh also turned to bolstering confidence in the future of the colony and to convincing incipient defectors to remain. To a gathering of freemen who swore loyalty oaths to the Swedish Crown and the company, he explained their rights and benefits, passed on to them the government's promises of future recruitment and supplies, and described the consultative role that ordinary settlers would have with the new ruling Council. He brought all of this home with special emphasis to the former Dutch people near Fort Trinity, whose loyalty he particularly hoped for despite their obvious desire to rejoin their countrymen in Manhattan as soon as possible.

And through all of this Risingh sought to stabilize official relations with the English, the Indians, and the Dutch. To a delegation from Maryland claiming title to the Delaware land he delivered a technical disquisition on international law as it related to Sweden's right to the land, and he gave a similar response to the claims of New Haven to the Delaware land. At the same time he made it a point to maintain good relations with the English merchants trading on the river, whose grain and other supplies were essential for the colony's survival.[26]

As to the Indians, though relatively good relations were maintained, and though the Rev. Johan Campanius, who believed they were the lost tribes of Israel, attempted to teach them Christianity through a catechism he wrote in what he believed was the Lenape language, derived from Hebrew (it was in fact a kind of trader's pidgin)—despite all of this, random clashes were unavoidable. Vandalism, thefts, and murders were committed almost casually by wandering Indians. Risingh himself had none of Printz's fierce animosity to the natives and conducted elaborate, careful negotiations with them to confirm the legality of Sweden's land purchases and to guarantee future deliveries of corn. His success was such that the Indians invited the Swedes to settle in their territory and to build trading stations there. But perhaps his greatest achievement was the purchase from the Susquehannock Indians of a huge block of land—over 250 square miles—that extended the colony's western boundaries to the head of Chesapeake Bay. He hoped by this to tap into the Susquehanna River trade at its approach to the upper Chesapeake and draw the furs from there through the Christina Kill into the fort near that river's mouth. Fort Christina would thereby, he hoped, become a major Atlantic entrepôt, an appropriate center for the craftsmen, builders, and artisans he hoped to attract to the colony. That fort and its surroundings were already beginning to take on the form of a small, orderly town, with new houses, one of them Risingh's own two-story structure, and planned land plots. And indeed by early 1655, the whole colony was becoming visually more coherent and physically more comprehensible by virtue of extended surveys and detailed maps made by the military engineer Peter Lindeström.

Lindeström, eager to see "the remotest nations and countries of the world," had volunteered to accompany Risingh on his voyage. Once in the colony, he quickly became New Sweden's cartographer, and he became too, in his *Geographia Americae*, which he wrote years later from his surveys and notes of 1654–56, the Delaware Indians' most vivid ethnographer. Seventeen of the twenty-nine chapters in that work describe the appearance, behavior, beliefs, customs, and economy of "the American savage people."[27]

4

In these strenuous efforts to revive the colony, Risingh was successful, but everything he accomplished was ringed around with the sense that there were forces at work—conspiracies—that would destroy the colony, indirectly by encouraging defections to the Dutch and the English, directly by military conquest. Though rational and constrained in most things, Risingh was ruthless and unforgiving in dealing with defections and those who encouraged deserters. When he learned that Andries Hudde, "a cunning Dutchman," formerly a Dutch official, had absconded, Risingh assumed "he had treachery in mind," sent out a posse to bring him back, arrested and interrogated him, searched his papers for incriminating evidence, and found just what he suspected: indications of "evil conspirations" by Virginians to entice the Swedes south. Hudde, though "a malicious man," was treated gently: he was forced to sign an oath "that he did not wish to conspire." Lars Olofsson, "the Finn," had no such luck. When he refused to confess that he had solicited people to leave the colony or to reveal his accomplices, "he was hanged up in handcuffs" until he confessed that most of the Finnish soldiers had talked of escaping to Virginia, where "it was good to live" and where one would not starve in the winter, as one would in New Sweden, nor be attacked by Indians. Risingh, morbidly sensitive to "dangerous plots," was determined to stop all this—to track down every deserter and to prosecute anyone, of whatever status, who conspired to depopulate the colony. To reinforce his authority to deal with this problem, he requested from home personal legal jurisdiction in all cases "higher and lower" and both a "law-reader" to assist in prosecuting such cases and "a hang-man" to handle punishments for secret plots in the future.[28]

But if Risingh could work to stem the tide of defections from the colony, there was nothing he could do to deflect the determination of the Dutch to retake Fort Trinity and ultimately recover the entire colony. Stuyvesant's actions as well as his silence were ominous. When Risingh's sister ship, the heavily laden *Golden Shark*, finally arrived in America, it landed, by a navigational error, not at Fort Christina but in Manhattan. Stuyvesant immediately confiscated the vessel and its entire cargo, persuaded its passengers to remain in New Netherland, and refused even to discuss Risingh's protests. Rumors of plans for a Dutch attack on New Sweden began filtering through from English and Indian sources, though knowledge of the real extent of the Dutch military buildup and the West India Company's flat orders to invade the Swedish colony remained secret.

In the summer of 1655, the worst rumors were confirmed when news arrived that Stuyvesant had left Manhattan with a large military force. On August 27 the army appeared: 317 soldiers and a contingent of sailors on seven armed ships. Risingh had a total of approximately 75 soldiers and armed farmers, whom he divided between his two main forts. Trinity, weakly held and beset by outright defectors within the garrison, quickly surrendered when locked in a tightening siege. The Dutch force then moved up to Fort Christina, where Risingh and his few men hoped to make a stand. The Dutch surrounded the fort on all sides and waited for the inevitable capitulation. Risingh refused to concede, however, hoping to convince Stuyvesant to allow the whole matter to be settled, not by arms in America but by negotiation in Europe. Sweden and the Netherlands, he explained to Stuyvesant in messages that passed between the lines, were allies and closely related in religion and culture; drastic action in the colony could have bad consequences at home. Stuyvesant replied that he had strict orders to deny all Swedish claims and to seize the colony.

So the siege went on, for three weeks. The idle Dutch troops, facing no opposition, lost all control. Joined by Indians from time to time, they overran the newly built farms and dwellings both below and above Christina, and at their leisure slaughtered the farm animals and looted the houses, confiscating or destroying everything they could lay their hands on. In the northern reaches of the river, Risingh wrote, "they plundered

many and stripped them down to their naked bodies." Printzhof on Tinicum Island was no sanctuary. Defying the wrath of Madame Papegoja,
they carried off "all that she owned there" and the possessions of others
she had stored, and broke into the nearby church. Meanwhile conditions
in Fort Christina worsened. Food and ammunition were scarce, the fortifications were clearly too weak to withstand the likely assault, and the
soldiers were becoming mutinous. By September sickness had overtaken
many of the defenders, and resistance was obviously futile. On September 15 the two governors met "in a large and beautiful tent erected for
that purpose," and Risingh capitulated. He set out, however, terms of surrender that were extremely favorable to the Swedes. Stuyvesant, informed
of the Indian war that was raging around Manhattan and urged by his
people to return with the army as soon as possible, quickly accepted Risingh's terms. But the devastation continued, despite the amicable legalities. Risingh wrote Stuyvesant that he "simply cannot believe" that the
Dutch authorities had ordered his troops to ravage New Sweden "as if
they were in the country of their archenemy . . . women were, sometimes
with violence, torn from their houses; buildings dismantled and hauled
away; oxen, cows, pigs and other animals slaughtered daily in large numbers; even the horses were wantonly shot, the plantations devastated and
everything thereabouts . . . taken away or otherwise consumed."[29]

5

But if as a consequence of the Dutch conquest the colony's formal status
was transformed and the boundaries of New Netherland now extended
from the upper Hudson to the lower Delaware, the social and demographic
situation in the former New Sweden continued to develop, almost by
inertial force, along familiar lines. The loss of the colony being unknown
in Sweden, the promised shipments of settlers and supplies continued. In
March 1656 the twelfth Swedish expedition, the *Mercurius*, arrived bearing 110 settlers. Significantly, at least 92 of them were Finns—listed as 33
men, 16 women, 11 maidens, and 22 children. Smaller groups of Finns
would continue to appear in the years that followed, culminating in 1664
in an entire shipment of Finns, 140 in all, who left from the Sundsvall
area, on the border of Medelpad and Hälsingland.[30]

   Apparently enticed by enthusiastic letters from relatives and friends
on the Delaware, and aware of the political changes in America, these

latest voyagers from the north lands, who had sold all their property to finance their emigration, had proceeded with caution. Determined to settle with kinsmen in what had become Dutch overseas territory, they had avoided Stockholm by traveling by sleigh southwest across Sweden to Christiana (Oslo), and from there had sailed to Amsterdam. In that sophisticated city, the forest Finns must have seemed, as one historian has put it, like the Goths in Rome, while the Swedish commissioner tried to stop their voyage on the grounds that they had been illegally recruited by the Dutch. Finally they were released and began their difficult ocean crossing. Significant additions to the population of the colony, these latest Finns to settle on the Delaware were part of a much larger group eager to join the exodus to America.

Their appearance in America was, in its small way, the result of the kind of "America fever" that would recur in various forms again and again in the generations that followed. It resulted then, and would result in the future, from a highly focused, suddenly developing expulsive force that dislodged certain groups of people from their familiar communities and caused them to look abroad for relief and renewal. But if the general phenomenon was typical, the Finns themselves were not. They were unique in the history of the North American settlements, and distinctive in the multi-ethnic settlements on the Delaware. Though at times and in certain ways conflated with the Saamis from Swedish Lappland, they retained their peculiarities, including their language, for at least two generations, while adapting with peculiar ease to the environment of this marchland world.[31]

For historically, anciently, they had always been marginal people. Considered by many to be half-pagan folk who lived barbarous lives on the fringes of European society, they had been highly mobile. From their original core locations around Lake Ladoga, they had first migrated north, in the fifteenth century, to Häme, Savo, and Karelia—stony, forested country, snow-covered for almost half the year. Then in the sixteenth century they had expanded even farther north, to Kainuu and Pohjanmaa, close to Lappland. And finally, in the late sixteenth and early seventeenth centuries, they had begun moving across the Gulf of Bothnia to central and southern Sweden. By the 1630s they had settled in the forests of sixteen Swedish provinces; there were close to ten thousand Finns in Värmland alone. And they brought with them a culture, a way of life,

FINNISH BURN BEATERS

Painting by Eero Järnfelt, 1893

Savo-Karelian in its origins, that was first thought by the Swedish authorities to be useful, then troublesome, finally intolerable if not criminal.

Finnic people, in whose folklife could still be heard echoes of the pagan, animist world of the mythic epic *The Kalevala*, ancient oral ballads until published together in the nineteenth century, they were hunters who trekked a hundred miles or more in subarctic climate in search of game and furs they could sell in the markets of Novgorod. They were also fishermen and gatherers of wild plants. Above all, they were burn-beating farmers—slash-and-burn farmers, whose cultivation was perhaps the most superficial form of agriculture then practiced. They did not plow, sow, and reap in settled fields, renewing the earth's nutrients in annual cycles. In virgin spruce forests they cultivated a few basic crops—rye particularly, but also barley and turnips—by cutting down or girdling trees in the spring, leaving them to dry through phases of rain and snow, until the midsummer of the third year. Then they burned the whole section, rolling blazing logs over deep leaf accumulations. When the area was sufficiently scorched, they planted rye seed in the ashes, "grain by grain, one seed under a footprint." The result was "the spectacular sight of soot-blackened, infernal-looking men and women rolling flaming tree trunks over the surface of the cleared areas to ignite all the leaf mold." The yield was high: "the old forest-rye could give up to a 12,000-fold harvest . . . one planted seed yielded 12,000 seeds in harvest." And the product was rich in nutrients: Finnish rye "had a 50% higher food value than other cereals." But this was a laborious and wasteful form of agriculture. Since a given plot could not be replanted in the same way for a full generation, a family needed at least 2,500 acres to continue their work for a substantial period of time. It was therefore a system that required the kind of nomadic forest life that had been theirs for generations.[32]

Their distinctive culture was resilient and forceful. Slash-and-burn farmers living on homesteads spaced far from each other, fiercely independent, defiant when need be—they were seen by such authorities as Brahe as licentious, rudely disrespectful of all government and law, superstitious, utterly lacking in regularity of work, and forever alternating between periods of gluttony and starvation. When hunting they took shelter in small, low, three-sided huts barely large enough for two or three people to huddle in; they could be mistaken for animal dens. For permanent residence, they built one- or two-room log cabins which served as living quarters, saunas, and farm sheds. These were not fine works of rural craftsmanship; the walls were made of whole logs notched together at the corners, the chinks sealed with smears of clay or moss. As these small, bare, dark log buildings multiplied and were surrounded by animal pens, bathhouses, and haybarns, they formed not coherent villages but sprawls of habitations randomly spread across the landscape.

The folkways of these forest Finns evoked the lives of the mythical Kalevalans whom their bardic singers had immemorially celebrated:

> free-spirited, boisterous, alcohol-guzzling, party-loving backwoods folk, capable of prodigious feats, bravery, foolhardiness, violence, and sundry foul deeds. Witches, wizards, and charms abound in a setting only dimly Christianized. Central authority and law rarely enter the epic.

They were outliers, pioneers in the swift surge of expansion out from Savo-Karelia, a diffusion that had been favored by the Swedish government as a way to render the hinterlands productive. It had been the same public interest that had led the authorities in the late sixteenth century to encourage the forest Finns to cross the Gulf of Bothnia and turn the undeveloped Swedish forest lands, as they had the Finnish, into useful, tax-paying territories. So from all over the Finnish lands, forest people had come to settle in central Sweden—in Värmland, Västmanland, Dalarna, Uppland, and Södermanland—moving from there west into the Norwegian borderlands and north into Hälsingland, Medelpad, and Ångermanland. Wherever they went they favored the forested hill districts, perching on heights overlooking the more regularly settled farmlands in the valleys below. There they worked their way through stands of virgin timber, bringing from their burned, smoldering, sloping fields surplus grain to lowland markets. And there, in the Swedish uplands, they reproduced their familiar log structures, took off on long hunts on which they lived in open-faced huts, often tearing the hides off their kill and leaving the flesh to rot. They avoided Swedish law and order in every way they could, but poaching, squatting, trespassing, and episodes of violence inevitably brought them into conflict with the settled Swedish villagers and royal law. The Swedish authorities, which had earlier encouraged their migration from Finland west to central Sweden, increasingly felt the need to control them and direct their energies elsewhere.[33]

By the 1630s the Finns in Sweden proper were coming under official pressure not only because of the disorder of their lives but also because the timber they were destroying had come to be seen as valuable for emergent industries. It was precisely in the area of their most populous resettlements—on the Dalarna-Värmland-Västmanland border—that new iron and copper industries were developing whose smelters needed increasing quantities of wood. Laws were passed to restrict the Finns' use of the forests, but "against our Edict and Prohibition [they] destroy the forests by setting tracts of wood on fire, in order to sow in the ashes, and [they] mischievously fell trees." In 1647 local authorities were told "to capture and as with other noxious animals, strive to get rid of them." They were expelled from Crown forests, and the most nomadic, boisterous, and violent among them, some condemned criminals, were rounded up and shipped overseas to the woodlands of New Sweden.[34]

The Delaware region was a natural environment for them. Land, especially forested land, was easily available. There was scarcely any public authority to constrain them; trading for furs was familiar to them; and the natives were similar in many ways to the Saamis of Lappland, whom some had dealt with and all had known about. Even the animals and fish seemed similar. By 1655 their settlements concentrated in the area north of the colony's center, which they called Finland, and in the south at Finn's Point. From these focus points they would eventually scatter to clearances on both sides of the river and would mark out areas for their "meat-wasting" hunts around the creeks at the entrance of the bay and in the north at the river's falls.

Though many of them spoke Swedish and had lived in Sweden proper, they stood out in this north European population. The records refer again and again to Finns as such: Askell the Finn, Anders Jurgen the Finn, Karin "the Finnish woman" forced to beg to support her children, Johan Fransson from Viborg, Finland, Mats Hansson from Borgå, Finland, Måns Månsson the Finn, and repeatedly—the records are full of him—that "miscreant, Iver the Fin."[35]

Iver—or Evert or Ivert or Ivar—Hindricksson had arrived in 1641 as a convicted criminal with a reputation as an "abandoned villain" and a "turbulent man" which he quickly justified. Hired as a farmhand, he was soon charged with violent assault—with sticks, knives, and an ax—and with threatening murder, stoning a canoeist, committing bigamy, and fornicating with the wife of another Finn. He was first banished from Upland and then ordered to leave the valley. Authorized to return to close down his affairs, he threatened an officer and fled to the woods. Drifting back into the colony, he joined in the petition against Printz and became a militia captain but did not change his ways. In 1669 he joined an incipient insurrection led by a more purposeful malcontent known as The Long Finn (Marcus Jacobsson) who, posing as a member of the aristocratic Königsmark family, ran through the settlements with the inflammatory message that a Swedish war fleet lay just offshore, preparing to overthrow the English regime. The cabal, such as it was—a noisy collection of forty-two resentful and alienated Swedes and Finns—collapsed when betrayed, but it was enough to frighten the new, insecure English regime. Its governor, Col. Francis Lovelace, newly arrived and unsure of the loyalty of the strange population on the Delaware, contemplated drastic reprisals but in the end settled for severe fines. The Long Finn himself, however, was whipped, branded on the face with the letter R, and shipped to Barbados to be sold into service.

This passing episode scarcely satisfied Iver's passion for defiance of authority and established civilities. Six years later he joined still another insurrection, and in 1680 he was charged once again with resistance to constituted authority.[36]

In his more extreme behavior the notorious Iver was not, of course, typical of the Finns in the colony. But they lived, a contemporary wrote, "a disorderly and riotous life," driven by instincts that seem to have been deeply bred in the forest culture of Savo-Karelia and sustained through the resettlements in Sweden and America. On the Delaware they were remarkably comfortable—that world, for a full generation, was theirs: it conformed to their way of life. For of necessity—as a result of poverty, neglect, isolation, instability, and fear in the alien American outback—the Finns' inherited culture became the norm for most Europeans in the Swedish colony. The records of the Delaware Valley under the Swedes, and then under the Dutch and English who followed,

> are filled with references to smuggling, assault, riot, obstruction of justice, tax evasion, rape, ignoring summons, adultery, army desertion, reckless use of firearms, flight to avoid prosecution, sale of liquor to Indians, murder of Indians, refusal to take an oath, vandalism, killing a neighbor's livestock, horse theft, prostitution, and insurrection on the part of local Finns and Swedes. . . . The ax was a favored assault weapon, but fists, knives, sticks, guns, and rocks also were used.

A later generation would idealize this barbarous existence. In 1759 the Lutheran preacher Israel Acrelius, deploring what he considered the effete, frivolous behavior of the American Swedes in his own time on the Delaware (1749–56), wrote admiringly of the founders' elemental lives and sorrowfully of the declension that had set in. A century earlier, in the colony's early years, he wrote, people would walk miles to get to church, servants and girls barefooted; now, in these later times, all must go on horseback. Once a good and honest man had only a piece of bearskin for a saddle; now one must have "a saddle-cloth with galloon and fringe" and the young must dress like people of quality, servants with "*perruques du crains* [horsehair wigs] and the like" and girls with hooped skirts, "fine stuff-shoes, and other finery." Once people lived in "low log-houses, where the chimney was made of sticks covered with clay"; now they must have "painted houses of stone and brick." Once they had only ale and brandy to drink; now they drink wine and punch. Once they ate grits and mush; now they live on tea, coffee, and chocolate.[37]

Acrelius's lament was a typical jeremiad against the corruption of later times—the New England Puritans would elevate such regrets to an art form. But if Acrelius idealized the crudeness, the barbarousness, of the lives not only of the Finns but of the Swedes and other northern Europeans in the Delaware Valley, his description came close to the truth. The Swedes adopted the burn-beating form of agriculture, and Finns and Swedes alike took on a "savage" appearance: for later observers, they "are like one people." When clothes wore out, they could not be replaced. There were reports that the soldiers were making shirts from sailcloth or simply going without shirts. More commonly the settlers reverted to the Savo-Karelian tradition, now neatly fused with the native Indians' practice, of wearing clothes made of animal skins. "Savage coats" of buckskin became common, as did elkskin trousers. Women adopted skirts and shirts of deerskin; both men and women began wearing clothes made of sheepskins from which the fleece had not been sheared; and blankets and bedcovers were made from the hides of bears and wolves. By the time Risingh began his revival of the colony, clothes made of animal skins had almost entirely replaced those of woven cloth. And for many, moccasins, stitched together from tanned deerskins—as familiar to the Saamis as to the Lenapes—and birch-bark shoes familiar to Finnish peasants, had replaced heeled shoes.

In other ways too there was a convergence between the lifestyles of the colonists and the Indians. The Finns adopted Indian corn mush thickened with meat as a staple food and used Indian herbal remedies. The Lenapes' animism, the spirit world that enclosed them, their reliance on guardian spirits, their shamanistic religion, their belief in the reality of dreams, their nomadism and hunting culture—all this was remarkably similar to the Saamis' world that the Finns knew well; they could easily relate to it. Miscegenation, though not intermarriage, came easily to them, and when children were exchanged for language learning, the Europeans much more often than the Lenapes resisted the return to their homes.

Conversely, as the Europeans increasingly adopted Indian ways, the Indians took on what they could of European external culture. Though shocked at the Europeans' clumsy boots, their hairy faces, their booming cannons, and the occupational inversion of men doing women's farmwork, they too practiced burn-beating agriculture and viewed the Finns "as a kindred people." They were especially intrigued by European clothes and wore what clothes they could get until they fell apart. They paid well, in trade, for caps made of scrap cloth topped with multicolored tassels, and they particularly favored knee-length coats half red and half blue—which amused the Swedes since they resembled the garments forced on Swedish orphans at home. And they quickly adopted the superior technology of firearms and the exciting and destructive power of alcohol.[38]

In dwellings too in the earliest years, the Europeans approached the natives' forms. The Finns' first habitations, modeled on the Lapplanders' huts, were strikingly similar to the Indians' wigwams—a circle of poles joined at the top, covered with skins or cloth, with a flap at one side for a door. From these tentlike structures they advanced to small log versions of the Finnish *pirtti:* low cabins that could be built without nails by two men using only axes. They were, typically, structures of round logs fitted together in notched ends, the chinks caulked with clay and the walls pierced by two or three windows closed by sliding boards or, later, isinglass. As in the most rural parts of Finland, the cabins had smoke holes but not chimneys, and when chimneys appeared they were built of hollowed tree trunks. The foundation stones, when they existed, were unmortared; the floors were usually of dirt, or at best of the flat sides of split logs; and the entrance door, cut into a gable end, was so low one had to stoop to enter. The interiors were utterly sparse. Beds of loose straw covered with sheepskins were set against the walls, and the furnishings were completed with freestanding tables, benches, and chairs of sections of tree trunks, with utensils of tin, iron, and wood. Dark even in bright daylight, lit less commonly by candles than by the ancient "lighting-splints" (smoking torches of pine sticks fixed diagonally to the walls, known even in the immemorial songs of *The Kalevala*), these cabins, huddled but warm, were serviceable if primitive shelters.[39]

By Risingh's time, despite the general decline in the quality of life, the dwellings, at least, had improved. The single-room cabins were larger, and some had crude porch-like entrances and small hallways and storerooms between the entrance door and the large main room. That central living quarter was large enough to be divided into sections by curtains or clothes draped over rails. Though roomier, with more separated spaces than their predecessors, these were still dark, crudely built dwell-

ings that housed family, strangers, and in the early years, barnyard animals. The kitchen equipment still clustered around the corner fireplace,
and the ceilings were still the roofs themselves, which were constructed
of flat-hewn timbers covered with birch bark held in place by rows of split
logs. By the late 1650s some two-story houses appeared. The most notable was Risingh Hall—not as grand as Printzhof which, though built of
hewn logs, had glass windows and brick ovens, fireplaces, and chimneys.
Risingh's residence was a simpler affair, probably a double log structure:
a two-story section set against a low one-story building. When such
houses were built, and there were few of them before 1660, the original
cabins were relegated to kitchens, sheds, or smokehouses, and small saunas appeared as well. But even for the officials who lived in such houses,
the level of comfort remained low, at best equal to that of prosperous
Swedish peasants. Many, especially the Finns, were still struggling with
the most elemental problems of physical existence.[40]

6

Such was the population the Dutch took over in 1655—some six hundred
souls in all, an almost equal number of Finns and Swedes and a variety
of other north European peoples, most of them peasants or laborers, still
lacking both a profitable crop or product and a major settlement center,
still scattering to new locations on the west side of the Delaware and into
the near backcountry, but also in very small numbers on the east (Jersey)
side as well. In the nine years of Dutch rule that followed, the population of the former Swedish colony grew rapidly, along with that of New
Netherland as a whole, and it became even more complex ethnically as a
result of a strange development that suddenly transformed the region's
governance.[41]

Immediately upon acquiring New Sweden, Stuyvesant set up a provisional government for the region and ordered the inhabitants to regroup
into towns of sixteen to twenty families and to pay taxes for the land
granted. The Swedes, "to prevent mischief," were to be protected, for "an
increase in population is the life of a state," the company had reminded
him. Living in towns among the Dutch instead of in scattered farms would
usefully reduce their ethnic identity and simplify the Dutch jurisdiction.
Thus relocated, "they will be less to fear," for these were "a sort of people
that must be kept under else they will rebell, and of that nation these here

are the worst sort." But this was a futile plan. The Scandinavians refused all orders and enticements to leave their farms and resettle among the Dutch, and they threatened to move off to Maryland, as some had already done, if pressed. And they were reinforced in their determination to live apart and in their own way by the arrival of the last of Sweden's emigrant ships, the *Mercury*, whose 110 passengers, 92 of them Värmland Finns in family groups, scattered defiantly among their countrymen in the northern districts. In the end Stuyvesant was obliged to grant "the Swedish nation," as he called the Scandinavians, limited local self-government to keep them from defecting.[42]

Meanwhile, in Europe affairs were taking an unexpected turn. The Dutch West India Company, whose North American mandate now stretched from New England to Maryland, was determined somehow to make New Netherland profitable, or at least keep it from becoming a further drain on the company's dwindling resources. Upon hearing of the conquest of New Sweden the company began negotiations with the city of Amsterdam, which had loaned the company funds to finance the conquest of New Sweden. To pay off that debt and to reinforce the colony generally the company, financially strapped by its losses in Brazil and Guinea, proposed to cede to the city the southern half of New Sweden—from the Christina River south to the mouth of the Delaware—to form a separate colony loosely attached to New Netherland's greater jurisdiction. The arrangement would be mutually profitable. The company would be relieved of a debt, with the prospect of increased revenues from a growing population's trade and customs duties, while the city could look forward to having supplies of North American grain, timber, and other products to replace those that could no longer be obtained from the usual Baltic and Polish sources.[43]

The thirty-five-point contract between the two parties that created the colony of New Amstel (Nieuwer Amstel) detailed the city's obligation to develop the new subcolony physically, administratively, and politically, and laid out a remarkable set of privileges—land grants, personal subsidies, and tax exemptions—that would be accorded the colonists: perhaps the most generous enticements ever offered prospective settlers. The response was immediate. On Christmas Day 1656, four shiploads of subsidized independent farmers and peasants, 167 people in all, recruited from Gulick (Jülich) in the duchy of Cleves on the Dutch-German border, and committed to at least four years of residence in the colony, sailed

off. They arrived on the Delaware, after vicissitudes that included a shipwreck on Long Island, four months later. The colony's new director,
Jacob Alrichs, led the debarkation of the passengers, seventy-six of them
women and children, together with forty soldiers and their wives and
children, and took over the management of New Amstel.[44]

Alrichs's travails, in the two years before his death, were agonizing
and unending. Settled in Fort Christina, now renamed Altona, he distributed lots to the newcomers, repaired the public houses, and saw to
the construction of a log town hall and "a goodly town of about one
hundred houses." But the first year was a nightmare. The population
of about six hundred souls, many of them "rough people . . . as poor as
worms, and lazy withal," only a few of them qualified farmers, fell victim
to the damp climate made more miserable by a sequence of heavy rains
that ruined the winter fodder. "A hot intermittent fever" and dysentery
became epidemic; about one hundred people, many of them children,
died. And the diseases were compounded by the arrival of 108 more settlers on the *Mill*, 11 of whose companions had succumbed to scurvy on
the passage, 3 of whom died on landing. The survivors, especially the
indentured orphan children taken from Amsterdam's almshouses, were
suffering from a variety of illnesses, some contagious, and they brought
with them no supplies. But recruitment continued, in Finland and especially in the farming districts of Gelderland in Holland, leading to the
arrival of 137 self-proclaimed artisans, most of them incompetent, 70
more soldiers, and approximately 300 more women and children. There
was no way Alrichs could properly provide for them. "Misfortune," he
wrote, "seldom comes alone. . . . We pray to God and hope that our sins
may cease, thus diminishing our punishment. This we desire from the
bottom of our hearts."[45]

But his prayers went unanswered. He never received the "industrious people" he fervently hoped for, nor the supplies necessary to sustain
the people he had. As the population grew, far outstripping the supplies
available to support them—several new arrivals sold their extra clothes
for food—the colony's resources declined. Worms destroyed much of the
first crop, seed corn had to be consumed, food prices soared, the hot, wet
summer was succeeded by a long bitter winter, and many of the muskets they had been given, when first used, "blew up, burst and became
useless." The place was being crushed "like a little willow in its beginning and sprouting." Then the Amsterdam authorities, fearing financial

losses, began cutting back on the subsidies promised the settlers, which further undermined the settlers' confidence in the future of the colony. By the second year, first the traders among the new arrivals, then others, petitioned to be allowed to remove to Manhattan, though they had not yet paid off their debts to the city. The poorest among them begged Alrichs "with clasped hands" to release them from their four-year commitments: "We have spent, in our hunger, wretchedness, and misery, all that we had saved from our small pittance. We have nothing left wherewith to pay." But Alrichs, who had lost six of his household, including his wife, in the epidemic, refused. The result of this "too great preciseness" (Stuyvesant)—despite Amsterdam's order that defection could bring the death penalty—was numerous secret departures for Maryland and Virginia, which Alrichs and his chief military officer, the pugnacious veteran of warfare in Brazil, Alexander D'Hinoyossa, failed to stop. In fact, the soldiers themselves were beginning to desert, especially when rumors began circulating that Maryland was preparing an army to take the place over, an impression greatly strengthened by the arrival of a threatening delegation from Maryland that flatly asserted that colony's right to all the Delaware lands. By then the entire region, it was said, had acquired "so bad a name that the whole river could not wash it clean."[46]

Alrichs, exhausting himself trying to solve these problems, sent a delegation to Maryland to settle relations between the two colonies and to bring back the Finns and Swedes who had defected. That embassy, led by Augustine Herrman, failed in both. But Herrman reported that the escaped Finns and Swedes had not run off because of wretchedness or ill treatment but because they were "entirely idle and lazy . . . even too lazy to wash their own spoons and plates from which they had eaten." They simply hoped, he said, "to gain the bread of idleness" in the Chesapeake lands. Meanwhile D'Hinoyossa and an ally, the sheriff Gerrit van Sweringen, were writing secretly to Holland accusing Alrichs of causing all the misery. In December 1659 Alrichs, worn out by his failing efforts in all directions—to provide for the prosperity and health of the colonists, to stem the flow of desertions, and to eliminate the threat of a takeover by the English—died.[47]

D'Hinoyossa and Van Sweringen took command and immediately tore into the scattered, fragile community in a rampage of exploitation and autocratic rule. D'Hinoyossa, who would ultimately die by execution for mutiny in the Dutch army, seized all of Alrichs's papers and, claiming that his predecessor had violated instructions, seized his personal property. When the magistrates refused to concur, D'Hinoyossa dismissed them, then charged Alrichs's executor and heir, a councilor and the colony's secretary, with mutiny, sacked him too, denied him Alrichs's papers, and drove him out of the colony. Inevitably he clashed with New Netherland's superior authority on the river, in the person of the mild-tempered, sensible Willem Beekman. None of the claims of Manhattan's authorities would be recognized, D'Hinoyossa declared, because he himself was "the head and fountain of justice." Beekman reported that D'Hinoyossa threatened to fine anyone who spoke ill of him, and charged him with having violently denounced the Dutch authorities in a tavern brawl. If the city of Amsterdam did not back his authority, D'Hinoyossa had declared, he would turn the place over to the English, the Portuguese, the Swedes, or the Danes. He might well get a commission from Portugal to go privateering along the Atlantic coast, in which case he would "do special damage to the people of Manhattan." "What the devil did he care," he was quoted as saying, "whom he served?"[48]

The conflict of jurisdictions continued, with the local populace driven by D'Hinoyossa into some degree of submission or alienation. When Beekman charged him with having sold for his own profit supplies intended for the settlers, D'Hinoyossa saw to it that the witnesses refused to testify against him. And when Beekman and Stuyvesant sought to bring D'Hinoyossa's ally Van Sweringen to justice for having shot one of the West India Company's soldiers, D'Hinoyossa pardoned him of any such crime before an investigation could be made. He seemed to have no scruples, no sense of moderation. When a runaway servant was captured after wounding two of his English captors, D'Hinoyossa ignored both English and Dutch authorities, appointed Van Sweringen judge, and when the man was convicted, hanged him, cut off his head, and displayed it on a post. People feared him. Beekman avoided him as much as possible, anticipating all sorts of false charges: "if you want to beat a dog, it is easy to find a club."[49]

Clearly the uneasy, overlapping jurisdictions on the Delaware were not working properly. In addition to the conflicts that erupted again and again between Beekman and D'Hinoyossa, there was the strange situation of the Swedes and Finns. Some enjoyed limited self-government because their farms fell within the company's jurisdiction; others, within New Amstel's boundaries, did not. In 1663, when the Amsterdam authorities, fearing further losses, attempted to return New Amstel to the West India Company, the company responded by granting the city the entire Delaware area, thus increasing for the Amsterdam merchants the prospect of eventual profits. And indeed, by the early fall of 1664, when an English force under Sir Robert Carr swept over the whole of New Netherland and put an end to Dutch colonization in North America, the prospects had brightened. Profitable cargoes of wheat, timber, and furs were beginning to be shipped from New Amstel, a sawmill was under construction, and the possible illegal marketing of Chesapeake tobacco, to be purchased by the sale of slaves and locally produced beer, was being planned. The population of the former New Sweden had grown to over a thousand, and the city of Amsterdam was actively and successfully recruiting more colonists—people who were "laborious and skilled in farming . . . Swedes and Fins (who are already there in reasonable numbers) being . . . particularly fitted, and of whom many families or households are . . . expected, as they have been notified by their countrymen . . . of the good opportunity there."[50]

In the summer of 1663 thirty-two Swedes were in Amsterdam waiting passage, and the city was preparing to send 130 more families willing to cover their own expenses. Meanwhile D'Hinoyossa himself returned from a trip to Holland with one hundred colonists, thirty-two of them Finns, and urged the dispatch of fifty slaves who, he believed, would be particularly useful in preparing the fertile but still uncleared valleys and doing "other heavy work." By then the former New Sweden had 110 farms, two thousand cows and oxen, twenty horses, eighty sheep, and several thousand swine. The whole of New Netherland, on the eve of its demise, had "*increased so much in population and commerce, as before they did not in 30 years.*" And then in July 1663 the *St. Jacob* arrived from Amsterdam. It carried, in addition to sixty farm laborers and unmarried women, a small group of radical utopians, most of them Mennonites, led by a remarkably articulate and energetic visionary, Pieter Cornelisz Plockhoy. A fringe, a sprig, a tiny offshoot of the vast growth of Protestant utopianism and messianic revivalism in western Europe, Plockhoy's conventicle settled on the lower Delaware amid the ruins of the West India Company's devastated settlement, Swanendael.[51]

THAT BLEAK RIVERSIDE CLEARING—long since renamed Whorekill—would soon again be the scene of ruin and destruction. But for a fleet-

ing moment—a year, more or less—Plockhoy's obscure, huddled, evanescent settlement lit up brilliantly the possibilities and dangers of life in North
America for those who hoped to live apart from the world, to achieve ideal,
rational lives, free of corruption, and to be a beacon for aspiring humanity.
In this most unlikely spot, witnessed by a few rustic Swedes and Finns,
some traders from Maryland, and an occasional wandering Indian, Plockhoy's people would, they hoped, begin the transformation of the world,
according to a plan elaborately designed by their leader.

The project that deposited this small group of believers on the
lower Delaware had had a long gestation. Plockhoy, born about 1620,
had known from childhood the passions of Protestant millenarianism,
the soaring utopianism and ecstatic visions that marked the efforts of
religious radicals to complete the work of the Reformation and restore
Christianity to its apostolic simplicity. It had been in his native Zierikzee,
the small commercial center of Zeeland in the far southwest of the Netherlands, that he had been touched by the fierce Biblicism and spirituality of the Mennonites and Anabaptists and had accepted their worldly
asceticism, their principles of adult baptism, pacifism, non-participation
in civil government, and personal responsibility for finding the way to
God's grace. But he remained neutral in the theological battles that split
the Dutch Mennonite community, and turned with increasing interest to
the "Collegiant" philosophy of his fellow townsman, Galenus Abrahams
de Haan, a prophetic herald of a new spiritual regime. Like Galenus,
Plockhoy came to seek a loose spiritual life guided not by doctrine or
credal discipline but by enlightened ideas and personal conscience.[52]

The Collegiants in Amsterdam were not an organized sect but a
convocation of various Christian groups who met together in Quaker-like
gatherings to discuss scripture and the spiritual life. Their passion for
religious freedom led them to a concern for social justice and, in Plockhoy's case, to a search for a comprehensive program that would embrace
"freedom of speech, absolute tolerance, and a universal Christendom."
Like Galenus, Plockhoy probed the inner structure of "the ideal Christian
commonwealth of love, equality, and freedom," testing his ideas in a society of poets who formed what they called "Parnassus on the Y,"* some of
whom would later write verses in support of his Delaware venture. With

---

* Amsterdam's bay is shaped like a Y. On the Pythagorean Y emblematic of the choice between
evil and virtuous ways, well known to European intellectuals of Plockhoy's generation, see
Frances A. Yates, *The Rosicrucian Enlightenment* (London, 1972), 56.

them, at the tavern they called "Sweet Rest" and that they thought of as an "art-school for the promotion of virtue," he discussed such meaningful and soul-searching questions as the abolition of "too deeply rooted customs," the possibility of an inclusive Christian "sheeps fold" that would embrace all sects, and the rights and wrongs of polygamy.[53]

By the 1650s Plockhoy was in search of a worldly venue for the Christian perfectionist ideas he was developing, some way to realize his utopian ideals. Inevitably he came into contact with that pan-European virtuoso of messianic reform, Samuel Hartlib, a Polish Prussian who had become a leader in the reformist ferment in republican England. Abandoning family and home, Plockhoy joined the self-appointed "universal secretary of the union of good men" in England, circulated among the English intelligentsia, and in time, in the final years of the Interregnum, found his way into the court of Oliver Cromwell. In those last months of the great man's regime, foundering though it was, a galaxy of social critics and prophetic seers was renewing the effort to realize the millennial aspirations of the early years of England's Revolution, when models of universal reform of all kinds had kindled hope for the transformation of the world and the proximate redemption of mankind. In 1657 and 1658 that earlier euphoria glowed once again, carrying forward into the late 1650s the utopian influences of Bacon's *New Atlantis*, Hartlib's *Kingdom of Macaria*, Comenius's prophetic tracts, and other, more ephemeral writings of the euphoric 1640s. In that world of soaring aspirations, the obscure, transported Zeelander flourished.[54]

He quickly managed to meet "God's Englishman" himself, and in a series of conversations ("I was heard several times with patience") Plockhoy urged Cromwell, failing in health though he was, to undertake the wholesale reformation of England as the first step in the rebirth of mankind, according to a few basic principles. There should be in England, he counseled the Lord Protector, a universal Christian state. Christian groups in every community should assemble together, in rooms where, seated, they could face each other, for regular, nondoctrinaire scripture readings. There should be an end to all "lording over consciences," and all ties of church and state and all tithes should be abolished. There should be total toleration for all Christian peoples, free of any support or influence by the financial or physical force of the state, whose only role would be to suppress, if necessary, all efforts of some to dominate others. In this situation most differences of doctrine or opinion would become reconciled, but if not, they should be left as they were, to be settled, if at all, at a later time. If Cromwell were to realize such a program in England, Plockhoy felt certain that "Holland, Denmark, Sweden, France and other kingdoms . . . will easily be brought to a firm bond of unity."

It may well have been that Cromwell was interested, but his death in September 1658 "obstructed" Plockhoy in his proceeding—though only temporarily. Four months later the Dutchman laid out the same ideas in an extensive letter to Parliament, enclosing two letters he had written to Cromwell, all of which he published in a pamphlet entitled *The Way to the Peace and Settlement of These Nations,* aimed "to awaken the publick spirits in England." And he followed that production with yet another letter along the same line, addressed to the new Lord Protector, Richard Cromwell.[55]

Though by the spring of 1659 nothing had yet come of his efforts, Plockhoy was only warming to the task of designing a utopian world. Social and economic ills were as much on his mind as religious oppression. He had ended his discourse to Parliament with the words, "Give ear to the poor, for the cry of them is exceeding great in these nations," and it was to that theme that he devoted himself in his next publication.

The message of that remarkable "*treatise*"—a plan for an ideal, Christian, semicommunistic community that anticipated the later Delaware settlement—is entirely contained in its sprawling title: *A Way Propounded To Make the Poor in These and Other Nations Happy, by Bringing Together a Fit, Sutable, and Well-Qualified People into One Household-government, or Little Common-wealth, Wherein Every One May Keep His Propriety, and Be Imployed in Some Work or Other, As He Shall Be Fit, without Being Oppressed. Being the Way Not Only To Rid These and Other Nations From Idle, Evil, and Disorderly Persons, but Also from All Such As Have Sought and Found Out Many Inventions, To Live upon the Labour of Others.* The title concluded with the words of the Psalms, "*Blessed Is He That Considereth the Poor . . . He Shall Be Blessed upon the Earth.*" And annexed to the pamphlet was a separate little publication entitled *An Invitation to This Society, or Little Common-wealth . . .* , which reflected a major shift in Plockhoy's thinking.

He had come to realize that he and his adherents might well prove to be "insufferable to the world, and [the world might] be incorrigible or unbetterable as to us." Therefore he and his people might have to "reduce our friendship and society to a few in number, and maintain it in such places as are separate from other men, where we may with less impediment or hindrance love one another and mind the wonders of God, eating the bread we shall earn with our own hands."[56]

He might indeed have thought that his ideas would be found insufferable by the world at large and that he and his brethren would have to withdraw to some remote spot in order properly to mind God's wonders. For his social and economic ideas were radical by any measure. The evils of inequality and disorder, he wrote, were everywhere. Not only do malevolent governors, greedy merchants, and lazy, idle, and negligent ministers bring slavery and thralldom to the common people everywhere, but ordinary artisans and laborers, to escape work, lie and deceive, throwing the burden of creative work on honest people. Let people join hands in brotherhood, he wrote, in righteousness and love. In the conventicles he now contemplated there would be a sharing of life's work with clear divisions of labor among farmers, artisans (seventy-two types were listed), mariners, and masters of arts and sciences. Specialization, hence interdependence, would increase; superiority in status would be temporary, revolving with the cycles of work; and in all things there would be a sharing of skills and experience for mutual benefit. Though private property would be preserved, there would be a pooling of effort in agriculture and industry as in education and management, and all of life would be carefully regulated by mutually agreed-on rules.

None of this, he assured his readers, was mere speculation. The first "little common-wealth," he wrote, was already in operation near London, and there were plans for more such settlements in Bristol and Ireland, where land and building materials were cheap. Applications were invited via Giles Calvert, who was also an agent for the Levellers. In the second edition of the pamphlet interested people were told where and when they might get in touch directly with Plockhoy himself. Nor were his schemes without prominent backers. Hartlib actively supported the cause and sent copies of *A Way Propounded* to the scientist John Beal, who approved of beginning Christian reform "in small models"; probably also to John Milton, whose views were not dissimilar on some points; and to Cambridge University's vice-chancellor, John Worthington, a major figure in reform circles, with whom Hartlib explored the similarity of Plockhoy's plans to the Hutterite conventicles in Hungary and Transylvania. Plockhoy himself referred to the similarities with the Hutterites, whose work he knew through the Dutch Mennonites if not through Comenius, then resident in Amsterdam.[57]

But fate once again blasted Plockhoy's hopes. Within a year of the publication of *A Way Propounded* Charles II was restored to the throne of England, and the reform era of the Protectorate came to an end. But Plockhoy pressed on, turning quickly to the possibility of a continental venue. In October 1660 he was reported to be leading a group to a safe territory in Germany, near Cologne, and a year after that he was back in his native Holland preparing to bring his campaign for justice, equality, and righteousness to a final, radical conclusion.

He had long known of New Netherland generally and of the Swanendael/Whorekill spot specifically. His friend Jacob Steendam, a member of the Parnassan club at the Sweet Rest tavern, had lived and prospered in the colony for a decade after 1652 and celebrated its wonders and vast potential, first in a 104-line rhapsodic poem, "The Complaint of New Amsterdam," and then in a metaphor-choked lyric of 288 lines, "The Praise of New Netherland," calculated to encourage emigration to that "noblest land of all," whose perfumed air was like that of the fields of Eden.

> *Nor turf, nor dried manure,—within your doors,*
> *Nor coal, extracted from earth's secret stores;*
> *Nor sods, uplifted from the barren moors,*
> *For fuel given;*
> *Which, with foul stench the brain intoxicate;*
> *And thus, by the foul gas which they create,*
> *The intellects of man, wise and great,*
> *Men are out-driven.*

Plockhoy was probably present when Steendam declaimed this rhapsody to the assembled Parnassans, but he had other reasons for believing that Whorekill could become the promised land.[58]

His brother Harmen in his late teens had moved to the colony and had served as a soldier in the small fort near Whorekill. Harmen probably knew Steendam in Manhattan, and he too urged his brother to consider the possibilities of settling on the scene of the Swanendael massacre. With such detailed information and encouragement from his friend and fellow

Parnassan and from his own brother, and with the Amsterdam merchants actively promoting emigration to New Amstel, Plockhoy began to think seriously of building his new Jerusalem on the Delaware. The place, a virtual paradise according to Steendam, seemed perfectly to satisfy his desire for a settlement "separate from other men." And in addition he had renewed his old contacts with Amsterdam's Mennonites, who too were seeking a refuge from the pressures and corruptions of the world.

Between 1661 and 1663 Plockhoy led the Mennonites in an extended series of negotiations with the Amsterdam authorities in which he explained his heart's desires. In seven letters written between November 1661 and May 1662, Plockhoy requested a land grant at Whorekill and a charter for a settlement for "the relief of many aggrieved and languishing families." In his colony there would have to be a "universal" church with no clergymen, laymen reading the scripture in rotation. The people would have to be free of tithes and have full civil though not criminal jurisdiction, the free exercise of all trades and crafts, total liberty of religion, and equality in political participation. Plockhoy's fourth letter was crucial. It listed 117 articles of association, in effect a constitution, that created a completely democratic regime. Equality of status and role would be the key to popular government. Every adult male would have to pledge never to "strive for any special power" and never quarrel over religion; and "the weaker members will always be protected as much as possible from oppression by the stronger ones." Laws would be enacted by two-thirds majority of votes of the people cast in ballots and enforced by a single popularly elected magistrate distinguished for "means, intelligence, and knowledge." The number of public servants, all of them accountable to the public, would increase only with the growth of the population. Mennonites were to be exempted from military service and from voting on military matters. People were to work together, in common, for the public good, for five years, laboring for no more than six hours daily. After that period the land and other property would be divided into parcels of private ownership by lot.[59]

This would be a welfare society: the sick, rich or poor, would have public health care; "all impotent men, women, and children"—the needy, orphans, sick, and old—would be looked after by the public. Youths would be counseled on marriage, and all quarrels, however personal, would be submitted to public servants for resolution. Troublemakers—stubborn slanderers and unruly quarrelers and such false believers as "obstinate papists . . . , parasitic Jews, Anglican headstrong Quakers and Puritans, and rash and stupid believers in the millenium . . . [and] present-day pretenders to revelation"—all these, who would threaten the basic toleration and rationality, would be counseled, and if necessary expelled by legal process. And well-disposed people who lived nearby, outside the community, would be treated with kindness so that they might be "saved from becoming degraded, and will become instead worthwhile members of our society."[60]

In April and June 1662 the burgomasters of Amsterdam granted Plockhoy and the Mennonites loans of passage money, cash subventions to settle on the Whorekill, and a contract to legalize the settlement. In October all the papers were published together in an eighty-four-page pamphlet, *Brief Account of New Netherlands Situation . . . and Peculiar Suitability for Colonization . . .*, which Plockhoy introduced with a discourse on what had turned out to be the most controversial issue that his utopian scheme had raised.

What did he mean by equality? Did he mean to abolish all differences among people—to level the whole society? For people familiar with the threatening claims of the Levellers, the Fifth Monarchy Men, the Diggers, and assorted radical agitators and for whom the memories of late medieval peasant rebellions were still fresh, this was an overwhelmingly important question, which Plockhoy struggled to answer. Equality, he insisted, was indeed to be the basis of his new society, but "we hope nobody will be so naive, much less malevolent, as to think . . . that we are attempting to remove all differences between people." Each person will always have special qualities, "comprising a universe in himself." Only a fool would try to confine everyone to a rigid, narrow set of rules without considering what they needed for their particular well-being. Yes, there must be general rules for the common welfare, but not such as to restrict anyone's "personal and natural liberty." If individuality is suppressed, it will surely, in the end, break out violently. The equality he sought as the basis for "a stable Christian civilian society, republic, or commonwealth" must be an equality among people, some of whom would be more intelligent than others, some more wealthy than others, some rulers and some ruled, some male and some female. But then, if there were to be these traditional differences between rich and poor, rulers and ruled, where was the equality? The equality, he wrote, lay in eliminating "all domineering amongst members of the society, or exercise of force . . . [and]

all complacent obedience, such as in the Roman Catholic way of imposing upon us, freedom loving Dutchmen." In other words, he sought to
eliminate not the natural differences among people and the differences in
the rewards of their personal accomplishments, but the differences created and maintained by force and intimidation—the arbitrary differences
shaped by the dead hand of custom, the church, or sheer force imposed
on subservient people.[61]

But Plockhoy was not finished explaining. In the summer of 1662 he
circulated his last publication, his *Brief and Concise Plan*. It was essentially
a recruitment pamphlet, but it was also a miscellany of documents. It
contained a copy of Plockhoy's contract with the city of Amsterdam, a
sonnet by one of the Parnassan group, Karel ver Loove, on the Netherlands' motto, "Union Makes Strength"; and an eleven-stanza poem by
Steendam praising the colony as "the flow'r, the noblest of all lands . . .
a pleasure garden" on the banks of the Delaware. There were also instructions on practical arrangements. But most important, there was a reprise
of Plockhoy's conception of an ideal commonwealth.[62]

With this, the years of thinking, planning, and explaining came to
an end, and the project was put into operation. Though Plockhoy had
contracted to transport only twenty-five adult males who would prepare
the way for others, including families to follow, he had hoped for an initial shipment of one hundred colonists, but in this he was disappointed.
On July 28, 1663, only forty-one souls disembarked from the *St. Jacob* at
Whorekill, among them his own family, to launch the community that
would usher in a new era in human history.

What happened in the months that followed, as the Dutch intellectual sought to realize his dreams and the hopes of his fellow Dutch and
English utopians, is not known. If a record of their lives at Whorekill was
kept, it has not survived. All that is known is that when in August 1664
Sir Robert Carr and his overwhelming English force assaulted the Dutch
colony, D'Hinoyossa—as opposed to Stuyvesant, who surrendered Manhattan without a shot—decided to fight for the defense of New Amstel.
As a result, blood was spilled in the colony's main area, and when Carr
swept south to Whorekill, he "there plundered and tooke possession of
all effects belonging to the Citty of Amsterdam, and alsoe what belonged
to the Quaking Society of Plockhoy *to a very naile*." Stuyvesant gave a
more lurid account of the fate of New Amstel: "they were invaded, stript
bare, plundered, and many of them sold as slaves in Virginia."[63] What can

be reconstructed from scattered sources is more commonplace and more in keeping with the general pattern of European population history in North America. The colony's corporate identity was destroyed, but the people remained and gradually dispersed through the region, mingling with people of quite different backgrounds, settling into a thinly populated polyethnic farming district—Finns, Swedes, English, Germans, and north Europeans of every description—whose distinctive vernacular culture would only gradually form.

A Whorekill census of 1671, reconstructed from genealogical sources, shows, in the careers of Plockhoy's immediate family members, the dispersal of his evanescent elysium. The leader himself died in his mid-forties, during that difficult first year or shortly thereafter. His wife, who remarried, also died before 1671. One of her daughters married an Englishman, as did Plockhoy's sister. His brother Harmen, long familiar with this frontier world, survived another twenty-five years, became an Indian trader, and obtained land for himself and Plockhoy's son, Cornelis, who was blind. It was this blind son who was the last survivor. In 1693 his stepfather, Willem Clasen, moved him to the Mennonite settlement in Germantown, Pennsylvania, where the blind young man was granted, as charity, a small house and a parcel of land. It was there that the last direct legacy of Plockhoy's experiment lived out his life.[64]

The whole of Plockhoy's adventure—from its origins in his euphoric vision within the intellectual ferment of metropolitan Europe to its squalid ending in the American woodlands—was a model for, an ideal type of, innumerable utopias to come. Like Plockhoy's peculiar embodiment of The Truth, they would be cities on the hill; they would flare up brilliantly in people's imaginations, take shape through bitter adversity, flourish briefly, and then as communities wither and die. But in this, Plockhoy's project was unique. Though his utopian village was obliterated, his ideas lived on, to inspire generations of European reformers, from the Quakers of his own time to Robert Owen, Karl Marx, Eduard Bernstein, and Joshua Rountree in the nineteenth century, and to economists and students of cooperative movements in the twentieth century.[65]

A different, almost mythological renown would be the fate of a more famous conventicle that had been established with passion equal to Plockhoy's some four hundred miles to the north. Its demise was more gradual than Plockhoy's utopia, but for those most intimately involved, it was no less tragic and far more eloquently lamented.

CHAPTER 11

God's Conventicle,
Bradford's Lamentation

1

THERE ARE STRIKING SIMILARITIES between Plockhoy's settlement at Whorekill on the Delaware and the Pilgrims' village at
Plymouth on the south shore of Massachusetts. Both had Anglo-Dutch
origins; both were deliberate and complete removals from a corrupt metropolitan world; both were designed as communes of equal sharing in
the initial years; both were convinced that they were the preservers, the
protectors and promoters, of pristine Christianity; and in the end both
were overtaken by forces they could not control, their people melding
into a diverse population whose distinctive folkways had not yet formed.

There were differences too. Plockhoy, born the year of the Pilgrims'
settlement in America, was critical but tolerant of diversity within the
Protestant confessions; the Pilgrim leaders feared toleration, which they
correctly saw would destroy their entire project, both church and sanctified society.[1] Plockhoy saw benefits in business enterprise; the Pilgrims
feared its corrosive effect. Plockhoy's program was elaborately articulated, the product of an intricate system of radical ideas expressed in enumerated rules and precepts; the Pilgrims lived in loose agreement on what

they took to be the true and simple principles of primitive Christianity and apostolic purity. Plockhoy's utopia ended in a sudden, fiery death that was barely recorded and entirely unlamented; the Pilgrims' utopia faded gradually, its demise documented in lamentations that would become classic texts in elegiac prose. But however different, both were products of the great churnings and burnings in radical Protestantism that account for population displacements throughout the Atlantic world.

WILLIAM BRADFORD, the leader of the Pilgrims' settlement in America and its great mythographer, would forever deny that his people were "Familists"—that is, devoted, like the notorious sixteenth-century German Family of Love, to the search for an ecstatic union with Christ—or that they were in any other way radical spiritists seeking exaltation that transcended the constraints of everyday life. They were much more earthbound, more pragmatic than that. Like other separatist groups, the Pilgrims, seeking to re-create what they believed had been the simple life of the earliest Christians, had despaired of the Church of England ever returning to that authentic spiritual state and had declared themselves independent of its discipline, its sacerdotal powers, and its secular sanctions. Following the lead of earlier separatists who had been forced into exile, they sought to narrow the distance between God's invisible church of the truly blessed and the visible church here below, by limiting membership in their conventicles to those who formally professed the doctrines of reformed Christianity, lived blameless lives, and submitted to the congregation's discipline. They shared much with the larger Puritan reform movement within the Church of England that was sweeping across England, but pressed on further, to deny any validity in the Episcopal establishment and to claim that their own small, independent congregation was the correct model of Christian organization. The demands on their members were simple—only a profession of faith, commitment to the covenant that bound the group together, and behavior appropriate for professing Christians. But in the context of the time, their views were considered to be not only defiant of church and state but subversive of social stability and likely to lead to the anarchic upheavals that had followed the original Reformation.[2]

In the face of Episcopal oppression on the one hand and the innate pressure toward even more radical and dangerous extremes, agreement within the group was essential. Solidarity was everything, and Bradford recorded with pride the Pilgrim leaders' description of their conventicle as "knit together as a body in a most strict and sacred bond and covenant of the Lord . . . straitly tied to all care of each other's good and of the whole, by every one and so mutually."[3] In fact, the emigrating community as a whole was never that. From the moment of its departure for America, it was a loose collection of people of many conditions, drawn from many places, with various degrees of devotion to the founding ideals. But the inner core, the central body of worshippers and the leadership, formed, as Bradford wrote, an independent church of true believers bonded together for their common good and the pursuit of pristine Christianity.

THE CONGREGATION FIRST TOOK FORM in a gathering of religious dissidents scattered through obscure villages in northern Nottinghamshire and the adjacent areas of western Lincolnshire and southern Yorkshire, 150 miles from London. There, in what has been called "the Pilgrim Quadrilateral"—an area of approximately ninety square miles that included thirty parishes, from the boggy grasslands of the Trent River valley west to the low-lying meadows and pastureland of Nottinghamshire—dissent from the ritual formalities and ecclesiastical structures of the Church of England had taken deep root. In Scrooby, a minor manor of the Archbishop of York, the bailiff's son, William Brewster, had brought back from the University of Cambridge something of the Puritan radicalism that was flaming through the colleges—especially Christ's, Emmanuel, Corpus Christi, Trinity, and Brewster's own Peterhouse. There, in the single year of his residence at age fourteen or fifteen, he had been singed by the fervent preaching of dissenters like William Perkins, Francis Johnson, John Udall, and John Greenwood, all of whom faced suppression and imprisonment, some of whom would die on the scaffold, martyrs to the reformist cause. And Brewster brought back to Scrooby also the worldly experience he had gained as an assistant to the chief English diplomat in the Netherlands, and a sense of that new nation's toleration and of its possibilities as a refuge for English dissidents.[4]

Assuming his father's positions and status—not quite of the gentry but above the rank of yeoman (he would acquire a personal library of 382 books, 64 in Latin)—Brewster drew to the modest Scrooby manor house some of the best known and most articulate opponents of the established church then living in retreat in villages within a radius of ten miles. Among these active and articulate dissenters were Richard Clifton, the dismissed rector of nearby Babworth; John Robinson, who had returned to his native Sturton-le-Steeple after stormy involvements in radical conventicles in Cambridge, London, and Norwich; and the notorious radical, already a formal separatist from the Church of England, John Smyth, of Gainsborough, a town six or seven miles north of Sturton-le-Steeple. Farther off but closely involved in a broad network of Puritan landowners and lawyers was the prosperous former law student Thomas Helwys, who had returned to his home, Broxtowe Hall, near Nottingham, where he assumed a leadership role in the spreading separatist movement. But however deeply involved he was with the work of Brewster, Robinson, Smyth, and the other dissident leaders, Helwys was yet unique in his secure gentry status. Almost all who came together to pray, to profess their convictions, and to debate the nature of the true church were ordinary farmers and artisans from the surrounding villages who were inflamed with the desire to worship "according to the simplicity of the gospel, without the mixture of men's inventions." Among these humble followers was the young William Bradford, an orphaned yeoman's son from the village of Austerfield, adjacent to Scrooby. A sensitive, rather bookish teenager when he met the mature Brewster, he had defied his family's practical expectations and had become Brewster's and Robinson's spiritual ward and ultimately the custodian of their memory and that of the enterprise they shared with a small, motley collection of their countrymen.[5]

By the time the clandestine congregation at Scrooby, Gainsborough, Austerfield, Sturton, and the other nearby villages had concluded that life was intolerable in England under what Bradford called the scoffing and scorn of the profane multitude and "the lordly and tyrannous power of the prelates" demanding conformity, they had become a company of about 125 souls. Depressed by recurrent waves of economic distress and the ordinary brutality of the world that surrounded their pious gatherings, as well as by the threatening demands of the overweening church, they were determined to defy the law and escape in secret to Amsterdam, where other Puritan radicals had preceded them. Their first, furtive effort, in 1607, to leave from an inlet near Boston, in Lincolnshire, was betrayed by the ship captain, and the entire group was taken into custody. A year later the community left Gainsborough on a coal barge for transfer to a small Dutch ship. The plan failed when the approach of the local militia forced them to sail off with only sixteen men aboard, leaving behind some eighty people, most of them women and children. Subjected to a long, stormy voyage across the North Sea, the men were badly "turmoiled" by the time they were reunited in Amsterdam with the rest of the devout "country village[r]s" they had left behind.[6]

Within a year they fled again, this time from the "grisly face of poverty coming upon them like an armed man" in the enterprising port city and from the sectarian controversies that developed with Smyth's people and other expatriated separatist groups that had long been settled there. The smaller, inland university city of Leiden was more congenial to them, and there, where they settled in 1609, they lived for a decade in what Bradford later recalled was "peace and love and holiness" under the tactful and humane leadership of Brewster and Robinson. But as the years passed and the demand for conformity increased in England, the Puritan diaspora spread, and the Leiden exiles were joined by so many others "from divers parts of England" as well as from the nearby French-speaking Walloon communities that their once-minuscule community grew to four or five hundred. The geographical sources of the newcomers to the Leiden congregation, a reflection of the spread of radical Puritanism in Jacobean Britain, were diverse. Of 123 members whose origins have been established, four came from the far north (Durham and Scotland), 68 from the eastern counties (eastern Yorkshire, Norfolk, Suffolk, Essex, and Kent), 24 from the middle counties (mid- and western Yorkshire, Lincolnshire, Nottinghamshire, Cambridgeshire, Leicestershire, Berkshire, and Wiltshire), 24 from the south (Somersetshire, Dorsetshire, Sussex, and Hampshire), and 17 from London. Contention within a group so large and so diverse was inevitable, as was the advent of people so alien to the Scrooby leaders, so "incurable and incorrigible" in their views and behavior, that after suitable warnings and counseling they had to be "purged off."[7]

By 1617 the Scrooby exiles and their new associates had settled into the daily life of the city as semiskilled and unskilled workers in some fifty-seven trades. There were among them tobacco workers and tobacco sellers, pipe makers, shoemakers, masons, silversmiths, cabinetmakers, brewers, coopers, lock makers, engravers, candle makers, and jewelers; but the great majority were workers at the lowest level in the production and retail sale of textiles—wool, fustian, say, bombazine, linen, baize, and camlet—or made small objects of them: gloves, ribbons, stockings, bunting, or hats. Few attained a modest prosperity (the well-educated Brewster taught English privately to highly placed locals and set up as a printer of polemical tracts); but most, having exhausted their savings, were desperately poor. And other problems began to appear. The Dutch language posed difficulties, especially for the adults, and it was not clear how best to educate the children. Occasionally there were riotous clashes with Dutch religious conservatives. The temptations of the enterprising world about them were pervasive, as was the tendency of their children to join in the pastimes and group life of the Dutch and be "drawn away by evil examples into extravagant and dangerous courses" as soldiers, sailors, or casual sinners. Increasingly it seemed that they would lose not only their language but their "name as English." A deepening erosion could be seen in their integrity as a separated conventicle, and with it came the fear that they would fail to become "stepping stones unto others for the performing of so great a work." Some lost heart and returned to England, but even the most committed came to believe that there was little hope that under these circumstances their desperate project in the service of God would survive into a second generation. It was the part of wisdom to consider migrating once again, to a more isolated, less worldly, less contaminating place.[8]

Guyana, for example. They knew about Guyana—the Wild Coast of South America at the Orinoco estuary, said by Raleigh and others to be a rich, fruitful place where nature produced such abundance that human effort was unnecessary. Some of the most prosperous among them favored a move to that exotic location, but others objected that the hot climate there "would not so well agree with our English bodies" and would breed grievous diseases—a caution that their Walloon neighbors in Leiden, who would settle in Guyana two years later, ignored at the cost of their lives. And if they prospered there, they feared that the Spanish would attack them and take over their settlement. They had offers from the Dutch to resettle in nearby Zeeland, and they knew of their predecessors' earlier efforts to relocate on the Magdalen Islands in the Gulf of the St. Lawrence River. But they knew most about Virginia, which, they had been told, had a more livable climate than Guyana and was safe from the Spanish and French. But there, in that English territory, they might once again be persecuted for their religion. That point was cleared up, however, when a patent for a private plantation in Virginia became possible and when the Crown assured them that they would be left in peace there to worship as they pleased.

But did they really wish to migrate to "those vast and unpeopled countries of America . . . where there are only savage and brutish men which range up and down, little otherwise than the wild beasts of the same"? They had to consider the unendurable length of the voyage, with its "unconceivable perils and dangers," and they had to consider too the likely miseries of the land ("famine and nakedness and the want . . . of all things"). And there was always the

> continual danger of the savage people, who are cruel, barbarous and most treacherous . . . not being content only to kill and take away life, but delight to torment men in the most bloody manner . . . flaying some alive . . . cutting off the members and joints . . . and broiling on the coals, eat[ing] the collops of their flesh in their sight whilst they live, with other cruelties horrible to be related.

Simply contemplating the voyage, Bradford wrote, caused "the very bowels of men" to grate within them and the weak among them to quake and tremble.[9]

But in the end they decided that the dangers, though great, were not desperate, nor were the difficulties insuperable. God, they believed, would bless them, and if they died in the removal, they would die honorably, while in Leiden they would die "in exile and in a poor condition." And the future in the Netherlands was darkened even more by the prospect of the resumption of warfare with the Spanish, who "might prove as cruel as the savages of America, and the famine and pestilence as sore here as there, and their liberty less to look out for remedy."

So they went ahead. They sent emissaries to London to negotiate with the Virginia Company and, after months of delays, obtained the patent to settle in that colony. But then they faced the more difficult problem of raising the necessary funds for the trip and resettlement. On this the Virginia Company was of no help, nor were the Dutch. Success came in the form of a London merchant named Thomas Weston, who had an interested investment group at hand, and the encouragement of the long-dormant Plymouth Company of Virginia whose pending patent would give them legal jurisdiction over New England. The attractions of that area were not only the available financing but also the sense of a more agreeable climate and the absence of a hovering Anglican presence.

In the end, Bradford wrote, "the generality was swayed" to New England. Weston's group—seventy London merchants and craftsmen, some more, some less sympathetic to the Pilgrims' religious views—raised a joint stock of approximately £7,000, of which the emigrating householders became partners by contributing their settlement efforts and labor. The next question became who should first undertake the move, and who should stay and follow later. Most of the congregation could not arrange their affairs quickly enough to join the immediate shipment; nor could the vessel they bought accommodate a large group. In the end it was agreed that about seventy-eight of the Leiden community would leave; the rest pledged that if the Lord gave them life, means, and opportunity, they would follow as soon as possible. The pastor, the charismatic John Robinson, would have to remain behind with the majority, despite his desire to "have borne my part with you in this first brunt," while the church's ruling elder, Brewster, took over the leadership of the exodus. All agreed that the migrants would not be alienated by their departure. The exiles would become "an absolute church of themselves," as would the group left behind, but if members of either group were able to join the other, they would be accepted fully "without any further dismission or testimonial."[10]

So, in late July 1620, on the eve of the emigrants' departure, the Leiden congregation, seeking a truly secure location in which to live safely apart from the world, gathered for a day of prayer, solemn humiliation, preaching, tears, and the singing of Psalms, "making joyful melody in our hearts, as well as with the voice, there being many of the congregation very expert in musick." The next day the voyagers, their close friends, and their household goods were loaded onto canal boats for the twenty-five-mile journey to Delftshaven where their ship, the *Speedwell*—a mere sixty tons—lay docked. The final parting from the Dutch world that had been their refuge and home for over a decade seemed unendurable. So doleful was the scene, Bradford would later recall—such "sighs and sobs and prayers did sound amongst them," such "tears did gush from every eye, and pithy speeches pierced each heart"—that the Dutch strangers standing on the quay "could not refrain from tears." At the final moment those who were left behind fired off their muskets, all raised their hands in salute, and Pastor Robinson fell to his knees, "and they all with him," to give his final blessing.[11]

2

He would never see them again, nor would many of the others who hoped to join the exodus. Families had divided. The Brewsters left three of their children behind, the Bradfords their five-year-old son, and at least eight of the men departed from their wives, hoping someday to be reunited. There was a reunion of sorts at their first stop, in Southampton, not with the Leiden people but with a contingent of co-religionists who had remained in England and who now wished to join the emigration. They had been brought from London in the chartered *Mayflower*, a commercial transport vessel most recently in the French wine trade, along with servants and artisans selected by the merchant backers to help in the fishing, hunting, and other lines of work by which they hoped to recoup their investment. After some days of greetings and further planning, the overall company was divided between the two vessels, and on August 5 the voyage began—disastrously, as it turned out for the 150 people on board. Twice they had to return to England when the *Speedwell* reported leaks and general weakness, perhaps exaggerated by the rather fearful crew. They had no choice but to abandon the smaller vessel, and stuff what they could of its provisions into the *Mayflower*, together with some of the *Speedwell*'s passengers—those who were still willing to face the dangers and those who were not considered to be too young or unfit to face the voyage.[12]

The *Mayflower*, "an ordinary pot-bellied merchantman" of 180 tons' burden, was a small vessel for the cargo it bore: perhaps 113 feet in length, twenty-six feet wide, with eleven-foot depth of hold. When it left Plymouth on September 6, it carried—in addition to barrels and crates of supplies of all kinds, piles of household goods, and some domestic animals—approximately 132 people, of whom about 30 were crew. The 102 passengers crowded into every available corner of the ship not occupied by the crew or cargo, sleeping in double bunks in the poop house, the cabin, and wherever they could find space—in hammocks in the 'tween decks beneath the grated hatch, in the shallop they carried aboard, on the gun deck, and among the goods and furniture. And of this jumbled, "ununited," undisciplined population, living "compact together" for over two months in a severely restricted space, the committed Pilgrim group was a minority: perhaps 44 souls in all—18 men, 11 women, and 15 children. They were a huddled, defensive cluster, harassed even by the vessel's official "governor," Christopher Martin, their own backers' agent, who, when in charge of purchasing and accounts in Southampton, "insulteth over our poor people," the Pilgrims' business agent Robert Cushman reported from Dartmouth, "with such scorn and contempt, as if they were not good enough to wipe his shoes. It would break your heart to see his dealing, and the mourning of our people."[13]

But Martin was only one of the many "strangers" who contested with the pious sect day and night for space, food, and the primitive sanitary facilities. Two-thirds of the passengers were servants or workmen hired by the merchant backers; they shared none of the Pilgrims' religious convictions and often mocked their piety. Among the many children aboard—thirty-four in all—seven were vagabonds who had been snatched up from the London streets and pressed into servitude; three were illegitimate children from Shropshire who had ended up servants in one of the merchants' houses; and among the hired workers and adult indentured servants were several vagrant journeymen, some of them respectable, some, in Bradford's eyes, profane, obscene, and arrogant. The worst person on board, Bradford reported, was a "lusty . . . haughty" seaman, always "contemning the poor people in their sickness and cursing them daily with grievous execrations," even threatening to throw them overboard. But such was "the just hand of God" that the sailor was smitten with a "grievous disease" that killed him, and so it was he and not the pious worshippers, Bradford wrote with some satisfaction, who ended in the sea.[14]

The sailors were always difficult, but they were a transient population. The hired help and independent workers aboard the *Mayflower* would be a more permanent part of the community, and some of them were little better than the sailors. They were drawn from every corner of the land, and they brought with them attitudes and experiences of all kinds. "One of the profanest families," Bradford would later recall, was the Billingtons, originally from Lincolnshire. The father, John, was trouble from the start; the son Francis, age eight in 1620, almost blew up the *Mayflower* when he fired a gun into a barrel of gunpowder in the main cabin; and John's wife, Eleanor, would be sentenced to time in the stocks and a whipping for slander. Stephen Hopkins, of a Gloucestershire family, alone of the people aboard had once lived in America, having arrived in Virginia after surviving the shipwreck of the *Seaventure* in Bermuda in 1609, where he had barely escaped hanging for defying the governor's authority. Sometime during his short stay in Virginia he had probably sailed along the New England coast and had become acquainted with the local natives, and so he would prove to be of great help to the Pilgrims in their relations with the Indians. But despite that, and despite the fact that

he would hold public office in the colony from time to time, he was forever in trouble with the authorities—at one point charged with battery, at
another with allowing excessive drinking on his premises, at still another
with contempt of court. Two of Hopkins's servants, Edward Doty and
Edward Leister, were so angrily at odds with each other on board ship
that they ended in a duel with swords and daggers, for which they were
condemned to be tied up neck and heels. Leister would ultimately escape
to Virginia, while Doty would spend much of his thirty-five years in the
colony defending himself from charges of assault, slander, and theft.[15]

Though the Pilgrims were harassed at times by the strangers aboard
and were always apprehensive of their contaminating influence, they
had supporters among them too. Their military leader, the tough
thirty-six-year-old veteran of the Low Country wars, Miles Standish,
who would be a rock and pillar of the settlement though some would
describe him as a small man with "a very hot & angry temper," had made
contact with the congregation's leaders before they left Leiden, yet he
was never of their church. And there was John Alden, the "hopefull"
twenty-one-year-old cooper, hired in Southampton for purely economic
reasons; in his sixty-seven years in the colony, he would prove to be not
only faithful to the Leideners' creed but one of the most rigorous in
enforcing it.

But however bedeviled the sectarians were by the profane majority
around them, the expedition in the end was theirs, its goal the realization of their dreams. To bring the miscellany of people into a purposeful
community were leaders of personal dignity, competence, and presence
if not of affluence or gentry status. The fifty-three-year-old Brewster, the
senior of the Leideners' project, the original organizer of the Scrooby
conventicle, was now the ruling elder. His capacities, Bradford would
write in an elegy after his death, were superior "above many." Perched
precariously on the cusp of gentry status, he was uniquely sensitive to the
despair of the suddenly dispossessed and the vulgarity of the nouveaux
riches. He was "wise and discreet," Bradford wrote,

and well spoken, having a grave and deliberate utterance, of a very cheer-
ful spirit, very sociable and pleasant amongst his friends, of an humble
and modest mind. . . . He was tenderhearted and compassionate of such
as were in misery, but especially of such as had been of good estate and
rank and were fallen unto want and poverty either for goodness and reli-

gion's sake or by the injury and oppression of others; he would say [that] of all men these deserved to be pitied most. And none did more offend and displease him than such as would haughtily and proudly carry and lift up themselves, being risen from nothing and having little . . . to commend them but a few fine clothes or a little riches more than others.

A modest, even humble man, his innate dignity was as impressive to contemporaries as was his lay preaching, which was capable of "ripping up the heart and conscience before God."

His former assistant in the Leiden printing trade, the twenty-five-year-old Edward Winslow, son of a salt merchant of Droitwich, Worcestershire, was not only well educated but exceptionally competent in public service. After twenty-two years as a diplomat, explorer, entrepreneur, pamphleteer, legislator, and executive in the Plymouth colony, he would find a larger role in England's foreign service and ultimately in the leadership of Cromwell's conquest of Jamaica. On board the *Mayflower* Winslow met Isaac Allerton, a tailor's son from London, already an imaginative, ambitious entrepreneur, clever and somewhat unscrupulous. With good connections in England and the Netherlands, he was one of the planners of the migration to America, where, after the death of his first wife, he would marry Brewster's daughter Fear and quickly assume a dominant role in the colony's trade and external affairs. But his enterprising flair as the colony's agent in London, his complex commercial adventures throughout the North American and Caribbean trading area, and his dubious mixing of personal and official accounts offended the colony's leaders, especially Bradford. Dismissed from the agency, he would thereafter engage in all sorts of enterprises in London and in the English, Swedish, and Dutch colonies, leaving an estate of £118 at his death in 1659.[16]

But of all the *Mayflower*'s leaders, John Carver had perhaps the most exceptional combination of talents. A Yorkshire tradesman born in Doncaster, less than ten miles from Scrooby, he moved to London where he prospered, and then to Leiden, where he was caught up in the separatists' congregation. By 1610, related by marriage and creed to Pastor Robinson, he was a deacon of the church. When in 1617 and again in 1620 negotiations for removal to America began, it was he, with another deacon, who was sent to England for discussions with the Virginia Company and to begin making arrangements for the move. And when the migration was finally under way it was he who was elected the prospective colony's governor. For it was in him above all other leaders, as his "dear brother" Robinson wrote in a moving farewell letter, that the congregation had its deepest confidence and rested its hopes for success. He had such "singular piety, rare humility, and great condescendency," and he was so selflessly devoted to the cause, so public spirited, and yet at the same time so competent. His wealth had become "a public purse, [he] having disbursed the greatest part of that considerable estate God had given him, for the carrying on the interest of the company." He had known the world and was fleeing from it, in search of higher, deeper goals.[17]

And then there was Bradford. He was thirty when the *Mayflower* left England, still in the shadow of his seniors in the search for the simple, uncluttered, austere Christian life. It could easily be seen that he was intelligent, thoughtful, pious, well read, and adept at languages—fluent in Dutch, familiar with French, a master (Cotton Mather later wrote) of Latin and Greek, and a student of Hebrew. But no one on board the *Mayflower* could have known that he had a heightened consciousness of the drama in which they were involved, the imagination to cast it all as a central passage in Christian history, and the literary capacity to express their fortunes as a heroic epic, in biblical cadences. He must have lived, even then, a deeply considered life, exquisitely responsive to the people around him, keenly aware of their and his own achievements and failures in what he took to be the eyes of God. Convinced of his people's transcendent mission and that they were finally, after many years of searching, approaching the ultimate realization of their dreams, he noted each fluttering motion, however slight, of progress or regression. The strangers' sins, vulgarities, and indifference aboard the *Mayflower* disturbed him deeply, seared his sensibilities; later he would recall them bitterly. So too would he rejoice in remembering the resolution, faithfulness, and sanctity of the truly pious in this travail of mind and soul and body.

3

He would never forget the voyage or its immediate aftermath. After a tranquil start the *Mayflower* hit storms that shook every timber in the ship, created leaks in the upper areas, and cracked one of the main beams. They had no choice but to reduce their sails and drift, pitching and tossing wildly. One of Carver's six servants, "a plain-hearted Christian," was thrown overboard as the ship tipped far over to one side, and was dragged underwater, clinging to a loose halyard until hauled back on board with a boat hook. The sailors panicked. They were willing, they said, to earn their wages but not to risk their lives. Their fear spread to the passengers. A group of them confronted the ship's officers demanding that they consider returning to England. But repairs, it was decided, could be made, and stress could be reduced by shortening sails, and so "they committed themselves to the will of God" and completed the voyage. On November 11 they dropped anchor in Provincetown harbor, in the northernmost tip of Cape Cod.

They had been at sea for nine weeks, and though only one passenger had died on the voyage, they were not only severely "weatherbeaten" but debilitated to an extent they did not yet know. Fresh food supplies had been consumed early in the voyage, firewood too, and signs of scurvy had appeared among both crew and passengers. Sickened and exhausted, when they came to the shore they were shocked by the scene before them. On one side, as Bradford would later write in one of his most vivid passages, there was "a hideous and desolate wilderness full of wild beasts and wild men . . . the whole country full of woods and thickets"; on the other side there was "the mighty ocean which . . . was now as a main bar and gulf to separate them from all civil parts of the world." The crew threatened not to budge from the temporary anchorage until the Pilgrims discovered a permanent location for their settlement, and if they delayed too long, the sailors said they would simply abandon them on the nearby sandy shore. And from the servants and other strangers came grim mutterings, to the effect that once ashore they would strike out on their own, which they said they were legally free to do since they were not in Virginia and hence not under any patented jurisdiction.

The shipboard community was thus riven by conflict, bereft of legitimate civil authority, and likely to splinter into fragments. It was to restore order, to counter the mutinous speeches, and to begin the construction by consensus of a governing structure, that the Pilgrim leaders drew up an agreement, a compact, to create a "civic body politic." The brief document, signed on shipboard, was simply a commitment by the signatories to obey the "just and equal laws, ordinances, acts, constitutions and offices" that would be promulgated by a government still to be formed. It was no constitution, only an effort to unite and direct to the public good the energies of the colony's diverse population—saints and sinners, servants and masters, the pious from Scrooby and Leiden and the profane from London and Southampton. It expressed in simple language the passion of the leaders finally to realize their pious hopes for the creation of a truly Christian community, and so it was ratified with some solemnity. Forty-one men signed the compact, pledging "all due submission and obedience" to whatever regulations would emerge. The first to sign were the main organizers and sectarian leaders, those who had carried the major burdens—Carver, Bradford, Winslow, and Brewster. They were followed by other respected figures—Allerton, Standish, Alden, Martin, and Hopkins; and they in turn were followed by some of the lesser members of the community, servants, and hired workers. The belligerent Billington signed, as did the feuding pair, Leister and Doty. Since the pledge of householders committed their dependents—wives, children, and servants—the forty-one signatories in effect committed the entire shipboard population, save for the sailors, to the Leideners' aspirations.

For Carver, endorsed as governor, and for the other leaders there was much to fear. In addition to the divisiveness of the community, there was the likely violence of the natives, possible abandonment by the crew, and starvation if their supplies ran out without help from the natives. But no one had imagined what the consequences would be of the malnutrition that had resulted from two months at sea, the accidents that could befall people coping with a strange environment, and above all the ferocity of a New England winter.[18]

There was a foretaste of things to come when, two days after their arrival, the passengers first went ashore. To get to dry land they had to wade through almost half a mile of shallow water, "which caused many to get colds and coughs, for it was . . . freezing cold weather." For a month thereafter scouting expeditions were sent out to explore the land, establish relations with the natives, forage for supplies, and identify a site for the permanent settlement. They were successful in making reasonably peaceful contact with the natives and, with their help, in locating and digging up some of the Indians' buried food supplies. But the cost was heavy. They had to dig into ground frozen a foot deep to reach the buried corn and beans, and to reach the ship after working on shore they had to wade "to the middle of the thigh, and oft to the knees . . . it brought to the most, if not all, coughs and colds . . . which afterward turned to the scurvey, whereof many died." The exploring teams faltered again and again in the face of driving winds and rain: "some of our people that are dead tooke the originall of their death here."

> **December 6:** "*the weather was very cold and it froze so hard as the spray of the sea lighting on their coats, they were as if they had been glazed*" (Bradford); "*like coats of iron*" (Winslow).
>
> **December 8:** *After some hours' sailing* [in the small shallop they had brought on the *Mayflower*] *it began to snow and rain, and about the middle of the afternoon the wind increased and the sea became very rough, and they broke their rudder . . . the storm increasing, and night drawing on, they bore what sail they could get in, while they could see. But herewith they broke their mast in three pieces and their sail fell overboard in a very grown sea. . . . And though it was very dark and rained sore, yet in the end they got under the lee of a small island . . . but were divided in their minds, some would keep [in] the boat for fear they might be amongst the Indians, others were so wet and cold they could not endure, but got ashore, and with much ado got fire (all things being so wet).*

Finally they found the pleasant hillside at Patuxet, the cleared, cultivated, well-watered site of a deserted Indian village which they would call Plymouth. Its advantages were obvious, but there were problems too, and they had to consider that other, as yet unknown sites might be better. When they weighed the pros and cons, one "especiall reason" convinced them to settle on that hillside:

> *The heart of winter and unseasonable weather was come upon us, so that we could not goe upon coasting and discovery, without danger of loosing men and boat, upon which would follow the overthrow of all. . . . Also cold and wett lodging had so taynted our people, for scarce any of us were free from vehement coughs, as if they should continue long in that estate, it would indanger the lives of many, and breed diseases and infection amongst us.*

In fact, the damage had already been done, and the ravages were beginning to mount.[19]

Death was everywhere. America, for these hopeful utopians, had become a graveyard, and the record keeper was the faithful Bradford. Day after day he registered in a small notebook the deaths as they occurred, along with the marriages and punishments. The young and the old died

first. On **December 4:** Edward Thompson, one of William White's servants; White himself would follow in February. On **December 6,** one of
Carver's young servants, the boy Jasper, died. On **December 7,** Bradford's own wife, then twenty-three, drowned, it was said, after a fall from
the *Mayflower.* On **December 8** the elderly James Chilton, who had survived a vengeful mob in Leiden, succumbed. And there were two other
deaths that month. **January** was worse: eight deaths were registered,
including Miles Standish's wife and the imperious Christopher Martin,
whose last act was to give Carver a report on the state of their accounts.
Early that month Bradford, who had caught cold on one of the expeditions, suffered such severe "griefe and paine" in his legs that his life was
despaired of: it was "Gods mercie," Winslow wrote, that he survived. By
February the dangerous illnesses had become so general that a special
house had been built as an infirmary, but in that month seventeen people died, among them Allerton's wife, Mary Norris, after a miscarriage.
And in **March** death took thirteen more, including Governor Carver,
who suffered a stroke (his "senses failed") after working in the fields. His
wife, "a weak woman," followed him a few weeks later. By then, Bradford
noted that

> *in two or three months time half their company died, especially in January and*
> *February, being the depth of winter, and wanting houses and other comforts;*
> *being infected with the scurvy and other diseases which this long voyage and*
> *inaccommodate condition had brought upon them. So as there died some times*
> *two or three of a day . . . that of 100 and odd persons, scarce fifty remained.*
> *And of these, in the time of most distress, there was but six or seven sound per-*
> *sons . . . [who] spared no pains night nor day, but with abundance of toil and*
> *hazard of their own health, fetched them wood, made them fires, dressed them*
> *meat, made their beds, washed their loathsome clothes, clothed and unclothed*
> *them. In a word did all the homely and necessary offices for them which dainty*
> *and queasy stomachs cannot endure to hear named.*

There was no such benevolence among the crew, who refused to help
each other or the passengers, muttering "if they died, let them die."
Almost half of the crew, including the "lustiest," were dead by early April,
when the *Mayflower* returned to England.

Families had been destroyed—not only Christopher Martin but his
wife and both servants had died; not only John Turner but both his sons

as well; both Carvers and three of their six servants; both Mullinses, their son, and a servant; both Tinkers and their son; Mrs. Winslow and two of their servants.

4

It was therefore a grieving remnant, settled in two rows of small, dark thatched houses on the slope leading down to Plymouth harbor, that assembled to greet the first relief vessel. The *Fortune*, almost four and a half months in passage from London, reached Cape Cod just a year after the *Mayflower* had arrived. Even smaller than the *Speedwell*, it carried among its thirty-five passengers several of the people who had been left behind in 1620, including a few who would become pillars of Plymouth's church and community, most notably Thomas Prence. The young son of a Gloucestershire carriage maker, in his fifty-two years in the colony Prence would become its most important public official after Bradford, serving as governor for seventeen years. He would also become one of the major landholders, and he would always be a battler for the maintenance of the church's apostolic purity. He was the complete separatist, remembered at his death as not only a pious gentleman and "well-wisher to all that feared God" but also "a terror to the wicked." And he was prolific. With his first wife, Patience Brewster, and the three wives who followed, he fathered nine children, whose careers trace the expansion of the town's population across southern New England.[20]

On board the *Fortune* too was Prence's future brother-in-law, Jonathan Brewster, William Brewster's eldest son, one of the very few survivors of the original Scrooby conventicle. A ribbon maker in Leiden, he would prove to be one of the colony's most active entrepreneurs, especially in developing the Indian trade, and at the same time he would engage in scientific experiments. The Cushmans, of a Kentish family who had been at the core of the Leiden group—Deacon Robert and his fourteen-year-old son Thomas—also arrived on the *Fortune*. The father quickly returned to England to continue his work on the Pilgrims' business problems, but the son remained, to be adopted by Bradford and eventually to succeed Brewster as the church's ruling elder. Two new arrivals who as children had been part of the Leiden community—Moses Simonson and the Walloon Philip Delano—quickly became members of the church and would remain faithful to it until their deaths six decades later. And there were a few others aboard the *Fortune* who were also prepared to live in close communion with the church, some of whose involvement was cut short by early deaths or sudden departures.

But the rest of the passengers, the majority on board, were work-men from London's labor market who had been hired for the colony by the Pilgrims' financial backers. A miller is listed, a journeyman mason, a leather seller (fellmonger), a vintner, a mariner, and an armorer; ten single young men gave no occupation. In no way committed to the church's ideals, these artisans and laborers would drift through and often out of Plymouth as they had through and out of London, leaving behind only occasional traces of their lives in America—traces that document mainly their resistance to the moral constraints of this piously disciplined community.

In the nine years that followed—before the beginning of the great migration to the Puritan colony in Massachusetts—only fourteen vessels came into Plymouth harbor, and only six of them—none between 1624 and 1629—carried passengers to supplement the colony's population. All of the ships, however, including the six that directly served the colony, brought an influx of just the kinds of "profane" people and the worldly corruptions that the Pilgrims had sought to escape.

Their struggle to maintain their identity and realize their hopes in this increasingly complex demographic situation was fierce, unending, and in the end unsuccessful. For a while, however, they seemed victori-ous. They could accommodate the sixty-seven "rough and unruly" men whom Thomas Weston sent over in 1622. For as expected, Weston's "rude fellows," led by his "heady . . . and violent" brother, moved off, after three months, to Wessagusset (Weymouth), thirty miles to the north, to establish a fishing station and trading post. Plymouth had been warned that these "are no men for us," indeed that they were "not fit for an honest man's company." In the event they proved to be worse than their reputation and the cause of the Pilgrims' most barbarous episode.

Throwing together a few log huts and a blockhouse surrounded by a stockade, Weston's men set out to extract what they could from the neigh-boring Indians, who had recently been devastated by a severe epidemic. Furs and food were not forthcoming, and as the group "neither applied themselves to planting of corn, nor taking of fish . . . but went about to build castles in the air . . . when winter came . . . many were starved to death, and the rest hardly escaped." The survivors (at least ten died that winter) scrounged for ground nuts, clams, and mussels for food and haunted the Indian encampments for help. When one of them was caught stealing the Indians' seed corn, thus threatening any future assistance the natives might give, he was hanged by his own people "to give the Indians content." By then the pressure on the natives had reached the point of brutality. In retaliation, the Indians began planning an assault that would wipe out the Wessagusset settlement altogether. Plymouth had recently heard of the Virginia massacre, and when word was received of a pending conspiracy at Wessagusset that might engulf them all, Standish, ruthless as were all of the veterans of the Netherlands' wars, and a small troop were sent off to repel the attack before it began.[21]

They did their work quickly and savagely. They lured the leading warriors into the blockhouse and then stabbed them to death, one after the other. It was incredible, Winslow wrote, how many wounds the chiefs suffered before they died, "not making any fearful noise, but catching at their weapons and striving to the last." The youngster who accompanied the warriors Standish "caused to be hanged." Then, apparently on instruction, Standish cut off the head of the "bloody and bold villain" believed to have inspired the conspiracy and brought it back to Plymouth in triumph, where it was displayed on the blockhouse together with a flag made of a cloth soaked in the victim's blood.

Standish was received "with joy" but not to universal acclaim. When word of the affair reached Leiden, the Reverend Robinson sent off a severe condemnation. Instead of murdering the Indians, why, he asked, had Standish not tried to convert them? And did he and his men have legal jurisdiction over them? It is not a question, he wrote, of what the Indians deserved but of what treatment was absolutely necessary. The murders were excessive. "Methinks one or two principals should have been full enough, according to that approved rule, the punishment to the few, and the fear to many." "To be a terror to poor, barbarous people" might seem "glorious" in men's eyes, but not in God's. And quite aside from the morality and legality involved, Robinson concluded, such behavior might well stimulate others to begin a "ruffling course in the world" to everyone's disadvantage.[22]

It was the end of this phase of Weston's search for quick profits. His half-starved, demoralized men scattered—one of them settled with the Indians—leaving the blockhouse and huts deserted. But not for long. Soon after they left, another group, under the leadership of the well-connected

Robert Gorges, resettled the abandoned site. Gorges, who sought some kind of palatinate for himself, some kind of private principality, came with a lieutenant's commission from the Council for New England, which claimed title to all of New England and had parceled out the entire area to its twenty patentees. Gorges's party was far more respectable than Weston's, consisting of gentlemen, soldiers, artisans, farmers, traders, and a preacher. But the expedition lasted only a year. Gorges "scarcely saluted the country," Bradford wrote, "not finding the state of things here to answer his quality and condition." His party, like Weston's, scattered after a single harsh winter. Some went back to England, some went on to Virginia, and some settled in isolated farms close by, eventually within, the expanding boundaries of the Plymouth colony.[23]

By then, in July 1623, more proper recruits to the colony had finally arrived among the ninety passengers on the *Anne* and the *Little James*. But the colony had been warned that this incoming group as a whole was "weak" in character, many of them having been selected not by Cushman but by the merchant backers for their financial interests. They and Cushman apologized for not sending over more of the Leiden congregation— "I hope ere long you shall enjoy them all" (Cushman)—and especially for failing to send over their charismatic leader, John Robinson. Still, though they were intermingled with people "so bad as they were fain to be at charge to send them home again the next year," a number of the wives and children who had been left behind in 1620 were aboard the two vessels. Among the "old friends" were two more of Brewster's daughters, Patience and the teenage Fear, who had been born during the flight from Scrooby; several of the Walloon wives, together with their Danzig-born compatriot, Godbert Godbertson; Deacon Fuller's wife; and that "godlie matron" from Somersetshire, Alice Southworth, who within a year would marry the widower Bradford.

Though faithful to the cause, the pious newcomers, when they arrived at Plymouth, found a scene that shook their confidence in God's favor. Some simply "fell a-weeping," Bradford later recalled, to see their predecessors in such a "low and poor condition." Many of those who came to greet them, survivors of the *Mayflower* and the *Fortune*, were "ragged in apparel and some little better than half naked." They seemed to have lost "the freshness of their former complexion," as a result, it was believed, of a diet consisting largely of fish without bread, washed down with spring water. "Daunted and dismayed . . . fancying their own misery in what they saw in others . . . all were full of sadness." And the future seemed grim. The spring and early summer of 1623 were hot and dry. For a time, with the ground "parched like withered hay," a near famine prevailed, until finally, after much prayer, the rain came "with such sweet and gentle showers as gave them cause of rejoicing and blessing God." The fading crops revived, and they gave thanks for a plentiful harvest.[24]

But no sooner had their food supply improved and the palisaded town began to seem secure than the settlers ran into a problem with a peculiar group among the recent arrivals. Ten of the passengers on the *Anne* had come "on their particular"—that is, as a separate group, to settle independently within Plymouth's territory. They were not separatists; nor were they religious in any significant way. Like so many adventurous spirits of the time, these "particulars," Bradford wrote, dreamed of "building great houses . . . they would be great men and rich all of a sudden." But they did have the right to settle and agreed, in exchange for land grants, to obey the colony's laws, share in the common defense, pay taxes, and keep away from the Indian trade, which was reserved to the Pilgrims and the merchants, who expected the profits from it to repay the costs of settlement.

They were trouble from the start. Their leader was John Oldham, a "trader" from Derbyshire who brought with him his wife and sister and several London tradesmen, among them the Devonshire-born Conant brothers, one a London grocer, the other a salter. Prickly, rambunctious, "a mad jack in his mood," Oldham, whose murder in 1636 would touch off the Pequot war, chafed at all restrictions and inspired a list of twelve charges against the Pilgrims that was carried to London by the "bad" newcomers whom Bradford sent back to England. The governor replied to all the charges, which ranged from religious heterodoxy to bad water, thievery, and too many mosquitoes. (Bradford: Those who cannot endure the biting of a mosquito "are too delicate and unfit to begin new plantations and colonies. . . . We would wish such to keep at home till at least they be mosquito-proof.") But he could not stamp out Oldham's discontents, which threatened to tear the colony apart when, in 1624, the Rev. John Lyford arrived.

An Irishman, once the Anglican minister of Loughgall in County Armagh, Lyford, his wife confessed to Bradford, had had "a bastard by another before they were married" and had never been able to keep his hands off the family maids. Later it emerged that he had been driven from Ireland after raping a young woman whose fiancé had sent her to him for religious counseling. In England Lyford had managed to worm his way into Puritan circles, and then "unhappily he was lit upon and sent hither." There was nothing accidental in this. He was apparently selected, over Winslow's and Cushman's objections, by a faction of the colony's financial backers opposed to transporting more of the pious Leideners to America, and especially opposed to sending over the powerful Reverend Robinson to lead the flock. Cushman was very apprehensive: be careful in electing Lyford preacher, he warned; "he knows he is no officer amongst you."

At first, in Plymouth, Lyford was all piety and docility. His reverence and humility were so extreme, Bradford wrote, that he embarrassed the Pilgrims. "He so bowed and cringed unto them, and would have kissed their hands . . . yea, he wept & shed many tears . . . admiring the things they had done in their wants &c. as if he had been made all of love." Moreover, he confessed his "former disorderly walking and his being entangled in many corruptions, which had been a burden to his conscience." But it was all a sham, Bradford discovered. Lyford had no intention of submitting what remained of his Anglican pride to the peculiar doctrines of the separatists. Soon there were "private meetings and whisperings" between Lyford and Oldham and among the faction they gathered. Oldham began picking quarrels everywhere, refused all requests for public service, threatened the captain of the watch with a knife, and "ramped more like a furious beast than a man, and called them all traitors and rebels and other such foul language." The climax came when the two attempted to introduce Anglican worship and sent off secretly to England a series of slanderous, accusatory letters, which Bradford intercepted. Confronted by these incriminating documents—calculated, Bradford believed, to bring about the Pilgrims' "ruin & utter subversion"—Lyford burst into tears, confessed his sins, and condemned himself as "unsavory salt" and not worthy of God's pardon. The two were tried and convicted in front of the entire colony, then expelled from the Pilgrims' jurisdiction. When Oldham reappeared without permission in 1625, denouncing the separatists once again in a "mad fury," he was confined and then forced to run a gauntlet of musketeers, each of whom gave him "a thump on the breech with the butt end of his musket." Expelled from the colony once again, he began wandering and trading on the New England and Long Island shores, until his bloody demise in 1636. Lyford turned south to Anglican Virginia, where, in 1628, he died.[25]

5

These two were gone, but still there was no peace or quiet. When the Lyford episode exploded, Plymouth was reported to have a population of only about 180 souls living in a village of thirty-two small, flimsy houses enclosed in a palisade and protected by a fort and watchtower. But the area was becoming better known. At least fifty English fishing vessels appeared annually off the coast, and small settlements were beginning to appear here and there on the islands and shores of Maine, New Hampshire, and Massachusetts. Plymouth itself had built trading stations at Aptucxet (modern Bourne) to the south, on Buzzard's Bay, on the Kennebec and Penobscot rivers in Maine, and on the Connecticut River north of Hartford. From all of these rough, unstable settlements, alien people were beginning to drift into the colony and to settle there, though under more restrictive conditions than the first "particulars." At the same time the English sponsors continued to send over in occasional shipments people more useful to themselves than to the Pilgrims, and indicated that they had little interest in transporting to the colony the remainder of the Leiden congregation. That community in any case was dwindling. Many of the original congregants, Bradford wrote, "being aged, began to drop away by death," and the survivors, "though their wills were good to come to them, yet they saw no probability of means how it might be effected." In 1625 two of the remaining lines of communication with the European sources of the Pilgrims' strength, spiritual and material, were severed with the deaths of both Robinson and Cushman. The likelihood increased that the remnants of the Leiden community would soon disappear into the Dutch population, while the Plymouth conventicle would be overwhelmed by profane influences.[26]

It was against such a fatal outcome that Winslow, on a return visit to England, fought in his *Good Newes from New England*, published in London in 1624. He warned those with unrealistic dreams of instant affluence against joining the colony, while welcoming those who "seriously, upon due examination, set themselves to further the glory of God, and the honor of our country." People who embarked for the colony "with too

great lightness," he wrote, will be doomed upon arrival to see "their foolish imagination made void." They would soon despair and would gladly
pay ten times the passage cost to get back home. For,

> can any be so simple as to conceive that the fountains should stream
> forth wine or beer, or the woods and rivers be like butchers' shops, or
> fishmongers' stalls. . . . If thou canst not live without such things . . . rest
> where thou art; for as a proud heart, a dainty tooth, a beggar's purse,
> and an idle hand, be here [in England] intolerable, so that person that
> hath these qualities there, is much more abominable.

But if one had the heart to bear the difficulties of the search for God's
glory, against which all other things in life are mere "accessories," he
would be received with thanks in the colony.[27]

Nothing, however, in Winslow's plea or otherwise, could divert the
demographic trend. Gentiles, dangerous spiritually if not physically,
seemed to be everywhere. The colony's young artisans and laborers who
had been sent by the merchant backers were beginning to gain their freedom from commitments and to seek independence from both religious
and secular authorities. But there were more immediate threats. The
most dramatic erupted in a strange commercial settlement that suddenly
appeared thirty miles to the north, on the near side of Boston Bay.

The original group of some thirty or forty workers that settled there
in 1625 under a Captain Wollaston had been a potential danger until
Wollaston became disillusioned and turned south to make what profit
he could by selling his servants in Virginia. But a small rump remained
at Mount Wollaston (modern Quincy) under one of the strangest, most
flamboyant, and most belligerently impious people ever to wander into
the coastal scene.

Thomas Morton had probably been in New England once before,
with Weston's group, and seems to have fallen in love with the region's
landscape, its flora and fauna—and also with its commercial possibilities. His English background is vague. At one point, he had probably
been a lawyer of sorts—at least he claimed some association with one of
London's Inns of Court—and as such his reputation, perhaps gained in
the West Country, was said to be rather shady. What is certain is that
he prided himself on being, if not a sportsman, at least a nature lover, a
pleasure seeker, and a Rabelaisian celebrant of secular rites. Uninhibited,

capable of high-spirited mockery of precisely such solemn pieties as those of the Pilgrims (whom he would lampoon in his *New English Canaan* in 1637), he was also a ruthless profiteer eager to squeeze every penny from the people and land around him.

When word reached Plymouth of his exploits, Bradford and the other leaders were appalled. The Lord of Misrule, as Bradford called him, was conducting, it was said, not only tumultuous revelries, perhaps orgies, together with the Indians both male and female, but also drunken, pagan, May Day celebrations performed around a huge beribboned maypole topped with antlers. ("Inviting the Indian women," Bradford wrote, "for their consorts, dancing and frisking together like so many fairies, or furies, rather; and worse practices . . . of the mad Bacchanalians.") Beyond that, he was "inveigling of men's servants away from them." And beyond even that, and more important, he had begun a trade with the Indians that threatened to destroy them all.[28]

His sale of liquor to the natives—proscribed in the formal regulations of every settlement—was dangerous enough, but his exchange of guns for furs threatened the very survival of the fragile European communities on New England's shores. Further, the position of his encampment, at the mouth of Boston Bay, was perfect for deflecting the outward flow of furs away from the Pilgrims. And finally there was the danger that Merrymount, as Morton called his profitable playground, would become a refuge for all sorts of profane characters—runaway servants and criminals, a "wicked and debauched crew" that would be more of a threat to respectable people than the Indians themselves.

Word of the physical danger of guns in the hands of the Indians and the economic danger of furs in the hands of this threatening entrepreneur came into Plymouth from a number of the scattered fishing and trading stations. It became clear, after negotiations with Morton failed, that drastic action would be necessary. In May 1628 Standish and eight armed men were sent to the offending settlement to take Morton by force. There, after a comic-opera escape which Morton related with exuberant embellishments ("he's gone, he's gone, what shall we do, he's gone! The rest . . . like rams ran their heads one at another full butt in the dark"), the half-drunken "host" at Merrymount was captured and carried off to Plymouth, then to the Isle of Shoals, where a passing vessel took him back to England. With him went a full bill of particulars and the assurance that if Morton had not been stopped, his group would have grown "by the access of loose persons" to such size that it would have been impossible to restrain them, living, as they did, "without all fear of God or common honesty, some of them abusing the Indian women most filthily, as it is notorious."[29]

So Morton was gone, at least temporarily, as were Oldham and Lyford, but the stain of corrupting influences could not be wiped clean. The colony's ideal image of itself as a community of pious believers dedicated to recovering the simple purity of pristine Christianity, and separated from the unregenerate world with all its churchly clutter, was becoming blurred, while those left behind in Leiden increasingly despaired of ever being able to join the church in exile. We are very weak, they wrote Bradford in 1625, and feared that reunion was "now as far off or farther than ever." Without Robinson they had no powerful leader to voice their concerns and focus their activities. And the majority of the backers were refusing to advance more funds to make further emigration possible. "If we come at all unto you, the means to enable us so to do must come from you." Everywhere, they felt, there was "frustration and disappointments." Vicious reports of life in Plymouth—"the passionate humors of some discontented men"—were circulating in England, discouraging any help they might receive. "Some say you are starved in body and soul; others, that you eat pigs and dogs that die alone; others, that . . . the goodness of the country are gross and palpable lies; that there is scarce a fowl to be seen or a fish to be taken." Above all, it was believed that no profitable returns would ever come from Plymouth. Those who were fit, it was said, were lazy, and those who were willing were weak.[30]

In 1626 the company of adventurers that had financed the colony finally broke up. None were very wealthy, and most felt that they could no longer sustain the losses and delays in profits; some were convinced that the colonists were "Brownists, condemning all other churches and persons but yourselves . . . contentious, cruel and hard hearted among your neighbors . . . And that you are negligent, careless, wasteful, unthrifty . . . and spend your time in idleness and talking and conferring." But a small core of the group—three in all—did remain faithful to the cause. Investing heavily again, they joined with eight of the colony's leaders as joint "undertakers" to buy out the company's assets and debts for £2,400, to be paid off by shipments of goods from Plymouth, especially furs, of which the new company had monopoly control for six years. Hoping to complete the emigration from Leiden, the London investors warned Bradford that his people must remain above reproach, avoid disputation over trivial points, work hard, and send over everything of possible value that would help reduce their debt. They should behave "so circumspectly" and "so uprightly . . . that no man may make just exceptions against you," and they should not be too strict and rigid in religion: "let all that fear God amongst you join themselves thereunto without delay." The faithful supporters still believed, they said, that the Pilgrims were in a position to "begin a new world and lay the foundation of sound piety and humanity for others to follow." They alone could "make a plantation and erect a city in those remote places when all others fail and return." And the still-devoted backers were prepared to do what they could to help.

But progress in uniting the Leiden and Plymouth congregations was painfully slow. In November 1625 the merchants repeated that only valuable goods shipped from Plymouth would make possible the realization of Robinson's dream that all of the remaining Leiden brethren, with their wives and children, would find their way to Plymouth. Goods were in fact shipped from Plymouth—furs and other local products—but not nearly enough to repay the colony's debt, let alone finance further emigration. Yet such was the "willing mindedness" of the colony's remaining backers in London that finally, in 1629—six years after the arrival of the *Anne* and the *Little James*—"divers of our friends of Leiden came to us," Bradford recorded, "as had been desired both of them and us." A second *Mayflower* carried most of the Leideners who left that year, followed by the *Talbot* with thirty-five servants. In 1630 the *Lyon* carried a few more of the original group, and the *Handmaid* perhaps sixty more—bringing the total population of Bradford's elysium to just under three hundred.[31]

Most of the arrivals of 1629–30 proved to be "the weakest and poorest" of the remaining Leideners, sent at this point on the assumption that those "of note and better discretion and government amongst them" would manage later on their own. And though they sailed on vessels of the Massachusetts Bay Company and bound themselves to repay their expenses, "some upon one condition and some upon another, as they could agree," the final costs of their transportation and supplies turned out to be fearfully high—a total of over £500. Further, since they brought nothing of value with them and arrived too late for planting, they were certain to be a net burden to the colony for at least a year—Bradford estimated their maintenance at another £500. Nevertheless, though most of these new arrivals were poor, and while in transit in London some found them annoyingly irritable at the treatment they felt they had received, they were the Pilgrims' own God-fearing people, Bradford wrote, hence welcome and useful—"for the most part."

Not all, however, were indigent or otherwise weak members of the congregation. Among the new householders and their families were some of the most spiritually gifted and most reliable of the "ancient friends" from the Dutch years. Thomas Blossom, originally from Cambridge, had been one of the *Speedwell*'s passengers of 1620 who had been left behind in the transfer to the *Mayflower*. For nine years thereafter, back in Leiden, he had been hoping to be able to complete the interrupted voyage, explaining to Bradford how it was that the Lord, "for reasons best known to himself" and apparently in anger, had not only thwarted their efforts but snatched Robinson away, "whom if tears could have held, he had remained to this day." Once finally in Plymouth, Blossom was immediately made a deacon of the church, and in the three remaining years of his life he would achieve the status in the eyes of the church of "a holy man and experienced saint, . . . competently accomplished with abilities." Richard Masterson, another of the arrivals of 1629, was a wool carder, originally from Sandwich, Kent, who had given part of his worldly goods for the community's welfare. In Plymouth he also became a deacon and not only a saint and holy man but something more than that. Masterson, they felt, was a second Saint Stephen. Like that first martyr of the primitive Christian church who had been so full of faith, wisdom, and spirit, Masterson defended the truth "by sound argument, grounded on the scriptures of truth." And also among the newcomers was Kenelm Winslow, Edward's brother, a cabinetmaker from their hometown in Worcestershire. He would contribute, not spiritual but artisanal virtuosity to the colony, becoming Plymouth's most accomplished crafter of fine furniture.[32]

So there were now a few more true saints in the leadership of the Pilgrims' small world, and more men of artisanal accomplishment. In all, in the decade of the 1620s, after which there were very few direct shipments of emigrants from Europe to Plymouth, the colony had received an estimated total of 362 people, of whom fewer than a third were members of the church.[33] By the early 1630s Bradford was beginning to record, and lament, the problems that were eroding the community's purpose and distinction: the difficulty of perpetuating a proper ministry, the constant danger of profane influences, and the first, portentous signs of the geographical dispersal that he knew would destroy the community's cohesion.

6

There was no hope of ever recruiting the likes of Robinson for the local ministry, but no one even approximate in quality appeared on the scene. The first appointment after the Lyford debacle was equally disastrous. In 1628 Allerton, without consultation, brought over at some expense as minister a Mr. Rogers, who proved to be, Bradford wrote, simply "crazed in his brain." Within a year he was sent back to England, where he was said to have become "quite distracted." He was followed by—in fact overlapped with—a Rev. Ralph Smith, whom the Pilgrims picked up at a forlorn encampment on nearby Nantasket, where he and his family had landed after having been forced out of the recently settled Puritan village of Salem because of Smith's separatist views. Housed in a flimsy shelter "that would neither keep him nor his goods dry," Smith begged the Pilgrims to rescue his family, servants, and supplies from the straggling fishing post. As a graduate of that Puritan center, Christ's College, Cambridge, and an experienced preacher, he had credentials for the vacant ministry. Soon he was "kindly entertained and housed" by the Pilgrims and appointed, at least temporarily, their "teacher." But it quickly became clear that he was no match, intellectually, pedagogically, or as a community leader, for such learned and experienced laymen as Brewster and "unable to discharge the trust committed to him with any competent satisfaction." All agreed that the responsibility was "too heavy a burden" for him, and he resigned his position, to drift about in various local ministries, finally to return to Salem with his second wife, who was Masterson's widow.[34]

One of Smith's problems in Plymouth must have been the extraordinary competition that suddenly appeared in the person of Roger Williams, who even then, still in his twenties, was a charismatic preacher and a subtle, learned, and combative intellectual. Harassed by the Puritan authorities in the Bay Colony for his separatist ideas and his belief in the separation of church and state, he assumed that the Pilgrims' conventicle would be a more congenial situation for him. Smith, with fitting modesty, shared his pulpit with him, but in the end Williams was no more acceptable to the Pilgrims than he had been to the Bay Colony's Puritans, who were still, in theory, members of the English church. That he was "godly and zealous, having many precious parts," no one in Plymouth doubted, and in later years Bradford would thank God for Williams's teaching even though at times he had been sharply critical of the Pilgrims' practices. For a while Williams worked easily with the dialogic formula of the Pilgrims' public worship, proposing the questions for discussion and "prohecying" (explicating) the issues with great effect. But he soon "began to fall into some strange opinions, and from opinion to practice, which caused some controversy between the church and him." Whether it was his insistence on the separation of church and state that caused the rift, or his publicized argument that the English had no right to seize the Indians' land, or his belief in absolute religious toleration—none of which the Pilgrims could accept—is not known. All these ideas, formulated with great acuity, probably played a role. Even so, some felt that compromises might be made to retain his services, until Brewster, fearful that Williams's views would splinter the fragile consensus that bound the community and that his ideas were heading toward the radical Anabaptism that twenty-five years earlier had split the church in Amsterdam, advised against his remaining.[35]

They never found a fully satisfactory "teacher" to assume the role they believed had been destined for Robinson. A Mr. Glover, engaged by Winslow in 1635, died on the eve of his departure from England. The learned, influential, and ambitious Rev. John Norton, who like Brewster had studied at Peterhouse, Cambridge, lasted only four months before he left for more important posts in the Massachusetts Bay Colony, eventually the powerful ministry of Boston's first church. Spurned also by the patriarchal Richard Mather, they had to settle for the "able and godly" John Rayner, a young Yorkshireman who had studied at Emmanuel College, Cambridge. Adequate but uninspired, he had all the secondary virtues: "a meek and humble spirit, sound in the truth and every way unreproveable in his life." He would serve as teacher for eighteen years, three of them together with the learned Charles Chauncy. That imperious and "very vehement" scholar from Hertfordshire, once a fellow and Greek lecturer in Trinity College, Cambridge, came to Plymouth as pastor in 1638; but he was no more likely than Norton to remain there. (He eventually became president of Harvard College.) If Chauncy's absolute insistence on baptism by full immersion had not brought him into conflict with the Pilgrims ("in this cold country not so convenient," Bradford wrote), something else would have driven him away.[36]

FOR THE MODEST Plymouth community, once the only beacon of Christian light in the northern coastal zone, was becoming deeply provincial, overwhelmed in the early 1630s by the vastly more populous, more sophisticated, and more prosperous Massachusetts Bay Colony of Puritans. Plymouth's confidence in the survival of its original mission, its faith in itself, seemed to be leaching away. A sensational murder trial of 1630 came to symbolize the growth of the profane influences creeping in among the saints, as well as the spiritual ordinariness of the majority of the people who had been drawn to the separatists' utopia.

The Billingtons, the troublesome family of the first *Mayflower* voyage, had become uncontrollable. Within a year of their arrival, the elder Billington's defiance of Standish's orders had led to his having to crave pardon to escape the punishment of being tied up neck and heels together. Soon thereafter he had joined Lyford's agitations, and in 1625 he had been reported to be railing against Cushman and threatening to have him arrested. It came as no surprise, therefore, that this "knave, and so will live and die," turned violent over a petty quarrel. His murder of John Newcomen led to his trial, the first of its kind, his conviction, and his execution by hanging.

Billington's crime was notorious but not unique; three others were hanged for robbing and murdering an Indian, and lesser crimes and abrasive social conflicts in this pious community were shockingly common. The first volume of the Plymouth court records covering the years 1633–40 documents cases of blasphemy, drunkenness, extortion, fornication, receiving stolen goods, and sedition. Servants were running away; there were charges of slander and accusations of witchcraft; and there was evidence of adultery and illegitimacy. The climax came in a bizarre case of bestiality "with a mare, a cow, two goats, five sheep, two calves, and a turkey," which followed closely on cases of attempted sodomy. The culprit, a teenaged servant boy, upon his confession and conviction by jury, was executed, and the animals concerned (they had trouble identifying which particular sheep had been involved) were ritually slaughtered "before his face," as required by Leviticus 20:15.

Bradford was utterly baffled, not only by the "foul nature" of such evil but also by where, and from whom, such practices could even have been learned. Perhaps, he said, the Devil had a greater animus against communities that were most successful in bridling and subduing man's corrupt nature. Perhaps, as with water that is dammed up, when there is a break, the flow is more violent, noisy, and disturbing. Perhaps it was not a matter of an excess of evil at all, but only the result of greater scrutiny, visibility, and punishment of evil. But these were large abstractions. There was a more specific issue involved: the nature of the specific people who had settled in the colony.

How could it have happened, he asked himself, that "so many wicked persons and profane people should so quickly come over into this land and mix themselves amongst them . . . seeing it was religious men that began the work and they came for religion's sake"? The answers, he believed, were, first, that the planters, the initial builders of the colony, had been desperate for help and so had brought over "many untoward servants" who, when their contracts expired, spawned families of their own that had no commitment to the church or even to decent behavior. Then, too, ambitious merchants, seeking to profit by the Pilgrims' market and the freightages of emigrants, sent over anyone who could pay the fare, among them "many unworthy persons who, being come over, crept into one place or other." Finally, the Pilgrims' material success, such as it was, their remoteness from metropolitan corruptions, and the stability of their community attracted some who were such burdens or embarrassments to people at home that they were happily disposed of to the colony; once here they followed "their dissolute courses." It was for these reasons, Bradford concluded, that the majority of his saintly community was becoming the "worser" part.[37]

But there was an even deeper problem, affecting more directly the core community of saints, and it emerged with what to some was tragic inevitability. The cohesiveness, the physical integrity, of the church community had been reinforced by the communal ownership of land and trade, except for a single acre for each individual. The plan had been that for seven years all would pool their efforts and productive goods to help pay off the debts to the sponsoring merchants. When the initial joint stock was dissolved in 1626, that arrangement ended. The colony's cattle were divided among the permanent residents (156 had claims), and land was distributed, twenty acres for each adult male who was not a servant. The resulting privately owned farms were needed to support the growing families and provide for approved newcomers. But every effort was made to keep the community together. The grants were not to be isolated in the interior but to front on the bay, spreading out equally on each side of the central village. And those who farmed the more distant plots were to reside, as far as possible, in Plymouth, or at least worship there. But such formal constraints were difficult to maintain. The land to the north and east was especially attractive, and by 1628 Miles Standish, who had claims to one hundred acres, had opened a farm eight and a half miles from Plymouth farther along the bay, which he worked in the summer. By 1632 he was joined by Alden, Prence, and the younger Brewster, whose claims reached farther north, ending at the end of Plymouth Bay in what became Duxbury. They promised to return to Plymouth in the winter, "that they may better repair to the worship of God." But the propulsive force was inexorable, especially since the initial recipients of land were entitled to portions of subsequent divisions when the colony expanded. Duxbury proved to be the first of a ring of satellite villages that within a decade spread out around the bay and inland: Marshfield and Scituate followed Duxbury to the north, then Sandwich, Barnstable, and Yarmouth to the south, and then Taunton, twenty-two miles inland.[38]

The first outliers, core figures among the saints, deeply committed to the conventicle's welfare, were responding to the need to provide for their growing families, but others had different motivations. The influx of the Puritans to the Boston Bay area immediately to the north of Plymouth created a huge new market for agricultural goods. An increasing number of Plymouth's settlers responded by maximizing their acreage and thus their yields, taking up new land grants whenever they could get them. So, Bradford explained,

> as their stocks increased and the increase vendible, there was no longer any holding them together, but they must of necessity go to their great lots. . . . And no man now thought he could live except he had cattle and a great deal of ground to keep them, all striving to increase their stocks. By which means they were scattered all over [Plymouth] Bay quickly, and the town in which they lived compactly till now was left very thin and in a short time almost desolate.

Their harvests improved year after year, but these were not the harvests of souls that Bradford sought. However well intentioned the outliers

were, they were serving Mammon, Bradford felt, and not God, destroying the integrity, the very heart, of the asylum he—and they—had fought
so hard to create. Worst of all, the church itself was splintering—"those
who had lived so long together in Christian and comfortable fellowship
must now part and suffer many divisions." Initially, this was not the work
of evil intentions. It was the elder Brewster himself who presided over
the forming of the Duxbury parish, the first of the separate congregations
within Plymouth's jurisdiction.

Bradford tried everything he could think of to stem the tide. Special
land grants were given to those who promised to live in Plymouth, wherever their fields might lie, and be helpful to the church and community.
"But alas," he reported, "this remedy proved worse than the disease; for
within a few years those that had thus got footing there rent themselves
away." Some simply marched off in defiance of their pledges; others so
noisily insisted on the need for their permanent removal that the town
faced the choice of letting them go or putting up with endless contention.
The future for Bradford was bleak: at the least, the ruin of the church;
ultimately, God's displeasure.

And then came the wrenching debate of the early 1640s on whether
to move the church itself, hence the central town, to a place called Nauset (later Eastham), a harbor town on the Atlantic side of Cape Cod fifty
miles from Plymouth. Surrounded by freshwater ponds, the site was
known to have some of the richest soil on the cape. So fierce was the
determination of some to make the move that the resisters, after arguing
that people should be satisfied with what they had instead of seeking to
enrich themselves elsewhere, finally gave in. But when a closer survey of
Nauset proved that it would be too small an area to accommodate the
whole of Plymouth, the vote was rescinded, and only the most insistent
broke away to settle there. But their departure was a significant loss. So it
was, Bradford wrote, that

> this poor church [was] left, like an ancient mother grown old and for-
> saken of her children, though not in their affections yet in regard of
> their bodily presence and personal helpfulness; her ancient members
> being most of them worn away by death, and these of later time being
> like children translated into other families, and she like a widow left
> only to trust in God. Thus, she that had made many rich became herself
> poor.[39]

But what for Bradford was ruin was for others a rising good fortune. By the late 1630s recruitment from the old Leiden congregation had come to an end, and direct seaborne immigration from other sources fell away. Yet the resident population, now in control of its environment, was growing rapidly by natural increase, supplemented by a small but continuous migration south from the Bay Colony. The total of approximately three hundred souls in 1630 had become at least a thousand by 1640, perhaps fifteen hundred by 1650, and about two thousand in 1660. And as the population grew, it showed signs of a remarkable demographic profile, utterly different from that of the Chesapeake south, different too from that of England, that would characterize New England's people throughout the seventeenth century. Settling families whose marriage partners lived to age fifty had seven or eight children who lived to adulthood. Infant and child mortality was not more than 25 percent, and the life expectancy of men who reached the age of twenty-one was approximately seventy. In a sample of 645 individuals, 30 percent of the men and 20 percent of the women lived into their seventies, 22 percent of them into their eighties. Remarkable figures whose full implications would become clear only in later years, they indicate the Pilgrims' success in controlling the environment and the general healthiness of the environment itself.[40]

7

But none of this was success for Bradford. For him, as he entered his sixties in 1650—still devoted to the ideals that had led him through the persecutions of Laudian England, the upheavals of Leiden, and the turmoils of resettlement in barren New England—it was all dross and loss. Looking back over the account of the colony's history he had compiled over the years, he came upon the glowing words that the Pilgrims had written at the outset of their great adventure, that they were "knit together as a body in a most strict and sacred bond and covenant of the Lord . . . straitly tied to all care of each other's good and of the whole, by every one and so mutually." It was precisely that solidarity and mutual commitment in behalf of the highest Christian ideals that had been lost, Bradford believed, and it was that that he most deeply lamented. Turning to the blank page opposite those confident words of 1617, he wrote his most heartfelt, elegiac lamentation.

O sacred bond, whilst inviolably preserved! How sweet and precious were the fruits that flowed from the same! But when this fidelity decayed, then their ruin approached. O that these ancient members had not died or been dissipated . . . or else that this holy care and constant faithfulness had still lived and remained with those that survived and were at times afterwards added unto them. But (alas) that subtle serpent hath slyly wound in himself under fair pretences of necessity and the like, to untwist these sacred bonds and ties, and as it were insensibly by degrees to dissolve, or in a great measure to weaken, the same. I have been happy, in my first times, to see, and with much comfort to enjoy, the blessed fruits of this sweet communion, but it is now a part of my misery in old age, to find and feel the decay and want thereof (in a great measure) and with grief and sorrow of heart to lament and bewail the same. And for others' warning and admonition (and my own humiliation) do I here note the same.

But his grief and lamentation at the loss of that "sweet communion" had deeper sources than the arrival of profane gentiles, the inexorable spread of settlement, and the forsaking of the ancient church. Something more profound and bewildering was at work. The greater world from which the Pilgrims had fled had been turned upside down, and their identity and the meaning of their strivings had been obscured. Once the Pilgrims had been convinced of their unique historic mission, to be a beacon in the recovery of pristine, primitive Christianity in the age of Episcopal persecution. But now, it seemed, their humble efforts had been overwhelmed by the great success of Cromwell's tolerationist Puritans in England—indeed, in the very counties from which the Pilgrims had fled—and by the defeat of the oppressive church. What now was the meaning of all their strivings in the greater scheme of things?[41]

To these ultimate questions Bradford turned in his final years, expressing himself no longer in history but in other literary forms. He composed what he called "sundry useful verses"—didactic poems directed to New Plymouth, to Boston, and to New England as a whole. Thus:

> *O New England, though canst not boast;*
> *Thy former glory thou hast lost.*
> *When Hooker, Winthrop, Cotton died,*
> *And many precious ones beside,*

Thy beauty then it did decay,
And still doth languish more away
...
Thy open sins none can them hide,
Fraud, drunkenness, whoredom and pride.
...
Repent, amend, and turn to God
That we may prevent his sharp rod.[42]

But though he prided himself on such verses, he must have known their limits as expressions of his search for meaning.

More important was his further study of Hebrew, which grew more urgent as he aged, and which he justified at length, in a heartfelt, strangely spaced paragraph.

Though I am grown aged, yet I have had a longing
desire to see with my own eyes something of that most
ancient language and holy tongue in which the Law
and Oracles of God were writ, and in which God
and Angels spake to the holy patriarchs of old
time; and what names were given to things
from the Creation. And though I cannot
attain to much herein, yet I am refresh-
ed to have seen some glimpse hereof,
as Moses saw the land of Can-
aan afar off. My aim and
desire is to see how the words
and phrases lie in the
holy text, and to
discern somewhat
of the same,
for my own
contente.

But it was difficult ever to reach "contente" with one's knowledge of the tongue with which God and the angels had spoken to the holy patriarchs.

A page from William Bradford's Hebrew glossary, part of his effort to grow closer to God through mastering His divine, biblical language. At the top Bradford lists eight names for God "expressing his nature, essence, power, and most glorious majestie."

He persisted, however, and in eight blank pages of his history of the colony he recorded something of the product of his Hebrew exercises: a glossary of more than a thousand Hebrew words, each painstakingly drawn, each with its English translation or transliteration; a list of eight Hebrew names for the deity; and twenty-five quotations in Hebrew from the Bible.[43]

But neither verse nor expression in the sacred language could satisfy Bradford's need to probe and reveal to the world the meaning of his people's epic. In the end he turned to direct discourse, in the form of an elaborate three-part "Dialogue" between "some yonge-men borne in New England; And sundry Ancient-men that came out of Holand and old England."[44]

Bradford began writing the Dialogue, a genre familiar in the polemics of the time, in 1648 and completed it four years later, when he was sixty-two. In these learned colloquies (only two of which survive, in part), Bradford attempted, first, to update and justify the separatist enterprise in general and his own congregation's distinctive accomplishments in the light of recent history. He felt too the need to make clear to the younger generation the great sacrifices his generation had made in an effort to reach its goals. And beyond that the Dialogue was something more personal—an *apologia* for his own humble life, now that the end was approaching, and an explanation of the meaning of his personal struggles in light of the unexpected result of the English Civil War and the settlement of the Puritans in Massachusetts Bay.

So much, he wrote, has been misunderstood, and so much could now, in the perspective of history, be clearly seen that earlier had been obscured in the clash of religious and political controversy. His people had never believed "none to be true churches but their own, and condemn[ed] all the churches in the world besides." That charge was a "foul blot." In fact, they had believed that all Protestant churches were "true churches" in some degree. The failure of the Church of England under Archbishop Laud lay in the ubiquity of its membership as a national institution—any sinner could belong—and in its hierarchical, coercive prelacy, which was the very opposite of pristine Christianity's simple, independent conventicles of true believers. Nor did they have fundamental differences with the Boston Puritans. They differed from them only in the process of admission to communion; otherwise there were only "words and terms" that separated them.[45]

ʃa: 26 · 8 ·

יְהוָה אָהַבְתִּי מְעוֹן בֵּיתֶךָ וּמְקוֹם מִשְׁכַּן כְּבוֹדֶךָ

יְהוָה מְנָת חֶלְקִי

pʃa: 16 · 5 ·

שָׂנֵאתִי קְהַל מְרֵעִים · pʃa: 26 · 5 · ז.

A' Dialogue

Or ·3· conference, betweene some
yonge-men borne in New-England;
And some Ancient-men, which came
out of Holand, and old England
concerning the
Church.

And the gouermente therof · ט · ט ט

— yonge-men —

Gentle-men, we hope you will pardon
our bouldnes, in that we haue ÿmpor=
tuned you to giue vs meeting once
more in this kind, for our ÿnstructi-
on, & establishmente in the truth.
We find that many, and great are the
controuersies, which haue risen in these
later times, about the Church, and ÿ
gouerments therof; and much trouble
and disturbance hath growne in the

FAC-SIMILE OF THE FIRST PAGE OF BRADFORD'S DIALOGUE.

First page of William Bradford's third Dialogue "betweene some yonge-men
borne in New-England; And some Ancient-men, which came out of Holand,
and old England." The three dialogues form an apologia for Bradford's own
life and for the Pilgrims' exile and settlement in New England.

The Pilgrims, Bradford explained to the imaginary young, had never been radical separatists like the "scandalous" Brownists or other extremists who refused all contacts with the ungodly. They had never cut themselves off completely; they had always been willing to commune "in all things in themselves lawful" with any group of reformed (Protestant) Christians, English, Dutch, French, Scotch, or German Lutheran, even though they were "not of the best mould." Nor had they completely rejected synods or other superior church structures, so long as they were merely consultative and not coercive—empowered only "to admonish one another of what is behooveful." Yes, they approved of lay prophesying—but so too had the ancient church, and in any case they mainly practiced it "in defect of public ministry," allowing only the few truly qualified members to engage in it. Were the young surprised that groups like his own and other reformers in England had so quickly become reconciled to the ecclesiastical regime of England's new Commonwealth? They should not be. In the sweep of history the two sides had grown closer to each other. The evils of the earthly church's intolerant, coercive prelacy had been exposed and destroyed, and the Pilgrims, who had been "in some things . . . too rigid," had modified their views. Rather than being "blasted with reproach to posterity" for their earlier rigidity, they should be pitied for the suffering they endured in those earlier, oppressive times. And suffering they had endured—far more than the Puritans. True, only six separatists had been executed in England (and the death of two of them Queen Elizabeth herself had regretted), but others had died in prison, and innumerable others had been stripped of their possessions and driven from the land, to live in impoverished exile. The Puritans, on the other hand, Bradford wrote, though they had here and there lost their ministries, had largely been protected and had managed to keep their property if not their offices.[46]

But if all of this were true, Bradford had his youths inquire, what role had the Pilgrims and their cosectarians played in Christian history? What had Bradford's people—not so radical, it now appeared, as one might have thought, not so cut off from the world as had been believed, and not so singular in their ecclesiastical and theological views—what had they accomplished? What difference had they made?

To answer this Bradford devoted his third Dialogue, which is a treatise on the history of Christianity, from the Apostles to Cromwell's saints. Citing authorities from Saint Augustine to Grosseteste, from Peter Martyr to Beza, and from Socrates to Petrarch, Calvin, and Whitgift, and quoting sources in Hebrew, Greek, Latin, French, and English, Bradford formulated the story around four ecclesiastical groups—the Catholics, Episcopalians, Presbyterians, and Independents—coming closer and closer to the true dispensation.

For the Catholics he had only seething contempt. The papacy, he explained to the young, had violated every principle of Christianity. They had imposed a tyrannical regime on their supine people and had sunk into a swamp of corruption. The Roman Church's history is a tale of "pontifical lasciviousness," the story of a world where "libidinous beasts" like John XIII were free to satisfy their "fleshly lusts" on captive youths until Rome became "an abominable warehouse of all spiritual and corporal fornications," where "deflowering, ravishing, incests, and adulteries are but a sport." Friars, swarming through the land, had followed suit, putting every clerical benefit up for sale and stocking their stately abbeys with whores and concubines, practicing incest and "filthy sodomitrie."

Episcopacy—that is, the English Church of the Reformation—had wiped out the unspeakable corruption of the Roman Church, but it retained the lordly hierarchy of bishops with coercive powers. No doubt many of the bishops had been worthy people, but the ecclesiastical structure was only a "human devise and intrusion" and had no sanction in scripture. There had been no diocesan bishops until the Council of Nicaea in the fourth century, and the only basis for them in England was the human, legal inventions of Henry VIII and Elizabeth.

The Presbyterian churches were true churches of Christ save for the jurisdiction of their councils, their synods and presbyteries, over local congregations. Some claimed to see advantages in being able to appeal local differences to higher authorities, but Bradford saw none. Appeals simply compounded the controversies at another level and led to "nothing but garboils & troubles in the world." And to the extent that the English church even now continued the practice of universal membership and a hierarchical structure, it was following the worst rather than the best elements of Presbyterian reform.

Only Independency—the Congregational way—had the sanction of antiquity and scripture. Clusters of believers adopted into fellowship after profession of their faith and commitment to the common good; congregations operating independently but in friendly concert with each other; sanctuaries for people fleeing Episcopal coercion for conscience's sake—these were the only apostolic churches. However obscure they might have seemed, they, in their suffering and persecution, had ignited concern for the nature of true ecclesiastical discipline all over England. God had used their faith and constancy as his instrument in the world. It had surely been their suffering, glowing in the dark tumultuous years just past, that had convinced Parliament to reform the ecclesiastical state and that had led, as a testimonial of God's blessing to the humble separatists, to Cromwell's successes in war.

Far from having been bypassed by the events of the greater world, the Pilgrims, Bradford explained to the young, had been at their very core. They had been the inner light, the flickering beacon, which in the end had illuminated the way. Now their mission seemed diffused, their physical unity was dissipated, the sordidness of profane life pressed against them, and their principles were no longer challenging. Yet their great historical role remained. As a church unique among the churches of the world, they would soon, Bradford recognized to his sorrow, disappear. But theirs had been a special, providential mission, he told the younger generation, and he charged them never to forget their scriptural mandate, the community's original beliefs and practices, and to follow the "best and most godly expositors . . . those shining lights that God hath raised up in the reformed churches . . . and help to propagate the same to generations to come, till the coming of the Lord."[47]

FIVE YEARS LATER, in 1657, Bradford died. By then Plymouth's population of 2,000 was spread out through eleven towns, and the population of New England as a whole exceeded 33,000.

CHAPTER 12

The New-English Sionists:
Fault Lines, Diversity, and Persecution

1

THUS THE INNER FLAME of the Pilgrims' conventicle had gradually dimmed until it had become only a faint point of light in a corner
of a populous, dynamic, disputatious world that had suddenly sprung up
around it. There were affinities between the Pilgrims' spiritual aspirations
and those of the seemingly multitudinous Puritans who poured into the
New England countryside after 1630, but these later comers were people
of a different order. Their leaders were anything but humble, and their
ambitions were the opposite of modest. They withdrew from the metropolitan world not, like the Pilgrims, to escape it but ultimately to transform it. Substantial gentlemen and merchants connected with some of the
movers and shakers in the political and ecclesiastical controversies that
were tearing England apart, and preachers of intellectual power, polemical skill, and reputation—they led one of the best organized and most
consequential displacements of European peoples that had yet taken place.

Consequential—but not simply because of numbers. The Puritan-led
"Great Migration" to New England was part, but only part, of a general
stirring and shifting of the British population that would end, by 1700,

in the emigration from Britain to the western hemisphere of approximately 400,000 people, with another 180,000 voyaging to and resettling in Ireland. Of all of these, somewhat fewer than 20,000 moved, permanently or temporarily, to New England, most in the single decade after 1630—years in which at least 100,000 English and Scots emigrated to Ireland.[1] Yet in its consequences, this relatively small migration to New England was utterly distinctive. It resulted in a world of villages not manifestly different from England's rural countryside. In outward appearance the Puritans' New England was similar to certain of the provincial areas of England that had been left behind. But the similarities were superficial and hid fundamental differences.

In this new English world of farms and small villages, the divisive forces in that earlier life, which had been confined by long-established institutions and deep structures of social control, were set free to work themselves out, to exfoliate, almost without restraint. The result was a provincial society that was full of creative energies but contentious, dedicated to the high ideals of reformed Protestantism but riven by conflicting views of how those ideals should be interpreted and realized, and abrasive as it sought to impose on ordinary people the demanding discipline of the Puritans' worldly asceticism. The fractious history of Puritan New England in its early years—the animosities, the conflicts, the reprisals, the community schisms and forced expulsions: all of this was a product of many conditions and forces—the geopolitical and cultural diversity of the population's origins, the personalities of the religious and secular leaders, the trauma of displacement and resettlement—but above all it was the result of the basic instability and the inner turbulence of Puritanism itself. And compounding all of these divisive forces was the savagery of race warfare.

MUCH INK HAS BEEN SPILLED on the question of whether or to what extent the Puritans' migration was principally a religious movement—whether it was a displacement of people who, like the Marian exiles fleeing a Catholic regime a century earlier, were a persecuted minority escaping a tyrannical state church to worship as they pleased, or whether it was chiefly a movement of economically insecure or desperate people, motivated less by religious aspirations than by the desire to resettle where they might find the land, employment, security, and opportunities denied them at home.[2]

The Great Migration was neither, exclusively, and in part it was both. The movement's initial leaders were committed church reformers, deeply devoted to the Puritan cause, convinced that in England their religious interests would not survive the Anglican Church's demand for conformity, and confident that they could create a model society shaped to their religious ideals. But from the start they had with them some who were only more or less sympathetic to the Puritan cause but not deeply committed to it, and many more—servants, artisans, farmworkers, and vagrant laborers—who were not involved at all in the religious passions of the time but who needed employment and some prospect of future security.

There is no way of knowing with any precision the numerical proportions of these groups, but it is clear that the leaders, the men who determined the goals, institutions, and norms of daily life in the resulting communities, were devoted to creating what they believed was a new Sion of God's desires. Most of the region's major difficulties were created not by those who cared little about religion and resisted it but by those who cared passionately.[3]

HOWEVER SMALL it was relative to the major population displacements in the British archipelago, the Puritans' exodus was concerted, collectively purposeful, and coherent. And it carried with it the expectation of replicating the social order of the world that had been left behind. For though the Puritans were reformist in their religious goals, they were conservative in their social views, and they expected to reconcile the fulfillment of their religious ideals with the maintenance of the social order familiar to them. The difficulties of doing this would appear in subtle forms throughout the history of their settlements; they appeared in obvious form at the start.

Very few of the Puritan migrants were drawn from England's titled aristocracy, and the few of that rank who did emigrate left little mark on the colony's life. Three siblings of the Puritan Earl of Lincoln were involved. One of the earl's sisters, Lady Arbella Fiennes, distinctive enough in status for John Winthrop to name his flagship after her, had married Isaac Johnson, a devout, wealthy merchant with estates in three counties who had contributed a major share of the financing of the Massachusetts Bay Colony. She and her husband both sailed with Winthrop in the fleet of 1630, together with Arbella's brother, Charles Fiennes. Later

Arbella's sister, Lady Susan, followed with her husband, John Humphrey, another affluent merchant and a lawyer, described by Winthrop as "a gentleman of special parts of learning and activity, and a godly man, who had been one of the first beginners in the promoting of this plantation, and had labored very much therein."[4]

Only slightly inferior in status to the Lincoln siblings was Sir Richard Saltonstall, of a well-established landowning Yorkshire family. He had studied at Cambridge and later at the Inns of Court. He had been knighted and had served as a justice of the peace before moving to London to join his merchant kinsmen in finance and overseas trade. There, increasingly devoted to church reform, he had flourished and began a series of substantial investments in the New England and other Puritan enterprises. Closely connected to the major financiers and promoters of the developing exodus—the Earl of Warwick, Sir Nathaniel Rich, and a cluster of influential second-tier London merchants, among them Samuel Vassall, Nathan Wright, and above all Matthew Cradock ("the center of one of the most powerful family-business networks in the American trades")—Saltonstall went further than almost all of the highly placed sponsors by joining Winthrop's fleet himself, taking with him five of his six children.[5]

Saltonstall and the Lincoln connections were exceptions among the initial settlers by virtue of their distinguished lineage. Only one other of similar status would follow: the young Sir Henry Vane, son and heir of the comptroller of the king's household. But however committed to the Puritans' cause these few of more elevated status may have been, they had neither the zeal nor the stamina for the harsh task of colonizing an undeveloped frontier or of dealing with the fierce contentions within Puritanism. Within a year Saltonstall left, with three of his children, discouraged by New England's climate, concerned about his family's finances, and repelled, it was said, by the heavy diet of "clams, and muscles, and ground-nuts, and acorns" he had endured in the first, desperate winter. Lady Arbella died, age twenty-nine, a few weeks after landing; her husband followed within a month, and her brother Charles never settled at all but returned to England on the first available vessel. As for Vane, shortly after his arrival in 1635 he was elected governor, at age twenty-three, pitched himself at once into the most bruising politico-theological battle ever to rock the colony, was defeated, and left hurriedly for home in 1637.[6]

By then a decisive moment had passed in the social history of the colony. Despite all the obvious discouragements for people "of great qualitye & estate" to join the migration, a few of such distinction had cautiously tested the waters. When Humphrey arrived in 1634 he carried with him "Certain Proposals" from Viscount Saye and Sele, father-in-law of the Earl of Lincoln and an early supporter of the Bay Colony, Baron Brooke, "and other Persons of quality, as conditions of their removing to New-England." The two lords, Saye and Sele and Brooke, leading Puritans but by no means religious utopians, were already deeply engaged in the Puritan colony on Providence Island in the Caribbean and in Puritan projects elsewhere, especially a new colony planned for establishment at the mouth of the Connecticut River, a site that would be known as Saybrook. For this they had organized a development plan, had begun sending supplies to the site, and had appointed John Winthrop, Jr., who had his own scientific interest in the project, to serve as governor. For that imagined community as well as for their knowledge of the Bay Colony, should they decide to migrate there, the "persons of great quality and estate" wrote to inquire what kind of a society New England actually was and whether it would be suitable for people like themselves.

So they asked: Did the colony have a bicameral legislature whose upper chamber was reserved for eminences like themselves and their heirs in perpetuity and had veto power over ordinary legislation? Was it true that any man could vote and serve in the lower house simply by virtue of church membership, without regard to wealth and standing? Surely, they wrote, men should be chosen for civil offices, even though "carnal" with respect to the church, if they had "eminent gifts of wisdom, courage, justice, fit for government."[7]

The colony's magistrates and its leading theologian, John Cotton, scrambled to respond. Eager for the support and if possible the presence in New England of such distinguished figures, they assured their lordships that there was no danger that the colony would ever become a "mere democracy." God, they hastened to say, never advised such a thing: "if the people be governors, who shall be governed?" Nothing in the colony's organization would "cast the commonwealth into distractions, and popular confusions." They were no levellers and no advocates of arbitrary rule of any sort. Nor was there a danger, they wrote, that the rule of the godly would lead to "excommunications." They simply believed, because they knew it was a "divine ordinance (and moral)," that no one should be trusted with public authority, either as voter or magistrate, who was not godly, and since godly people were "fit materials for church fellowship," it followed that membership in the church should be, and would continue to be, a qualification for political participation. But though the magistrates would be church members, they would govern by civil laws enacted by civil legislatures and executed by normal courts of law. As for social distinctions, they would be fully respected, as would all the privileges natural to them. Indeed, they wrote, the colony had already established a Standing Council whose members would serve for life, though membership in that body would not be hereditary. There was no biblical sanction for hereditary governance, nor was it reasonable. To exalt to high places heirs lacking "gifts fit for magistracy," simply because they were heirs, would be to violate God's clear intention. Hereditary honors and titles would of course be respected, but hereditary authority and power would be taking God's name in vain, just as would hiding "under a bushel" the abilities of any members of noble families who had in fact been blessed by God "with a spirit and gifts fit for government."[8]

The language was somewhat complicated, but the message was clear. The colony would be ruled by members of the church who qualified for leadership. Hereditary distinctions would be respected but not deemed qualification for office. While there would be no levelling of the social order, rank or wealth would not in themselves be qualifications for political participation.

Thereafter Lord Saye and Sele, while leading the opposition forces in Parliament, concentrated on the Puritans' colony on Providence Island, even attempting, to the mortification and deep resentment of Winthrop and his assistants, to lure some of the Bay Colony's settlers to that remote Caribbean spot. Brooke joined him in this and in the Connecticut venture, which languished for lack of funds and attention. Ultimately Brooke would gain fame as an officer in the military struggles against the royal forces, until he was killed in battle in 1643.[9]

But however fruitless the two nobles' approach to the Puritan leadership in Massachusetts had been, it forced the leaders to consider what kind of community they were creating and what form the peopling of the colony should take. A popular democracy the colony would certainly not be. Nor would it be a theocracy. It would be a society of traditional social ranks below the level of the titled aristocracy and nobility, with a majority of farmers, artisans, and laborers, dominated by affluent, or once-affluent, well-educated, godly, competent gentlemen and merchant-entrepreneurs, together with a powerful cohort of England's clerical intelligentsia.[10]

And so it was. While in Ireland English and Scottish settlements were being imposed on an indigenous population of Christians to form garrisoned enclaves of conquest; while in the scattered plantation world in the American south immigrants were forming an overwhelmingly male population of agricultural laborers violently displacing the native population; and while in the mid-Atlantic coastal region a polyglot mix of north Europeans was struggling with fiercely contesting natives for control of agricultural lands and the fur trade—in the same years greater New England was being transformed. English village communities appeared in increasing numbers, radiating inland from initial settlements on the Atlantic coast, from estuaries on Long Island Sound, and along the Connecticut River. In the process clusters of native Indian villagers were scattered into new, diminished, unstable groupings in more remote locations.

THE MIGRATION BEGAN, after the establishment of the Massachusetts Bay Company's preliminary settlement at Salem and the transfer of the company's government to Massachusetts, with the Winthrop fleet of 1630. That formidable flotilla, the largest single shipment of emigrants ever to have left England, consisted of eleven vessels carrying approximately 700 passengers. Six other vessels followed in the weeks thereafter, bringing the total within the single year to approximately 1,000 migrants, most of whom landed at the ramshackle fishing village of Salem, where 80 of the company's 180 servants had died during the previous winter. The flow continued, at a diminished rate, for the next three years, bringing annual increments of approximately 500 men, women, and children. Then in 1633, which marks the advent of William Laud to the Archbishopric of Canterbury and the beginning of determined repression of active nonconformists, the numbers soared.

Annually thereafter, until 1640, dozens of vessels left ports in southern England bearing well over a thousand migrants to Massachusetts; in 1638 no fewer than three thousand arrived. At docks in Boston, Salem, and a few lesser New England harbors and inlets the passengers, hundreds at a time, after long, exhausting, often frightening voyages, unloaded their personal belongings, their supplies, and equipment of all sorts, sought out kin, acquaintances, and church and neighborhood leaders who had gone before, and crowded together in whatever shelters they could find. In 1631 the future Charlestown, at the confluence of the Mystic and Charles rivers, was a "sprawling tent community," Boston a disorderly scattering of shacks, huts, wigwams, and small, half-built timber-frame houses. Once secured in whatever makeshift shelters they could devise, the new arrivals began the difficult process of organizing quasi-normal communities and of learning to cope with the local environment. At the same time preliminary structures of church and state were improvised, and some elementary regulations of economic life, especially the distribution of land, were agreed upon. It was a frantic, contentious, and remarkably creative time, but also dangerous and threatening. Diseases spread, many died (two hundred, it was said, between April and December 1630), and at least one hundred of the thousand who arrived in 1630—despairing, disillusioned, and fearful for their lives—returned to England. But the region's population grew with astonishing speed. Before the decade was out, it had reached more than eleven thousand men, women, and children, in villages scattered from Boston and a ring of neighboring communities in the east to clusters of settlements on the Connecticut River and Long Island, and to a string of fishing villages stretching north along the Atlantic coast to the mouth of the Kennebec River.[11]

Peculiarly derived from English antecedents, these villages, as they developed, were social amalgams, hybrids in English terms, variations on known community models, demographically dynamic to an extraordinary degree, and remarkably contentious.

2

The demographic complexity of New England's population derived in part from the geographical diversity of the English sources from which it was drawn and from the resulting variety of the migrants' socioeconomic and cultural backgrounds.[12]

There was no singular sociogeographic source of the Puritan migration. The largest number of settlers came from the east-central area of England, between the Humber River on the north and the Thames on the south—that is, from East Anglia proper (Norfolk and Suffolk) and its surrounding counties (Essex, Cambridgeshire, Lincolnshire, and Hertfordshire),[13] and in addition from London and Kent. But New England was not simply a greater East Anglian or east-central England transplant. The scope and reach of the recruitment was far broader than that. Though the passengers in the initial Winthrop fleet were locally recruited and as far as possible were personally screened by Winthrop and the Bay Company's incorporators, among them were people whose origins lay in no fewer than twenty counties of England: from the north (Yorkshire and Lancashire), from the west (Cheshire), and from the south (Hampshire); five of the voyagers, though English, came from Holland. And Winthrop's fleet had been preceded by the arrival of an independent shipment of 140 emigrants from the West Country (Devon, Dorset, and Somerset).[14]

Every relevant record repeats this pattern of regional and subcultural diversity in the origins of New England's population. Of Boston's residents in the 1630s, the English origins of 141 are known: though 60 percent came from the East Anglian counties of Suffolk and Essex, the rest were drawn from ten other counties, and from London and the Netherlands. Of the 669 emigrants known to have left the port of London for New England in 1635, 48 percent were residents of London and greater East Anglia, but the rest came from twenty-eight other counties as far distant as Northumberland and Devon, Yorkshire and Lancashire. In the most comprehensive listing of the origins of all known emigrants to New England before 1650, almost the whole of England, plus Holland and Ireland, are represented. Of the 4,282 people whose residential origins are known (approximately one-fifth of those known to have emigrated to New England in those years), the largest number (1,302, or 30 percent) came from Suffolk, Essex, and Norfolk, followed by London and Kent (608, or 14 percent). But 687 (16 percent) came from the West Country (Somerset, Wiltshire, Devonshire, and Dorset), and there were significant numbers from Yorkshire (136), Lincolnshire (113), Lancashire (54), Northumberland (37), and Sussex (33). The only county that was not represented was Westmoreland, though not because of its remoteness: Northumberland, Cumberland, and Durham in the north sent 42. And there were also residents of Ireland (11) and Wales (34) as well as 80 people, no doubt English in origin, who began their journey to New England from the Netherlands.[15]

These regional differences, in the still deeply decentralized England of the early seventeenth century, defined distinct variations in local cultures, in economic experiences, and in the expectations of the settlers.

. . .

IN THE BROADEST GEOPHYSICAL and climatological terms, England as a whole was divided between pastoral highlands in the north and west and arable lowland areas of mixed husbandry in the east. The former was a cool, wet land of mountains and moors and thin, poor soils good mainly for animal raising—sheep and cattle—and grass growing. The south and east were a drier region of gentle slopes, open pastures, and a richer, deeper soil excellent for grain cultivation and mixed farming as well as pasturage. In the highlands, enclosure of the land into separate farmsteads was widespread, and mining and quarrying were important parts of the economy. But in the south and east, enclosure was still in the process of development, in many places incomplete and a matter of controversy; open-field mixed farming and "large-scale commercial dealings in food" predominated, and everywhere there were nucleated villages whose inhabitants lived within the control of manorial institutions. And the "social framework of community life in upland and lowland England was as distinct as the farming arrangements." Partible inheritance, for example, was more widely practiced in the highlands than in the south and east where primogeniture was common.[16]

But these gross distinctions mask a great variety of specific, local differences that were vital in shaping the experiences, customs, and expectations of the migration's people. "When an Englishman in the early seventeenth century said 'my country,'" Lawrence Stone has written, "he meant 'my county,'" and there was "an emotional sense of loyalty to the local community, and also . . . institutional arrangements to give that sentiment force." But "country" could also mean "immediate neighborhood, one's farming region or 'pays.'" For not only were there significant differences in the social structure, the political temper, and the economic fortunes of adjacent counties, but even within counties there were "sudden changes of scenery and society." "Geographically, few counties were homogeneous"; nor were all local areas unitary in character. Individual communities within them were peculiarly shaped by the impact of a particularly charismatic preacher, sudden rent increases, or personal struggles in politics. And throughout these years there was something subtler and more general at work: a deepening introversion, an intensifying insularity and sense of parochial self-consciousness.[17]

Thus greater East Anglia, from which the largest number of emigrants

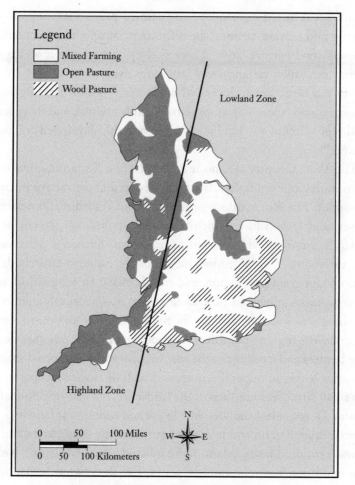

Legend

☐ Mixed Farming
■ Open Pasture
▨ Wood Pasture

Lowland Zone

Highland Zone

N
W—✦—E
S

0   50   100 Miles
0   50   100 Kilometers

Farming regions of England, 1500–1640

came, while it shared certain general characteristics of the southeastern region, had its own economic and cultural diversity. The core counties of Norfolk and Suffolk were given over to grassland and dairying, but its broad western and northern circumference had long been a major supplier of grain to the great London and northern European markets as well as to its own coastal fishing areas. Sheep breeding supplied a cloth industry centered in Norfolk, especially in its shire town, Norwich. In addition there were wood-pasture districts, in which small hamlets and isolated dairy and horse-breeding farms were scattered among extensive woodlands that nourished a long-established timber industry. Neighboring Essex and Kent too were complex worlds, containing as they did in some areas mixed husbandry and enclosed pasture farming, in others dairying and market farming, in still others sheep and pig breeding in enclosed wood-pasture lands. There as elsewhere economic and agrarian differences shaped variant social structures even at the most local level. Society was more hierarchical and oligarchic in mixed farming regions; in pastoral areas there was more clan or family control, and there was less social regulation of any kind in districts of highly developed commercial farming.[18]

The West Country was no less complex, no less a region of diverse communities and multiple relationships rooted in distinctive microlocal economies. The four southwestern counties of Wiltshire, Somersetshire, Dorset, and Devonshire, which together supplied 16 percent of New England's migrants whose origins are known, formed a patchwork of local variations. The Wiltshire chalklands were almost entirely devoted to sheep and grain production, and in this mixed farming world, manorial institutions remained powerful, society was peculiarly hierarchical, and there was a steady increase in the holdings of the major farmers. Somerset, the region's most densely populated county, was crowded with dairy farmers and clothiers in the east but elsewhere supported a range of industries based on mineral resources. Much of Dorset was pastureland, with small farms scattered across the landscape, but dairying flourished in its vales. Devon, bleak and desolate in fall and winter, was largely pastoral country, though grain and fruit were grown in the south, and cloth making was a major industry. Many of the isolated inland farmsteads had little communication with the outside world, but the coastal lowlands were closely tied to the metropolitan markets.[19]

Similarly varied was the northern area of recruitment, Yorkshire primarily, but also Lincolnshire, Lancashire, and Northumberland. Yorkshire's emigrants came from both the West and East Ridings, but the majority were from the East, which was a countryside "of nucleated villages, common fields, and stinted, shrinking commons" that produced grain of various kinds and raised mixed herds of cattle. Most of the vales in southeastern Yorkshire and northern Lincolnshire were held within tight manorial control; open fields were worked under regulations made by common consent and managed by manorial stewards; population size was steady; most individual holdings were small; society was more static and more highly stratified than it was in East Anglia; and change was slowly paced. In the upland vales of Yorkshire and Lincolnshire, there were contrasts in wealth between squires and large farmers on the one hand who knew how to reach metropolitan markets, and ordinary yeomen and husbandmen who did not. While the hills of the two adjacent counties "were a fertile field for the development of large-scale farming by the capitalist farmer," the forests and fens of both counties were centers of chronic poverty. There landless cottagers struggled to survive, and fenland peasants fought large-scale drainage schemes that threatened their use of the commons.[20]

SUCH WAS the complexity of England's diversified ecology from which New England's population was drawn. Not only did the familiar patterns of their daily lives differ from region to region and from place to place in the worlds they knew, but so too did their expectations in settling New England's distant, largely uncultivated land. The mere diversity of their geo-ecological backgrounds and the shifting forms of their associations would be sources of friction, but the likelihood of conflict among them was heightened by the stressful conditions that had precipitated their emigration.

3

The communities from which the emigrants came, varied and multifaceted as they were, were deeply rooted, even in modernizing areas like East Anglia. There, as elsewhere, long-established webs of kinship, economic function, and neighborhood association, however complex, were dense, and the structure of social authority, in its variant forms, was widely respected. Though relative to its own past and to most of contemporary Europe, England was a mobile society, social cohesion served to brake the more extreme centrifugal forces. In such a world it would take what have been called "seismic shocks" to disrupt the interpersonal networks sufficiently to propel people in large numbers out of the sockets of customary life and into dangerous overseas voyages and resettlement in a land they could only imagine—to undertake a radical adventure certain to disrupt the delicate patterns of multilevel relationships.[21] And there were sudden shocks, not least among them the economic recession that had hit much of greater East Anglia and parts of the West Country in the early 1620s and that continued for over a decade.

The severe downturn was the result of long-term population growth and increasing pressure on land use brought to a crisis by a collapse in the cloth trade, which devastated the prospects, indeed the livelihood, of much of the workforce in East Anglia and the West Country, and a series of poor harvests. The result had been plummeting wages, rising rents, widespread unemployment, increased vagrancy, and escalating food prices which led to near famine among the poor. Rural drifters joined with town workers to protest the shortages, high prices, and lack of employment, and to demand protection and increases in charitable relief.

Yet severe as these regional depressions were, and dangerous as was the increase in the "restless fringe" of drifters and the unemployed, there was no general breakdown of community organization, no broad-based, panicked uprising. "Simmering discontent" that broke out into occasional riots was familiar, especially in the more dynamic parts of the realm, which were closely tied to fluctuating European markets and dependent on erratic food supplies to provide for a growing population. And familiar too were the means of alleviating, or at least containing, popular distress until the economic cycle moved upward once again.[22] What was not familiar, however, what created the shocks that precipitated the large-scale emigration to New England, were the near apocalyptic decisions made by local leaders in the countryside, clerical and lay, who were not only disillusioned by diminished economic prospects but also fearful of what was clearly a rising wave of religious repression by a newly aggressive, radically conformist ecclesiastical hierarchy. For the areas most severely affected by the economic collapse were also the regions of the highest incidence of Puritanism.

BY 1629, when Charles I dissolved Parliament—after having struggled with it since his accession, having imprisoned its most forceful leaders, and having continued to tax without consent—the nation's public life was in turmoil and the danger of monarchical autocracy was palpable. The likelihood of a total convulsion in religious life was less predictable, but threatening signs were multiplying throughout the realm.

During her long reign, Elizabeth had maintained in the Church of England a careful, compromised balance between the extremist pressures of right and left—between the zeal of certain Catholics who dreamed of returning England to the Church of Rome, with all that that implied for the nation's foreign alliances, and the fervor of those who felt that the

English Church had barely begun its reformation and should be purified of its ritualistic formalism, institutional hierarchy, and emotional sterility. Both extremes had persisted, but while the threat from the Catholic right, implicitly unpatriotic, had diminished under savage repression, the pressures from the purifiers on the left increased and took doctrinal form. From a general impulse to carry England's reformation to its logical conclusion, which would ground the experience of religion more squarely and solely on personal faith and the authority of the Bible, "Puritanism" became a cluster of doctrines bearing on worship, ecclesiology, preaching, and the ultimate goals of spiritual life. The differences mattered, in England as they would in New England. There the fault lines in the English reform movement would become fissures that led to bitter conflicts.

For some in the "feathering-out of the reform movement into an increasing host of sects and factions," reform meant principally a change in ecclesiastical structure: the abolition of Episcopacy in favor of popularly elected preachers and elders organized from the bottom up into a hierarchy of synods and presbyteries culminating in a national assembly free of state control. Others concentrated on a transformation of preaching, seeking to go beyond routine instruction and exegesis to stir people's emotions, hoping by exuberant exhortations to wring their souls in the search for salvation and to encourage them to adopt a rigorous discipline of sanctified behavior and spiritual striving. Others isolated the phenomenon of baptism as the key reform issue, its essential role in distinguishing the visible from the invisible church of God's election. Still others demanded the isolation of those who experienced God's grace into congregations of their own, independent of the overall church yet part of the larger world. And there were some—such were the Pilgrims—for whom there could be no stopping in the escape from the institutionalized life of a formal, national church until one reached exclusive conventicles of saints, withdrawn from the larger world, devoted to their own righteous living and the attainment of their personal salvation. And beyond even such isolates, there were small groups whose fervor carried them into an absolute resolution where one could tolerate no organization whatever—where individuals became churches in themselves, unbound in their sanctity by any constraints of the profane world. These were condemned, even by—especially by—others within the Puritan movement, as Brownists, Familists, antinomians, later Fifth Monarchy Men and Quakers; they were considered to be not merely religious radicals but social anarchists, reeling out of control, beyond the farthest reaches of respectable reform.[23]

Amid all these stirrings and strivings of reform, these complex and intermingled dreamings, designs, and exaltations, the Elizabethan state and its ecclesiastical arm had played a cautious role. Drastic suppression had been reserved for those whose religion could be considered a threat to the state itself, hence traitorous; more than 250 Catholics were executed or died in prison under Elizabeth, and many more suffered torture. This savagery was well known and lingered as a threat to all challengers to the authority of the established church and state, left as well as right. But though the Puritan movement in its far extremities might be considered anarchic, it was not traitorous, and only the wildest extremists challenged the belief that there could be only one true religion. So under Elizabeth there had been no systematic effort to stamp the reform movement out.[24]

To be sure, there had been, from time to time, well-publicized sanctions imposed on the most egregious reform agitators, and these episodes burned like flares in the awareness of later Puritan leaders. But since most of the reformers only barked and did not bite, they were not driven to the wall, and their voices were increasingly heard in pamphlets and manifestos and in Parliamentary declamations.

So Richard Rogers, in Wethersfield, Essex, one of the most fervent, famous, and effective of the early Puritan preachers, whose kin would play major roles in New England's history, was forbidden to preach in 1583 but was restored to his pulpit by the intervention of highly placed Puritan patrons; they rescued him once again in 1589. But while prominent Puritans like Rogers could escape debilitating censure because of their influential patrons and the Crown's reluctance to stir up trouble over the struggle for people's souls, even they lived in fear of persecution. Humbler Puritans, devoid of influence, could be tossed into prison and otherwise seriously punished. At one point Rogers apprehensively visited the prisoners in Bridewell and returned troubled by the prospect that he too was "like to loose my liberty" and end up in such a fearful bedlam.[25]

For many, that likelihood rose sharply in Elizabeth's last years and under her immediate successor, and not merely because of the activities of autocratic prelates. A peculiar social force was at work that intensified the Puritans' conflict with church and state. The reform movement's leaders, its publicists and formulators, were for the most part academic and clerical intellectuals, and that clerisy in the early seventeenth century was growing in number and influence. For increasingly, gentry and mercantile wealth flowed into the universities, creating more and better opportunities for the higher education of poor, able youths; but their careers could no longer be fulfilled within England's national church or in the universities themselves. The best connected and luckiest, if not the ablest, of these professional intellectuals were appointed to established pulpits, but many, an increasing number, were not, and became journeymen preachers, chaplains, and above all "lecturers" ("the people's creatures," the Church called them) who were supported not by church funds but by temporary stipends or private endowments donated by lay patrons or congregations. The University of Cambridge was the major producer of this growing rootless intelligentsia, and its most vibrant and prolific centers were its Puritan colleges; Christ's was "the greatest Puritan seminary of them all" until in 1584 Emmanuel was founded. From Christ's, from Emmanuel, and from others—Sidney Sussex, Trinity, and Clare Hall—came a phalanx of well-educated, sophisticated, and ambitious young men who naturally, inescapably, were led "by the circumstances of their positions," William Haller has written, "as well as their convictions to become the critics and opponents of authority, of custom, of accepted ideas and vested interest."[26]

The pressure of their numbers and the notoriety of their preaching grew in the early years of James I's reign. And in the decade that followed, under Charles I, with the advent to supreme power in the Anglican Church of William Laud—an ecclesiastical disciplinarian possessed of demonic energy and burning with zeal to rid the land of its dissidents—the tense mingling of forces exploded in bitter confrontations, which would shape New England's history.

While still only Bishop of London, from 1628 to 1633, Laud became the dominant force in both of the most powerful coercive courts, the church's Court of High Commission and the Privy Council's criminal Court of Star Chamber. His influence swept across the land. In instructions to all twenty-five bishops of England, which he sent out in 1629 over the signature of the aged Archbishop of Canterbury, he ordered lecturers to substitute catechizing for afternoon sermons and to read, in hood and surplice, from the church's Prayer Book before sermonizing. Itineracy was restricted, and the law limiting to high dignitaries the right to appoint chaplains was to be enforced. Laud was especially insistent that clerics and their parishioners adhere to all of the church's rituals: wearing proper clerical vestments, bowing at appropriate moments, and returning the communion table to its traditional form as a railed altar before which one kneeled to receive the sacrament. And he began the process of eliminating the London trust (the Feoffees) that was buying up income-bearing properties (impropriations) to support Puritan preachers who were not otherwise provided for.[27]

Much of this could not be enforced, but though the cleansing Laud sought could not be fully achieved, even after his elevation to the Archbishopric of Canterbury in 1633, and he had to accept from many dissenting lecturers only the vaguest pledges of conformity, he was unrelenting in his efforts. For all its incompleteness, his campaign had a transforming effect on the Puritans. It created fear and a sense of desperation, forged a mutually supportive community of previously scattered dissidents, steeled their resistance, propelled many from a "loose conformity" to outright nonconformity, and precipitated a willingness on the part of certain of the Puritan leaders to contemplate flight.[28]

What stirred the Puritan community most deeply was Laud's sweeping "visitations" of suspect dioceses to flush out even the mildest signs of nonconformity before they could fester and spread contamination, and his selective targeting of certain of the most influential and popular Puritan leaders. Laud's inquisitors scoured the religious landscape with such intensity, especially in the Puritan regions of greater East Anglia and the West Country, that one of his chaplains could happily report that the nonconformists "shrink away at the very name of Visitation."[29]

The visitation of the heavily nonconformist diocese of Norwich under Bishop Matthew Wren was especially severe: the House of Commons later concluded that as a result of his and his successor's work "both ministers and tradesmen were driven to fly to Holland and New England." God's true church, one of the bishop's victims wrote, is now "under hatches, the walls of Jerusalem beaten down; poor Suffolk and Norfolk lying desolate by that cursed, wretched Wren." Fear grew as preacher after preacher and lecturer after lecturer was suspended from his clerical role for failing to preach orthodox doctrine and to observe the prescribed rituals of the church.[30]

But such general visitations, though they raised fears and created upheavals throughout the Puritan world, could not reach what Laud considered the most alarming sources of the Puritan malignancy. That lay in the work of a few powerful preachers, whom he and his aides were determined to silence. It was not so much isolated troublemakers who stirred Laud's reprisals—pastors like Charles Chauncy of Marston St. Lawrence, Northamptonshire, and Ware, Hertfordshire, who was accused of committing doctrinal omissions and denouncing kneeling for communion at railed altars. Such a solitary scholar could be dealt with, especially since he seemed irresolute in his opposition. What troubled Laud most profoundly was the growing influence of a single large but tightly bound network of eloquent, well-connected, and increasingly popular "inconformists" deeply rooted in affluent parishes in the very heart of metropolitan England. At the center of this dangerous web of subversion was the interrelated clerical dynasty of the Rogers and Ward families, whose destinies, like Chauncy's, would be fulfilled in New England.[31]

4

The patriarch of the deeply Puritan Rogers family, Richard, had survived his conflicts with authorities in the 1580s to publish in 1603 his *Seven Treatises*, one of the Puritans' most popular works on the conduct of everyday life "leading and guiding to true happiness." He died in 1618, but his progeny seemed to be everywhere, and to Laud they were everywhere incendiary. One of Richard's sons, Daniel, followed him in the Wethersfield, Essex, pulpit, where he matched him in eloquence if not charisma, and another, Ezekiel, who would be known for his "passionate distemper," settled in Yorkshire where his influence radiated far beyond his East Riding parish of Rowley. But the most powerful of the second-generation Rogerses was Richard's nephew John, of Dedham, Essex. Revered by his followers as "the prince of all the preachers in England," he was a "plain" preacher but enormously and theatrically eloquent. Clutching the canopy of the pulpit with both hands "and roaring hideously to represent the torments of the damned," he reduced many of his auditors to tears. Mobs flocked to his blistering sermons, catching sparks from his legendary fire. His brother Nathaniel commanded large if not tumultuous audiences in nearby Bocking, and his stepbrothers, the Wards—the Reverends Samuel, John, and Nathaniel Ward—were at least as influential in their own constituencies; Samuel, of Ipswich, was particularly singled out by Laud's agents as a veritable "breeder" of discontent, his preaching one of the causes of all "this giddiness."[32]

But the Rogers-Ward network, which was such a threat to Laudian conformity, was not limited by consanguinity. One of the most gifted Puritan preachers, intellectuals, and counselors—and one of Laud's prime targets—was Thomas Hooker, no blood relation of the Rogers-Ward cousinage but closely involved in their lives, in England as, later, in New England. After many vicissitudes, Hooker had settled near John Rogers for the express purpose of studying with him and sharing in his fierce Puritan commitment. There, in Chelmsford, Essex, in close collaboration with Rogers, he developed into a renowned healer of souls. Received by many as "a teacher sent from God," he was a major force in the region's monthly meetings of Puritan preachers, and his eloquence overwhelmed the people who heard his stern sermons. A close member of the Rogerses' extended clan, he soon formed his own secondary circle of "bold and fiery spirits." Among them were Thomas Shepard, Hugh Peter, Thomas Weld, and Nathaniel Ward, all of whom would carry their distinctive doctrines to New England, where their mentor would elaborate and apply his own views, to the discontent of many.[33]

Laud, increasingly concerned for the growing influence of the Rogers circle, soon learned that Hooker's genius was penetrating the region's pulpits and stirring up people far and wide. Hooker had become, he was told, a veritable oracle and the "principal library" of young preachers. One by one the others in the East Anglian Puritan cousinage were identified, and after Parliament was dissolved in 1629 the crackdown, the most severe since the reign of the Catholic Queen Mary, began in earnest.

Secret lists were drawn up of leading nonconformists: an Essex list of nine, in 1630, included John Rogers, Samuel Rogers, Nathaniel Ward, and Thomas Shepard. Within months John Rogers and both of his sons, Daniel and Nathaniel, were suspended from their offices, as were in time Samuel Ward and his brother Nathaniel. The latter, having been singled out as an "absolute inconformitarian," was subjected to court proceedings that lasted for two years. The accusations against him were summarized in forty-three articles, which included charges that he had denounced ritualistic prayers as something "a parrot might be taught" and that one could get "a jack-an-apes or a baboon" to bow as prescribed. Adamant, defiant, he was suspended from his lectureship and ordered to recant and to pay all the court expenses.

The Rogerses and the Wards were major "breeders" of nonconformity, but Hooker was clearly preeminent. Despite warnings that suppressing him would enrage the local population and create "great heart-burnings," Laud deprived him of his Chelmsford lectureship. But Hooker's voice was not so easily stilled. He quickly established a grammar school, employing as his assistant the young John Eliot, whom he led to conversion, and he continued counseling the local ministers, preaching informally in laymen's houses, and in the process drawing off whole congregations from the authorized churches. In 1630 he was summoned to the Court of High Commission. Forty-nine Essex clergymen protested on his behalf, testifying to his basic conformity and that he was "no ways turbulent or factious." But counterpetitions by conforming churchmen citing his "licentious irregularities" carried more weight. His prospects were hopeless, and he fled to Holland, to join Hugh Peter, leaving his family under the protection of the Puritan Earl of Warwick.[34]

By then all of Hooker's protégés were under attack. Thomas Weld was excommunicated and then summoned for admonition before the High Commission. In Yorkshire, where various Puritan "exercises" and conferences were shut down, Ezekiel Rogers was excommunicated for holding "secrete assemblies or conventicles," expounding "dangerous and schismatic" views, and refusing to read to his people the official Book of Sports, which permitted what the Puritans believed to be the profanation of the Sabbath and which prevented them from restricting their servants' engagement in undue "sports and pastimes." In London, John Davenport, vicar of the vast parish of St. Stephens, found himself subject to sixteen charges of impropriety brought to Laud by Davenport's own curate, and though he answered the accusations fully, and though he had the patronage of the powerful Vere family as well as Secretary of State Conway, he knew he could not long continue in his Puritan ministry in the heart of the nation's metropolis. He was quite willing, he wrote Lady Vere, "to lye and dye in prison, if the cause may be advantaged by it," but it was clearly more useful "to preserve the liberty of my person and ministry for the service of the church elsewhere if all dores are shutt against mee here." So, forced by Laud from a rather loose nonconformity to a highly specified, rigid dissent, he disguised himself "in a grey suit and an overgrown beard" and fled to the Netherlands.

Far to the west, in Dorchester, Dorset—an area "deeply imbued," the historian Clarendon would write, "with the rigid piety of the Puritans"—the Rev. John White was charged by the High Commission with opposing orthodox theology and formal rituals as well as main-

taining "secret and sly practices" against church and state; he escaped
prosecution only by the wiles of his most respectable parishioners. But
the young Thomas Shepard, "a poore, weake, pale complectioned man"
who had not yet decided whether or not he was "a nonconformable man,"
was forced to present himself to Laud personally, to face the Episcopal
wrath alone. That dramatic confrontation, on the eve of the Winthrop
fleet's departure, perhaps embellished in the telling, cleared up Shepard's
uncertainty and became a warning to others to seek refuge in any way
possible.[35]

The bishop, Shepard reported, seemed at the start of the encounter to
be in "a fit of rage" and immediately warned Shepard "to deal plainly with
him, adding withal that he had been more cheated and equivocated with
by some of my malignant faction than ever was man by Jesuit." Laud's
anger seemed to grow with every effort Shepard made to defend himself: "he looked as though blood would have gushed from his face and
did shake as if he had been haunted with an ague fit . . . by reason of
his extreme malice and secret venom." His "railing" became bitter: "You
prating coxcomb! Do you think all the learning is in your brain?" And his
verdict on the twenty-five-year-old cleric was sweeping:

> I charge you that you neither preach, read, marry, bury, or exercise any
> ministerial function in any part of my diocese, for if you do, and I hear
> of it, I will be upon your back and follow you wherever you go, in any
> part of the kingdom, and so everlastingly disenable you. . . .You have
> made a company of seditious, factious Bedlams. . . . I will have no such
> fellows prate in my diocese. Get you gone, and now make your com-
> plaints to whom you will!

With that malediction upon his head, Shepard fled, and, hoping for a refuge "so remote and strange" as to be out of Laud's reach, ended in Yorkshire, and there he began "to listen to a call to New England." Should he
leave all behind and join in that radical venture? He struggled with the
question and in the end found five good reasons why remaining in Yorkshire and exercising his talent privately, secretly, was dubious and eight
stronger reasons why he should commit himself to the refuge in the wilderness. First, he wrote in his autobiography, he "saw no call to any other
place in old England, nor way of subsistence in peace and comfort to me
and my family." Second, many of his friends were already there or en

route; further, God seemed to him to have left England with the departures of such luminaries as Hooker; in addition, participating in any way
in a church of empty ceremonies was surely not lawful; and beyond that,
only in New England, it seemed, could he fulfill "all God's ordinances."
His wife, he noted, favored the move, and surely Christ had deliberately
provided this escape. Though he admitted that his "ends were mixed"
and that the search for physical security and personal comfort mingled
with loftier motives, God had revealed to him "the glory of these liberties
in New England" and that for him to join in that holy enterprise, weak as
he was, would be to "come out from the dead, to his praise."[36]

Other clergymen, many others, pondered the question, organized
their thoughts in similar syllogisms, but came to different conclusions.
Some, like Samuel Rogers, agonized for months, probing the issues again
and again, and finally decided against the move—largely in deference to
the wishes of his father, Daniel, a man of "a most woeful temper," who
had opposed Winthrop's leaving because he was dissatisfied with the
governor's closely wrought reasoning. Still others, who had turned first
to the Netherlands as a more accessible asylum, had discovered that the
English churches there were no less conflicted than England's and were
well within the reach of Laud's influence. How many churchmen in all
actually emigrated to New England in the decade of the 1630s cannot
be precisely known—98, according to one estimate, 103 or 113 according to another, 129 according to still another. Many of them—at least
43—returned to England after 1640, when the Puritan revolution top-
pled Laud and his entire ecclesiastical regime; but the clergy's presence
nevertheless dominated the exile community in New England, and not
only because of numbers.[37]

The clerics who did emigrate had been steeled by adversity—stripped
of their offices, silenced, harassed, and threatened by the highest powers of church and state. These were not gentle souls. The timid, the
unsure, and the malleable found means of accommodation, adopting
loose forms of outward conformity while practicing their beliefs in private: they remained at home. Those who left were tougher, more defiant,
more self-assured, more self-absorbed. They had been tempered by their
refusal to buckle under to what Ezekiel Rogers, in his bristling Last Will
and Testament of 1661, would recall as "the hottest persicution of that
bloody hierarchy." Their nonconformity, like Nathaniel Ward's, had
been "absolute," and so they were not easy men, unlikely, in any circum-

stances, to compromise for peace. They had risked too much, had known too much of "persecution, frustration, defiance, and fear."[38]

For Richard Mather, suspended from his pulpit in Toxteth Park, near Liverpool, the fear of persecution had a vivid, dramatic meaning. As he considered the future of life under the present repressive church-state regime, he turned to John Foxe's martyrology, *Actes and Monuments of . . . the great persecutions . . . practised by the Romishe Prelates. . . .* With the third volume open before him, he read of the fearful torments that had been inflicted on Bishop Nicholas Ridley and the Rev. John Bradford in 1555. Then he came on the advice those martyrs had given others as they prepared themselves to be burned at the stake for heresy. For Mather, contemplating the world in 1635, nothing could have been more relevant. Those who fear they might not be able to stand firm before the ultimate violence, John Bradford had written—those who might dishonor God when *in extremis*—should "fly . . . if you feel such infirmity in yourselves." Bradford, who had been, as Mather then was, a Lancashire preacher, had phrased the issue especially well, and Mather, in his elaborate "Arguments" justifying his removal from "a corrupt church to a purer," partly quoted and partly paraphrased the exact words he found on pages 518 and 319 of Foxe's third volume. "In respect of your infirmity," Bradford, facing death at the stake, had written to friends whose ultimate courage he doubted, "God will never tempt you above your ability; fly and get you hence . . . your home here is no home, but that ye look for another." Had not God told Joseph that he should fly rather than stay and in his weakness disgrace His name? "Go," Bradford had instructed his "infirm" friends, "go where you may with free and safe conscience serve the Lord." Mather went.[39]

But he had not needed Foxe's *Actes* to justify his fears. The terrible sufferings of those who had died for their faith under Queen Mary were living, personal memories in Lancashire; and so they were elsewhere—in Hingham, Norfolk, for example, where the Rev. Robert Peck's grandfather had been driven underground in Mary's reign and had been forced to flee for his life and to preach "in woods and forrest places." Was it so different now? True, Mather, Peck, and the other suppressed Puritan activists had not themselves been physically tormented or savagely martyred, as their predecessors had been, but might that not be their eventual fate? They had been forced to consult and collaborate secretly and to protect themselves against spies; some had gone into hiding and were moving about in disguise. Having faced intimidation, they were unbending and defiant in spirit. Seasoned controversialists, articulate and well informed on doctrinal points, and capable of mobilizing arguments quickly to defend their positions, they were braced for further contention. Not all were as severe, as commanding and imposing, as the "choleric," "condescending" Hooker who, Cotton Mather later wrote, was "able to do more with a word, or a look, than most other men could have done by a severer discipline." But they all left England embattled—uncompromised in spirit, fortified by adversity.[40]

5

Tranquillity would forever elude them. For the Puritanism that defined them collectively was a cluster of latently divergent views and commitments. As they boarded the vessels for New England these differences were suppressed in their common defense of church reform and their mutual struggle to survive. At the point of their departure, differences were as yet "nuances of temperament and thought within the framework of a more cohesive Puritanism."[41] But the fissures that would become conflicts when the pressure was relieved could, even then, be seen. And none of these differences would be more important, more central to the lives of the migrants and the entire New England community, than those that divided Hooker from his shipmate aboard the *Griffin* in June 1633, John Cotton. Their experiences in England before they left—Hooker at age forty-seven, Cotton at age forty-nine—and the development of their thought from the time they left the University of Cambridge to the time they made their decision to emigrate, explains much of the tumultuous history of the colony's early years.

COTTON, for twenty-one years vicar of the largest parish church in England, the notoriously Puritan St. Botolph's in Boston, Lincolnshire, was the intellectually gifted son of an obscure Derbyshire lawyer.[42] He had a brilliant academic career in Cambridge, and as a fellow of Emmanuel College, amid clerics of learning and disputational skills, he became famous for his mastery of languages, elegant preaching, and piety. There he came to embrace the fundamental tenets of Puritanism, and there too, in association with Richard Sibbes, master of St. Catharine's College, and John Preston, master of Emmanuel and a great intriguer in public affairs, and together too with other like-minded scholars, clerics, and patrons, he turned to the spiritist side of Puritanism, the more pietist emphasis within the broad ambit of the reform movement.

Having himself experienced to his great satisfaction a profoundly moving, exalting conversion to God's grace, Cotton became convinced that only such shattering, radically transforming, direct, and unmediated infusions of divinity ultimately mattered. He could express the overwhelming experience that ruled his life best in metaphors. Conversion, he wrote, was "a melting of stone, a warming of ice, a quickening of paralyzed will"; it was not a mere *wading* in grace, but such a *drenching* that one would never thereafter be dry. With respect to such a profound experience— a marriage with Christ heavy with erotic implications[43]—all external trappings, rational calculations, willful strivings for redemption, and clerical ministrations were worthless. So like the others who have been called the Spiritist Brethren within the Puritan movement, he could tolerate some of the church's demands as simply irrelevant—"indifferent things"—and he could in good conscience avoid confrontation with the church by evasions while nourishing his and his parishioners' deepest spiritual ambitions. Seeking to reach into his parishioners' souls, he abandoned the academic elegance of preaching and learned to speak simply, plainly, but with powerful effect as he exhorted his listeners to receive the infusion of the Lord's transforming power.

In St. Botolph's, to whose vicarage he had been preferred in 1612, he practiced what he preached—not blatantly, not defiantly, but softly, subtly, diplomatically, and persistently, clinging to the belief that the Church of England, for all the corruptions of its rituals and its stultifying hierarchies, was still the true church. Rather than restricting participation in the parish church to those who gave convincing evidence of a saving grace, he gathered those palpable converts together into an informal, semisecret inner group, a congregation of the truly converted within the broader eclectic congregation, and to this cluster of visible saints he ministered separately and quietly. This small, exclusive church within the church flourished, without excluding from ordinary worship the majority, who were unredeemed, and without alienating the local conformists or unduly antagonizing the Episcopal powers.

Thoughtful, mild in manner, never confrontational, professing conformity to just the minimal degree needed to avoid collision with the church authorities, Cotton turned his parish toward the spiritist tendency within Puritanism. At this stage he had no need to probe the deep, tangled implications of his instinctive spiritism. As the years passed, he grew ever more certain that the heart and soul of true Christianity lay in the inward, personal experience of saving grace, in the direct visitation of God's mercy, which owes nothing to human effort or to contractual relations with divinity, or even to the sanctity of one's daily life.

In part his long survival within England's ecclesiastical establishment, which was growing ever more rigid in its demands for conformity to institutional rituals, was the result of the protection he received from sympathizers among the nobility—not only the Earl of Lincoln, whose estate was becoming a refuge for harassed and deposed Puritan clergymen, but also Viscount Dorchester, a principal secretary of state and supporter of the Massachusetts Bay Company, the Earl of Dorset, the Earl of Lindsey, admiral of the fleet and privy councilor, and others among the powers in the land—the Pembrokes and the Veres; Warwick; Say and Sele; and even at one point the king's favorite, the Duke of Buckingham.[44] Insulated in part from the more rigorous demands of the church, Cotton extended his reach farther and farther into the world, accepting for his tutelage a flow of Cambridge students sent to him by Emmanuel College's master as well as groups of young Germans who sought his instruction. And to the world at large he preached with extraordinary diligence: both mornings and afternoons on Thursdays and Saturdays, and also mornings on Wednesdays.

His fame spread through Puritan circles, in Lincolnshire and beyond. For one contemporary he was "one of England's glories," for another he was a man "of admirable candor, of unparalleled meekness, of rare wisdom, very loving even to those that differed in judgment from him." His radiating influence shed light for many perplexed people on what the ultimate experience of justification might be, how far to discount the rituals of the church, and in the end what to think about the ultimate survival of true religion in England and what to do if all hope faded.

The possibility of flight was in the minds of many of his personal followers. Some had left for New England in the first wave; many were actively planning their emigration; and Cotton himself, though so far sheltered, grew close to the Massachusetts settlement in his correspondence with Samuel Skelton, the Earl of Lincoln's former chaplain who in 1629 had settled with the advance party in Salem, Massachusetts. As Cotton's fame spread, so too did his vulnerability, and when after 1633 the pressure from church authorities mounted, Cotton's protectors' influence waned, and he was summoned to the ecclesiastical Court of High Commission.

Since from that inquisitorial body he could expect nothing but "scorns and prison," he fled to London, and there, in hiding, he considered various alternatives. He might live with the church's demands as merely "indifferent things" and continue the struggle for reform, though at the risk of imprisonment. He could escape to the familiar refuge of Holland, where he might secretly influence events in England and be poised to return quickly when and if a great reformation occurred. Or he could join the migration west across the ocean, serve the saving remnant that had settled there, and share in the life of the apostolic churches he believed the colonists were creating. In June, urged on by his former parishioners already committed to emigration—substantial people like the Boston alderman Thomas Leverett, who had protected him in the past, and the town's former mayor Atherton Hough—and disillusioned with prospects in Holland, Cotton joined two hundred other emigrants on the *Griffin* and left for Massachusetts.[45]

It could not have occurred to him, as he sailed to America, that in that distant land, free from the constraints of an oppressive church, the implications of his belief in an unmediated saving grace, as yet but an emphasis within the complex, still inchoate body of Puritan piety, would evolve, would become engrossing and rancorous, and would generate destructive animosities. Nor could he have anticipated that in these altered circumstances he would find it necessary to limit the quasi-pietistic tendency of his thought, and that in the end he himself, who had pressed so persistently against the establishment in England, would become a constraining force against other enthusiasts of "graceful" inner experience, whose ideas in their origins were similar to his own. And he certainly could not have imagined that on fundamental issues one of his strongest opponents, directly or indirectly, would be his respected shipmate, Hooker, with whom, four years earlier, he had discussed plans for the Puritan colony; with whose deeply pondered reasons for abandoning England he concurred; and with whom he had secretly consulted before departing for New England.[46]

HOOKER, so brilliantly successful in Chelmsford and so fiercely condemned by Laud, had also been shaped by his experiences in Cambridge, where he had remained for fourteen years, deeply immersed in the liberal arts and religious studies in that hotbed of Puritan spirituality.[47] And it was there, in his late twenties, that he had undergone the deepest experience of his life, which set him on a path that would fundamentally diverge from Cotton's. His conversion followed an extended spiritual crisis in which he lamented his miseries before God, suffered terrors ("O Lord, I am distracted"), and yearned for that "restructuring of experience, willed by a human will that could not will." Despite all his efforts his redemption was very long in coming. Again and again he meditated in anguish, confessed his sins, begged for Christ's mercy, and accepted damnation for the glory of God. When finally, after an agonizing trial of his soul, he felt the vast transformation he had sought, he was assured of his clerical vocation and the basic tendency of his ministry.

His search for personal redemption and its ultimate resolution had been "so intense, so difficult that he was never able to shake the memory of it, and the work of his pastoral career is marked by a tender consideration for the spirits of men and women undergoing like experiences." And this bent of his thought, this pastoral orientation of his clerical role, was strongly reinforced by the strange circumstances of his first ministerial appointment.[48]

In the years when Cotton was enjoying his great popularity at St. Botolph's and in effect sensitizing a broad constituency to the possibility of emigration, Hooker, upon leaving Cambridge, found employment only as rector of an obscure parish in Esher, Surrey, and as the personal counselor to the patron's agonized wife who was distracted near to the point of insanity by fears of damnation and her incapacity to find salvation. For years Joanna Drake and her husband had sought the help of preachers, but none had been able to help her resolve her torments. Hooker, who lived in the Drake household for seven years while attending to the parish in general and Mrs. Drake in particular, applied the lessons of his own travail to Mrs. Drake's affliction and in the process developed a model of the preparation for grace within the boundaries of predestinarian Calvinism.[49] There were techniques involved (a "new answering method" framed by Ramist logic), specific steps to be taken to eliminate hindrances, and distinct stages to be reached before any help could be expected. It was not a matter of what one *could* do to reach a state of possible acceptance of grace, but what one *must* do, despite the fact that no human action could in the end be efficacious. And for success in this seemingly impossible effort, instruction was necessary, the minister's work as guide was crucial, and the institutions of the church formed the context of correct procedure. By the time Mrs. Drake was "cured" and Hooker had accepted a lectureship in Chelmsford, he had become an expert in leading troubled souls to redemptive peace through an elaborate process of preparation, a guide through the labyrinth that led to a saving grace. In his four years in Chelmsford, before Laud deprived him of his lectureship, it was the doctrine of preparation that he mainly preached, and he made common cause with many who would share his views in New England's later struggles. But committed as he was to the externals of worship and hence uncompromising in his demand for the reform of the church, he could sustain his success neither there in Chelmsford's St. Mary's parish nor in the refuge he sought in the Netherlands.[50]

The English churches there, he found, were convulsed with the question of church organization in general and congregational autonomy in particular, and he was immediately caught up in the struggle. Hugh Peter, "rash and hasty," who had arrived in Holland four years earlier, could do little to secure a ministerial post for Hooker, especially when, upon inquiry, Hooker denied the authority of the ruling *classis* and justified the cause of what was in effect full congregational autonomy. Refused appointment in Amsterdam, Hooker moved to Delft and again became embroiled in a bitter dispute. Having failed twice in Holland to find the peace and stability he sought in order to continue his ministry, he was more convinced than ever of the truth of "unconformity," even if it required the Puritans to fly "unto the Indians for safety, to say nothing of their losse of life itselfe, by cruell imprisonments." Returning secretly to England, he retrieved his family and, evading the agents sent to find him, joined Cotton in boarding the *Griffin* bound for New England.[51]

COTTON AND HOOKER WERE major figures in the Puritan migration, famous in England long before they emigrated: inspired leaders, spiritual guides, formulators of basic doctrine, and ultimately adversaries. For them, as for others of the extraordinary phalanx of clerics who joined and helped lead the exodus from England, the decision to migrate was impelled by the deepest sources of their religious commitment. Given their insistence on reform, for them to remain within the immediate embrace of the "corrupted" church would be to call into question their integrity, their sincerity, ultimately the effectiveness of their ministry.

But to leave England, especially under duress, was, as David Hall has written, to reject all worldly expectations and "to strike a prophetic stance." To lead thousands of laymen across the ocean was surely "proof of the 'regard' for their ministry." And thousands did follow, especially as New England came to be seen more clearly as the primary site of religious renewal.[52]

In leading their flocks abroad, the major figures—Cotton and Hooker most prominently—were never isolates within the ministry. Each brought with them, or rejoined, affiliates who shared their views. Closest to Cotton in religious doctrine was Davenport, thirteen years his junior, whom Cotton had guided to conversion. A kindred spirit too was John Wheelwright, who had fallen under Cotton's sway in Lincolnshire, where Wheelwright had preached in Bilsby, a parish near Alford. To Hooker's early clerical affiliates in Essex who would join in the migration—Weld, Ward, Peter, Eliot, and above all Shepard, more rationalist in doctrine than Cotton, more concerned with ministerial agency and church organization, and more devoted to the articulated preparatory staging of redemption—was later added John Wilson, a contemporary of both Cotton and Hooker at Emmanuel College and a former student at the Inns of Court. Like so many others, Wilson, who had close family ties to the church's hierarchy and to London's politicians, had found his way to Puritanism and to Hooker's allegiance through the influence of Richard Rogers, whose instruction he had sought and whose neighbor he had become when he settled in Sudbury, Suffolk.[53]

But the divergences of thought within militant Puritanism that would find clashing expression in New England were not confined to the differences between Cotton's radical spirituality and Hooker's temperate preparationism, the one veering toward the extreme of antinomian disregard for external, ecclesiastical constraints, the other tending toward institutional demands that would enhance the role of the clergy and restrict access to full church membership. Neither position was "orthodox" Puritanism. There was no Puritan orthodoxy as the migration began—only a broad field of force, within which there were many uncoordinated impulses.

If such respected and famous figures as Cotton and Hooker did not represent orthodoxy in Puritanism, still less did others of less renown or public acceptance whose instincts would lead in various directions: congregational-separatists like Samuel Skelton; quasi-Presbyterians like

James Noyes and Robert Peck; proto-Anabaptists like Hanserd Knollys; radical spiritists like Samuel Gorton; and brilliant millennialist seekers like Roger Williams.

Williams was entirely unique. The perfectionism and driving logic of his radical Puritanism, which would lead him in the end away from all settled groups to isolation in a church of his own, might have been foreseen in his brief career in England. Fresh from the university in his early twenties, he had become the spiritual guide to Cromwell's aunt, the melancholic Lady Joan Barrington. But his remorseless attack on what he believed was her unsatisfactory spiritual condition, his insistence that all her travails (her illnesses, her husband's death, her children's afflictions) were God's "thunderclaps" and "quarrel" against her, and his constant dwelling on her "gray hairs," her impending last days "like the close of some sweet harmony," her candle "twinckling and glass near run" (in fact she lived another twelve years), so enraged the grieving widow that she banished Williams from her sight and in addition sharply rebuked him for his presumption in seeking a relationship with her niece. It was the same "unlambelike" stiffness, relentless pursuit of absolute resolutions, and self-assertive disregard for conventional norms that led Williams to join the migration to New England and thereafter to challenge the boundaries of the colony's fragile civility.[54]

6

The religious leadership was thus as diverse, as potentially conflicted, as the ordinary settlers, drawn as they were from different regional backgrounds and habituated to different forms of customary life. No less diverse in their views than the clergy and at least as prone to discord was the secular leadership. Of that remarkable group much is known—of their intelligence, their ambition, their boldness, their imagination and ingenuity in facing unforeseen problems, and also their tenacity and obstinacy, fortified by religious conviction, their abrasiveness in human relations, and what seems to have been an elemental propensity for contention.

A few were pivotal figures, uniquely influential or peculiarly representative. First among them was John Winthrop, a man of exceptional ability: adept as a land manager, lawyer, lay theologian, and politician, whose personal agency became critical in precipitating the Great Migration. His personal concerns, his tormented state of mind, exemplify and vivify—convey in dilated form—the deep perplexities and worries of much of the Puritan gentry, and the "seismic" dimensions of the decision that many of them made amid agonizing doubts.[55]

He was the son and grandson of prosperous Suffolk gentlemen active in the Puritan reform movement since the early years of Elizabeth's reign. His father was a barrister and manor lord with close connections to the Puritan leaders in Cambridge University, and Winthrop grew up in the "godly commonwealth" of East Anglia's Stour Valley, a center of aggressive Puritanism. After studies at Trinity College, Cambridge, and Gray's Inn, London, he returned to his native village of Groton.

JOHN WINTHROP, SR.

The dominant, successful leader in the establishment of
Puritan society in New England, he sought compromises
within a narrow range of toleration.

There he became the soul of managerial worldliness. He managed his family's properties, served as a justice of the peace, and in addition took on the office of attorney in the royal Court of Wards in London. At home in Suffolk, as he immersed himself in estate management, local administration, and the spiritual life of the intense Puritan community, he observed the disordered state of ordinary lives. When in London he saw about him the corruptions of the cumbersome legal system and the fierce turmoils of the metropolitan city. By the late 1620s, a man just over forty with seven children, he had failed to exceed, at times to maintain, the role he had inherited and had begun to despair of his prospects for a reasonably successful and secure life. He was in debt, he was worried about his children, he was tied up in a lawsuit, he had given up his lucrative office in the Court of Wards, and in the background of these personal problems, he was increasingly aware of the growing autocracy of the English Crown. Anticipating a divine "affliction upon this land and that speedily," he believed that God would provide "a shelter and hiding place for us and ours." Perhaps that refuge could best be found overseas, in New England. But such a deracination would be a momentous event and could be undertaken only after the deepest consideration and with convincing justification.

In his "General Observations for the Plantation of New England," which circulated in several manuscript drafts, and in his private letters, Winthrop not only laid out the conditions that led him to consider uprooting himself, his family, and his "company," but also probed his own motivations, sought divine approval, and answered his critics point by point.[56] England, he believed, was a world out of joint, corrupted, sinful, and in need of redemption. "The land groaneth under her inhabitants," he wrote, "so that man, the best of creatures, is held more base than the earth they tread on." Though the earth was the Lord's garden, given to mankind for its improvement, people struggled to live on the cultivation of an acre or two when vastly more was freely available elsewhere. The "intemperancy" of the time—the extravagance, the feckless prodigality, the passion for cheap satisfactions—all that had grown to the point that "no man's estate will suffice him to keep sail with his equal," and if one fails to keep up with the high-flying excesses, one "must live in contempt." So avarice is rampant and trades are carried on so deceitfully and unrighteously that "a good upright man [cannot] maintain his charge and . . . live comfortably in his profession." Even the "fountains of learning"—the schools and universities—ruinously expensive, were so corrupted by the evil examples and "licentious government" within them that "the best wits and fairest hopes" of the youth were "perverted, corrupted, and utterly overthrown." Above all, the true religion lay under heavy threat. The Jesuits' "kingdom of antichrist" had brought all the European churches but England's to desolation, and it could not but be that the like judgment would soon descend on England. To sit at home waiting for that to happen would result in just the ruin that had overtaken the true churches on the continent. That "woeful spectacle" should teach one to avoid the plague before it struck, before one was overcome by force and led into the temptation to backslide and abjure the truth.

Not all, even of Winthrop's intimates, agreed. Specific, practical doubts were raised as Winthrop approached a decision. Would not the departure of the godly make an evil judgment on England more likely? Why hurry, when one could wait and see what happened? Was not England still a plentiful land? Suppose one died along the way, or died there quickly, of hunger or the sword: could one imagine "how uncomfortable would it be to see our wives, children, and friends come to such a misery by our occasion"? What warrant was there for seizing others' land—land that "had been so long time possessed by other sons of Adam"? Why not send just the young and expendable people rather than "our best number and magistrates"? And was not the record of recent plantations overseas dismal? Had they not uniformly failed of their purpose?

These were reasonable questions, raised not only by his friends but by Winthrop himself. They were answerable, and Winthrop replied to them systematically; but they did not go to the essential point. Behind all of Winthrop's arguments and reasoning that led to his great decision lay something larger, something grander, than these specific problems. His thinking was illuminated by a desire to construct freshly, on distant shores, a society reformed not merely in religion but also in human relations, relieved not only of ecclesiastical tyranny but also of the hurt and grief of everyday conflicts. He yearned for wholeness, for a peaceful, unconflicted life in godly communities whose people were bound together in mutual support and obligation, and where the abrasions of competition and clashing desires would be softened and one could hope for generosity of spirit and goodwill from one's neighbors.

It was this elemental hope and vision that he developed most fully in the lay sermon he delivered on the deck of the *Arbella* just before her departure for New England. His "Model of Christian Charity," little remarked on at the time but destined for fame in later generations as a core statement of Puritan aspirations, cast his personal longings and his personal despair in familiar Christian terms. He longed for a community of decency, he said, of generosity, charity, and kindness—a community where the God-given order of society would be maintained in stable equilibrium, where "the rich and mighty should not eat up the poor nor the poor and despised rise up against their superiors," where one loved one's neighbors as oneself, where one helped another in want or distress, where "the care of the public must oversway all private respects," where we and our posterity might be "the better preserved from the common corruptions of this evil world"—all of this "to serve the Lord and work out our salvation under the power and purity of his holy ordinances."

It was this longing for a softer, more benign existence that would lead him as magistrate away from the hard edge of Puritanism, its restrictive precisionism, toward its softer humanity and generosity of spirit. So again and again, in years to come, he would be accused by his opponents of excessive leniency when severity was needed, of being indulgent when excessive "enthusiasm" threatened the colony's coherence. For while he was always zealous, his latest biographer has written, "he was not a zealot," and he instinctively reached for moderation in the fierce religio-ideological struggles that would ensue. Aware of his own sinfulness, he sought to treat his opponents with charity, confident that in the end God would ensure the wholeness of life that he sought.[57]

It was in the end this vision—of a more harmonious, more organic, more godly community—and not merely the mounting practical problems and fears he faced that led Winthrop to the wrenching decision to leave the land of his birth. By 1629, when he joined with others similarly disposed to reorganize the Massachusetts Bay Company and arrange for its transfer to New England, where it would serve as a government overseas, his general desires and frustrations had fused into an irrevocable determination to begin the world anew. As the company's governor, he threw himself into the myriad practical tasks of extricating himself and his family from their deep local roots, recruiting a population of settlers who would form not simply a labor force but a fully constituted society, hiring and supplying the fleet of vessels needed to transport hundreds, perhaps thousands, of people overseas, and keeping the entire venture clear of the authorities of church and state.

As his determination steeled and he took on the managerial burdens of the evolving project, the strength and complexity of his personality became a force in itself. In outward manner he was cool, austere,
constrained, unbending, proud, and remorselessly purposeful, but his
interior self was passionate, fervent, and sensuous. Though unbending
in his belief that it was proper for women's roles to be restricted, his
heart-wrenching, prayerful deathwatch over the demise of his second
wife—an exultation of piety and love which he recorded almost hour by
hour for two weeks—and his deeply affectionate letters to his third wife,
Margaret, testify to the force and warmth of his private emotions, however discreet and sober he appeared in public. When he and Margaret
were separated for extended times they pledged to commune with each
other telepathically—"to meet . . . in spirit before the Lord"—each Mon-
day and Friday between five and six. Severely self-disciplined, he knew
the truth and sought to engender it in a world mired in error and corruption. He had the vigor, intelligence, and passion for the achievement of a
commander, a leader of men, but he was a leader with a rigorously logical
mind capable of fine discriminations in theological debate and a sense of
human frailty. His greatest virtues were the clarity of his vision, his resolution, and his managerial skills; his weakness was his single-mindedness,
which made him seem at times self-righteous. But he was always a commanding figure, and he dominated the circle of able men who shared in
the leadership of the Puritans' Great Migration.[58]

For while many of the decisions that propelled the project forward
were his, they were not his alone. Others, equally competent and equally
committed, joined him in triggering the exodus, which was never a silent
Völkerwanderung, a mute, undirected milling and drifting of people overseas. From the start it was a deliberate, well-organized, and purposeful
mobilization of the idealistic, the discontented, the frustrated, and the
fearful into a structured project—for some, renewal; for others, evasion.
Some who shared in the migration's initial leadership were of the gentry like Winthrop, some were merchant entrepreneurs, some were local
leaders of ordinary status. They were all, like Winthrop, experienced in
practical affairs and, also like him, forceful and resolute.

THE MOST ACCOMPLISHED among them, the most cosmopolitan,
worldly, sophisticated, and intellectually adventurous, was Winthrop's
son, John, Jr. Only twenty-five when he joined the migration in 1631, he

had already completed his studies at Trinity College, Dublin, had spent three years at the Inns of Court, had served in the military campaign to relieve the siege of La Rochelle, had traveled to Constantinople, and had visited major cultural centers in Italy and the Netherlands. The impetus behind much of his traveling was the desire to advance his knowledge of the world in general and of science in particular, especially the advances in alchemy, one of the frontiers of scientific advancement at the time, and medicine associated with it. He had discovered the lure and importance of alchemical science in London, and it merged in his mind with the semisecret Rosicrucian movement, dedicated to the universal betterment of mankind. He had found in "alchemical culture," his most recent biographer writes, "an intellectual and Christian natural philosophy to which he could fully commit and through which he could seek knowledge and material gain while fulfilling his Christian duty to improve the world." But what for his colleagues and mentors in advanced intellectual circles in London were largely theoretical matters became for Winthrop highly practical concerns, since in New England he found the ideal setting for the realization of the meliorist dreams of the alchemical experimentalists, the pansophists, and the Rosicrucian healers.

> Over the next half century, Winthrop [Jr.] would found three colonial towns, serve as a Bay Colony assistant for nearly two decades, govern the colony of Connecticut for eighteen years, secure that colony a charter from the Restoration court of Charles II granting it virtual independence, found several New England iron foundries, serve as a physician to nearly half the population of Connecticut, and become a founding member of the Royal Society. Alchemical knowledge and philosophies factored, often essentially, into each of these accomplishments.

A "Christian alchemist" and the most successful and renowned physician in New England, he never deviated from his commitment to the Puritan cause, but his world was broader than his father's, more complex, more closely attuned to the new and exciting intellectual waves that were sweeping across Europe and the entrepreneurial possibilities they inspired. So broad were his interests, so serious his commitment to advancement in whatever form, that in the end he could not avoid deviating from his revered father on the question of toleration, and indeed he

JOHN WINTHROP, JR.

A modernizing, worldly Puritan, he was an aspiring
scientist and entrepreneur, open to the emerging world,
tolerant of religious dissent.

became an outspoken advocate of liberty of conscience, so long as it did
not lead to social or political unrest.

A well-traveled, talented intellectual, he was also a practical manager,
and he shouldered much of the heavy burden of arranging the departure
and resettlement of the large Winthrop family on the shores of Massachusetts. Clearly, a contemporary wrote, young Winthrop was "a very ingenious Gent" who would prove to be "of speciall use to the Plantation."[59]

But though Winthrop, Jr. was impressively energetic and enterprising, he was a junior among the migration's initial leaders, and he was
uncharacteristically genial and conciliatory in difficult situations. His
seniors in the settlement were, almost to a man, stubborn, self-willed,
and sharply competitive when challenged.

Thus Thomas Dudley, who would prove to be the elder Winthrop's chief competitor for dominance in governing the colony, had been brought up in the household of the Earl of Northampton and had clerked for a judge before serving as an army officer in France and then, for over a decade, as manager of the Earl of Lincoln's estates, which he helped rescue from debt. Like so many others, he found in and around Boston in Lincolnshire in the late 1620s the direction he would follow in nonconformist politics and in devotion to the Puritans' ideals. A natural leader, he would be elected governor of Massachusetts four times, deputy governor thirteen times. But his would never be a peaceable kingdom. "Proud and overbearing, irascible and argumentative," he was a rigid precisionist whose rule was always abrasive. Hating heresy, it has been said, "was the largest component of his piety."[60]

His belligerence, his assertiveness, and his argumentativeness seem typical of New England's first leaders. If Dudley was a hard man, the hardest, the genealogist James Savage wrote, was Richard Bellingham, who would serve for twenty-three years as either governor or deputy governor of the Bay Colony. A lawyer, recorder of the town of Boston, Lincolnshire, and in 1628 a member of the House of Commons (the only migrant to have held that office), he was close to Lincolnshire's social and political leadership, including the Earl of Lincoln, and he was a man who never doubted his worth. Secure in the social and political status he brought with him from England, he would prove to be a relentless foe of the Winthrops and a skillful political infighter—a populist of sorts, promoting the cause of the town representatives against the magistracy of which he was himself a part. But however populist he became in politics, he was never remotely beholden to public opinion. "Very very greedy for more money," a contemporary wrote, short-tempered and truculent, he would scandalize everyone, high and low, by officiating at his own wedding—in effect marrying himself—to a girl twenty-six years his junior and then refusing to withdraw as judge of the court that was to try him for the offense.[61]

William Pynchon also came from a well-connected English family and also became a controversialist. An inheritor of substantial properties in Essex, "on the fringe of the social class which usually held manors and served as justices of the peace," and a churchwarden in his native town of Springfield, he was like Dudley a precisionist in secular affairs as in religion. When at the age of forty he, his wife, four children, and some servants arrived in New England with the Winthrop fleet, he was long experienced in commercial land management and trade and as alive to the possibilities of material profit as he was to the nuances of theological debate. While his experience in estate management in the most commercialized part of rural England would pave the way for his remarkably successful exploitation of the fur supplies and the land that he would acquire on the Connecticut River—which in time would make his heir a wealthy frontier rentier—so too his close associations with his Puritan neighbors in Essex, especially Hooker, and his acquaintance with Latin, Greek, and Hebrew, predisposed him to enter freely, and contentiously, into the doctrinal debates that would threaten the colony's stability.[62]

There were other secular leaders—a remarkable number of them—of background and standing similar to those of Dudley and Pynchon, who were equally experienced in practical affairs, equally contentious, equally contrary-minded, equally argumentative, sensitive to slights, and relentless in following through on their opinions.

William Coddington, the son of a wealthy Lincolnshire merchant, was another adherent of the Earl of Lincoln. His Puritanism reinforced by the preaching of his Lincolnshire neighbor Cotton, he arrived in New England with Winthrop in 1630. He would soon thereafter oppose the colony's establishment and join with the opposition; in the end he would defect from the colony altogether. But his respectability and affluence were never in doubt; for Winthrop he was, at least initially, "a godly man and of good estate."[63]

William Vassall, also a challenger for the colony's leadership, was no less respectable, no less affluent, no less godly, and no less prickly. The son of a London alderman and brother of one of the founders and financiers of the Massachusetts Bay Company who was also a Parliamentary leader in the resistance to the Crown, Vassall was always, Winthrop would later write, "a busy and factious spirit . . . a man never at rest but when he was in the fire of contention." Yet he was undeniably a man of substance, with powerful political connections.[64]

And some of the colony's most substantial people, who would themselves prove to be peaceable, enterprising, and orderly, brought with them sources of profound disorder—none more so than the Hutchinsons.

They arrived as a virtual clan in 1633–34. A sprawling Lincolnshire family anchored in part in their native village of Alford, near Boston, and in part in London, where their kinsman Richard was a prosperous ironmonger, they sent over to New England two forerunners and then followed in a party of seventeen: William and his wife Anne, ten of their children (Anne, age forty-three, had borne fourteen children in twenty-three years of marriage), three kinswomen, and two male servants. They quickly settled in, began organizing an Atlantic-wide network of trade linking London, Boston, Rhode Island, and Barbados, and entered into the colony's political and religious life. But while William and his enterprising sons and in-laws worked quickly and quietly to develop their stake in the colony's economy, Anne—fiercely defiant, verbally clever, and a zealot in her religious beliefs—had already begun her journey into radical dissent which would, within two years of her arrival in the colony, force into the open the deepest, most contentious implications of Puritan thought, and in the process traumatize the colony's religious life.[65]

Her sensational career in New England emerged from within the context of East Anglia's pious, prosperous tradesmen and London's newly affluent, rising merchants. Robert Keayne was not as respectable or sophisticated as the Hutchinson men nor as penetrating a thinker as Anne, but he was a successful tradesman, had acquired wealth above that of most of the prosperous migrants, and was fierce and passionate in his piety.

Keayne was a product of the lesser world of London's shopkeepers and small-scale money dealers—an inhabitant of the narrow, crowded, clangorous lanes and alleyways that radiated out from the main artery of the medieval city—Cheapside, Cornhill, and Leadenhall streets. There aspiring, marginal people lived intense, bristling lives, elbowing their way forward by careful calculation, taking while the taking was good. By 1635 when he left for New England, Keayne, a butcher's boy from Windsor, had greatly succeeded. Said to be a "gentleman," admitted to the freedom of the Merchant Tailors' Company and of the city of London, he had married the daughter of London's Lord Mayor and hence become kinsman of the highly respectable preacher John Wilson, and he was a member of the Honourable Artillery Company of London. As his prosperity had grown, so too had his piety and commitment to the Puritan cause, and that commitment had both reinforced his drive for material success and at the same time acted as a moral constraint on it. For God's sake alone, he believed, one must work industriously in this world and profit from it wherever and whenever possible, but not for display, not for sensuous satisfaction. Carefully, delicately, one must balance avarice and benevolence, enterprise and morality; one must prosper but not exhibit, and calculate profit and loss in one's spiritual as well as material life.

When Keayne appeared in Massachusetts, acquisitive and ascetic, ardent and calculating in everything he did, he carried with him, besides "two or 3000 lb in good estate," both a reputation for "covetous practice" and a bundle of sermon notes he had taken down over the years that testified to his passionate piety and the fierce tension of his inner life. His standing as a fervently pious and enterprising, if not avaricious, tradesman devoted to the Puritan cause was typical of a significant group within the migration's leadership, men whose names feature in the economic history of early New England and who became mainstays of the developing community. Such were the new Bostonians: Valentine Hill, John Hewes, John Cogan, Henry Shrimpton, Edward and William Tyng, John Cogswell, Anthony Stoddard. Such too were the enterprising founders of the New Haven colony, almost all of them ex-inhabitants of Coleman Street, London, in Davenport's parish, adjacent to Cheapside and Cornhill: Theophilus Eaton, his son-in-law Edward Hopkins, Richard Malbon, and David Yale.[66]

And such too were the leaders from other parts of the realm. The West Country contribution to the migration of 1630 was initially inspired by the embattled Rev. John White, rector of Dorchester, Dorset. As early as 1622 he had sought to transform the West Country's seasonal fishing stations in New England into permanent settlements that would serve both Dorset's economy and the propagation of the gospel to the fishermen and the native Americans they might encounter. When his plans failed they were taken over by the Dorchester Company, funded by substantial Dorset and Devon gentry and merchants, together with a scattering of London investors and local men "in a small way of business." By 1628, as that company was being absorbed first by the New England Company and then by the Massachusetts Bay Company, it had on the ground, at Salem, a governor of their own in John Endecott and an agent of some experience in Roger Conant; and they were discovering leadership qualities in Roger Ludlow and Henry Wolcott.[67]

Endecott, who would serve for at least fifteen years as governor of Massachusetts, would soon become famous, notorious, for his fierce Puritanical fervor. Suppressor "of a pestilent generation . . . called Quakers" (he would hang three), given to fistfights on occasion and enthusiastic assaults on Indians, he would embarrass the colony by tearing the red cross from the royal flag as a symbol of the pope and the Antichrist. Conant, the son of a prosperous Devonshire yeoman and a brother of a clerical associate of White's, would have a less prominent, more tranquil career, but even he showed some of the characteristics of this hard, adventurous generation. Having prospered in the London salters trade, supplying ships with provisions and supplies, he had ventured with his family to the Pilgrims' colony as members of the unassociated "particular" settlement, along with the notorious Oldham and Lyford. He made no friends there. Bradford found him to be "an ignorant, foolish, selfwilled fellow" who failed to establish a necessary salt manufacture. He soon moved off to Boston's North Shore where, first at Cape Ann and then at Salem, he secured the West Country's foothold in the Bay Colony. Thereafter he withdrew from the colony's leadership to a magistrate's role in county and town government.[68]

But the major group from the West Country had settled in 1630, not on Conant's Cape Ann or Salem, but on a spur of land that jutted into Boston harbor that they called, in honor of the Reverend White, Dorchester. The lives of the 140 men, women, and children who disembarked from the *Mary and John* of Devon were desperate at first, as they sought shelter in hastily erected canvas tents and wigwams and in timber-framed earthen dugouts and unloaded their crates, barrels, and bundles of clothes, food, drink, equipment, and firearms. But their leadership was strong. Chief among them—typical in many ways of the Great Migration's secular leaders—was Roger Ludlow.

Scion of a prominent family of Wiltshire landowners and lawyers, Ludlow had studied at Balliol College, Oxford, then had had legal training at the Inner Temple and had practiced law in London. Married into the family of prominent West Country merchants, he was drawn by White, and probably Endecott, his brother-in-law, into the settlement project. He personally funded the purchase of the *Mary and John* and became the official leader of the expedition. Well educated, politically informed, sophisticated in the law, and enormously energetic, Ludlow had all the qualities needed for the task except an even temper and a conciliatory spirit. Contemporaries found him "arrogant, overbearing, and opinionated." When in 1632 it was proposed that the magistrates and governor be elected by more popular procedures, Ludlow flew "into passion," declared that all government would then be at an end, and that under those conditions he would return to England. His impatience and restlessness were matched by his ambition. When in 1635, having served as Massachusetts' deputy governor, he would fail of election to the magistracy, in part because of intemperate remarks to the town representatives, he would break with the community he had helped found and lead many of his people westward, to Connecticut—first to Windsor, then to Fairfield. For a time the challenges of creating a settlement in the wilderness, devising a new, remarkably innovative code of law, serving in a magistracy of his own creation, and leading troops against the Dutch—all this would absorb his energies. But when the political-ecclesiastical world turned in England, his ambition would overcome him and he would return, to serve in Ireland on Cromwell's commission on forfeited estates.[69]

There were more peaceable, less restless leaders of the West Country contingent—notably Henry Wolcott and Edward Rossiter. But the latter died within months of his arrival, and Wolcott, who emigrated with his family from Somerset at age fifty-two, would devote his considerable energy and cunning to land development in Windsor, Connecticut, and in connection with his Somerset kin, he established a trading network that would launch the fortunes of an affluent family. Like Conant, Wolcott and his sons and grandsons would never forget their West Country origins, which continued to shape their lives. Less fervently Puritan than the East Anglians who dominated Boston and its satellites, they remained different in style and folkways: "softer in speech," their historian has written, "slower in tempo, and distinct in . . . rural habits and allegiances."[70]

7

Such was the leadership of the migration that would populate New England—clerics resolute in refusing to concede to the church's demands for conformity and determined to realize their hopes for a fulfilled, apostolic Protestantism, and pious laymen familiar with land management and the law, and familiar too with commerce and the mobilization of resources. There is abundant record of their frantic efforts to launch the exodus and establish the settlements. The problems they faced, starting in 1629 and in the decade that followed, were enormous. Besides dealing with the details of disposing of their own personal property, they had to decide how much and what kinds of food would be needed for the voyage and for the year thereafter, what clothes, tools, building materials, fishing and hunting equipment, arms, and kitchenware; what cattle could be transported; what craftsmen, tradesmen, artisans, and physicians—indeed what preachers—should be brought along,[71] and how many sailors and soldiers. What would be the transportation cost—per person, per family, for the fleet as a whole—and how should it be paid for? Above all, they had to decide how the settlers were to be recruited and how they should be organized for departure.

Many left as members of informal, loosely associated "companies" under clerical leadership, drawn to the migration by the magnetism of major figures like Cotton and Hooker. These were not stable, durable communities whose members were bound together in networks of shared rights and obligations. They came together only as associates in migration, and their group identity therefore was fragile and transitory. Thus Anne Hutchinson, who had been deeply touched by Cotton's preaching, traveled in his entourage.[72] So too did the Boston (Lincolnshire) alderman Thomas Leverett, who had protected Cotton in his need, and the town's former mayor, Atherton Hough, who was linked by marriage to the extensive Bedfordshire clan of the Rev. Peter Bulkeley. In all, fifty-nine emigrants have been identified as having been in Cotton's initial "company," and many more, in subsequent years, would follow in his path. John Davenport led his own large and important contingent from Coleman Street, London, ultimately to New Haven, Connecticut, which became a refuge for spiritists of Cotton's persuasion. Wheelwright, Anne Hutchinson's brother-in-law, led twenty-nine of his followers to Boston. Nathaniel Rogers, son of "the mighty thunderer of Dedham," inspired the migration of twenty people to Ipswich, Massachusetts; his stubborn, domineering cousin Ezekiel brought twenty families from his Yorkshire parish in Rowley and its surroundings to Massachusetts, where they joined thirty others in settling a new Rowley, close by the new Ipswich.

Hooker's personal influence on the migration was even greater, numerically, than Cotton's. Fifty-eight of his Essex devotees preceded him to New England; later fifty-three others followed. Among them were people of some wealth and standing. John Haynes, of Copford Hall, Essex, whom Winthrop described as "a gentleman of great estate," traveled with Hooker and would serve first as governor of Massachusetts and then, when he followed Hooker to Connecticut, as governor or deputy governor of that colony for the rest of his life. Shepard's "company" of thirty-eight included the young, affluent Roger Harlakenden, son of the manor lord of Earls Colne, Essex, whose family had attempted to shield Shepard from Laud's attacks. Harlakenden traveled in some style, with his wife, sister, eight servants, and an associated family of five.[73]

Such ministerial "companies" gathered wherever Puritanism was under heavy attack and where there were forceful preachers determined to lead the way. From parishes in northeastern Suffolk came the John Phillips and John Young groups of forty-nine, along with the John Allen and John Fiske "company" of sixty-two. The largest single ministerial "company" known to have moved to New England came from Hingham, Norfolk, and its surroundings. Between 1633 and 1640, 143 people migrated from that district with the blessings of both "the old fox," the Rev. Robert Peck, who had been excommunicated as "a very violent schismatical spirit" and emigrated at age fifty-eight, and the Rev. Peter Hobart, twenty-seven years his junior. Together they would organize and dominate the settlement of Hingham, Massachusetts.[74]

The total population of the ministerial "companies"—some of them loose groupings of scattered parishioners, some actual congregations— that left from the five counties of greater East Anglia has been calculated at 667.

The fabric of the Great Migration was much more, however, than a patchwork of ministerial-led clusters. Equally a part of the complex pattern were other associations independent of clerical leadership—groups related not so much by shared religious experiences and commitments as by kinship, friendship, and geographical proximity. One of the subtlest statistical analyses of the migration from London to New England reveals disproportionate numbers from different inland locations sailing together—statistics that identify them as voyagers who had gone to London not to take the first transport available but to wait, according to plan, for others to join them—family, neighbors, and friends—with whom "to brave the uncertainty of an Atlantic crossing."[75] Not all such groups survived the migration intact. Some of these conglomerates broke up at the start, their subunits traveling sequentially. Men often preceded their families; adult children sometimes led the way for their parents, siblings, and in-laws. But once settled in New England the scattered elements at times rejoined their association supplemented by strangers.

Thus John Winthrop's extended kin group of twenty-eight individuals included, through marriage ties, members of the Tyndal, Fones, Sampson, Doggett, Firmin, Downing, and Goad families, who arrived at various times and settled in Boston, Ipswich, Salem, and Watertown and yet retained a sense of commonality; the ties among them survived years of physical separation. The relationship between the large nuclear families of the two Winthrops, father and son, remained especially close, even when the younger Winthrop lived in Connecticut and traveled abroad. Similarly, the Hutchinson clan, which by in-law extension and other relationships has been counted at forty people scattered through Massachusetts and Rhode Island, managed to maintain its ties through many vicissitudes and geographical distances. And so too the prosperous Tuttle family, who traveled from the market town of St. Albans, Hertfordshire, as a cluster of at least twenty-five that included the couple's children, stepchildren, in-laws, and servants.

In genealogical terms, much of the emigration, especially from greater East Anglia, the West Country, and eastern Yorkshire, can be conceived of as tangles of such extended kinship groups. In the case of greater East Anglia, fifty-five such networks have been identified. Together they appear to account for over a third of all emigrants from that region of southeastern England.[76]

BUT SUCH CONGLOMERATES ARE only the outer manifestations of the central role of family organization in the history of the Great Migration. For at the core of such galaxies were nuclear families and their immediate households. In number they were unique in the migration history of the era. No other displacement of the English people—to Ireland, the West Indies, or elsewhere in North America—involved so many stable, complete, traditional nuclear families. But their importance cannot be measured by numbers alone. While the family basis of the Puritan migration accounts for much of the cohesion of the New England communities, it also accounts for a deep fault line in New England's social structure that would prove to be the source of persistent conflict.

FAMILIES—nuclear families—were everywhere in the migration of the 1630s, and everywhere they proved to be the source of both stability and instability in the emerging social order. A meticulous study of the seven emigrant vessels of the 1630s whose passenger rosters are complete reveals that almost nine-tenths (87.8 percent) of the 680 passengers aboard were traveling in family groups, most of them nuclear units of married couples, generally in their thirties, who had been married for approximately a

decade and who brought with them three or more children. "These were
families-in-progress, with parents who were at most halfway through
their reproductive years and whose continued fertility would make possible New England's remarkable rate of population growth."

But there were important ambiguities. Twelve percent of the emigrants in this sample were traveling not in full family groups but alone
or with siblings, and most of these eighty-three individuals were young
males, mainly tradesmen and semiskilled artisans. More than half of the
families aboard these seven vessels brought with them servants, predominantly male. Of the seventy-four married couples who came with
their children, over half (forty-two) also brought servants as members
of their families. The servants totaled 17 percent of the entire group (as
opposed to 13.4 percent of the English population) and 37 percent of the
male emigrants, and they were present in perhaps twice as many families among the migrants as among the English population generally. In
the disorienting circumstances of transatlantic travel and resettlement
in unfamiliar and difficult circumstances, young male servants restive
within the constraints of disrupted families, and unattached laborers and
tradesmen anxious for the future, could be the source of severely destabilizing tensions.

Their origins mattered. These seven vessels left from the outports—
Great Yarmouth (Norfolk), Sandwich (Kent), Southampton (Hampshire),
and Weymouth (Dorset). The complexities of families in the migration
become more apparent when one turns to the metropolitan port of London.[77] Of the 4,878 voyagers to the colonies whose names are entered in
the London port register of 1635, 1,169 boarded seventeen vessels bound
for New England. In some ways the characteristics of that group match
those of the previous sample; they too resembled, roughly, the attributes
of the society from which the migrants had come. The sex ratio of those
who left through London (1.5 males for each female) is almost as well
balanced as that of the outport emigrants (1.3), and the age distribution
is similar. But the anomalies stand out more clearly. Only 60 percent of
these 1,169 migrants, as opposed to almost 90 percent, traveled in family
groups, and a third, as opposed to 17 percent, of those whose occupations or statuses are known were servants. Their presence accounts for a
notable bulge in the age group 15–24.[78]

Thus in the London register of 1635, as in the previous compilation
of vessels leaving the outports, the incidence of families among the emi-

grants to New England is far greater than that of groups destined for
other colonies, but in both cases the families are accompanied by large
numbers of solitary travelers and servants, some attached to families,
some not. The same configuration is found in the comprehensive compilation of almost ten thousand people known to have migrated to New
England between 1620 and 1650. Here the lines are broader, the details
far fewer, but once again there is a higher incidence of families traveling
to New England than to any other colonial destination, and yet here too
one finds that "one third of the adult males . . . were single, young, and
without family connection in their new land."[79]

It is a complex picture—of cohesive families and unaffiliated workers,
of patriarchal householders and self-directing isolates, of exalted utopians
and pedestrian toilers, of deeply rooted, prosperous gentry and wandering, unemployed laborers. The complexity is compounded—the discrepancies deepened—by the dominant groups' remarkable cultural level. In
this remote, uncultivated, disarrayed frontier world the educational level
of New England's population in the 1630s was utterly distinctive, and
discordant with the crudeness and primitiveness of everyday life. It was
not simply that some 60 percent of the region's adult male population
was fully literate (as opposed to 30 percent in rural England) and that
perhaps "a major part" of the rest could to some extent read—or indeed,
that in the mid-seventeenth century New Englanders "were the equals in
literacy of the citizens of Amsterdam and of the best-educated sectors of
pre-industrial England."[80]

More important was the cultural accomplishments of the settlements'
leadership. At least 130 of the migrants to New England before 1646
had matriculated in Oxford or Cambridge university; eight had attended
other European universities. And if the range of years is expanded to
1660 and the definition of "university men" is broadened to include Harvard graduates and those "informally tutored" in preparation for clerical
careers, the number of highly educated men rises to 266. By 1640 there
was probably one university educated man in New England for every
thirty-two families, a ratio similar to that of England itself and astonishing in a frontier world.[81] And few of these had been simply casual students, attending university only to acquire a literate or social polish. The
ministers who emigrated were not average clergymen. They were better educated than the average and more effective as preachers. Many,

like Hooker and Cotton, had been scholars of considerable attainments. Charles Chauncy, besides having held the Greek lectureship at Trinity College, Cambridge, was also a student of Hebrew and Arabic. John Wilson, Boston's future pastor, was gifted in writing Latin poetry; as a young man, he had scoured the abstruse literature on conformity and dissent, then had spent three years at the Inns of Court before returning to Cambridge University and committing himself to a clerical career. John Winthrop, Jr.—the notable scientist, alchemist, industrial entrepreneur, and physician—would be the first American member of the Royal Society. Everyone, even his opponents, recognized that Roger Williams, for all his restless and rebarbative ways, was a brilliant intellectual, relentless in pursuing to their logical extremes the subtlest and at times the most dangerous implications of his and his opponents' ideas. "Never," Edmund Morgan has written, "was a man of action more an intellectual."[82]

The discrepancy between this highly educated, articulate clerisy, extraordinary in such a crude marchland world, and the growing mass of ordinary settlers intent on material security, intensified conflicts endemic in Puritan society. It was not so much a matter of who or how many would gain technical membership in the Puritan churches as who and how many would conform to the demands of rarified social ideals brought to a point of refinement by learned, sophisticated, aspiring, contentious minds freed from external constraints and determined to design a new world. The incongruities were glaring—between intellectuals attuned to the advanced ideas of metropolitan Europe and an insecure laboring population, pragmatic, individualistic, vagrant, responding in the most parochial terms to the possibilities of immediate satisfaction.

THIS STRIKING INCONGRUITY compounded other discrepancies and anomalies within a migrant population that only in romantic retrospect could be seen as a congruent whole. The settlers of Massachusetts and its satellite colonies were in fact people from many different English subcultures, and brought with them many different folkways and differing expectations. They would be ruled in public life by hard and abrasive personalities in constant competition for dominance and guided in spiritual matters by clerics who differed increasingly on fundamental principles. They would be drawn between the magnetic poles of sophisticated, cosmopolitan ideals and the mundane realities of an uncultivated world. The resulting conflicts, the clangor and disaffections, would set in early in the settlements' history and would last for two generations before a consistent and integrated regional culture evolved. That end product of the Great Migration would prove to be far different, in its peculiar provincialism, from anything the founders had imagined.

CHAPTER 13

Abrasions, Utopians, and Holy War

1

SOCIAL DISAGREEMENTS, personality conflicts, and theological controversies within this carefully managed exodus to the New World emerged quickly as the thousands of settlers, drawn from every region of England and committed to various shades of religious reform, disembarked and began the tortuous process of settling into the land. Winthrop had hoped that the outcome of this wrenching enterprise and its ultimate justification would be a single harmonious community ruled by a unified magistracy and guided in spiritual matters by clerics in agreement on the essentials of reformed Protestantism. He was the first of the Great Migration to know the bitterness of ideals betrayed. It immediately became clear that the Puritans' world would consist not of a single integrated community devoted to carefully defined Christian goals but a sprawl of small settlements scattered across the countryside and dominated by contentious magistrates and clerics of increasingly divergent views. In the end Winthrop would live to see, not the maturing of an integrated Puritan community, but the development of a society of divergent opinions and discordant modes of behavior—differences and antagonisms that would be resolved, to the extent that they were resolved, at times by persuasion, at other times by intimidation, and at moments of crisis by vengeful brutality.

THE FIRST AND most vital question the settlers faced was how the land— so vast, so apparently boundless, so providentially open for exploitation— would be possessed and used. They had lived in a realm where every acre was preciously possessed and where whole domains were preserved for landlords' recreation while tenants and subtenants cultivated plots whose yields were shared in rents. In the varieties of their regional origins they had had different experiences in crop selection and land use. Now, in New England, cling as they might to the practices they had known, they had no choice but to reconsider the foundations of land distribution and exploitation.

At first, all was confusion. Displeased with the original landing site at the earlier settlement at Salem—a scene of death and desolation—the Winthrop fleet's leaders turned south and explored the Boston Bay area, only to disagree on a permanent location for the future city. With Dudley stubbornly insisting on a site inland along one of the two rivers empty- ing into the bay, the Charles, and Winthrop favoring a site on the other, the Mystic, they compromised on a temporary encampment between the two, at what became Charlestown. There, on the sloping shore, the hundreds of disoriented, exhausted voyagers threw together temporary shelters—tents, huts, and wigwams—and dragged their supplies, live- stock, and equipment to safety above the waterline. It was a desperate, crowded, helter-skelter huddle, lacking sanitation, sufficient food, and medical supplies. Dysentery swept through the encampment, and the set- tlers were forced to disperse. While Dudley continued to demand that the entire colony follow him up the Charles to "Newtown" (Cambridge), Sir Richard Saltonstall led one group farther up the Charles to what would become Watertown, William Pynchon led another a short distance south to Roxbury, and Winthrop, though conceding enough to Dudley to build a house at Newtown, led his personal following to the small, narrow pen- insula jutting into the bay that became known as Boston, in recognition of the Lincolnshire town where John Cotton had inspired a generation of Puritans. By the end of 1630, six months after the fleet's arrival, there were seven settlements scattered on the shores and inlets of Boston Bay, and Winthrop's dream of a single, organic community, a model of disciplined Christian civility free of the corruptions of the world left behind, had begun to fade.[1]

None of these initial communities had rules to follow for the distribution of land. But as the settlements multiplied, the General Court devised, not by theory but by pragmatic adjustments to demographic, cultural, financial, and ecological pressures, a procedure that would determine the process of land distribution for generations to come. Well before 1650, by which time forty-four towns had been founded, it had become clear that the complicated process began with the gathering of a group—ecclesiastical or secular—with the will and resources to choose a site, obtain permission from the General Court, purchase the land from the Indians, survey the plot in approved form, and design not only the lots for distribution (home lots, fields for cultivation, and meadowland) but also the roads and bridges that would be needed by the initial settlers. The allocation of land was necessarily a subtle process. There was nothing egalitarian about it. The more a family was believed to be able to contribute to the community's welfare, the greater its entitlement to grants among the several parcels to be divided. Prestige had to be taken into account, as well as professional skills and wealth. And the entitlements based on these social measures had to be cross-calculated with the quality of land in the several parcels: a mediocre town lot could be balanced by a generous grant of rich meadowland. And decisions had to be made on which sections of land would be held in reserve for later distribution and who would be entitled to share in the later grants.[2]

The entire process, from the initial gathering of people hoping to found a new town to the allocation of land to the last of the founding group, was laborious and expensive. And it required, besides the farming families who would actually settle and work the land, affluent and influential sponsors, resident or absentee, who could provide the necessary financial and political backing. As the process went forward it became peculiarly confusing because of the diversity of the settlers' regional backgrounds.

For they brought to the process of land distribution and cultivation a variety of habits and expectations drawn from their earlier lives. Though the settlers sought to join with people they knew personally or who came from the same region, no part of New England and very few towns were populated exclusively by migrants from a single ecological, agricultural district of England. Everywhere people were faced with "strangers very unlike themselves despite their common nationality"; people, Winthrop wrote, who originally had been "absent from eache other many miles, and had [had] . . . imploymentes as farre distant" were now obliged to live together and collaborate in a common enterprise. If in some areas settlers of a common background were dominant, often their dominance did not last. Neighborhood groups, even those that had arrived together, broke up as families moved in search of permanent locations. Dissident factions split off from parent communities to join with other dissidents and with later immigrants to form new towns; and servants, once freed from their obligations, had no choice but to move on until they found steady employment or their own stake in the land.[3]

Movement, a constant shuffling, was everywhere. Of the 693 heads of household who arrived on the seven ships whose complete passenger lists are known, only 115 remained in their first locations. Though most of these families moved only once, some seemed peripatetic, moving four, five, even six times before settling down permanently. Similarly, of the 939 migrants from London to New England in 1635, only just over one-third remained in the town of their arrival; an equal number moved once before settling, 154 made two moves, and 106 moved three times or more; two can be traced as residents of no less than seven communities. Three-fifths of all those who arrived before 1634 left their original habitations. Roxbury's settlers, for example, two-thirds of whom came from Essex and East Hertfordshire and were closely related by kinship, "moved in and out of Roxbury at a dizzying rate." Half of that town's original free adult males moved on—seven to Rhode Island, one to New Hampshire, three to Salem and its surroundings, nine to Connecticut or Long Island, and two to the West Indies.[4]

All of this settlement and resettlement compounded the complexity of the communities' subcultural blendings. An indication of how intricate the pattern became is shown on the map of the English origins of the settlers in a significant number of New England areas as of 1650. In each of the three main areas around Boston Bay, for example, there are people from all five major regions of England. Though the Bay's North Shore settlements have a preponderance of West Country people; though the people in the mid-Bay area (Middlesex and Suffolk counties) are mainly from England's southeast coast; and though on the South Shore East Anglians were in the majority, there were people from all parts of England

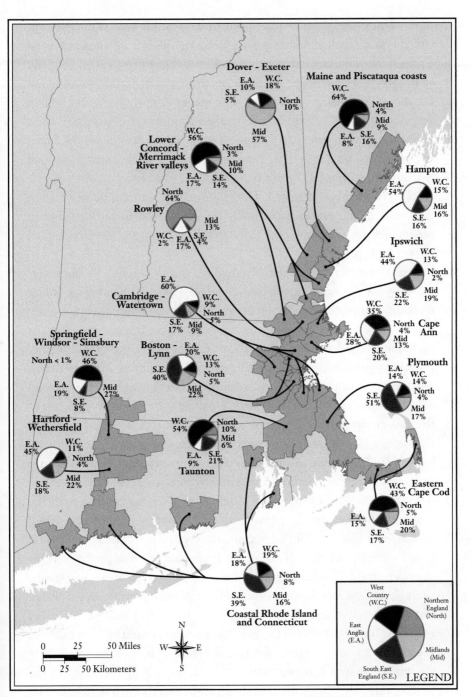

Dover - Exeter
E.A. 10%
W.C. 18%
S.E. 5%
North 10%
Mid 57%

Maine and Piscataqua coasts
W.C. 64%
North 4%
Mid 9%
E.A. 8%
S.E. 16%

Lower Concord - Merrimack River valleys
W.C. 56%
North 3%
Mid 10%
E.A. 17%
S.E. 14%

Rowley
North 64%
Mid 13%
W.C. 2%
E.A. 17%
S.E. 4%

Hampton
E.A. 54%
W.C. 15%
Mid 16%
S.E. 16%

Ipswich
E.A. 44%
W.C. 13%
North 2%
S.E. 22%
Mid 19%

Cambridge - Watertown
E.A. 60%
W.C. 9%
North 5%
S.E. 17%
Mid 9%

Cape Ann
W.C. 35%
North 4%
Mid 13%
E.A. 28%
S.E. 20%

Springfield - Windsor - Simsbury
W.C. 46%
North < 1%
E.A. 19%
Mid 27%
S.E. 8%

Boston - Lynn
E.A. 20%
W.C. 13%
North 5%
S.E. 40%
Mid 22%

Plymouth
E.A. 14%
W.C. 14%
North 4%
S.E. 51%
Mid 17%

Hartford - Wethersfield
E.A. 45%
W.C. 11%
North 4%
S.E. 18%
Mid 22%

Taunton
W.C. 54%
North 10%
Mid 6%
E.A. 9%
S.E. 21%

Eastern Cape Cod
W.C. 43%
North 5%
Mid 20%
E.A. 15%
S.E. 17%

Coastal Rhode Island and Connecticut
E.A. 18%
W.C. 19%
North 8%
S.E. 39%
Mid 16%

LEGEND
West Country (W.C.)
Northern England (North)
East Anglia (E.A.)
Midlands (Mid)
South East England (S.E.)

0 25 50 Miles
0 25 50 Kilometers

N
W - E
S

English origins of New England settlers: distribution by regions in all of these areas. There were jarring juxtapositions and shifts in domi-nance even in such a limited area as the sparsely settled Cape Cod: West Country men dominated the eastern Cape, though not exclusively, but southeasterners were the majority on the western Cape. Similarly, in the mix of peoples in the isolated settlements along Long Island Sound, the majority were drawn from England's southeastern coast, but a few miles to the north along the Connecticut River, one cluster around Hart-ford was predominantly East Anglian in origins, while another, around Springfield, was largely drawn from the West Country.

The differences mattered. In certain places distinctions created by English regional origins were easily reconciled and soon faded, but in others they persisted and led at times to difficult community relations and bitter controversies.

For two generations Salem's public life was dominated by the strug-gle between the original, pre-Puritan West Country men led by Roger Conant, who settled on the north side of the town's harbor (Cape Ann), and the later influx of East Anglians, who established themselves across the harbor and on inland farms. Every aspect of the town's life—landholding, church organization, social order, and political power—reflected that rivalry. The town's problems rose and fell, but through all the turmoil of the town's early years, the West Country men clung to their iden-tity as a group apart. By the 1660s, when commerce began to dominate the largely East Anglian port sector and when as a consequence prob-lems of land use and taxation led to sharp differences, the West Country men simply walked off and formed their own town of Beverly. Nothing, it seemed, could dim the West Country men's identification with the region of their origins. In 1671, forty-six years after Conant had settled on the part of Salem that had become Beverly, he petitioned the General Court on behalf of himself and thirty-four others to change the name of the town to the "western name of Budleigh, a market towne of Devon-sheer ... where myself was borne." His request, he wrote, was a "littell Privelidg," but at the age of seventy-nine, it was important to him. He reminded the Court that all the first comers who had settled with him had been "from the western part of England," and that in his long life this was the only request he had ever made of the authorities.[5]

Nothing in the settling of the towns was more clearly influenced by regional background than the question of whether the granted town lots would be owned and worked in common, as in England's open or common field system, or whether individual grants would form separate enclosed farms worked independently by individual families. And nothing was more complex, since the two forms had overlapped in certain areas. Further, in many regions the process of enclosure had been in flux, spreading rapidly in modernizing areas in East Anglia, where open-field agriculture had once been dominant, while scarcely penetrating large parts of the Midlands.[6]

Often at the start of settlement the physical need to collaborate in building new villages and in opening virgin land to cultivation, as well as the desire to keep church communities together, led to some form of communal cooperation. But frequently counterpressures in the end prevailed, and not always peaceably.[7]

A common experience was that of the village of Andover. Its founders were West Country men who devised an open-field system similar to what they had known in their earlier lives, and they imposed fines on people who moved away from the core settlement. But when some of the most influential of the original leaders died and newcomers arrived from enclosed regions of England, the controls were relaxed and the system was compromised—not fully, to a complete scattering of autonomous family farms, but to the distribution of parcels of land within several large divisions, each held privately by families whose residences remained in the central village while they farmed the outside fields. Then later, in the 1670s, the transition was completed when the villagers began relocating their residences out of the village to their distant farms.[8]

A more complex picture can be seen in the early years of the South Shore village of Hingham. Founded as Bear Cove by West Country men, it was soon populated overwhelmingly by East Anglians, most of them from Hingham, Norfolk. The town's agriculture came to resemble the "mixed system" of that East Anglian town: a scattering of private smallholdings in several fields and cooperative efforts in dairy farming and small-scale textile production. But the minority elements from the West Country and Midlands retained their own traditions of open-field agriculture, whose regulation fell naturally into the hands of the town's selectmen as custodians of the community's common obligations. For a decade, as new arrivals further complicated the picture, the town lived with the anomalies of its mingled traditions, until gradually the more abrasive differences softened, memories lost some of their grip, children of founding West Country families married East Anglians, and the scattering of autonomous farms began to form a pattern that to many of the rising generation seemed normal.[9]

It was a typical transition as regional differences melded into a common form. But in some places such a transition was long delayed, and in others it led to conflicts and community ruptures. The contrast between two immediately adjacent North Shore villages, Rowley and Ipswich, and the history of Watertown's offshoot Sudbury are exemplary of the varieties of ways that regional differences became absorbed into an emerging vernacular culture.

Rowley, Massachusetts, was a Yorkshire village, its "very laborious [industrious] people" drawn largely from the East Riding and led to New England by their imperious, exacting, stubborn, cantankerous, socially conservative preacher Ezekiel Rogers, the son of the charismatic Richard Rogers who had so intensified the Puritans' zeal. The Yorkshire villagers were conservative in their agricultural practices and quickly devised an open-field system in which most landholders had between seven and ten strips of land in several fields; their total allocations seldom exceeded twenty acres. Further divisions of the town's property were slow in coming, while Rogers battled with the General Court for the expansion of the town's boundaries. The system survived almost intact through the founding generation, partly because of the strength of the English inheritance, partly because of Rogers's fierce domination of the community ("I am the man who rules here," he was supposed to have said), and partly because of the villagers' youth. An estimated 90 percent of the original adult males were under forty upon arrival, 40 percent under thirty, hence few were in a position to challenge the system and the imperious Rogers's ideas until after his death in 1661. Rowley remained through those years a model not only of open-field farming in an ecologically complex situation but of the political and social characteristics commonly associated with it. Its town meeting met frequently and in effect assumed the role of a manorial court; the town's social order was stable and sharply stratified, with little outmigration; and there was little entrepreneurship despite the townsmen's English background in textile production.[10]

All of this was strikingly different from the lifeways of the adjoining village, Ipswich, presided over, briefly, by Rogers's lawyer-preacher stepbrother Nathaniel Ward, and then by his cousin Nathaniel Rogers.

Ipswich was an East Anglian village, its people drawn largely from the Winthrops' homeland of the Stour River area, the Suffolk and Essex border region that was involved, directly or indirectly, with overseas trade and the booming London food market. There, as opposed to what Cotton Mather called "those drowsy corners of the north," land values had soared and parcels were bought, sold, and exchanged in a constant flow of transactions. New England's Ipswich (originally Agawam) was established by the modernizing, enterprising John Winthrop, Jr., and from the start individual, enclosed farms were carved out of the large town grant (14,505 acres). The individual allotments averaged ninety-seven acres, quadruple the size of the average Rowley grants, and they became the basis of a lively market in land transactions, as parcels were exchanged, sold, and resold in full or in part. In this volatile real estate market Ipswich men filed 104 land deeds before 1660, over ten times the number filed in Rowley. More than half of the Ipswich deeds related to sales of town houses or house lots in the village, reflecting considerable mobility within the town. When parcels of farm land were sold, the average transaction involved twenty-nine acres; in Rowley the equivalent figure was slightly over six acres. By 1670 at least twenty-eight individuals in Ipswich had bought or sold parcels of over one hundred acres, and almost every one of these men had origin in Suffolk or the adjacent home counties.

In Ipswich, where most householders could claim considerable property, leadership was tied to wealth; crafts and commercial activities were actively promoted; and a wide economic disparity developed quickly. Ten percent of the original settlers came to control almost half of the town's wealth, the bottom 50 percent only 12 percent. And the same oligarchic tendency shaped the town's politics. The town was ruled not by a broadly representative, cooperative town meeting but by a small band of selectmen, and a few families dominated that elite group. Some selectmen in effect served for life; sixteen men held 62 percent of the positions on the board between 1636 and 1687; seven held almost 40 percent of the total.

Thus the differences in regional backgrounds between the adjacent towns of Rowley and Ipswich, separated by no more than fences, had dramatic consequences: in one, a cooperative community; in the other, a community of separate, enclosed farms quickly becoming competitive, volatile, and commercial. But however different they were, these patterns developed separately in the two towns, and neither was conflicted within itself. But where these divergent regional traditions came together within a single town, there were clashes, sometimes with splintering effect.[11]

Watertown, though initially led by the Yorkshireman Sir Richard

Saltonstall, his family, and his clients, was even more completely an East Anglian town than Ipswich. Almost all of its original people were derived from a thirty-five-mile-wide band from northern Essex to southern Suffolk, an area long since given over to enclosure and commercial farming. Since the town proved to be a staging area for incoming migrants of other backgrounds, all of them seeking land of their own, and since the General Court might well seek to create new towns out of existing grants, Watertown's allocation of 23,456 acres was threatened with subdivision. Resisting this danger to their interests, the founding proprietors in the course of six years granted over four-fifths of the entire township to themselves, thus closing off the possibility of having to share land in later divisions with ambitious newcomers of different views. The resulting family parcels were large, an average of 124 acres, and the proprietors quickly began the development of their handsome grants.

But if they controlled the land they could not control the inflow of migrants. By the late 1630s competitive claims by new arrivals were increasing, some by immigrants from open-field regions. Arguments arose between the establishment and the newcomers, tempers flared, and the protesters' numbers grew. When the proprietors held firm and denied the claimants satisfaction, the latter formed a founding group of their own and petitioned the General Court for a separate town where they could work out their own way of life. The result was the town of Sudbury, thirteen miles to the west, and there the potential for bitter discord between different lifestyles and different generations was fully realized.[12]

Sudbury's arrangements, by "joint consent," reflected those of the conservative open-field village of Sudbury, Suffolk. The size of each proprietor's holdings in each category—town lots, meadowland, arable—was determined by a scale of age, rank, and wealth, with grazing rights in the commons in the same proportion. Thus, typically, John Goodnow, an immigrant from the open-field village of Donhead St. Andrew, on the Wiltshire-Dorset borderland, had grants totalling ninety-one acres, but divided into eleven plots ranging in size from four and a half to twenty acres. He would travel eleven miles to collect the hay from his various meadow allotments.

For fifteen years—a time of initial land clearing and experimental crop regulation—the cooperative, interwoven open-field system held firm. There was general participation in the town meeting, from which flowed annual regulations determining grazing rights, the selection of fields for plowing and fallow, the types and location of fences, and the officials to supervise all of this work. And the townsmen conceded to the social hierarchy that was built into the system, according special deference to the authority of the town's preacher, Edmund Brown, a Cambridge graduate with fourteen years of experience in the church of Sudbury, Suffolk, and a man with a sharp eye for personal advantages in the life here below.

By the late 1640s, with the town's farmland expanding and the population growing, tremors of discontent were heard. There had always been a minority of East Anglian commercial farmers and enterprising tradesmen in the community, and now the founders' sons were reaching maturity. Many of them had no provision of land nor any prospect of it. When in 1649 the town acquired a new strip of land, 6,400 acres, the entire land policy came into question. Should the new plot be divided equally or follow the previous distribution system? The town split sharply on the question, with the younger generation and their sponsors favoring not only an equal division of the land but the building of an expensive new meetinghouse to accommodate the entire town in its increasingly contentious meetings. The two issues ignited passions; the town meetings were packed and acrimonious, with charges flying back and forth. Would access to the use of the undivided common land follow the formula of the original rankings, hence exclude the noisy protesters who were turning more and more toward a system of equal rights and enclosed farms? The struggle came to a head in an uproarious town meeting in which the town's "peace and comfort" were thoroughly "despoiled."

A spokesman for the protesters declared that the selectmen's position was sheer "oppression"; that when oppressed, the poor will certainly "cry out"; and prophetically, that "if you persecute us in one city, wee must fly to another." When a vote was taken on access to the commons, it was claimed that some of the votes, especially those of absentees who had contributed to the town's original expenses, were illegal, and that the conservative pastor, who had his own material interests to protect, had meddled too much in the process, thus dishonoring God and the ministry and hindering "the conversion and building up of souls." Ignoring the preacher's threat to return to England, the "expansionist" party in the town meeting purged the board of selectmen of the conservatives and voted to divide the new plot of land in equal lots, thus turning away from the long-established open-field system toward individual, competitive farming. The Reverend Brown, "with great violence," led the opposition to change and sought the support of an outside committee appointed by the General Court to look into the controversy. At the same time a self-appointed investigating committee of neighboring clergy met, despite the refusal of the town to cooperate with it. Undeterred, it issued a ten-point report charging the head of the "expansionists," John Ruddock, with nine violations of the fifth and ninth commandments, and with having committed "a great sin" in expunging a selectmen's order that had been reversed.

If Ruddock was disturbed by these charges there is no record of it; nor did he respond to Goodnow's declaration that "right or wrong" the old system would prevail, and that "if we can have it no other way, we will have it by club law." It did not come to physical violence, but the split was irrevocable, and the result was predictable. Ruddock and twelve others petitioned the General Court for their own township, supporting their appeal by reference to God's blessing in having increased the number of children to be provided for. With such an endorsement—and also with help from allies in the General Court—they succeeded. The new town, Marlborough, eight miles to the west, proved to be an "East Anglian suburb" of Sudbury, in which all the constraints of Sudbury's open-field system were cast off.[13]

THIS COMMUNITY GENEALOGY—Watertown begetting Sudbury begetting Marlborough—is an example of a process at work in the European resettlement of New England. Everywhere in the open countryside there were conflicts stemming from differences in background cultures. And everywhere generational phasing was crucial. Where the initial settlers were young, as in Rowley, the earlier English practices were likely to persist; where the founders were older, the transition was often quicker, as successors soon took control and fell more readily into the emerging pattern of scattered independent family farms.

But the process was irregular, jolted by disputes and confusions. It would be three generations before the pattern of individual, enclosed farms fully evolved. Anomalies in fact survived into the eighteenth century—vestiges of fading memories and peculiar circumstances. But the normalization into a world of independent family farms was irresistible, driven by the universal passion for privately held and independently worked land, despite the inherited constraints that worked against it.[14]

2

But another divisive force was at work as well—a force so powerful that it threatened to destroy New England's fragile, still-forming community life. In the region's open countryside, Puritanism's turbulent inner core of radical potentialities, which had been constrained in the struggle for survival in England, burst out toward what for some was ultimate perfection, for others anarchic degradation.

No more in New England than in old England was there a well-defined original Puritan "orthodoxy," an accepted configuration of Puritan thought and church polity from which deviation could be measured and by which dissent might be controlled. If in New England there were to be a Puritan orthodoxy against which dissent could be defined, it would have to be constructed and fought for against competing strains. And in fact there never would be an uncontested orthodoxy. From the start and for the three decades that followed, New England was a scene of conflicting enthusiasms, a hothouse of holy rage, as Puritanism's inner force, in Edmund Morgan's phrase, "hurl[ed] itself outward to its ultimate limits." The struggles were fierce and unending. Not a year went by in the lifetime of Winthrop's generation when the moderate majority was not under assault by radical dissenters, perfectionists of one sort or another who fought against the compromises of an emerging orthodoxy. By the time New England's delicately balanced moderate Congregationalism was established, it could no longer exclude all other strains, and its inner contradictions were leading to its own declension.[15]

How far the ultimate limits of Puritanism could stray from respectable religion and ordinary civility, how close to the abyss of chaos a society in which religion was the source of morality and order, could be seen in the elemental fears of the colony's leaders. Though there were differences among them on precise points of doctrine and church organization, they shared the fear that the fierce passion for spiritual satisfaction and the irrepressible antiauthoritarianism that lay at the heart of Puritanism might erupt into wild, destructive excesses: of "Familism," antipedobaptism, "Fifth Monarchy" anarchy, radical spiritism, and a pervasive antinomianism that would lead God-besotted enthusiasts to all kinds of "phanatic doctrines and practises." Though they could not have anticipated how in England these impulses would soon produce the Leveller, Ranter, and Digger movements and the radical sectarianism that would threaten to turn English society upside down, they were haunted by the common memory of the devastation of Münster a century earlier, when tens of thousands of Anabaptist zealots, led by a Dutch tailor who claimed authority direct from God, had instituted rule by the saints, abolished property, and sanctioned polygamy—only to be slaughtered en masse by enraged armies encouraged by Luther himself. To mention Germany, or Münster, in the context of religious extremism and possible revelations from God was to conjure up scenes of social turmoil, ultimately carnage. The colony's leaders were certain that the integument of civility that stretched over the turmoils of religious passions was thin and easily ruptured, and when that happened—when people's passions erupted into civil strife—when as Winthrop put it, the sword of spirit turned into the sword of steel—the result was "always . . . tragicall and bloudy." Practical men of affairs like Winthrop and Dudley, however devout, were determined somehow, while establishing a devotional community, to rein in such excesses before they became dangerous.[16]

But how could they? Where was the line between dangerous fanaticism and benevolent zeal? Once Puritanism was released from traditional ecclesiastical and social constraints, an inexorable logic took over that could sweep one through deepening stages of sectarian radicalism. The transition points in this surging process were subtle. To stop the logical flow from benign reform to chaotic excess that might lead to "German" devastation would take intellectual skills of a high order; and in the end, if dialectical power and persuasion failed to keep New England from degenerating into "a Colluvies [filth pit] of wild Opinionists," responsible authorities would have to resort to force, despite the fact that, as England would soon discover, coercion brought with it the likelihood of civil war.[17]

Therefore, the colony's moderate leaders argued: start at the beginning. Keep the dangerous zealots from entering the City on the Hill. But there was no way of identifying in advance the bearers of dangerous doctrines and prevent them from migrating to the Puritan refuge. Most of those who would soon be condemned as malignant sectarians—advocates of what Ezekiel Rogers called "Base Opinnions" and "Phrenticke dotages" whom God would undoubtedly "cause to be as doung on the earth"; people, Peter Bulkely wrote, with "itching eares, itching mindes, and itching tongues also, itching to be . . . venting novelties"—such dangerous dissidents differed at the start from the moderate Puritan mainstream only by their temperament, their emotional susceptibilities, or the intensity of their spiritual needs.[18]

It was into the controls of a nascent centrist system, still theoretically within the Church of England, that the cautious leadership of the early 1630s, both lay and clerical, sought to channel unbounded religious enthusiasms of all kinds. Their aim was to create autonomous, disciplined congregations of visible saints within the ostensible purview of the Church of England—groups of individuals who could convincingly testify to an experience of saving grace but who would nevertheless commit themselves in their piety to worship and behave according to the dictates of the clergy and accepted norms of conduct. But for some this was an illogical and indefensible compromise, and it came under attack even before it was fully formulated. In fact the ultimate definition of New England's moderate Congregationalism was in part the product of efforts to deflect the forces of extremism and reinforce the system at its most vulnerable points. The major dissidents began by concentrating on specific fault lines within the emerging system, and then swept on to what were for many strange and disturbing conclusions.

THE FIRST TO CAUSE serious concern was Roger Williams, one of the most respected and learned but in some ways the most dangerous of all those who challenged New England's emerging system. The ultimate source of Williams's stubborn individualism, his utter refusal to compromise with what he saw as the truth, and the creative imagination that led him to anticipate a liberalism in human relations that would become publicly acceptable only generations later, had first appeared in the "godly terrorism" he had visited on the distraught Lady Barrington. By his mid-twenties he had clearly developed into a stubborn personality, assertive, self-confident, imaginative, and yet attractive to almost everyone who knew him ("a man lovely in his carriage"), though insensitive to the consequences of his actions as he followed out the logic of his principles wherever they might lead.

Williams's spiky, uncompromising assertiveness (some in New England would call him "selfe-willed," others "self-conceited, unquiet, turbulent, and uncharitable," a man of "unmoveable stiffnesse" of spirit) became notorious almost from the moment he landed in Massachusetts. On his arrival early in 1631, he was quickly offered the leadership post of teacher in the Boston church, which he just as quickly declined.

For however independent of the Church of England the Boston church was, and however reformed its worship, it was still officially and in principle "non-separating," hence ostensibly Anglican. For Williams, "non-separating congregationalism" was the devil's work—a dishonest dodge to have things both ways. The English Church had never, he believed, thrown off its quasi-papist past. It was still a "national" institution, comprehensive in its inclusion of sinners as well as saints. It had a bureaucratic hierarchy, the very opposite of the simple, independent, humble apostolic congregations of his yearnings. Its preachers were appointed by religious and secular authorities, not elected by autonomous worshippers. Its discipline lay in the hands of ecclesiastical courts he believed to be corrupt, not congregational communities. It forbade emotional prophesyings of lay preachers—the untutored voices of the authentically redeemed. Above all, it made no attempt to identify the visible church here below with God's invisible church of the saved; and in addition, it glittered with the false gold of worldly wealth and power. Not only, Williams argued, should proper congregations of visible saints separate themselves from this contaminated institution, but they should publicly declare their separation from it and express remorse for ever having been associated with it.[19]

Winthrop and the church leaders were shocked by Williams's extremism and fearful that his zeal would bring their fragile refuge to ruin. But they could not ignore the logic of his argument—its consistency, as opposed to the compromise they had made based on the convenience of the colony's geographical removal; and they recognized therefore the likelihood that others, perhaps many others, would respond to Williams's arguments and form a bloc of dissidents. They knew the dangers of separatism. They knew the grim fate of such zealots of Elizabethan separatism as Robert Browne and his followers, whose spirit had lived on into their own time; and they knew too that "Brownist" separatism was the kind of disorder that opened one up to all sorts of other, malignant diseases. To be sure, the neighboring Pilgrims' religious community was ostensibly separatist, but it had never been rigorously so, and for the Puritans it constituted no threat. Elsewhere, though, scattered throughout the region and in process of immigration, were others inclined to more rigorous separatist views. The largest group was in Salem, under the tutelage of the Rev. Samuel Skelton, and it was to Salem, therefore, that Williams moved once he had burned his bridges in Boston.

He had been called by the Salemites to consider appointment as the teacher in their church. Once there he immediately raised the question of separatism, but before any conclusion could be reached the General Court warned Salem of the danger Williams represented, and the appointment failed. Williams thereupon moved off to Plymouth, where his "strange opinions" and unwelcome "admonitions and reproofs" quickly led to his departure. In 1633, he returned to Salem and accepted appointment as assistant pastor, convinced that many there agreed with his views.[20]

In the two years that followed, Williams's opinions grew into what the Massachusetts authorities considered a tangle of poisonous weeds. Stirring up a separatist revival among the East Anglians in that divided community, he challenged the validity of the colony's charter, hence its right to the Indians' land; he denied that civil authorities had any right to enforce the first four commandments; he denied the validity of loyalty oaths administered to unregenerate men by government since it involved the wicked in the works of God; he denied too the propriety of a man's worshipping with an unregenerate wife; and following the dictum of Salem's preacher Skelton, he insisted that women wear veils in public "under penalty of non-communion, urging the same as a matter of duty and absolute necessity." And indeed, "through his and others' influence, veils were worn here abundantly," until Cotton, visiting Salem, declared the custom "not to be tolerated," and Winthrop, when the issue got to Boston, "interposed and so brake it off."[21]

But veils were the least of the problems. The clerical establishment challenged Williams on all the major points, summoned him again and again to defend himself before the General Court, and finally, in 1635, banished him from the colony and ordered him to return to England. But he eluded the colony's agents, and after spending a bitter winter in an Indian camp, he drew together his family and a small group of followers and with them opened a new settlement on the shores of Narragansett Bay.

Williams's radicalism, emerging from his critical separatist views, continued to deepen and to be the center of fierce debate. By 1638 he had embraced Anabaptism, the baptism not of infants but of adults, which he insisted followed logically from the Puritans' own belief that that sacrament should be enjoyed only by those who consciously experienced and fully understood the experience of saving grace. Associated with the "German" upheavals and anathema to the Bay Colony authorities,

Anabaptism spread throughout the Narragansett area and beyond, into Massachusetts, where by 1644 it was considered so great a threat that its advocates were banished from the land. Who could doubt the dangers of the spread of this contamination? Not only had Anabaptists long been known as "incendiaries of Common-wealths & the Infectors of . . . religion & the Troubles of Churches," but they "usually held other errors or heresies" which they hid "until they espied a fit advantage." There was no knowing how far this infection might spread: it could reach to challenges to constituted law, to the right to make war, to the enforcement of the first table of the Decalogue. No one, it seemed, was immune. In 1654 the president of Harvard College resigned his post when, after deep and troubled study of the subject and despite labored discussions with his fellow ministers, he decided he could no longer deny the logic of the Baptists' position. By then, despite the fact that Anabaptism had been banned by law for a decade, there were at least twenty-six known cases of Baptist conversion in the Bay Colony.[22]

But even Anabaptism proved to be but a transition for Williams in his relentless and fiercely logical pursuit of the ultimate form of apostolic Puritanism. Leaving both separatism and Anabaptism behind, he swept on to the absolute resolution of his struggle against impediments to true religion. In the end he abandoned all institutional worship, however simple, prayed alone, or privately with his wife, and immersed himself in the primitive world around him—the "natural" world of the Narragansett Indians, his closest neighbors. Contrary to almost all other observers, he found among these "wild Americans . . . a savor of civilitie" superior to the ways of the "civiliz'd world," a discovery that became the source of the extended meditations on the Indians' natural humanity, the common nature of all mankind, and the sinfulness of ostensible Christians which he included in the "observations" in his Indian phrasebook, *A Key into the Language of America* (1643).

Yet while Williams—sympathetic to the Indians' civility, ruthlessly logical, incapable of compromise with his vision of the primitive church—was forever the subject of bitter condemnation, he was always personally respected. Winthrop himself had assisted him in his escape from Massachusetts, and in his trips to England to gain legal protection for Rhode Island he immediately became a consultant to the heads of the Commonwealth government, and entered into discussion with John Milton and his associates. In fact it was his respectability, his dignified "carriage," and his skill in debate that made him so menacing to the Puritan establishment. Had he been crude, ignorant, or deliberately bent on the destruction of the Bible Commonwealth he might have been easier to deal with. Even his ultimate, most heretical argument, for full liberty of conscience and the free practice of religious professions—a position for which posterity would honor him but for which contemporaries almost universally condemned him—deserved and received formal debate. For however subversive of the Puritan leaders' vision Williams may have been, however "divinely mad" he may have been considered and "beside himself" from too much zeal and learning, he was one of them—well educated, well connected, and rational. No such feelings were extended to most of the other Rhode Island factionalists who challenged the Bay Colony's principles and practices, least of all Samuel Gorton.[23]

A CLOTHIER BY TRADE, without formal education but steeped in the half-mystical, fiercely antiauthoritarian, and recondite theology of London's underground extremists, Gorton arrived in Boston in 1637 and immediately began his contemptuous challenge to the colony's establishment. "Warm-hearted, hot-tempered, energetic, irrepressibly cocksure and jaunty, pugnacious, endowed with a scathing humor and political horse sense, capable of attracting passionate disciples . . . and given to spending hours in meditation and religious ecstasy," he was no rational explorer of Puritanism's inner logic and of the Bible's dicta. For him the Puritans' delicate theory of nonseparating Congregationalism was the duplicitous invention of an overeducated social elite intent on enhancing its power and wealth at the expense of ordinary souls. What mattered were none of the bookish clerisy's subtle deductions and complicated institutions but the pulsations of Christ's animating presence within every believing being. "*We are complete in Christ,*" Gorton declared: through Christ's indwelling presence we hear God's voice daily; we are bound not to any law or any magistrate's rule but only to the Holy Spirit within. There could be no differences between saints and sinners: the concept of "sin" itself was but a link in the chain of oppression imposed by those in power. All the niggling restrictions designed by learned priests should be eliminated. Anyone—male or female, ignorant or informed—could properly preach; a learned ministry was superfluous, and parochial boundaries meaningless. All that mattered was that "God is *all in all* in every one of the Saints," and those who disagreed were consumed by the Antichrist, chief among whom were the colony's leading magistrates. Winthrop himself was but an "Idol General."[24]

This, the authorities agreed, was blatant anarchy drawn from the dark, submerged recesses of Puritan lore. Not merely defiant of everything that was holy, Gorton's views were destructive of civil order. A priesthood of all believers each "complete in Christ" would surely be a jungle where "every Christian . . . must be King, and Judge, and Sheriffe, and Captaine." A literal equality of men? Everyone knew the obvious good sense of Winthrop's words, that God had ordained that "some must be rich some poore, some highe and eminent in power and dignitie, others meane and in subieccion." There would be no mercy for Gorton and his anarchic band of like-minded spiritists.

Within a year he was hounded out of Plymouth for encouraging lay preaching, defying the authorities, and proclaiming the universality of the indwelling Holy Spirit. He fled first to Aquidneck (Portsmouth), one of Rhode Island's multiplying settlements of Bay Colony refugees. But the dissidents there, while rebellious too in their ultra-Puritanism, were led by William Coddington, a Lincolnshire gentleman versed in law and practiced in commerce, who had been a magistrate in Massachusetts and the colony's treasurer. For Coddington's respectable if radical villagers, Gorton, the self-styled "professor of the mysteries of Christ," in direct communion with the Holy Spirit, was a dangerous crank capable of creating anarchy within dissent. For his seditious behavior he was whipped and banished from the town. He and his small, faithful band, still enthralled by their leader's charismatic ecstasies, then fled to Williams's tolerant Providence, but they found no welcome there either once they began their "bewitching and bemadding" of the local population. In the end the Gortonites—full-blown spiritists determined to live by their leader's passionate teachings—settled in a primitive clearing on a tract called Shawomet, which they purchased from the Indians.[25]

But there was no peace for such as they. The Indians challenged the zealots' claim to the land, and the nearby settlers, themselves exiles from ordered society but intolerant of strange and quarrelsome neighbors, were so disturbed by Gorton's preaching and bizarre behavior that they called on Boston's authorities for help. A military guard was forthwith sent to disarm and capture the troublesome band. Its members were brought to trial in Boston and convicted of "horrible and detestable blasphemies against God, and all Magistracie." Some were dismissed with warnings, but Gorton and his chief associates were distributed among the towns to work in shackles at hard labor. There they remained, committed to wear "an iron chaine upon one leg," and not "by word or writing to maintaine any of their blasphemous or wicked errours upon paine of death." After four months, however, concern for their wives and children, and even more for reactions at home, led to the commutation of their sentences to banishment. Shipped off to England, they were warned that if they ever returned they would suffer "death by course of lawe."[26]

But there would be no riddance of this bristling spiritist and his notorious troop. England in the mid-1640s was no longer the world Winthrop had left. Puritan reformers of one sort or another were now in charge, and in its triumph the defiant movement that the New Englanders had once shared at their peril had produced strange, exotic fruit. For four years Gorton immersed himself in London's perfervid sectarian underground, preaching universal salvation to the General Baptists in the Bell Alley conventicle of the Leveller Thomas Lamb and sharing the pulpit with inspired enthusiasts, male and female. By the time he returned to New England in 1648, he was a veteran exhorter of "illiterate mechanicks" and a fiery pamphleteer; his antiauthoritarianism and his hatred of book learning and of an educated, ordained ministry had been heightened by his encounters with London's Levellers and Ranters. Bearing a letter from the Earl of Warwick that gave him safe passage through Massachusetts, he rejoined his parishioners in his Rhode Island village, now called Warwick, and there he remained, firing off blistering pamphlets for publication in London and preaching, as an instrument of the Holy Spirit, "such a luminous understanding of God as to pass beyond human comprehension."

By then Rhode Island was confirmed in the Puritans' mind as "a cesspool of vile heresies and irreligion" whose foul waters were seeping constantly northward. Williams and Gorton, united, if in nothing else, in their dissociation of church and state, had long since been joined by other dissident bands—William Aspinwall's Biblicist utopia in Aquidneck, and John Clarke's "Particular" Baptists in Newport, convinced that only some would ever be saved. Like Coddington's people, they were refugees from, victims of, the explosive struggle to establish and secure the Bay Colony's moderate Congregationalism.[27]

3

In its origins that great effort, inflamed by its involvement with a genocidal racial war, arose in effect from the basic differences in theological
and ecclesiastical principles between John Cotton's and Thomas Hooker's approaches to Puritan theology, which had been developing latently
in the years before their emigration. Once released in New England, the
disagreements quickly escalated and acquired hard, abrasive lines. Before
the controversy had run its course, it would split Boston's small community and much of the rest of New England into warring factions, disrupt
congregations and alienate them from their pastors, and generate bitter
personal confrontations.

That these disagreements would become conflicts that would dominate religious life in New England might have been predicted, but the
savagery of the struggle, the bitterness of the main contenders, and the
deep stain it left on the region's collective memory could not have been.
For the Antinomian Controversy evoked elemental fears peculiar to what
was experienced as a barbarous environment—fears of what could happen
to civilized people in an unimaginable wilderness and fears of racial conflicts in which God's children were fated to struggle with pitiless agents of
Satan, pagan Antichrists swarming in the world around them.[28] The two
were one: threats from within merged with threats from without to form
a heated atmosphere of apocalyptic danger.

AT THE START Cotton was the major figure in the emerging conflict.
Famous as he was, he quickly became a leader in the new Boston, and as
teacher of the town's First Church, he began in sermons to expound his
views. Neither a relentless theo-logician like Williams nor a passionate
spiritist like Gorton but a mild-tempered, left-leaning moderate, he was
more responsive than most to the belief in the unmediated grace of God,
to the idea of Christ as the gentle bridegroom who would of his own
benevolence shed "the seeds of his grace" into passive, receptive hearts.
Slowly, as Cotton found his authentic voice in New England's unconfined
environment, the peculiar slant of his views became more pronounced,
and some began to detect disturbing implications in his preaching. Was
he not suggesting an immediacy of God's presence that might bypass
both the church's mediation and the necessary labor of preparation, the
personal striving for sanctity appropriate for one's redemption? Did this

renowned preacher mean to trivialize the Bible's Word and destroy the
efficacy of both church and clergy? Was his preaching not implicitly antinomian, even potentially anarchic? Preparationists like Hooker and his
future son-in-law Thomas Shepard, who were devoted to an elaborately
articulated, multistage process of conversion and the clergy's powerful
role in it, sensed danger below the surface of Cotton's sermons and cautiously began an inquiry.[29]

It started privately, early in 1636, with a tightly written, probing letter from Shepard to Cotton. Was Cotton, Shepard asked, not separating
the inner assurance of redemption from the outward signs of piety and
behavioral sanctity? Was not the personal revelation he extolled "a thing
beyond and above the woord [of the Bible]"? Even the Familists, Shepard
pointed out, those devilish Dutch mystics "Godded with God," whose
"glorious estate of perfection" had once attracted Shepard himself—even
they respected the Bible as a necessary guide to redemption. A quick
reply to these queries, Shepard wrote, would be important, for while he,
Shepard, had no intention of beginning a quarrel with the revered Cotton, there were others whose secret suspicions "I feare will flame out
unles they be quenched in time."[30]

Cotton lost no time in replying. He hoped to avoid all "differences,
and jarres," he wrote, "especially with Brethren," but in fact he saw none
in what Shepard had written. It was simply "misexpression" on his part,
he wrote, or "misconstruction, or misreport" by others. Some of the
views attributed to him he had in fact actively opposed. Redemption, he
wrote, was indeed beyond human striving, beyond institutions, works,
or sheer effort. What was essential and only essential was to "close with
Christ." Did true redemption therefore nullify the importance of pious
behavior? Not quite: sanctified behavior was necessary too, but it was
secondary evidence of redemption. Could the redeemed not sin? They
could, but if God's true children fell into "divers grosse, and scandalous
sinnes" while claiming God's fatherly love, surely the effect would be to
renew the doubts of these "gracious" people about the state of their souls.

> I would not wish christians to build the signes of their Adoption upon
> [any] sanctification but such as floweth from faith in christ jesus; for all
> other holynesse and righteousnes . . . may be . . . a [mere] mortall seede
> and fall short of perseverance: whereas the least seede of fayth, and of
> that holynes which floweth from it, abideth for ever.

Have no fear, Cotton concluded. So long as we understand each other it will be clear that there are no real differences between us. And if he were truly in error, "God forbid I should shutt mine eyes against it."[31]

It was a vigorous reply, but subtle—for some, too subtle. The distinctions were fine and the metaphors elegant, but Cotton's meaning remained elusive. Where would his beliefs lead? Were there no steps to the altar? How might such ideas affect less scrupulous thinkers than he? Perhaps, given the shadings and complexities of his thought, he himself might maintain a "semi-Familist" position without falling into antinomianism or worse, but could others, his disciples, maintain the same discipline? Doubts grew, and deepened.

In May, with Cotton still under suspicion, Wheelwright arrived in the colony. A vigorous, bold, uncompromising man whose athleticism was remarked on, he was proposed for appointment as coteacher with Cotton in the Boston church. But was his theology sound? There were serious doubts. His "spirit," Winthrop recorded, "they knew not," and what was known of his technical views—that, for example, a true believer actually unites with the Holy Ghost and becomes, like Christ, more than a simple creature—was disturbing. Was this not a doctrine that excluded the church and ethical striving? Wheelwright's appointment failed.[32]

At the same time another of Cotton's zealous followers, Anne Hutchinson, came under deep suspicion. She had arrived in 1634 carrying with her a passion for Cotton's teachings and the reputation of a busy "lay prophesier." Supremely self-confident, worldly wise, and learned in theological discourse, she suffered, Winthrop wrote, from "two dangerous errors: 1. That the person of the Holy Ghost dwells in a justified person. 2. That no sanctification [behavior, piety, zeal] can help to evidence to us our justification." Together these views could form a node of malignancy that Winthrop and the clerical establishment feared might spread wildly and with deadly effect.[33]

By the fall of 1636 their fears seemed to be realized as Hutchinson, inspired and oblivious to external authority, cultivated the familiar practice of gathering together groups of women to discuss recent sermons, she presiding "(gravely) sitting in the chaire" and commenting freely. At first these meetings could be excused as an extension of her role as midwife and herbalist, and her opinions did not appear to be dangerous. But soon her constituency broadened to include men, and as Winthrop noted with alarm, she was presiding over two "public lectures" each week attended by sixty to eighty devotees who appeared to support her increasingly strident condemnation of all the clergy but Cotton for preaching a covenant of works, not grace.

By October word of these teachings had circulated widely, and when the colony's ministers gathered for the General Court's meeting they held a private session with Cotton, Wheelwright, and Hutchinson. Cotton, ever conciliatory, "gave satisfaction." But Wheelwright and Hutchinson, while conceding that sanctification "did help to evidence justification," stuck to their belief in the "indwelling of the person of the Holy Ghost," to the extent, in Hutchinson's view, of "a personal union."[34]

This was no satisfaction. While Cotton's parishioners became more and more excited in their "free grace" enthusiasms, conservatives like Winthrop and Boston's pastor, the Rev. John Wilson, felt more embattled, and the clergy elsewhere were increasingly convinced that they were faced with nothing less than a "Familist" upsurge in Boston that would blast away the theory and practice of preparatory stages toward redemption and end all respect for customary norms and the law and authority of both church and state. By December, with the young, emotional governor Henry Vane, respectable as the son of the comptroller of the king's household but close to Cotton in his theology, threatening to leave the colony if the "free grace" views were not endorsed, a formal clerical convocation was summoned to settle the disputed issues.

The December 1636 meeting of the colony's elders was a formal board of inquiry, and they issued to Cotton a list of sixteen interrogatories probing his views once more and requesting "humbly and earnestly" that he return "a short and plaine Answer."[35]

An answer they soon did receive, but it was neither short nor plain. To explain whether the doctrine of sanctification was or was not "a Covenant of Works" (question XIII) required an answer of seven complex "propositions," in all some five thousand words. When the elders sorted through this tangle, they conceded that "some doubts [were] well cleared," but others were not. So they went at it again, replying point by point in some six thousand words to Cotton's responses, which in turn elicited a final rejoinder by Cotton. This document was a virtual treatise of some twenty-seven thousand words that stretches over seventy-two pages in modern print and includes references not only to innumerable biblical passages but to the writings of Calvin, Piscator, Foxe, Ames, Perkins, Augustine, and the Catholic controversialists Catharinus and Bellarmine.

How convincing all this was to the elders is not clear, but by late January 1637 the troubles had escalated. On the nineteenth of the month, Wheelwright struck out boldly in a Fast Day sermon aflame with violent language. Christ's own people, he declared, those under a covenant of grace, base their faith on direct revelation; those who do not, those whose faith rests on behavioral sanctification and contractual relations with God, no matter how holy their behavior, were under a covenant of works and therefore ultimately enemies of true religion. They were, in fact, he declared with rising passion, nothing less than partisans of the Antichrist, and therefore it was the obligation of the children of God to take up arms against them. There would be—there would have to be— a decisive struggle between them. God's true, "graceful" children must have their "loynes girt and be redy to fight" for Christ. Despite the odds, true Christians "must lay load" upon the unredeemed: "we must kill them with the word of the Lord . . . breake them in peeces as shivered with a rod of yron." Truth cannot prevail by "peace and quietnes . . . we must be willing to lay downe our lives, and shall overcome by so doing." Thus "Moses seeing an Egiptian striving with his brother, he came and killed him. Acts 7.24.25.26."

But will this not cause "a combustion in the Church and comon wealth"? Yes, Wheelwright declared, but "never feare combustions and burnings." For Christ came "to send fire upon the earth," and as it is prophesied in Malachi 4.1, "the day shall come that shall burne like an oven and all that do wickedly shall be stubble." "The whore must be burnt, Revelation 18.8." Nothing else will serve the Lord: "this way must Antichrist be consumed."[36]

It was a sweeping and portentous judgment. Not only was Wheelwright condemning the entire magistracy and all the clergy save Cotton, but he seemed also to be threatening some kind of violent action. Was he not stirring up another Münster? Later he would insist that he had been speaking only of spiritual combat and that his language was figurative. But some did not take it so. The Rev. Thomas Weld, introducing Winthrop's summary account of the antinomian struggle (his *Short Story*, 1644), epitomized the common clerical reaction. Wheelwright, Weld wrote, spoke for those who sought "a faire and easie way to Heaven, that men may passe without difficulty," and who would live without law or concern for sin or prayer. His sermon cast dung on the clergy; it was as if he had discharged "halfe a dozen pistols" at their faces. And beyond even that, he was urging violence. He may have spoken in figurative terms of spiritual not physical combat, but Münster proved how close the two in fact were. And—Weld added in a sentence that went to the heart of the deepest anxieties at work—"We had great cause to have feared the extremity of danger from them, in case power had beene in their hands."

Winthrop's attack was even more severe and his language, usually moderate, more vivid. Wheelwright, he wrote, claimed that all who disagreed with him on the path to salvation were Antichrists, Herods, Pilates, and persecuting Jews; and in his Fast Day sermon, he had urged his followers "to fight with [their opponents], to lay load on them, to burne them, to thresh them, to bind them in chaines and fetters, to kill them and vexe their hearts," and those who refused to get involved would suffer the "paine of the curse of *Meroz.*" Wheelwright might have spoken spiritually, but he should have known "how dangerous it is to heat peoples affections against their opposites." The bloody wars in Germany may have originated in different beliefs, but the sword of spirit had turned into the sword of steel. So it had been in Switzerland, in the Netherlands, and between Calvinists and Lutherans. Such violence might be reasonable in confronting Turks or papists, but those who opposed Wheelwright were Christian compatriots sharing in the establishment of this Puritan refuge. There could be no doubt about it: Wheelwright "did intend to trouble our peace, and hee hath effected it." "All things are turned upside down among us"—the church, family, decorum, even civil order.[37]

4

And in this Wheelwright was not alone. Others too were disturbing the peace with even more blatant violence. His inflammatory sermon, all fire and combat, came at a time when troops were being assembled in Connecticut and Massachusetts to put down the Pequot Indians and their allies, and these, everyone knew, were truly agents of the Antichrist. They fought like beasts, they were both cowardly and merciless, and despite the offering of Christian redemption, they remained irremediably pagan. Their ferocity had been mounting. Skirmishes with the settlers were commonplace, and in 1634 the Indian trader Capt. John Stone and his crew had been murdered along the Connecticut River. Though in life something of a miscreant—privateer, smuggler, drunkard, and adulterer—who had been banished from the Bay Colony, Stone had become notable in his death, which the Puritans were determined to avenge. More recently the more respectable Capt. John Oldham was murdered and partly dismembered by the Narragansetts on Block Island, precisely when doubts about Cotton and Wheelwright were beginning to disturb the colony. An expedition to the island (August 1636) to revenge Oldham's murder failed, but news of bloody attacks continued, and fears grew that the Pequots, who refused to give up Stone's murderers, were planning an attack. In October, just when the first of the clerical confrontations with Cotton took place, word reached Boston of the fate of the river trader Joseph Tilly. The Pequots had captured him and had "tied him to a stake, flayed his skin off, put hot embers between the flesh and the skin, cut off his fingers and toes, and made hatbands of them." Somehow, in agony, he had survived for three days, yet, Winthrop proudly noted, "he cried not in his torture." Surely, the Puritan Capt. John Underhill wrote, this barbarous cruelty was enough to move "the hearts of men to hazard blood, and life, and all they had, to overcome such a wicked, insolent nation."

The savagery of the Indians, undoubtedly in league with Satanic powers, and the challenge of the antinomians, Shepard would later recall, were conjoined in their malevolence. Both were manifestations of the Antichrist. They rose together, he noted, and in the end they were doomed to fall together. And both reached climaxes in 1637. In February there were more bloody encounters, this time at the fort in Saybrook, Connecticut—half a dozen settlers badly wounded by arrows; hand-to-hand combat in a tangle of burning weeds; captures and torture; and from the Indians, taunting defiance: we can blot out Englishmen like mosquitoes and will "kill men, women, and children, and we will take away the horses, cows, and hogs."[38]

By March, when from without the very existence of the settlements seemed to be threatened, from within the foundations of civil life were under withering attack. The erosive effects of Wheelwright's and Hutchinson's preaching were spreading. Preachers in Boston and elsewhere were being condemned as "legalists" and their ordinations shunned. Church services were being interrupted by questions of the soundness of the ministers' views; similar challenges were beginning to disturb town meetings; cordial personal relationships were turning rancorous. And the newborn civil state was in turmoil. Governor Vane entered the struggle directly, challenging Winthrop's argument that banishing the likes of Wheelwright from the colony was justified, indeed necessary. Surely,

Winthrop declared, "we are bound to keepe off whatsoever appears to tend to our ruine or damage" and may therefore "refuse to receive such whose dispositions suite not with ours and whose society (we know) will be hurtfull to us." If, he said, the laws were made specifically to exclude "such as are of Mr. Wheelwright his judgment . . . where is the evill of it?" The magistrates must have the right to keep out those whose opinions "cannot stand with externall peace" and who would "infect others with such dangerous tenets . . . and make people looke at their magistrates, ministers and brethren as enemies to Christ and [therefore] Antichrists."

But note the effect, Vane replied. Such exclusionary laws would reject not the profane but "those, that are truly and particularly religious, if the magistrates doe not like them." And furthermore no such power of exclusion is given by the colony's royal charter, and so the banishment of preachers like Wheelwright was not sanctioned by either king or God.

But in the end Winthrop and his associates prevailed. At the March meeting of the General Court Wheelwright was convicted of seditious contempt of authority and fomenting discord, and he was ordered upon sentencing to leave the colony.[39]

The community was sundered—split as if, Winthrop wrote, "between Protestants and Papists." And the tumult did not subside. At the Court of Elections in May Vane brought forward a petition on Wheelwright's behalf and, fearful of losing a majority in the Court, insisted that it be heard before the election votes were cast. Winthrop's supporters, who expected to prevail in the new election, objected and left the meeting-house in protest. Congregated out of doors, they were urged on by the Rev. John Wilson (aloft in a tree, it was said). The votes were cast. Winthrop's group swept the offices, and Winthrop himself resumed the governorship. Vane and his supporters were defeated, but not persuaded or eliminated. They withdrew, Winthrop correctly noted, only because they were outnumbered. The scars were deep. The colony, barely a half-dozen years old, had split into bitterly warring parties whose differences had produced not only "fierce speeches" but riot. Some, Winthrop recorded, "laid hands on others."[40]

VIOLENCE, IT SEEMED, was everywhere. In April word arrived that the Pequots had attacked Wethersfield, Connecticut, killed nine men and women and several animals, and abducted two young girls. At the end of May the colony's leaders, having succeeded for a time in putting down the enemy within, turned to the enemies without, with results that could properly be called apocalyptic.

The recruitment of troops had proceeded in both Connecticut and Massachusetts, though claims were made that Wheelwright's and Hutchinson's challenges to the authority of church and state had reduced recruitment in Boston to a trickle. Massachusetts, with a hundred or more Narragansett allies and a small troop of militia soldiers under Capt. John Underhill, and Connecticut with a similar number under Capt. John Mason, another veteran of the continental wars, took the battle to the enemy. After a series of treks and feints, the Pequots retreated to an earth-and-timber fort in Mystic, Connecticut, and there the English, ninety in all, surrounded the inhabitants—not warriors alone but several hundred men, women, and children. Surely "the Finger of God" was in all this, Mason later wrote. For the situation was perfectly prepared for what Shepard called a "divine slaughter." The English cut their way through the tree branches that blocked the entrances, and then, convinced that they must "burn them," set the brush huts and timbered walls afire and stationed men at the exits to kill anyone who attempted to escape. In what Mason called the "dreadful Terror" that followed, those who ran back, away from the English, went straight "into the very Flames, where many of them perished," while those who fled through the exits—forty, Mason estimated—"perished by the Sword." Thus God's judgment: "in little more than one Hour's space was their impregnable Fort with themselves utterly Destroyed, to the number of six or seven hundred."

There was something strangely ecstatic, trance-like, in the soldiers' experience, something mystical and transcendent. "We were like Men in a Dream," Mason wrote, "then was our Mouth filled with Laughter, and our Tongues with Singing; thus we may say the Lord hath done great Things for us among the Heathen, whereof we are glad. Praise ye the Lord!"[41] Underhill was equally transported, equally entranced with the ways of God's vengeance against evil. But he knew enough about warfare to recognize the Indians' bravery, so he felt the need to ask, "Why should you be so furious? . . . Should not Christians have more mercy and compassion?" The answer was clear: "when a people is grown to such a height of blood, and sin against God and man," there will be "no respect to persons, but [God] harrows them, and saws them, and puts them to the sword, and the most terriblest death that may be." And terrible it was. "Great and doleful was the bloody sight to the view of young soldiers that

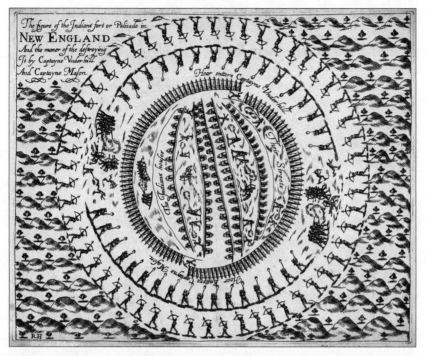

Schematic diagram of the English attack on the Pequot fort, 1637. The two blocked exits are shown top and bottom; the English are using guns, the Indians bows and arrows.

never had been in war, to see so many souls lie gasping on the ground, so thick, in some places, that you could scarcely pass along."

But it was left to the gentle Pilgrim leader Bradford to pronounce the most doleful requiem. He too praised God, "who had wrought so wonderfully for them, thus to enclose their enemies in their hands and give them so speedy a victory over so proud and insulting an enemy." But the horror of the charred and bloody corpses could not be disguised; he could not get it out of his mind. "It was a fearful sight to see them thus frying in the fire," he wrote, "and the streams of blood quenching the same, and horrible was the stink and scent thereof."[42]

Yet even with God's bloody vengeance at Mystic, the struggle was not over. The surviving Pequots, demoralized and bewildered, took what vengeance they could on Indian allies of the English, then fled for protection to other tribes, mainly to the dangerous, warlike Mohawks. But they left behind several contingents of their people, who were hunted down relentlessly. One group huddled in a swamp in southern Connecticut. There they were attacked by fresh troops from Massachusetts led by Capt. Israel Stoughton, who flushed them out of their retreat. All the adult males were slaughtered on the spot, and the women and children seized. Some of those spared were handed over to friendly tribes, others were sold to Caribbean slave traders, a few ended up with the settlers. Roger Williams, while he too rejoiced in God's vengeance on this "miserable drove of Adams degenerate seede," argued against killing or enslaving innocent captives ("2 Kings 14:5, 6"). Spare the women and children, he urged, use the captives "kindly," act "like the mercifull Kings of Israell," have a "humane Consideracion of so much blood spilt," and note the likelihood that when enslaved, the captives might "turne wild Irish." For himself he picked out one small boy—the one "with the red about his neck"—promising to keep him and bring him up personally. But such benevolence was rare, and Stoughton's troops persisted.

The main body of survivors, led by their chief Sassacus, struggled on along the Connecticut coast, ending in a "hideous swamp, so thick with bushes and so quagmiry, as men could hardly crowd into it." Surrounded, some two hundred surrendered, begging mercy, but the rest fought on until most of them were killed by musket fire systematically raking through the thicket. Of the captives, the adult males were killed (by drowning, Cotton Mather said); thirty were given to the Narragansetts; and the rest were divided between the two colonies, the girls to be distributed among the towns, most of the boys sold into slavery in the West Indies. Sassacus escaped, but two months later his body parts and those of his closest companions, victims of the Mohawks' ferocity, were brought into Boston. Friendly tribes continued to seek protection by delivering the severed heads and hands "of divers other Pequods" that they happened to encounter. Winthrop estimated that in all between eight hundred and nine hundred Pequots had been slain.

Even so, it was not enough. Obliteration—total and final annihilation—of the Satanic enemy was the ultimate if unobtainable object. Friendly tribes, well rewarded by gifts of captured noncombatants, promised never to shelter enemies of the English and to cut off and deliver the heads of any Pequots they found who were suspected of having killed Englishmen. And all Pequots were then and forever barred from returning to their native country.[43]

CHAPTER 14

Defiance and Disarray

1

THE PEQUOTS' THREAT had been eliminated in genocidal slaughter. Yet fears of Indian conspiracies persisted, for Satanic influences
could never be finally defeated here below—not in the world at large and
not in one's hearth and home.

Thus Stoughton's troops had no sooner returned from the war than
the struggle with threats from within was resumed.

Since Wheelwright's condemnation, the elders, fearful of the insidious spread of Familist or antinomian views, had started the process of
barring from immigration into the colony all who "might be dangerous
to the commonwealth," especially since, Winthrop wrote, "it was very
probable" that some particularly dangerous people would soon be arriving from what was considered to be the true pit of English Familism, the
notorious village of Grindleton, in Yorkshire. In fact, no Grindletonians
ever migrated to New England. The main effect of the restrictive statute
was to deny entrance to Hutchinson's quite inoffensive brother-in-law
Samuel and "some other of Mr. Wheelwright's friends," which was "taken
very ill" by Winthrop's opponents and touched off "many hot speeches."
And it led Cotton, who believed the ban would bar from entrance "godly
passengers" who saw the truth as he did, to consider leaving the colony

for another. But the real danger, the leaders knew, lay not at the port of entry but deep within the hearts of Hutchinson's and Wheelwright's resident sympathizers. And it was to cauterize their dangerous errors before they spread further that a synod of the colony's clerics and elders was assembled, charged with identifying and refuting every one of the theological nodes of malignancy.[1]

With so many fears circulating in the colony, so many wild and unfocused dangers believed to be lurking, the investigators let their imaginations soar and quickly produced a list of no less than eighty-two errors, "some blasphemous, other erroneous, and all unsafe." No sooner had the list been presented than trouble erupted. Some of the Bostonians and others demanded to see names. Who, they said, had ever subscribed to such wild notions? Where were the documents, the witnesses? When Winthrop told the dissenters that the synod was dealing with doctrines, not people, and to desist in their objections or the magistrates would "interpose," the opponents challenged the right of civil authorities to interfere in religious matters and walked out of the meeting.[2]

But the enumeration of errors—which, Winthrop believed, were spreading like a plague—was not the only, or the most important, of the synod's accomplishments. Once the catalog of abominations marking the outer limits of possible error had been established and the devilish means by which they had been insinuated into unsuspecting worshippers were revealed, the synod turned to more immediate and practical matters. It formulated the central points of contention between Cotton and Wheelwright on the one hand and the other clerics, led by Hooker and Shepard, on the other. The central question, stated and restated in several forms, was by then only too familiar: the correct priority between justification and sanctification—that is, direct, inner assurance of salvation or the articulated process of striving, which involved belief, personal sanctity, theological correctness, and the church's ministrations.[3]

The discussion and resolution of this inflamed question in early September 1637 were memorable and decisive. The outcome determined the ultimate character of New England's Puritanism. For in the midst of the discussion, John Cotton, the central figure, always conciliatory, always determined to avoid "differences, and jarres," and proud if uncertain of his role as the community's most respected preacher and counselor, came to believe that the radicals, and especially Wheelwright and Hutchinson, had taken advantage of his goodwill and deliberately distorted the delicate balance of his thought to promote their own extremist views, which, he said, he had never endorsed. They had advanced their distended opinions behind the shield of his reputation. He had been duped, misused, by his most fervent followers, made to appear to be something he never was, and now was exposed to criticism he did not deserve. The "iniquities" of these people grated on him. They had "without my Privety . . . harboured & secretly disseminated such Erroneous & daungerous Opinions, as (like a Gangrene) would have corrupted & destroyed Faith & Religion had not they bene timely discovered, & disclaymed both by our owne & other Churches." His own views, he explained, were subtle indeed. Faith, he now agreed, was not simply a passive element in joining with Christ, not simply "habitual" in that ultimate union. While faith and sanctification might not be determinative of redemption, they were at least coexistent with it. If therefore the soul must consent through faith, faith and all its behavioral attributes must play a necessary if not sufficient role in the achievement of salvation.

It was a careful change of phrasing if not a change of mind—indeed, "a masterpiece of equivocation." Some—Shepard especially, who had himself once flirted with radical ideas until he withdrew in panic—never believed that Cotton had really changed his mind; he had simply changed his appearance for quite pragmatic reasons. But however delicate it was and however unconvincing to some, Cotton's reformulation was enough to separate him from the "sectaries" and to associate him with the emerging mainstream. Before the synod met he had promised his colleagues that if the suspects' errors could be proved by two witnesses he would "bear witness against them." And now, having cleared himself, he did exactly that. He named the "Ringleaders" who had deceived him, and he repudiated their "Bastard-opinions."

He would never forget those decisive moments at the synod. Later he would explain again and again—to colleagues in New England, to Wheelwright in a long exculpatory letter, and to his English correspondents—how slow he had been "to see [the radicals'] windings, and subtile contrivances, and insinuations . . . whilst they propagated their Opinions under my Expressions . . . as if they had held forth noething, but according to the doctrine publickly taught by me." How naïve he had been, he would recall, to have thought that the errors they had promoted had been mere "misexpressions" or "misconstructions." And how trusting he had been to think that by private counseling he could reclaim from their errors such confirmed "Familists" as William Aspinwall, John Coggeshall, and William Coddington, once his trusted friends from Lincolnshire. But he knew now how corrupt their judgments had become and the extent of "their fraudulent pretence of holding forth no other, but what they received from me."

There was profound satisfaction behind Winthrop's quiet note in his account of the synod, that on the questions propounded, "Mr. Cotton and [the Elders] agreed, but Mr. Wheelwright did not."[4]

The unrepentant Wheelwright and the other leading dissidents, now stripped of Cotton's protection and denounced by him as dangerous schemers, were isolated and defenseless against formal prosecution. It proceeded quickly and thoroughly. On November 2 Aspinwall, for having signed a petition, itself a "seditious libell," in support of Wheelwright, and for his "insolent & turbulent carriage," was dismissed from his seat in the General Court, disfranchised, and banished from the colony. Coggeshall was similarly deprived of position and "enjoyned not to speake any thing to disturbe the publike peace, upon paine of banishment." Wheelwright's sentence was phrased more elaborately. Rejecting a last chance to repent, he was—for having declared magistrates, ministers, and most of God's people "enemies to Christ and Antichrists"; for having preached sedition, by which now "all things are turned upside down among us"; and for having made the differences between himself and the establishment "as wide as between Heaven and Hell"—for all of this he was banished—"put out from among us"—and given fourteen days to leave the colony.

Other punishments, most commonly disfranchisement, were imposed on nineteen others, though ten, acknowledging their sin, were reprieved on the spot. It was at that point, as the climax of this general purge of the "opinionists" whose views had been so thoroughly condemned by the synod, that they turned on Anne Hutchinson—"the head of all this faction, (*Dux fœmina facti*)," Winthrop wrote in a steaming indictment, "the breeder and nourisher of all these distempers," a woman "of a haughty and fierce carriage, of a nimble wit and active spirit, and a very voluble tongue, more bold then a man, though in understanding and judgement, inferiour to many women."[5]

Fierce, voluble, and bold she certainly was in the criminal trial before the General Court that stretched over two full days. Again and again, in the swirling debate between the unintimidated woman and the phalanx of interrogators, she was challenged—for having held illegal conventicles in which she instructed men as well as women; for having condemned all the clergy except Cotton as soul-dead preachers of works; for having exceeded her proper role as a woman; for having violated the fifth commandment in failing to honor the legal authorities; for having said things "very prejudicial to the honour of the churches"; and for having encouraged those who supported Wheelwright.

But again and again she eluded their grasp. Anything can be alleged, she said; but can anything be *proved*? Where were the witnesses? Conscience is surely free: had she *done* anything wrong? Religious meetings were common and had always been proper: why were hers improper? "Can you find a warrant for yourself and condemn me for the same thing?" Where is the rule that required her to reject men who came to her for instruction? Why will her accusers not testify under oath—were they afraid that untruths would be revealed? What authority was there for applying the fifth commandment to civil affairs? If she had in fact "countenance[d]" Wheelwright's supporters, did that make her guilty of their crime?

Winthrop, who as governor chaired the trial, grew increasingly irritated, increasingly impatient with the deft evasions and the unwavering defiance of this "proud dame, that . . . makes havocke of all that stand in the way of her ambitious spirit." She was by no means "so simple a Devill" as had been the rustic instigator of the bloody tragedy of Münster, the catastrophe that always haunted his imagination. Satan had surely used the "utmost cunning" in commissioning her "to undermine the Kingdome of Christ here." For by her clever maneuvers, she seemed at times to be turning the whole trial on its head. Remember, he felt obliged to insist, "we are your judges, and not you ours."[6]

Winthrop was in fact outpointed in sparring with Hutchinson, so others took over. *Simon Bradstreet:* Would she now give up her meetings? As far as she was personally concerned, yes, she said, "but for others I do not yet see light but shall further consider of it." *Deputy Governor Dudley:* Had she not charged all the clergy but Cotton with preaching nothing but a covenant of works? *Nothing but . . . ?* she asked. Prove that I ever said that—but if I did, "I proved it by God's word" and only in private, and not in public. And in any case it is not a matter of black and white: "one [person] may preach a covenant of grace more clearly than another," and the weakest such account might fade into works.

Then the ministers were brought in: *Wilson, Peter, Phillips, Weld, Symmes, Shepard, Eliot.* All testified against her, but still she saw only assertions, not proof. And with the clergy she could, and did, confidently dissect the subtlest issues. Did they not see the difference between preaching a covenant of works and being under a covenant of works? Could they not see the distinction, made clear in the sixteenth-century Geneva translation of Romans 3 and 2 Corinthians 3, between the letter of the law and the letter of the gospel, and that one could be under the letter but not the spirit of the gospel and by virtue of that be under a covenant of works? Finally, *Cotton* was brought in, somewhat embarrassed, but no doubt privately gratified, by her repeated assertion that he alone was under a covenant of grace. Though he had repudiated Wheelwright and several of his supporters, he could not bring himself to do the same for his disciple Hutchinson, whose arguments were more elusive and whose dialectical skills were more intimidating. He temporized. He could not definitely confirm, he said, that he knew for a fact that she had explicitly said that the clergy were under a covenant of works. In fact, it was not clear what precisely she had said to him, nor, in what he had heard of her wrangles with others, what exactly she had said to anyone else, and when.

Given such an opening Hutchinson felt her confidence rising, and turning broadly to her audience she lectured them freely on the growth of her spiritual state, on the voices she had heard, and on the ability God had given her to discern which ministers were preaching what and with what effect. But how, it was asked, had such knowledge come to her? It came, she said, just as the word had come to Daniel, that is, "by an immediate revelation" (*Dudley:* "How! an immediate revelation"), and furthermore she knew that she would be delivered out of their hands "by miracle as *Daniel* was." Dudley challenged Cotton to condemn her talk of miracles and revelations. Cotton equivocated, distinguishing between God's deliverance by the Word (reasonable, scriptural) and outright miracles (delusive and sinful). *Dudley:* "Sir, you weary me": did Cotton not realize that all the atrocities in Germany had stemmed from just such revelations? There the deluded prophets "stirred up their hearers to take up arms against their prince and to cut the throats of one another. . . . Mrs. Hutchinson is deluded by the devil." *Winthrop:* "The revelation she brings forth is delusion." *All the Court but two or three:* "We all believe it—we all believe it."[7]

The ordeal was over. Her confession of immediate revelations, Winthrop wrote with great relief, had gone beyond scripture and all church authority; Hutchinson had "freely and fully discovered her selfe." And that she had done this by "her owne mouth" was surely a special providence, for in fact, he had to confess, the Court had not been "furnished with proofe sufficient to proceed against her." She had done the work for them, and so, exuberantly, the Court was able to pronounce the sentence of banishment. When she asked, "Wherefore I am banished?" Winthrop replied, "Say no more, the Court knows wherefore and is satisfied."[8]

But simply to banish Hutchinson along with Wheelwright and the other "opinionists" was not enough. The specter of a violent uprising of a millennial frenzy leading to a bloody rebellion against constituted authority—the ultimate threat that burned in the deep recesses of Puritan radicalism—could not so easily be dissipated. The fear of a satanic conspiracy in the guise of fanatical religion persisted—the fear of precisely the kind of murderous, suicidal rampage that the Fifth Monarchy zealots were capable of. Drastic, precisely targeted measures were necessary to head off such violent prospects. On November 20 the Court—noting that Wheelwright's and Hutchinson's "opinions & revelations" had "seduced & led into dangerous errors many of the people heare" and that there was as a consequence "just cause of suspition that they, as others in Germany in former times, may, upon some revelation, make some suddaine irruption upon those that differ from them"—ordered seventy-five men, chiefly Bostonians, to surrender all their "guns, pistols, swords, powder, shot, & match" to designated authorities. Failure to do so would incur a fine of £10 for each weapon concealed. And further, the same suspects were denied the right to buy or borrow such weapons, though magistrates might exempt from the order any who "acknowledg their sinn in subscribing the seditious libell" or at least "acknowledg it evill."

But even that did not satisfy the worried authorities. The Court, "sensible of the great disorders growing" and the "contempts wch have of late bene put upon the civill authority," ordered that anyone who defamed a court of law, its proceedings or its judges, would be fined, imprisoned, disfranchised, or banished. And if the Court itself became corrupted and magistrates abused their own colleagues for their opinions or rulings, such offenders were to be "sharply reproved" by the governor; if they persisted they were to be punished by fines or imprisonment.[9]

But the Antinomian Controversy, as it would be known, was not yet at an end. After seven months of confinement and intense, isolated biblical study, Hutchinson, pregnant and physically weak, was brought before the church of Boston to be tried for her "divers errors and unsound opinions." The exhausting, two-day inquisition focused primarily on the charge of "mortalism"—that Hutchinson denied the soul's immortality, hence endorsed "familistical" libertinage ("let us eate and drinke and doe any Thinge, tomorrow we shall dye"), which led quickly to the further charge that she misunderstood and deluded others on the doctrine of resurrection, a delusion, Cotton charged, that led inescapably to "that filthie Sinne of the Comunitie of Woemen and all promiscuus and filthie cominge togeather of men and Woemen without Distinction or Relation of Marriage." And further, she was accused of falsely attributing her "errors" ("mistakes," she insisted) to the effects of the debilitating confinement she had suffered.[10]

Amid the confusion of charges and countercharges and the tangles of biblical citations, a partial recantation that she had crafted with Cotton's help was ignored. Her accusers, agreeing that they could no longer allow her to go on "seducinge to seduce, and in deaceivinge to deceave, and in lyinge to lye," closed in on her as her fortitude faded. With Cotton's reluctant agreement to condemn his *"puft up"* disciple, whose revelations and theology seemed to be increasingly independent of scripture and church authority and who persisted, he believed, in falsifying when she had adopted such ideas, they reached the scripted verdict on her "groce and damnable Heresies." For having disturbed the church's tranquillity, for having misled "many a poor soule," for having persisted in her revelations, and for having lied in her testimony, Hutchinson was finally and totally "cast out" of the church. "*I doe deliver you up to Sathan,*" the Rev. John Wilson, on behalf of the church, declared. And "*I command you in the name of Christ Jesus and of this Church as a Leper to withdraw your selfe out of the Congregation.*"[11]

2

Though efforts to retrieve the exiled Hutchinson from the clutches of Satan would continue, she never repented and was still defiant at her violent death in 1643 in New Netherland at the hands of marauding Indians—devils, Cotton said, who had been appropriately sent to punish one who had herself been the devil's advocate. Cotton, having repudiated his embarrassing disciple, recovered his cherished role as the colony's leading cleric, though in subtle ways he continued to argue the case against Shepard and Hooker. Shepard never slackened in his zeal

and never believed that Cotton's concession had been sincere. Most of
the outspoken dissidents, including Wheelwright, sooner or later came
to terms with the establishment, and those who did not left the colony,
mainly to settle in Rhode Island, where they joined Gorton or turned
Quaker or simply lived in isolated hamlets where they were free to practice their esoteric faiths. And so, though Boston's churchmen still felt
threatened by the "wandring sheepe" to the south, the center, saved
from implosion by the colony's open boundaries, had held. And from
the turmoil of those critical years, an orthodoxy supple enough to absorb
some of the radicals' aspirations emerged in the form of New England's
nonseparating Congregationalism, which would be codified in the Cambridge Platform of 1648.[12]

But the cost had been high. Abroad, as word of the struggle reached
England, the colony gained a reputation for both extreme radicalism and
suppressive intolerance. And at home, the rupture revealed, as nothing
else could have done, the failure of Winthrop's dream of an organic community disciplined by the encompassing commitment to Puritan ideals.

The ostensible struggle had been fought over doctrine, over the most
exquisite details of attaining salvation and the role of human intermedia-
tion in that great effort. But while the clerics and the more learned laymen understood the issues in those terms and felt the world tremble when
they believed a word or phrase of scripture had been misconstrued, the
majority of the participants, as Winthrop knew, had no such understanding, however sincere their beliefs. Yet they too were fervently engaged,
equally willing to commit themselves to abstruse theological positions
that put them at risk. For they, no less than the most abstracted theologian, had much at stake. In a culture so deeply permeated by religion,
personal interests were naturally expressed in theological terms. And
though, as R. H. Tawney has written, "the vulgar categories of class and
income" do not as such shape religious zeal and moral enthusiasm, "experience proves, nevertheless, that there are certain kinds of environment
in which they burn more bravely than in others, and that, as man is both
spirit and body, so different types of religious experience correspond to
the varying needs of different social and economic *milieux*."[13]

It was precisely the varying needs of different social and economic
groups, derived from the complex demography of the Puritan migration,
that shaped the divisions in the antinomian struggle. The numbers are
striking. In all, 187 men (and there were at least as many women) can be

said to have been sympathetic to the Hutchinsonian movement—no less than 12 percent of Massachusetts's entire adult male population; half of them (96) were residents of Boston. Of the 187 male sympathizers, 38 can be said to have been deeply involved—a core group formally committed by word or deed to the antinomian cause. That the English origins of both the overall group and the core participants were centered not in central East Anglia and the West Country, as was the migration as a whole, but in Lincolnshire and London (32 percent overall, 53 percent of the core) may not be surprising. Cotton's and Hutchinson's connections and influence were strongest in Lincolnshire, and there were more Londoners in Boston than in any other New England town. But it is surprising that, while the occupations of the overwhelming number of the immigrants to Massachusetts were in agriculture or in labor in some form, 40 percent of the antinomian group as a whole were merchants or craftsmen, and more than half (55 percent) of the core group can be similarly classified. And almost all of the core group and over half of the larger group were church members, most of them also freemen; several of them were magistrates.[14] This was no collection, like Gorton's sect, of enraptured zealots, ignorant laborers, or feckless wanderers. Though among them were excitable, impressionable, hot enthusiasts who thrilled at Hutchinson's eloquence and Cotton's prophetic flair without considering the implications of their arguments, most of the antinomians were well-established, respectable men and women, substantial if not affluent members of the community—merchants, like Hutchinson's husband William, who was deeply involved in developing networks of Atlantic commerce, tradesmen at various levels, and "many of the most wise and godly" people in the community. In turning to Hutchinson and Cotton rather than to the mainstream "preparationist" clerics "for counsel about matter of conscience," they were responding less to the technical substance of antinomian doctrines than to the aura the movement carried of a looser, more personal, more individualistic, and more self-expressive form of worship.

This was especially true for the women, who had been Hutchinson's initial and most numerous constituents. For them her doctrines, exemplified in her personal prominence, fortitude, and independence of mind and spirit, were inspirational in equating men and women as recipients of God's revelations and in expressing freely and flagrantly otherwise suppressed aspirations. Again and again in her trials she had been reproved for violating the constraints appropriate for women's lives. *Hugh Peter:* "*You have rather bine a Husband than a Wife and a preacher than a Hearer; and a Magistrate than a Subject.*" *John Winthrop:* Your assemblies are "a thing not tolerable nor comely in the sight of God nor fitting for your sex." Indeed, "we do not mean to discourse [debate] with those of your sex." *John Cotton:* Though you may not as yet have been unfaithful to your marriage, such is the "*highth of your Spirit . . . that will follow upon it.*" *Shepard:* With your "fluent Tounge and forwardnes in Expressions" you "seduce and draw away many, Espetially simple Weomen."[15]

The dangers to the social order of "simple Weomen" transcending the mildness, meekness, and subservience expected of their sex to enter masculine domains were obvious, and every effort was made to suppress the disorders they threatened. Cotton told the "sisters" of the church that they had been "too much seduced and led aside by [Hutchinson]." No doubt she had some good to offer. Then take whatever good she may have given you, but do not think everything of hers is good, "for you see she is but a Woman and *many unsound and dayngerous principles are held by her.*" Therefore "if you have drunke in with this good any Evell or Poyson, make speed to vomit it up agayne and to repent of it."[16]

Others took more direct action against overly assertive or strangely affected females. Jane Hawkins, Hutchinson's closest friend, a midwife and herbalist given to trance-like states in which she spoke Latin, was declared to be familiar with the devil and "a prime Familist"; the General Court ordered her never again to meddle with medicines of any kind and never "to question matters of religion." Eventually she would be banished, to join Hutchinson in exile. Mary Oliver, said to be more eloquent and zealous even than Hutchinson, was imprisoned for insisting on being made a member of the Salem church, and when she argued for open membership and other "very dangerous" opinions, she was whipped and clapped in the stocks, her tongue clamped with a cleft stick.

And a series of other prosecutions followed in Hutchinson's wake: the maidservant Smith, cast out of the church for persisting in "sundry Errors"; Katherine Finch, whipped for disrespect to the authorities; Phillipa Hammond excommunicated for defending Hutchinson and for slandering and reviling church and state; and Sarah Keayne, Dudley's daughter, excommunicated for "irregular prophesying in mixed assemblies." There seemed to be no end to the women who responded to Hutchinson's inspiration. The Salem church expelled four "sisters" who denied the validity of the colony's churches. And Dorothy Talby, for justifying rebellion by an "immediate revelation" similar to Hutchinson's and for beating her husband "to the danger of his life," was cast out of the church, chained to a post, and whipped. When, on instructions from heaven, she murdered her young daughter, whom she had named Difficult, to save her from future misery, she was hanged (though she preferred beheading)—whereupon the Rev. Hugh Peter "gave an exhortation to the people to take heed of revelations."[17]

3

But the suppression of the antinomian dissenters and the agitators inspired and energized by them was one phase of a bitter and extended struggle. An orthodoxy had emerged from the turmoil of the mid-1630s, but there was no final stability. Such was the protean, fluid character of Puritanism, so strong were its inner dynamics, and so broad the range of its possible interpretations that the fragile structure of "the New England way" would continue to come under pressure from both left and right, as newcomers to the region brought with them competing claims and as developments in England fed back across the Atlantic. So long as New England was not physically sealed off from the world, so long as new ideas, challenging ideas, could be borne into the community by arriving voyagers, the new orthodoxy would be embattled, forced to defend itself, by whatever means: by persuasion if possible, by force if necessary.

FOR WINTHROP and his first-generation allies in the mid-1630s, antinomianism, seemingly indistinguishable from anarchic "Familism," had measured the dark and deadly depths to which Puritanism could sink under the pressure of semimystical enthusiasm. But their immediate successors soon discovered that there were depths below depths—a truly absolute debasement of their faith, with respect to which Williams's disagreements were rational explorations, Wheelwright's challenges were verbal exaggerations, and Hutchinson's heresies were manageable if dangerous aberrations.

Winthrop, Dudley, Cotton, Hooker, and even Shepard were safely dead when in 1656 the first of the itinerant Quakers—two Englishwomen from Barbados—arrived in Boston harbor to spread the word of the impending end of the world and the need for all to recognize the Inner

Light that God had instilled in them. The Puritan authorities, like the
Dutch, were horrified, but for them the dangers of Quakerism were more
profound and their reaction was far more severe than Stuyvesant's. For
New England's leaders knew that in the great cacophony of factions and
sects that had exploded in the upheaval of England's civil war, Quakerism had emerged as the ultimate descent from rational, Biblicist, clerical
Protestantism into subjective, anticlerical, nonscriptural millennialism
that threatened the basic institutions of civilized life—church, family, and
social hierarchy—that they were struggling to preserve. However deviant
the dissidents of the 1630s had been, they had not challenged such fundamentals as the sanctity of Scripture, the principles of predestination and
original sin, and the propriety of religious "ordinances": the sacraments,
scripted orders of worship, structured preaching, and the formalities of
prayer. With all of this the Quakers had broken, substituting belief in
a universally shared Inner Light of God's benevolence as the ultimate
guide, wide-open participation in unstructured worship, and contempt
for both parochial jurisdictions and the hierarchy of deference and social
organization. Yet—and in this lay their ultimate threat—despite their
rejection of the substance and structure of organized Protestantism, they
shared with the more radical Puritans a mystical strain and a fervent millennialism that blurred the boundaries between them, and that for some
could make translation to the new faith attractive. Quakerism for them
was therefore doubly dangerous: utterly defiant and disparaging of organized, rational religion, yet associated with familiar radical doctrines of
the immanence of the Holy Spirit. The Quakers were thus as demonic as
the devilish Indians, to whom they were frequently compared, and as ter-
rifying in their "spiritual phrenzy" and "frantick passions" as the bloody
anarchists of Münster, who, some said, were their exact predecessors in
promoting chaos. And the worst of it, for the local authorities, was that
some of the Quakers' seeds fell on fertile ground.[18]

　　Despite the formal success of the new and tenuous Congregational
orthodoxy, there were here and there groups peculiarly susceptible to
the Quakers' message. In Salem, amorphous radicalism had smoldered
below the surface ever since Roger Williams had left the town, and it
had flared up repeatedly—in the agitations of the "wise and anciently
religious woman" Lady Deborah Moody, who in her resettlement in
New Netherland would provide refuge for persecuted Quakers; in the
outbursts of the obstreperous Mary Oliver, silenced and exiled in 1648;

and in the fierce egalitarian protests of the town's alienated farmers and artisans. Plymouth's separatist, sectarian tradition with its emphasis on the indwelling Spirit, spreading out through its satellite towns on Cape Cod, made that sprawl of pious communities also "ripe" for Quaker revelations. And in Rhode Island the self-intensifying radicalism of its exiled population had long since anticipated Quaker-like forms of worship. Led by such once-respectable but now fallen Puritans as Coddington and inspired by such free spirits as Hutchinson's devoted friend Mary Dyer and the "bold, though ignorant" Nicholas Easton, who believed in man's natural unity with God, many in the hamlets around Narragansett Bay had forsaken organized forms of worship for extemporized expressions of their individual spiritual yearnings. Some were professed Anabaptists, some Gortonish spiritists, some isolated advocates of free grace, but all were prepared to welcome the itinerant Friends, to identify with them, and to endorse their assault on the fortress of the Bible Commonwealth.[19]

That assault proceeded rapidly, despite the treatment of the first two women missionaries, whom the authorities had strip-searched for signs of demonism, had deprived of books and pamphlets, and had isolated in a windowless cell for five weeks before shipping them out of the colony. Eight more missionaries followed as the two women left. The reprisals now were savage, inflicted upon self-sacrificial devotees alight with Truth and burning with zeal by men fearful of impending chaos. Repressive laws of increasing severity were passed in most of the New England colonies. In Massachusetts, anyone professing the "pernitious opinions & practices" of those "quaking and trembling anthusiasts" who

> take uppon them to be immediately sent of God, and infallibly asisted
> by the spirit to speake & write blasphemouth opinions, despising gov-
> ernment & the order of God in church & commonwealth, speaking
> evill of dignities, reproaching and reviling magistrates and ministers,
> seeking to turne the people from the faith, & gaine proselites to theire
> pernicious wayes

—all such blasphemers were to be severely whipped, locked up in jail, and then shipped out of the colony. Those who returned would have an ear cut off; those who appeared yet again, another ear; and the women among them would be "severely whipt." For a third offense "they shall have theire toungues bored through with a hot iron." If after all of that and other punishments they still persisted, they would be banished "on paine of death."[20]

And so it was. Half-naked women were flogged, men's ears cropped and their bodies savagely beaten. Finally, with Boston patrolled by a special guard of thirty-six soldiers, four of the proselytizing Quakers, defiantly testifying to the Truth in Boston and passionate for martyrdom, were taken from jail and hanged—among them Mary Dyer, after she had deliberately rejected a "benevolent" reprieve and had defiantly appeared in Boston for the fourth time.[21]

By then, in the early 1660s, at least forty-three Quakers, from England, Barbados, and Rhode Island, had invaded the Bible Commonwealth, and though battered and bruised and repeatedly jailed and banished, in their prophetic zeal they had sufficiently convinced dozens of New England radicals to see the beauty of the Quakers' absolute subjectivity and creedless illumination and to profess the prohibited faith. Many if not most of Rhode Island's population who were not biblical literalists embraced the new confession and began to organize their community's business in the distinctive style of monthly and yearly meetings, the latter a gathering of Quakers from all over New England. Faced with this spreading contamination, the Massachusetts authorities felt driven not only to increase the severity of the punishments but also, sensitive to New England's reputation at home, to publicly justify their persecution.[22]

After commissioning the Rev. John Norton to write and publish a formal refutation of "the evill of [the Quakers'] tenets and dainger of theire practises," the General Court itself issued a vindication of its proceedings against "the cursed sect." Their punitive laws, they wrote, were simply efforts to secure peace and order in the face of people known "by the example of theire predecessors, in Münster," to be determined to destroy both. The Quakers' destructive purpose was clear: "to chainge and alter the received laudable customes of our nation in giving civill respect to aequalls or reverence to superiors ... also to destroy the order of the churches, by denying all established formes of worship." Banishment on pain of death was nothing new in English law, the General Court pointed out; it had been used against a similarly destructive and demonic cabal, the Jesuits. Accusations of excessive severity were unjustified, for the Quakers had become "felons de se," against whom the sovereign law of "salus populi" should properly prevail. What was at stake were the fundamentals of Christian civilization: "the sacred Trinitie, the person of Christ, & the Holy Scriptures, as a perfect rule of faith & life." The Quakers' shocking belief that they were

> perfectly pure & without sinne, tends to overthrow the whole gospell & the very vitalls of Christianitie, for they that have no sinne have no neede of Christ, or of . . . his blood to cleanse them from theire sinne . . . no neede of repentance . . . no neede of growing in grace . . . no neede of Christian watchfulnes against sinne . . . no need to purify themselves dayly, as all Christians should.

Therefore, the General Court concluded, "the commandment of God is plaine . . . he that presumes to speake lyes in the name of the Lord, & turne people out of the way which the Lord hath commanded to walk in, such an one must not live, but be put to death."[23]

However consistent this draconian policy may have been with Puritan views, Governor Endecott and the General Court realized that it was suspect by the Restoration court of Charles II, and in a long, eloquent appeal to the king for the continuation of their chartered privileges they included an explanatory passage on the treatment of the Quakers. The colony had acted in self-defense. The Quakers were such "malignant & assiduous promoters of doctrines directly tending to subvert both our churches & state . . . [that] wee were at last constreined, for our oune safety, to passe a sentence of bannishment . . . upon paine of death." The executed Quakers had died not because of their seditious crimes or their blasphemous sins but because of their "breaking in upon us, notwith-standing theire sentence of bannishment made knoune to them." They had died, in effect, by "theire oune act . . . bringing theire blood on theire oune head."

But though the Crown was willing to tolerate the colony's charter, it could not concede the power of life and death or concur in this degree of intolerance. Orders were sent from London to stop the executions and return the condemned to England.[24]

Punishments, however, continued. Recidivist Quakers were to be tied half naked to a cart's tail and whipped from town to town until out of the colony, and upon successive returns to be branded on the shoulder. (In New Haven they were to be branded on the hand.) So three women in Maine—"vagabond Quakers"—were whipped, bleeding, through several miles of knee-deep snow. Women who appeared in church in sackcloth, their faces smeared with ashes ("the greatest and most amazing uproar that I ever saw"—Samuel Sewell), were frantically suppressed; and men who interrupted sermons by smashing bottles together in symbolic demonstration of the Puritans' ultimate demise were dragged off to prison by the hair. But the suppression could not long survive the advice of the royal commission of 1664, that the Quakers should be allowed to "pass about their lawful occasions."

Gradually the fury slackened, and by 1674 the sect was able to establish a regular meeting in Boston itself, despite bitter protests. At the end of the century, Cotton Mather could look back indulgently on his grandparents' fury against the Quakers. He agreed that the first generation of Quakers had been "*Madmen*, a sort of *Lunaticks*, *Daemoniacks* and *Energumens*," fitter for a madhouse than a gallows; but in time they would have "come to nothing if the *Civil Magistrate* had not inflicted any *Civil Penalty* upon them." It would have been enough, he thought, if, as a Plymouth councilor had proposed, they had been forced *to have their Heads Shaved*—a "*Capital*" punishment to be sure (Mather could not resist the pun) that "would have both Sham'd and Cur'd them."[25]

4

But if the Quakers constituted an effective assault from without on the establishment of New England's Puritanism, changes from within—erosion, disillusion, and the lure of opportunities abroad and of more worldly goals—had a greater, more transformative effect. As the region's life settled into stable forms the tensions within Puritanism became increasingly difficult to maintain; the lure of exile dimmed when escape was no longer necessary and return was safe and beguiling, and when commercial prospects in a burgeoning Atlantic world became clear.

IN THE STRUGGLE to maintain Puritanism's inner balances, the sufferings of the pious merchant Robert Keayne—that frenetic product of London's spiritually burnt-over inner city—and the turmoils of the country-bred perfectionist Roger Williams were opposite ends of the same spectrum. Both were profoundly pious, but the one could not maintain the delicate balance of pressures within the system; the other would not. Both became pariahs, the one condemned for avarice, the other for an excess of zeal.

Keayne, as devoted to his spiritual life as to his business dealings, had quickly established his religious and commercial credentials after his arrival in 1635. Within a few months, he was received into the communion of Boston's first church and soon thereafter, while perfecting both his economic and spiritual bookkeeping, he resumed his practice of keeping detailed notes on the sermons he heard, especially those of Cotton, and recording certain of the church's proceedings. Three volumes of his sermon notes, covering the years 1638–46, survive and are testimonials to the passion of his religious life. He was, it seemed, the soul of integrity and Christian charity. As his business success increased, so too did his gifts to the public. He contributed generously to the building of Boston's fort and laid aside a regular percentage of his profits to distribute to the poor. He served the public: he sat on town committees, was elected deputy to the General Court, and joined in the founding of the Ancient and Honorable Artillery Company. Such was his public prominence and respectability that it was he who was designated, in November 1637, to receive the surrendered weapons of the seventy-five disarmed antinomians.[26]

Two years later all of this structure of prominence and respectability came crashing down. He was publicly charged with excessive profiteering: "taking above six-pence in the shilling profit; in some above eight-pence; and, in some small things, above two for one." The General Court fined him for this offense £200, but then reduced the fine to £80. The church then took up the matter. The elders studied "how farr I was guilty of all those claymors and rumors that then I lay under" and, after an "exquisite search" into Keayne's defense, condemned him "in the Name of the Church for selling his wares at excessive Rates, to the Dishonor of Gods name, the Offence of the General Cort, and the Publique scandall of the Cuntry." Keayne lived under this ban until the following May, when "upon his penetentiall acknowledgment thereof . . . and pr[o]mise of further satisfaction to any that have just offence against him, He is now become Reconciled to the Church."

The horror of this fall from grace, the embarrassment and, he believed, the injustice of it, was something he would never forget. Fourteen years later, when he came to write his will, the wound was still raw, and he poured out his bitterness and self-justification in a passionate fifty-thousand-word *apologia* that filled 158 pages of the Suffolk County probate records and that reveals as no other document of the time the inner tensions of Puritan life.

> It was the greife of my soule . . . that any act of mine (though not justly
> but by misconstruction) should be an occasion of scandall to the Gospell
> and p[ro]fession of the Lord Jesus or that my selfe should be looked at as
> one that had brought any just dishonor to God . . . if it had beene in my
> owne power I should rather have chosen to have p[e]rished in my cradle
> than to have lived to such a time.

It had all been a misunderstanding, he wrote, compounded by the vicious-
ness of his enemies, and bewildering in view of the strict orthodoxy of his
beliefs. He had renounced—had never indulged in—all "knowne errors,
all Popish and Prelaticall superstitions, all Anabaptisticall inthusiasms
and Familisticall delusions, with all other fayned devises, and all Old
and New upstart opinions, unsound and blasphemous errors, and other
high imaginations." Of course, he knew that nothing he had ever done
or ever could do—all his "righteousness, sanctific[ati]on and close walking with God if it were or had bin a thousand times more exact than ever
I attayned too"—could secure for him God's justification. Still, the fact
that he had been blessed with worldly success was surely a sign of God's
approval. And why should he not have been blessed?

> I have not lived an idle, lazie or dronish life nor spent my time wantonly,
> fruitlessly or in company keeping [nor] . . . had in my whole time either
> in Old England or New, many spare houres to spend unprofitably away
> or to refresh myselfe with recreations, *except reading and writing hath
> beene a recreation to me which sometimes is mixt with paine and labor enough,*
> but have rather studyed and endeavored to redeeme my time as a thing
> most deare and precyous to me.

He had lived a disciplined life of self-denial and devotion to the word of
God in order to reach the greatest measure of success in the work of this
world and the next. And were they not the same? The self-denial, careful
accounting, and passion for attainment that were mandated by Keayne's
religion were the same virtues that ruled his business life. And yet while
they impelled him forward, at the same time they limited and challenged the righteousness of his success. He was caught between the two
impulses: the God-given passion to succeed, to profit, by infinite care and
calculation, and the need to adhere to moral constraints. The same body
of religious precepts that had systematized the virtues making for busi-

ness success checked their free play in behalf of the community good and the avoidance of excess, self-indulgence, vanity, and sensuality. He was at once driven and constrained, and the tensions had proved insupportable.

And so it continued. Restored to his offices if not to public approval, busy as before in his meticulous note taking in church, he fell foul of the authorities again, in a notorious court case of 1642—important in con-stitutional history—that grew from the charge that he had robbed the widow Sherman of her sow. And when that was settled and he was once more restored to official acceptance, he relieved his tensions in other ways: in belligerent challenges to those who opposed him, in slackening attention to his public duties. Finally, in 1652, his lifelong self-discipline entirely failed, and his disgrace was complete:

> Whereas Capt Robert Keayne beinge acused to this Court for drunk-
> enes . . . and findinge that he is proved to have been three times drunke
> and to have drunke to excesse two times, for which offenses the Court
> doth fine him thirty six shillings and eyght pence

—to which was added fifty-five shillings two pence in Court expenses and dismissal from his judicial post.

Keayne's career, in its prominence and profuse documentation, con-cluding in the *cri de coeur* of his testimonial lamentation, is unique, but the problems he faced were not. They lay at the heart of the region's religious culture. The doctrine of the just price, which he was accused of having violated and which conflicted head-on with the entrepreneurial instincts fortified by Puritanism's worldly asceticism, was integral to the medieval substratum of Puritan belief, and it was discussed in elaborate colloquies by both Cotton and Winthrop. Others too were caught in this cultural contradiction, which extended beyond individual cases of avarice into broad ranges of social behavior where legal restraints proved futile. Price controls had to be imposed, but they failed; wage ceilings had to be mandated, but they were largely ignored; and sumptuary laws, reflect-ing the Puritans' horror of display, vainglory, and economic waste—and reflecting also the social disarray, the disordering of traditional statuses, inherent in a borderland society—were passed, but they had very little effect.[27]

So in 1651, in the most poignant expression of the erosion of val-ues that had shaped the Puritan mission and the confusion of inherited statuses on the American frontier, the General Court of Massachusetts, led by a remnant of the ancient fathers (Endecott, Dudley, Bellingham), lamented the corruption of the world the founders had struggled to create. It was a matter of grief, they declared, that "intollerable excesse and bravery hath crept in uppon us, and especially amongst people of meane condition, to the dishonnor of God, the scandall of our profession, the consumption of estates, and altogether unsuiteable to our povertie." It was their duty, therefore, to declare their

> utter detestation and dislike that men or weomen of meane condition should take uppon them the garbe of gentlemen, by wearing gold or silver lace or buttons, or points at their knees, or to walk in great bootes, or weomen of the same rancke to weare silke or tiffany hoodes or scarfes, which though allowable to persons of greater estates, or more liberall education, yett wee cannot but judge it intollerable in persons of such like condition.

They therefore prohibited anyone "whose visible estates, reall and personall, shall not exceed the true and indifferent valew of two hundred pounds, shall weare any gold or silver lace, or gold and silver buttons, or any bone lace above two shillings per yard, or silk hoods or scarfes, uppon the pœnaltie of tenn shillings for every such offence." Those who defied this ruling would be taxed at the level of wealth they pretended to—*provided,* they added in an elegiac conclusion that went to the heart of their discontents, that the law would not apply to anyone "*whose education and imployments have binn above the ordinary degree, or whose estates have binn considerable, though now decaied.*"[28]

5

Excess, pretension, and "bravery" in dress and behavior on the part of people of "meane condition" were signs enough that the Bible Commonwealth was in disarray. But problems suddenly appeared that chiefly affected not so much those of "meane condition" as those "of greater estates" and "more liberall education," those who lived the most considered lives.

In 1640 the Puritan colonists were pitched into turmoil by events abroad. The oppressive world from which they had escaped had suddenly been transformed. Charles I was forced to recall Parliament, which quickly took charge of public affairs. It impeached Strafford and Laud, passed the Triennial Act obliging the king to convene Parliament every three years, dismantled the structure of Episcopacy, and eliminated the oppressive courts of Star Chamber and High Commission. The Puritans' spiritual kinsman Cromwell led the Parliamentary forces to victory against the royalists in the first phase of the Civil War and was poised for greater conquests not only in England but in Ireland and Scotland as well. And above all, the religious scene had changed from coercive conformity to open toleration.

The effect of all of this on New England was transformative. Impulses were set in motion that together shaped the future of the Puritan colonies.

THE UPHEAVAL IN ENGLAND inverted the migration pattern. Relieved of oppression and the threats of a coercive regime, the Puritans in England felt increasingly secure, and the westward flow of desperate emigrants quickly dwindled and then came to a stop. At the same time New England's prominent people, those of "quality," were being welcomed back, to contribute to England's revolution, to resume their old positions, and to consider opportunities unknown in earlier years. An eastward remigration began that lasted in different phases of intensity for the next twenty years and that led to a renewed search for justification and identity.[29]

The effect of discovering that their people at home had triumphed— those who had stood their ground against oppression while they themselves had fled—and that much of what could only have been done in the wilderness could now be done at home, raised disturbing questions. In the 1630s they had raked their consciences, measured their resolve, and tested their fortitude before they had joined the exodus to New England, and they had pledged themselves to share in the preservation of threatened values and in the creation of a truly reformed Christianity. Could they now, in good conscience, withdraw from that whole endeavor and return to their former lives relieved of oppression? Could they simply abandon their friends and neighbors with whom they had shared the burden of bringing Christianity and civilization to a barbarous world? They had no choice but to reconsider and reassess the decisions they once had made in the light of present circumstances.

For some, of course, return was inconceivable: secular leaders like

Winthrop and Dudley, whose commitment to the new Jerusalem had consumed their lives; leading clerics like Hooker, Cotton, and Shepard, who were responsible for defining New England's Puritanism; and prospering farmers now possessed of land of their own and deeply invested in its cultivation. Conversely, others at either end of the spectrum were only too eager to leave and could do so without much consideration—those on the "left" who had been ostracized for their radicalism and those on the "right" who had resisted the compromises of New England's Congregationalism. But for many, especially those of "greater estates" and "more liberall education," there was no obvious response. Return was something to consider carefully. It had obvious attractions. Clerics with years of service before them were excited by the tolerant religiosity of England's new regime and the prospect of appointment to pulpits suddenly purged of Anglicans, and this at a time when vacancies in New England were becoming scarce. Soldiers and public officials could imagine roles for themselves in the reformed government; and all those who had never learned to cope with the harsh environment could look forward to more comfortable lives at home.[30]

But if return was an option to consider, it was an option fraught with moral ambiguities. There were doubts, hesitations, a sense of guilt and betrayal. Many felt the need for a "just call" to sanctify such a change of course and the sudden departure from friends and a great cause—some indication that Providence concurred in a decision that might be construed as simply the search for crass betterment: future employment, the recovery of property and inheritance, the welcome of friends, and escape from poverty and a harsh climate. John Davenport, in poor health and fearing another winter in New Haven, glossed the admonition "thou shalt not kill" as an argument to leave for England since doing so would preserve a life—his own. Nathaniel Ward, who had been expelled from his ministry in 1632 and for twelve years thereafter had preached in Ipswich, Massachusetts, explained, in his rollicking, satirical *Simple Cobler of Aggawam* (1647), with appropriate reference to Hebrews 11:9, that while "no man ought to forsake his own country but upon extraordinary cause . . . when that cause ceases he is bound in conscience to return if he can." Ward could and did. He ended his notable career in England, as rector of a church some four miles from his original parish. Some found moral refuge in obtaining official certificates of release from their church covenant, charitably donated by their pastors, friends, and neighbors.[31]

The moral pressures could be intense. Did England's reformation cast doubt on God's intentions for New England? Richard Saltonstall, whose father and sisters had fled the colony within a year of their arrival in 1630, was so conflicted in 1640 that he felt it necessary to bind himself by solemn oath never to desert Massachusetts, so long as the purity of the colony's religious life continued. But when he heard that his wife, recovering her health in England, was advised not to return to America, he went to John Cotton for advice. What should he do? Abandon his wife or violate his oath? Cotton, ever the compromiser (in his will he would himself restrict his benefactions to those who remained in the colony), replied that a Christian may be called by God to leave a country even if it remains in a state of purity "upon sundry just grounds," in this case to preserve the sanctity of marriage—so long, that is, that he comes back when he can. Similarly, the son of Governor George Wyllys of Connecticut was required by his father to sign an oath, with God as witness, before leaving for England pledging to return to the colony without fail. As the years passed with no return, Wyllys berated his son for violating his oath. The son replied that there was no need for him to return since England now had "many churches gathered . . . and the purity of God's ordinances may there be enjoyed." Arguments went back and forth between the two, until the governor, refusing to "quit" his son from his engagement, returned the signed oath to him with the admonition: "seriously consider of it."[32]

Such small dramas played themselves out throughout the 1640s and 1650s, especially in the calm years 1646–48 between the two phases of the Civil War, and after the downfall of the monarchy, years when the remigration was at its height. The elders, Winthrop above all, were shocked and embittered by the growing apostasy. "Such as come together into a wilderness," Winthrop wrote angrily, "where are nothing but wild beasts and beastlike men and there confederate together in civil and church state . . . do implicitly at least, bind themselves to support each other." How could one desert New England and the covenanted cause? Think of it, he wrote: Would you have "plucked up thy stakes, and brought thy family 3,000 miles," if you had expected to be forsaken? How can one grant liberty to leave to some and not to others? "And so church and commonwealth may be left destitute in a wilderness, exposed to misery and reproach, and all for thy ease and pleasure."[33]

How many responded to the upheaval at home, overcame their scruples, and found the means to return to a world turned upside down is not known. But reasonable estimates indicate something of the magnitude of the remigration. At least 600 colonists who have been identified by name returned to England in the 1640s and 1650s, most of them permanently. If, as seems likely, at least 450 of the 600 were adult men, by extrapolating from complete passenger lists that include women and children, one finds, the most recent student of the subject concludes, "a fairly secure figure of a minimum of 1,500 settlers . . . returned to England."

How significant is this number? If the total immigrant population to New England before 1640 had been 21,000, the proportion of the immigrants who returned to the total migration of the 1630s would have been one in fourteen; if the Massachusetts population had been 12,500 in 1640, as is widely believed, the proportion for that colony would have been one in eight. More reliable, and perhaps more significant, are the figures for the clerics who returned. Of the seventy clerical immigrants known to have been alive in 1640, twenty-five (more than one in three) left for England. And no fewer than half of the 108 Harvard graduates before 1660 ended their careers in England, Ireland, or Scotland; few of them ever returned to the colonies.

A broader study identified all those who might be called "university men" or "intellectuals" in the Puritan colonies—those who matriculated in any college or university, had been informally tutored for clerical careers, or had held positions contingent on higher education (lawyers, doctors). Of the total of 266, nearly half of those alive in 1640 left for England, only 5 percent of whom ever returned to the colonies. And the majority of all of these remigrating groups were the younger among them, those less likely to find secure positions in view of their elders' establishment. Many faced underemployment at best while Cromwellian England suddenly seemed a world of opportunity.[34]

SOME, PERHAPS MOST, of those who left—even some of the most notorious in the colonies—fell comfortably back into unremarkable and undocumented lives "at home." Wheelwright, so embroiling and belligerent a figure in Massachusetts, slipped silently into a Lincolnshire parish a few miles from Bilsby, where he had presided for a decade before leaving for New England. And the notorious William Aspinwall carried forward his erratic and polemical career to London, where he became a leading publicist for the Fifth Monarchist belief that the only valid laws were those of God not man (views that led his New England colleague Thomas Venner to stage a murderous revolt in the back streets of London, for which he was hanged, drawn, and quartered); but in the end Aspinwall settled for a parish in County Kildare, Ireland, where he did what he could to advance the Puritan cause.[35]

But while few of the returnees became major players in the turmoils of the war years and the Cromwellian regime, a significant number of them entered actively into England's political and military struggles and became prominent in midlevel positions; in their ambitious outreach they brought New England's presence out from its deepening provincialism into the greater world. For in Britain they were not anonymous. "'Tis a notion of mighty great and high respect to have been a New-English man," Nathaniel Mather wrote from England in 1651, "'tis enough to gain a man very much respect, yea, almost any preferment." He exaggerated, in his enthusiasm, but the success of some of the returnees bore him out.[36]

Saltonstall, liberated by Cotton's kind advice, became a trustee of confiscated estates in Scotland and later a commissioner there for customs and excise. Stephen Winthrop served as a captain in his brother-in-law Thomas Rainsborowe's regiment in Ireland, ending a colonel with a seat in Parliament and substantial landed property. John Leverett of Boston also served as one of Rainsborowe's captains, and Israel Stoughton, of Pequot War fame, led a group of Boston's Artillery Company to join that regiment; he became Rainsborowe's lieutenant colonel. When Rainsborowe died, command was taken by George Cooke, once of Cambridge, Massachusetts, who participated in the savage sack of Wexford, of which he then became the military governor. George Fenwick, one of the leaders of the Connecticut River project at Saybrook, twice held seats in Parliament, commanded a regiment in the north, and became governor first of Berwick then of Leith and Edinburgh, ending in 1651 as one of the commissioners to govern Scotland. The pious Edward Hopkins, once a "Turkey merchant in London, of good credit and esteem," who served for years as governor of Connecticut, returned to London in 1652, where he became a member of Parliament, commissioner of the Navy, and keeper of the palace of Westminster. The New England ship captain Nehemiah Bourne saw action as a British naval commander in the 1650s and also was appointed a commissioner of the Navy. Robert Sedgwick, of Charlestown, prominent merchant, commander of Massachusetts's Artillery Company, and major general of the colony, was commissioned by Cromwell, along with his son-in-law Leverett, to lead an amphibious attack on New Netherland; when that project was terminated by the conclusion of the Dutch war in 1654, Sedgwick went on to lead a large naval expedition to reinforce Cromwell's Western Design in the Caribbean. The commission in charge of that vast and disastrous project was chaired by the Pilgrims' old negotiator, Edward Winslow, who had come to Cromwell's attention as a spokesperson for New England in London and had chaired a commission to adjudicate England's wartime claims against the Dutch. Though the Western Design failed in its main purpose, it did result in the capture of Jamaica, which Sedgwick, briefly, helped govern and whose economy he helped organize for further trade with New England. He died there in 1656.[37]

While a few became prominent, even famous, some became infamous. Hugh Peter had arrived in Boston in 1635, to work first with Winthrop, Jr., his son-in-law, thereafter to serve as minister at Salem, where he proved to be a popular preacher and a stalwart of the colony's nascent establishment. He returned to England in 1641 as one of the colony's agents, charged with burnishing the Puritans' darkening reputation and advancing the cause of their special church form. Frenetic in everything he did, Peter flung himself into endless rounds of preaching, organizing, negotiating, planning, publicizing, and counseling on Cromwell's and the colony's behalf. Distinguishing himself particularly as an inspiring army chaplain and tireless defender of Puritan reform, he disagreed with his American sponsors from time to time, especially on the question of toleration, but generally preached their Congregational version of reformed Christianity.

Often Peter and his colleague in the colony's agency, Thomas Weld, discussed returning to New England ("ah sweet New England," Peter wrote to Winthrop, Sr., while pleading for greater toleration), but caught up in the exciting swirl of great affairs, neither man did. Peter, however, never lost contact with the Puritan colony, and he did what he could to advise ambitious young New Englanders finding their way in Britain. An "eloquent, resolute, bustling little man," he was semiretired at the Restoration, and while he was not technically a regicide, he was widely hated by royalists and religious conservatives and was promptly charged with and convicted of treason and executed. His head was posted on display on London Bridge. Two years later Sir Henry Vane—the disfavored governor of Massachusetts in 1635–37 but always, as Winthrop wrote, "a true friend of N.E. & a man of noble & generous minde"—was similarly executed after a major career at the heart of England's revolutionary politics. As politician, diplomat, political and ecclesiastical theorist, official at various levels, and able administrator, for twenty years after he left Boston Vane had lived at the heart of British public life, ending, as did Hugh Peter, consistent in following the vision of his early years.[38]

But by far the most successful and famous—to many Puritans the most villainous—of the returnees was Winthrop's nephew, George Downing, a member of Harvard's first graduating class (1642), who was brought up under Hugh Peter's tutelage in Salem. At age twenty-two he left the colony to become a chaplain in the New Model Army. From there he rose in prominence and was appointed scoutmaster general of the English army in Scotland—in effect, head of army intelligence. Married to "a very beautiful Lady of a very Noble Extraction," he served in the Parliaments of the 1650s and began a series of diplomatic missions of increasing importance, developed a network of spies, and became a valued adviser on the fiscal power of state building. At the Restoration he deceitfully disowned his Puritan background and was taken on by the Crown for his skill in diplomacy, political economy, and intelligence gathering. Knighted in 1660, he received a baronetcy in 1662 and a plethora of lucrative offices. But his reputation as "a most ungrateful villaine" (Pepys) followed him as he organized the apprehension and execution of three regicides. Ruthless, ambitious, shrewd, and energetic, he served the Crown as "one of the most remarkable legislative entrepreneurs of his time" and as a designer of the fiscal-military state. Ultimately he became the wealthiest landowner in Cambridgeshire. In New England, however, Thomas Hutchinson later wrote, "it became a proverbial expression, to say of a false man who betrayed his trust, that he was an arrant George Downing."[39]

THE REMIGRATION HAD HAD a double effect. While it brought New England out into the mainstream of Cromwellian Britain insofar as some of its leading members contributed to the politics, religious life, and military efforts of the new regime, it drained from the colonies not only most of the outspoken dissidents but also many of the most broad-minded, innovative, and imaginative minds of the younger generation. Their instinct was to broaden the colony's culture, bring it out from its deepening provincialism into the modernizing world. "While old *England* is becoming new," the banned Baptist John Clarke declared, in his rollicking, satirical *Ill News from New-England*, "New-England is become Old." To many of its most sympathetic returnees, New England looked "more and more conservative, particularly in light of the political gains of the radicals during the years of the Long Parliament."[40]

Again and again the returnees wrote back pleading for greater toleration in the colonies they had left, for a loosening of the tight restrictions that had defined the New England Way. In 1645, a year after Massachusetts had banished all Baptists from the land, George Downing wrote John Winthrop, Jr., that the "law banishing for conscience . . . makes us stinke every wheare." At the same time Stephen Winthrop was writing his brother John from London that "heere is great complaint against us for our severitye against Anabaptist[s]. It doth discourag any people from coming to us for feare they should be banished if they discent from us in opinion." And Sir Richard Saltonstall, whose stay in Massachusetts had been so short, reacting to the persecution of three prominent Baptists of Rhode Island, expressed his grief at the "sadd things [that] are reported dayly of your tyranny and persecution"; these "rigid wayse," he insisted, "have layd you very lowe in the hearts of the saynts."[41]

But none were more insistent in seeking a broader, less restrictive society than the merchants, especially the young among them. For them the shock of the Civil War and the transformation of England, with its devastating effect on New England's economy, was a stimulus for new, imaginative, and innovative enterprises that would make Boston and its environs a hub of Atlantic commerce. But the transition from the gnarled world of Robert Keayne to the soaring amplitudes of the new commercial entrepreneurs would not be easy.

6

The economic situation after 1640 was desperate. Lacking the cash and credit supplied by incoming heads of families, the colonists' purchases of necessary goods from abroad could not be funded. Their credit in England dried up, the price of cattle collapsed, the markets for agricultural products became glutted, debts could not be discharged, and grain ceased to have monetary value. Friends in England warned that "if there not be some course taken for beter payments of our creditors our tradeing will utterly cease."

Facing disaster, the leaders moved in two directions: short term, to relieve the pressure on debtors, and long term, to create a permanent, self-sufficient economy free of the encroachments of the philistine world. Debtors could be helped, it seemed, simply by benevolent legislation. Laws were passed to prevent the ruinous valuation of foreclosed property; the pricing of seized property would thereafter be determined not by market forces but by the arbitration of "3 understanding and indifferent men." Further, all debts could thereafter be paid in "corne, cattle, fish, or other commodities," at rates also determined "by apprizment of indifferent men." Such decrees did ease some of the debtors' burdens, but they were weak gestures that could not in the long run loosen the grasp of creditors or pay for goods bought from abroad. What was needed was a local commodity valuable enough in England to serve as a direct means of payment, and beyond that, large-scale local production of essential goods that would relieve the burden of imports.[42]

There was hope—there had been from the start—that the fur trade could be developed to serve the European markets in immaculate exchanges—exchanges, that is, that did not embroil the Puritans in foreign dealings or draw to New England's shores crowds of riotous sailors, peddlers, and dock hands. New Haven's merchants—Theophilus Eaton, his son-in-law Edward Hopkins, and Daniel Yale—were among the most affluent immigrants, and they were especially well situated to draw on the furs available in western and northern New England and to tap into Manhattan's hinterland. There was hope that they might go beyond that, to reach the primal source of furs said to be somewhere around a great lake in the north, which the Laconia Company of 1629 had searched for in vain. But in fact the local sources had largely been exhausted. The furs they were able to collect were insufficient to contribute in any significant way to the balance of payments, and the "great Mediterranean sea" was never found, even by a newly licensed company of traders chartered to discover it. Nor did a scheme to penetrate north through the Delaware River succeed; that effort was quickly blocked by the Dutch. Scattered efforts to collect furs indirectly from Great Lakes sources continued, but with little success. Even the Pynchon family, who had become the landed gentry of western Massachusetts thoroughly versed in local geography and who for a while did profit from the pelts they acquired, could not produce anything like the furs needed to supply the needed remittances. By the 1650s the fur trade was in deep decline; by 1660 it was defunct.[43]

There remained the possibility that New England's economy could be rescued and would remain as independent as its churches and government if native manufactures could be created that would supply at least the two most vital imports: cloth goods and iron products.

In 1640 the General Court of Massachusetts offered a bounty on every shilling's worth of linen and woolen and cotton cloth spun and woven by the settlers, and required all servants and children to use their free time working on hemp and flax, which Connecticut ordered all families to plant. But it was wool that had the greatest promise, especially with the growing flocks of sheep in various areas of the region. But if there was enough wool, there were not enough cloth workers. And so Massachusetts prohibited all exports of sheep and lambs and ordered the towns to count up the number of spinners each family had available and ordered the designated spinners to turn out three pounds of linen, cotton, or wool threads every week for thirty weeks each year. The town of Rowley, settled by Yorkshire cloth workers, was productive and built a fulling and cloth-processing mill, but the legislation greatly exaggerated the effectiveness of government regulation in frontier communities. The laws could not be enforced, and it quickly became clear that New England would not develop a textile industry sufficient for its needs.[44]

But if furs and the production of textiles failed, some degree of self-sufficiency might be gained by a domestic iron industry, and for this there was a major effort—highly financed, technically sophisticated, and for a while productive. Its failure was not only an economic defeat but the source of a bitter ideological struggle that reached into the basics of Puritan belief and that created tension between Winthrop, Sr. and his son.

It had long been believed that ores of various kinds were abundant in New England, and Winthrop, Jr., like most of the pansophists of Hartlib's circle in London, was devoted to the study of minerals, their qualities and possibilities. He soon discovered excellent iron ore (bog iron) deposits near Braintree and Saugus, Massachusetts.

He had everything he needed to launch New England's iron industry: entrepreneurial skills; excellent contacts among scientists, technicians, and financiers; and above all energy and enthusiasm, generated by the belief that this project would realize some of the theories of the advanced thinkers of Europe. He shared their belief that in applied scientific knowledge, drawn from esoteric sources, lay hope for the true betterment of mankind. The ironworks project was not therefore merely a business enterprise that might help rescue New England's economy; it was also a demonstration that from hitherto unknown religio-scientific sources could come what the Rosicrucians believed would "regenerate the whole world." And he also had the collaboration of a remarkable young panso-phist thinker, agronomist, and ebullient "projector," Dr. Robert Child.[45]

The Cambridge-educated son of a prosperous landholder in Kent, Child had completed an extensive tour of Europe, touching base with circles of advanced scientific and commercial thinkers from Amsterdam to Rome, when he completed his medical studies in Padua in 1638. Then twenty-five, he joined Hartlib's circle and immersed himself in advanced alchemical, agricultural, and commercial studies. His focus was not on theories alone, however, but on the possibilities of putting them to work in practical affairs. Like many of the theorists, he saw in the *tabula rasa* of America in general and New England in particular a unique site for the practical application of the most advanced ideas. Within a year of his return to England, he left for America and made a survey of the colonies from the Chesapeake to Maine, assessing the possibilities in applied sci-ence and commercial development. He noted with approval the Puritan colonies' cultural advantages, especially the newly founded college in Cambridge to whose library he contributed books on science, the newly installed press, and the spread of local schools. In 1641 he returned to London with a comprehensive report on his findings and the determina-tion to follow words with deeds.

It was in London in 1641 that he probably met young Winthrop, then serving as an agent of the Bay Colony. The two had much in common. Both were entrepreneurial reformers devoted equally to science and religion. Both believed in the delicately balanced principles of worldly asceticism—commitments to industry and frugality, personal profit and the public good, the exploitation of God's benefactions and the stew-ardship of wealth. And both were pragmatists yet deeply engaged in the study of esoteric lore.

They quickly joined forces and together returned to New England. There Child immediately launched a series of projects ranging from the search for the Lake of the Iroquois to experiments with fruit and wine production in Maine, the development of a timber industry, expanded fisheries, and mining. But Child's major venture was the Saugus Iron-works, of which he became a major investor.[46]

The ironworks project had been initiated four years earlier when the younger Winthrop, fund-raising in England, had gathered twenty investors—men "of good rank and quality," some with extensive knowl-edge of iron manufacturing—into a Company of Undertakers for the Ironworks in New England. Upon his return to New England with a ship-load of miners, foundrymen, and laborers, he had launched the construc-tion at Saugus of a highly subsidized bloomery for smelting ore, a rolling and slitting mill, and a forge for crafting finished ironware products. He had extracted important concessions from the General Court—land grants, tax exemptions, a marketing monopoly, and the relaxation of legal and religious constraints on the labor force of "prophane persons" he had recruited. By 1645 the project was capitalized at over £15,000, the plant had a labor force of 135 workers, and its ironware was beginning to enter the local markets.[47]

But there were problems, and they quickly grew in severity. The company's profits were limited by the low market prices set for its prod-ucts by the government in exchange for its concessions, by the high cost of labor in the frontier economy, and by the difficulties of transporting supplies and products. The General Court was beginning to complain that the level of production was not matching the value of its subsidies, and the imported workers—strangers, the elder Winthrop wrote, "no members of churches . . . some of them corrupt in judgment, and oth-ers profane"—were proving to be increasingly obnoxious to the Puritan regime. Few of them, Winthrop discovered, were being "cured of their distempers" by the Puritans' admonitions, as he had hoped they would be. Massachusetts's immigration restrictions, believed to be necessary if the colony was to maintain its religious integrity, were proving to con-flict directly with the labor needs of the new enterprises. With Baptists, among other dissidents, flatly banned from the colony and Presbyterians, like Child himself, suspect despite the fact that Presbyterianism was now in the mainstream of post-Laudian England, the relationship between the Puritan governments and Child's enterprises grew bitter. The bitterness intensified when the ironworks' chief manager, Richard Leader, was cen-sured and fined for "slander and sedition" and for violating "Christianity, morality, and civility."

Child, shocked at discovering "lawes banishing and punishing all schismaticks," even those who had poured out their blood and estates in the service of Parliament, began a campaign of protest. Voicing the concerns of many of his coinvestors, he declared that nothing would ever prosper in New England unless there were liberty of conscience and unless the Puritan colonies relaxed their rules against "strangers."

Frustrated in many ways—as an investor in the ironworks, as a manager seeking a useful labor force, and as a Presbyterian "sojourner" barred from direct engagement in both church and state—Child found the situation intolerable. There was bitterness everywhere in New England, he reported to Hartlib, "breach upon breach"—between ministers and people and between members and nonmembers of the official community. Truly, he wrote, if things remained for long the way they were, everything would be lost. The situation had become so bad, he wrote, that to escape the Puritans' jurisdiction, he had decided to move to Maine, which he assumed was beyond Massachusetts's jurisdiction.

Other investors, even some close to the Puritan leadership, agreed, and the result was an open challenge to the Bay Colony's basic structure in the Remonstrance of May 1646.[48]

The Remonstrance was signed by seven men of varied religious background: two were Presbyterians, one was faithful to the Church of England, and the rest were Congregationalists of somewhat unsure commitment. All of the signers, and those who supported them, had grievances against the Puritan regime. Most, like Child, were reacting to the restrictions on the new enterprises; some were associated with agitators like William Vassall, who was petitioning Parliament to quash the Massachusetts charter; some came from towns that had controversies with the General Court; and some resented the disabilities of nonfreemen. Thus Thomas Burton, one of the signers, a churchman sympathetic to Presbyterianism and a lawyer of sorts, had been involved with the town of Hingham's explosive charge that the colony's magistrates had exceeded their legal powers, and another, David Yale, kin of the merchant founders of the New Haven colony, had suffered from the church trial and excommunication of his mother for "divers scandalous offences."[49]

The Remonstrance brought into sharp focus all of these grievances and all of Child's resentments of the restrictions he had endured personally and those that had been imposed on the enterprises he had designed for the betterment of mankind. The seven signers, representing, they said, "divers others," presented themselves, in an elaborate, ironic metaphor, as being "under decks, being at present unfit for higher employ-ments," but in that lowly position in the Bay Colony's ship of church and state, they were in a good position to "perceive those leaks which will inevitably sink this weake and ill compacted vessell."

Obviously, they wrote, God's hand, which had preserved the colonists in their settlement in New England, had turned against them, blasting all their carefully planned designs and excellent prospects. Instead of the "staple commodities" and "comfortable subsistance" the complainants had looked forward to, they had been devastated by "unwonted malig-nant sicknesses" and brought to the brink of poverty. Despite their best efforts, "even to the exhausting of our estates and spirits," things were getting worse all the time, "threatening (in our apprehensions) of no less than finall ruine." And why? What were the "special leaks" that were leading them and New England to catastrophe?

First: though they were all English, they had been denied the "sure and comfortable enjoyment of our lives, libertyes, and estates, accord-ing to our due and naturall rights, as freeborne subjects of the English nation." What was needed was the establishment of "the fundamentall and wholesome lawes of our native country . . . agreeable to our English tempers" in place of the peculiar ordinances of the Bible Commonwealth.

Second: the limitation of the colony's franchise and officeholding to church members was odious, and in this they spoke for the "many thou-sands," including friends of the victorious reform Parliament of England, who had been disbarred from "all civill imployments" in the colony, though they were freely taxed and their goods seized at will. Massachu-setts, they pointed out, was not a sovereign state but merely "a colonie or corporation of England." The denial of English rights had led to "secret discontents, murmurings . . . discouragements in their callings, unset-tlednes in their minds, strife, [and] contention . . . The Lord only knows to what a flame in time it may kindle."

And third: the "sober, righteous and godly" members of the Church of England, even those agreeable to the "latest and best reformation of England, Scotland, &c" (i.e., Presbyterians) were denied communion in New England's churches. And they were compelled "under a severe fine, every Lords day to appear at the congregation" and to attend the baptism of other men's children but not their own. Give liberty to the Church of England members, they wrote; take them into your congregations, that they may enjoy all of Christ's liberties and ordinances.

All of this, the Remonstrants insisted, must be done or, they concluded portentously, we "shall be necessitated to apply our humble desires to the honourable houses of parliament, who we hope will take our sad conditions into their serious considerations."[50]

The threat was not lost on the colony's magistrates. The General Court immediately appointed a committee, which included Winthrop, Sr., Dudley, and Bellingham, to respond to the challenge.

Their response was uncompromising. They denied all the allegations and denounced the Remonstrants for their "dareing presumption" in invoking God's name to serve their "corrupt project." The petitioners spoke of leaks that will sink New England's civil and ecclesiastical government, "houlding us forth as the scumme and off-scouring" that our English brethren "avoyde as a pest." But in fact Massachusetts's government is framed by its charter, which includes the fundamental and common laws of England, making allowance for the disproportion between the populous, wealthy kingdom and the poor infant colony and for provincials' understandable ignorance of the niceties of English law.

On every point the Remonstrants are wrong, the magistrates continued. *Is it offensive, as they claim, that the magistrates [upper house] have a veto power in the legislature?* That structure follows perfectly the model of mixed government. *Oaths and covenants are arbitrary?* There are none that are not allowed by the charter and that were practiced when the company was still in England. *Unjust taxes?* Nothing is charged but what is absolutely necessary and which all freemen and officers pay equally. And did the Remonstrants say *they speak for all nonfreemen?* Not one had joined them in their protest. And all nonfreemen should know from their experiences elsewhere—Virginia, London—that "Englishmen may live comfortably and securely under some other lawes besides the common and statute lawes of England" and that the privileges of freeborn Englishmen do not include the right to vote, even if they pay taxes. Yet here as in England nonfreemen received the same justice as freemen, and they have the same right to property and the same access to church, assembly, and trade.

And who, in any case, are these Remonstrants? What stake do they have in the colony? One, Child, is but a sojourner here who has never paid a penny in taxes. A second chooses not to be a freeman in order to escape burdens. A third is a freeman but chooses not to be a church member. A fourth is also a sojourner and has no estate. A fifth is too young to know of commonwealth affairs. A sixth is in fact a resident of Rhode Island, not Massachusetts. And the seventh is "an ould grocer of London" who is so ancient and so infirm that he has forgotten the laws of London and the duties one owed government.

As for the complaint that "sober, righteous and godly men" are barred from sharing in the church covenant: such charges are misrepresentations. The truth is that many of those who are not admitted to church communion are "fraudulous" in their testimonials of faith, or corrupt in their opinions, or ignorant of the principles of religion, or simply refuse publicly to profess their convictions. Few have ever been denied simply because they refused to testify to their faith. And those who refuse, if they agree to commit to the ordinances of Christ, will be admitted.

Do the Remonstrants object to compulsory church attendance? Surely "sober and godly" men, such as they profess to be, need no compulsion to attend church: only the "loose and irreligious" need to be compelled. Should *all* be allowed into full communion, as they demand? Some certainly need to be "fitted" for communion by instruction before they are admitted; otherwise ignorant and profane people will populate the congregations. As to the ban on Baptists, such was their contentiousness that the colony had to provide for its own safety by keeping them out. Anyone we consider "in charity . . . to be beleevers" are freely admitted to private prayers and are visited in times of sickness "&c," unless they refuse this benevolence. Finally, as to the denial of baptism to nonmembers' children, that matter is now under discussion and will soon be decided.

There is no general issue, the General Court wrote. The Remonstrants' belief that everyone should be allowed unfettered liberty and that no distinctions should ever be drawn among people has been utterly refuted by experience. Eight years ago we had just such claimants "who out of theire tendernes of libertie of conscience, and civill libertie . . . made greate disturbance both in church and civill state." They predicted, as now do the Remonstrants, that without these total liberties there will be ruin in the land, and so they fled to Rhode Island, where they established the regime of their desires. "But alas! it was but a dreame . . . For this liberty and equallity so fomented [men's] naturall corruption" that they fell out among themselves, split off into three or four groups, and ended by destroying both church and state. From such a fate "the Lord deliver us, and all the seed of Israell to the comeing of Christ Jesus."[51]

But the Lord, they knew, saves those who save themselves, and the

Puritan establishment wasted no time in taking action to provide for New England's deliverance from this peril. Two of the petitioners, attempting to leave Massachusetts, were apprehended and forced to post bond for their good behavior before being released. The remaining Remonstrants were formally charged with twelve counts of defamation, slander, sedition, and denying the jurisdiction of the Court. Despite the point-by-point denial that the petitioners quickly composed, they were all convicted—Child for threatening an appeal to Parliament and for contemptuous speeches—and fined until they repented.

Once freed, Child busied himself preparing documents to present to Parliament, but he failed to anticipate the Puritans' vigilance. His papers were seized before his ship sailed, and they were publicly examined. To the magistrates' horror, they included not only a petition from nonfreemen for liberty of conscience and for the appointment of a royal governor, but also the Remonstrants' tale of mistreatment and their demands that a Presbyterian church system be established and that oaths of loyalty to England be extracted from the colonists. And beyond even that, they requested the forfeiture of Massachusetts's charter and raised the question of whether treasonous statements had not been uttered in both church and state in Massachusetts.[52]

Nothing could have been more inflammatory. Child was hauled before the governor and Council with little ceremony. Denounced, the Baconian scientist, rationalist, and world reformer flew into "a great passion, and gave big words." He calmed down only when told to behave himself like the person of quality he was or he would be clapped in irons and thrown into prison. He then agreed to post bonds of £800 to guarantee his remaining in Boston until his trial, and settled in with the manager of the ironworks to await the verdict—two verdicts, in fact: one for his involvement in the Remonstrance and another for his role in writing the inflammatory documents that had been discovered.

The first judgment came in November 1646, when his colleagues were variously punished for their crimes; Child was fined £50. Months passed until in June 1647 he was tried again and this time fined £200 for conspiring to subvert the government of the Bay Colony. Once the verdicts were in, there followed a blur of payments, refusals, jailings, and abatements that lasted into the 1650s. Child himself paid his £200 fine, but when in October 1647 he returned to England, he left the £50 fee to be drawn out of his investments in the ironworks.[53]

Upon his arrival in London he discovered that while he had been fighting the charges in Boston, Massachusetts had dispatched to England the "Smothe tounged Cunning" Edward Winslow to represent its interest before Parliament's Commission for Plantations. The notorious Gorton had preceded him and was petitioning Parliament on behalf of Rhode Island and against Massachusetts; in August 1646 he had published his elaborate indictment of the Puritans, *Simplicities Defence . . . or Innocency Vindicated.* In his campaign against the Bay Colony Gorton had been joined by the well-connected, cantankerous William Vassall, always a thorn in Winthrop's side ("a man of a busye & factious spirit, & allwayes opposite to the Civill Governmentes of the Countrye"), who had left New England with the Remonstrants. The two demanded universal toleration in New England, as did Maj. John Child, Robert's brother, determined to justify the Remonstrants' charges and redeem his brother's reputation. Winslow quickly replied to Gorton's assault in his own fiery *Hypocracie Unmasked,* to which John Child replied in *New-England's Jonas Cast up at London,* a narrative of New England's persecution of "divers honest and godly persons" for merely seeking "Ministers and Church-government according to the best Reformation of England and Scotland."

The charges and countercharges were prolix, ponderously documented, bitter, and vivid. But what mattered in the end was the judgment of Parliament's plantation commissioners, and for them the issue proved to be clear. They had no interest in entertaining endless appeals from Massachusetts and no interest in narrowing the compass of the powers granted in the colony's charter. We leave the colony, they wrote, "with all that freedom and latitude that may, in any respect, be duly claimed by you; knowing that the limiting of you . . . may be very prejudicial (if not destructive) to the government and public peace of the colony."[54]

Massachusetts could have asked for no more. Its establishment had been vindicated. But it was a costly victory. Not only had the ironworks failed but something essential had been lost in Child's departure, besides the prospect of imaginative, large-scale projects. He had never been an enemy of Puritan reform. He represented, in fact, the magnification of its most exalted aspirations, the transformation of mankind in the approach to the final days. And there was no contradiction between the Puritans' concept of work and Child's sphere of activity, which, like Hartlib's and Winthrop, Jr.'s, was devoted to the exploitation of the resources with which God had endowed mankind. He too operated, Margaret Newell writes, "within an organic, hierarchical social structure inimical to notions of possessive individualism, domestic consumption, and competition. . . . For Child, economic progress and Protestantism were inextricably intertwined." Yet though intimately involved in Puritanism, Child—age thirty-three, confronting the sixty-year-old Winthrop—was responding too to an impulse that would supersede both his and the governor's world. At the heart of his efforts, though still mingled with and dominated by the moral imperatives of reformed Protestantism, lay a more ruthless force that in the next generation would emerge freely: the force of entrepreneurship for its own sake, of profiteering for profit's sake, of avarice unencumbered with moral obligations. For Child the moral integument of his enterprise was essential. His struggle had been with the external constraints and institutional structures of a peculiar Puritan regime, whose essential purpose he could only endorse.[55]

Freed from New England, Child continued his redemptive entrepreneurship in Ireland, where he actively and happily communed with Hartlib's "invisible college," occasionally recalling his frustrated efforts in New England.[56] So too Winthrop, Jr. continued his studies, his experiments, his widespread medical practice, and his collaboration with the illuminati in London, and he turned also to public service. In 1659 he accepted the governorship of Connecticut, a position he held until his death nineteen years later. But the failure of the ironworks project and the troubles of his colleague Child had been trials for him too, in a deeply personal way.

His respect and affection for his father, who had led the proceedings against his friend Child and the other Remonstrants, never diminished. He remained dutiful, respectful, and caring. But increasingly, and especially at this time, the two Winthrops differed on the limits of toleration, the father deeply entrenched in defense of his carefully delimited domain, the son reaching out more and more broadly to the open-ended world of science, arcane experimentation, and energetic entrepreneurship. All magistrates, the younger Winthrop wrote, must defend the profession of the Gospel and maintain civil order. But when "men exercising a good conscience" differ in interpreting the ways of worship or the meaning of doctrine without disturbing others, "there is no warrant for the magistrate under the Gospell to abridge them of their liberty."

The tension between father and son led to sadness and concern, and also to the respectful avoidance of confrontation. Winthrop, Jr. had remained silent during the Antinomian Controversy, busying himself with private matters, and he had been absent also at the trials of Child and the Remonstrants. He knew, as Richard Dunn has written, that his father's "operating Massachusetts like a sovereign state, dissociated from Parliament as well as the King, was harming New England's development," but he did not say so. Similarly, Winthrop, Sr. did not object to his son's takeover of Pequot land for his experimental settlement in New London, though he had reason to do so. At the end he did not counsel his son but only asked him to respect authority, hoping that he would do the right thing.[57]

7

By 1649, when Winthrop, Sr. died, New England's economy was beginning, slowly, to recover, despite all the early failures, but in ways that the great Puritan magistrate would not have approved. While schemes for a self-enclosed, self-sustaining domestic economy had come and gone, while government subsidies had been devised and discarded and ordinary people had hoped and despaired, small traders had been busy feeling their way into the elaborating trading circuits of the Atlantic basin. They were obscure men of the first Puritan generation, none of them very wealthy, few of them greatly daring, but most of them well connected at home. All were convinced that New England had to "learn commerce or perish." Later the question would arise how, if at all, their involvement in the intractable world of Atlantic commerce might be accommodated within the Puritan scheme of things. But in the 1640s the main problem was simply how they might engage with the Atlantic trading system and profit from it.

The rudiments had long been evident, in trading connections with the chaotic West Indies in general and Barbados in particular. Despite the tumultuous, often bloody conflicts among the European powers for control of the increasingly valuable islands, trade with New England had been established in the 1630s. Indeed, the possibility of such contacts had been evident even before the Great Migration. Winthrop's "scrapegrace" second son, Henry, had been one of the first colonists on Barbados, serving the powerful Courteen syndicate there as early as 1627, while the Winthrop family's good friend from Suffolk, Sir Thomas Warner, settled in as the long-serving governor of the English part of the divided St.

Kitts. Later the possibilities of a lucrative trade with the Caribbean would be explored in a letter to Winthrop, Jr. by his cousin George Downing, then a wandering twenty-two-year-old, in which he shrewdly assessed the economic potential of each of the main islands, concluding from Barbados that "Negroes [are] the life of this place." The more the settlers bought them, "the better able they are to buye, for in a yeare and halfe they will earne . . . as much as they cost." He had a receptive reader. John, Jr., like others in the family, especially Stephen and Samuel, would eventually be involved in the slave trade, as they would be in all aspects of West Indian commerce.[58]

The essence and starting point of the Caribbean trade were New England's fisheries. The region's fishing grounds had long been known to be fertile, close to shore, and easily workable. The value of the fish—cod, mackerel, bass, and sturgeon—for Catholic Europe and the plantations in the Atlantic and Caribbean islands was obvious, as were the markets there for the produce of New England's farms—beef, pork, bread, flour, and timber products, especially pipestaves, and horses to power the sugar mills.[59]

Simple bilateral trade with the Caribbean islands had sprung up quickly. Between 1630 and 1640 at least twenty ships are known to have sailed between New England and Barbados, Bermuda, Providence Island, St. Kitts, and Tortuga, returning with cotton, tobacco, sugar, slaves, and tropical produce. In 1640 alone eleven ships loaded with lumber sailed from New England's ports to the West Indies, and it was at that point, as New England's economy plummeted, that the potential of this commerce began to be fully appreciated and its benefits realized. Like the English and French traders, the Puritan merchants "poured like flies," a leading historian of the West Indies writes, "upon the rotting carcase of Spain's empire in the Caribbean."[60]

In all of the expanding trade to the Caribbean they were not acting alone. English merchants were eager for a share of the trade and the profits of freightage, and they had the capital, shipping, and potential markets needed for complex, expensive, and risky ventures. Often they worked within family networks, for the most reliable partners and agents were kinsmen. Brothers, sons, and in-laws became key cogs in the commercial mechanism. Together, in shifting patterns of shares, partnerships, and agencies, they joined in ventures that spread across large areas of the Atlantic. So Valentine Hill drew bills of exchange on his brother

John, "merchant at the Angell and Starre in Cheapside." Joshua Hewes received shipments of merchandise from his uncle Joshua Foote, who became so interested in the American trade that he sent over his son Caleb to join his Hewes cousins in the family's transactions. The success of Henry Shrimpton, who left property worth £12,000 at his death in 1666, was based on the credit he received from his brother Edward, a London merchant. John Hull built up a flourishing business with the help of his uncle, Thomas Parris, a haberdasher, and his "coz Edw" Hull at the "Hatte-in-Hand" within Aldegate, London. When young Samuel Winthrop moved from Tenerife to Barbados and eventually Antigua, the Winthrops, centered in England and Massachusetts, extended their trade from Rhode Island and Connecticut to the West Indies. So too the troublesome William Vassall, together with his wealthy merchant brother Samuel in London, was careful to keep in touch with his commercial agents in New England and to protect his extensive landholdings there. Settled permanently in Barbados, he joined with Samuel in far-flung enterprises, but the connection with New England remained vital; its produce was essential for the development of his West Indian properties. For others of the business elite in London whose religious views had brought them into the Puritans' orbit—Maurice Thompson, Matthew Craddock—New England's West Indian trade became a normal part of the networks of Atlantic commerce they personally controlled.[61]

But the Hutchinson network was the most complete such trading unit of which we have knowledge. It was based on the continuous flow of manufactures sent from London by the affluent Richard Hutchinson to his brothers Samuel and Edward and his nephews Elisha and Eliakim, in Boston, who worked together with Richard's brother-in-law Thomas Savage. All five marketed the imported goods in the bay area and in inland communities, whose products they shipped out to the West Indies in exchange for cotton and sugar, which were shipped back to London. Much of the family's trade was managed by Peleg Sanford in Portsmouth, Rhode Island, a nephew of Richard, hence cousin and nephew of the family's Boston merchants. Peleg ran the family's cattle farms in Rhode Island and shipped horses, provisions, and manufactured goods to his brothers, the Barbadian merchants William and Elijah Sanford. Richard in London, the Hutchinson kin in Boston and Rhode Island, together with their Barbadian relatives, operated in a constantly shifting series of combinations, as partners or agents or as customers to each other. They formed a self-conscious family group that considered it unfortunate but not unnatural that Edward Hutchinson should go to jail, as he did in 1667, as a consequence of his support of his nephew Peleg in a lawsuit.[62]

The ties of kinship mattered most, however, in the more dynamic, riskier, more volatile, less predictable ventures that reached out south and east into the farther reaches of the Atlantic trading system. Such far-flung exchanges were initiated in 1641 by Massachusetts's stubborn Anglican, Samuel Maverick, who paid for purchases in Bristol by sending clapboards to Málaga, on Spain's Mediterranean coast, whence his agent sent remittances back to his creditors in England. The New Havenites made similar exchanges through the Canaries, and a small group joined to send fish, oil, and pipestaves to Fayal in the Azores for similar remittances. In 1643 no fewer than five vessels left New England with shiploads to Fayal, Bilbao, Málaga, and Madeira. In April 1645 a ship left Massachusetts for the Canaries loaded with pipestaves; from there it turned to the Cape Verde islands, where it took on "Africoes," who were sold in Barbados for wine, sugar, salt, and tobacco. The ship's principal owner was listed simply as "Winthrop," probably John, Jr., whose uncle Emmanuel Downing had written enthusiastically about the value of importing slaves. "I doe not see," he wrote, "how wee can thrive untill wee gett into a stock of slaves suffitient to doe all out buisnes." For indentured servants, he explained, will "desire freedome to plant for them selves, and not stay but for verie great wages." It is cheaper to maintain twenty "Moores," he concluded, than one English servant.[63]

THUS IN ITS ENGAGEMENT with the greater Atlantic world, New England found its economic bearing, which would remain secure for the next century and beyond. As a result, while the country towns multiplied in stable and familiar form, increasingly provincial and rustic, the main commercial centers—Charlestown, Salem, and especially Boston—were transformed into dynamic economic hubs. Their expanding businesses required wharves and storehouses, shops and marketplaces. The preparation and disposition of their cargoes called for laborers, handicraftsmen, and roadways into the interior; and the equitable conduct of trade called for official regulation of markets and of weights and measures, the care and protection of the harbors, and easily accessible courts of law. In thirty years the makeshift hamlet on the peninsula in Massachusetts Bay had grown into a thriving commercial community of three thousand souls that could muster "fouer companys of Foote and a Troope of horse."[64]

But this was not Winthrop's world, and its development was marked by repeated clashes with the custodians of the City on the Hill. Piety was not incompatible with commerce, not then and not later. In the smaller port towns of Marblehead and Gloucester, "the coming of commerce did nothing to alter the character of local religious belief and practice." But in general the spiritual health of the Puritan community required isolation from the contamination of Old World sin and respect for the domination of the Puritan magistrates. By performing their indispensable economic function, the merchants, most of whom did not seek the destruction of Puritan society, deprived the community of its isolation and challenged its patriarchalism. Trade required the free movement of people and goods and a rising population. Should strangers come freely to New England shores? Should the sailors and merchants of all nations traffic in Massachusetts ports? In 1645 four prominent merchants, including Robert Sedgwick, led a group that protested the laws limiting residence of unaccredited strangers in Massachusetts to three weeks and banishing the Anabaptists. The General Court, under pressure from the clergy, rejected the protest, refusing not only to alter the laws but even to explain them. In 1651, well after the struggle over Child's Remonstrance, the General Court required every stranger over sixteen years of age to present himself upon arrival to two magistrates, who would pass on his fitness to remain. The next year the Court required a written oath of fidelity to Massachusetts from all those suspected of disloyalty and from any stranger who had lived in the colony for two months or more.[65]

Though the merchants sympathized with all efforts to maintain civil order, they tended to side with the dissidents in the attacks, small and large, directed at the reigning magistracy. For the establishment, the future, as seen in the behavior of the rising generation, looked bleak. The children of the founders, however well intentioned, knew nothing of the fire that had steeled the hearts of their fathers. They seemed to their elders to be frivolous, given to excess in dress and manners, lacking in fierceness of belief, and only too receptive to some of the most alien among the incoming strangers.

As the original Puritan tradesmen and merchants died off in the 1650s and early 1660s, new men began to appear. Some were utter strangers, entirely alien to the Puritans' culture—men like the supercargo Thomas Breeden, whose interests were exclusively commercial. Even his dress was outlandish, defiant—a four-cornered hat and breeches hung with ribbons from the waist downward, "one row over the other like shingles on a house." The children in the street made such a commotion at the sight of him that people came out of their houses to see what the trouble was. Breeden was after big game in the commercial hunt, but he was himself a small figure next to Richard Wharton, who also arrived in the 1650s. To this "economic imperialist, interested in business as a source of private wealth, of public prosperity, and of national expansion," whose interests would expand into large-scale land speculation, monetary policy, commercial warfare with the Dutch, naval stores, and mining, and who favored a royal government for Massachusetts, the attitudes and institutions of Puritanism were archaisms, alien to his interests, which he sought relentlessly to pursue.

That pursuit was greatly enhanced by the Restoration in 1660. The restored monarchy projected powers that, while restrictive for some, created opportunities for others that led to advancement and profits at a new, elevated level. For those so favored, royal preferment and its benefits meant not only economic and political advantages unknown before but a new form of social distinction. At the same time, the influence and institutions of the Puritan elders were crumbling. The mere passage of years, attended by a "declension" of religious fervor, splintered the ecclesiastical unity within the Bible Commonwealth and weakened the position of its church. Continuously through the post-Restoration years, the voices of the guardians of the Puritan virtues were heard, shrill and anxious, pleading with the sons and grandsons of the founders to remember the rock whence they were hewn. But stronger forces were at work. In 1663 the powerful Salem preacher John Higginson cried out, in his election day sermon, against the notion that God's purpose in establishing New England was "the getting of this world's good." Never forget, he declared to his congregation and to the world at large, "that *New England is originally a plantation of religion, not a plantation of trade.*" Nine years later his daughter Sarah married Richard Wharton.[66]

PART III

Emergence

CHAPTER 15

The British Americans

T HEY LIVED CONFLICTED LIVES, beset with conflicts experienced, rumored, or recalled—unrelenting racial conflicts, ferocious and savage; religious conflicts, as bitter within as between confessions; conflicts with authority, private and public; recurrent conflicts over property rights, legal obligations, and status; and conflicts created by the slow emergence of vernacular cultures, blendings of disparate subcultures adjusting to the demands of heightened aspirations and local circumstance.

1

There was never a time, over a half century of settlement, when there was not a racial conflict in one or another of the European colonies in coastal North America—not only random killings on isolated border lands and deadly attacks by ruthless traders, but concerted wars of devastation different from the precontact Indian wars and beyond the rules of civilized warfare, the principles of just war, and Christian moderation, which in some degree had softened the impact of military conflict in Europe. If there were familiar precedents for the Indian wars in seventeenth-century North America, they were the exceptions to the normal practices of European warfare: the merciless slaughter and devastation reserved for conquered towns and cities that refused to surrender when sieged; domestic rebels who openly challenged established regimes; or heretics whose radical doctrines threatened to destroy the stability of civil society. For these, in the wars of the sixteenth and early seventeenth centuries, there had been, and was, no mercy. So in Elizabethan Ireland, where the conquering English were convinced that the natives were utter barbarians who lived like beasts, "more uncivill, more uncleanly, more barbarous, and more brutish . . . than in any other parts of the world" and that their warriors were mere rebels and traitors, there were no limits on the conquerors' savagery. Again and again whole garrisons were massacred, hundreds of men, women, and children slaughtered whether or not they resisted, and terror tactics were unrestrained. Humphrey Gilbert famously lined up on both sides of the path to his tent the severed heads of some of those he had killed so that those who came to speak with him were forced to see "the heddes of their dedde fathers, brothers, children, kinsfolks and freindes lye upon the grounde before their faces." Rebels in England suffered similarly brutal fates. And nothing had been more devastating, and better known throughout Protestant Europe, than the Duke of Alba's savagery in his efforts to suppress the Dutch revolt. The retaliatory executions in the conquered city of Mons, in Hainault, proceeded at a leisurely pace: for a full year "ten, twelve, twenty persons were often hanged, burned, or beheaded in a single day."[1]

The experience and knowledge of such extreme but not uncommon events were carried to North America by the many veterans of the Dutch rebellion and the Thirty Years War who were sent to the colonies to protect the settlements and to suppress the Indians' resistance to presumably legitimate authority. Hundreds of hardened "hammerours," they were led by professional officers: De La Warr, Kendall, Martin, Wingfield, Ratcliffe, and Smith, in Virginia; Printz in New Sweden; Endecott, Underhill, Mason, Standish, and Gardiner in New England. So closely linked were the incidences of racial conflict, so extended their deadly aftermaths, that one can conceive of a single, continuous Euro-Indian war—precisely the Virginia Company's hoped-for "perpetuall Warr without peace or truce"—that lasted from 1607 to 1664 and beyond, to reach its climax in the ferocious upheavals, north and south, in the 1670s.

The lines were blurred; encounters merged. So the devastating "feed fights" that followed the bloody massacre in Virginia of 1622—looting and destroying by fire the Indians' crops in the fields and in storage—were still in progress when the Puritans' small but efficient army, backed by Narragansett and Mohegan allies, burned alive the hundreds of unsuspecting Pequot men, women, and children, slaughtered all those they found attempting to escape, and hunted the rest down as they fled into swamps and the deepest woods. When the native survivors of that war drifted westward and south they found themselves caught up in the beginning of Kieft's War, which tore like wildfire through the Anglo-Dutch population. The four years of that eviscerating conflict, in which Underhill repeated his bloody successes of the Pequot War, seared the countryside from the upper Delaware to Manhattan and the settlements on the upper Hudson and touched off revenge assaults on isolated settlements like that of the exiled Anne Hutchinson. At the same time Maryland and its allies, the Piscataways, came under savage attack by the feared Susquehannocks, whose continuous raids wiped out the Jesuit communities and led to severe retaliation by the settlers that in turn helped precipitate the massacre of 1644 in Virginia.[2] That bloody effort of the last of the major Powhatan chiefs, Opechancanough, to repel the encroaching English failed, after murdering four to five hundred settlers, but it led to two years of the same kind of retaliatory village burnings, contrived famines, and killings that had followed the massacre of 1622. The Dutch war subsided, but there was no peace, only a respite before the resumption of warfare in the 1650s, now focused on defending New Netherland's northern communities and the pursuit of the Indians to the west.

Only twice in the long litany of wars, raids, and scorched-earth retribution were there moments of serious doubt and reflection among the Europeans about the moral grounds of the conflicts they were engaged in. For the Virginians, war against the Indians was a matter of survival in a world of treacherous savages who threatened their existence. For the Puritans, war with the natives was a struggle with satanic forces whose "extirpation" was a Christian duty. Only for the Dutch, arguably the most ferocious of the Indian fighters, were the moral issues confronted as such. Mindful that they themselves had been victims of a conqueror's savagery and proud of their humanist tradition, they could not evade the ethical implications of what was happening in their settlements and on their distant frontier. The Dutch West India Company's blistering condemnation of Kieft's War, in which every word carried a freight of distinct meaning—*unnatural, barbarous, unnecessary, unjust, and disgraceful*"—was sincere. So too was Stuyvesant, the former theology student, in twice convening his council for formal debates on whether war against the Esopus Indians was justified. Would this be a just war? he asked in 1655. By what reasoning? He spoke of the issues at length and demanded written responses of the councilors. Ideas were exchanged; "just and sufficient causes" were searched for and found. At this point Stuyvesant opposed the war, was outvoted, then equivocated, until pressure from the panicked settlers, fearful for their lives, forced him to launch the war, which, like its predecessors, was fought barbarously and mercilessly—yet not without a sense of guilt and self-reproach. By 1660, after waves of raids and murders on both sides, he justified aggressive, unbounded war on the grounds that the natives were "barbarous savages," "a species apart," incapable of, and unfettered by, laws, governance, and rational negotiation. "The story of New Netherland is not a tale of tragedy," Donna Merwick writes in exploring the moral dilemmas of the Dutch, but "the record of the Dutch encounter with the native population is a tragedy. . . . The Dutch acted out a betrayal of ideals and accepted values: betrayal of themselves and others. They reaped the shame and the sorrow."[3]

By 1664 the Indians' world in coastal North America had been utterly transformed, their lifeways disrupted and permanently distorted. The demographic losses had been catastrophic. By the 1630s the Algonquian population of Virginia, which once had numbered between 14,000 and 22,000, "was nearing a state of collapse"; by 1656 the once proud overlords of the Virginia plain were reported to be "in absolute subjection to the English"; by 1669 a census revealed that the population had been literally decimated; two thousand survivors, banished from their ancestral lands, were huddled on reservations, tributaries to some twenty-five thousand Europeans. By then 90 percent of the estimated 125,000 Algonquian-speaking natives of southern New England had been wiped out by epidemics related to contact with the Europeans (1616–19, 1633–39) and by warfare that had destroyed at least 10 percent of the rest.[4]

Less palpable, less easily identified, but more widespread—radiating out into the interior—were the indirect effects of contacts with the Europeans, which had begun even before there were permanent settlements: unaccustomed migration patterns due to pressure on land, intertribal warfare in the near backcountry, mergers among displaced groups of Indians, the loss of tribal identity, and the disruption of customary behavior. The natives' universe of balance and reciprocity in exchanges, material and spiritual, was undermined, and the attempts to Christianize the Indians introduced conflicts within the tribes that reached into the foundations of certainty and generated factions based on variant responses to what has been called "the invasion within."[5] Nor within these altered conditions was a new stability reached in these years. By the end of the period change in the natives' world was accelerating, not diminishing, stability was increasingly fragile, and one looked to the future with bewilderment and foreboding.

For the settlers, who suffered less in terms of fatalities, the constant violence, the unpredictability of sudden attacks, and the sight of atrocities reminiscent of the worst excesses of European wars bred an ever-present anxiety, a sense of dread and apprehension that permeated everyday existence. Twenty years after the Pequot War, Lion Gardiner, one of New England's most experienced soldiers, a veteran of the wars in Europe, prayed for a "naturall" and honorable death, "not [in captivity] to have a sharp stake . . . thrust into my fundament and to have my skin flaid of[f] by piecemeale and cut in pieces and bits and my flesh rosted and thrust down my throat as thes[e] people have done." Beyond such manifest fears lay a general anxiety, that in this perilous borderland world the normal rules of civility were being suspended, that human relations were being reduced to atavistic struggles, and that the Europeans were threatened with what Cotton Mather would call "creolian degeneracy."[6]

So in the New Haven colony, a cluster of eight hamlets in southern Connecticut, elaborate provisions were made to arm and train every man sixteen to sixty years of age. Watchmen were on the alert all through the night. The colony was divided into squadrons commanded by captains elected for "all martiall affayres," one squadron designated to attend every Sabbath meeting "completely armed, fitt for service with att the least 6 charges of shott and pouder" and with the matches of the patrolling sentinels' muskets lit at all times. Fines were liberally imposed to strengthen military preparedness—fines for any citizen's "defect in armes," for coming to prayer without guns, for sleeping on the watch, for coming late to military exercises.[7]

There was much to suggest to future chroniclers of early British America that this was a bucolic world of peaceful settlers at work in a quickly developing economy, effectively re-creating European folkways. There were flourishing plantations in the upper south, which boasted orchards and gardens; public offices and institutions were being created in all of the colonies; and the elaboration of kinship and neighborhood networks, especially on the Eastern Shore of Chesapeake Bay, suggested a stable, structured world. Similarly, well-organized villages were multiplying in the north, fields were being cleared, crops were being sown and harvested, livestock were increasing, and capital was being created that would result, eventually, in new wealth and remarkable productivity and population growth. Further, sermons were being preached, written, published, and discussed, ideas were circulating, and in places the life of the mind was flourishing. But this was not a peaceful world, evolving steadily and naturally into the civil society of the eighteenth century.[8]

The sense of stability and confidence in the future were shaken by the fear of lurking plots and sudden upheavals. Sensibilities coarsened when brutality grew commonplace. The desecration of bodies, so much a part of the Indians' search for reciprocity in warfare and diplomacy, became for the Europeans a search for domination. Just as the Indians in Virginia were seen "defacing . . . and mangling [the colonists'] dead carcasses into many pieces, and carrying some parts away in derision," so the Virginians "ransaked their Temples, Tooke downe the Corpes of their deade kings from of[f] their Toambes," engaged freely in scalping, and did not hesitate to decapitate their enemies in campaigns of terror. (Percy, casually: "I cawsed the Indians heade to be Cutt of[f]"; Kiefft, coolly: ten fathoms of wampum for a Raritan's head, twenty for a suspected murderer's.) Extreme episodes were not forgotten. Just as Captain Davis in Virginia, under pressure from his superiors, had stabbed an Indian "queen" to death as a merciful alternative to burning her alive, so Captain Underhill was thought to have been considerate when he shot to death at point-blank range a captive Pequot being torn to pieces, limb from limb, by vengeful Mohegans. There was no peace after the slaughter of the Pequot War, whose bloody climax had left Captain Mason in a dream-like state of jubilation. The colonists' victory in that "contest of terror" sentenced them to "years of fear and paranoia" and a legacy of "suspicion, fear, and additional violence." Massachusetts claimed that some of the murderers of Englishmen, undoubtedly Pequots, were still at large (the tolerant Roger Williams, who knew the local tribes intimately, kept a private list of suspected killers deserving of punishment) and offered bounties for their capture and execution. Day after day native allies seeking to demonstrate their fidelity and mutuality of interests with English power appeared in Boston with the severed heads and hands of their common enemies, gestures that the English took as signs of submission and of the legitimacy of their conquest. Dismembered body parts—heads, hands, scalps, and torn-off strips of skin—had become commonplace objects among such gentle people as the Pilgrims, as they had been for centuries among such militant people as the Narragansetts. The well-informed Roger Williams, who understood the Indians' elemental passion for balance and reciprocity, dutifully passed on to Winthrop the severed hands of three Pequots because failure to do so, he believed, would be an insult to the donors.[9]

2

Conflicts with the native Americans had been continuous, barbarous, and degrading for both peoples. Conflicts with authority, public and private, had been problems distinctive to the settlers' world. But they too had been continuous and destabilizing—sources of bitter personal disputes and communal disarray.

In Virginia, no public authority had been sustained for long in the eighteen years of the Virginia Company's existence. The contentious, erratic rule of aristocratic adventurers had given way to that of hard-bitten soldiers of fortune, which had been superseded by a military regime, which in turn had been followed by the dominance of would-be reformers. Magistracy had been unsettled, transitory, ineffective. Personal disputes among competing officials had become public challenges that led to arbitrary trials, drumhead convictions, and at least one public execution. The chaos of authority under the company's jurisdiction subsided when the Crown took over the colony directly. But its authority had not prevailed. The first royal governor, Sir John Harvey, cautious, conservative, and faithful to his charge to rein in the planters' excesses, was "thrust out" of office by a phalanx of ambitious planters seeking ruthless expansion of settlements, aggression against resistant natives, and absolute guarantees of titles to the property they claimed. Harvey's immediate successors prevailed to the extent that they conceded to such demands. The longest-serving governor, Sir William Berkeley, was dismissed by the commonwealth government and returned to England, only to end his career back in Virginia in the great upheaval of Bacon's rebellion.

The Calverts' authority in Maryland was never secure, often vacant, challenged by the Protestant majority in the colony, by various claimants to their land, and by shifting powers at home. Legitimate authority collapsed entirely during Ingle's devastating raids, which were succeeded by open civil war against the Calverts' surrogates, four of whom were executed. When some degree of stability had been restored, the colony's leadership remained a contentious assortment of Catholic associates of the Calverts, newly arrived relatives and agents of London merchants, quarrelsome local Protestants, and scheming Virginians. The "instability, incoherence, and frequent turnovers" in Maryland's leadership continued unabated.[10]

In New Sweden the "furious and passionate" disgraced military commander Johan Printz, having quashed a murderous rebellion that denounced him for brutality and avarice by executing the supposed ringleader by firing squad, quit and, without authorization, left the colony in the hands of his overbearing daughter Armegot and her compliant husband Papegoja. When the competent and enterprising Johan Risingh finally arrived to begin a complete renewal of the colony, the small settlement was so factious, conflicted, and defiant that Risingh succumbed to morbid paranoia before acceding to the Dutch conquest. There never had been a stable authority in Sweden's colony; nor was there in New Netherland before Stuyvesant. Until then, the exercise of public authority had been erratic and arbitrary, as one incompetent and dictatorial director followed another, tolerating elective councils (the Twelve, the Eight, the Nine) only when it pleased them, which was seldom. Three such directors had preceded the disastrous Kieft, who barely escaped assassination. Stuyvesant—bolder, more competent, more rational and decisive than his predecessors—was in power only two years before he was faced with the formidable challenge of Van der Donck's elaborate Remonstrance, which, voicing the fears and complaints of the colony's main leaders, condemned him personally and brought into question the entire jurisdiction of the West India Company. That body, it was claimed, stood between the people and the rights they deserved as loyal Dutch citizens. And there were other challenges as well: in 1653 both the formal, contemplative Remonstrance of the Long Island villagers and Underhill's rash and insurrectionary "Vindication"; in 1657 the eloquent Flushing Remonstrance, in defiance of Stuyvesant's suppression of the Quakers; and through the entire seventeen years of Stuyvesant's directorship, a seething resentment at his authoritarian rule despite his co-optation of his main opponents.

But though Stuyvesant managed to bring the colony to a degree of order and civility and to defeat his enemies at The Hague, the ultimate disruption of public authority lay just over the horizon, in the outcome of the war with England. When Stuyvesant surrendered to the English troops, the formal structure of Dutch authority collapsed, leaving the Dutch and Anglo-Dutch merchants and officials scrambling to find their footing in the new regime. And no sooner had some of them managed to do so than, eight years later, the Dutch reconquest in the Third Anglo-Dutch War restored the old Dutch authorities, now complicated by the presence of recently arrived English officials and merchants. But that readjusted, patchwork system, such as it was, disappeared too when, fifteen months later, the English reacquired, by the terms of the treaty that ended the war, the province they had once conquered and restored England's authority. By then new elements had appeared in the population, who would increase the demographic tensions and rivalries to a dangerous pitch.

In New England, the antinomian upheaval was not the only or the most threatening challenge to the successful Puritan authorities. For all its notoriety and fervor, that episode was confined; it was a domestic struggle over theological and ecclesiastical principles. Child's Remonstrance of 1646 was different. It mobilized and brought into the open various strains of dissent and discontent that lay just below the surface of the colonies' public order. The Remonstrants went over the heads of the Puritan authorities to declare to officials at home that the entire Puritan government, under cover of its charter, was depriving England's loyal subjects of their native rights and imposing on them a sectarian regime that sacrificed the general good to the benefits of a minority faction. And just as Van der Donck's challenge to the West India Company's chartered jurisdiction could be adjudicated only by the ultimate authorities in The Hague, so Child's challenge to the legitimacy of the Puritans' chartered rights was directed to the highest powers in England, who ultimately decided the issue. But while vindicated in this episode, the Bay Colony's authorities were never free from the possibility of fundamental challenge to the legitimacy and autonomy of their vulnerable jurisdiction.

A more subtle but more threatening challenge to the Puritan authorities than Child's lay in the principles behind John Eliot's Indian Praying Towns, which, for safety's sake if not for sheer survival, they were forced utterly to repudiate.

The origins of Eliot's mission to the Indians had lain not only in the desire to convert these benighted people to Christianity and civility but to prepare all mankind for the approaching millennium. In a series of lectures in the 1640s John Cotton had discoursed vividly on the twenty-two chapters of the Book of Revelation and left a searing impression on Eliot that the predestined end of history was approaching and that the entire drama of Christ's deliverance would soon be enacted, beginning with the prophesied destruction of all earthly monarchies and the presage of the rule of Christ. A new, millenarian polity would be required, and it would be extrapolated from the small-scale model that he, Eliot, would create among the Indians in New England. The Algonquians, gathered into settled towns, would be governed by elected rulers of tens, of fifties, of hundreds, and of thousands as prescribed in Exodus 18, and they would be able to lead perfected Christian lives within covenanted churches, in preparation for Christ's deliverance.

"I doubt not," Eliot wrote to Cromwell, "but it will be some comfort to your heart, to see the kingdom of Christ rising up in these western parts of the world, a blessed kingdom that will in time 'fill all the earth.'" In his *Christian Commonwealth*, written in 1651 at the height of his apocalyptic fervor, Eliot laid out the full vision that gripped his imagination. With the Praying Towns templates of what could prevail in England, and given the likelihood that the Indians, ripe for utopian molding, were descendants of the lost tribes of Israel, their conversion, followed by that of all gentiles, would indicate that the kingdom of Christ was nigh.

But his ecstatic message and the reports of his Praying Towns reached an England in turmoil over the proper form of republican government. His urgent advice was taken to mean that England should give up ransacking law, history, and constitutional theory to find proper forms of government and draw on scripture alone, for, he wrote, "Christ is your King and Soveraign Lawgiver . . . set the Crown of *England* upon the head of Christ . . . Let him be your *Judge*, let him be your *Law-Giver,* Let him be your *KING!*" England's constitution should, like the Indians', consist of elected rulers with suffrage for all self-sufficient males. This, he wrote, is the form of government, infinitely expandable, "by which Christ meaneth to rule all the Nations on earth according to Scriptures."

All of this was a deadly embarrassment to the Massachusetts authorities. It would surely bring down on the colony the wrath of the restored royal government. As the Restoration approached, they forced Eliot to recant, officially condemned the book, and confiscated every copy they could lay their hands on.[11]

But their authority was never secure. How insecure, how liable their authority was to outright confiscation in the Restoration world, became clear with the arrival in 1664 of a royal commission sent to examine and constrain their corporate existence. Staffed by representatives of disaffected New Englanders, of merchants with designs on New England's economy, and of ambitious royalists, they were led by the Puritans' most committed enemy, Samuel Maverick, still smarting from the indignities he had suffered in Massachusetts. The commission's mandate in effect restated the charges of Child's Remonstrance, compounded with demands that New England comply with the restrictions of the newly enacted navigation laws. The colony mobilized its legal and constitutional defenses, refused to acknowledge the commission's existence, and denied them access not only to officials and records but even to suitable housing. (Breedon's house became their working headquarters.) The commission failed, but New England's authorities were on notice that the legal basis of their corporate existence in the reign of Charles II was no longer secure, as it had been under Cromwell and the Protectorate, and that other, later commissions might well be more effective.[12]

3

Contention and insecurity in British North America were not confined to public authorities. The structures of private authority were no less insecure.

In the 1660s the immigrant flow to the Chesapeake was continuing unabated. No one at the Restoration had any reason to think it would slacken, especially as the 1650s had seen the largest inflow to date. The region's population rose by 12,000 during that decade—literally doubling the population as of 1650—mainly due to the arrival of new indentured servants. And in the 1660s the population grew by 15,000—more than half again the total population as of 1660. Between 1640 and 1670 the total European population in the Chesapeake area more than quadrupled: from 8,000 to 38,500—an annual growth of 7.5 percent, the product of improved survival rates and greatly increased inflow of indentured servants.

The difficulties, the confusion, of absorbing in two decades thousands of bound servants of different backgrounds and conditions into the unfamiliar life of tobacco farms, were compounded by the arrival in the same years of steadily increasing numbers of slaves. By 1660 they numbered approximately nine hundred, brought in mainly from the West Indies. Though they formed only 3.6 percent of the total population, their numbers were rising at almost three times the rate of the rest of the population. Further, by 1650 perhaps 150 convicted felons had arrived, and by 1661 they were coming in a steady flow—a small flow, but enough to cause grave concern, especially after a servant uprising in Virginia in 1663. In 1670 the colony legislated a complete ban on the further importation of "*jaile birds* or such others who for notorious offenses have deserved to dye in England," a move that Maryland followed six years later. Given the relative respectability of many of the ordinary indentured servants, the convicted felons, drawn from London's underworld and slums as well as from among the vagabonds and petty thieves who infested the English countryside, constituted a peculiarly contentious element in so small a population. And further compounding this social and ethnic mix were shipments of Irish vagrants who had begun to appear as bond servants in large numbers in the 1650s, the same years that saw the arrival of Cromwell's war prisoners, a small contingent of the thousands sent out to where they would do the most good and the least harm.[13]

This heterogeneous population—indentured servants from a variety of English subcultures, Africans from the West Indies, English convicts, Irish vagabonds, and Scottish war prisoners—formed in the Chesapeake lands a labor force that was restive, quarrelsome, ill disciplined, and latently rebellious.

With the new servant population beset, as their predecessors had been, by recurrent waves of disease, unaccustomed climate conditions, and exhausting work schedules, master-servant relations remained uncertain, often tumultuous, at times violent. For "the work was unceasing, seldom relieved by amusement or relaxation, and shelter or provisions were frequently lacking. Loneliness broke the spirit, work weakened the body, disease contributed to ill health, and many servants died before they fulfilled their indentures." Some rebelled, ran off, stole from their masters and from the common stores. Masters swung between bursts of reprisals and concessions necessary to keep servants working. Runaways and the many unmarried servant women who bore children continued to be fined or whipped and forced to serve an extra year or two to make up for the lost labor. Not much notice was taken when a manservant who attempted to escape with stolen guns and a canoe was severely beaten and given five and a half years of extra labor, nor even when another died of a beating with a rake handle. It seemed obvious, when a servant hanged himself, for suspicious neighbors to examine his body for bruises. The records, Warren Billings writes, document "a dreary litany of privation, overwork, beatings, harassment, and other abuses," and the court dockets were "clogged by cases of runaways, bastard bearings, petty thievery, and other infractions." It is hardly surprising that there were two servant uprisings in the early 1660s and that Virginia was obliged to pass a statute defining the rights of servants. For, the Assembly stated in 1662, "the barbarous usage of some servants by cruell masters bring soe much scandal and infamy to the country . . . that people who would willingly adventure themselves hither are through fear thereof diverted." "Barbarous"—the word appears again and again in contemporaries' descriptions of the treatment of servants.[14]

But solutions to the problems of master-servant relations could not be legislated, any more than upheavals in marital relations or child abuse, both of which are constant reminders, in the records of time, of the breakdown of accepted modes of social relations.

The Chesapeake colonies, with their constant inflow of new servants, white and black, bound to labor under brutal circumstances, had special problems. But social disorder and contention in the 1650s and 1660s were not confined to the tobacco lands. New Netherland, polyglot, polyethnic, and polysacral in its origins, grew ever more complex as the years passed, its population more fragmented, its clangorous diversity more abrasive and more dangerously volatile.

It is impossible fully to classify the ethnic complexity of that outpost of the Dutch maritime empire. But an effort has been made to list the places of origin of 904 of the estimated 5,700 immigrants from the Dutch Republic to New Netherland, who, with their families, represent well over half of the population of the colony and the adjacent settlements on the Delaware River at the time of the English conquest. The colony of approximately six thousand people in 1664 was a mosaic of peoples from all over northern Europe. Half of the settlers known to have emigrated from the Netherlands had not originated there. Of the non-Dutch who had come through the Netherlands, the largest group was of German origin, people not only from the German principalities on the borders of the

Netherlands—Cleves, East Friesland, Oldenburg, Osnabrück, Emden, Münster, and Hamburg—but from as far southwest as Württemberg, near French Lorraine; from as far southeast as Nuremberg in Bavaria; and from as far east as Pomerania, soon to be absorbed into Prussia. But the non-Dutch from the Netherlands were by no means all Germans. There were French among them too—from Calais, Amiens, Dieppe, Paris, and even Languedoc and the Pays de Vaud in present-day Switzerland. And there were major components from the French-speaking Walloon and Flemish provinces, from the Channel Islands, from Schleswig-Holstein, and in relatively large numbers from Denmark, Sweden, and Norway. Three of the immigrants in the sample were from Poland. And there were in addition an increasing number of English throughout Long Island and in the Hudson River settlements, a small and evanescent community of Jews, and an estimated six hundred blacks, 12 percent of the total population, imported largely from Brazil and, after 1654, from Curaçao. There was little sign by the 1660s that New Netherland's mixed multitude was converging into a coherent and stable civil society, but many signs that it was increasingly fractious, unstable, riven with contending interests.[15]

Even New England, though ethnically more homogeneous and dominated by able, well-informed magistrates, its public institutions so carefully devised and so advanced for their time that in modified form they have survived to this day,[16] was no oasis of tranquil social relations, its villages peaceable kingdoms. Dissension appeared repeatedly in the eastern Massachusetts towns. The inhabitants of Sudbury were not alone in fighting bitterly over the division of common land, over farming procedures, and over church organization. As in that town, dissenters frequently rose against the initial leadership, formed schisms that ruptured the small communities, and went off to found new, more harmonious villages.

The courts were sensitive reflectors of social reality. David Konig's examination of the Essex County, Massachusetts, court records reveals an extraordinary incidence of litigation—"literally thousands of cases," at least two hundred a year—in a population that never exceeded two thousand adult males. His study concentrates on the integrative function of the court system, the way it channeled, contained, and absorbed many of the myriad conflicts of a contentious society—but not all of the conflicts. The court could not resolve all of the animosities, feuds, claims, and counterclaims, especially when increasingly valuable property rights were in question. Some contestants simply ignored the court and resorted to malicious mischief, violence, and vandalism to gain advantage, even turning, at times, to malefic magic.[17]

The more isolated Puritan settlements, deep in the interior, were even less stable than the eastern villages. The standard study of the Connecticut River towns, ninety miles west of Boston, is called *Valley of Discord*. "Dissension," we read, "was a bitter fact of life in the seventeenth century, and the more [Connecticut] Valley Puritans sought to control it, the more they fostered ideological conflict and widened the gap between ideals and behavior." Their struggles to establish consensus and to shape behavior by ideal values "left an institutional order weakened by dispute and torn by a growing argument over the locus of authority in church and society." The history of Springfield, in western Massachusetts, is replete with accounts of "physical assaults, slander, family feuds, fraud, and witchcraft accusations." Personal animosities escalated into fistfights and "hair-pulling, rib-kicking" brawls. The Scottish war prisoners allocated to the town compounded the disorder. Accused of chronic drunkenness, card playing, and slander in this remote Puritan village, they were universally despised. New Haven was no less disordered, its social pathology intensified by what has correctly been called the "fierce communion" of these devout villages—villages in which every man was his brother's keeper, every neighbor a moral guardian. "People," it has been remarked, "spent a good deal of time saying no to each other in New England towns."[18]

4

By the 1660s, when England's government first took serious notice of what had been achieved in its overseas lands in the west and began to draw the elements together into a western empire, the North American communities had existed for two or three generations, and distinctive, persistent patterns of life were beginning to emerge. The patterns were not entirely clear, the trajectories unpredictable, but certain fundamental lines could be perceived that framed the colonies' place in the world.

New England had fallen victim to the forces that reshaped English life after the Restoration. The settlement of the great issues of church and state that had inspired the founding of the Puritan colonies had come quickly. The monarchy was restored in 1660, and the conflicts of religion that had torn the realm apart were resolved by the reestablishment of the Church of England as the nation's official church, but toleration had been conceded to those who could not conform. In the new pattern of establishment and nonconformity, New England found itself a minor cluster of distant nonconformists, no longer generative of challenging new ideas and exciting socio-religious experiments. The fierce religious intensity, the sense that theirs was a daring and risky enterprise of great relevance to the whole informed Protestant world, had passed. They had turned in upon themselves and were deeply engaged in devising their own parochial way of life.

John Winthrop, Jr., had seen it all, had lived it all, dramatically. A founding Puritan, scientist, and entrepreneur, he had contributed to the vitality of both the Massachusetts Bay project and Hartlib's circle of advanced intellectuals in London. He had worked at the frontier of experimental knowledge and social reform, and he alone had attempted to bring the Hartlib circle's theories and speculations into practice in the providential setting of New England—all this in the years of Laudian persecution and Cromwellian revolution. The Restoration changed his world. As governor of Connecticut, he became keenly aware of the royalists' threat to his colony's autonomy and left for England to defend Connecticut's charter. He remained in London for two years—busy, active, productive years which would prove to be his last direct contact with the metropolis.

Well respected in London, he worked through a court-connected "scientific patronage network" and succeeded not only in securing his colony's charter but in extending its geographical boundaries. But his deepest engagement in those exciting years was with the Hartlib circle and the nascent Royal Society, of which at that point he became a member and whose meetings he attended faithfully. The Society was immensely important to him: "It offered high-level political patronage, potential access to private and public capital, elevated personal status, intellectual stimulation, and an opportunity to play a part in an organization that seemed on the verge of accomplishing at least some of the goals of world reformation." He was recognized by the leading members not only for his scientific skills but especially, and increasingly, for his knowledge of New England's natural history, its flora and fauna, specimens of which he produced for discussion, its resources, productive capacity, and potential wealth. But he was never a major figure in the Society, and disappointments set in. His proposals for two major projects—to organize Indians as producers of commercial products and to establish a land bank in New England—proved to be of little interest to the Society, and increasingly he found himself, in the words of his latest biographer, "a kind of colonial curiosity," whose peculiar knowledge of New England might be the basis for a useful natural history of the region, something consistent with the Society's search for useful knowledge.

Back in Connecticut he engaged in all the detailed affairs of his colony and his medical practice, supported the English conquest of New Netherland, and worked cautiously and diplomatically with the Commission of 1664. Sensitive to the threats to his colony by the Restoration government's zeal for imperial consolidation, he saw the possibility that the natural history he was urged to write would enhance England's incentives for exploiting or taxing New England's resources and extending the Crown's control of the region. The book was never written. But ever regretful that he was "at such a distance from that fountaine whence so many rivelets of excellent things do streame forth for the good of the world," Winthrop tried to keep in touch with the Royal Society. He continued to send them scientific specimens—barnacles, a hummingbird's nest and eggs, an earless hog, horseshoe crabs, milkweed fibers. He studied the Society's *Transactions* and reports of Boyle's experiments, and to those concerned with the propagation of the Gospel he sent over John Eliot's Algonquian translation of the Bible and two essays written in Latin by Indian students at Harvard. But his patronage network in London was evaporating. Caught up in the minutiae of Connecticut's problems, he felt drawn and isolated, yearning for one more visit to the metropolis. He died in 1676, in the midst of New England's most devastating Indian war and the arrival of a new royal commission, both of which threatened the existence of his colony. He was venerated in the villages along the Connecticut River—themselves changing like autumnal leaves from vital, experimental religious communities to sere, old-fashioned backwoods towns, largely forgotten in the greater world at home. His sons, provincial land speculators and politicians, "selfish, petty, and confused," were native to the land, and their cultural horizons had narrowed to its practical demands. For them the founders' accomplishments were an inheritance they were born into—honored and respected but familiar and routine. And for *their* children, what had once been rebellious, liberating, and challenging had become a fading memory they were enjoined to keep alive. Their interests centered on the struggle to profit from and extend their farms; on the conduct of trade; and on the consequences of extraordinary population growth.[19]

The New England population—lacking in major accretions from abroad—was doubling every twenty-seven years. This phenomenal growth had the effect of propelling the boundaries of Anglo-American settlements farther and farther out from the original coastal and riverbank enclaves. In the half century between 1620 and 1670 New Englanders staked out spacious townships that would by the twenty-first century subdivide into 297 towns.[20] And each new settlement represented severe dislocation, required the brutal labor of breaking open uncultivated lands and building housing, and involved complex problems of community organization and property claims.

Behind this remarkable spread of settlement lay a propulsive force that would grow in strength in future years. By the third generation—that of the first Winthrop's grandsons—pressure was beginning to be felt on the progressive subdivisions of parental properties to provide for adult children. By then, and clearly in the fourth generation, the sense of relative deprivation was strong enough to lead some to leave the family domain and create new settlements, new towns, for themselves, elsewhere—often on land earlier acquired, speculatively, by farsighted kin. There was no precise level of morcellation at which ambitious sons would break away, but there was a general sense that thirty acres, more or less, was the minimum needed for a viable farm.

There was no pattern in this expansion, nor were the villages neatly nucleated. It was a progressive scattering of isolated family farmsteads which formed communities loosely, as social webs very different from the "individual town distinctiveness inherited from England." Only later would the confusion of initial settlements fall into stable spatial forms and the classic image of nucleated farming villages reflect reality. Only then would New England's landscape resemble "a great mosaic of equal sized communities."[21]

But none of this involvement with population growth and land distribution was incompatible with the serious way of life instinctive to these latter-day Puritans. New England, nonconformist to the greater British world, had developed its own vernacular culture. Though nostalgia for remembered distinctiveness, like Roger Conant's passion to commemorate his West Country origins, lingered, the awareness of the subcultural

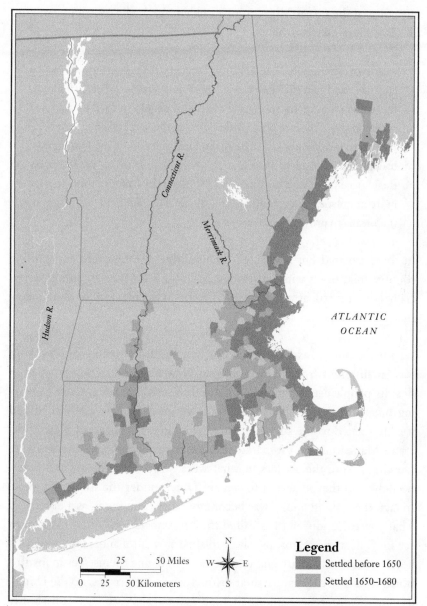

Expansion of New England settlements, 1650–80

ATLANTIC
OCEAN

Connecticut R.

Merrimack R.

Hudson R.

0   25   50 Miles

0   25   50 Kilometers

N
W   E
S

diversity of the Great Migration had faded. As the historical geographer R. Cole Harris writes, the

> wealth of different local superstitions, accents, dialects, languages, social customs, and material cultures . . . [did] not survive where, suddenly, there was no longer a sustaining society of people steeped in the same traditions. . . . Microregional differences in the settlers' collective heritage were quickly lost. . . . The many local cultures of the immigrants' backgrounds collapsed into one. . . . A society in which people knew their social place within a finely graded hierarchy had given way to a far more atomistic society built around the nuclear family in possession of the means to provide its subsistence.[22]

In these isolated but associated communities lived austere and prolific country folk, pious without passion, ambitious for worldly things, especially land, yet still attuned in some degree to the memory of their ancestors' spiritual quest.

IN THE LATE 1660S AND 1670S the new English province of New York was far different from its neighboring New England. It was a world in flux, its people caught up in complex ethnic tensions, its economy growing but shifting in organization, its government newly established and weakly related to the society it ruled. The great majority of New Yorkers in Manhattan (an estimated 76 percent of a significant sample) were Dutch, as were the settlers in what were now called Albany and Schenectady, and they expected to remain Dutch under the English regime. In fact, their "Dutchness" was becoming more prominent, as a process of what Joyce Goodfriend has called the "crystallization" of ethnic groups set in. The various groups, she explains, now in a more open society, became more self-aware and felt the need to define themselves in institutional form and to preserve their distinctive characteristics. So the Dutch, despite the differences among them, began to "coalesce"—to consciously value their distinctive common ground: in their language, religion, customs, and values. So too other groups sought their own places in this province of tolerated diversity.[23]

But crystallized "ethnicization," even in this more open world, was a slow, halting, and controversial process. The French, whose numbers began to rise as the pressure on the Huguenots increased in France, had the advantage of group awareness as a result of persecution, flight, and exile, and could easily organize their church in New York. But though fervently Protestant, the Huguenots came from a Catholic nation, and the perpetuation of French culture in Manhattan could only be suspect, especially as it became generally known that the colony's proprietor, the Duke of York, was himself a Catholic, in fact if not yet in public profession, and might well attempt to sponsor or favor his co-religionists in his new domain. The renewed Jewish congregation, superseding the few Jews who had so disturbed Stuyvesant, was distinct in its well-defined religious culture, but its establishment as a community within the colony required the merging of its Sephardic and Ashkenazic elements. And the growing population of Africans, scattered among the city's households, farms, and dockside shops, and on small properties along the Broadway, sought, but could only partly find, common ground amid the diversity of their origins, religions, and customs.

The most tortuous "ethnicization" within the European population was that of the English, a minority group, though the dominant power in the land. New York had become an English province. But who were the English? Were the Scots and Irish English? They were not English "at home." Did they become so in New York? If not, would they have separate cultural expressions? And how could the English coalesce around religion when among them were Lutherans, Presbyterians, Baptists, Quakers, Anglicans, and even Catholics—or around politics when some were Parliamentarians and an increasing number were royalists? It took thirty-three years after the conquest of 1664 for the first Anglican church, Trinity, to be founded; the first Presbyterian meeting gathered in 1716.[24]

They had little support from fresh immigration until late in the century. The first two English governors made every effort to attract English settlers. They offered generous terms for community settlements with guarantees of religious freedom, special dispensations for Scottish migrants, unusual enticements for religious groups in Bermuda—but all such schemes failed. Some English migrants did appear, especially in the years immediately following the English conquest and reconquest (1664–66, 1674–75), but they were few in number, diverse in origins, and often transitory. Further, it was at times difficult to distinguish actual settlers from among the incoming officials, soldiers, sailors, and business agents. When in 1674 a considerable number of middle-level London merchants saw the possibilities of profitable trade with New York and created new lines of commerce with the colony, they drew on family and other ties to the settled English population but had no intention of permanently joining them.[25]

The English in Manhattan, perched precariously on a bristling Dutch majority, represented the sovereign power and had access to the benefits of public office and the perquisites of royal favor. This combination of social rootlessness and political power dominated New York's life in the post-Restoration years. Anomalous in a world where political power was expected to emanate from and express the natural organization of society—where the attributes of social authority were naturally associated with political dominance—this condition was the source of fears of arbitrary authority, of lawlessness within law, and of personal rivalries and bitter factionalism, which would persist until, gradually, the splintered social order would stabilize, in part through interethnic marriages, and the political system would find more natural roots in the community at large.

Commerce, coastal and oceanic, flourished in the colony's hub; fur trading and farming in the upriver settlements continued despite persistent threats of Indian raids; and the scattered villages on Long Island— the five western Dutch towns, ethnically mixed by the 1680s, the twelve eastern towns mainly English—prospered, with relatively equitable wealth distributions. But the sociopolitical tensions deepened as affiliations with royal authority shifted and turned. Some of the major figures from the Dutch years—especially Van Cortlandt and Philipse—swung adroitly with the political winds, managed to maintain their dominant positions in trade and politics, and shared the benefits of what became a powerful "court" party that formed around successive governors. Others, most notably Steenwyck, of similar origins, fell back at times into an opposition "country" party, scattered and weak and of shifting composition. Anxieties bred misperceptions. Despite the fact that the English taxables in Manhattan rose from a scattered few to one-third of the total and that half of the most "substantial" people in the city were English, the English on Long Island continued to believe that the city was still Dutch and that Dutch merchants were exploiting special benefits at their expense. Cultural stereotypes deepened the tension. While the English officials, civil and military, respected such highly placed, wealthy, and sophisticated Dutchmen as Steenwyck, they mocked ordinary Dutch farmers and tradesmen as "boors," ignorant, uncivilized, unlettered, and ludicrous in manners. Language mattered. The Dutch, one official reported with dismay, "can neither speak nor write proper English." Even the well-educated Leisler would be ridiculed and condemned as vulgar for his freewheeling grammar in English and amusingly phonetic spelling. In this strained situation, tensions repeatedly broke into open conflict.[26]

There was trouble from the first years of English rule. The first English governor, Nicolls, moved cautiously, since he knew that "wee cannot expect they love us." But he hit a wall when he tried to extract an oath of loyalty to the king and duke and their officials. Ultimately he succeeded, but only after stormy sessions with the Dutch leaders, whom he excluded from his government, and after he officially conceded that nothing in the oath abrogated the generous terms of the surrender agreement. But there was little he could do to restrain the violence of his idle garrison troops, who stole from the Dutch and fought them in the streets. His presumably shrewd plan to constrain the violence by quartering some of the troops in Dutch households was flatly opposed until he agreed to pay the host burghers an exorbitant fee for their hospitality. On Long Island, Dutch townsmen refused to pay taxes issued from Manhattan, insisting that only the local communities themselves could levy taxes on their people, and they did not hesitate to drive off the English tax collectors.

Relations in the Hudson River towns were especially abrasive. The troops stationed there, cooped up through the long winters, took out their frustration on the townsmen, whose resentment was compounded by having to pay for the troops' upkeep. Street fights and verbal battles multiplied, and in Kingstown animosities came to a head in a full-scale riot. When the local brewer was jailed for threatening to assassinate the resident army captain, the town rose in protest, then exploded when a soldier killed a local tradesman. The verdict of a special commission convened to end the furor was acquittal for the soldier on grounds that he had faced an armed uprising, and the banishment from the colony of four burghers. The brief but bitter encounter left the Dutch with burning resentments.[27]

The most important and revealing episode in the slow, grinding accommodation to English rule took place in Albany in 1676. Originally a simple case of slander, it became a major public scandal that revealed the core elements of New York's social and political life. Nicholas van Rensselaer, a wayward and thoroughly disrespected son of the Dutch branch of the family, had floundered his way into a ministerial career, without the ability or credentials to succeed. Failed of ordination by the Classis of Amsterdam, he sought and won the patronage of the exiled Charles Stuart in Brussels. When Stuart returned to England as Charles II, he had Van Rensselaer ordained in the Church of England and instructed his new governor in New York, Edmund Andros, to find Van Rensselaer a position in the Dutch church in the colony. The appointment, in support of the respected but failing Dominie Gideon Schaets in Albany, was especially propitious, since the resident head of the Van Rensselaer family's great property around Albany, Rensselaerswyck, had recently died and Nicholas was due to succeed him.

In May 1676 the newly installed preacher delivered a sermon on the traditional problem of original sin and the possibilities of salvation. In attendance was the merchant Leisler—suspicious of the dominie's theology and status and fearful of his Anglo-Catholic sponsors—and his young colleague Jacob Milborne. The sermon was barely over when they declared that the preacher's views were heterodox and condemned him personally and publicly as both sinful and incompetent. Van Rensselaer immediately sued for slander, claiming that Leisler had brought him into contempt and destroyed his standing with his congregation. When the Albany court failed to give him satisfaction, Van Rensselaer enlisted his kinsman Stephanus van Cortlandt to bring the matter to Governor Andros's court in Manhattan since Andros, he knew, would support him. And indeed, the governor took the matter to his council and the local ministers, while requiring all the participants to post expensive bonds. When Leisler refused to do so, Andros had him arrested. Ultimately, the combatants agreed to desist, but all the costs of the court procedures in Albany and Manhattan were charged to Leisler.

Such was the public narrative. But all the participants knew that the underlying conditions were what mattered. There were substantial theological issues involved that generated their own heat. Leisler's fierce Calvinist orthodoxy, an inheritance that went back three generations, had come to focus on the strict scholasticism of Gybertus Voetius, in passionate opposition to the more tolerant theology of Johannes Cocceius, whose views, the Voetians believed, could open the way to Catholicism and "the damn'd Doctrins of Passive Obedience and Non-resistance." For the zealous Calvinist Leisler, Van Rensselaer's theology was dangerously Cocceian, consistent with his clientage to the Catholic Andros and his proto-Catholic master the Duke of York and ultimately the king himself. To Leisler, whose parents and grandparents had suffered from Catholic persecution, both fearful and bold and now truly alarmed, the danger was clear. The English rulers of the colony embodied the ultimate menace. Slowly but surely they would impinge on the autonomy of the Dutch, corrupt the theological basis of their culture, break up the unity of their church, and reduce the Dutch population to a weak dependency of England's royal power. None of this was publicly discussed, but all of it was clear to those like Leisler who were sensitive to the slightest tremors that might portend upheavals to come.[28]

The growing dangers were all around him. The Dutch pastors were required to preach in English, and the new appointees were more Anglicized and cooperative with the Crown officials than their staunch predecessors had been. In the months when Leisler was struggling with the Van Rensselaer affair, the governor issued a new loyalty oath to be signed by all. When the entire Dutch merchant leadership, led by Steenwyck, rose in protest demanding the rights they had been given at the surrender, Andros jailed them all, convicted them, in a court of English officials, of promoting rebellion, and seized all their property. With no hope of appeal or redress, the Dutch leaders eventually capitulated, but at the cost of one-third of their property. Their trial left deep scars in the Dutch community and such fears of biased English juries that they withdrew from the official courts whenever they could and sought justice among themselves in the consistory of their Reformed church.[29]

There was no settled pattern of life in New York, only a slow and at times contentious process by which the mixed multitude of the Dutch years, soon to be supplemented by Huguenots and German Pietists, grew into a new community dominated by the English. Slowly and persistently English laws, language, and institutions were beginning to penetrate the lives of the minor ethnic groups and to press against the majority Dutch who clung to their inherited ways. The consolidation of economic interests and kinship among the major merchant families, Dutch and English, tended to weaken ethnic differences, as did the shared interest of the most successful merchants in establishing great estates on the Hudson, suitable properties for landed gentlemen of whatever ethnic origin and excellent soils for valuable grain production. Philipse lived to see his tenants—one hundred or more—on his 90,000-acre manor, Philipsburg, loading his sloops with grain for bolting in Manhattan and shipment overseas as flour.

By 1700 his 200-square-mile estate had acquired two baronial neighbors to the north: the Hudson River estate of the American-born Dutchman Stephanus van Cortlandt and that of the recently arrived Scotsman Robert Livingston, whose marriage into the Schuyler and Van Rensselaer families was a notable event in ethnic relations.[30]

IN THE LAND to the south—the Chesapeake region, stretching from the Delaware River south to the James and from the Atlantic coast to the Piedmont—the distinctive social order that had been forming took on, in the post-Restoration era, not steadily and peacefully but haltingly and contentiously, its permanent characteristics. Though still fluid in composition, it was deeply hierarchical in structure. At the base of the free population, in the immediate post-Restoration period, was a restive underclass of freedmen. Of the fortunes and misfortunes of this fast-growing part of the free population in Virginia—the most powerless of the Europeans, the most viciously exploited, and the most combative—Edmund Morgan has written eloquently. Most were rootless, impoverished, and faced with a grim fact of life. Land, which they sought above all else, continued to rise in price as the population grew, as established households expanded and spread across the land, and as large-scale land speculation became increasingly common.

The freedmen of Virginia, Morgan writes, were bound to be "losers." To the relatively secure, ambitious small and middle-level planters seeking to expand their holdings, as well as to the rising gentry, the freedmen, land poor and desperate, became competitors and constituted a threat that the planters sought to contain. Through their representatives in the House of Burgesses, the planters passed laws that extended, by all sorts of devices, the length of servants' bondage; imposed penalties for idleness and bastardry; and granted loans that tied the freedmen in webs of debt. In desperation, the newly released servants either moved west to poor lands often directly exposed to Indian threats or drifted footloose from county to county in search of security. Commonly they simply bowed to the immediate pressures and became tenants, often of the planters who had been their masters and who were now their landlords and creditors. In 1642 more than half of Maryland's freedmen were tenants, and they were often indebted. For a man alone, Morgan writes, "whose next year's crop would be the result only of his own labor, debt might be a road back to servitude." Often those who did manage to get an edge on the system and acquire a piece of land found that their plot was located so far from a river or navigable stream that marketing a crop was especially difficult and expensive.[31]

But while the industrious, prospering small and middle-level planters were beset by threats from the freedmen—those "terrible young men," Morgan calls them, capable of all kinds of incivility, from thievery to tax dodging and support of servant uprisings—the gentry class was forming in large part from among the recently arrived claimants to established properties (the Byrds, the Masons, the Carters, the Blands), together with the successful survivors of the pioneering generations who had money to invest and the desire to build substantial estates. Prominent by the 1670s, they were firmly in control of county affairs as local magistrates and major entrepreneurs, with influence in the colony's government through their deputies in the House of Burgesses. Some—but only a few—had ties to the highest circle, the Governor's Council, and to the newly arrived royal officials responsible for tax collection, customs regulations, and the management of land grants. Loosely associated, they formed a dominant political and economic group, the Green Spring faction, named after Berkeley's plantation, bound together by patronage, shared interests, and above all, kinship.

So Thomas Ludwell, Berkeley's cousin, became the colony's secretary of state; he was succeeded by his brother Philip, who would marry Berkeley's widow. Lady Berkeley, in turn, the second cousin of Thomas Lord Culpeper, who would become governor in 1675 (but who arrived, temporarily, only in 1680), was the sister of Alexander Culpeper, whom Berkeley appointed surveyor general, a post he held for twenty-three years while resident in England and exercised through deputies. William Byrd's growing affluence was in large part the result of his officeholding, which derived from his wife's connections with Lady Berkeley.

Officials, often in tandem with the new gentry, scoured the land for properties to reserve for future use, including territory beyond the Indian treaty line, which Berkeley fervently sought to preserve. Clashes with the aggressive Susquehannocks were looming possibilities; clashes with the resident small planters were inevitable. The most notorious and complex struggle was over the disposition of the Northern Neck, the vast domain between the Rappahannock and Potomac rivers, at least one million acres. In 1649 the exiled Charles II had granted that princely territory to a group of his supporters, despite the fact—no doubt ignorant of the fact—that much of it had already been patented by prescient speculators. By 1653 there were approximately thirteen hundred people at work on the land; by 1674 they would be close to six thousand. The immensely tangled legal struggle that resulted between the new proprietors—among whom were Berkeley's brother and brother-in-law, his wife's cousin Thomas Lord Culpeper, and her father, Thomas Culpeper—and the resident planters and earlier speculators would drag on well into the eighteenth century. And it was further complicated by the king's grant in 1674 of all of Virginia's remaining public lands for thirty-one years to two loyal friends, one of them the ubiquitous Thomas Lord Culpeper.[32]

The Northern Neck controversy was only the most famous of the struggles created by the great wave of land speculation that was leading to the patenting and hence removing from the market of great swaths of otherwise accessible land in expectation of lucrative rents and sales at elevated prices.

By the 1650s most of the valuable land in the lower James, York, and Rappahannock river areas had been patented, and much of it brought under cultivation. Speculators had begun patenting land along the Potomac River, where several new counties had been quickly formed. By 1660 thirty individuals held patents for one hundred thousand acres along the Potomac. At the same time the inland areas of the York and Rappahannock rivers were being reserved, and plots in the range of ten to fifteen thousand acres were being patented on the Eastern Shore. The years 1650–75 were the boom period of Chesapeake land speculation. In that quarter century Virginians patented 2,350,000 acres, only small portions of which were being farmed.[33]

Of the speculators, the most flamboyant and high-flying were the new Crown officials and their associates among the rising gentry. And it was they, consistent with their avaricious land dealings, who led the way to the profoundly consequential transformation of the labor force. The widespread adoption of slavery in the post-Restoration years, as the key force in tobacco production, completed the transformation of the Chesapeake world. It had been widely understood, well before 1650, that in the long run slaves were more profitable laborers than servants. Planters in Maryland and Virginia knew as well as Emmanuel Downing in Massachusetts that it was cheaper to maintain twenty "Moores" than one English servant.

But only in the long run. Slaves were expensive—a healthy adult male was priced at about £23 at midcentury—and required at least a modicum of lifelong care. Ordinary planters could seldom afford them and could not easily include them within the family structure of their farms. But increasingly slaves appear in the records of the more affluent, and by 1675, as the result of hundreds of private, unrecorded decisions, they became common on the region's plantations. The change was rapid. By the 1650s slaves could be found almost everywhere on the larger plantations on the lower James and York rivers, often working side by side with servants; by the 1660s, 15 percent of York County's population was black. By 1670 over half of the estates in both Virginia and Maryland had slaves, and thereafter their importation boomed, not uniformly across the region but differentially, according to affluence and influence. The councilors and officials took the lead, Lorena Walsh writes, in buying slaves, "followed by burgesses and other county-level officeholders. . . . Overall, officeholders controlled between two-thirds and three-quarters of enslaved bondpeople." Two-thirds of all officeholders in both Virginia and Maryland owned slaves, while only 6 percent of nonofficeholding planters did. The majority of the tobacco producers rarely owned any. So the rich and politically powerful grew more powerful and more expansive. The record of the growth and distribution in the ownership of slaves reflects the emergence of a racist, patriarchal culture. But in the 1670s it was newly formed, strange, uncertain, and taut with inner tensions.[34]

By 1675 the stress lines in Chesapeake society had become clear. A restive, footloose, unsettled population of land-hungry former servants exposed to Indian assaults pressed against an established population of small-scale planters and farmers active in the local courts and, through their deputies, in the Burgesses. They in turn were sensitive to pressure from increasingly aggressive gentry families intent on creating great estates that required demanding personal management. The most successful of the newly risen gentry collaborated, when they could, with the powerful and erratic Crown officials, none of whom were native to the land, few of whom spent much time in the land, and all of whom took office for the profits that might result. And feverish land speculation was driving up land values, to the spectacular benefit of some but for many a keen sense of real and relative deprivation.

With opportunities apparently—and distractingly—everywhere, with so much more that might be gained, discontents became heated and stirrings became explosive. A sudden destructive event could threaten the entire structure of social and political authority.

5

Thus, in the barbarous years of the British and Dutch conquest of North America, commercial ambitions, the search for religious perfectionism, environmental circumstances, and the great flow of migrants, free and unfree, from Europe and Africa, had combined to produce variant ways of life, different from what had been known before. There were resemblances to earlier, familiar lifestyles, and most settlers clung, at times desperately, to what they had known and remembered. But physical circumstances and the constant mingling of peoples of varied backgrounds forced to live together created new cultural worlds. The emergent Chesapeake gentry might yearn for the stable structure of English county life and attempt to imitate it, but lacking a permanent and reliable tenancy, which was the economic foundation of the English landowning aristocracy, even the most affluent of the planters found themselves bound down to the personal management of dusty tobacco fields, responsible for a burdensome and worrisome labor force, and dependent on unpredictable incomes. Village life in nonconformist New England bore resemblances to what had been known before, but the culture of post-utopian Puritanism was unique in its pious austerity, its access to what seemed to be infinite quantities of land, and the extraordinary fecundity of its population. And the human complexity of the town on Manhattan was something new even for the residents of the cosmopolitan cities of the Netherlands, in the multiplicity of the town's ethnic groups, in its polylingualism, in the variety of its religious confessions, and in its jarring dissonance between society and the state.

BUT THESE COASTAL SETTLEMENTS, scattered from Maine to Carolina, were not isolated from the greater world. Just as in the years before the arrival of the Europeans, the native Americans living in the same coastal territory had vital ties to far distant, powerful networks of communities deep in the interior north and west, so now the British Americans were bound to intricate networks in the far exterior south and east—to the Atlantic complex, the first "hemispheric 'community,'" David Eltis writes, in human history.[35]

The Atlantic, transnational dimensions of their lives had been pervasive from the start, but it broadened out, as Carla Pestana has written, into the Atlantic community in the tumultuous decades of England's Civil War and Interregnum. Decisions in Amsterdam and Rotterdam had sent small fleets of trading vessels to the Chesapeake, especially in the Civil War years, to profit from the marketing of the almost unmanageably large tobacco crop. (Exports rose from 365,000 pounds annually in the early years to 17.6 million in 1672.) Dutchmen had formed close personal ties with leading planters and stationed their own middlemen in Virginia to collect goods for rapid loading and shipping. When the navigation laws forced the Dutch out of the direct trade, their contacts had survived in other forms, especially in the coastal trade and in the hugely successful smuggling operations that became a basic component of the entire Atlantic economy. After 1664 major English merchants took over much of the tobacco trade, trans-shipping great quantities of the plant to the seemingly insatiable European markets, whose intricate movements, driven by remote political and economic forces, could shape and reshape the Chesapeake economy. (One group of powerful English merchants probed the vast Russian tobacco market; others negotiated entry into the French state monopoly.) But the trade was open to all, and when tobacco prices fell, many of London's and the outports' small traders, retailers, and ship captains flocked to the trade of North America and the West Indies. At least 1,304 individual traders are known to have participated in the Virginia trade, almost all of whom were involved in three or fewer voyages. And as their ships and boats moved slowly into the waterways to locate and trade with the scattered planters, social connections soon developed. As April Hatfield has explained in rich detail, it took weeks to dispose of the inbound cargoes and more weeks to gather the necessary consignments of tobacco. During those weeks and months the supercargoes, ship masters, and crews, drawn from far different parts of the Atlantic world, mingled with the planters, brought word of things abroad, formed friendships and useful associations, and helped overcome the Virginians' isolation. So constant were these sojourns of mariners from abroad, so frequent were these dockside transactions, that the Chesapeake colonies can be said to have developed, Hatfield writes, a "pervasive maritime culture," contributing "to the creation of an Atlantic world that was of necessity international, not fractured into national bailiwicks." And what can be said of the social history of Chesapeake commerce can be said in even greater detail of the elaborate trading systems of the north.[36]

By the 1660s transnational, intersecting Atlantic trading networks, which were the primary sources of west European economic growth, had long since linked New York, Boston, their satellite towns, and the Chesapeake ports to western Europe, West Africa, the Wine Islands, the West Indies, and ports on the Hispanic-American mainland. By the 1670s the tangles of the overlapping trade routes were too intricate, too volatile, and too often extemporized to be described in clear, schematic form. New England merchants were carrying fish from the coastal waters and the Grand Banks to ports in Spain and the Caribbean islands, often together with provisions and cattle from their farms, and returning, legally or illegally, with sugar for trans-shipment and for the local production of molasses and rum, the profits paying in complex ways for European goods imported in constant flows. New York progressed far beyond its earlier role as a producer and marketer of furs and grain. Its many middle-level merchants (two-thirds of the 112 identifiable wholesale merchants in 1664) swarmed into the North American coastal ports north and south, trading the produce of the colony's hinterlands for tobacco, sugar, and other exotic goods. At the same time New York's great merchants, in all sorts of high-level transactions, roamed the distant ports of Europe, West Africa, and mainland Hispanic America, maintaining, despite political obstacles, their profitable contacts with the broad reaches of the Dutch-Atlantic trading network. They had grown rich in this Atlantic system. Philipse, in the post-Restoration era, built on his earlier successes to create a commercial empire beyond most colonists' imagining. In addition to his manor on the Hudson, he owned houses and warehouses in New York, scores of slaves and tenants, "mills, cattle, and sloops . . . and at least four solely owned ships for the external trade." A few other formerly Dutch merchants followed, but rather far behind—Steenwyck, for example, with an estate of £15,841, Loockermans, worth 520,000 guilders. All the major merchants prospered by transnational ties, legal and illegal, maintaining affiliations not only with English creditors and suppliers but with the credit, supplies, and contacts of the Low Country's Atlantic trading patriciate.[37]

And the flow was not only material. The British Americans were informed, though often belatedly and in fragments, about events abroad, about the politics of the great states whose casual permutations could affect them directly, about the clangorous discourse of English political and religious thought in this fraught century, and about the long struggle for the grounds of legitimate authority.

They were provincials, listening for messages from abroad, living in a still barbarous world, struggling to normalize their own way of life, no less civil, they hoped, than what had been known before.

Acknowledgments

HISTORIANS BUILD on the work of their predecessors, and this book rests heavily on the original scholarship of several distinct groups of historians who in recent years have transformed their fields of interest: the Chesapeake historians, led by Lois Green Carr, James Horn, Karen Kupperman, Russell Menard, and Lorena Walsh, who have revealed in their studies a social and economic world of the upper South never seen before; three generations of New England scholars led by Perry Miller, Edmund Morgan, and David Hall, who have found in Puritanism an astonishing richness of life and thought; and the Dutch archival scholars, editors, and translators led by Charles Gehring, Joyce Goodfriend, Jaap Jacobs, Donna Merwick, Oliver Rink, and David Voorhees, who have transcended linguistic barriers to explore the complexity of New Netherland's multi-ethnic community. None of them bear any responsibility for what I have written, but like so many others I have greatly benefited from their scholarship and that of the other historians who in recent years have helped transform these fields.

On a more personal level, I am enormously indebted to Elizabeth McCormack, whose interest in the Peopling project as an officer in the Rockefeller Brothers Fund led to grants from the Fund and from the National Endowment for the Humanities that have made much of the research possible. I am deeply grateful to her and to the Fund's and the Endowment's support.

Jane Garrett, my old friend, early collaborator, and editor at Knopf has been wonderfully patient and encouraging over the years. I have relied on her judgment in many ways, and appreciate all she has done to bring history to a broad audience. In her absence, Leslie Levine took over at Knopf, and did everything she could to help bring the book to completion.

Barbara DeWolfe worked with me in searches through the vast archive of materials, in this country and abroad, bearing on early North American population history, and contributed especially to the complex documentation, literary and electronic, that went into *Voyagers to the West*. She continues her discerning scholarship in her present position, as curator of manuscripts at the Clements Library at the University of Michigan.

I am grateful to Ginger S. Hawkins for her ingenious assistance, especially in data collection and analysis, and to C. Scott Walker, cartographer at the Harvard University Map Collection, who generously set aside his other work to devise and adapt, with skill and imagination, the basic maps for this book. Jennifer Nickerson bore with me patiently and cheerfully through long, complex stints of research and revision while keeping track of books, files, and notes. Her assistance was indispensable.

Lotte Bailyn has listened, read, re-read, and corrected endlessly. Her forbearance, encouragement, and blessed optimism have kept the entire project alive, and made this book possible.

B.B.

Notes

ABBREVIATIONS USED IN NOTES

CSPC	W. Noël Sainsbury, ed., *Calendar of State Papers, Colonial Series, 1574–1660* (London, 1860)
Docs. Rel.	E. B. O'Callaghan et al., eds., *Documents Relative to the Colonial History of the State of New-York* (Albany, N.Y., 1856–87)
Kingsbury, *VC Records*	Susan M. Kingsbury, ed., *The Records of the Virginia Company of London* (Washington, D.C., 1906–35)
Md. Archives	William H. Browne et al., eds., *Archives of Maryland* (Baltimore, Md., 1883–1972)
MHM	*Maryland Historical Magazine*
NEQ	*New England Quarterly*
NYHM: Dutch	A. J. F. van Laer, trans. and ed., *New York Historical Manuscripts: Dutch* (Baltimore, Md., 1974)
Smith, *Works*	Philip L. Barbour, ed., *The Complete Works of Captain John Smith (1580–1631)* (Chapel Hill, N.C., 1986)
VMHB	*Virginia Magazine of History and Biography*
Winthrop, *Journal*	Richard S. Dunn, James Savage, and Laetitia Yeandle, eds., *The Journal of John Winthrop 1630–1649* (Cambridge, Mass., 1996)
WMQ	*William and Mary Quarterly*, 3rd ser.

CHAPTER 1
The Americans

1. Rosemary R. Finn, "The Belief System of the Powhatan Indians," *Quarterly Bulletin of the Archaeological Society of Virginia*, 42, no. 3 (1987), 152.

2. Thomas L. Altherr, "'Flesh Is the Paradise of a Man of Flesh' . . . ," *Canadian Historical Review*, 64 (1983), 269–71; William A. Haviland and Marjory W. Power, *The Original Vermonters* (Hanover, N.H., 1981), 178–79.

3. Calvin Martin, *Keepers of the Game: Indian-Animal Relationships and the Fur Trade* (Berkeley, Calif., 1978), 74, 76, 36; Haviland and Power, *Original Vermonters*, 196, 187–88; Dean R. Snow, in Bruce G. Trigger, ed., *Handbook of North American Indians, XV: Northeast* (Washington, D.C., 1978), 139.

4. Martin, *Keepers of the Game*, 36; Altherr, "'Flesh Is the Paradise,'" 269.

5. Neal Salisbury, *Manitou and Providence: Indians, Europeans, and the Making of New England, 1500–1643* (New York, 1982), 37–39; Martin, *Keepers of the Game*, 34, 74.

6. Salisbury, *Manitou*, 10–11, 35–36, 43–44, 49, 53; Daniel K. Richter, *The Ordeal of the Longhouse: The Peoples of the Iroquois League in the Era of European Colonization* (Chapel Hill, N.C., 1992), 20–22, 32–38; Haviland and Power, *Original Vermonters*, 193–94. On "mourning wars": Jill Lepore, *The Name of War* (New York, 1998), 117. On the pivotal significance of body parts: Andrew Lipman, "'A meanes to knit them togeather': The Exchange of Body Parts in the Pequot War," *WMQ*, 65 (2008), 3–15. On "bride price": Helen C. Rountree, *The Powhatan Indians of Virginia: Their Traditional Culture* (Norman, Okla., 1989), 90; Trigger, ed., *Handbook*, 140, 167, 262.

7. William S. Simmons, "Southern New England Shamanism: An Ethnographic Reconstruction," in William Cowan, ed., *Papers of the Seventh Algonquian Conference, 1975* (Ottawa, 1976), 218–56; Martin, *Keepers of the Game*, 37–38, 73, 92–93; Haviland and Power, *Original Vermonters*, 184–87; Finn, "Belief System of the Powhatan Indians," 154–55.

8. Anthony F. C. Wallace, "Dreams and the Wishes of the Soul: A Type of Psychoanalytic Theory Among the Seventeenth Century Iroquois," *American Anthropologist*, 60 (1958), 234–48, quotation at 236; Martin, *Keepers of the Game*, 75–76. For an excellent example of the importance of dreams, even in warfare, see the account of Champlain's dream revelation in the battle he led between rival Indian groups (1609); Matthew Dennis, *Cultivating a Landscape of Peace: Iroquois-European Encounters in Seventeenth-Century America* (Ithaca, N.Y., 1993), 71–72.

9. Rountree, *Powhatan Indians*, 84, 77, and chap. 4 ("Manliness") generally. On the remarkable significance of color in the inner lives of native Americans, see George R. Hamell, "The Iroquois and the World's Rim: Speculations on Color, Culture, and Contact," *American Indian Quarterly*, 16 (1992), 451–69, and his "Mythical Realities and European Contact in the Northeast During the Sixteenth and Seventeenth Centuries," *Man in the Northeast*, 33 (1987), 63–87.

10. Rountree, *Powhatan Indians*, 80–84; Jeffrey P. Blick, "The Huskanaw and Ossuary Rituals of . . . Southeastern Virginia," *Quarterly Bulletin of the Archaeological Society of Virginia*, 42, no. 4 (1987), 193–204; J. Frederick Fausz, "The Powhatan Uprising of 1622 . . . Ethnocentrism and Cultural Conflict" (Ph.D. diss., College of William and Mary, 1977), 85–86. On the warrior cult in Powhatan culture, see ibid., 115–18; Martin, *Keepers of the Game*, 74–75; William S. Simmons, *Spirit of the New England Tribes: Indian History and Folklore, 1620–1684* (Hanover, N.H., 1986), 47. On the Pokanokets' ritual

abandonment of adolescents through long, bitter winters and their harsh treatment of them thereafter, see Salisbury, *Manitou*, 39–40. On the Wabanaki pubescent boys' search for guiding visions and spirit helpers, see Haviland and Power, *Original Vermonters*, 179.

11. Alvin H. Morrison, "Dawnland Dog-Feast: Wabanaki Warfare c. 1600–1760," in William Cowan, ed., *Papers of the Twenty-First Algonquian Conference* (Ottawa, 1990), 267–69; William A. Starna and Ralph Watkins, "Northern Iroquoian Slavery," *Ethnohistory*, 38, no. 1 (1991), 34–57; Rountree, *Powhatan Indians*, 84; Richter, *Ordeal of the Longhouse*, chaps. 2, 3. On the rites of prisoner sacrifice among the Hurons, see Bruce G. Trigger, *The Children of Aataentsic: A History of the Huron People to 1660* (Montreal, 1976), I, 68–75.

12. E.g., Rountree, *Powhatan Indians*, 96–99.

13. Ibid., 96, 85, 87.

14. Ibid., 80; Philip L. Barbour, *Pocahontas and Her World* (Boston, 1970), 6; Simmons, *New England Tribes*, 46.

15. This necessarily loose approximation was developed along two lines wherever alternative figures were available: on the one hand, the average of the range of regional estimates, and on the other, the upper limits of these estimates. Since in my opinion all estimates for the precontact population are likely to be low, I have discarded the estimated lower boundaries. The regional estimates I have used are the following. **Southern New England and Long Island:** average 135,000; upper limit 144,000, in Salisbury, *Manitou*, 30. **Northern and Western New England (Eastern and Western Abenakis):** 21,900, in Dean R. Snow, *The Archaeology of New England* (New York, 1980), 31–42, table p. 34. **Middle Region:** middle and upper Hudson, 5,300; lower Hudson, average 23,800, upper limit 32,300; upper Delaware, average 14,000, upper limit 19,000, in Snow, *Archaeology of New England*, 33, table 2.1; Susquehannocks, 8,000, in J. Frederick Fausz, "Merging and Emerging Worlds," in Lois G. Carr et al., eds., *Colonial Chesapeake Society* (Chapel Hill, N.C., 1988), 60. **Chesapeake:** Maryland, 12,000, in Trigger, ed., *Handbook*, 242; Virginia, average 22,500, upper limit 25,000, in Russell Thornton, *American Indian Holocaust and Survival: A Population History Since 1492* (Norman, Okla., 1987), 68, adopting Mooney's figure of 1907. (Cf. average 18,300, upper limit 22,300, in Christian F. Feest, "Seventeenth-Century Virginia Algonquin Population Estimates," *Quarterly Bulletin of the Archaeological Society of Virginia*, 28 [1973], 66–79). **North Carolina:** 7,000, in Trigger, ed., *Handbook*, 272. **Iroquois:** average 25,000, upper limit 30,000, in Richter, *Ordeal of the Longhouse*, 17. **Nova Scotia and Cape Breton:** average, 3,750, upper limit 5,000, in R. Cole Harris, ed., *Historical Atlas of Canada*, vol. 1 (Toronto, 1987), plate 18.

The total of the averages is 278,250; the total of the upper limits is 309,500. Rough as these figures, developed from regional estimates, are, they correspond reasonably well to such large-scale estimates as that of Douglas H. Ubelaker, in John W. Verano and Douglas H. Ubelaker, eds., *Disease and Demography in the Americas* (Washington, D.C., 1992), 173: for the entire northeast, including trans-Appalachia and southeastern Canada—345,700 in 1600.

16. Alfred Cammisa, "A Comparison of Settlement Patterns and General Land Use . . . in Southern New England . . . ," *Bulletin of the Massachusetts Archaeological Society*, 45 (1924), 68; Richter, *Ordeal of the Longhouse*, 17; Fausz, "Powhatan Uprising," 92; Snow,

Archaeology of New England, 88, 96, 87 (converting population per km^2 to mi^2 by a multiplier of 2.6); Rountree, *Powhatan Indians*, 15; E. Randolph Turner, "A Re-Examination of Powhatan Territorial Boundaries and Population, ca. A.D. 1607," *Quarterly Bulletin of the Archaeological Society of Virginia*, 37 (1982), 57, table 3; Marshall J. Becker, "A Summary of Lenape Socio-Political Organization and Settlement Pattern . . . ," *Journal of Middle Atlantic Archaeology*, 4 (1988), 82; Becker, "The Boundary Between the Lenape and Munsee . . . ," *Man in the Northeast*, 26 (1983), 2; Becker, "Cultural Diversity in the Lower Delaware River Valley," in Jay F. Custer, ed., *Late Woodland Cultures of the Middle Atlantic Region* (Newark, Del., 1986), 94.

17. For typical seasonal movements of Indian villagers, see the charts in Snow, *Archaeology of New England*, 76, 79, 89, 92; Richard W. Wilkie and Jack Tager, eds., *Historical Atlas of Massachusetts* (Amherst, Mass., 1991), 13; Harris, ed., *Atlas of Canada*, plate 34; Cammisa, "Comparison," 68, 70; William A. Starna, "Aboriginal Title and Traditional Iroquois Land Use . . . ," in Christopher Vecsey and William A. Starna, eds., *Iroquois Land Claims* (Syracuse, N.Y., 1988), 33–34; Peter A. Thomas, *In the Maelstrom of Change . . . The Middle Connecticut River Valley, 1635–1665* (New York, 1990), 106–8. For an interesting account of relative stability within the Iroquois League of Peace in the precontact period, see Dennis, *Landscape of Peace*, chap. 2. But even the more stable Iroquois communities changed locations "at intervals of approximately twelve to twenty years." Richter, *Ordeal of the Longhouse*, 23.

18. Starna, "Aboriginal Title," 42, 31; Fausz, "Powhatan Uprising," 95; Starna, "The Pequots in the Early Seventeenth Century," in Lawrence M. Hauptman and James D. Wherry, eds., *The Pequots of Southern New England* (Norman, Okla., 1990), 35. The abandonment of overworked fields in some cases constituted a regular fallow system: Thomas, *Maelstrom of Change*, 111–12.

19. Snow, *Archaeology of New England*, 45, 76, 79.

20. Starna, "Aboriginal Title," 43–44; Dean R. Snow, "Wabanaki 'Family Hunting Territories,'" *American Anthropologist*, 70 (1968), 1148.

21. Emerson W. Baker, ". . . Anglo-Indian Land Deeds in Early Maine," *Ethnohistory*, 36 (1989), 239; Helen C. Rountree, *Pocahontas's People: The Powhatan Indians of Virginia Through Four Centuries* (Norman, Okla., 1990), 6, 7; Becker, "Summary," 79–81; Haviland and Power, *Original Vermonters*, 155; Snow, "Wabanaki 'Family Hunting Territories,'" 1146–47.

22. Starna, "Aboriginal Title," 40, 41; Baker, "Anglo-Indian Land Deeds," 239; William Cronon, *Changes in the Land* (New York, 1983), 60–66. On the strange, numinous places, see George R. Hamell, "Mythical Realities and European Contact in the Northeast . . . ," *Man in the Northeast*, 33 (1987), 69:

> In the deep gloomy forest far beyond the village clearing and in the dark waters far beyond the village shoreline, the hunter, the fisherman, and the berrypicker are apt to stumble across or into . . . numinous places [which] include mighty hollow trees and logs, caves and rocky places generally, deep springs, waterfalls and whirlpools, and the foreboding waters surrounding rocky islands, floating or otherwise, and such islands themselves at the world's rim. These are known thresholds to the other world and to the under(water)world particularly.

Those real human man-beings who desired an exchange with the under(water) world . . . since time immemorial, with (the) *grandfathers*, sought such places out. All those real human man-beings who encountered such places and these grandfathers offered gifts, the consecrating purposiveness of mind and heart through song (prayer), sacred tobacco, trussed dog man-beings, wampum, and other precious things.

23. Rountree, "The Powhatans as Trackers," in Helen C. Rountree, ed., *Powhatan Foreign Relations, 1500–1722* (Charlottesville, Va., 1993), 29–39; Rountree, *Pocahontas's People*, 4; C. G. Holland, "A Northern Neck Indian Path Complex," *Quarterly Bulletin of the Archaeological Society of Virginia*, 43 (1988), 108–24; Francis Jennings, " 'Pennsylvania Indians' and the Iroquois," in Daniel K. Richter and James H. Merrell, eds., *Beyond the Covenant Chain* (Syracuse, N.Y., 1987), 76; Jennings, *The Ambiguous Iroquois Empire* (New York, 1984), 74–78; Paul A. W. Wallace, *Indian Paths of Pennsylvania* (Harrisburg, Pa., 1965), passim, esp. endpaper maps; comparison with Scotland, 1–2; Wilkie and Tager, eds., *Historical Atlas of Massachusetts*, Native Settlements and Trails, c. 1600-1650, 12.

24. Ibid., 27–30; Rountree, ed., *Powhatan Foreign Relations*, 33–34; Elizabeth A. Little, "Inland Waterways in the Northeast," *Midcontinental Journal of Archaeology*, 12 (1987), 55–63. For the "maze of intervillage contacts" in the southeastern regions, and the "trails and canoe routes over distances of several hundred miles, extending in the case of war parties and diplomatic missions to 1,000 or 1,500 miles," see Helen H. Tanner, in Peter H. Wood et al., eds., *Powhatan's Mantle* (Lincoln, Neb., 1989), 6–17. For an exhaustive account of the Indian trail system of the southeast, mainly in the eighteenth century, see William E. Myer, "Indian Trails of the Southeast," *Forty-second Annual Report of the Bureau of American Ethnology . . . 1924–1925* (Washington, D.C., 1928), 727–854.

25. Rountree, ed., *Powhatan Foreign Relations*, 25–26; Fausz, "Powhatan Uprising," 109–10; George R. Hamell, "The Iroquois and the World's Rim . . . ," *American Indian Quarterly*, 16 (1992), 458; Morrison, "Wabanaki Warfare," 267; Little, "Inland Waterways," fig. 4.

26. Rountree, ed., *Powhatan Foreign Relations*, 21, 50–52.

27. Trigger, ed., *Handbook*, 70ff., 282, 334ff.; Snow, *Archaeology of New England*, 27–31, 63–64; Rountree, *Powhatan Indians*, 7, 8; Fausz, "Powhatan Uprising," 64. On the vexed question of the linguistic-ethnic identity of the Piedmont tribes of Virginia, see Rountree, *Powhatan Indians*, 8; Jeffrey L. Hantman, in Rountree, *Powhatan Foreign Relations*, 95–96; Nancy O. Lurie, "Indian Cultural Adjustment to European Civilization," in James M. Smith, ed., *Seventeenth-Century America* (Chapel Hill, N.C., 1959), 43.

28. Haviland and Power, *Original Vermonters*, 156: "The 'sense of place' of these peoples seems to have been a good deal stronger than that of modern North Americans, who for the most part show far more tendency to move about from one place to another than did Abenakis prior to the Historic period." The definition of *tribe* I have used is that of L. Daniel Mouer, in *Quarterly Bulletin of the Archaeological Society of Virginia*, 36 (1981), 1. (Cf. Jennings, *Ambiguous Empire*, 37.) On tribal names: Herbert C. Kraft, "Settlement Patterns in the Upper Delaware Valley," in Custer, ed., *Late Woodland Cultures*, 106; C. A. Weslager, *The Delaware Indians* (New Brunswick, N.J., 1972), 31, 45–46; Rountree, *Powhatan Indians*, 11; Trigger, ed., *Handbook*, 137, 235, 236, 478, 489–90, 516; Richter, *Ordeal*, 1.

29. Fausz, "Powhatan Uprising," 62, 63, 80, 87–89, 106, 113; Rountree, *Powhatan Indians*, 114–21 and chap. 6; Rountree, ed., *Powhatan Foreign Relations*, 7, 8, 10–11, 13, 18.

30. E. Randolph Turner, in Rountree, ed., *Powhatan Foreign Relations*, 92; Lewis R. Binford, *Cultural Diversity Among Aboriginal Cultures of Coastal Virginia and North Carolina* (New York, 1991), 241–42; Becker, Custer, and Kraft, in Custer, ed., *Late Woodland Cultures*, 94, 111, 144; Marion F. Ales, "A History of the Indians on Montauk, Long Island," in Gaynell S. Levine, ed., *The History and Archaeology of the Montauk Indians (Readings in Long Island Archaeology and Ethnohistory*, 3 [1979]), 15, 24; John Strong, "The Evolution of Shinnecock Culture," in Gaynell Stone, ed., *The Shinnecock Indians* (Lexington, Mass., 1983), 36–38; Snow, *Archaeology of New England*, 76–77, 97, 336, 342; Starna, "Pequots in Early Seventeenth Century," 39–43; Peter A. Thomas, in William Fitzhugh, ed., *Cultures in Contact . . . 1000–1800* (Washington, D.C., 1985), 135, 137–38; Thomas, *Maelstrom*, 29–44, 96ff.; Ted J. Brasser, "Riding on the Frontier's Crest: Mahican Indian Culture and Culture Change," *National [Canadian] Museum of Man*, Mercury Series, Ethnology Division, Paper no. 13 (Ottawa, 1974); Trigger, ed., *Handbook*, 137, 156–57.

31. Richter, *Ordeal*, 17, 31, 32, 36, 17, 18, 39–43, 46, 44, 40. On the Abenakis' fear of the Iroquois, see Morrison, "Dawnland Dog-Feast," 270.

32. Richter, *Ordeal*, 42–43, 35; Salisbury, *Manitou*, 40–42; Jack Campisi, *The Mashpee Indians* (Syracuse, N.Y., 1991), 71–72; Starna, "Pequots in Early Seventeenth Century," 39–43; Snow, *Archaeology of New England*, 72, 77; Weslager, *Delaware Indians*, 64–65; Rountree, *Powhatan Indians*, 93, 117, 119–20.

33. Rountree, ed., *Powhatan Foreign Relations*, 217ff.

34. Patrick M. Malone, *The Skulking Way of War: Technology and Tactics Among the New England Indians* (Lanham, Md., 1991), 15–19; Karen O. Kupperman, *Settling with the Indians* (Totowa, N.J., 1980), 102; Snow, *Archaeology of New England*, 98; Dennis, *Landscape of Peace*, 69, 70, with illustrations of Iroquois woven reed armor. Lescarbot reported seeing in 1606–7 Wabanaki warriors with shields that covered their whole bodies: Morrison, "Wabanaki Warfare," 267.

35. C. Keith Wilbur, *The New England Indians* (Chester, Conn., 1978), 63–67; Kupperman, *Settling with the Indians*, 103; Rountree, ed., *Powhatan Foreign Relations*, 32; Haviland, *Original Vermonters*, 166–67.

36. Ibid., 167. Illustrations of typical dwellings, in Carl Waldman, *Atlas of the North America Indian* (New York, 1985), 51.

37. Wilbur, *New England Indians*, 60–62; Rountree, *Powhatan Indians*, 34–35; on the whale fishery of Long Island, Strong, "Shinnecock Culture," 32–34; Ales, "Indians on Montauk," 82; Weslager, *Delaware Indians*, 60; Kraft, "Settlement Patterns," 107; Sarah Clayton, "The Potomac (Patawomeke) Indians," *Quarterly Bulletin of the Archaeological Society of Virginia*, 27 (1973), 180–81; C.A. Weslager, *The Nanticoke Indians—Past and Present* (Newark, N.J., 1983), 43.

38. Rountree, *Powhatan Indians*, 39–42; Haviland and Power, *Original Vermonters*, 161–64; Wilbur, *New England Indians*, 56–57; Clayton, "Potomac Indians," 180; Fausz, "Powhatan Uprising," 102–4.

39. Haviland and Power, *Original Vermonters*, 157–59; Weslager, *Delaware Indians*, 51; Kraft, "Settlement Patterns," 111–12; Ales, "Indians on Montauk," 16; Haviland and Power, *Original Vermonters*, 159.

40. Clayton, "Potomac Indians," 183; Trigger, ed., *Handbook*, 306; Hamell, "Iroquois and the World's Rim," 459–61; Hamell, "Mythical Realities," 67; Wilbur, *New England Indians*, 84–85; Weslager, *Nanticoke Indians*, 45.

41. On the Powhatans' great diversity of resources: Binford, quoted in Fausz, "Powhatan Uprising," 105; Rountree, *Powhatan Foreign Relations*, 68–69, 218; Weslager, *Delaware Indians*, 53–54, 57–58; Martin, *Keepers of the Game*, 33; Kraft, "Settlement Patterns," 106–8; Snow, *Archaeology of New England*, 334; Haviland and Power, *Original Vermonters*, 156.

42. E.g., Rountree, ed., *Powhatan Foreign Relations*, 38:

When Indian people set out to walk along their trails or paddle along the waterways, they traveled fast by European standards. Woodland Indian people of both sexes were physically fit and very proud of being so. When they ran, their speed and endurance seemed almost miraculous. . . . That sort of endurance helps to explain how the "Tomahitans" could cover 2,200 miles on foot and by canoe in five months, with only short rest stops, and consider such efforts merely to be ordinary.

43. Ubelaker and Rountree, ibid., 64–65, 207; Fausz, "Powhatan Uprising," 46; Starna, "Pequots in Early Seventeenth Century," 44–45; Cronon, *Changes in the Land*, 24, 85. On infant mortality and life expectancy in Europe, see Louis Henry and Pierre Goubert, in D.V. Glass and D. E. C. Eversley, eds., *Population in History* (London, 1965), 444, 468; and Pierre Goubert, "Legitimate Fecundity and Infant Mortality in France During the Eighteenth Century," *Daedalus*, 97, no. 2 (1968), 599.

44. Lurie, "Indian Cultural Adjustment," 38.

45. Rountree, *Powhatan Indians*, chap. 1; Rountree, *Pocahontas's People*, chap. 1; Turner, "Re-examination of Powhatan Territorial Boundaries," 47–49.

46. Dennis, *Landscape of Peace*, chap. 2; Richter, *Ordeal*, 50–54; Ann F. Ramenofsky, *Vectors of Death: The Archaeology of European Contact* (Albuquerque, N.M., 1987), 100–2; Hamell, "Iroquois and the World's Rim," 459.

47. T. J. Brasser, "Early Indian-European Contacts," in Trigger, ed., *Handbook*, 82–88; Thomas S. Abler and Michael H. Logan, "The Florescence and Demise of Iroquois Cannibalism . . . ," *Man in the Northeast*, 35 (1988), 1–17.

CHAPTER 2

Death on a Coastal Fringe

1. Frederic W. Gleach, *Powhatan's World and Colonial Virginia: A Conflict of Cultures* (Lincoln, Neb., 1997), chap. 2, 40, quotation (Genesis 2: 26) at 63.

2. D. M. Palliser, *The Age of Elizabeth: England Under the Later Tudors, 1547–1603*, 2nd ed. (London and New York, 1992), 236, 13, 201, 84, 202, 6, 106; Charles Wilson, *England's Apprenticeship, 1603–1763* (London, 1965), 7–9.

3. R. A. Houston, *The Population History of Britain and Ireland, 1500–1750* (London, 1992), 64; E. A. Wrigley and R. S. Schofield, *The Population History of England 1541–1871* (Cambridge, Mass., 1981), 224–28.

4. Charles M. Andrews, *The Colonial Period of American History* (New Haven, Conn., 1934–38), I, chaps. 2, 3; Karen O. Kupperman, *The Jamestown Project* (Cambridge, Mass., 2007), chaps. 1, 2, 4, 6, quotations at 43, 44; David Armitage, *The Ideological Origins of the British Empire* (Cambridge, England, 2000), chap. 1; Peter C. Mancall, *Hakluyt's Promise: An Elizabethan Obsession for an English America* (New Haven, Conn., 2007), esp. 137–55; Kupperman, "Controlling Nature and Colonial Projects in Early America," in Hans-Jüngen Grabbe, ed., *Colonial Encounters* (Heidelberg, 2003), 69–88.

5. Theodore K. Rabb, *Enterprise & Empire... 1575–1630* (Cambridge, Mass., 1967), 29ff.; Robert Brenner, *Merchants and Revolution... 1550–1653* (Princeton, N.J., 1993), chaps. 1, 2, 92.

6. Ibid., 108.

7. Nicholas Canny and Anthony Pagden, eds., *Colonial Identity in the Atlantic World, 1500–1800* (Princeton, N.J., 1987), 66–67, 72–74; Robert F. Berkhofer, Jr., "White Conceptions of Indians," in William C. Sturtevant, ed., *Handbook of North American Indians*, IV (*History of Indian-White Relations*, Washington, D.C., 1988), 523ff.; Anthony Pagden, *The Fall of Natural Man: The American Indians and the Origins of Comparative Ethnology* (Cambridge, England, 1982), chap. 4, esp. 75–90; J. H. Elliott, *The Old World and the New, 1492–1650* (Cambridge, England, 1970), chap. 2; Elliott, *Empires of the Atlantic World: Britain and Spain in America 1492–1830* (New Haven, Conn., 2006), 240–41.

8. Paul Hulton, *America 1585: The Complete Drawings of John White* (Chapel Hill, N.C., 1984), plates 65–69, fig. 28.

9. Nicholas P. Canny, "The Ideology of English Colonization: From Ireland to America," *WMQ* 30 (1973), 584, 588; David B. Quinn, *The Elizabethans and the Irish* (Ithaca, N.Y., 1966), chaps. 7–9.

10. Keith Thomas, *Religion and the Decline of Magic* (London, 1971), esp. chaps. 21, 22; Edward L. Bond, "Source of Knowledge, Source of Power: The Supernatural World of English Virginia," *VMHB*, 108 (2000), quotations at 114, 116, 120; cf. David D. Hall, *Worlds of Wonder, Days of Judgment: Popular Religious Belief in Early New England* (New York, 1989).

11. Palliser, *Age of Elizabeth*, 7, 18, 20, 32, 55, 57; Paul Slack, *The Impact of Plague in Tudor and Stuart England* (Oxford, England, 1985), passim.

12. Gleach, *Powhatan's World*, 3, 44–45, 60.

13. Palliser, *Age of Elizabeth*, 360–67, 397–98, 19, 20, 381; J. M. Beattie, *Crime and the Courts in England, 1660–1800* (Princeton, N.J., 1986), 451; Lionello Puppi, *Torment in Art: Pain, Violence and Martyrdom*, trans. Jeremy Scott (New York, 1991), 7, and the illustrations that follow; G. R. Elton, *England Under the Tudors* (London, 1955), 220, 308; Keith Wrightson, *English Society, 1580–1680* (London, 1982), 202–3.

14. William Haller, *The Elect Nation: The Meaning and Relevance of Foxe's Book of Martyrs* (New York, 1963), 13–14, 194. For the influence of Foxe's *Actes and Monuments* in seventeenth-century New England, see Anne G. Myles, "Restoration Declensions... John Foxe in 1664 Massachusetts," *NEQ*, 80 (2007), 35–68, and Francis J. Bremer, "Foxe in the Wilderness...," in David Loades, ed., *John Foxe at Home and Abroad* (Aldershot, England, 1988), chap. 9.

15. Brenner, *Merchants and Revolution*, 109; Andrews, *Colonial Period*, I, chap. 4.

16. Warren M. Billings, ed., *The Old Dominion in the Seventeenth Century: A Documentary History of Virginia, 1606–1700* (rev. ed., Chapel Hill, N.C., 2007), 19–21; John W. Shirley, "George Percy at Jamestown, 1607–1612," *VMHB*, 57 (1949), 227–30; Bernard Bailyn, "Politics and Social Structure in Virginia," in James M. Smith, ed., *Seventeenth-Century America* (Chapel Hill, N.C., 1959), 92; James P. C. Southall and Samuel M. Bemiss on John Martin: *VMHB*, 54 (1946), 21–67; 65 (1957), 209–21; Smith, *Works*, I, xxix, xxxvi; Warner F. Gookin, "Who Was Bartholomew Gosnold?" *WMQ*, 6 (1949), 398–415; Warner F. Gookin and Philip L. Barbour, *Bartholomew Gosnold* (Hamden, Conn., 1963), part I. On Harriot, see John W. Shirley, *Thomas Harriot: A Biography* (Oxford, England, 1983), and Joyce E. Chaplin, *Subject Matter: Technology, the Body, and Science on the Anglo-American Frontier, 1500–1676* (Cambridge, Mass., 2001), 28–34 passim.

The laborers, Smith later recalled, "were for the most part footmen, and such as they that were adventurers brought to attend them . . . that never did know what a dayes work was." Like the "poore gentlemen, tradsmen, serving-men, libertines, and such like," the laborers, Smith said, were "ten times more fit to spoyle a common-wealth, then either to begin one, or but helpe to maintaine one. For when neither the feare of God, nor the law, nor shame, nor displeasure of their friends could rule them here [in England], there is small hope ever to bring one in twentie of them to be good there." Smith, *Works*, II, 225.

17. Bailyn, "Politics and Social Structure," 92–93; Lyon G. Tyler, ed., *Narratives of Early Virginia 1606–1625* (New York, 1907), 281, 286; Kupperman, *Jamestown*, 64–70, 112, 129, 290; William S. Powell, *John Pory, 1572–1636* (Chapel Hill, N.C., 1977), chaps. 1, 2; James Horn, *A Land As God Made It: Jamestown and the Birth of America* (New York, 2005) [hereafter: Horn, *Jamestown*], 251–52; Richard B. Davis, *George Sandys, Poet-Adventurer: A Study in Anglo-American Culture in the Seventeenth Century* (London, 1955); James Ellison, *George Sandys: Travel, Colonialism, and Tolerance in the Seventeenth Century* (Cambridge, England, 2002).

18. Philip L. Barbour, "Captain George Kendall, Mutineer or Intelligencer?" *VMHB*, 70 (1962), 298–313; Kupperman, *Jamestown*, 219–20; K. R. Andrews, "Christopher Newport of Limehouse, Mariner," *WMQ*, 11 (1954), 28–51, quote at 40; Gookin, "Gosnold," 413; Smith, *Works*, I, liii; Gookin and Barbour, *Gosnold*, 198; Horn, *Jamestown*, 34–35, 46.

19. Laura P. Striker, "Captain John Smith's Hungary and Transylvania," in Bradford Smith, *Captain John Smith: His Life and Legend* (Philadelphia, 1953), app. 1; Striker, "The Hungarian Historian, Lewis L. Kropf, on Captain John Smith's True Travels," *VMHB*, 66 (1958), 22–43; Smith, *Works*, I, lv–lviii; Philip L. Barbour, *The Three Worlds of Captain John Smith* (Boston, 1964), 112; Horn, *Jamestown*, 42–43; George Percy, "A Trewe Relacyon . . . [1609–1612]" (text as transcribed from Mark Nicholls, *VMHB*, 113, no. 3 [2005]), 246. For an excellent survey of Smith's early career, based on his jumbled *The True Travels . . . of Captaine John Smith* (1630, in Smith, *Works*, III, 153–241), see Kupperman, *Jamestown*, 51–60; for the complex relationship between Smith and Newport that later developed, see Daniel K. Richter, "Tsenacommacah and the Atlantic World," in Peter C. Mancall, ed., *The Atlantic World and Virginia, 1550–1824* (Chapel Hill, N.C., 2007), 47–59.

20. Philip L. Barbour, ed., *The Jamestown Voyages under the First Charter, 1606–1609* (Cambridge, England, 1969), I, 49–54, quotation at 51. The Don and Dvina rivers were identified in the instructions as the "Tan[a]is and Dwina."

21. Philip L. Barbour, "The First Reconnaissance of the James," *Virginia Cavalcade*, 17 (1967), 35–41; Barbour, *Jamestown Voyages*, I, 133–35.

22. Ibid., 134, 136, 137, 138; Barbour, *Three Worlds*, 125; Ivor N. Hume, *Martin's Hundred* (New York, 1982), 27.

23. The narrative that follows is based in part on Barbour, *Three Worlds*, Part II; in part on Smith's *Generall Historie of Virginia, New-England, and the Summer Isles. . .* (1624), in Barbour's edition of Smith's *Complete Works;* and in part on the portion of George Percy's *Discourse of . . . Virginia . . .* in Barbour, *Jamestown Voyages*, I, 129–46. I have been guided too by the detailed account in Horn, *Jamestown*, and by Kupperman, *Jamestown*, 217–55. For the figures on the living and the dead, see Virginia Bernhard, "'Men, Women and Children' at Jamestown: Population and Gender in Early Virginia, 1607–1610," *Journal of Southern History*, 58 (1992), 599–618 [hereafter, Bernhard, "Population and Gender"].

24. Dennis B. Blanton, "Drought as a Factor in the Jamestown Colony, 1607–1812," *Historical Archaeology*, 34, no. 4 (2000), 74–81; David W. Stahle et al., "The Lost Colony and Jamestown Droughts," *Science*, 280 (April 24, 1998), 564–67.

25. Carville V. Earle, "Environment, Disease, and Mortality in Early Virginia," in Thad W. Tate and David L. Ammerman, eds., *The Chesapeake in the Seventeenth Century* (New York, 1979), chap. 3.

26. Percy, *Discourse*, 144–45; Bernhard, "Population and Gender," 603.

27. Smith, *Works*, II, 160–62; Barbour, *Three Worlds*, 174; Horn, *Jamestown*, 75, 76.

28. Smith, *Works*, II, 181, 184, 190–91; I, 240–42. Ann Burras, servant to a "Mistress Ferrar," is known to have married John Laydon, a carpenter who had arrived on the *Susan Constant*. Their daughter Virginia is recorded as the first child born in the colony of English parents. Annie L. Jester and Martha W. Hiden, comps. and eds., *Adventurers of Purse and Person, Virginia, 1607–1624/5* (3rd ed., revised by Virginia M. Meyer and John F. Dorman, Richmond, Va., 1987), 389.

29. Barbour, *Three Worlds*, chaps. 14, 15. For the details of the limits of Smith's expeditions and the specific Indian villages and rivers he identified, see *Works*, I, 185–90.

30. Horn, *Jamestown*, 14–17.

31. Kupperman, *Jamestown*, 223, 225.

32. Gleach, *Powhatan's World*, 11, 36, 51, 57.

33. Barbour, *Three Worlds*, 141, 223.

34. Louis B. Wright and Virginia Freund, eds., *The Historie of Travell into Virginia Britania* (1612) by William Strachey, gent. (London, 1953), 56–58.

35. Smith, *Works*, I, lix, 47–57, 213; II, 150–51; Gleach, *Powatan's World*, 114–22; Horn, *Jamestown*, 70–71, 78–79. Cf. Everett Emerson, *Captain John Smith* (rev. ed., New York, 1993), 77; Barbour, *Three Worlds*, 443–44. Smith's most elaborate version is in his letter to the Queen, 1616, quoted in Barbour, *Pocahontas and Her World . . .* (Boston, 1969), 156. On the ritual and symbolic significance of establishing Smith's "fictive kinship" with Powhatan and his people: Cynthia J. Van Zandt, *Brothers Among Nations: The Pursuit of Intercultural Alliances in Early America, 1580–1660* (Oxford, England, 2008), 74–78.

36. Smith, *Works*, I, 237; Horn, *Jamestown*, 105–8; Van Zandt, *Brothers Among Nations*, 76–81.

37. Kupperman, *Jamestown*, 232; Horn, *Jamestown*, 79.

38. Barbour, *Jamestown Voyages*, I, 95; Smith, *Works*, I, 175; II, 127; Percy, "A Trewe Relacyon," 247–48.

39. Smith, *Works*, II, 201–2.

40. Bernhard, "Population and Gender," 605–6.

41. Smith, *Works*, I, 259–60, 263–65; Barbour, *Three Worlds*, 264, 248, 266.

42. Percy, "Trewe Relacyon," 248–49. Of the cannibalized woman, Smith later wrote, rather archly, "whether shee was better roasted, boyled or carbonado'd [i.e., grilled], I know not, but of such a dish as powdered [i.e., salted] wife I never heard of." Smith, *Works*, II, 232–33.

43. Percy, "Trewe Relacyon," 250–51; Governor and Council of Virginia to the Virginia Company of London, July 7, 1610, in Alexander Brown, comp. and ed., *The Genesis of the United States* ([1890], New York, 1964), I, 405–6.

CHAPTER 3

The "Hammerours'" Regime

1. George Percy, "A Trewe Relacyon . . . [1609–1612]" (text as transcribed by Mark Nicholls, *VMHB*, 113, no. 3 [2005]), 251–52.

2. Charles M. Andrews, *The Colonial Period of American History* (New Haven, Conn., 1934–38), I, 37, 45, 102–3; Wesley F. Craven, *The Southern Colonies in the Seventeenth Century, 1607–1689* (Baton Rouge, La., 1949), 82–92; Theodore K. Rabb, *Enterprise & Empire . . . 1575–1630* (Cambridge, Mass., 1967), 378.

3. Alexander Brown, comp. and ed., *The Genesis of the United States* (1890; New York, 1964), I, 352, 342, 340. On the supposed "surplus" of population, see Mildred Campbell, "'Of People Either Too Few Or Too Many' . . . ," in William A. Aiken and Basil D. Henning, eds., *Conflict in Stuart England* (London, 1960), 171–201.

4. William Strachey, comp., *For the Colony in Virginea Britannia. Lawes Divine, Morall and Martiall, etc.* ([London, 1612] David H. Flaherty, ed., Charlottesville, Va., 1969), xvi; Brown, ed., *Genesis*, I, 342, 350, 353.

5. Ibid., 241–43, 260–77, quotations at 263, 272–73.

6. William R. Scott, *The Constitution and Finance of . . . Joint-Stock Companies to 1720* (Cambridge, England, 1910–12), II, 251–52; Rabb, *Enterprise and Empire*, 90; Craven, *Southern Colonies*, 102–3; Brown, ed., *Genesis*, I, 317.

7. Andrews, *Colonial Period*, I, 113n; Brown, ed., *Genesis*, I, 355, 356, 354, 252, 248; Darrett B. Rutman, "The Virginia Company and Its Military Regime," in Rutman, ed., *The Old Dominion* (Charlottesville, Va., 1964), 6–8; J. Frederick Fausz, "An 'Abundance of Blood Shed on Both Sides': England's First Indian War, 1609–1614," *VMHB*, 98 (1990), 30, 37–38, 41; Geoffrey Parker, *The Military Revolution* (Cambridge, England, 1988), 49, 50, 52, 53, 55, 57.

8. James Horn, *A Land As God Made It: Jamestown and the Birth of America* (New York, 2005) [hereafter: Horn, *Jamestown*], 189; Brown, ed., *Genesis*, I, 409, 410, 412.

9. Horn, *Jamestown*, 184–85.

10. Ibid., 185–86; Percy, "Trewe Relacyon," 252, 253–54; Fausz, "'Abundance of Blood,'" 34.

11. Percy, "Trewe Relacyon," 255; Fausz, "'Abundance of Blood,'" 35–37.

12. Figures for ships and passenger arrivals are based on a comprehensive list of annual arrivals, 1607–60, compiled by Barbara DeWolfe from all available sources; file retained by author.

13. On the spread of settlement, see Charles E. Hatch, Jr., *The First Seventeen Years: Virginia, 1607–1624* (Baltimore, Md., 1993), 34ff. On Dale's grand design, see Warren M. Billings, ed., *The Old Dominion in the Seventeenth Century: A Documentary History of Virginia, 1606–1689*, rev. ed. (Chapel Hill, N.C., 1975), 41–43.

14. Darrett B. Rutman, "The Historian and the Marshall," *VMHB*, 68 (1960), 284–94.

15. *Lawes Divine, Morall and Martiall*, 34, 35.

16. Billings, ed., *Old Dominion*, 44; *Lawes Divine, Morall and Martiall*, 3–25; E. R. Adair, "English Galleys in the Sixteenth Century," *English Historical Review*, 35 (1920), 510–12; Craven, *Southern Colonies*, 106–7.

17. *Lawes Divine, Morall and Martiall*, 40–101; David T. Konig, "'Dale's Laws' and the Non-Common Law Origins of Criminal Justice in Virginia," *American Journal of Legal History* 26 (1982), 356.

18. Ibid., 357–69; Konig, "Colonization and the Common Law in Ireland and Virginia, 1569–1634," in James A. Henretta, Michael Kammen, and Stanley Katz, eds., *The Transformation of Early American History* (New York, 1991), 81–92; William E. Nelson, *The Common Law in Colonial America*, I (Oxford, England, 2008), 14–18.

19. Billings, ed., *Old Dominion*, 43.

20. A. Roger Ekirch, *Bound for America: The Transportation of British Convicts to the Colonies, 1718–1775* (Oxford, England, 1987), 27; Sigmund Diamond, "From Organization to Society: Virginia in the Seventeenth Century," *American Journal of Sociology*, 63 (1958), 467; Craven, *Southern Colonies*, 107; Percy, "Trewe Relacyon," 262.

21. Billings, ed., *Old Dominion*, 41; Nicholas P. Canny, "The Ideology of English Colonization: From Ireland to America," *WMQ*, 30 (1973), 582; Fausz, "'Abundance of Blood,'" 3–4, 33. Frederic W. Gleach, *Powhatan's World and Colonial Virginia* (Lincoln, Neb., 1997), 11, 36.

22. Louis B. Wright and Virginia Freund, eds., *The Historie of Travell into Virginia Britania* (1612) by William Strachey, gent. (London, 1953), 24; Melanie Perreault, "'We Washed Not the Ground with Their Bloods': Intercultural Violence and Identity in the Early Chesapeake," in Debra Meyers and Melanie Perreault, eds., *Colonial Chesapeake: New Perspectives* (Lanham, Md., 2006), 30–33.

23. Fausz, "'Abundance of Blood,'" [6], 40–42; Percy, "Trewe Relacyon," 261.

24. Fausz, "'Abundance of Blood,'" 44–48, 50, 53. For an elaborate discussion of the practical and symbolic significance of Pocahontas's supposed reprieve of Smith, her

marriage to Rolfe, and her conversion to Christianity, see Cynthia J. Van Zandt, *Brothers Among Nations: The Pursuit of Intercultural Alliances in Early America, 1580–1660* (Oxford, England, 2008), 74ff.

25. For the fortunes and transformation of the Virginia Company in the paragraphs above, see Craven, *Southern Colonies*, 108–9, 114, 116, 118, 121; Wesley F. Craven, *Dissolution of the Virginia Company* (New York, 1932), 33–35; Andrews, *Colonial Period*, I, 124–26.

26. Craven, *Southern Colonies*, 109, 115, 121–24.

CHAPTER 4

Recruitment, Expansion, and Transformation

1. Wesley F. Craven, *Dissolution of the Virginia Company* (New York, 1932), 46, chap. 3.

2. *A Declaration of the State of the Colonie and Affaires in Virginia* . . . (London, 1620), in Peter Force, comp., *Tracts and Other Papers Relating Principally to . . . the Colonies in North America* . . . (Washington, D.C., 1836–46), III, no. 5, 3–5. On land distribution, Craven, *Dissolution*, 56–57. Praise of Sandys's program and of the great prospects for Virginia was privately circulated in high places, as in John Pory's letter (1619) to Sir Dudley Carleton, the English ambassador to the Netherlands, in Lyon G. Tyler, ed., *Narratives of Early Virginia, 1606–1625* (New York, 1907), 282–87.

3. Ibid., 282, 284–85.

4. Kingsbury, *VC Records*, I, 220; III, 115–17, 240, 278, 279, 102, 161, 470; "Old Kecoughtan," *William and Mary College Quarterly*, 9 (1900), 86; Frederick W. Gookin, *Daniel Gookin, 1612–1687* (Chicago, 1912), 38–42; Alexander Brown, *The First Republic in America* (Boston and New York, 1898), 474, 562, 335–36. For a summary of Capt. William Norton's complicated negotiations to bring over Italians to man the glassworks, see Craven, *Dissolution*, 188, 191 (details in Kingsbury, *VC Records*, I, 484, 499, 507, 512–13, 566). For the highly funded, short-lived effort at iron manufacture, see Charles E. Hatch and Thorlow G. Gregory, "The First American Blast Furnace, 1619–1622," *VMHB*, 70 (1962), 259–77.

5. Kingsbury, *VC Records*, III, 240, 278, 314; IV, 23–24; *CSPC*, 498; Robert C. Johnson, "The Transportation of Vagrant Children from London to Virginia, 1618–1622," in Howard S. Reinmuth, Jr., ed., *Early Stuart Studies* (Minneapolis, 1971), 137; Robert Hume, *Early Child Immigrants to Virginia, 1619–1642* (Baltimore, Md., 1986), 1–30.

6. *CSPC*, 23; Johnson, "Transportation of Vagrant Children," 139–40, 142, 143–44; Peter W. Coldham, comp. and ed., *The Complete Book of Emigrants, 1607–1660* (Baltimore, Md., 1987), 16.

7. Johnson, "Transportation of Vagrant Children," 142–43, 146, 150; "Kidnapping Maidens to Be Sold in Virginia, 1618," *VMHB*, 6 (1899), 228–30.

8. Coldham, ed., *Complete Book*, 18, 20, 23; Thorpe to John Ferrar [May 15, 1621?], Ferrar Papers, FP239, Magdalene College, Cambridge (Virginia Company Archives Online, http://www.virginiacompanyarchives.amdigital.co.uk).

9. Craven, *Dissolution*, 96–97; Kingsbury, *VC Records*, III, 115–16.

10. Tyler, ed., *Narratives*, 286; Irene W. D. Hecht, "The Virginia Colony, 1607–1640:

A Study in Frontier Growth" (Ph.D. diss., University of Washington, 1969), 335–36, lists fourteen vessels that left England for Virginia in 1619; Avery E. Kolb, "Early Passengers to Virginia: When Did They Arrive?" *VMHB*, 88 (1980), 412, 409, 408. On the arrival of the Africans, see Wesley F. Craven, *White, Red, and Black: The Seventeenth-Century Virginian* (Charlottesville, Va., 1971), 77–82; Engel Sluiter, "New Light on the '20. and Odd Negroes' Arriving in Virginia, August 1619," *WMQ*, 54 (1997), 395–98; John Thornton, "The African Experience and the '20. and Odd Negroes' . . . ," ibid., 55 (1998), 421–34; Martha W. McCartney, "An Early Virginia Census Reprised," *Quarterly Bulletin of the Archaeological Society of Virginia*, 54 (1999), 178, 179. The various accounts of the arrival dates and numbers of passengers arriving in Virginia differ. I have used Hecht's list (App. II), which is documented, checked against Kolb's, which is not.

11. Hecht, "Virginia Colony," 335–45, App. IV.

12. David R. Ransome, " 'Shipt for Virginia': The Beginnings in 1619–1622 of the Great Migration to the Chesapeake," *VMHB*, 103 (1995), 447–449, 451–52.

13. David R. Ransome, "Wives for Virginia, 1621," *WMQ*, 48 (1991), 7–15; Ferrar Papers, FP306; Kingsbury, *VC Records*, III, 493, 505, 640; IV, 231.

14. *A Declaration*, 5.

15. On the fierce polemics of Lawne and Bennett in the sectarian struggles of the English exiles in the Netherlands, see John B. Boddie, *Seventeenth Century Isle of Wight County Virginia* (Chicago, 1938), chaps. 2, 3; on their establishment and fate in Virginia, Charles E. Hatch, Jr., *The First Seventeen Years* (Baltimore, Md., 1957), 85–89. On the Bennett family in Virginia: Annie L. Jester and Martha W. Hiden, comps. and eds., *Adventurers of Purse and Person, Virginia, 1607–1624/5* (3rd ed., revised by Virginia M. Meyer and John F. Dorman, Richmond, Va., 1987), 109ff. Babette M. Levy, *Early Puritanism in the Southern and Island Colonies* (Worcester, Mass., 1960), 92ff., traces Puritan elements in much of the religious life of the colony during the company years and stresses the company's tolerance of "Genevan" influences.

16. William Bradford, *Of Plymouth Plantation, 1620–1647* (S. E. Morison, ed., New York, 1967), 356–57.

17. Craven, *Dissolution*, 158–61, 163, 174, 179; Kingsbury, *VC Records*, IV, 151, 161, 162, 174–75, 451; III, 297, 299, 302; I, 513.

18. Hatch, *First Seventeen Years*, map of plantations and the dates of their founding, 32–33; Kingsbury, *VC Records*, III, 104; Ulrich B. Phillips, quoted in J. Frederick Fausz, "Patterns of Settlement in the James River Basin, 1607–1642" (M.A. thesis, College of William and Mary, 1971), 53. The fatal effects of dispersal are a major theme in the letters written home from Virginia.

19. J. E. Gethyn-Jones, "Berkeley Plantation, Virginia," *Transactions of the Bristol and Gloucestershire Archaeological Society*, 94 (1976), 7; Hatch, *First Seventeen Years*, 44–46, 39; William M. Kelso, *Kingsmill Plantations, 1619–1800* (New York, 1984), 57; Theodore K. Rabb, *Enterprise and Empire . . . 1575–1630* (Cambridge, Mass., 1967), 174, 407; Robert Brenner, *Merchants and Revolution . . . 1550–1653* (Princeton, N.J., 1993), 98; Ivor N. Hume, *Martin's Hundred* (New York, 1982), 67, 154–55; Craven, *Southern Colonies*, 123n.

20. Brenner, *Merchants and Revolution*, 95, 103ff.; Craven, *Southern Colonies*, 161–62; Hecht, *Virginia Colony*, App. III; James Deetz, *Flowerdew Hundred* (Charlottesville, Va., 1993), 20–24.

21. Theodore R. Reinhart, ed., *The Archaeology of Shirley Plantation* (Charlottes-ville, Va., 1984), 215; Jester and Hiden, eds., *Adventurers*, 12–16, 353, 595; William T. Buchanan, "The Browning Farm Site . . . ," *Quarterly Bulletin of the Archaeological Society of Virginia*, 35 (1981), 139, 146; H. R. McIlwaine, ed., *Minutes of the Council and General Court of Colonial Virginia*, 2nd ed. (Richmond, Va., 1979), 149, 150, 145.

22. Hume, *Martin's Hundred*, 256–58, 237–39, 46–49, 51. Besides the excellent illus-trations in Hume's book, Richard Schlecht's paintings of the plantation as he imagined it before and during the massacre of 1622 are reproduced in *National Geographic*, 155 (June 1979), 735–67, and 161 (Jan. 1982), 53–77. The fort (1621) is visualized in Ivor N. Hume, *The Virginia Adventure* (New York, 1994), 366. On the hundred's resemblance to an Irish bawn village, see ibid., 155.

23. Hume, *Martin's Hundred*, 195; Kingsbury, *VC Records*, III, 197–98, 417; Cold-ham, *Complete Book*, 31; Smith, *Works*, II, 295.

CHAPTER 5
"A *Flood,* a *Flood* of *Bloud*"

1. J. Frederick Fausz, "The Powhatan Uprising of 1622: A Historical Study of Eth-nocentrism and Cultural Conflict" (Ph.D. diss., College of William and Mary, 1977), 322–25, 327, 342–46, 303ff., 265, 273; Lyon G. Tyler, ed., *Narratives of Early Virginia, 1606–1625* (New York, 1907), 240, 242; Smith, *Works*, II, 251. My interpretation of Opechancanough's intentions follows Frederic W. Gleach, *Powhatan's World and Colonial Virginia: A Conflict of Cultures* (Lincoln, Neb., 1997), 34, 35, 37, 51, 156, 158, rather than Fausz's view that he intended to "annihilate the English" ("Powhatan Uprising," 351).

2. Kingsbury, *VC Records*, III, 102; Fausz, "Powhatan Uprising," 334–335 (cf. Smith, *Works*, II, 294–95), 295–97, 300–2, 307, 310.

3. Kingsbury, *VC Records*, I, 504; III, 584; Fausz, "Powhatan Uprising," 328, 332–41, 349; Ferrar Papers, FP247, Magdalene College, Cambridge (Virginia Company Archives Online, http://www.virginiacompanyarchives.amdigital.co.uk); Smith, *Works*, II, 295; Helen C. Rountree, *Pocahontas's People* (Norman, Okla., 1990), 73.

4. Fausz, "Powhatan Uprising," 362–63; Kingsbury, *VC Records*, III, 551, 554–56.

5. Rountree, *Pocahontas's People*, 71–72, 73, 302; Fausz, "Powhatan Uprising," 346–439, 353–55; Smith, *Works*, II, 293; John Donne, "A Sermon Preach'ed to the Honour-able Company of the Virginian Plantation . . . ," in George R. Potter and Evelyn M. Simpson, eds., *The Sermons of John Donne* (Berkeley, Calif., 1953–62), IV, 271.

6. Rountree, *Pocahontas's People*, 73–74, 303–4; Fausz, "Powhatan Uprising," 366–67, 370ff., 386, 394, 396–97, 399, App. B (an alphabetical list of the victims); Kingsbury, *VC Records*, III, 555, 551, 552, 553, 670. The number of survivors at Martin's Hundred is disputed. Ivor N. Hume (*Martin's Hundred* [New York, 1982], 66) sees the planta-tion's population of about 140 reduced to 62, all of whom fled; later, 20 returned. One of the survivors listed "butt 22 lefte alive" (Kingsbury, *VC Records*, IV, 41). Fausz, "Powhatan Uprising," table VI, 1, lists 42 settlers known by name to have been at Mar-tin's Hundred before the massacre, of whom 22 (52 percent) died before August. On the symbolic importance of Thorpe's death and mutilation, Fausz, "Powhatan Upris-ing," 379–80.

7. Smith, *Works*, II, 295; I, xxxii, 222, xxxvii, 296 (Causey apparently later told his story directly to Smith: III, 215); Kingsbury, *VC Records*, III, 542ff., 551, 553; Fausz, "Powhatan Uprising," 390.

8. Ibid., 403; Kingsbury, ed., *VC Records*, IV, 24, 25, 66, 70–71, 160, 74 (italics in original).

9. Ibid., III, 554, 556–58, 672; Fausz, "Powhatan Uprising," 427–28, 422n, 434, chap. 6, pt. 1 passim.

10. Ibid., table V, 1 (after 400), 448, 450, 457, 458; Kingsbury, *VC Records*, IV, 221–22; Ivor N. Hume, *The Virginia Adventure* (New York, 1994), 382–85.

11. On ship and passenger arrivals, see above, chap. 3, n12; Fausz, "Powhatan Uprising," 464–65. On the *Abigail*: Kingsbury, *VC Records*, IV, 65, 228ff. (Lady Wyatt quotation at 232), and Frethorne letters, ibid., 41–42, 58–62.

12. Butler's "Unmasked face of our colony in Virginia as it was in the winter of ye yeare 1622," in Kingsbury, *VC Records*, II, 374–76. On the document's provenance, see Wesley F. Craven, *Dissolution of the Virginia Company* (New York, 1932), 255n; Kingsbury, *VC Records*, IV, 94.

13. Tyler, ed., *Narratives*, 412–18; Kingsbury, *VC Records*, II, 397–99; IV, 231.

14. Ibid., IV, 41–42, 58–62; Emily Rose, "The Politics of Pathos: Richard Frethorne's Letters Home," in Robert F. Appelbaum and John Wood Sweet, eds., *Envisioning an English Empire: Jamestown and the Making of the North Atlantic World* (Philadelphia, Pa., 2005), 92–108.

15. Craven, *Dissolution*, 176–81. On George Sandys's detestation of tobacco ("I loath it and onelie desire that I could subsist without it"), typical of the views of the company's leadership, and on the king's fervent desire that the planters concentrate on producing wine and silk rather than tobacco, "which, besides much unnecessary expence, brings with it many disorders and inconveniences," see Kingsbury, *VC Records*, IV, 65, 125; III, 662, 663.

16. Irene W. Hecht, "The Virginia Muster of 1624/5 As a Source for Demographic History," *WMQ*, 30 (1973), 70; Fausz, "Powhatan Uprising," 472; William S. Powell, "Aftermath of the Massacre: The First Indian War, 1622–1632," *VMHB*, 66 (1958), 58; Rountree, *Pocahontas's People*, 77–84.

17. Hecht, "Virginia Muster," 78. Fifteen of the twenty-three were located in only two households.

18. Richard B. Davis, *George Sandys, Poet-Adventurer* (London, 1955), 231, chap. 9 passim. On this and the following two paragraphs, see Bailyn, "Politics and Social Structure in Virginia," in James M. Smith, ed., *Seventeenth-Century America* (Chapel Hill, N.C., 1959), 93–96.

19. Robert Brenner, *Merchants and Revolution: Commercial Change, Political Conflict, and London's Overseas Traders* (Princeton, N.J., 1993), 103–12, figures at 105.

20. After receiving his knighthood, Yeardley, it was reported in London, "hath set him[self] up so high that he flaunts it up and down the streets in extraordinary braverie, wiuth fourteen or fifteen fayre liveries after him." William S. Powell, *John Pory, 1572–1636* (Chapel Hill, N.C., 1977), 74. His arrival in Virginia touched off a protest by some of the "ancient planters" of higher status who feared that his lack of eminence

would discourage settlement. "Great actions," they wrote, "are carryed wth best successe by such comanders who have personall aucthoritye & greatness answerable to the action, sithence itt is nott easye to swaye a vulgar and servile nature by vulgar & servile spiritts." Bailyn, "Politics and Social Structure," 94n.

21. Of nearly a million acres patented by 1625, fewer than fifteen thousand were actually under cultivation. Even if the eight hundred thousand acres "alledged" to have been patented by the associates of Martin's Hundred and the hundred thousand acres claimed by Southampton Hundred are both reduced by half, only 2½ percent of the registered land was under cultivation. Kingsbury, *VC Records*, IV, 551–59; J. Frederick Fausz, "Patterns of Settlement in the James River Basin, 1607–1642" (M.A. thesis, College of William and Mary, 1971), 61–63.

22. Ibid., 58–61. Thus, for example, the peregrinations of the French Protestant Nicholas Martiau, who arrived in Virginia in 1620 as an agent of the Earl of Huntington. After the massacre he moved off, first, west far up the James River, and then, in 1630, north to the York River, where he opened a new area to English settlement and where in 1640 he patented thirteen hundred acres for himself and his household. Jester and Hiden, eds., *Adventurers*, 417–18. On the palisade of 1634: Philip Levy, "A New Look at an Old Wall," *VMHB*, 112 (2004), 226–66.

23. On the Susquehannock-Claiborne association and the role of the Susquehannocks in the tangled networks of tribal rivalries in trade and war, see Cynthia J. Van Zandt, *Brothers Among Nations: The Pursuit of Intercultural Alliances in Early America, 1580–1660* (Oxford, England, 2008), 118ff.

24. Nathaniel C. Hale, *Virginia Venturer: A Historical Biography of William Claiborne 1600–1677* (Richmond, Va., 1951), 101–30, chap. 8; Brenner, *Merchants and Revolution*, 121–24.

CHAPTER 6
Terra-Maria

1. R. A. Houston, *The Population History of Britain and Ireland, 1500–1750* (London, 1992), 64; E. A. Wrigley and R. S. Schofield, *The Population History of England, 1541–1871* (Cambridge, Mass., 1981), 224–28.

2. R. J. Dickson, *Ulster Emigration to Colonial America, 1718–1775* (London, 1966), 3; Ruth Dudley Edwards, *An Atlas of Irish History* (2nd ed., London, 1981), 172–73; M. Perceval-Maxwell, *The Scottish Migration to Ulster in the Reign of James I* (London, 1973), 313–14; cf. L. M. Cullen, "Population Trends in Seventeenth-Century Ireland," *Economic and Social Review*, 6 (1975), 153–54.

3. Bernard Bailyn, *Voyagers to the West: A Passage in the Peopling of America on the Eve of the Revolution* (New York, 1987), chap. 1.

4. John Bossy, in Alan G. R. Smith, ed., *The Reign of James VI and I* (New York, 1973), 101–2; and Bossy, *The English Catholic Community, 1570–1850* (Oxford, England, 1976), chap. 8, esp. 188, 193; Wrigley and Schofield, *Population History*, table A3.3, 532.

5. John D. Krugler, *English and Catholic: The Lords Baltimore in the Seventeenth Century* (Baltimore, Md., 2004), chaps. 2, 3; G. P. V. Akrigg, *Jacobean Pageant . . .* (Cam-

bridge, Mass., 1962), 366, 358–59, 170–71; R. J. Lahey, "The Role of Religion in Lord Baltimore's Colonial Enterprise," *MHM*, 72 (1977), 498, quotation at 499n.

6. Theodore K. Rabb, *Enterprise and Empire: Merchant and Gentry Investment in the Expansion of England, 1575–1630* (Cambridge, Mass., 1967), 259; Krugler, *English and Catholic*, chap. 4.

7. Lahey, "Role of Religion," 495–501; Gillian T. Cell, *English Enterprise in New-foundland, 1577–1660* (Toronto, 1969), 92, 93.

8. Gillian T. Cell, ed., *Newfoundland Discovered . . . 1610–1630* (London, 1982), 53; Lahey, "Role of Religion," 505–8.

9. Krugler, *English and Catholic*, chap. 4, quotation at 98; Thomas M. Coakley, "George Calvert and Newfoundland: 'The Sad Face of Winter,'" *MHM*, 71 (1976), 12–15; Cell, *English Enterprise*, 94, 95; Lahey, "Role of Religion," 511. "From the mid-dest of October to the middest of May there is a sadd face of wynter upon all this land, both sea and land so frozen for the greatest part of the tyme as they are not penetrable, not plant or vegetable thing appearing out of the earth untill it be about the beginning of May, nor fish in the sea, besides the ayre so intolerable and cold as it is hardly to be endured." Baltimore to Charles I, Newfoundland, Aug. 19, 1629, quoted in Cell, *English Enterprise*, 95.

10. Krugler, *English and Catholic*, chap. 5, quotation at 106; Lahey, "Role of Religion," 509; Andrews, *Colonial Period*, II, 279; Vera F. Rollo, *The Proprietorship of Maryland* (Lanham, Md., 1989), 37ff.

11. Wesley F. Craven, *The Southern Colonies in the Seventeenth Century, 1607–1689* ([Baton Rouge, La.], 1949), 189–90; Andrews, *Colonial Period*, II, 281–83; Krugler, *English and Catholic*, 125–26.

12. Russell R. Menard, *Economy and Society in Early Colonial Maryland* (New York, 1985), 430–31, 25–30; *A Declaration of the Lord Baltimore's Plantation in Mary-land . . .* (London, 1633; facsimile, ed. Lawrence C. Wroth, Baltimore, Md., 1929), 8; *Woodstock Letters: A Historical Journal of Jesuit Educational and Missionary Activities*, IX (1880), no. 2, 90; no. 3, 168; Krugler, *English and Catholic*, 112–15, 156. On White, his contributions to the Maryland promotional tracts, and the writings about him, see J. A. Leo Lemay, *Men of Letters in Colonial Maryland* (Knoxville, Tenn., 1972), 8–27, 349–54.

13. *A Declaration of the State of the Colonie and Affaires in Virginia . . .* (London, 1620), in Peter Force, comp., *Tracts and Other Papers Relating Principally to . . . the Colonies in North America . . .* (Washington, D.C., 1836–46), III, no. 5, 3.

14. Lawrence C. Wroth, "The Maryland Colonization Tracts," in William W. Bishop and Andrew Keogh, eds., *Essays Offered to Herbert Putnam . . .* (New Haven, Conn., 1929), 539–55; "Objections answered touching Mariland," in Thomas A. Hughes, *History of the Society of Jesus in North America, Colonial and Federal* (London and New York, 1907–10), documentary vol. I, 10–15; text vol. I, 257–59.

15. Craven, *Southern Colonies*, 191; Menard, *Economy and Society*, 22–23.

16. "Instructions 13 Novem: 1633 . . .," in Clayton C. Hall, ed., *Narratives of Early Maryland, 1633–1684* (New York, 1910), 16–23.

17. "A Short Treatise sett downe in a letter written by R. W. to his worthy freind J.C.R. Concerning the new plantation now erecting . . . in Maryland" ([London, Sep-

tember 12, 1635] printed in facsimile and transcription by John D. Krugler, Baltimore, 1976, under the title *To Live Like Princes*), 12, 14–16, 18, 26–31, 33, 34, 37, 38; Thomas Copley to Lord Baltimore, "St. Maries," April 3, 1638, in John W. Lee, ed., *The Calvert Papers* (Maryland Historical Society Fund Publication, no. 28, Baltimore, Md., 1889), 161–62. The inventory of Wintour's estate, Sept. 4, 1638, is in William H. Browne et al., eds., *Archives of Maryland* (Baltimore, Md., 1883–1972) [hereafter *Md. Archives*], IV, 85–89. For Wintour's arrival in Maryland, Jan. 12, 1637, with seven people, including a fifteen-year-old boy, see "Land Notes, 1634–1655," *MHM*, 5 (1910), 167. For an extended discussion of Wintour's "Short Treatise," see John D. Krugler, *English and Catholic*, 135ff.

18. Harry W. Newman, *The Flowering of the Maryland Palatinate* (Washington, D.C., 1961), 155–58; Menard, *Economy and Society*, 30–32; Garry W. Stone, "Manorial Maryland," *MHM*, 82 (1987), 6; James Axtell, "White Legend: The Jesuit Missions in Maryland," *MHM*, 81 (1986), 1. Cornwallis, lamenting his "poore younger brothers fortune," feared that his expenses in establishing himself in Maryland would impoverish him unless some kind of profits were quickly forthcoming. Lee ed., *Calvert Papers*, I, 176.

19. Hall, ed., *Narratives*, 40; Stone, "Manorial Maryland," 6–7; Aubrey C. Land, *Colonial Maryland* (White Plains, N.Y., 1981), 16–21; *Woodstock Letters*, II (1873), no. 1, 3; J. Frederick Fausz, "Present at the 'Creation': The Chesapeake World that Greeted the Maryland Colonists," *MHM*, 100, no. 1 (Spring, 2005), 42.

20. Ibid., 34, 35, 36, 42; Harold S. Bowen, "Henry Fleete," *Northern Neck Historical Magazine*, 40 (1990), 4633–34, 4636; Newman, *Flowering*, 204–9; Henry Fleete, "A Brief Journal of a Voyage . . . ," in Edward D. Neill, *The English Colonization of America During the Seventeenth Century* (London, 1871), 237.

21. Hall, ed., *Narratives*, 41.

22. Menard, *Economy and Society*, 43; Hall, ed., *Narratives*, 42, 44.

23. Henry C. Forman, *Jamestown and St. Mary's* (Baltimore, Md., 1938), 196–99, 206–7; Stone, "Manorial Maryland," 6–9, 11; Lois G. Carr, "'The Metropolis of Maryland' . . . ," *MHM*, 69 (1974), 124–26; Menard, *Economy and Society*, 430–31; Lois G. Carr, Russell R. Menard, and Lorena S. Walsh, *Robert Cole's World: Agriculture and Society in Early Maryland* (Chapel Hill, N.C., 1991), 5, 120ff., 256.

24. Menard, *Economy and Society*, 27–29; Newman, *Flowering*, 188–89, 226–29; Garry W. Stone, "Society, Housing, and Architecture in Early Maryland: John Lewger's St. John's" (Ph.D. diss., University of Pennsylvania, 1982), 155; Lee, ed., *Calvert Papers*, I, 172. Biographical information not otherwise documented is taken from Edward Papenfuse et al., *A Biographical Dictionary of the Maryland Legislature, 1635–1789* (2 vols., Baltimore, Md., 1979, 1985).

25. Newman, *Flowering*, 163. On Lewger: Stone, "Society, Housing, and Architecture," chap. 2, 92; on Brent and Gerard, in addition to Papenfuse et al., *Biographical Dictionary*, see Axtell, "White Legend," 5; and Carr et al., *Cole's World*, 5, 119ff. For the Jesuits' account of the adoption, by Margaret Brent, of the much-loved seven-year-old Indian "princess" "to be washed in the sacred font of baptism; she is beginning to understand the Christian mysteries," see *Woodstock Letters*, XI (1882), no. 1, 13; Nuran Çinlar, "'Come Mistress Margarett Brent': Political Representation, Power, and Authority in Early Maryland," *MHM*, 99 (2004), 405–27; Lois C. Green, "Margaret Brent—A Brief

History," manuscript, Maryland State Archives (available online at www.mdarchives .state.md.us).

26. Baltimore issued some two dozen manors by 1655, only a quarter of which were developed as planned. Donnell M. Owings, "Private Manors: An Edited List," *MHM*, 33 (1938), 311ff. The social profile is drawn from a biographical file of 715 settlers (manuscript in author's possession) compiled from information in *Md. Archives*, vols. I, III, IV (esp. the tax list of August 1642: I, 142–46), and the Provincial Court records [Judicial and Testamentary], 1637–1650 (IV); "Land Notes, 1634–1655," in *MHM*, 5 (1910) and 6 (1911); Papenfuse et al., *Biographical Dictionary;* Newman, *Flowering;* Carr et al., *Cole's World;* and genealogical material scattered through *MHM*. On the distribution of property, see Menard, *Economy and Society*, 60, 61, 65.

27. Carr et al., *Cole's World*, 9; Menard, *Economy and Society*, 60, 41. Formal land titles were deceptive; of thirty-seven thousand acres patented in St. Mary's County by 1642, only 5 percent (1,920 acres) were actually improved.

28. Stone, "Manorial Maryland," 11; Henry M. Miller, "Archaeology and Town Planning in Early British America," in Geoff Egan, ed., *Old and New Worlds: Historical Post-Medieval Archaeology* (Oxford, England, 1999), 75–83; table 9.1.

29. Stone, Society, Housing, and Architecture, 191; Lee, ed., *Calvert Papers*, I, 174; and Henry C. Forman, *Maryland Architecture: A Short History from 1634 through the Civil War* (Cambridge, Md., 1968), 1, 8; Jason D. Moser et al., "Impermanent Architecture in a Less Permanent Town," *Perspectives in Vernacular Architecture*, 9 (2003), 197–214; Julia A. King, "A Comparative Midden Analysis of a Household and Inn in St. Mary's City, Maryland," *Historical Archaeology*, 22 (1988), 17–20; *Md. Archives*, IV, 110.

30. James Horn, *Adapting to a New World: English Society in the Seventeenth-Century Chesapeake* (Chapel Hill, N.C., 1994), 302–4.

31. Thomas Cornwallis to Lord Baltimore, "St. Maries," April 16, 1638, in Lee, ed., *Calvert Papers*, I, 174, 176; Vertrees J. Wyckoff, *Tobacco Regulation in Colonial Maryland* (Baltimore, 1936), 49. The following paragraphs on credit and debt, property transactions, and boundaries are drawn from the biographical file, esp. the Provincial Court and land records, cited above, n26.

32. Carr et al., *Cole's World*, 128.

33. John Bartholomew, ed., *Gazetteer of the British Isles* (Edinburgh, 1887), 373.

34. Erich Isaac, "Kent Island, Part I: The Period of Settlement," *MHM*, 52 (1957), 104; Stone, "Society, Housing, and Architecture," 163.

35. "Land Notes," *MHM*, 5 (1910), 167; Kenneth B. Murdock, *The Sun at Noon: Three Biographical Sketches* (New York, 1939), chap. 2, quotation at 6. Lady Falkland's shipping servants to Maryland was no doubt part of a broad pattern of benevolence, recounted by one of her daughters in a memoir, *The Lady Falkland: Her Life* (London, 1861), 19. The devout viscountess, her daughter reported, brought over from Ireland to England more than eight score "beggar children (with which that country swarms)" and distributed them to masters and mistresses who would teach them whatever trades they were capable of learning.

36. Russell R. Menard, "British Migration to the Chesapeake Colonies in the Seventeenth Century," in Lois G. Carr et al., eds., *Colonial Chesapeake Society* (Chapel Hill,

N.C., 1988), 122; Menard, "Maryland's 'Time of Troubles': Sources of Political Disorder in Early St. Mary's," *MHM*, 76 (1981), 135; Menard, *Economy and Society*, 56; Stone, "Society, Housing, and Architecture," 179. For Snow's "outhouse necessary for servants lodging," see *Md. Archives*, IV, 110. On the scarcity of black servants/slaves in the early years, see Menard, *Economy and Society*, 68; cf. chap. 7.

37. Lois G. Carr, "From Servant to Freeholder: Daniel Clocker's Adventure," *MHM*, 99 (2004), 287–311; Papenfuse et al., *Biographical Dictionary*, I, 319, 98; Newman, *Flowering*, 200–3; "Land Notes," *MHM*, 5 (1910), 167; Menard, *Economy and Society*, 67, 72, 58; Menard, "From Servant to Freeholder . . . ," *WMQ*, 30 (1973), 47–48, and that essay in general for the remarkable rise of the original indentured servants.

38. David Peterson de Vries, quoted in April Hatfield, *Atlantic Virginia* (Philadelphia, 2004), 65; *Md. Archives*, IV, 83, 74, 121, 98, 143, 201, 47, 244, 208, 306, 195. For Canedy's remarkable contract with Gerrard, see ibid., 214. Three and a half months later Canedy ran off to Virginia, where Gerrard sold his remaining time for "a valuable consideracion." There apparently he flourished. Nine years later he contracted with Cornwallis to supply sixty thousand bricks for a house he was building on the Potomac. Forman, *Jamestown and St. Mary's*, 255.

39. Thus Lewger to Baltimore, Jan. 5, 1639: "negros I heare of none come in this yeare." Lee, ed., *Calvert Papers*, I, 199.

40. *Woodstock Letters*, IX, no. 2, 90.

41. Menard, "Maryland's 'Time of Troubles' . . . ," 127.

42. Axtell, "White Legend," 5; *Woodstock Letters*, IX, no. 2, 74–89; Edwin W. Beitzell, "'Thomas Copley, Gentleman,'" *MHM*, 47 (1952), 209–23; Hughes, *Society of Jesus*, text vol. I, 423, 472–75. Rigbie's letter of application to join the Maryland mission is especially fervent. He conceived of the mission not only as "happy and glorious" but "withal hard and humble in regard of the raw state things as yet are in; yet the love of Jesus neither fears labor nor low employments." He had, he wrote the Provincial of England, "a great desire of this voyage . . . very much strengthened, this time of holy exercises, both in prayer, Holy Mass, and other occasions which I have taken to deliberate of this point." *Woodstock Letters*, IX, no. 2, 78. Rigbie, "who had great influence among the Indians" in part because of his linguistic skills, "died of hardship," the Jesuits reported, in exile in Virginia in 1646. *Woodstock Letters*, XV (1886), no. 1, 90.

43. Hughes, *Society of Jesus*, text vol. I, 336.

44. *Woodstock Letters*, XI, no. 1, 5, 7–12.

45. Ibid., 12–13; X (1881), no. 3, 220; XI, no. 1, 1, and no. 2, 119; Hughes, *Society of Jesus*, text vol. I, 480–82; Axtell, "White Legend," 4.

46. *Woodstock Letters*, XI, no. 2, 119–20.

47. Debra R. Boender, "Our Fires Have Nearly Gone Out: A History of Indian-White Relations on the Colonial Maryland Frontier, 1633–1776" (Ph.D. diss., University of New Mexico, 1988), 61; Bishop Benedict J. Fenwick's "Brief Account," in *Woodstock Letters*, IX, no. 3, 171. Cf. Menard, *Economy and Society*, 66.

48. Krugler, *English and Catholic*, 166–78, quotation at 167; *Woodstock Letters*, XI, no. 2, 122, 123–27; Hughes, *Society of Jesus*, text vol. I, 482, 556–59; Andrews, *Colonial Period*, II, 313.

49. *Md. Archives*, III, 191.

50. Boender, "Indian-White Relations," 68, 105; Hall, ed., *Narratives*, 75; James H. Merrell, "Cultural Continuity Among the Piscataway Indians of Colonial Maryland," *WMQ*, 36 (1979), 560–61.

51. Merrell, "Cultural Continuity," 550–54; J. Frederick Fausz, "Merging and Emerging Worlds: Anglo-Indian Interest Groups and the Development of the Seventeenth-Century Chesapeake," in Carr et al., eds., *Colonial Chesapeake Society*, 47–48, 57; Fausz, "Profits, Pelts, and Power . . . 1620–1652," *Maryland Historian*, 14 (1983), 18; cf. Fausz, "Present at the 'Creation,'" 29–43.

52. Boender, "Indian-White Relations," 137–44, 163, 170–72, 181, 187–88; "Land Notes," *MHM*, 6 (1911), 61; Gene Williamson, *Chesapeake Conflict* (Bowie, Md., 1955), 27, 110.

53. Of the many writings on Claiborne (including Nathaniel C. Hale's romantic *Virginia Venturer . . . William Claiborne, 1600–1677* [Richmond, Va., 1951]), see especially, in this connection, Fausz, "Merging Worlds," 58ff.; Isaac, "Kent Island," 104, 106–19; Fausz, "Profits, Pelts, and Power," 19, 20; and Robert Brewer, *Merchants and Devotion: Commercial Change, Political Conflict, and London's Overseas Traders, 1550–1653* (Princeton, N.J., 1993), 120–24. At the end of his life, still hoping to reclaim his property in Maryland, Claiborne submitted a comprehensive documentary account of his entire struggle with the Calverts and of the grounds for all his claims: *Md. Archives*, V, 157 ff. On the Susquehannocks, see John Smith's vivid description in Smith, *Works*, II, 106: people attired in "Cassacks made of Beares heads and skinnes," with wolves' heads "hanging in a chain for a jewell," and who carried tobacco pipes three-quarters of a yard long with carved ends "sufficient to beat out ones braines."

54. *Md. Archives*, IV, 22; I, 23–24; III, 64–73; V, 187, 191, 219; Raphael Semmes, *Captains and Mariners of Early Maryland* (Baltimore, Md., 1937), 152–54, 156; Boender, "Indian-White Relations," 135; Hale, *Venturers*, 196–97, 200–5; Fausz, "Profits, Pelts, and Power," 21; Fausz, "Merging Worlds," 72–73, 75–76; Hall, ed., *Narratives*, 58, 61.

55. Boender, "Indian-White Relations," 95–96, 135–36, 147ff., 169–71, 190–95; Fausz, "Merging Worlds," 76, 77; Alice L. L. Ferguson and Henry G. Ferguson, *The Piscataway Indians of Southern Maryland* (Accokeek, Md., 1960), 32–34; Peter Lindeström, *Geographia Americae, with An Account of the Delaware Indians . . . 1654–1656* (Amandus Johnson, trans. and ed., Philadelphia, 1925), 242–44.

56. Boender, Indian-White Relations, 145–50, 190–92; Fausz, "Merging Worlds," 78.

57. Timothy B. Riordan, *The Plundering Time: Maryland and the English Civil War, 1645–1646* (Baltimore, Md., 2004), 32, 95–97, 131, 139, 141, 163; *Md. Archives*, III, 165.

58. Riordan, *Plundering Time*, 174, 175, 189, 211, 220ff. Further biographical details in Papenfuse et al., *Biographical Dictionary*.

59. Riordan, *Plundering Time*, 210–11, 293–95, 193–95, 206, 221. For a full accounting of the contents of Cornwallis's plundered Cross House and their value, see Appendix, 331–34.

60. Ibid., 205, 215, 217, 210, 221, 236, 238, 253, 201, 268, 306, 185; Fausz; "Merging Worlds," 80.

61. Krugler, *English and Catholic*, 164–65, 185–88, 214–23; Andrews, *Colonial Period*, II,

310–12. The text of the act is in *Md. Archives*, I, 244–47. In practice Baltimore's toleration would ultimately extend not only to Quakers—pacifists who refused to take oaths—but also to a Jew accused of blasphemy for his views on Christ and the resurrection.

62. Krugler, *English and Catholic*; 183–84; Al Luchenbach, *Providence 1649* (Maryland State Archives, 1995); Babette M. Levy, *Early Puritanism in the Southern and Island Colonies* (*Proceedings of the American Antiquarian Society*, 70, pt. 1, 1960), 130–31; Andrews, *Colonial Period*, II, 312, 314–17.

63. Fausz, "Merging Worlds," 82–83; Andrews, *Colonial Period*, II, 318–21; Hall, ed., *Narratives*, 238–44, 250, 264, 266. On Calvert's struggle to control Lewis's passionate Catholicism: Krugler, *English and Catholic*, 104–5. For a detailed account of Baltimore's adroit maneuvering in England in defense of his charter, which involved questions of the status of Parliamentary laws overseas, see ibid., chap. 8.

64. Carr et al., *Cole's World*, 122, 130–31.

CHAPTER 7

The Chesapeake's New World

1. Lorena S. Walsh, *Motives of Honor, Pleasure, and Profit* (Chapel Hill, N.C., 2010), 131; James Horn, *Adapting to a New World: English Society in the Seventeenth-Century Chesapeake* (Chapel Hill, N.C., 1994), 137, 25–31 [hereafter: *New World*]; James Horn, "'To Parts Beyond the Seas': Free Immigration to the Chesapeake in the Seventeenth-Century," in Ida Altman and James Horn, eds., *"To Make America": European Emigration in the Early Modern Period* (Berkeley and Los Angeles, 1991), chap. 4, table 4.1.

2. Lois G. Carr, Russell R. Menard, and Lorena S. Walsh, *Robert Cole's World* (Chapel Hill, N.C., 1991), chap. 2; Walsh, *Motives*, 128–30.

3. Karen O. Kupperman, *Settling With the Indians . . . 1580–1640* (Totowa, N.J., 1980), 188.

4. Darrett B. Rutman and Anita H. Rutman, *A Place In Time: Middlesex County, Virginia, 1650–1750* (New York, 1984), 40–41; Walsh, *Motives*, 91ff., 155–61.

5. Ann Kussmaul, *Servants in Husbandry in Early Modern England* (Cambridge, England, 1981), 62–63; Russell R. Menard, "British Migration to the Chesapeake Colonies in the Seventeenth-Century," in Lois G. Carr, Philip D. Morgan, and Jean B. Russo, eds., *Colonial Chesapeake Society* (Chapel Hill, N.C., 1988), 114 [hereafter: Menard, "British Migration"].

6. E. A. Wrigley and R. S. Schofield, *The Population History of England, 1541–1871* (Cambridge, Mass., 1981), 528, table A3.1; Horn, *New World*, 63, 137; Menard, "British Migration," 102–3, 116, 125, 131; Rutman, *Middlesex County*, 71.

7. David Souden, "'Rogues, Whores and Vagabonds'? Indentured Servant Emigrants to North America, and the Case of Mid-Seventeenth-Century Bristol," *Social History*, 3 (1978), 29–34, tables 3, 4; Menard, "British Migration," 123, 127; Horn, *New World*, 90, 185–87.

8. Horn, *New World*, 74, 62, 64; Abbot E. Smith, *Colonists in Bondage: White Servitude and Convict Labor in America, 1607–1776* (Chapel Hill, N. C., 1947), 69, 71–73, chap. 4;

Peter W. Coldham, "The 'Spiriting' of London Children to Virginia, 1648–1685," *VMHB*, 83 (1975), 282–83.

9. Smith, *Colonists in Bondage*, 152–57, chap. 5; Butler, "British Convicts Shipped to American Colonies," *American Historical Review*, 2 (1896), 16–17; *CSPC*, 360; Alexander Moray, "Letters Written by Mr. Moray, a Minister . . . February 1, 1665," *WMQ*, 2nd ser., 2 (July 1922), 160.

10. James Horn, "Servant Emigration to the Chesapeake in the Seventeenth-Century," in Thad W. Tate and David L. Ammerman, eds., *The Chesapeake in the Seventeenth Century* (Chapel Hill, N.C., 1979), 53–54; David W. Galenson, *White Servitude in Colonial America: An Economic Analysis* (Cambridge, England, 1981), 16–17, App. A.

11. Menard, "British Migration," 128–29; Gloria L. Main, *Tobacco Colony: Life in Early Maryland, 1650–1720* (Princeton, N.J., 1982), 14; Horn, *New World*, 38; Hilary McD. Beckles, "A 'Riotous and Unruly Lot': Irish Indentured Servants and Freemen in the English West Indies, 1644–1713," *WMQ*, 47 (1990), 505–20.

12. Horn, *New World*, 272.

13. Ibid., 138; Russell B. Menard, "The Growth of Population in the Chesapeake Colonies: A Comment," *Explorations in Economic History*, 18 (1981), 402, 399; Rutman, *Middlesex County*, 130; Lorena S. Walsh and Russell B. Menard, "Death in the Chesapeake: Two Life Tables for Men in Early Colonial Maryland," *MHM*, 69 (1974), 222; Menard, "Population, Economy, and Society in Seventeenth-Century Maryland," *MHM*, 79 (1984), 71–73 [hereafter: Menard, "Population"]; Main, *Tobacco Colony*, 14–15.

14. Darrett B. Rutman and Anita H. Rutman, " 'Now Wives and Sons-in-Law': Parental Death in a Seventeenth-Century Virginia County," in Tate and Ammerman, eds., *Chesapeake*, 153, 158, 162, 167, 168; Menard, "Population," 72; Lorena S. Walsh, " 'Till Death Us Do Part': Marriage and Family in Seventeenth-Century Maryland," in Tate and Ammerman, eds., *Chesapeake*, 132, 143; Horn, *New World*, 245, 247; Lois G. Carr, Russell B. Menard, and Lorena S. Walsh, *Robert Cole's World: Agriculture and Society in Early Maryland* (Chapel Hill, N.C., 1991), 124, 138–39, 159 [hereafter: *Cole's World*].

15. Ibid., 91, 93, 102–3, 105, 107, 108, 311; Horn, *New World*, 293–95, 302, 303, 333, 306–307; Main, *Tobacco Colony*, 141 (and chap. 4 generally), 217–19, 222; Menard, "Population," 83; "Answer of the Lord Baltimore to the Querys About Maryland," Mar. 26, 1678, in *Md. Archives*, V, 266; extended quotation from Barbara and Cary Carson, unpublished paper, in Horn, *New World*, 314–15; Louis B. Wright, *The First Gentlemen of Virginia* (San Marino, Calif., 1940), 191.

16. Carr et al., *Cole's World*, 108–11; Horn, *New World*, 271–72, 275–76; Menard, "Population," 72.

17. Russell Menard, "From Servants to Slaves: The Transformation of the Chesapeake Labor System," *Southern Studies* 16 (1977), 355–90; Horn, *New World*, 151, 154–57.

18. For precise, detailed accounts of the pressures behind the transition to slavery in specific localities, see Rutman, *Middlesex County*, 72ff.; Paul G. E. Clemens, "The Settlement and Growth of Maryland's Eastern Shore During the English Restoration," *Maryland Historian*, 5 (1974), 69ff.

19. Engel Sluiter, "New Light on the '20 and Odd Negroes' . . . ," *WMQ*, 54 (1997), 395–98; John W. Lee, ed., *The Calvert Papers*, I (*Maryland Historical Society Fund Publica-*

tion, no. 28, Baltimore, 1889), 149, 249; *Md. Archives*, IV, 189, 304; John J. McCusker and Russell R. Menard, *The Economy of British America, 1607–1789* (Chapel Hill, N.C., 1985), 136; Winthrop D. Jordan, *White Over Black* (Chapel Hill, N.C., 1968), 74; Whittington B. Johnson, "The Origin and Nature of African Slavery in Seventeenth Century Maryland," *MHM*, 73 (1978), 239–40; J. Douglas Deal, *Race and Class in Colonial Virginia* ... (New York, 1993), 167, 177; Menard, "Population," 86; Ira Berlin, *Many Thousands Gone* (Cambridge, Mass., 1998), 17–46.

20. Deal, *Race and Class*, 177; Edmund S. Morgan, "Slavery and Freedom: the American Paradox," *Journal of American History*, 59 (1972), 17–18; Morgan, *American Slavery, American Freedom* (New York, 1975), 154–57; Johnson, "Origin and Nature," 217–50. For a full exploration of the lives of the black achievers on the Eastern Shore, see T. H. Breen and Stephen Innes, *"Myne Owne Ground": Race and Freedom on Virginia's Eastern Shore, 1640–1676* (New York, 1980); for a broad interpretation, in the general context of the history of American slavery, see Berlin, *Many Thousands Gone*.

21. Ibid., 38; biographical details in Deal, *Race and Class*, pt. 2; Jordan, *White Over Black*, chap. 1; Alden T. Vaughan and Virginia M. Vaughan, "Before *Othello*: Elizabethan Representations of Sub-Saharan Africans," *WMQ*, 54 (1997), 18–44 (quotations at 44). Cf. James H. Sweet, "The Iberian Roots of American Racist Thought," ibid., 143–66.

22. On the ambiguities in the use of the word *slave*: Robert McColley, "Slavery in Virginia: 1619–1660: A Reexamination," in Robert H. Abzug and Stephen E. Maizlish, eds., *New Perspectives on Race and Slavery in America* (Lexington, Ky., 1986), 12–15; Helen T. Catterall and James J. Hayden, eds., *Judicial Cases Concerning American Slavery and the Negro* (Washington, D.C., 1926–37), IV, 2 n7 (the petition of the father of an indentured servant girl, "crav[ing] that his daughter may not be made a slave, a terme soe scandalous that if admitted to be the condicion or tytle the apprentices in this province will be so distructive as noe free borne Christians will ever be induced to come over [as] servants").

23. Jordan, *White Over Black*, 81 ("Certainly it was the case in Maryland and Virginia that the legal enactment of Negro slavery followed social practice, rather than vice versa ... slavery was less a matter of previous conception or external example in Maryland and Virginia than elsewhere"); April L. Hatfield, *Atlantic Virginia* (Philadelphia, 2004), 154–55.

24. Deal, *Race and Class*, 176, 254; Jordan, *White Over Black*, 81–82.

25. William D. Phillips, Jr., "The Old World Background of Slavery in the Americas," in Barbara L. Solow, ed., *Slavery and the Rise of the Atlantic System* (Cambridge, England, 1991), chap. 2; for an excellent short summary of the global background of North American slavery, see Philip D. Morgan, "Origins of American Slavery," in Organization of American Historians, *Magazine of History*, July 2005, 51–56, with references to the master works on the history of slavery by David B. Davis. Cf. Robin Blackburn, *The Making of New World Slavery* ... *1492–1800* (London, 1997), chaps. 1–5.

26. For a detailed discussion of the law of 1664, see Jonathan L. Alpert, "The Origins of Slavery in the United States—the Maryland Precedent," *American Journal of Legal History*, 14 (1970), 197–98; Johnson, "Origin and Nature," 238–39. The text of the law of 1664 is in *Md. Archives*, I, 183–84.

27. William W. Hening, *Statutes at Large ... Laws of Virginia* ... (Richmond, Va., 1809–1823), III, 87–88, II, 260; Deal, *Race and Class*, 180, 258; Jordan, *White Over Black*,

78–79; William W. Wiecek, "The Statutory Law of Slavery and Race . . . ," *WMQ*, 34 (1977), 264. The logic of Virginia's relief of felony charges against masters, the result of whose "correction" of a slave was such that the slave "should chance to die," rested on the presumption that "it cannot be presumed that prepensed malice (which alone makes murther [a] felony should induce any man to destroy his owne estate." Hening, *Statutes*, II, 270. On the repeal of the Act of 1664, see Catterall and Hayden, *Judicial Cases*, 2, 49.

28. Bailyn, "Politics and Social Structure," 98; Menard, "Population," 83–85; Peter W. Coldham, *The Complete Book of Emigrants, 1607–1660* (Baltimore, Md., 1987), 173, 190, 191, 193, 211, 217, 233; Annie L. Jester and Martha W. Hiden, comps. and eds., *Adventurers of Purse and Person: Virginia, 1607–1624/5* (3rd ed., revised by Virginia M. Meyer and John F. Dorman, Richmond, Va., 1987), 442–45, 607, 581; Main, *Tobacco Colony*, 225–39; William A. Reavis, "The Maryland Gentry and Social Mobility, 1637–1676," *WMQ*, 14 (1957), 425–26.

29. Warren M. Billings, *Sir William Berkeley and the Forging of Colonial Virginia* (Baton Rouge, La., 2004), chaps. 1–3, quotation at 256; Billings, "Sir William Berkeley—Portrait by Fischer: A Critique" and Fischer's "Rejoinder," *WMQ*, 48 (1991), 598–611.

30. Edward [Hyde], Earl of Clarendon, *The History of the Rebellion and Civil War in England . . .* , ed. W. Dunn Macray ([1702–4]; Oxford, U.K., 1888), V, 263; Anon., "Ingrams Proceedings," in *A Narrative of the Indian and Civil Wars in Virginia in the Years 1675 and 1676* (Boston, 1814), in Peter Force, comp., *Tracts and Other Papers . . .* (Washington, D.C., 1836–46), I, no. 11, 34.

31. James Horn, "Cavalier Culture? The Social Development of Colonial Virginia," *WMQ*, 48 (1991), 238–45.

32. Basil Morgan, "Sir Thomas Lunsford," in *Oxford Dictionary of National Biography*; P. R. Newman, ed., *Royalist Officers in England and Wales, 1642–1660: A Biographical Dictionary* (New York, 1981), 242; Rutman, *Middlesex County*, 211.

33. Newman, *Royalist Officers*, 69; *CSPC*, 337; Rutman, *Middlesex County*, 46; Billings, *Berkeley*, 216; Culpeper to William Blathwayt, Mar. 20, 1682–3, quoted in Morgan, *American Slavery, American Freedom*, 253.

34. P. H. Hardacre, "The Further Adventures of Henry Norwood," *VMHB*, 67 (1959), 271–72; Stephen S. Webb, "Henry Norwood," in *American National Biography Online*; Colonel [Henry] Norwood, *A Voyage to Virginia*, in Force, *Tracts*, III, x, 3–4, 49; Newman, *Officers*, 195, xvi; Webb, *The Governors-General . . . 1569–1681* (Chapel Hill, N.C., 1979), 15.

35. Horn, *New World*, 58. For a romantic exaggeration of the royalists' numbers and influence, which shaped popular views, see Philip A. Bruce, *Social Life of Virginia in the Seventeenth Century* (Richmond, Va., 1907), 76ff. Cf. David H. Fischer, *Albion's Seed: Four British Folkways in America* (New York, 1989), 207ff.; Horn's critique, note 31 above, and Fischer's reply, *WMQ*, 48 (1991), 277–89.

36. [Sir William Berkeley,] *A Discourse and View of Virginia* [London, 1663], 3, 9; Billings, *Berkeley*, 143–46.

37. Bailyn, "Politics and Social Structure," 98–99; Douglas S. Freeman, *George Washington* (New York, 1948–54), I, 15–16.

38. Christopher Johnston, "Neale Family of Charles County," *MHM*, 7 (1912), 202;

Edward C. Papenfuse et al., comps., *A Biographical Dictionary of the Maryland Legislature, 1635–1789* [hereafter: *Biographical Dictionary*] (Baltimore, Md., 1979–85), II, 609; Thomas J. Peterson, *Catholics in Colonial Delmarva* (Devon, Pa., 1996), 18; Beatriz B. Hardy, "A Papist in a Protestant Age: The Case of Richard Bennett, 1667–1749," *Journal of Southern Studies*, 60 (1994), 206.

39. Papenfuse et al., *Biographical Dictionary*, II, 724; I, 187.

40. Ibid., I, 250–51; II, 830; L. G. Shreve, *Tench Tilghman: The Life and Times of Washington's Aide-de-Camp* (Centreville, Md., 1982), 10, 12, 13.

41. Bailyn, "Politics and Social Structure," 99; Papenfuse et al., *Biographical Dictionary*, II, 609.

42. Bailyn, "Politics and Social Structure," 107; Main, *Tobacco Colony*, 225, 233.

43. Warren M. Billings, "Imagining Green Spring House," *Virginia Cavalcade*, 44 (1994), 85–95; Billings, *Berkeley*, 60–62; Horn, *New World*, 307.

CHAPTER 8
The Dutch Farrago

1. Jan Lucassen, "The Netherlands, the Dutch, and Long-Distance Migration in the Late Sixteenth to Early Nineteenth Centuries," in Nicholas Canny, ed., *Europeans on the Move: Studies on European Migration, 1500–1800* (Oxford, England, 1994), 156, 159–60; Oliver A. Rink, *Holland on the Hudson: An Economic and Social History of Dutch New York* (Ithaca, N.Y., 1986), 155–56.

2. Lucassen, "Long-Distance Migration," 160, 166, 167.

3. Rink, *Holland on the Hudson*, 29, 32–35, 47.

4. Ibid., 62–63; C. R. Boxer, *The Dutch Seaborne Empire, 1600–1800* (Harmondsworth, England, 1965), 24–25.

5. Ibid., 48–50; Henk den Heijer, "The Dutch West India Company, 1621–1791," in Johannes Postma and Victor Enthoven, eds., *Riches from Atlantic Commerce . . . 1585–1817* (Leiden, 2003), chap. 4, esp. 85; *Docs. Rel.*, I, 66; Pieter Geyl, *The Netherlands Divided (1609–1648)* (S.T. Bindoff, trans., London, 1936), 191–96; Johannes M. Postma, *The Dutch in the Atlantic Slave Trade, 1600–1815* (Cambridge, England, 1990), 19.

6. Ibid., 29; Charles Wilson, *Profit and Power; A Study of England and the Dutch Wars* (London, [1957]), 45, 115.

7. Rink, *Holland on the Hudson*, 73, 76–79. For a full discussion of the reluctance of the Dutch and especially the Dutch West India Company to engage in territorial conquest and their concentration on commerce and the empire of trade, see Donna Merwick, *The Shame and the Sorrow: Dutch-Amerindian Encounters in New Netherland* (Philadelphia, 2006), 87–88, 107, 117, 194, 204.

8. Ibid., 79–80; Emily J. de Forest, *A Walloon Family in America* (Boston, 1914), I, 17–20; II, 422, 424; Johanna W. Tammel, comp., *Pilgrims and Other People from the British Isles in Leiden, 1576–1640* (Isle of Man, 1989), passim; Charles W. Baird, *History of the Huguenot Emigration to America* ([1885] Baltimore, Md., 1966), I, 160–61, 351–53.

9. De Forest, *Walloon Family*, I, 21, 38ff., 45, 50; Cornelis C. Goslinga, *The Dutch in the Caribbean and on the Wild Coast* (Gainesville, Fla., 1971), 75ff.

10. J. Franklin Jameson, ed., *Narratives of New Netherland 1609–1664* (New York, 1909), 75, 47; Rink, *Holland on the Hudson*, 79–80; Van Cleaf Bachman, *Peltries or Plantations: The Economic Policies of the Dutch West India Company in New Netherland, 1623–1639* (Baltimore, Md., 1969), 81–83.

11. Ibid., 85n35; Rink, *Holland on the Hudson*, 143; Thomas J. Condon, *New York Beginnings: The Commercial Origins of New Netherland* (New York, 1968), 101, 102, 106, 78; Richard Pares, *Merchants and Planters (Economic History Review Supplements*, 4, Cambridge, England, 1960), 15–16.

12. Condon, *New York Beginnings*, 105, 86; Bachman, *Peltries*, 84–85, 87, 93; Jameson, *Narratives*, 79, 83, 85, 89–90; Rink, *Holland on the Hudson*, 81ff., 85n34.

13. Ibid., 89–91, 94–109; Boxer, *Dutch Empire*, chap. 7; Bachman, *Peltries*, 5–108. The text of "Freedoms and Exemptions" is in A. J. F. van Laer, trans. and ed., *Van Rensselaer Bowier Manuscripts* (Albany, N.Y., 1908) [hereafter *RB MSS*], 137–53. For Van Rensselaer's complicated claims to feudal rights, ibid., 530–31 and his "Memorial" of 1633, 235ff. For the term *patroon*: S. G. Nissenson, *The Patroon's Domain* (New York, 1937), 26–27.

14. Rink, *Holland on the Hudson*, 107ff.; Bachman, *Peltries*, 161–67.

15. Charles M. Parr, *The Voyages of David de Vries* (New York, 1969), 109, 111–13; Rink, *Holland on the Hudson*, 113.

16. Ellis L. Raesly, *Portrait of New Netherland* (New York, 1945), 22–25; Albert C. Myers, ed., *Narratives of Early Pennsylvania, West New Jersey, and Delaware, 1630–1707* (New York, 1912), 15–17; Parr, *De Vries*, 119–22. C. A. Weslager, *The Siconese Indians of Lewes, Delaware* (Lewes, Del., 1991), 16–19, casts doubt on the accuracy of De Vries's account of the Swanendael massacre.

17. Parr, *De Vries*, 124, 130, 151, 154, 156, 159; *RB MSS*, 335; David P. de Vries, "Voyages from Holland to America, A.D. 1632 to 1644," *Collections of the New-York Historical Society*, 2nd ser., III, pt. I (1857), 78, 129.

18. *RB MSS*, 428–29, 615, 805–46 ("Settlers of Rensselaerswyck"); Rink, *Holland on the Hudson*, 146–50, 154–55; Ernst van den Boogaart, "The Servant Migration to New Netherland, 1624–1664," in Pieter C. Emmer, ed., *Colonialism and Migration: Indentured Labour Before and After Slavery* (Dordrecht, 1986), 73n23; Condon, *New York Beginnings*, 141.

19. Jameson, *Narratives*, 262; Rink, *Holland on the Hudson*, 156, 143, 118, 128–30; Joyce D. Goodfriend, "Burghers and Blacks: The Evolution of a Slave Society at New Amsterdam," *New York History*, 59 (1978), 128, 130; Edmund B. O'Callaghan, *History of New Netherland . . .* (New York, 1846–48), I, 384–85; Edmund B. O'Callaghan, ed., *Voyages of the Slavers . . . Illustrative of the Slave Trade Under the Dutch* (Albany, N.Y., 1867), vi, xii–xiv. Cf. Robert J. Swan, "First Africans into New Netherland, 1625 or 1626?" *de Halve Maen*, 66, no. 4 (1993), 75–82.

20. George O. Zabriskie and Alice P. Kenney, "The Founding of New Amsterdam: Fact and Fiction. Part IV. The Disgrace of Willem Van Hulst," *De Halve Maen*, 51, no. 3 (1976), 11–13; "Instructions for Willem Van Hulst," in A. J. F. van Laer, ed. and trans., *Documents Relating to New Netherland, 1624–1626* (San Marino, Calif., 1924),

36–79, esp. 39, and his "Further Instructions," 82–129; "Special Instructions for Cryn Fredericksz," ibid., 132–68.

21. Rink, *Holland on the Hudson*, 84–85, 88, 91; Van Laer, ed., *Documents Relating to New Netherland*, 187–88; Zabriskie and Kenney, "Verhulst," 13; Jameson, ed., *Narratives*, 84–85; James H. Williams, "Peter Minuit," *American National Biography Online* (Feb. 2000).

22. Jameson, ed., *Narratives*, 88, 89, 104; Rink, *Holland on the Hudson*, 87, 127–28, 83; A. Eekhof, ed., *Jonas Michaëlius* (Leiden, 1926), 110 (Wim Klooster suggests that "hovels and cabins" seems a more reasonable translation of *hutten ende coten* than Eekhof's "hovels and cots"); *Docs. Rel.*, I, 368.

23. Versteeg, *Manhattan*, 185; Van Laer, ed., *Documents Relating to New Netherland*, 176, 192, 195, 196, 199, 236, 200, 212, 235, and on Van Krieckenbeeck, 264; Jameson, ed., *Narratives*, 84–85, 105–6.

24. *RB MSS*, 169–70.

25. Eekhof, *Michaëlius*, chap. 7, 130–37, 68–70, 75; Rink, *Holland on the Hudson*, 128; Jacobs, *New Netherland*, 276, 277.

26. Jacobs, *New Netherland*, 277; E. B. O'Callaghan, *New Netherland*, I, 167; *RB MSS*, 267, 272, 271. Cf. Jaap Jacobs, "A Troubled Man: Director Van Twiller and the Affairs of New Netherland in 1635," *New York History*, 85 (2004), 213–32.

27. Jacobs, *New Netherland*, 277, 279; *NYHM: Dutch*, IV, 291–98; J. H. Innes, *New Amsterdam and Its People* (New York, 1902), 25.

28. Raesly, *New Netherland*, 62, 65, 74–75; Rink, *Holland on the Hudson*, 132, 133; *Docs. Rel.*, I, 153. Raesly describes Kieft, for all his brutality, as "a man of intelligence and culture," noting some (lost) literary work "with water-color illustrations" and his suggestion to Roger Williams, on the basis of apparent linguistic similarities, that the Indians were derived from Icelandic peoples. O'Callaghan, *New Netherland*, I, 394. For details on Doughty's affairs, ibid., App. Ff.

29. Rink, *Holland on the Hudson*, 135; *Docs. Rel.*, I, 110ff. (cf. 106–7), 495–502; O'Callaghan, *New Netherland*, I, 220–22.

30. Merwick, *Shame and Sorrow*, 115; Boogaart, "Servant Migration," 61, 77; Jameson, ed., *Narratives*, 259–60; O'Callaghan, *New Netherland*, I, 220, 433–41, 223–24, 238–39; Condon, *Beginnings*, 152–54; Allen W. Trelease, *Indian Affairs in Colonial New York: The Seventeenth Century* (Ithaca, N.Y., 1960), 61, 63; *Docs. Rel.*, I, 181ff. (quotation at 182); Rink, *Holland on the Hudson*, 215, 218.

31. Frederick W. Bogert, "Long Island Settlements Prior to 1664, Part III," *De Halve Maen*, 39, no. 1 (1964), 11; Trelease, *Indian Affairs*, 65; Rink, *Holland on the Hudson*, 217; E. B. O'Callaghan, trans. and ed., *Laws and Ordinances of New Netherland, 1638– 1674* (Albany, N.Y., 1868), 28–29; *Docs. Rel.*, I, 150–51. For a dramatic account, in nine "scenes," of this early phase of Kieft's War, see Merwick, *Shame and Sorrow*, chap. 10. For a different account of the events of Kieft's War than what follows, see Evan Haefeli, "Kieft's War and the Cultures of Violence in Colonial America," in Michael A. Bellesiles, ed., *Lethal Imagination: Violence and Brutality in American History* (New York, 1999), 17–46.

32. Jameson, ed., *Narratives*, 208, 211, 226, 214; *Docs. Rel.*, I, 150, 183; XIII,

7; O'Callaghan, *New Netherland*, I, 240, 266; *NYHM: Dutch*, IV, 124–25; Innes, *New Amsterdam*, 103.

33. Jameson, ed., *Narratives*, 226–28, 273–74; Rink, *Holland on the Hudson*, 217, 222; O'Callaghan, *New Netherland*, I, 270, 269; *Docs. Rel.*, I, 151, 190, 187, 139, 210; Trelease, *Indian Affairs*, 72ff.; Henry C. Murphy, trans. and ed., [Cornelis Melyn?] *Broad Advice to the United Netherland Provinces . . .* (Antwerp, 1649), in *Collections of the New-York Historical Society*, 2nd ser., III, pt. 1 (1867), [237]–79, quotation at 257–58. Merwick, *Shame and Sorrow*, chaps. 11 ("The Indian War Seen") and 12 ("The Indian War Given Words"), drawing on Benjamin Schmidt's *Innocence Abroad: The Dutch Imagination and the New World, 1570–1670* (Cambridge, England, 2001), esp. chap. 5, explores with great subtlety the cultural context of atrocity tales like Melyn's. She explains their popular appeal and notes the inversion of roles (Dutch in New Netherland are like savage Spanish, Indians are like innocent Dutch), hence their contribution to collective guilt. She does not question the truth of the narratives and notes their acceptance by the authorities in The Hague. On Underhill: Merwick, *Shame and Sorrow*, 109, 179.

34. *NYHM: Dutch*, IV, 189–92; Innes, *New Amsterdam*, 103, 292–94. For another threat to assassinate Kieft, by the Frenchman Michiel Picquet, and the discussion of the use of torture to force his confession, see ibid., 446–52.

35. Jameson, ed., *Narratives*, 374–76; David M. Riker, "Govert Loockermans: Free Merchant of New Amsterdam," *de Halve Maen*, 54, no. 60 (June 1981), 4–10; Dennis J. Maika, "Commerce and Community: Manhattan's Merchants in the Seventeenth Century" (Ph.D. diss, New York University, 1995), 51–59; Russell Shorto, *The Island at the Center of the World* (New York, 2004), 139–40; Henry H. Kessler and Eugene Rachlis, *Peter Stuyvesant and His New York* (New York, 1959), 68–69; Dennis J. Maika, "Leadership in Manhattan's Merchant Community," Atlantic History Seminar Papers, Harvard University (2002), 10.

36. In his first approach to Van Rensselaer, Van der Donck proposed simply to sponsor the migration to Rensselaerswyck of two or three farmers and their families. *RB MSS*, 527.

37. Ibid., 608, 554–55, 557, 573–75, 603, 608, 547–50.

38. Shorto, *Island*, 109, 132; the letter of admonition, Mar. 9, 1643, is in *RB MSS*, 630–44; quotations at 644, 636–37. On Van der Donck's failure as *schout*, see Stefan Bielinski, "The *Schout* in Rensselaerswijck: A Conflict of Interests," in Nancy Zeller, ed., *A Beautiful and Fruitful Place: Selected Rensselaerswijck Seminar Papers* (New York, 1991), 6–10.

39. Shorto, *Island*, 138–39.

40. Adriaen van der Donck, *A Description of New Netherland* [1655] (Charles T. Gehring and William A. Starna, eds., Diederik W. Goedhuys, trans., Lincoln, Neb., 2008) is discussed more fully below, pp. 236–37; quotations here at 80, 75.

41. Bielinski, "*Schout*," 10; Shorto, *Island*, 163. Van Curler's struggle with Van der Donck grew out of Van der Donck's claim that Van Rensselaer should pay for the loss of his house: O'Callaghan, *History*, I, 345, with details in App. O: "he gave me the lie," Van Curler alleged, "Here came the wolf out of sheep's clothing! Here hypocrisy removed the mask from her own face!" 469.

42. Innes, *New Netherland*, 284–86, 290; Christian J. Koot, "The Merchant, the

Map, and Empire: Augustine Herrman's . . . Trade, 1644–73," *WMQ*, 67 (2010), 609, 612ff.; Earl L. W. Heck, *Augustine Herrman* (Englewood, Ohio, 1941), chaps. 1, 2; Jacobs, *New Netherland*, 358. It seems reasonable that Herrman, a skilled draftsman in close touch with the engraver of his map, would have drawn the quite distinctive portrait that appears on the map.

43. *Docs. Rel.*, I, 209–13; Jacobs, *New Netherland*, 140.

44. Jaap Jacobs, "Like Father, Like Son: The Early Years of Petrus Stuyvesant," in Joyce Goodfriend, ed., *Revisiting New Netherland* (Leiden, 2005), 221ff. (fifty-five of the books Stuyvesant auctioned are listed, 237–42); Shorto, *Island*, 149–50, 153; Kessler and Rachlis, *Stuyvesant*, 45–50; O'Callaghan, *New Netherland*, II, 25.

45. Shorto, *Island*, 151, 154, 174, 176ff.; *NYHM: Dutch*, IV, 370–71, 405–11; *Docs. Rel.*, I, 205–9 (cf. 213, 214).

46. Jameson, ed., *Narratives*, 259–60; Arthur E. Peterson and George W. Edwards, *New York as an Eighteenth-Century Municipality* (New York, 1917), 93–94; Innes, *New Netherland*, 81–82; Carl Bridenbaugh, *Cities in the Wilderness* (New York, 1938), 111.

47. Kessler and Rachlis, *Stuyvesant*, 66–67, 96.

48. Jacobs, *New Netherland*, 488; *NYHM: Dutch*, IV, 600–1, 586; Kessler and Rachlis, *Stuyvesant*, 97–99.

49. *Docs. Rel.*, I, 259–61, 262–70, 275–318. The Remonstrance is also in Jameson, ed., *Narratives*, 293–354. Quotations at ibid., 320, 342, 340; *Docs. Rel.* I, 317–18.

50. Van Tienhoven's "Answer": *Docs. Rel.*, I, 422ff., and Jameson, *Narratives*, 359ff.

51. Shorto, *Island*, 217, 224, 227, 240–42, 279, 226; Charles T. Gehring, trans. and ed., *Correspondence, 1647–1653* (*New Netherlands Documents Series*, XI, Syracuse, N.Y., 2000), 82.

52. Van der Donck, *Description*, 95–97, 103.

53. Gehring, ed., *Correspondence*, 203; O'Callaghan, *New Netherland*, II, 550–51.

54. Heck, *Herrman*, 49; *Docs. Rel.*, I, 497–98; Koot, "The Merchant, Map, and Empire," 635; Jacobs, *New Netherland*, 305. For Herrman's journal account of his mission to Maryland, *Docs. Rel.*, II, 88–98; William G. Duvall, "Smuggling Sotweed: Augustine Herrman and the Dutch Connection," *MHM*, 98, no. 4 (2003), 399.

55. Bartlett B. James and J. Franklin Jameson, eds., *Journal of Jasper Danckaerts, 1679–1680* (New York, 1913), xviii–xx, 112–16.

56. *Docs. Rel.*, II, 99; Koot, "The Merchant, Map, and Empire," 615–30, emphasizing the map's design as a statement of Herrman's transnational, trans-imperial view of the world; J. Louis Kuethe, "A Gazetteer of Maryland, A.D. 1673," *MHM*, 30 (1935), 310–25; Karel J. Kansky, "Augustine Herrman: the Leading Cartographer of the Seventeenth Century," *MHM*, 73 (1978), 352–359.

CHAPTER 9

Carnage and Civility in a Developing Hub of Commerce

1. *Docs. Rel.*, I, 246, 318; Russell Shorto, *The Island at the Center of the World* (New York, 2004), 226.

2. Dixon R. Fox, *Yankees and Yorkers* (New York, 1940), 59–62; Winthrop, *Journal*, 325–27; James T. Adams, *History of the Town of Southampton* (Bridgehampton, N.Y., 1918), 53; Evarts B. Greene and Virginia D. Harrington, *American Population Before the Federal Census of 1790* (New York, 1932), 93 note g.

3. Fox, *Yankees and Yorkers*, 61; Frederick W. Bogert, "Long Island Settlements, Part I," *de Halve Maen*, 38 (1963), 6.

4. Jessica Kross, *The Evolution of an American Town: Newtown, New York, 1642–1775* (Philadelphia, 1983), 13, 111; *Docs. Rel.*, I, 181, 44; George L. Smith, *Religion and Trade in New Netherland: Dutch Origins and American Development* (Ithaca, N.Y., 1973), 172n38, 224–25; Winthrop, *Journal*, 475n13; Emery Battis, *Saints and Sectaries* (Chapel Hill, N.C., 1962), 248.

5. Winthrop, *Journal*, 462–63; Lucille L. Koppelman, "Lady Deborah Moody and Gravesend, 1643–1659," *de Halve Maen*, 67, no. 2 (1994), 38–43; Cotton Mather, *Magnalia Christi Americana: or the Ecclesiastical History of New England . . .* [1702] (facsimile ed., New York, 1972), bk. III, chap. 9; Frederick W. Bogert, "Long Island Settlements, Part II," *de Halve Maen*, 38, no. 4 (1964), 12, 15; Smith, *Religion and Trade*, 224–25; Frederick Zwierlein, *Religion in New Netherland* (Rochester, N.Y., 1910), 160–62; Jaap Jacobs, *New Netherland* (Leiden, 1999), 152–54.

6. [Benjamin D. Hicks, ed.,] *Records of the Towns of North and South Hempstead, Long Island, N.Y.* (Jamaica, N.Y., 1896), I, 8. The paragraphs that follow, on the struggle between the Dutch and English for control of southern Connecticut, are drawn from Oliver A. Rink, *Holland on the Hudson* (Ithaca, N.Y., 1986), 122–23, 125, 247; Fox, *Yankees and Yorkers*, 84–85; and Donna Merwick, *Possessing Albany, 1630–1710: The Dutch and English Experiences* (Cambridge, England, 1990), 68.

7. Rink, *Holland on the Hudson*, 246–49; Ronald D. Cohen, "The Hartford Treaty of 1650 . . . ," *New-York Historical Society Quarterly*, 53 (1969), 311–22. Cf. Claudia Schnurmann, *Atlantische Welten: Engländer und Niederländer im amerikanisch-atlantischen Raum, 1648–1713* (Cologne, 1998), 86–90.

8. Simon Middleton, "Order and Authority in New Netherland: The 1653 Remonstrance and Early Settlement Politics," *WMQ*, 67 (2010), 52–55, 58–66; *Docs. Rel.*, II, 151–52.

9. Martha D. Shattuck, "A Civil Society: Court and Community in Beverwijck, New Netherland, 1652–1664" (Ph.D. diss., Boston University, 1993), 51ff.; Donna Merwick, *Possessing Albany*, 77–78.

10. Shattuck, "Civil Society," 73–74, 240ff., 251, 255, 285–91, 198, 196, 227; Merwick, *Possessing Albany*, 79–81, 90–91.

11. Shattuck, "Civil Society," 249, 78ff.; Merwick, *Possessing Albany*, 77; John J. McCusker, *Essays in the Economic History of the Atlantic World* (London, 1997), 116, with correction to £30,429 by Professor McCusker in correspondence.

12. Boogaart, "Servant Migration," App. I; Firth Haring Fabend, *A Dutch Family in the Middle Colonies, 1660–1800* (New Brunswick, N.J., 1991), 265.

13. Rink, *Holland on the Hudson*, 233; Charles R. Boxer, *The Dutch in Brazil, 1624–1654* (Oxford, England, 1957), 242–45. For the fortunes of one Dutch-Brazilian refugee

of note in New Amsterdam, the Rev. Jacob Polhemus, see Ellis L. Raesly, *Portrait of New Netherland* (New York, 1945), 226–28.

14. Jacob R. Marcus, *The Colonial American Jew, 1492–1776* (Detroit, Mich., 1970), I, 205, 209–11, 216ff.; Boxer, *Dutch in Brazil*, 243; Johannes M. Postma, *The Dutch in the Atlantic Slave Trade 1600–1815* (Cambridge, England, 1990), 19. Two recent collections of essays explore in detail the history of the Jews in the early modern Atlantic world: Paolo Bernadini and Norman Fiering, eds., *The Jews and the Expansion of Europe to the West, 1450 to 1800* (New York, 2001), esp. the essay by James H. Williams; and Richard L. Kagan and Philip D. Morgan, eds., *Atlantic Diasporas: Jews, Conversos, and Crypto-Jews in the Age of Mercantilism, 1508–1800* (Baltimore, Md., 2009).

15. Rink, *Holland on the Hudson*, 230–33; Smith, *Religion and Trade*, chap. 12.

16. Marcus, *Colonial Jew*, I, 219–21, 224–26, 238–40; Rink, *Holland on the Hudson*, 233–34; J. Franklin Jameson, ed., *Narratives of New Netherland, 1609–1654* (New York, 1909), 392–93.

17. Rink, *Holland on the Hudson*, 235–37; Smith, *Religion and Trade*, 220–30, quotation at 230; Kross, *Newtown*, 45. For the text of the "Flushing Remonstrance," Smith, *Religion and Trade*, 225.

18. Postma, *Dutch Slave Trade*, 16–17, 21; Rink, *Holland on the Hudson*, 169, 163–64; Joyce D. Goodfriend, "Burghers and Blacks: The Evolution of a Slave Society at New Amsterdam," *New York History*, 59 (1978), 126, 133, 134. For an opposing view, that the West India Company never contemplated making New Netherland an entrepôt for the distribution of slaves, see Pieter Emmer, "The History of the Dutch Slave Trade, a Bibliographical Survey," *Journal of Economic History*, 32 (1972), 735.

19. Robert J. Swan, "First Africans into New Netherland, 1625 or 1626?" *de Halve Maen*, 66, no. 4 (1993), 75–83; Boogaart, "Servant Migration," 58; Goodfriend, "Burghers and Blacks," 130.

20. Boogaart, "Servant Migration," 58–59; Goodfriend, "Burghers and Blacks," 128–29, 138, 139, 141–44; Joyce D. Goodfriend, *Before the Melting Pot: Society and Culture in Colonial New York City, 1664–1739* (Princeton, N.J., 1992), 13, 10; Rink, *Holland on the Hudson*, 129, 163. Goodfriend, who makes clear that the blacks of this period did not become skilled workers, gives higher estimates of their percentage of the population in 1664 than the estimates (Boogaart's) cited. For evidence of another full slave ship arrival and of slave auctions, see Raesly, *Portrait of New Netherland*, 160.

21. Peter R. Christoph, "The Freedmen of New Amsterdam," in Nancy A. M. Zeller, ed., *A Beautiful and Fruitful Place: Selected Rensselaerswijck Seminar Papers* ([Albany, N.Y.,] 1991), 158, 166; Edgar J. McManus, *A History of Negro Slavery in New York* (Syracuse, N.Y., 1966), 13, 43–45; Graham R. Hodges, *Root & Branch: African Americans in New York & East Jersey* (Chapel Hill, N.C., 1999), 41–43; E. B. O'Callaghan, comp., trans., and ed., *Laws and Ordinances of New Netherland, 1638–1674* (Albany, N.Y., 1868), 36–37; Vivienne Kruger, "Born to Run: The Slave Family in Early New York, 1626–1829" (Ph.D. diss., Columbia University, 1985), 165.

22. Kruger, "Born to Run," 261ff.; Christoph, "Freedmen," 161–62, 157; McManus, *Negro Slavery*, 12, 16, 22.

23. Rink, *Holland on the Hudson*, 165–71; Boxer, *Dutch in Brazil*, 246; *Docs. Rel.*, XIII, 205; Jaap Jacobs, *New Netherland* (Leiden, 1999), 54. Rink is inconsistent in his figures. In his table 6.4 (p. 166) he leaves out the ship *Purmerlandkerk* to correct O'Callaghan's list in his *Documentary History of the State of New-York* (Albany, N.Y., 1849–51), III, 52–63 (not 33–42); but in the figures he uses in his text explaining the table, he does use that ship. Hence the table lists 167 families but the text refers to 176 families. All the figures here are taken from the table, not from his text.

24. Ibid., 166, 168, 169; Goodfriend, *Before the Melting Pot*, 15–17; [Mariana G.] Van Rensselaer, *History of the City of New York in the Seventeenth Century* (New York, 1909), I, 421.

25. Donna Merwick, *The Shame and the Sorrow: Dutch Amerindian Encounters in New Netherland* (Philadelphia, 2006), 216; Shorto, *Island*, 266; Van Rensselaer, *City of New York*, I, 455–56; E. B. O'Callaghan, *History of New Netherland; or, New York Under the Dutch* (New York, 1846–48), II, 540; Jameson, ed., *Narratives*, 421, 423; Claudia Schnurmann, "Seventeenth-Century Atlantic Commerce and Nieuw Amsterdam / New York Merchants," in Hermann Wellenreuther, ed., *Jacob Leisler's Atlantic World in the Later Seventeenth-Century* (Berlin, 2009), 65.

26. Dennis J. Maika, "Commerce and Community: Manhattan Merchants in the Seventeenth Century" (Ph.D. diss., New York University, 1995), 39–58, 322–27; Jameson, ed., *Narratives*, 374–77; Maika, "Leadership in Manhattan's Merchant Community," Working Paper, Atlantic History Seminar (Harvard University, 2002), 1–5. On denization, oaths to English sovereignty, and the transfer of allegiance as "more of a transition point . . . than a distinct end or beginning" for the leading merchants, see Maika, "Commerce and Community," 132–35, 147, 155, 158, 348–89; Maika, "Leadership," 16–17, 31. On figures of shipping from the Netherlands to New Netherland, see table 4.5 in Johannes Postma and Victor Enthoven, eds., *Riches From Atlantic Commerce: Dutch Transatlantic Trade and Shipping, 1585–1817* (Leiden, 2003), 94.

27. Maika, "Commerce and Community," 158; Rink, *Holland on the Hudson*, 177–206.

28. E. B. O'Callaghan, ed., *The Register of New Netherland, 1626–1674* (Albany, N.Y., 1865), 176; Linda B. Biemer, *Women and Property in Colonial New York: The Transition from Dutch to English Law, 1643–1727* (Ann Arbor, Mich., 1983), 33–43; Jean Zimmerman, *The Women of the House: How a Colonial She-Merchant Built a Mansion, a Fortune, and a Dynasty* (Orlando, Fla., 2006), prologue, chaps. 1–11. Loockermans's marital connections formed a remarkably tight kinship network. He married a niece of Gillis Verbrugge, who was a sister-in-law of Jacob van Couwenhoven. His sister married Oloff Stevensen van Cortlandt, his daughter married Stuyvesant's nephew, and his stepdaughter married Leisler. Maika, "Commerce and Community," 160.

29. Claudia Schnurmann, "Representative Atlantic Entrepreneur: Jacob Leisler, 1640–1691," in Postma and Enthoven, eds., *Riches from Atlantic Commerce*, 267–73, 278; Maika, "Leadership," 16–17, 31; David W. Voorhees, "The 'Fervent Zeale' of Jacob Leisler," *WMQ*, 51 (1994), 452–57.

30. Maika, "Leadership," 7–9, 14; Maika, "Securing the Burgher Right in New Amsterdam . . . ," in Goodfriend, *Revisiting New Netherland*, 108–16.

31. Victor Enthoven, "An Assessment of Dutch Transatlantic Commerce, 1585–1817," in Postma and Enthoven, eds., *Riches from Atlantic Commerce*, 445.

32. Rink, *Holland on the Hudson*, 258; Jameson, ed., *Narratives*, 172ff. For Van der Donck's sympathetic account, see his *Description*, passim; for De Vries's, see the journal of his travels, in Jameson, ed., *Narratives*, 216ff., in Raesly, *New Netherland*, 174, and in Parr, *De Vries*, passim.

33. Cynthia J. Van Zandt, *Brothers Among Nations: The Pursuit of Intercultural Alliances in Early America, 1580–1660* (Oxford, England, 2008), 171–86. As an illustration of the "intercultural alliances" that are the subject of her book, Van Zandt, developing a suggestion of Trelease (*Indian Affairs*, 139), argues that New Sweden, on the upper Delaware River, had replaced Claiborne's Kent Island settlement on Chesapeake Bay as the Susquehannocks' main trading outlet with the Europeans; that the weak Swedish settlement had become a client colony of the powerful Susquehannocks; and that in a swirl of rumors about the impending Dutch attack, the Swedes or their affiliates, deliberately or not, may have instigated the Susquehannocks' assault on Manhattan as a diversion or in reprisal, the Susquehannocks in any case resenting the Dutch contacts with the Iroquois. The ubiquitous Isaac Allerton, she explains, in his complex intercolonial maneuvering, found himself a special target of the Indians' attack on the town.

34. Merwick, *Shame and Sorrow*, 185–92, 219–22, 225–28; Trelease, *Indian Affairs*, 138–48; Raesly, *New Netherland*, 98. For the widely shared view of Van Tienhoven's culpability and a higher estimate of the numbers of colonists killed in the Indians' revenge, see Capt. Nicasius de Sille's account, quoted ibid., 299.

35. Merwick, *Shame and Sorrow*, 231, 232–34, 237; *Docs. Rel.*, XIII, 84; Trelease, *Indian Affairs*, 150.

36. Merwick, *Shame and Sorrow*, 241ff.; Trelease, *Indian Affairs*, 160ff.; Raesly, *New Netherland*, 224–25; Edward T. Corwin, ed., *Ecclesiastical Records, State of New York* (Albany, N.Y., 1901–16), I, 534–35, 546.

37. Trelease, *Indian Affairs*, 163, 165, 168; *Docs. Rel.*, XIII, 339; Merwick, *Shame and Sorrow*, 249–50; *RB MSS*, 442; O'Callaghan, ed., *Documentary History*, III, 70–71.

CHAPTER 10

Swedes, Finns, and the Passion of Pieter Plockhoy

1. Terry G. Jordan and Matti Kaups, *The American Backwoods Frontier: An Ethnic and Ecological Interpretation* (Baltimore, Md., 1989).

2. Michael Roberts, ed., *Sweden's Age of Greatness, 1632–1718* (New York, 1973), 60, 104, 22, 267, 106–7, chap. 2; Margareta Revera, "The Making of a Civilized Nation . . . ," in Carol E. Hoffecker et al., eds, *New Sweden in America* (Newark, Del., c. 1995), 30; Gunlög Fur, *Colonialism in the Margins: Cultural Encounters in New Sweden and Lapland* (Leiden, 2006), chap. 1; on Sweden's interactions with its own frontier peoples, chap. 2.

3. Stellan Dahlgren and Hans Norman, *The Rise and Fall of New Sweden . . . Risingh's Journal, 1654–1655 . . .* (Uppsala, 1988), 47. The book includes the text, in Swedish and English, of *Risingh's Journal*, 130ff., which will be cited as such hereafter.

4. Amandus Johnson, *The Swedish Settlements on the Delaware, 1638–1664* (Philadelphia, 1911), I, 53–55, 68, and chap. 8 generally.

5. C. A. Weslager, *Dutch Explorers, Traders and Settlers in the Delaware Valley, 1609–1664* (Philadelphia, 1961), 84ff.; Van Cleaf Bachman, *Peltries or Plantations: The Economic Policies of the Dutch West India Company in New Netherland, 1623–1639* (Baltimore, Md., 1969), 161–64; Michael Roberts, *From Oxenstierna to Charles XII* (Cambridge, England, 1991), 12; Johnson, *Swedish Settlements*, II, 675–76, 695–96.

6. Ibid., I, 103–7.

7. Sten Carlsson, "The New Sweden Colonists, 1638–1656: Their Geographical and Social Background," in Hoffecker, ed., *New Sweden*, 173. For a listing of the voyages, based on Johnson's *Swedish Settlements*, see Dahlgren and Norman, *New Sweden*, 126.

8. Ibid., 59–61; Carlsson, "Colonists," in Hoffecker, ed., *New Sweden*, 173.

9. Johnson, *Swedish Settlements*, I, 16, 125–26, 149–50, 239, 243; II, 699.

10. Dahlgren and Norman, *New Sweden*, 62; Jordan and Kaups, *Backwoods Frontier*, 61; Johnson, *Swedish Settlements*, I, chaps. 18, 25, 26.

11. Ibid., I, 151–54; Peter S. Craig, *1671 Census of the Delaware* (Philadelphia, 1999), 18–19; Carlsson, "Colonists," in Hoffecker, ed., *New Sweden*, 174, 176, 180. Many of the place names assigned to settlements on the Delaware reflect specific places of the settlers' origins. Thus Fort Tarne (Torne), erected after the abandonment of the blockhouse at Vasa (which had been named after Vasa in northern Finland), was named after Tarne at the northern point of the Bay of Bothnia: Johnson, *Swedish Settlements*, I, 328; II, 715.

12. Ibid., I, 197, 202–3, 198.

13. Amandus Johnson, trans. and ed., *The Instruction for Johan Printz* (Philadelphia, 1930), 47; *Docs. Rel.*, XII, ix; Winthrop, *Journal*, 480.

14. *Instruction for Printz*, 120, 3–15.

15. Richard Waldron, "New Sweden: An Interpretation," in Joyce D. Goodfriend, ed., *Revisiting New Netherland* (Leiden, 2005), 80; Johnson, *Swedish Settlements*, II, 700–10; Dahlgren and Norman, *New Sweden*, 72; *Instruction for Printz*, 116–18.

16. Johnson, *Swedish Settlements*, I, 378–79.

17. On Printz's request for artisans of all kinds, as well as for bricks and other supplies, echoed by his son-in-law Johan Papegoja, the vice-governor ("there is a great cry for people, for here are few"), ibid., I, 321. The colony's population as of Mar. 1, 1648, is enumerated ibid., II, 710–16.

18. Charles T. Gehring, trans. and ed., *Delaware Papers (Dutch Period) . . . 1648–1664 (New York Historical Manuscripts: Dutch, XVIII–XIX)* (Baltimore, Md., 1981), 1–2, 7 [hereafter: Gehring, *Delaware Papers*]; Dahlgren and Norman, *New Sweden*, 65, 69, 70; Johnson, *Swedish Settlements*, I, 328.

19. Ibid., I, 435–36, 445, 447, 448.

20. Dahlgren and Norman, *New Sweden*, 73, 157.

21. Ibid., 10; *Instructions for Printz*, 41.

22. Johnson, *Swedish Settlements*, I, 462–63, 243; II, 703, 714, 69; Dahlgren and Norman, *New Sweden*, 185, 78, 79. On Papegoja's background in Västergötland and his tormented marriage with the cantankerous, "tyrannical and ill-disposed" Armegot, see

Evert A. Larsson, "The Papegojas of Old and New Sweden," *Swedish-American Historical Quarterly*, 39 (1988), 64–69. Papegoja left the colony and his wife in 1656, joined the Swedish army, and retired to his native Västergötland. But he could not escape Armegot, who joined him in Sweden in 1662. He sued unsuccessfully for divorce, while Armegot devoted herself to regaining her properties on the Delaware, in which, after many years and a period back in America, she succeeded. She outlived Papegoja by twenty-eight years. For a romantic view of Armegot, including the claim that she was a champion of women's rights, but with useful quotations from the legal documents, see Esther C. Meixner, *The Governor's Daughter* (Chester, Pa., 1965).

23. Dahlgren and Norman, *New Sweden*, 33, 14–15, 28–29, 64ff., 285–87; Johnson, *Swedish Settlements*, II, 693–94.

24. Dahlgren and Norman, *New Sweden*, 85, 92, 161, 157; Johnson, *Swedish Settlements*, II, 514.

25. Dahlgren and Norman, *New Sweden*, 151, 155, 87–90.

26. Ibid., 92, 93, 95, 97, 98, 181; Johnson, *Swedish Settlements*, II, 515–19.

27. Ibid., II, 560, 520–21; Thomas Campanius Holm, *A Short Description of the Province of New Sweden . . .* [1759] (Peter S. Du Ponceau, trans., Historical Society of Pennsylvania, *Memoirs*, III [1834]), 113–15; Fur, *Colonialism*, 189–90, 199–200; Dahlgren and Norman, *New Sweden*, 107; E. P. Richardson, "Peter Martensson Lindström . . . and the Delaware Indians," *American Art Journal*, 12 (1980), 62. On Campanius and his catechism, see articles by Trygve Skarsten and Isak Collijn in *Lutheran Quarterly*, 2 (1988), 47–87, 89–98.

28. *Risingh's Journal*, 215–23, 201, and Johnson, *Swedish Settlements*, II, 511–13.

29. Dahlgren and Norman, *New Sweden*, 113; *Risingh's Journal*, 253; Johnson, *Swedish Settlements*, II, 604–7; Gehring, *Delaware Papers*, I, 44.

30. Johnson, *Swedish Settlements*, II, 634, 667; John H. Wuorinen, *The Finns on the Delaware, 1638–1655* (New York, 1938), 79–80; Jordan and Kaups, *Backwoods Frontier*, 55, 57. For the disposition of the *Mercurius*, see *Docs. Rel.*, XII, 120ff.

31. Jordan and Kaups, *Backwoods Frontier*, 57, 55; A. R. Dunlap and E. J. Moyne, "The Finnish Language on the Delaware," *American Speech*, 27 (1952), 85.

32. Jordan and Kaups, *Backwoods Frontier*, 50, 40; Johnson, *Swedish Settlements*, II, 528; Per Martin Tvengsberg, "Slash-and-Burn Cultivation . . . ," *New Jersey Folklife*, 16 (1991), 16; M. Soininen, "Burn-beating as the Technical Basis of Colonization in Finland in the 16th and 17th Centuries," *Scandinavian Economic History Review*, 7 (1959), 150–66. Soininen describes several forms of burn-beating besides the common *huuhta* method summarized here.

33. Johnson, *Swedish Settlements*, II, 677–78; Fur, *Colonialism*, 38; Jordan and Kaups, *Backwoods Frontier*, 43, 46–47, 51–53.

34. Ibid., 57–58; Fur, *Colonialism*, 94–95; Wuorinen, *Finns*, 16–19.

35. Jordan and Kaups, *Backwoods Frontier*, 58, map on 54, 229; Peter Lindeström, *Geographia Americae . . .* (Amandus Johnson, trans. and ed., Philadelphia, 1925), 173; Dunlop and Moyne, "Finnish Language," 81–83; Johnson, *Swedish Settlements*, II, 547; Dahlgren and Norman, *New Sweden*, 221.

36. Jordan and Kaups, *Backwoods Frontier*, 72, 73; *Docs. Rel.*, XII, 425–26; Gehring,

Delaware Papers, 319–20, 335; Johnson, *Swedish Settlements*, I, 151; II, 705, 711. For a list of the Long Finn's confederates and the fines imposed, see Charles T. Gehring, ed., *New York Historical Manuscripts: Dutch, Volumes XX–XXI (Delaware Papers, English Period . . . 1664–1682)* (Baltimore, Md., 1977), 7–10. For an exhaustive account of the incipient rebellion of 1669 and also the events of 1675 and 1680, see Evan Haefeli, "The Revolt of the Long Swede: Transatlantic Hopes and Fears on the Delaware, 1669," *Pennsylvania Magazine of History and Biography*, 130 (2006), 137–80; Robert C. Ritchie, *The Duke's Province . . . 1664–1691* (Chapel Hill, N.C., 1977), 74.

37. Jordan and Kaups, *Backwoods Frontier*, 71; Israel Acrelius, *Description of the Former and Present Condition of the Swedish Churches, in What Was Called New Sweden . . .* [Stockholm, 1759] (William M. Reynolds, trans., *Historical Society of Pennsylvania, Memoirs*, XI [1874]), 310.

38. Jordan and Kaups, *Backwoods Frontier*, 214, 88–92; Johnson, *Swedish Settlements*, II, 527–28, 533–35, 541; Fur, *Colonialism*, 201, 205ff., 196–97, and chap. 6 generally; Lorraine E. Williams, "Indians and Europeans in the Delaware Valley, 1620–1655," in Hoffecker, ed., *New Sweden*, 118–19.

39. Johnson, *Swedish Settlements*, I, 345, 348–49, 346–47, 351–52, 358; Patricia I. Cooper, "The Log Cabin . . . ," *Pennsylvania Folklife*, 43 (1993–94), 77–79; C. A. Weslager, "Log Structures in New Sweden . . . ," *Delaware History*, 5 (1952), 87; Tvengsberg, "Slash-and-Burn Cultivation," 17.

40. Johnson, *Swedish Settlements*, II, 537ff.; I, 348, 358; Weslager, "Log Structures," 84, 90–91; Cooper, "Log Cabin," 78.

41. Revera, "Making of a Civilized Nation," in Hoffecker, ed., *New Sweden*, 37; Carlsson, "Colonists," ibid., 180 (cf. Hans Norman, "The New Sweden Colony and . . . Swedish and Finnish Ethnicity," ibid., 189–90). The population figures are only approximate throughout since the sources differ and almost all figures they cite are estimates.

42. E. B. O'Callaghan, *History of New Netherland . . .* (New York, 1848), II, 324, 326; *Docs. Rel.*, XII, 233, 271; Charles T. Gehring, "*Hodie Mihi, Cras Tibi*: Swedish-Dutch Relations in the Delaware Valley," in Hoffecker, ed., *New Sweden*, 81; Carlsson, "Colonists," ibid., 180; Norman, "Ethnicity," ibid., 194. On the Dutch struggle to get the Swedes and Finns to resettle, see Gehring, *Delaware Papers*, I, 191–95, 197, 201.

43. C. A. Weslager, "The City of Amsterdam's Colony on the Delaware, 1656–1664 . . . ," *Delaware History*, 20 (1982), 5–7; O'Callaghan, *New Netherland*, II, 327–33.

44. Weslager, "Amsterdam's Colony," 8–10; O'Callaghan, *New Netherland*, II, 334, 336; Gehring, *Delaware Papers*, I, 97–98; *Docs. Rel.*, XII, 163; Simon Hart, "The City-Colony of New Amsterdam . . . ," *de Halve Maen*, 39 (1965), 13 col. B.

45. Weslager, "Amsterdam's Colony," 5, 11 and n34; O'Callaghan, *New Netherland*, II, 337, 375, 374; *Docs. Rel.*, XII, 231, 225, 227; Gehring, *Delaware Papers*, I, 130, 138; Hart, "New Amstel," 8 col. A, 13 col. B. The complex character of the colony's population is well illustrated by the geographical origins of six of the deserting soldiers: one from Stockholm, one from Jutland (Denmark), one from Winseren (Sweden), one from Antwerp, and two from the Netherlands (Utrecht and Amersfort).

46. Gehring, *Delaware Papers*, I, 174, 86; *Docs. Rel.*, XII, 277, 228–229, 231, 236–37, 293, 277, 249; O'Callaghan, *New Netherland*, II, 377 (for a different translation: Gehring,

Delaware Papers, I, 167), 380, 375; Weslager, "Amsterdam's Colony," 13; C. A. Weslager, *The English on the Delaware, 1610–1682* (New Brunswick, N.J., 1967), chap. 11.

47. Ibid., 163; Gehring, *Delaware Papers*, I, 214, 231; O'Callaghan, *New Netherland*, II, 388.

48. Ibid., 459, 464–65; Gehring, *Delaware Papers*, I, 188, 187, 237, 238, 244, 279, 276; Weslager, "Amsterdam's Colony," 12, 14.

49. Gehring, *Delaware Papers*, I, 274, 279, 316, 321, 309, 311, 341; O'Callaghan, *New Netherland*, II, 465.

50. Weslager, "Amsterdam's Colony," 2, 4, 14, 12, 17, 20; Gehring, *Delaware Papers*, I, 327; Hart, "New Amstel," 8 col. A, 7 col. B; *Docs. Rel.*, II, 211.

51. Gehring, *Delaware Papers*, I, 321, 338, 327; *Docs. Rel.*, II, 212, 213, 210; XII, 272.

52. Leland Harder, "Plockhoy and His Settlement at Zwaanendael, 1663," *Mennonite Quarterly Review*, 23 (1949), 188; Leland Harder and Marvin Harder, *Plockhoy From Zurik-zee* (Newton, Kan., 1952), 81–82. The Harders' book contains the texts of Plockhoy's chief writings, the two English pamphlets of 1659—*The Way to the Peace . . . of These Nations . . .* and *A Way Propounded . . .* —plus a translation of his *Kort en Klaer Ontwerp* [*Brief and Concise Plan*] . . . and the 117 articles of association in the *Kort Verhael* [*Brief Account*] . . . , both of 1662.

53. Harder, *Plockhoy*, 16, 83, 17; Ellis L. Raesly, *Portrait of New Netherland* (New York, 1945), 290.

54. Harder, *Plockhoy*, 108, 85; H. R. Trevor-Roper, *The Crisis of the Seventeenth Century: Religion, the Reformation and Social Change* (New York, 1968), 251.

55. Harder, *Plockhoy*, 25, 31, 109–11, 114, 27, 29. For Plockhoy's remarkably vigorous and clear defense of freedom of religion, see especially his letter to Cromwell, which he reprinted in his *Way to the Peace*: Harder, *Plockhoy*, 113–20.

56. Ibid., 31–32.

57. Ibid., 103, 32, 34, 36, 37.

58. Ibid., 48; Raesly, *New Netherland*, 281ff. The texts of Steendam's poems are in Henry C. Murphy, trans., *An Anthology of New Netherland . . .* (New York, 1865), [37]–75.

59. Craig, *1671 Census*, 80–81; Harder, *Plockhoy*, 52–55, 57, 189, 191 (quotations from articles 1, 15, 104).

60. Ibid., 105, 56; quotations from articles 112, 78–82.

61. Ibid., 51, 58–59, 86, 90.

62. Ibid., 174ff., quotation at 185.

63. *Docs. Rel.*, II, 176; XII, 429; III, 346; Harder, "Plockhoy . . . at Zwaanendael," 197n38, emphasis added.

64. Ibid., 188; Craig, *1671 Census*, 74–77.

65. Plockhoy's ideas were adopted by the Quakers later in the century and through them transmitted to Robert Owen, whose utopian social programs of the early nineteenth century they profoundly influenced. They were thereafter incorporated into Marx's labor theory of value and cited at length by the Marxist revisionist Eduard Bernstein. He devoted a chapter of his 1895 *Cromwell and Communism* (H. J. Stenning, trans.,

London, 1930) to "Plockboy" [sic], finding in the Dutchman's *A Way Propounded* a clear anticipation of his own ideal of social reform combined with modified market economics. "Socialism," he wrote, "has to take account of a commercialized state of society, which Plockboy is the first whose guiding principle is to anticipate developments rather than lag behind. . . . Plockboy may well rank among the pioneers of the modern idea of co-operation." Subsequently the English reformer Joshua Rowntree endorsed Plockhoy's ideas, which have also interested modern economists, and in 1934 the Manchester Co-operative Union (U.K.) declared that if their movement had a father, Plockhoy "has an excellent claim to that distinction." In 1968, three hundred years after Carr obliterated Plockhoy's community "to a very naile," all of the Dutchman's publications were translated into French at the École Pratique des Hautes Études to support a study of cooperative utopianism. Bernard Bailyn, "The Search for Perfection: Atlantic Dimensions," *Proceedings of the British Academy*, 151 (2007), 150–53, 156–57; Jonathan Israel, *Radical Enlightenment: Philosophy and the Making of Modernity, 1650–1750* (Oxford, England, 2001), 177. Israel explores at length Plockhoy's influence on his contemporary, the radical free thinker Franciscus Ven den Eden, whose influence, in turn, on Spinoza may have been important.

CHAPTER 11
God's Conventicle, Bradford's Lamentation

1. The proposal to allow "full and free tolerance of religion to all men that would preserve civil peace," backed by most of Plymouth's deputies in 1645, horrified Bradford and the other leaders. They refused to allow it to come to a vote, so certain were they that it "would eat out the power of Godliness." Edward Winslow to John Winthrop, Nov. 24, 1645, in *Winthrop Papers*, V (Boston, 1947), 56.

2. Philip F. Gura, *A Glimpse of Sion's Glory: Puritan Radicalism in New England, 1620–1660* (Middletown, Conn., 1984), 53–54; Edmund S. Morgan, *Visible Saints: The History of a Puritan Idea* (New York, 1963), 53.

3. William Bradford, *Of Plymouth Plantation, 1620–1647* (Samuel E. Morison, ed., New York, 1952), 33 [hereafter: Bradford, *Plymouth*; other editions will be specifically cited].

4. Nick Bunker, *Making Haste from Babylon: The Mayflower Pilgrims and Their World* (New York, 2010), 103, 125ff. [hereafter: Bunker, *Pilgrims*]; Robert C. Anderson, *The Pilgrim Migration: Immigrants to Plymouth Colony, 1620–1633* (Boston, 2004), 67–68; Henry M. Dexter and Morton Dexter, *The England and Holland of the Pilgrims* (Baltimore, Md., 1978), 40, 154–57, 215ff., 259ff., 320–29, 395; B. R. White, *The English Separatist Tradition: From the Marian Martyrs to the Pilgrim Fathers* (Oxford, England, 1971), 91–92; M. M. Knappen, *Tudor Puritanism* (Chicago, 1939), 313–14 and chap. 15 generally.

5. For book collection, James Deetz and Patricia Scott Deetz, *The Times of Their Lives* (New York, 2000), 195; Bunker, *Pilgrims*, 129, 170–77, 106–10; 165–66; Bradford, *Plymouth*, 326, 9–10; Dexter, *England and Holland*, 377ff., 239; Timothy George, *John Robinson and the English Separatist Tradition* (Macon, Ga., 1982), iii; White, *Separatist Tradition*, vi; Bradford Smith, *Bradford of Plymouth* (Philadelphia, 1951), 36–38, 55, 57. On Bradford's family background, his peripatetic childhood, and his defiance of his family's expectations, see Bunker, *Pilgrims*, 115–17.

6. Bradford, *Plymouth*, 8, 11, 14; Bunker, *Pilgrims*, 113, 187, 191. For Cushman's description of the economic distress that contributed to the Pilgrims' determination to leave England ("each man is fain to pluck his means, as it were out of his neighbour's throat . . . There is such pressing and oppressing in town and country . . . so as a man can hardly any where set up a trade, but he shall pull down two of his neighbors"), see ibid., 269.

7. George D. Langdon, Jr., *Pilgrim Colony . . . 1620–1691* (New Haven, Conn., 1966), 6; Bradford, *Plymouth*, 20n, 19n. Bradford in his "First Dialogue" (Alexander Young, ed., *Chronicles of the Pilgrim Fathers . . . 1602 to 1625* [Boston, 1841], 455–56) estimated the Leiden congregation at "not much fewer" than three hundred; Dexter, *England and Holland*, 648, estimates the number at 473. On the geographical distribution, ibid., 650. On the "purging," Bradford, *Plymouth*, 18. For a comprehensive account of the Pilgrims in Leiden—the city, the circumstances, and the fortunes of the Pilgrims there—see Jeremy Bangs, *Strangers and Pilgrims, Travellers and Sojourners: Leiden and the Foundations of Plymouth Plantation* (Plymouth, Mass., 2009).

8. Ibid., 17n, 25; Johanna W. Tammel, comp., *Pilgrims and Other People from the British Isles in Leiden, 1576–1640* (Isle of Man, 1989), 57, 6; Dexter, *England and Holland*, 601–41, 565–67.

9. Bradford, *Plymouth*, 28, 30–31, 25–26; Edward Winslow, *Hypocrisie Unmasked . . .* (London, 1646, reprint ed., Providence, R.I., 1916), 91; David B. Quinn, *England and the Discovery of America, 1481–1620* (New York, 1974), xiii.

10. Bradford, *Plymouth*, 27, 36, 368; Ruth A. McIntyre, *Debts Hopeful and Desperate* (Plymouth, Mass., 1963), 20, 32–33, 45.

11. Winslow, *Hypocrisie*, 90, 91; Smith, *Bradford*, 113–14; Dexter, *England and Holland*, 587–88; Bradford, *Plymouth*, 48.

12. William Bradford, *History of Plymouth Plantation, 1620–1647* (Worthington C. Ford et al., eds., Boston: Massachusetts Historical Society, 1912), I, 142n, 145 [hereafter: MHS, ed., Bradford, *History*]; W. Sears Nickerson, *Land Ho!—1620* (1931; rev. ed., East Lansing, Mich., 1997), 16; Bradford, *Plymouth*, 53.

13. Nickerson, *Land Ho!*, 17, 19–28; Eugene A. Stratton, *Plymouth Colony* (Salt Lake City, 1986), 21, 31n, 323–24; Smith, *Bradford*, 121–22; Bradford, *Plymouth*, 55. Martin called the Pilgrims "froward and waspish, discontented people." McIntyre, *Debts*, 19. Bunker, *Pilgrims*, 55, identifies twenty-four households aboard the *Mayflower*, of whom at least fifteen were led by men who had lived in Leiden.

14. George F. Willison, *Saints and Strangers* (New York, 1945), 454; Stratton, *Plymouth Colony*, 328; Bradford, *Plymouth*, 58.

15. Willison, *Saints*, 440, 441; Stratton, *Plymouth Colony*, 245, 308–9, 283–85; Henry M. Dexter, ed., *Mourt's Relation or Journal of the Plantation at Plymouth* [London, 1622] (Boston, 1865), 42–43; Annie L. Jester and Martha W. Hiden, comps., *Adventurers of Purse and Person* (3rd ed., revised by Virginia M. Meyer and John F. Dorman, Richmond, Va., 1987), 374–75; Charles E. Banks, *The English Ancestry and Homes of the Pilgrim Fathers* (New York, 1929), 61–63.

16. MHS, ed., Bradford, *History*, I, 394n; Stratton, *Plymouth Colony*, 357–59, 373; Bradford, *Plymouth*, 327–28 and chap. 33 generally; Anderson, *Pilgrim Migration*, 10–15; Cynthia J. Van Zandt, *Brothers Among Nations: The Pursuit of Intercultural Alliances in Early*

America, 1580–1660 (Oxford, England, 2008), passim. On Allerton's jumbling of private and community affairs, McIntyre, *Debts*, 52–58.

17. Banks, *English Ancestry*, 44; Bradford, *Plymouth*, 42n, 367; Stratton, *Plymouth Colony*, 259, quoting William Hubbard's *General History of New England . . .* [1682] (Cambridge, Mass., 1815).

18. Cotton Mather, *Magnalia Christi Americana, Books I and II* [London, 1702] (Kenneth B. Murdock, ed., Cambridge, Mass., 1977), 207; Bradford, *Plymouth*, 58–59, 61–63, 75, 76; Nickerson, *Land Ho!*, 11; *Mourt's Relation*, 7–9.

19. Ibid., 5, 27, 46, 39; Bradford, *Plymouth*, 68, 70–71; Deetz and Deetz, *Times of Their Lives*, 57.

20. Thomas Prince, *A Chronological History of New-England in the Form of Annals* [1736–1755] ([Boston], 1826), xviii; *Mourt's Relation*, 70, 72–73, 66, 137–41; Bradford, *Plymouth*, 77–78; Robert C. Anderson, *The Great Migration Begins: Immigrants to New England 1620–1633* (Boston, 1995), III, 1522. [hereafter Anderson, *Immigrants*]. For a dismissal of the idea that Dorothy Bradford may have committed suicide "after gazing for six weeks at the barren sand dunes of Cape Cod" (Morison, in Bradford, *Plymouth*, xxiv), see Stratton, *Plymouth Colony*, 324–25. Cf. Deetz and Deetz, *Times of Their Lives*, 305.

21. Charles F. Adams, *Three Episodes of Massachusetts History* (rev. ed., 1892), 55–57, 65–66, 73, 76–79; Phinehas Pratt, "A Declaration of the Affairs of the English People That First Inhabited New England" [1662], *Collections of the Massachusetts Historical Society*, 4th ser., IV (1858), 479–87.

22. Young, *Chronicles*, 331–32, 339; Adams, *Three Episodes*, 92–93, 97, 99; Bunker, *Pilgrims*, 328–30.

23. Ibid., chaps. 7, 9, 139–40; Bradford, *Plymouth*, 138.

24. Ibid., 127–30, 132; Willison, *Saints*, 446–50. On the "great cheer" at Bradford's wedding feast, see Emmanuel Altham's report, in Sydney V. James, Jr., ed., *Three Visitors to Early Plymouth* (Plymouth, Mass., 1963), 29–30.

25. Bradford, *Plymouth*, 133, 142–44, 148ff, 165, 167, 168, 373–74. Bradford indicates that Oldham brought with him his wife "and family" (157). Details on Oldham's and Lyford's backgrounds and careers are in Anderson, *Immigrants*, II, 1350–53 and 1214–17.

26. John Smith, in his description of the colony, probably based on information Winslow brought back to England late in 1623, summarized here, estimated the value of Plymouth's goods at hand at £500 and noted that the community still lived "as one family or household, yet every man followeth his trade and profession both by sea and land." John Smith, *The Generall Historie of Virginia, New-England, and the Summer Isles . . .* (London, 1624), in Smith, *Works*, II, 472. Altham, writing from Plymouth in September 1623, estimated only twenty houses but otherwise agreed with Smith's description (*Three Visitors*, 24). McIntyre, *Debts*, 49, 50; Langdon, *Pilgrim Colony*, 36; Bradford, *Plymouth*, 193n, 140–41, 180. For an extended discussion of the housing in Plymouth—the initial pit or cave houses, the predominant, small, simple "earthfast" dwellings, impermanent and fragile, typical of rural England, see Deetz and Deetz, *Times of Their Lives*, chaps. 5, 4.

27. Young, *Chronicles*, 373–74.

28. Adams, *Three Episodes*, 162, 168, 163, 169, 171, 177, 182; Bradford, *Plymouth*, 205–6; *Governor Bradford's Letter Book* (Boston, 1906), 41.

29. Adams, *Three Episodes*, chap. 8; Bradford, *Plymouth*, 208–9; Bradford, *Letter Book*, 42–43; Thomas Morton, *New English Canaan, or New Canaan* . . . (Amsterdam, 1637), reprinted in *Publications of the Prince Society*, XIV (Boston, 1883), 284, 286–87. Michael Zuckerman, in "Pilgrims in the Wilderness: Community, Modernity, and the Maypole at Merry Mount," *NEQ*, 50 (1977), 255–77, argues that Morton and his Merrymount crew have been misinterpreted as a result of the Pilgrims' animus against them. Morton, Zuckerman claims, a nature lover, simply delighted in the "sensual splendor" of the New England landscape, believed that the Indians were innocents, "full of humanity," and sought to share food, drink, and sex with them. That frightened the Pilgrims, who "could not countenance carnal pleasure for its own sake," evoking their fear that intimate association with the natives "would weaken the discipline they maintained so tenuously over their own impulses." For another sympathetic view of Morton, based on his intercultural familiarity with the Indians, see Van Zandt, *Brothers Among Nations*, 96–97.

30. Bradford, *Letter Book*, 17, 18, 19, 1; Bradford, *Plymouth*, 374.

31. McIntyre, *Debts*, 31–32, 47, 48; Bradford, *Letter Book*, 4, 9, 6, 21–22, 45, 50; Bradford, *Plymouth*, 382; Stratton, *Plymouth Colony*, 47, 40, App. F.

32. Bradford, *Letter Book*, 50, 45; Stratton, *Plymouth Colony*, 38, 246, 324; Young, *Chronicles*, 481, 483n, 73n.

33. Willison, *Saints*, 454.

34. Bradford, *Plymouth*, 210–11; Gura, *Sion's Glory*, 39–40; Willison, *Saints*, 346; Stratton, *Plymouth Colony*, 353, 42.

35. Bradford, *Plymouth*, 257; Winthrop, *Journal*, 82, 50; Willison, *Saints*, 349; Gura, *Sion's Glory*, 40–41.

36. Willison, *Saints*, 355; Bradford, *Plymouth*, 293, 313; MHS, ed., Bradford, *History*, II, 302.

37. Nathaniel B. Shurtleff, ed., *Records of the Colony of New Plymouth in New England . . . Court Orders*, vol. I, *1633–1640* (Boston, 1855), 177, 97; Deetz and Deetz, *Times of Their Lives*, chaps. 3, 4; Stratton, *Plymouth Colony*, 245; Bradford, *Plymouth*, 316, 320–21.

38. Stratton, *Plymouth Colony*, App. G; McIntyre, *Debts*, 47; John Demos, *A Little Commonwealth: Family Life in Plymouth Colony* (New York, 1970), 9, 11n; Dorothy Wentworth, *Settlement and Growth of Duxbury, 1628–1870* (Duxbury, Mass., 1973), 4; Stratton, *Plymouth Colony*, 58ff.

39. Bunker, *Pilgrims*, 301; Bradford, *Plymouth*, 253, 254, 333–34.

40. *Historical Statistics of the United States, Colonial Times to 1970* (Washington, D.C., 1975), II, 1168; John Demos, "Notes on Life in Plymouth Colony," *WMQ*, 22 (1965), 269–71; Demos, *Little Commonwealth*, 192, 193, tables I, II, III.

41. Bradford, *Plymouth*, 33n; Mark L. Sargent, "William Bradford's 'Dialogue' with History," *NEQ*, 65 (1992), 396–97.

42. William Bradford, "A Dialogue or 3d Conference," *Proceedings of the Massachusetts Historical Society*, [XI] (1869–70), 465–82; Smith, *Bradford*, 300–4.

43. Bradford, *Plymouth*, xxviii; Isidore S. Meyer, "The Hebrew Preface to Bradford's History of the Plymouth Plantation," *Publications of the Jewish Historical Society*, 38 (1948–49), 296–303. For a full account of Bradford's Hebrew studies, see Meyer, *The Hebrew Exercises of Governor William Bradford* (Plymouth, Mass., 1973).

44. Young, *Chronicles*, 414–58, quotations at 414; *Publications of the Colonial Society of Massachusetts*, XXII (1920), 115–41. For the complicated provenance and bibliography of the Dialogue, see Sargent, "Bradford's Dialogue," 391n.

45. Ibid., 390; Young, *Chronicles*, 457, 415.

46. Ibid., 415–17, 421, 422, 427–32, 436–40, 457; Bradford, *Plymouth*, 171–72 (cf. Winslow, *Hypocrisie*, 93–98); David S. Lovejoy, *Religious Enthusiasm in the New World: Heresy to Revolution* (Cambridge, Mass., 1985), 48–61.

47. Bradford, "A Dialogue or 3d Conference," 407–64, quotations at 420, 421, 423, 424, 428, 452, 464.

The New-English Sionists: Fault Lines, Diversity, and Persecution

1. For a summary of statistical estimates of English emigration in the seventeenth century, see Nicholas Canny, "English Migration into and Across the Atlantic During the Seventeenth and Eighteenth Centuries," in Canny, ed., *Europeans on the Move ... 1500–1800* (Oxford, England, 1994), 54–56, 64. The first figure of the size of the migration to New England was that of the contemporary, Edward Johnson, in his *Wonder-working Providence of Sion's Saviour in New England* [London, 1653] (J. Franklin Jameson, ed., New York, 1910), 58. His estimate of 21,200 "or thereabout" arrivals in New England 1628–43 in 298 ships (corrected to 198 ships, 61) is undoubtedly too high. Richard Archer, "New England Mosaic: A Demographic Analysis for the Seventeenth Century," *WMQ*, 47 (1990), 478, working with the standard genealogical listings, finds records for 9,314 migrants before 1650 and 4,981 who were either migrants to New England or were born there, hence a maximum of 14,295 to 1650. Robert C. Anderson, "A Note on the Changing Pace of the Great Migration," *NEQ*, 59 (1986), 407, based on his own exhaustive genealogical study, in progress (eleven volumes to date: *The Pilgrim Migration: Immigrants to Plymouth Colony 1620–1633* [Boston, 2004]; *The Great Migration Begins: Immigrants to New England 1620–1633* [3 vols., Boston, 1995]; *The Great Migration: Immigrants to New England 1634–1635* [7 vols., Boston, 1995–2011, vols. 1 and 2 in collaboration with George F. Sanborn, Jr., and Melinda L. Sanborn]) estimates 2,500 before 1634 and "somewhere between 15,000 and 20,000" in 1634–40. Virginia D. Anderson, *New England's Generation: The Great Migration and the Formation of Society and Culture in the Seventeenth Century* (Cambridge, England, 1991), 15, estimates "13,000 men, women, and children."

2. For a summary of the question and a forceful argument in favor of primary religious motivation, see Virginia D. Anderson, "Migrants and Motives: Religion and the Settlement of New England, 1630–1640," *NEQ*, 58 (1985), 339–83 (followed by discussion with David G. Allen, ibid., 59 [1986], 408–24), and her *New England's Generation*, 37–46. For a contrary view, see David Cressy, *Coming Over: Migration and Communication Between England and New England in the Seventeenth Century* (Cambridge, England, 1987), esp. chap. 3.

3. Janice Knight, *Orthodoxies in Massachusetts: Rereading American Puritanism* (Cambridge, Mass., 1994), 30. V. Anderson, *New England's Generation*, 39.

4. R. Anderson, *Great Migration Begins*, II, 1105; James Savage, *Genealogical Dic-*

tionary of the First Settlers of New England ... [Boston, 1860–62] (Baltimore, Md., 1965), II, 157; Thomas Hutchinson, *The History of the Colony and Province of Massachusetts-Bay* (Lawrence S. Mayo, ed., 3 vols., Cambridge, Mass., 1936), I, 409; Alexander Young, *Chronicles of the First Planters of the Colony of Massachusetts Bay* ... (Boston, 1846), 317, 106; Michael J. Canavan, "Isaac Johnson, Esquire, the Founder of Boston," *Publications of the Colonial Society of Massachusetts*, XXVII (*Transactions*, 1927–1930), 272–85; Charles E. Banks, *The Planters of the Commonwealth* (1930; Baltimore, Md., 1979), 109–10; Winthrop, *Journal*, 323.

5. Robert S. Moody, comp., *The Saltonstall Papers, 1607–1815*, in *Collections of the Massachusetts Historical Society*, 80–81 [1972–74]), I, 3–8; Robert Brenner, *Merchants and Revolution ... 1550–1653* (Princeton, N.J., 1993), 135–40, 150.

6. Banks, *Planters*, 161; J. H. Adamson and H. F. Folland, *Sir Harry Vane* ... (Boston, 1973), chaps. 4, 5; James K. Hosmer, *The Life of Young Sir Harry Vane* ... (Boston, 1889), pt. 1.

7. Winthrop, *Journal*, 120; Francis J. Bremer, *John Winthrop, America's Forgotten Founding Father* (Oxford, England, 2003), 255–59; Hutchinson, *History*, I, App. II.

8. Ibid., App. III.

9. Alison Games, *Migration and the Origins of the English Atlantic World* (Cambridge, Mass., 1999), 136; Karen O. Kupperman, *Providence Island, 1630–1641: The Other Puritan Colony* (Cambridge, England, 1993), 265–66, chap. 6. For Winthrop's bitter rebuke to Lord Saye and Sele and others for their efforts to divert settlers from Massachusetts to Providence Island, and for Saye and Sele's equally bitter, rambling reply denying that God had intended only Massachusetts as a refuge for His people, see Winthrop, *Journal*, 323–25; *Winthrop Papers, 1498–1654* (Boston, 1929), IV, 263–67.

10. The appeal to people of high status continued, however fruitlessly. Thus John Masters, a settler in Watertown, Massachusetts, wrote the pious and distressed Lady Joan Barrington (see p. 396), who was deeply devoted to the Puritan cause, and her son Thomas, of the excellence of New England's bounty, urging them "or any of yours" to come to the colony; it was a land, he said, "fitt to receive lords and ladies," though more houses were needed. The land was there, the water, the "good creatures to hunt and to hawke, and for fowling and fishing, and more also our natures to refresh in." And he pointed out that Sir Richard Saltonstall's family was there, investing in the development of the land. But if the Barringtons themselves were tempted, they gave no sign of it. Similarly uninterested in migrating was Lady Joan's youngest son, John, who was casting about for suitable employment. A possible involvement in New England seems to have been proposed to him, but that, he wrote his mother, was something "I do utterly dislike." Arthur Searle, ed., *Barrington Family Letters, 1628–1632* (London, 1983), 183, 122, 168. There is a rather wistful mention by Cotton Mather that Sir William Constable, the future regicide, Parliamentary leader, and successful military commander, and Sir Matthew Boynton would have accompanied Ezekiel Rogers from Yorkshire to New England "if some singular Providences had not hindred them." Cotton Mather, *Magnalia Christi Americana* ... [London, 1702] (facsimile ed., New York, 1972), III, 102. Thomas Hutchinson had heard that various "persons of figure and distinction" had been expected to come over, among them Pym, Hampden, Sir Arthur Haslerigg, Oliver Cromwell "&c," some of whom had been prevented "by express order of the King." *History*, I, 38–39.

11. Richard S. Dunn, "Experiments Holy and Unholy, 1630–1," in K. R. Andrews et al., eds., *The Westward Enterprise* ... (Liverpool, England, 1978), 283; Banks, *Planters*, 65–92; Young, *Chronicles*, 311–12; R. Anderson, "Note on the Changing Pace"; Darrett B. Rutman, *Winthrop's Boston* ... *1630–1649* (Chapel Hill, N.C., 1965), 25–28, 36–37, 178–79; Frank Thistlethwaite, *Dorset Pilgrims* ... (London, 1989), 80–82; Cressy, *Coming Over*, chap 8; David G. Allen, *In English Ways* ... (Chapel Hill, N.C., 1981), 221–22; John Farmer, ed., *Governor Thomas Dudley's Letter to the Countess of Lincoln, March, 1631*, in Peter Force, comp., *Tracts and Other Papers Relating Principally to ... the Colonies in North America* ... (Washington, D.C., 1836–46), I, no. 4, 9, 10.

12. Allen, *English Ways*, 8, 14–18.

13. East Anglia, for Roger Thompson, in *Mobility and Migration: East Anglian Founders of New England, 1629–1640* (Amherst, Mass., 1994), 14, is "Greater East Anglia," which includes five counties: Lincolnshire, Norfolk, Suffolk, Cambridgeshire, and Essex. For N. C. P. Tyack, "Migration from East Anglia to New England before 1660" (Ph.D. diss., University of London, 1951), East Anglia is only Essex, Suffolk, and Norfolk. For Allen, *English Ways*, xvi, East Anglia includes Norfolk, Suffolk, Essex, and Hertfordshire. The usage here will vary according to context, but will be specified where there is any doubt.

14. Rutman, *Winthrop's Boston*, 136–38; Tyack, "Migration," 50–51; Cressy, *Coming Over*, 132–33; Charles E. Banks, *The Winthrop Fleet of 1630* ... (Boston, 1930), 50–51; Thistlethwaite, *Dorset Pilgrims*, chaps. 1–4; Frances Rose-Troup, *John White* ... (New York, 1930), chaps. 6–16.

15. Rutman, *Winthrop's Boston*, 138; Games, *Migration*, 28–29 (table 1.4); Archer, "New England Mosaic," 483.

16. Allen, *English Ways*, 14–18; Joan Thirsk, "The Farming Regions of England," in Thirsk, ed., *The Agrarian History of England and Wales*, IV (Cambridge, England, 1967), 2–10, 15.

17. Lawrence Stone, *The Causes of the English Revolution, 1529–1642* (London, 1972), 106; Alan Everitt, *Change in the Provinces: The Seventeenth Century* (Alan Everitt, ed., Department of English Local History, *Occasional Papers*, 2nd ser., no. 1, Leicester, England, 1969), 7, 48, 30, 10; Ann Hughes, "Local History and the Origins of the Civil War," in Richard Cust and Ann Hughes, eds., *Conflict in Early Stuart England* (London, 1989), 235, 230, 229, 233; Alan Macfarlane, *Reconstructing Historical Communities* (Cambridge, England, 1977), 11–13, 18, 19.

18. Thirsk, "Farming Regions," 41, 45–47, 53, 65, 9, 14, 15.

19. Ibid., 64–65, 68, 72–73, 78–79.

20. Ibid., 21, 28–33, 38, 46, 47, 200; Allen, *English Ways*, 19; Thirsk, "Farming Regions," 34, 36–39.

21. Thompson, *Mobility*, 98–100.

22. Tyack, "Migration," chaps. 5, 6, quotations at 101, 157. ("The great outpouring from Essex and Suffolk, particularly between 1631 and 1636, was in large measure the outcome of East Anglia's agrarian problems, particularly the agrarian depression of 1629, 1630, and 1631 ... [Yet there was] in all three counties a broad stability in the structure of rural society and in the distribution of land during the first half of the seventeenth century," 185–86). Thompson, *Mobility*, 23 and chap. 5.

23. William Haller, *The Rise of Puritanism* . . . (New York, 1938), 15, 19, 20, 23, 25, 35–36; G. R. Elton, *England Under the Tudors* (London, 1955), 310–11.

24. Ibid., 307–8; Haller, *Rise*, 9, 14, 19.

25. Ibid., 12–13, 35ff., 42–43; Elton, *England*, 458, 313, 310. For the imprisonment in Norfolk in 1612 of one William Sayer for remarks deemed heretical, a case that "stands out as a first flash of lightning in the storm that was brewing in the Norwich diocese between Puritans and episcopal authority," and for similar imprisonments of obscure dissidents—impoverished weavers and dyers—which "were the first mumblings of a religious storm in East Anglia that undoubtedly in later years drove many to seek shelter in New England," see Tyack, "Migration," 242–44.

26. Ibid., 244ff., 249, 272, 257–58, 262; M. M. Knappen, *Tudor Puritanism* . . . (Chicago, 1939), 219, 470–72; Haller, *Rise*, 40. On Laud and the lecturers, see Paul S. Seaver, *The Puritan Lectureships* . . . *1560–1662* (Stanford, Calif., 1970), chap. 8; H. R. Trevor-Roper, *Archbishop Laud, 1573–1645* (London, 1940), 106–7.

27. Ibid., 81, 104, 106–9; Francis J. Bremer, *Congregational Communion: Clerical Friendship in the Anglo-American Puritan Community, 1610–1692* (Boston, 1994), 83–84.

28. Trevor-Roper, *Laud*, 119; Haller, *Rise*, 20, 230–31, 262; Bremer, *Communion*, 82–91. Thus John Davenport, who considered himself well within the church in his views, believed that he had been driven into nonconformity by Laud's and the High Commission's pressure on such technical points as standing rather than kneeling at communion and insisted on his absolute loyalty to the state and his orthodoxy in opposing heresies, schisms, and "all sectaries, as Familists, Anabaptists, and Brownists." Isabel M. Calder, ed., *Letters of John Davenport, Puritan Divine* (New Haven, Conn., 1937), 41 [hereafter: Davenport, *Letters*].

29. Bremer, *Communion*, 83–86; William Hunt, *The Puritan Moment: The Coming of the Revolution in an English County* (Cambridge, Mass., 1983), 109.

30. Bremer, *Communion*, 87–88; Kenneth W. Shipps, "The Puritan Emigration to New England: A New Source on Motivation," *New England Historical and Genealogical Register*, 135 (1981), 90; "An Abstract of the Metropolitan Visitation . . . 1635" [of Norwich, Peterborough, Lichfield, Worcester, Gloucester, Winchester, and Chichester], in John Bruce, ed., *Calendar of State Papers, Domestic Series* . . . *1635* (London, 1865), xxx–xlv [hereafter: *CSP, Dom, 1635*]; Tyack, "Migration," 303.

31. *CSP, Dom, 1635*, 489; Allen, *English Ways*, 192–93. In a personal communication, Mark Peterson, author of the *American National Biography* [*ANB*] sketch of Chauncy, explains that Chauncy served first in Marston St. Lawrence, then went to Ware, where he was first charged by the High Commission, and returned to Marston, where he was finally suspended, mainly because he objected to installing rails around the altar and to kneeling at communion. He recanted but continued to preach secretly as well as officially until he departed for New England.

32. Haller, *Rise*, 35–38; Hunt, *Puritan Moment*, 110–11, 254; Mather, *Magnalia*, III, 59; Bremer, *Communion*, 39–40; David D. Hall, *The Faithful Shepherd* . . . (Chapel Hill, N.C., 1972), 51–52, 65; John Bruce, ed., *Calendar of State Papers, Domestic Series* . . . *1633–1634* (London, 1863), 450. For details on the fortunes of the Rogers-Ward network, see Tyack, "Migration," 248–55, 260. The funeral of the charismatic John Rogers was a sensational, apparently a providential, event in the regional history of Puritan-

ism. At Rogers's funeral, Emmanuel Downing reported to Winthrop, "there were more people than 3 such churches could hold: the gallery was soe over loaden with people that it sunck and crackt and in the midle where it was joynted the tymbers gaped and parted on[e] from an other soe that there was a great cry in the church: they under the gallery fearing to be smothered, those that were upon it hasted of[f], some on[e] way some an other, and some leaped downe among the people into the church: those in the body of the church seing the tymbers gape were sore afrighted, but it pleased God to honour that good man departed with a miracle at his death, for the gallerie stood . . . had it faln as blackfryers did under the popish assembly, it would have ben a great wound to our religion." Downing to Winthrop, Mar. 6, 1637, *Collections of the Massachusetts Historical Society*, 4th ser., VI (1861), 47.

33. Hunt, *Puritan Moment*, 196–97, 254; Frank Shuffelton, *Thomas Hooker, 1586–1647* (Princeton, N.J., 1977), 73–74, 125; Mather, *Magnalia*, III, 59.

34. Tyack, "Migration," 256–57, 260–61, 290–92, 297, 307, 353; Trevor-Roper, *Laud*, 260; Hunt, *Puritan Moment*, 253–57; Shuffelton, *Hooker*, 128–30; Richard W. Cogley, *John Eliot's Mission to the Indians before King Philip's War* (Cambridge, Mass., 1999), 45; Bremer, *Communion*, 94–95, 97–98.

35. Hunt, *Puritan Moment*, 257, 253; Allen, *English Ways*, 166–67; Bremer, *Communion*, 88–90, 96; Davenport, *Letters*, 33–38 (on Davenport, in this connection, see Knight, *Orthodoxies*, 45ff.); Rose-Troup, *White*, chap. 23, 302; Thistlethwaite, *Dorset Pilgrims*, 31; Johnson, *Wonder-Working Providence*, 136; Michael McGiffert, ed., *God's Plot: Puritan Spirituality in Thomas Shepard's Cambridge* [1972] (Amherst, Mass., 1994), 50.

36. Ibid., 51n, 53, 57, 58.

37. Shipps, "Puritan Emigration"; Hunt, *Puritan Moment*, 120; *Winthrop Papers*, II, 163. Estimates of the number of clerics who emigrated: Samuel E. Morison, *The Founding of Harvard College* (Cambridge, Mass., 1935), 360, lists ninety-eight who had had university training in Europe; Waterhouse, "Reluctant Emigrants: The English Background of the First Generation of the New England Puritan Clergy," *Historical Magazine of the Protestant Episcopal Church*, 44 (1975), finds seventy-six who had been ordained in the Church of England, twenty-seven who had not been ordained but who had had appropriate clerical education at Oxford or Cambridge and became Puritan ministers, and ten others who had had neither qualification but who were ministers in New England in any case. Allen, *English Ways*, 13, relying on Frederick L. Weis, *The Colonial Clergy and the Colonial Churches of New England* (Lancaster, Mass., 1936), lists 129. Waterhouse finds that of the seventy-six who had been ordained in the Church, sixty-eight survived to the outbreak of the Civil War, and of those, twenty-six (38 percent) returned. Susan Hardman Moore, in her *Pilgrims: New World Settlers and the Call of Home* (New Haven, Conn., 2007), identifies seventy-six ministers who came to New England in the 1630s; of the seventy who survived to 1640, twenty-five (36 percent) returned (22, 55). The criteria of choice in her extended list, App. 3, are not clear. In her discussion of remigration in general (55–56) she writes that one in four or one in six of the settlers returned to England, depending on whether the total migration is best calculated at thirteen thousand or twenty-one thousand. For other discussions of remigration see William L. Sachse, "The Migration of New Englanders to England, 1640–1660," *American Historical Review*, 53 (1947–48), 251–78, and Harry Stout, "The Morphology of Remigration . . . ," *Journal of American Studies*, 10 (1976), 151–72.

38. Waterhouse, "Reluctant Emigrants," 484; Tyack, "Migration," 344. Rogers's remarkable will—an elegy for the Puritans' original, defiant faith and a lamentation for the "base opinions" and "evil fashions" that had overtaken the purity of New England's life by the 1660s—centers on the "three special blessings" of his life: the education he received from his father, Richard; the capture of his soul by Christ in the course of a near-fatal illness; and his calling to be a minister of the Gospel, "the most glorious calling in the world." Henry F. Waters, *Genealogical Gleanings in England* (Boston, 1885–89), II, 227.

39. Increase Mather, *The Life and Death of That Reverend Man of God, Mr. Richard Mather* . . . [Cambridge, Mass., 1670] (facsimile ed., Benjamin Franklin V and William K. Bottorff, eds., Athens, Ohio, 1966), 12–19; specific page references to Foxe are at p. 14, where Mather quotes the letter Bradford wrote to "a godly couple, Erkinalde Rawlins and his Wife." George Townsend, ed., *The Acts and Monuments of John Foxe* . . . (London, 1843–49), VII, 212–14.

40. B. R. Burg, *Richard Mather* (Boston, 1982), 13–14; Allen, *English Ways*, 171; Games, *Migration*, 63, 72; Mather, *Magnalia*, III, 59.

41. Knight, *Orthodoxies*, 31.

42. Except where otherwise cited, biographical information on Cotton is drawn from Larzer Ziff, *The Career of John Cotton* . . . (Princeton, N.J., 1962); Ziff's edition of Cotton's writings, *John Cotton and the Churches of New England* (Cambridge, Mass., 1968); Sargent Bush, Jr., ed., *The Correspondence of John Cotton* (Chapel Hill, N.C., 2001), esp. Introduction; Knight, *Orthodoxies*, passim, esp. 37ff.; and "John Cotton's Life and Letters," in Young, *Chronicles*, 417–44.

43. The affection with Christ, Cotton wrote, was like that between husband and wife. When you come to the congregation, he asked rhetorically, do you have "a strong and hearty desire to meet him in the bed of loves . . . and desire you to have the seeds of his grace shed abroad in your hearts, and bring forth the fruit of grace to him, and desire that you may be for him and for none other?" Knight, *Orthodoxies*, 116.

44. Ibid., 19, 45; Ziff, *Cotton*, 44; Charles M. Andrews, *The Colonial Period of American History* (New Haven, Conn., 1934–38), I, 366–67. In his memoir of Cotton, *Abel Being Dead, Yet Speaketh* . . . (London, 1658), the Rev. John Norton, Cotton's successor in the Boston church, wrote that "according to report," King James himself, despite his opposition to nonconformity, having been informed of Cotton's "great learning and worth," allowed him to "have his liberty without interruption in his ministry." Enoch Pond, ed., *Memoir of John Cotton by John Norton* (New York, 1842), 39.

45. Ziff, *Cotton*, 67. On Leverett and Hough, among Cotton's prominent connections: R. Anderson, *Great Migration Begins*, II, 1175–78, 1005–10. Cotton's account of his reasons for emigrating, written a year after his arrival in New England and stressing "our Saviour's warrant . . . that when we are distressed in our course in one country (*ne quid dicam gravius*) we should flee to another" and suggesting that in New England people like Hooker and himself might provide much more service to their people than they could "in prison (especially in close prison, which was feared)"—arguments both different from and similar to those of Mather—is in Young, *Chronicles*, 438–44. For his letter of resignation to the Bishop of Lincoln, May 7, 1633, written with apparent sadness: Bush, ed., *Cotton Correspondence*, 178–80.

46. George H. Williams et al., eds., *Thomas Hooker: Writings in England and Holland, 1626–1633 (Harvard Theological Studies,* XXVIII, Cambridge, Mass., 1975), 17–18; Shuffelton, *Hooker,* 156–57; Bush, ed., *Cotton Correspondence,* 181–88.

47. Biographical information on Hooker, unless otherwise cited, is from Shuffelton, *Hooker;* Williams et al., eds., *Hooker: Writings;* and Knight, *Orthodoxies.*

48. Shuffelton, *Hooker,* 23–25.

49. The difference between Hooker's procedures in seeking to alleviate the soul-killing melancholy of this distressed woman fearful of damnation, and Roger Williams's efforts with the equally afflicted Lady Joan Barrington (see p. 396) is striking. The contrast anticipates the differences in the major phases of the two clerics' later careers in New England.

50. Shuffelton, *Hooker,* chap. 2; Norman Pettit, *The Heart Prepared: Grace and Conversion in Puritan Spiritual Life* (New Haven, Conn., 1966), 87–101.

51. Bremer, *Communion,* 94–98; Shuffelton, *Hooker,* chap. 4, quotation at 156.

52. Hall, *Shepherd,* 78; Bremer, *Communion,* 104, 107–8.

53. Ibid., chaps. 1–4; on Davenport, ibid., 89–92, Knight, *Orthodoxies,* 45ff.; on Wheelwright, Emery Battis, *Saints and Sectaries . . .* (Chapel Hill, N.C., 1962), 110–14; on Wilson, sketch by Francis J. Bremer in *American National Biography* [ANB].

54. Hall, *Shepherd,* 79–80, 89; Allen, *English Ways,* 171–74; Thompson, *Mobility,* 188; David S. Lovejoy, *Religious Enthusiasm in the New World: Heresy to Revolution* (Cambridge, Mass., 1985), 62–63; Philip F. Gura, *A Glimpse of Sion's Glory . . .* (Middletown, Conn., 1984), 40–41, 164–65, 188–92, chap. 10; *Correspondence of Roger Williams,* ed. Glenn LaFantasie (Providence, R.I., 1988), I, 2–7; Hunt, *Puritan Moment,* 222–33; Ola E. Winslow, *Master Roger Williams* (New York, 1957), 81–83; *Barrington Letters,* 63–68, 15, 19; Arthur Searle, "'Overmuch Liberty': Roger Williams in Essex," *Essex Journal,* 3 (1968), 85–92; "Master John Cotton's Answer to Master Roger Williams," ed. J. Lewis Diman, in *Publications of the Narragansett Club,* 1st ser., 2 (1867), 14.

Williams was not one to retreat silently when rebuked. "Woe unto me if I hold my peace," he wrote relentlessly to the distressed Lady Barrington, "and hide that from you which [though it] may seeme bitter at present, it may be sweeter then hon[e]y in the latter end." LaFantasie, ed., *Correspondence of Roger Williams,* 5.

In later years Williams must have encountered his first love (Lady Barrington's niece, Joan Whalley) again since she and her husband, Rev. William Hooke, emigrated to New England in the late 1630s, to return to England in 1656, when Cromwell appointed Hooke his chaplain. James Savage, *A Genealogical Dictionary of the First Settlers of New England . . .* ([1860–62], Baltimore, Md., 1965), II, 458.

55. Superseding all of the many biographical studies of Winthrop is Francis J. Bremer, *John Winthrop: America's Forgotten Founding Father* (Oxford, England, 2003). Bremer's earlier summary of the family's religious culture and the context of Winthrop's decision to emigrate—"The Heritage of John Winthrop: Religion Along the Stour Valley, 1548–1630," *NEQ,* 70 (1997), 515–47—is fully amplified in the book. Bremer, *Winthrop,* chaps. 7, 8; *Winthrop Papers,* II, 106–149.

56. Bremer, *Winthrop,* chaps. 7, 8; *Winthrop Papers,* II, 106–49.

57. Bremer, *Winthrop,* 175ff.; *Winthrop Papers,* II, 282–95 (text of Winthrop's "Model of Christian Charity"), quotations at 283, 293.

58. Bremer, *Winthrop*, 103–4, 169, 200.

59. Walter W. Woodward, *Prospero's America: John Winthrop Jr., Alchemy, and the Creation of New England Culture, 1606–1676* (Chapel Hill, N.C., 2010), 36, 43, 52–53, chap. 6; Richard S. Dunn, *Puritans and Yankees: The Winthrop Dynasty of New England, 1630–1717* (Princeton, N.J., 1962), 62.

60. Young, *Chronicles*, 304n; Rutman, *Winthrop's Boston*, 25; Morgan, *Puritan Dilemma*, 87, 103. Details on officeholding in this and subsequent paragraphs: Robert E. Wall, *The Membership of the Massachusetts Bay General Court, 1630–1686* (New York, 1990); Michael P. Winship, *Making Heretics: Militant Protestantism and Free Grace in Massachusetts, 1636–1641* (Princeton, N.J., 2002), 137.

61. Savage, *Dictionary*, I, 161; Wall, *Membership*, 161–63; sketch of Bellingham by William Pencak in *ANB*; Winthrop, *Journal*, 131, 367; R. Anderson, *Great Migration*, I, 243–50.

62. Joseph H. Smith, ed., *Colonial Justice . . . The Pynchon Court Record . . .* (Cambridge, Mass., 1961), 6–7; Stephen Innes, *Labor in a New Land . . . Seventeenth-Century Springfield* (Princeton, N.J., 1983), [3]; John F. Martin, *Profits in the Wilderness . . .* (Chapel Hill, N.C., 1991), 47–52; R. Anderson, *Great Migration Begins*, III, 1536–38; Gura, *Sion's Glory*, chap. 11; Samuel E. Morison, *William Pynchon . . .* (Boston, Mass., 1932), 39.

63. Wall, *Membership*, 210–12; R. Anderson, *Great Migration Begins*, I, 395–401; *Winthrop Papers*, III, 22.

64. Wall, *Membership*, 549–50; Charles M. Calder, "Alderman John Vassall and His Descendants," *New England Historical and Genealogical Register*, 109 (1955), 94–95; Games, *Migration*, 86, 205; Winthrop, *Journal*, 624, 709.

65. Banks, *Planters*, 113; Wall, *Membership*, 362–64; Battis, *Saints and Sectaries*, chaps. 1, 2, 4, and genealogical chart [16]; Bernard Bailyn, *The New England Merchants in the Seventeenth Century* (Cambridge, Mass., 1955), 35, 40, 88–90; R. Anderson, *Great Migration*, III, 477–84.

66. Bailyn, "The *Apologia* of Robert Keayne," *WMQ*, 7 (1950), 568–72; Helle M. Alpert, "Robert Keayne: Notes of Sermons . . ." (Ph.D. diss., Tufts University, 1974), 381; Bailyn, *Merchants*, 35–37, 29, and illustration of Cheapside-Cornhill district, following 130; Stephen Innes, *Creating the Commonwealth: The Economic Culture of Puritan New England* (New York, 1995), chap. 4.

67. Thistlethwaite, *Dorset Pilgrims*, 34ff.

68. R. Anderson, *Great Migration Begins*, I, 645, 456; Morgan, *Puritan Dilemma*, 86–87, 102–3; Andrews, *Colonial Period*, I, 414–15; Clifford K. Shipton, *Roger Conant . . .* (Cambridge, Mass., 1944), 8; William Bradford, *Of Plymouth Plantation (1620–1647)* (Samuel E. Morison, ed., New York, 1952), 146.

69. Thistlethwaite, *Dorset Pilgrims*, 78ff., 100–2; Winthrop, *Journal*, 66–67, 174; John M. Taylor, *Roger Ludlow, the Colonial Lawmaker* (New York, 1900), chaps. 6–16.

70. Thistlethwaite, *Dorset Pilgrims*, 211–16, 99.

71. For discussion of the Winthrop group's circular letter to prominent divines seeking their help "to judge of the persons and corses of such of their brethren of the Ministery whom we shall desire to single out for this employ" (*Winthrop Papers*, II, 163–64), see Darren Staloff, *The Making of an American Thinking Class* (New York, 1998), 18.

72. Battis, *Saints and Sectaries*, chaps. 3–5.

73. Knight, *Orthodoxies*, 44–45; R. Anderson, *Great Migration Begins*, II, 1005–10; Anderson, *Great Migration*, III, 221–25; Thompson, *Mobility*, 165, 200, 186–89; Winthrop, *Journal*, 194n. On the interesting case of the Harlakendens, see Macfarlane, *Historical Communities*, 143–48; Macfarlane, *The Family Life of Ralph Josselin, a Seventeenth-Century Clergyman* ... (Cambridge, England, 1970), passim; Games, *Migration*, 45–46.

74. Thompson, *Mobility*, 188–89, 199–200, 261; Allen, *English Ways*, 169–80; John J. Waters, "Hingham, Massachusetts, 1631–1661 ... ," *Journal of Social History*, 1 (1967–68), 351ff.

75. Games, *Migration*, 56–57.

76. Thompson, *Mobility*, table 27 (190–96), 200–201; Games, *Migration*, 53–54.

77. V. Anderson, *New England's Generation*, 24–25, tables 2–4 (222–23), 23; Peter Laslett and Richard Wall, eds., *Household and Family in Past Time* ... (Cambridge, England, 1972), 152; Ann Kussmaul, *Servants in Husbandry in Early Modern England* (Cambridge, England, 1981), chaps. 1, 2. Cf. Michael L. Fickes, ". . . The Captivity of Pequout Women and Children . . . ," *NEQ*, 73 (2000), 64.

78. Games, *Migration*, tables 1.1, 2.1, 2.4, 2.3, p. 53.

79. Archer, "New England's Mosaic," 481.

80. Kenneth A. Lockridge, *Literacy in Colonial New England* (New York, 1974), 13; David Cressy, *Literacy and the Social Order: Reading and Writing in Tudor and Stuart England* (Cambridge, England, 1980), 72, 183; Cressy, *Coming Over*, 217, 98n; Samuel E. Morison, *The Intellectual Life of Colonial New England* (New York, 1956), 85.

81. Morison, *Founding*, App. B; Harry S. Stout, "University Men in New England, 1620–1660: A Demographic Analysis," *Journal of Interdisciplinary History*, 4 (1974), 377.

Lawrence Stone ("Literacy and Education in England 1640–1900," *Past and Present*, 28 [July 1964], 54) estimates that between 1600 and 1630 approximately 30,100 Englishmen entered Oxford, Cambridge, the Inns of Court, or foreign universities. If all survived to 1630, or if the deaths were balanced by survivors of earlier years, in a population of 5 million (or 1,052,632 families of mean size 4.75 (Laslett and Wall, eds., *Household and Family*, table 1.6), there would have been one man of higher education for every thirty-five families. These figures are of course crude, perhaps only informed guesses. But they do provide at least a very rough measure of the high incidence of well-educated men among the migrants of the 1630s—a phenomenon unique among the settlement colonies in the western hemisphere.

82. Waterhouse, "Reluctant Emigrants," 481; Morison, *Founding*, 89–91, 113–15 (for the text of Wilson's Latin elegy to John Harvard, 224–25); Morison, *Harvard in the Seventeenth Century*, I, 320–21; Mather, *Magnalia*, III, 42; Edmund S. Morgan, *Roger Williams: The Church and the State* (New York, 1967), 4.

CHAPTER 13

Abrasions, Utopians, and Holy War

1. Darrett B. Rutman, *Winthrop's Boston: Portrait of a Puritan Town, 1630–1649* (Chapel Hill, N.C., 1965), chap. 2.

2. William Macphail, "Land Hunger and Closed-Field Husbandry on the New England Frontier, 1635–1665: The First Generation of Settlement in Watertown, Massachusetts" (Ph.D. diss., Brown Univ., 1972); Virginia D. Anderson, *New England's Generation: The Great Migrations and the Formation of Society and Culture in the Seventeenth Century* (New York, 1991), 90; Gloria L. Main, *Peoples of a Spacious Land: Families and Cultures in Colonial New England* (Cambridge, Mass., 2001), 42.

3. V. Anderson, *New England's Generation*, 105; John F. Martin, *Profits in the Wilderness: Entrepreneurship and the Founding of New England Towns* (Chapel Hill, N.C., 1991), chap. 1; Richard Archer, *Fissures in the Rock: New England in the Seventeenth Century* (Hanover, N.H., 2001), 150; Main, *Peoples of a Spacious Land*, 13; Rutman, *Winthrop's Boston*, 8–9, cf. 138.

4. V. Anderson, *New England's Generation*, 4, 114, 117, 118; Main, *Peoples of a Spacious Land*, 46.

5. Richard P. Gildrie, *Salem, Massachusetts, 1626–1683: A Covenant Community* (Charlottesville, Va., 1975), chaps. 1, 2, 8, pp. 59, 61, 67, 100–105, 171; Robert C. Anderson, *The Great Migration Begins: Immigrants to New England, 1620–1633* (Boston, 1995), I, 455–56. Conant had another reason for wanting the town's name changed: "Beverly," he wrote, sounded too much like "beggarly," which had become the district's nickname.

How profoundly regional differences shaped the contours of public conflicts is reflected in the origins of the notorious Hingham Militia Case, which exploded into a challenge to John Winthrop's authority and touched off struggles between the deputies and magistrates and between local town rights and the powers of the colony's government. It also led Winthrop to write his famous "Little Speech" on the just powers of magistrates. At issue originally was the determination of the town's East Anglian majority to oust the lone West Country man from the captaincy of the town's militia. See Robert E. Wall, Jr., *Massachusetts Bay: The Crucial Decade, 1640–1650* (New Haven, Conn., 1972), 94–95, chap. 3.

6. Joseph S. Wood, "New England's Exceptionalist Tradition: Rethinking the Colonial Encounter with the Land," *Connecticut History*, 35 (1994), 152–55, 157, 160, 179; Wood, *The New England Village* (Baltimore, 1997), chap. 2.

7. Glenn T. Trewartha, "Types of Rural Settlement in Colonial America," *Geographical Review*, 36 (1946), 568–80.

8. Darrett B. Rutman, *Husbandmen of Plymouth: Farms and Villages in the Old Colony, 1620–1692* (Boston, 1967), 5–6, 12; Philip J. Greven, Jr., *Four Generations: Population, Land, and Family in Colonial Andover, Massachusetts* (Ithaca, N.Y., 1970), 49–55.

9. John J. Waters sees a deeper West Country–East Anglia split: "Hingham, Massachusetts, 1631–1661: An East Anglian Oligarchy in the New World," *Journal of Social History*, 1 (1968), 351–70; David G. Allen, *In English Ways: The Movement of Societies and the Transferal of English Local Law and Customs to Massachusetts Bay in the Seventeenth Century* (Chapel Hill, N.C., 1981), 81, 75.

10. Winthrop, *Journal*, 270–71, 338; Patricia T. O'Malley, "Rowley, Massachusetts, 1639–1730: Dissent, Division, and Delimitation in a Colonial Town" (Ph.D. diss., Boston College, 1975), 3, 121, 43–44; Allen, *In English Ways*, 30–36, 44, 38; Samuel Maverick, "A Briefe Discription of New England . . . ," *Proceedings of the Massachusetts Historical Society*, 2nd ser., 1 (1884–85), 235.

11. Roger Thompson, *Divided We Stand: Watertown, Massachusetts, 1630–1680* (Amherst, Mass., 2001), chap. 3; Allen, *In English Ways*, 128, 124, 31, 129, 130–37, 142.

12. Thompson, *Watertown*, 14, 12, 19, 6, 54, 58, chap. 2.

13. Sumner C. Powell, *The Puritan Village: The Formation of a New England Town* (New York, 1963), 152, 153, 120, 121, 150, 156, 159, 160, 161, 164, 166, 169, 173.

14. Herbert B. Adams, "Origin of Salem Plantation," *Historical Collections of the Essex Institute*, 19 (1882), 241–53; Wood, "New England's Exceptionalist Tradition," 176.

15. Philip F. Gura, *A Glimpse of Sion's Glory: Puritan Radicalism in New England, 1620–1660* (Middletown, Conn., 1984), 5; Theodore D. Bozeman, *To Live Ancient Lives: The Primitivist Dimension in Puritanism* (Chapel Hill, N.C., 1988), esp. 345; Edmund S. Morgan, *Roger Williams: The Church and the State* (New York, 1967), 4.

16. [Nathaniel Ward], *The Simple Cobler of Aggawam* . . . (1647), in Peter Force, comp., *Tracts and Other Papers Relating Principally to . . . the Colonies in North America . . .* (Washington D.C., 1836–46), III; David D. Hall, ed., *The Antinomian Controversy, 1636–1638: A Documentary History*, 2nd ed. (Durham, N.C., 1990) [hereafter Hall, *AC*], 294.

17. Gura, *Sion's Glory*, 29. [Ward], *Simple Cobler*, 6.

18. Ezekiel Rogers's will, in Henry F. Waters, *Genealogical Gleanings in England* (Boston, 1888), I, pt. 2, p. 227; Gura, *Sion's Glory*, 22.

19. William Hunt, *The Puritan Moment: The Coming of Revolution in an English County* (Cambridge, Mass., 1983), 222; Edward Winslow, *Hypocrisie Unmasked: A True Relation of the Proceedings of the Governor and Company of Massachusetts Against Samuel Gorton of Rhode Island* ([1646] Providence, R.I., 1916), 65; William Hubbard, *A General History of New England* . . . ([1680] Boston, 1848), 203; "Cotton's Answer to Williams," 14; Morgan, *Williams*, 25, 18–22, 27.

20. *Correspondence of Roger Williams*, ed. Glenn LaFantasie (Providence, R.I., 1988), I, 12–23.

21. Gildrie, *Salem*, 21; Winthrop, *Journal*, 111; Hubbard, *General History*, 117, 202–13. Williams's preaching on veils, Hubbard wrote, was "as if he meant to read them a lecture out of Tertullian, *De velandis Virginibus*."

22. Samuel E. Morison, *Harvard College in the Seventeenth Century* (Cambridge, Mass., 1936), I, 305–14; Carla G. Pestana, *Quakers and Baptists in Colonial Massachusetts* (Cambridge, England, 1991), 5; Gura, *Sion's Glory*, 20.

23. Roger Williams, *A Key into the Language of America* (London, 1643) (John J. Teunissen and Evelyn J. Hinz, eds., Detroit, 1973), introduction and text; J. Patrick Cesarini, "The Ambivalent Uses of Roger Williams's *A Key into the Language of America*," *Early American Literature*, 38 (2003), 471, 477–79, 484–87; Gura, *Sion's Glory*, 74–75; W. Clark Gilpin, *The Millenarian Piety of Roger Williams* (Chicago, 1979), 50; [Ward], *Simple Cobler*, 6; Hubbard, *General History*, 206.

24. Sydney James, *Colonial Rhode Island: A History* (New York, 1975), 28–29; Gura, *Sion's Glory*, 295, 294, 299, 296.

25. Ibid., 280, 266, 296; James, *Rhode Island*, 25, 28; R. Anderson, *Migration Begins*, I, 395–401; [Samuel Gorton], *Simplicities Defence against the Seven-Headed Policy* . . . (London, 1646), 47 (as reprinted in Force, *Tracts*, IV).

26. [Gorton], *Simplicities Defence*, 56, [6]; Gura, *Sion's Glory*, 291–92; Winslow, *Hypocrisie Unmasked*, 8; Nathaniel B. Shurtleff, ed., *Records of the Governor and Company of the Massachusetts Bay in New England* (Boston, 1853–54), II, 52, 57.

27. John Donoghue, "'Hell Broke Loose': London's Coleman Street Ward and the Atlantic World of Radical Republicanism, 1624–1661," Atlantic History Seminar, Harvard University, Working Paper, no. 03–02 (2003), 13; Gura, *Sion's Glory*, 102, 132–33, 284, 285, 296, 299; A. L. Morton, *World of the Ranters: Religious Radicalism in the English Revolution* (London, 1970), 59; James, *Rhode Island*, 36–37. On Aspinwall, R. Anderson, *Migration Begins*, I, 55–60.

28. Ann Kibbey, *The Interpretation of Material Shapes in Puritanism: A Study of Rhetoric, Prejudice, and Violence* (New York, 1986), chap. 5; Michael Winship, *Making Heretics: Militant Protestantism and Free Grace in Massachusetts, 1636–1641* (Princeton, N.J., 2002), 194; Weld's preface to Winthrop's "Short Story," in Hall, *AC*, 201ff.

29. Janice Knight, *Orthodoxies in Massachusetts: Rereading American Puritanism* (Cambridge, Mass., 1994), 20–21; Richard Godbeer, "'Love Raptures': Marital, Romantic, and Erotic Images of Jesus Christ in Puritan New England, 1670–1730," *NEQ*, 68 (1995), 355–84; Winship, *Heretics*, 73, 84; George Selement and Bruce C. Woolley, eds., *Thomas Shepard's Confessions* (*Publications of the Colonial Society of Massachusetts*, 58 [1981]), figs. 1 and 2, pp. [16, 17].

30. Winship, *Heretics*, 70, 81–82, 34, 22, 24, 253n56; Sargent Bush, Jr., ed., *The Correspondence of John Cotton* (Chapel Hill, N.C., 2001), 225–30; Hall, *AC*, 24–29; Gura, *Sion's Glory*, 54, 55. On the origins of "Familism," Jean D. Moss, "'Godded with God': Hendrik Niclaes and His Family of Love," *Transactions of the American Philosophical Society*, 71, pt. 8 (1981), esp. 63–65.

31. Hall, *AC*, 29–33; Winship, *Heretics*, 54.

32. Ibid., 71, 45, 49; On Wheelwright: David S. Lovejoy, *Religious Enthusiasm in the New World: Heresy to Revolution* (Cambridge, Mass., 1985), 72–74; Winthrop, *Journal*, 195–97; [Thomas Hutchinson, comp.], *A Collection of Original Papers . . . [1769],* reprinted as *Hutchinson Papers* (*Publications of the Prince Society*, Albany, N.Y., 1865), I, 79–113, esp. 84–85.

33. Gura, *Sion's Glory*, 242, 241; Winthrop, *Journal*, 193.

34. Hall, *AC*, 264, 208; Winship, *Heretics*, 56; Winthrop, *Journal*, 240, 194, 195.

35. Gura, *Sion's Glory*, 187; Winship, *Heretics*, 86ff.; Hall, *AC*, 43ff. On Wilson: Samuel E. Morison, *The Founding of Harvard College* (Cambridge, Mass., 1935), 173.

36. Hall, *AC*, 52, 60, 158, 163, 166, 168, 165; William K. B. Stoever, *"A Faire and Easie Way to Heaven": Covenant Theology and Antinomianism in Early Massachusetts* (Middletown, Conn., 1978), 28; Morgan, *Williams*, 143–44.

37. Hall, *AC*, 203, 204, 209, 210, 293, 294, 253. Cotton never believed Wheelwright was an antinomian or Familist: Gura, *Sion's Glory*, 268.

38. Alfred A. Cave, *The Pequot War* (Amherst, Mass., 1996), 76, 72–74, 104–8 (Oldham's murder), 98–99, 131–34; Francis Jennings, *The Invasion of America: Indians, Colonialism, and the Cant of Conquest* (Chapel Hill, N.C., 1975), 189, 206; Charles Orr, *History of the Pequot War: The Contemporary Accounts of Mason, Underhill, Vincent and Gardener* (Cleveland, 1897), 51, 66–67; Winthrop, *Journal*, 193; Michael McGiffert, ed., *God's*

Plot: The Paradoxes of Puritan Piety, Being the Autobiography and Journal of Thomas Shepard (Amherst, Mass., 1972), 70.

39. Stoever, *"Faire and Easie Way,"* 28, 29; John Winthrop, "A Defence of an Order of Court Made in the Year 1637," in Perry Miller and Thomas H. Johnson, eds., *The Puritans: A Sourcebook of Their Writings* (1938; rev. ed., New York, 1963), I, 199, 200, 202; Gura, *Sion's Glory*, 187–88.

40. Winthrop, *Journal*, 209, 214n, 215.

41. Cave, *Pequot War*, 139, 137, 143, 149, 148, 150; McGiffert, *Autobiography and Journal of Shepard*, 67; Orr, *History of Pequot War*, 45.

42. Orr, *History of Pequot War*, 81; William Bradford, *Of Plymouth Plantation, 1620–1649*, ed. Samuel E. Morison (New York, 1952), 296.

43. Cave, *Pequot War*, 158–59, 161; *Correspondence of Williams*, I, 88, 73, 86–87, 118; Winthrop, *Journal*, 226–27, 231, 229; Cotton Mather, *Magnalia Christi Americana . . .* ([1702]; facsimile ed., New York, 1972), book VII, 44; Almon W. Lauber, *Indian Slavery in Colonial Times Within the Present Limits of the United States*, Columbia University, Studies in History, Economics and Public Law, 54, no. 3 (1913), 123–24.

CHAPTER 14
Defiance and Disarray

1. John Winthrop, "A Defence of an Order of Court Made in the Year 1637," in Perry Miller and Thomas H. Johnson, eds., *The Puritans: A Sourcebook of Their Writings* ([1938]; rev. ed., New York, 1963), I, 199–202; Michael Winship, *Making Heretics: Militant Protestantism and Free Grace in Massachusetts, 1636–1641* (Princeton, N.J., 2002), 137; Nathaniel B. Shurtleff, ed., *Records of the Governor and Company of the Massachusetts Bay in New England* (Boston, 1853–54) [hereafter: Shurtleff, ed., *MR*], I, 196; Winthrop, *Journal*, 219, 226. On Grindleton, see Geoffrey F. Nuttall, *The Holy Spirit in Puritan Faith and Experience* ([1946] Chicago, 1992), App. I; Stephen Foster, "New England and the Challenge of Heresy, 1630 to 1660: The Puritan Crisis in Transatlantic Perspective," *WMQ*, 38 (1981), 645; Philip F. Gura, *A Glimpse of Sion's Glory: Puritan Radicalism in New England, 1620–1660* (Middletown, Conn., 1984), 252, 54–56; James F. Maclear, "'The Heart of New England Rent': The Mystical Element in Early Puritan History," *Mississippi Valley Historical Review*, 42 (1956), 629; Winthrop, *Journal*, 226; David D. Hall, ed., *The Antinomian Controversy, 1636–1638: A Documentary History* (2nd ed., Durham, N.C., 1990) [hereafter: Hall, *AC*], 414.

2. Winthrop, *Journal*, 232–33; Foster, "Challenge of Heresy," 647.

3. Hall, *AC*, 202, 219–43; Winthrop, *Journal*, 233.

4. Sargent Bush, Jr., ed., *The Correspondence of John Cotton* (Chapel Hill, N.C., 2001), 50, 51, 161, 53, 52, 54; Winship, *Heretics*, 160, 162.

5. Hall, *AC*, 257–63, 254, 253; Shurtleff, ed., *MR*, I, 205–9.

6. Winship, *Heretics*, 226; Hall, *AC*, 314, 315, 275, 276; Jean Cameron, *Anne Hutchinson, Guilty or Not?: A Closer Look at Her Trials* (New York, 1994), 145, 147, 148. On Anne Hutchinson's private meetings, see Mary Beth Norton, *Founding Mothers and Fathers: Gendered Power and the Forming of American Society* (New York, 1996), 362–65.

7. Hall, *AC*, 317, 318, 319, 326, 333–38, 273, 342, 343; Cameron, *Hutchinson*, 149, 151–53, 161.

8. Hall, *AC*, 74, 341, 276, 348.

9. Gura, *Sion's Glory*, 138–43; Shurtleff, ed., *MR*, I, 211–13.

10. Hall, *AC*, 350–88; Emery Battis, *Saints and Sectaries: Anne Hutchinson and the Antinomian Controversy in the Massachusetts Bay Colony* (Chapel Hill, N.C., 1962), chap. 16; Jesper Rosenmeier, "New England's Perfection: The Image of Adam and the Image of Christ in the Antinomian Crisis, 1634 to 1638," *WMQ*, 27 (1970), 435–59.

11. Battis, *Saints and Sectaries*, 245; Hall, *AC*, 372, 364, 388; Foster, "Challenge of Heresy," 644–45.

12. Battis, *Saints and Sectaries*, 248; Helle M. Alpert, "Robert Keayne: Notes on Sermons by John Cotton and the Proceedings of the First Church of Boston from 23 November 1639 to 1 June 1640" (Ph.D. diss., Tufts University, 1974), 41–43, 7; Winship, *Heretics*, 235, 237, 241.

13. R. H. Tawney, *Religion and the Rise of Capitalism: A Historical Study* ([1926] New York, 1937), 202.

14. Battis, *Saints and Sectaries*, 258ff.

15. Lyle Koehler, "The Case of the American Jezebels: Anne Hutchinson and Female Agitation During the Years of the Antinomian Turmoil, 1636–1640," *WMQ*, 31 (1974), 63, 64, 68; Hall, *AC*, 312, 314, 370, 365.

16. Ibid., 370.

17. Ibid., 281; Koehler, "American Jezebels," 62, 69, 70; [Edward Johnson], *A History of New-England. From the English Planting in the Yeere 1628 until the Yeere 1652 [Wonder-working Providence of Sions Saviour]* [1654], ed. J. Franklin Jameson (New York, 1910), 132; Shurtleff, ed., *MR*, I, 224, 329; Winthrop, *Journal*, 275, 276, 271, 272; Robert C. Anderson, *The Great Migration . . . 1634–1635* (Boston, 1999–), II, 850, 856. On Talby's murder, see Peter C. Hoffer and N. E. H. Hull, *Murdering Mothers: Infanticide in England and New England, 1558–1803* (New York, 1981), 40–41.

18. Carla G. Pestana, *Quakers and Baptists in Colonial Massachusetts* (Cambridge, England, 1991), 10, 12; Nuttall, *Holy Spirit*, esp. chap. 10, p. 151; Maclear, " 'The Heart of New England Rent,' " 624, 625; Carla G. Pestana, "The City upon a Hill Under Siege: The Puritan Perception of the Quaker Threat to Massachusetts Bay, 1656–1661," *NEQ*, 56 (1983), 336–37, 345, 347; John Norton, *The Heart of N-England Rent at the Blasphemies of the Present Generation* (Cambridge, Mass., 1659), 52; Richard P. Hallowell, *The Quaker Invasion of Massachusetts* (2nd ed., Boston, 1883), 45.

19. Gura, *Sion's Glory*, 146, 148; Winthrop, *Journal*, 462–63, 363; Richard P. Gildrie, *Salem, Massachusetts, 1626–1683: A Covenant Community* (Charlottesville, Va., 1975), 130ff.; Shurtleff, ed., *MR*, II, 283; Maclear, " 'The Heart of New England Rent,' " 627, 645–51, 637.

20. Rufus Jones, *The Quakers in the American Colonies* (New York, 1911), 36; George Bishop, *New England Judged by the Spirit of the Lord . . .* ([1661] London, 1703), 42ff., 55; on Plymouth laws, Meredith B. Weddle, *Walking the Way of Peace . . .* (New York, 2001), 84–85; Norton, *Heart of N-England Rent*, 8; Shurtleff, ed., *MR*, IV, pt. 1, 277, 309, 383. Cf. J. Hammond Trumbull et al., eds., *The Public Records of the Colony of Connecticut* (Hart-

ford, Conn., 1850–90), I, 283–84, 303, 308, 324; Charles J. Hoadly, ed., *Records of the Colony or Jurisdiction of New Haven . . .* (Hartford, Conn., 1858), 238–41.

21. Jones, *Quakers*, 66, 72, 75, 91–92; Shurtleff, ed., *MR*, IV, pt. 1, 383, 384; Sydney James, *Colonial Rhode Island: A History* (New York, 1975), 65.

22. Pestana, "City upon a Hill Under Siege," 347n; James, *Rhode Island*, 39, 41, 42; Jones, *Quakers*, 53–56.

23. Shurtleff, ed., *MR*, IV, pt. 1, 348, 385–90, 308, 345–46; Norton, *Heart of N-England Rent*, 2, 7, 53ff.; Carla G. Pestana, "The Quaker Executions as Myth and History," *Journal of American History*, 80 (1993), 463.

24. Shurtleff, ed., *MR*, IV, pt. 1, 451. For text of the king's order: Jones, *Quakers*, 98.

25. Listed in Hallowell, *Quaker Invasion*, 183–86; Jones, *Quakers*, 102, 104–5, 108; Shurtleff, ed., *MR*, IV, pt. 2, 2; M. Halsey Thomas, ed., *Diary of Samuel Sewall, 1674–1729* (New York, 1973), I, 44; Cotton Mather, *Magnalia Christi Americana . . .* ([1702]; facsimile ed., New York, 1972), Book VII, 23.

26. The following paragraphs on Keayne are drawn from Bernard Bailyn, "The *Apologia* of Robert Keayne," *WMQ*, 7 (1950), 569–87. See also Alpert's interpretation in "Keayne: Notes on Sermons," 1–92. For the detail and importance of Keayne's note taking, see Sargent Bush, Jr., ed., *The Correspondence of John Cotton* (Chapel Hill, N.C., 2001), 71, 320, 331, 382. The text of Keayne's will appears in Bernard Bailyn, ed., *The Apologia of Robert Keayne . . .* (New York, 1965).

27. Bernard Bailyn, *The New England Merchants in the Seventeenth Century* (Cambridge, Mass., 1955), 32, 33, 48, 49, 207–8 nn68 and 70; Stephen Innes, *Creating the Commonwealth: The Economic Culture of Puritan New England* (New York, 1995), chaps. 3, 4.

28. Shurtleff, ed., *MR*, IV, pt. 1, 60–61, emphasis added.

29. The most thorough study of the remigration is Susan H. Moore, *Pilgrims: New World Settlers and the Call of Home* (New Haven, Conn., 2007), especially chap. 5 and the four detailed Appendixes. See also David Cressy, *Coming Over: Migration and Communication Between England and New England in the Seventeenth Century* (Cambridge, England, 1987), chap. 8.

30. Moore, *Pilgrims*, chap. 4.

31. Ibid., 80, 95, 54, 55, 12, chap. 5. Ward was paraphrasing the "celebrated divine" William Perkins: ibid., 72.

32. Ibid., 88–90. On Cotton's will: Robert C. Anderson, *The Great Migration Begins: Immigrants to New England, 1620–1633* (Boston, 1995), I, 485.

33. Moore, *Pilgrims*, 92; Winthrop, *Journal*, 416.

34. Moore, *Pilgrims*, 55–56; William L. Sachse, "Harvard Men in New England, 1642–1714," *Publications of the Colonial Society of Massachusetts: Transactions 1942–1946* (Boston, 1951), 119–44; Harry S. Stout, "University Men in New England 1620–1660: A Demographic Analysis," *Journal of Interdisciplinary History* 4 (1974), 394.

35. Moore, *Pilgrims*, 77, 119, 120, 111; Gura, *Sion's Glory*, 138–43.

36. William L. Sachse, "The Migration of New Englanders to England, 1640–1660," *American Historical Review*, 53 (1948), 257.

37. Moore, *Pilgrims*, 113, 65, 66; Walter W. Woodward, "George Fenwick"; Richard P. Gildrie, "Robert Sedgwick"; and Richard P. Gildrie, "Edward Winslow," *Oxford Dictionary of National Biography* [www.oxforddnb.com, hereafter *ODNB*]; Jeremy D. Bangs, *Pilgrim Edward Winslow* (Boston, 2004), chaps. 9–11; Bailyn, *Merchants*, 94.

38. Raymond P. Stearns, *The Strenuous Puritan: Hugh Peter, 1598–1660* (Urbana, Ill., 1954), pt. 3; Carla G. Pestana, "Hugh Peter," in *ODNB* (quoting C. V. Wedgwood); *Winthrop Papers* (Boston, 1929–), V, 158; Winthrop, *Journal*, 608; Ruth E. Mayers, "Sir Henry Vane the Younger," *ODNB*.

39. Jonathan Scott, "Sir George Downing," *ODNB*; Thomas Hutchinson, *The History of the Colony and Province of Massachusetts-Bay* [London, 1765], Lawrence S. Mayo, ed. (Cambridge, Mass., 1936), I, 97n.

40. Gura, *Sion's Glory*, 143.

41. Sachse, "Migration," 254; *Winthrop Papers*, V, 13.

42. Bailyn, *Merchants*, 47–48.

43. Ibid., 49–60; on the New Haven merchants, 29.

44. Ibid., 72, 73.

45. Ibid., 62ff.; Walter W. Woodward, *Prospero's America: John Winthrop, Jr., Alchemy, and the Creation of New England Culture, 1606–1676* (Chapel Hill, N.C., 2010) 62–63.

46. Margaret E. Newell, "Robert Child and the Entrepreneurial Vision: Economy and Ideology in Early New England," *NEQ*, 68 (1995), 227–30, 233–37; George E. Kittredge, "Doctor Robert Child, the Remonstrant," *Publications of the Colonial Society of Massachusetts*, 21 (*Transactions*, 1919), 5–7; E. N. Hartley, *Ironworks on the Saugus . . .* (Norman, Okla., 1957), chaps. 3, 4.

47. Hartley, *Ironworks*, 64; Bailyn, *Merchants*, 62; Newell, "Child," 237–38. For a full account of the workers, including Scottish prisoners of war, their recruitment, and their lives in Massachusetts, see Hartley, *Ironworks*, chap. 10.

48. Ibid., 135; Newell, "Child," 240, 243, 244, 246; [G. H. Turnbull], "Robert Child," *Publications of the Colonial Society of Massachusetts*, 38 (*Transactions*, 1947–51), 51. For an exhaustive account of the Remonstrance and the reaction to it, see Robert E. Wall, Jr., *Massachusetts Bay: The Crucial Decade, 1640–1650* (New Haven, Conn., 1972), chaps. 5 and 6.

49. Kittredge, "Child," 20–28.

50. "A Remonstrance and Petition of Robert Child, and others," in [Thomas Hutchinson, comp.] *A Collection of Original Papers . . .* [1769], reprinted as *Hutchinson Papers* (*Publications of the Prince Society*, Albany, N.Y., 1865), I, 215–19.

51. Ibid., 224, 225, 237, 239–47.

52. Kittredge, "Child," 32–33, 37–38, 41.

53. Ibid., 41, 43, 56. John Winthrop, Jr., saw to it that Child never had to pay the £50 fine. Richard S. Dunn, *Puritans and Yankees: The Winthrop Dynasty of New England, 1630–1717* (Princeton, N.J., 1962), 92.

54. [Gorton], *Simplicities Defence*, 19, 20, 26; Winslow, *Hypocrisie Unmasked*, 102; and John Childe, *New-Englands Jonas Cast up at London . . .* (London, 1647), 21, 24, as reprinted in Peter Force, ed., *Tracts and Other Papers Relating Principally to . . . the Colonies*

in North America . . . (Washington, D.C., 1836–46), IV; Kittredge, "Child," 49. For Vassall's role in the Remonstrance, see Wall, *Crucial Decade*, chap. 5. On Winthrop's view of Vassall: Winthrop, *Journal*, 624.

55. Newell, "Child," 227, 254.

56. For Child's later career, see [Turnbull], "Child," 20–53.

57. Woodward, *Winthrop, Jr.*, 134–35, 51, 53, 135; Robert C. Black III, *The Younger John Winthrop* (New York, 1966), 106; Dunn, *Winthrop Dynasty*, 64, 92.

58. Bailyn, *Merchants*, 86, 33–38, 84; Newell, "Child," 231; Lawrence S. Mayo, *The Winthrop Family In America* (Boston, 1948), 59–61; *Winthrop Papers*, V, 43–44. For a general view of New England's emerging commercial economy, see John J. McCusker and Russell R. Menard, *The Economy of British America, 1607–1789* (Chapel Hill, N.C., 1985), chap 5.

59. Bailyn, *Merchants*, 76ff.; McCusker and Menard, *Economy of British America*, 98–101.

60. William B. Weeden, *Economic and Social History of New England, 1620–1789* (Boston, 1890), I, 142; Bailyn, *Merchants*, 84.

61. Ibid., 35, 87–90. On Vassall: see John C. Appleby in *ODNB*; on Thompson and Cradock, London's two most powerful entrepreneurs in New England's commerce, see Robert Brenner, *Merchants and Revolution: Commercial Change, Political Conflict, and London's Overseas Traders, 1550–1653* (Princeton, N.J., 1993), passim.

62. Bailyn, *Merchants*, 88–90.

63. Ibid., 83; Winthrop, *Journal*, 573; *Winthrop Papers*, V, 38.

64. Bailyn, "Communications and Trade: The Atlantic in the Seventeenth Century," *Journal of Economic History*, 13 (1953), 384; Bailyn, *Merchants*, 96–97; Rutman, *Winthrop's Boston*, chap. 7, esp. 186, 190.

65. Christine L. Heyrman, *Commerce and Culture: The Maritime Communities of Colonial Massachusetts, 1690–1750* (New York, 1984), chaps. 5, 11, quotation at 411; Bailyn, *Merchants*, 105–6; Winthrop, *Journal*, 611–12.

66. Bailyn, *Merchants*, 109–11, 140; Viola Barnes, "Richard Wharton . . . ," *Publications of the Colonial Society of Massachusetts*, 26 (*Transactions*, 1924–26), 250.

CHAPTER 15

The British Americans

In referring to material that appears in previous chapters, the annotation is not repeated. But quotations and extensions of previous material are documented.

1. Ronald D. Karr, " 'Why Should You Be So Furious?': The Violence of the Pequot War," *Journal of American History*, 85 (1998), 884–87; John L. Motley, *Rise of the Dutch Republic* [1856] (New York, 1906), II, 331.

2. J. Frederick Fausz, "Merging and Emerging Worlds: Anglo-Indian Interest Groups," in Lois G. Carr, Philip D. Morgan, and Jean B. Russo, eds., *Colonial Chesapeake Society* (Chapel Hill, N.C., 1988), 74–79; Helen C. Rountree, *Pocahontas, Powhatan, Opechancanough* (Charlottesville, Va., 2005), 231–35.

3. Donna Merwick, *The Shame and the Sorrow: Dutch-American Encounters in New Netherland* (Philadelphia, 2006), 232–34, 252–56, 266–67; *Docs. Rel.*, XIII, 51–57, 135–42.

4. Christian F. Feest, "Seventeenth Century Virginia: Algonquian Population Estimates," *Quarterly Bulletin of the Archaeological Society of Virginia*, 28 (Dec. 1973), 74; E. Randolph Turner, "Socio-Political Organization Within the Powhatan Chiefdom and the Effects of European Contact, A.D. 1607–1646," in William Fitzhugh, ed., *Cultures in Contact . . . 1000–1800* (Washington, D.C., 1985), 216; Neal Salisbury, *Manitou and Providence . . . 1500–1643* (New York, 1982), 22–30; Dean Snow and Kim M. Lamphear, "European Contact and Indian Depopulation in the Northeast: The Timing of the First Epidemics," *Ethnohistory*, 35 (1988), 15–33.

5. James Axtell, *The European and the Indian* (New York, 1981), chap. 3.

6. Andrew Newman, ed., "'Relation of the Pequot Warres,' by Lion Gardiner," in *Early American Studies*, 9 (2011), 483. On Mather's fear of a "rushing" degeneracy, "a visible *shrink* in all orders of men among us," and his hope to stem the decline by recalling to contemporaries "that *greatness* and that *goodness* which was in the *first grain*": *Magnalia Christi Americana: or the Ecclesiastical History of New-England . . .* [London, 1702] (facsimile ed., New York, 1972), Book III, 11.

7. Charles J. Hoadley, ed., *Records of the Colony and Plantations of New Haven from 1638–1649* (Hartford, Conn., 1857), 40, 119, 122–23.

8. James R. Perry, *The Formation of a Society on Virginia's Eastern Shore, 1615–1655* (Chapel Hill, N.C., 1990), esp. chaps. 7–9; Jon Kukla, *Political Institutions in Virginia, 1619–1660* (New York, 1989), esp. xviii–xx; Kukla, "Order and Chaos in Early America . . . ," *American Historical Review*, 90 (1985), 275–98.

9. Andrew Lipman, "'A meanes to knit them togeather': The Exchange of Body Parts in the Pequot War," *WMQ*, 65 (2008), 3–28 (on the "asymmetry" of the exchange, 22); Mark Nicholls, ed., "George Percy's 'Trewe Relacyon,'" *VMHB*, 113 (2005), 245, 253, 254; Helen C. Rountree, *The Powhatan Indians of Virginia* (Norman, Okla., 1989), 133–35; Philip Vincent, *A True Relation of the Late Battell Fought in New-England . . .* (London, 1638), in Charles Orr, ed., *History of the Pequot War* (Cleveland, 1897), 101; Henry C. Shelley, *John Underhill* (New York, 1932), 193–94; Joyce E. Chaplin, *Subject Matter: Technology, the Body, and Science . . . 1500–1676* (Cambridge, Mass., 2001), 269; Katherine A. Grandjean, "The Long Wake of the Pequot War," *Early American Studies*, 9 (2011), 393, 391, 410, 400.

10. Russell R. Menard, "Maryland's 'Time of Troubles': Sources of Political Disorder in Early St. Mary's," *MHM*, 76 (1981), esp. 136; David W. Jordan, "Maryland's Privy Council, 1637–1715," in Aubrey C. Land et al., eds., *Law, Society, and Politics in Early Maryland* (Baltimore, Md., 1977), 73.

11. Richard W. Cogley, *John Eliot's Mission to the Indians before King Philip's War* (Cambridge, Mass., 1999), chaps 4–5 (quotation at 93); J. F. Maclear, "New England and the Fifth Monarchy: The Quest for the Millennium in Early American Puritanism," *WMQ*, 32 (1975), 225, 229, 231–34, 244–47, 255; James Holstun, "John Eliot's Empirical Millenarianism," *Representations*, 4 (1983), 131, 143–47; James Holstun, *A Rational Millennium: Puritan Utopias of Seventeenth-Century England and America* (N.Y., 1987), 104–9, 111–15, 131–32, 158–59.

12. Bernard Bailyn, *New England Merchants in the Seventeenth Century* (Cambridge, Mass., 1955), 114–15, 119–26.

13. John J. McCusker and Russell R. Menard, *The Economy of British America, 1607–1789* (Chapel Hill, N.C., 1985), 136; Abbot E. Smith, *Colonists in Bondage* (Chapel Hill, N.C., 1947), chaps. 5, 7, 8, p. 104; William W. Hening, ed., *The Statutes . . . of Virginia* (Richmond, Va., 1809–23), II, 509–10. For a detailed analysis of Virginia's population growth, see Edmund S. Morgan, *American Slavery, American Freedom* (New York, 1975), 395–432.

14. Russell R. Menard, "Population, Economy, and Society in Seventeenth-Century Maryland," *MHM*, 79 (1984), 82–83; Warren M. Billings, "The Law of Servants and Slaves in Seventeenth-Century Virginia," *VMHB*, 99 (1991), 50–52; Karen O. Kupperman, *Settling with the Indians . . . 1580–1640* (Totowa, N.J., 1980), 137; examples in H. R. McIlwaine, ed., *Minutes of the Council and General Court of Colonial Virginia* (2nd ed., Richmond, Va., 1979), 22, 23, 105, 148; Act of 1662: Hening, *Statutes*, II, 117.

15. David S. Cohen, "How Dutch Were the Dutch of New Netherland?" *New York History*, 62 (1981), 43–59; Oliver A. Rink, *Holland on the Hudson* (Ithaca, N.Y., 1986), chap. 6.

16. David D. Hall, *A Reforming People: Puritanism and the Transformation of Public Life in New England* (New York, 2011), chaps. 1, 4, esp. pp. 47–52.

17. David T. Konig, *Law and Society in Puritan Massachusetts: Essex County, 1629–1692* (Chapel Hill, N.C., 1979), xi, chaps. 2, 6, esp. pp. 193–94.

18. Paul R. Lucas, *Valley of Discord: Church and Society Along the Connecticut River, 1636–1725* (Hanover, N.H., 1976), 204, 206; Stephen Innes, *Labor in a New Land: Economy and Society in Seventeenth-Century Springfield* (Princeton, N.J., 1983), chap. 5, quotations at 128, 133, 143; Helena M. Wall, *Fierce Communion: Family and Community in Early America* (Cambridge, Mass., 1990); John Frederick Martin, *Profits in the Wilderness* (Chapel Hill, N.C., 1991), 304.

19. Walter W. Woodward, *Prospero's America: John Winthrop, Jr., Alchemy, and the Creation of New England Culture, 1606–1676* (Chapel Hill, N.C., 2010), 261, 269, 293, 274, 279, 302, quotation at 265; Robert C. Black, *The Younger John Winthrop* (New York, 1966), 312, 313; Richard S. Dunn, *Puritans and Yankees: The Winthrop Dynasty of New England, 1630–1717* (Princeton, N.J., 1962), Part III, quotation at 191.

20. Daniel Scott Smith, "The Demographic History of Colonial New England," *Journal of Economic History*, 32 (1972), 165–83. Township figures are derived from the working papers of A New England Settlement Map Series, compiled by Lee Shai Weissbach, Harvard University, 1977, based on individual town records; Secretary of the Commonwealth, *Historical Data Relating to Counties, Cities, and Towns in Massachusetts* (Boston, 1920); Lois K. Mathews, *The Expansion of New England* (Boston, 1909); and Joseph B. Felt, "Statistics of Towns in Massachusetts," *Collections of the American Statistical Association*, I (1843).

21. For a meticulous study of the limits of the morcellation of landholdings in New England, see Philip J. Greven, Jr., *Four Generations: Population, Land, and Family in Colonial Andover, Massachusetts* (Ithaca, N.Y., 1970) chaps. 5–8. On the dispersal of New England villages: Joseph S. Wood, "Village and Community in Early Colonial New England," *Journal of Historical Geography*, 8 (1982), 340, 343. Cf. Sumner C. Powell, *Puritan Village* (Middletown, Conn., 1963), 160.

22. R. Cole Harris, "The Simplification of Europe Overseas," *Annals of the Association of American Geographers*, 67 (1977), 474, 479–80.

23. Joyce D. Goodfriend, *Before the Melting Pot: Society and Culture in Colonial New York City, 1664–1730* (Princeton, N.J., 1992), 40, 58, 219.

24. Ibid., chaps. 3, 6. For an argument that the blacks in New Netherland formed, remarkably, "a new and vibrant community" by 1660, despite the fact that "they may have spoken different languages, belonged to several distinct ethnic groups, and come from diverse places in Africa and the Atlantic littoral," see Cynthia Van Zandt, *Brothers Among Nations: The Pursuit of Intercultural Alliances in Early America, 1580–1660* (Oxford, England, 2008), 144, 138, and chap. 6 generally.

25. Robert C. Ritchie, *The Duke's Province: A Study of New York Politics and Society, 1664–1691* (Chapel Hill, N.C., 1977), 78–81, 114–16; Cathy Matson, *Merchants and Enterprise: Trading in Colonial New York* (Baltimore, Md., 1998), 55.

26. Ritchie, *Duke's Province*, 131, 136, 98, 100, 107, 125, 140, 57; Donna Merwick, *Possessing Albany, 1630–1710* (Cambridge, England, 1990), 235–40.

27. Ritchie, *Duke's Province*, 68, 71–73.

28. Claudia Schnurmann, "Merchants, Ministers, and the Van Rensselaer-Leisler Controversy of 1676 as a Dress Rehearsal for 1689," in Hermann Wellenreuther, ed., *Jacob Leisler's Atlantic World in the Later Seventeenth Century* (Piscataway, N.J., 2009), 77–88; David W. Voorhees, "The 'fervent Zeale' of Jacob Leisler," *WMQ*, 51 (July 1994), 447–72; Lawrence H. Leder, "The Unorthodox Dominie: Nicholas Van Rensselaer," *New York History* 35 (1954), 166–76.

29. Ritchie, *Duke's Province*, 148, 140–43.

30. *Philipsburg Manor* (Tarrytown, N.Y., 1969), 13–21, 23.

31. Morgan, *American Slavery, American Freedom*, chap. 11, quotations at 225, 244–45; Lorena S. Walsh, *Motives of Honor, Pleasure, and Profit* (Chapel Hill, N.C., 2010), 109.

32. On the Green Spring faction and the networks of officials connected to Governor Berkeley and his wife, Frances Culpeper, see Mary Beth Norton, *Separated by Their Sex: Women in Public and Private in the Colonial Atlantic World* (Ithaca, N.Y., 2011), 9–34. On the Northern Neck: Douglas S. Freeman, *George Washington: A Biography* (New York, 1948), I, App. I, p. 1.

33. Morgan, *American Slavery, American Freedom*, 219–20.

34. Walsh, *Motives of Honor*, 140–43. For a study of Virginia's black population: Morgan, *American Slavery, American Freedom*, 420–32.

35. David Eltis, "Free and Coerced Migration from the Old World to the New," in Eltis, ed., *Coerced and Free Migration* (Stanford, Calif., 2002), [33]: "Community in the sense . . . that everyone living in it had values that if they were not shared around the Atlantic were certainly reshaped in some way by others living in the Atlantic basin, and, as this suggests, where events in one geographic area had the potential to stimulate a reaction—and not necessarily just economic—thousands of miles away."

36. Walsh, *Motives of Honor*, 149; Jacob M. Price, *The Tobacco Adventure to Russia . . . 1676–1722* (*Transactions of the American Philosophical Society*, NS 51, 1961), pt. 1; Price, *France and the Chesapeake* (Ann Arbor, Mich., 1973), I, pt. 2; Jacob Price and Paul G. E. Clemens, "A Revolution of Scale in Overseas Trade: British Firms in the Chesapeake Trade, 1675–1725," *Journal of Economic History*, 47 (1987), 37, 3–4; Price, "Merchants and Planters: The Market Structure of the Colonial Chesapeake Reconsidered,"

in *Tobacco in the Atlantic Trade* (Aldershot, England, 1995), IV, 11; April L. Hatfield, *Atlantic Virginia: Intercolonial Relations in the Seventeenth Century* (Philadelphia, 2004), chap. 3, quotations at 181, 80.

37. Daron Acemoglu, Simon Johnson, and James Robinson, "The Rise of Europe: Atlantic Trade, Institutional Change, and Economic Growth," Centre for Economic Policy Research, *Papers*, no. DP3712 (2003), 550, 552, 562: "West European growth after 1500 was due primarily to growth in countries involved in Atlantic trade or with a high potential for Atlantic trade. . . . The rise of Europe reflects not only the direct effects of Atlantic trade and colonialism but also a major social transformation induced by these opportunities." Bailyn, *New England Merchants*, 126–34, 143ff.; Christian J. Koot, *Empire at the Periphery: British Colonists, Anglo-Dutch Trade, and the Development of the British Atlantic, 1621–1713* (New York, 2011), pts. 1, 2; Matson, *Merchants and Empire*, 26–29, 54, chaps. 1–4; Claudia Schnurmann, *Atlantische Welten: Engländer und Niederländer im amerikanisch-atlantischen Raum, 1648–1713* (Cologne, 1998), summarized briefly in English in "Migration and Communication: Relations between Inhabitants of English and Dutch Colonies in the New World, 1648–1713," Working Paper No. 96-03, Atlantic History Seminar, Harvard University (1996).

Index

A Note About the Author

BERNARD BAILYN did his undergraduate work at Williams College and his graduate work at Harvard, where he is currently Adams University Professor and James Duncan Phillips Professor of Early American History, emeritus. His previous books include *The New England Merchants in the Seventeenth Century; Education in the Forming of American Society; The Ideological Origins of the American Revolution*, which received the Pulitzer and Bancroft Prizes; *The Ordeal of Thomas Hutchinson*, which won the National Book Award for History; *Voyagers to the West*, which won the Pulitzer Prize; *Faces of Revolution; Personalities and Themes in the Struggle for American Independence; To Begin the World Anew: The Genius and Ambiguities of the American Founders;* and *Atlantic History: Concepts and Contours*. In 2011 he received the National Humanities Medal.

A Note on the Type

This book was set in Janson, a typeface long thought to have been made by the Dutchman Anton Janson, who was a practicing typefounder in Leipzig during the years 1668–87. However, it has been conclusively demonstrated that these types are actually the work of Nicholas Kis (1650–1702), a Hungarian, who most probably learned his trade from the master Dutch typefounder Dirk Voskens. The type is an excellent example of the influential and sturdy Dutch types that prevailed in England up to the time William Caslon (1692–1766) developed his own incomparable designs from them.

Composed by North Market Street Graphics,
Lancaster, Pennsylvania

Printed and bound by Berryville Graphics,
Berryville, Virginia

Designed by Cassandra J. Pappas